The Affirmative Defense of Qualified Immunity for Law Enforcement

Contemporary Decisions

Volume 1

* * *

D1279866

A LandMark Publication

Criminal Law Series

The Affirmative Defense of Qualified Immunity for Law Enforcement
Contemporary Decisions
Volume 1

Published in the United States of America
by LandMark Publications.
www.landmark-publications.com

Publication Date: June 2020;
Subject Heading: Criminal Procedure;
Audience: Law Professionals.

Character Set: ISO 8859-1 (Latin-1);
Language Code: EN;
Interior Type: Text; Monochrome.

Help us serve you better.
Write to landmarkpx@live.com with
your requests, comments and suggestions.

ISBN: 979-8656953597

Summary of Contents

PROLOGUE

Qualified immunity is a doctrine aimed at providing government officials (including police officers) a modicum of protection from civil damages liability for actions taken under color of state law. *See Harlow v. Fitzgerald,* 457 U.S. 800, 818, 102 S.Ct. 2727, 73 L.Ed.2d 396 (1982); *McKenney v. Mangino,* 873 F.3d 75, 80 (1st Cir. 2017), *cert. denied,* ___ U.S. ___, 138 S.Ct. 1311, 200 L.Ed.2d 475 (2018). This p.10 protection attaches "to all but the plainly incompetent or those who knowingly violate the law." *Malley v. Briggs,* 475 U.S. 335, 341, 106 S.Ct. 1092, 89 L.Ed.2d 271 (1986). Thus, a government official may invoke the defense of qualified immunity when his actions, though causing injury, did "not violate clearly established statutory or constitutional rights of which a reasonable person would have known." *Conlogue v. Hamilton,* 906 F.3d 150, 154 (1st Cir. 2018) (quoting Harlow, 457 U.S. at 818, 102 S.Ct. 2727).

The qualified immunity analysis has two facets: "[t]he court must determine whether the defendant violated the plaintiff's constitutional rights" and then must determine "whether the allegedly abridged right was 'clearly established' at the time of the defendant's claimed misconduct." Id. at 155 (*quoting McKenney,* 873 F.3d at 81). [. . .]

[The question whether the allegedly abridged right is clearly established] has two facets. First, the plaintiff must "identify either 'controlling authority' or a 'consensus of cases of persuasive authority' sufficient to send a clear signal to a reasonable official that certain conduct falls short of the constitutional norm." *Alfano v. Lynch,* 847 F.3d 71, 75 (1st Cir. 2017) (*quoting Wilson v. Layne,* 526 U.S. 603, 617, 119 S.Ct. 1692, 143 L.Ed.2d 818 (1999)). Second, the plaintiff must demonstrate that "an objectively reasonable official in the defendant's position would have known that his conduct violated that rule of law." Id. This latter step is designed to achieve a prophylactic purpose: it affords "some breathing room for a police officer even if he has made a mistake (albeit a reasonable one) about the lawfulness of his conduct." *Conlogue,* 906 F.3d at 155. Taken together, these steps normally require that, to defeat a police officer's qualified immunity defense, a plaintiff must "identify a case where an officer acting under similar circumstances was held to have violated the Fourth Amendment." *City of Escondido v. Emmons,* ___ U.S. ___, 139 S.Ct. 500, 504, 202 L.Ed.2d 455 (2019) (per curiam) (*quoting District of Columbia v. Wesby,* ___ U.S. ___, 138 S.Ct. 577, 590, 199 L.Ed.2d 453 (2018)); *see Anderson v. Creighton,* 483 U.S. 635, 639-40, 107 S.Ct. 3034, 97 L.Ed.2d 523 (1987). Although such a case need not arise on identical facts, it must be sufficiently analogous to make pellucid to an objectively reasonable officer the unlawfulness of his actions. *See City of Escondido,* 139 S.Ct. at 504; *Ashcroft v. al-Kidd,* 563 U.S. 731, 741, 131 S.Ct. 2074, 179 L.Ed.2d 1149 (2011).

Gray v. Cummings, 917 F. 3d 1 (1st Cir. 2019)

Foreword

THIS CASEBOOK contains a selection of U. S. Court of Appeals decisions that analyze and discuss issues raised when law enforcement officers assert the affirmative defense of qualified immunity. Volume 1 of the casebook covers the District of Columbia Circuit and the First through the Fifth Circuit Court of Appeals.

On January 26, 2015, Gerald Simpson, a mentally infirmed man, was walking in the middle of Highway 12 in Kosciusko, Mississippi. Around 5:00 p.m., an individual witnessed Simpson walking and contacted the authorities. The Kosciusko Police Department responded to the dispatch call. Officer Steve Allan arrived and stopped Simpson and "asked [him] to step out of the highway." He determined that Simpson was outside the city limits and within Attala County's jurisdiction so he alerted the Attala County Sheriff's Department. Waiting for Attala County law enforcement to arrive, Officer Allan attempted to question Simpson, but he was unable to understand Simpson due to his incoherent speech. Simpson continuously pointed westward down the highway. *See Keller v. Fleming*, 952 F. 3d 216 (5th Cir. 2020).

Kosciusko Police Officer Maurice Hawthorne arrived and replaced Officer Allan, who left to respond to another call. Simpson then began to resume his walk down the highway. "Officer Hawthorne followed him in his patrol vehicle until he was able to convince Simpson to sit in the backseat of his vehicle." Simpson sat with his feet on the ground with the door still open.

Deputy Fleming of Attala County arrived on the scene, "at which point the officers purportedly decided to take Simpson to his residence, though both officers acknowledge that Simpson was still incoherent." Deputy Fleming put Simpson in the back seat of his vehicle and asked Simpson where he resided. He was unable to articulate the location of his residence and instead pointed west on Highway 12, in the direction of Durant, Mississippi. Deputy Fleming did not ask for Simpson's exact address or identification card. Based on Simpson pointing west, Deputy Fleming transported Simpson in that direction until he reached the Attala County line which was sometime after 5:00 p.m. Deputy Fleming then pulled over, opened the back door of his patrol vehicle, Simpson exited the vehicle, and Simpson continued walking toward Durant on County Road 4101, outside of Attala County's jurisdiction. "Deputy Fleming testified that there was barely enough daylight to see someone walking, but that it was not dark yet." Later that night, Simpson was struck by a vehicle and killed as he "was walking east, back toward Kosciusko."

Plaintiffs filed this wrongful death action against City of Kosciusko, Officers Allan and Hawthorne, Attala County, and Deputy Fleming. They alleged, pursuant to 42 U.S.C. § 1983, that the officers' actions violated Simpson's constitutional rights under the Fourth Amendment for wrongful seizure and the substantive due process clause of the Fourteenth Amendment. The district court granted summary judgment in favor of the City of Kosciusko and Officers Allan and Hawthorne. As to Attala County and Deputy Fleming, the court granted only partial summary judgment, finding that genuine issues of material fact existed as to Plaintiffs' constitutional claims. Deputy Fleming appealed.

Reversed — Fleming's qualified immunity defense as to Plaintiffs' Fourth Amendment claim prevails because Plaintiffs failed to prove that a reasonable officer in Fleming's position would have understood his actions violated clearly established law. *Keller v. Fleming, ibid.*

* * *

Plaintiffs bear the burden to rebut Deputy Fleming's qualified immunity defense and demonstrate that there were Fourth and Fourteenth Amendment rights that were clearly established at the time of the constitutional violation. *See, e.g., King v. Handorf,* 821 F.3d 650, 653-54 (5th Cir. 2016) (noting that a "good-faith assertion of qualified immunity alters the usual summary judgment burden of proof") (quoting *Cass v. City of Abilene,* 814 F.3d 721, 728 (5th Cir. 2016)).

In evaluating the qualified immunity defense, the familiar two-step analysis controlling our review is whether (1) "'the facts alleged show the officer's conduct violated a constitutional right'; and [(2)], 'whether the right was clearly established.'" *Trammell v. Fruge,* 868 F.3d 332, 339 (5th Cir. 2017) (quoting *Saucier v. Katz,* 533 U.S. 194, 201, 121 S.Ct. 2151, 150 L.Ed.2d 272 (2001)). [. . .]

We first "answer the constitutional violation question by determining whether the officer's conduct met the Fourth Amendment's reasonableness requirement." *See Lytle,* 560 F.3d at 410.

* * *

Plaintiffs' wrongful seizure claim implicates the Fourth Amendment's prohibition on unreasonable seizures as the basis for a constitutional violation. U.S. Const. amend. IV.

Our Fourth Amendment de novo analysis begins with whether Simpson was seized, and assuming a seizure has occurred, we then evaluate the seizure's reasonableness and the clearly established law prong. *McLin v. Ard.,* 866 F.3d 682, 691 (5th Cir. 2017) (reviewing whether a seizure occurred under the qualified immunity framework de novo); *United States v. Cooper,* 949 F.2d 737, 744 (5th Cir. 1991) (stating that "the ultimate question of the legality of the ... seizure is a question of law alone [that this court must answer]" subject to a de novo review).

Seizure. The district court determined that Simpson was seized.

Fleming's position is that the district court erroneously considered his subjective intentions of his encounter with Simpson, rather than applying an objectively reasonable standard. Irrespective of the court questioning Fleming's motive during these events, Fleming is silent on the issue of seizure. Plaintiffs, on the other hand, contend that Fleming improperly seized Simpson in placing Simpson in the back of his patrol vehicle and not allowing him to exit the car without Fleming's authority or assistance. While Fleming is correct that the court analyzes seizure using an objectively reasonable test, it is Plaintiffs who are ultimately correct.

Under the Fourth Amendment, a seizure occurs when, under the totality of the circumstances, a reasonable person would have thought he was not free to leave. *Michigan v. Chesternut,* 486 U.S. 567, 572, 108 S.Ct. 1975, 100 L.Ed.2d 565 (1988) (citation omitted). "[W]henever a police officer accosts an individual and restrains his freedom to walk away, he has seized that person." *Terry v. Ohio,* 392 U.S. 1, 16, 88 S.Ct. 1868, 20 L.Ed.2d 889 (1968) (internal quotations omitted).

Assuming the district court's version of the events to be true, Simpson's freedom of movement was restrained and a reasonable person in Simpson's position would not have felt free to leave. The officers' collective supervision and actions support this finding. Here, when Simpson tried to walk down the highway again, Officer Hawthorne followed him in his patrol car until he had to pull off because there was "no room." Once the vehicle was pulled off to the side, Officer Hawthorne persuaded Simpson to stop and sit in the backseat of his patrol car. In other words, Officer Hawthorne interrupted Simpson's path and "intercept[ed] him to prevent his progress"—which is "probably decisive" in assessing seizure. *United States v. Berry,* 670 F.2d 583, 597 (5th Cir. 1982) (blocking defendant's path at an airport constituted a seizure) (citation omitted). This is likely when the seizure began, and it likely did not end until Simpson was dropped off because as the district court stated, "Fleming [subsequently] put Simpson in the backseat of his vehicle" and drove for several miles, and finally just "pulled over and opened the door of his patrol vehicle" when he reached the county line. *Keller,* 2018 WL 615681, at *1. This is an example of a show of authority restraining Simpson's freedom to leave, triggering the Fourth Amendment. *Florida v. Bostick,* 501 U.S. 429, 434, 111 S.Ct. 2382, 115 L.Ed.2d 389 (1991). ("The encounter will not trigger Fourth Amendment scrutiny unless it loses its consensual nature ... 'Only when the officer, by means of physical force or show of authority, has in some way restrained the liberty of a citizen may we conclude that a 'seizure' has occurred.'") (quoting *Terry,* 392 U.S. at 16 n.16, 88 S.Ct. 1868).

Consequently, we affirm the district court's seizure finding.

Unreasonableness. We now determine whether this seizure was reasonable under the Fourth Amendment.

Absent probable cause, warrantless searches and seizures are presumptively invalid or "*per se* unreasonable under the Fourth Amendment—subject only to a few specifically established and well delineated exceptions." *Katz v. United States,* 389 U.S. 347, 357, 88 S.Ct. 507, 19 L.Ed.2d 576 (1967); *compare with United States v. Morris,* 477 F.2d 657, 663 (5th Cir. 1973) ("A warrantless arrest is nevertheless valid if the arresting officer has probable cause to believe that the person arrested has committed or is in the act of committing a crime."). As such, Deputy Fleming now bears the burden in proving that the seizure of question was either supported by probable cause or falls within one of the few well-delineated exceptions to the warrant requirement. *United States v. Roch,* 5 F.3d 894, 897 (5th Cir. 1993) ("While in general ... the defendant has the burden of proving ... that the material in question was seized in violation of his constitutional rights, there are several situations where the burden shifts to the government.") (citation omitted).

Here, Deputy Fleming's appellate brief is unclear as to what warrant exceptions justified the seizure of Simpson. Fleming does not contend that he had probable cause to believe that Simpson was guilty of criminal activity nor does he state that he had a reasonable suspicion of such criminal activity. He continues to rely on his subjective mindset. He also maintains that he was only giving Simpson a courtesy ride and his brief states that "Attala County Sheriff's Department has a history of offering to give pedestrians courtesy rides if there is a need for it or for their own safety." But he goes no further into how this policy or this specific courtesy ride fits within the prism of our well-delineated warrant exceptions. Therefore, Deputy Fleming did not satisfy his burden in justifying this stop because any argument to that effect was forfeited. *See Cinel v. Connick,* 15 F.3d 1338, 1345 (5th Cir. 1994) ("A party who inadequately briefs an issue is considered to have abandoned the claim.").

Accordingly, without a valid exception to the probable cause requirement, the seizure is therefore presumptively unreasonable, and a constitutional violation is present.

Clearly Established Law. Plaintiffs must still demonstrate that there was a clearly established right at the time of the challenged actions. Thus, the question becomes whether there is precedent that put Deputy Fleming on notice that he was committing a constitutional violation when he drove Simpson several miles to the county line and dropped him off.

For purposes of determining whether the right was clearly established, "[t]he relevant question ... is ... whether a reasonable officer could have believed [his or her conduct] to be lawful, in light of clearly established law and the information the ... officers possessed." *Anderson v. Creighton,* 483 U.S. 635, 641, 107 S.Ct. 3034, 97 L.Ed.2d 523 (1987). In other words, Plaintiffs must point this court to a legislative directive or case precedent that is sufficiently clear such that every reasonable official would have understood that what he is doing violates that law. *Reichle v. Howards,* 566 U.S. 658, 664, 132 S.Ct. 2088, 182 L.Ed.2d 985 (2012) (citing *Ashcroft v. al-Kidd,* 563 U.S. 731, 741, 131 S.Ct. 2074, 179 L.Ed.2d 1149 (2011)).

Here, Plaintiffs' burden is not met. Plaintiffs' clearly established law contentions in their briefing are in fact a narrative as to why Deputy Fleming's seizure was unreasonable. Plaintiffs' narrative argument is of no import of a pre-existing or precedential case. *Kovacic v. Villarreal,* 628 F.3d 209, 214 (5th Cir. 2010) ("Plaintiffs have not referenced a single case in either the district courts or the court of appeals of this circuit in which state actors were held liable for private harm caused to an individual after he was released from custody."). In turn, there is no binding Supreme Court or Fifth Circuit precedent to anchor our de novo review of whether a similarly situated officer violated a constitutional right acting under similar circumstances. *See White v. Pauly,* ___ U.S. ___, 137 S. Ct. 548, 551, 196 L.Ed.2d 463 (2017) (per curiam) ("[F]or a right to be clearly established, 'existing precedent must have placed the statutory or constitutional question beyond debate.'") (quoting *Mullenix v. Luna,* ___ U.S. ___, 136 S. Ct. 305, 308, 193 L.Ed.2d 255 (2015)). Without setting forth a clearly established right for which the analysis can continue, Plaintiffs have not defeated

Deputy Fleming's qualified immunity defense. *Cass,* 814 F.3d at 732-33 (granting qualified immunity because plaintiffs failed to show an existing precedent of the constitutional violation).

Of note, the dissent cites to *Hope v. Pelzer* for the proposition that "general statements of the law are not inherently incapable of giving fair and clear warning" and "general constitutional rule already identified in the decisional law may apply with obvious clarity to the specific conduct in question." 536 U.S. 730, 741, 122 S.Ct. 2508, 153 L.Ed.2d 666 (2002). The dissent argues that Deputy Fleming was on clear notice that the reasonableness of the seizure of Simpson would be subject to a Fourth Amendment balancing test (weighing individual intrusion against legitimate government interests). Weighing the cognizable interests of Simpson against the government interests here, the dissent's position is that the scale tips starkly in Plaintiff's favor in light of *Papachristou v. City of Jacksonville*'s holding that "anti-vagrancy" laws are void for vagueness as they permit "unfettered discretion" in seizing an individual like Simpson. 405 U.S. 156, 171, 92 S.Ct. 839, 31 L.Ed.2d 110 (1972).

Assuming that general statements (under *Hope*) may suffice, the balance of interests here are not so lopsided. As stated herein and by the district court, there is an argument for the community caretaker function (for example) which would be a legitimate government interest as to public safety. *See, supra,* Sect.III n.17 (collecting cases); *see also Keller,* 2018 WL 615681, at *5 ("[T]he initial interaction between Simpson and Deputy Fleming may have been reasonable, given the fact that Simpson possibly posed a danger to himself and the community by standing in oncoming traffic."). Because there are legitimate interests on both sides, this is not a one-sided balancing test where the officer "do[es] not have any relevant, legitimate interests to put on their side of the[] scales." *Kinney,* 367 F.3d at 372; *cf.* Sect. III n.17.

Accordingly, Deputy Fleming's qualified immunity defense as to Plaintiffs' Fourth Amendment claim prevails because Plaintiffs failed to prove that a reasonable officer like Fleming would have understood his actions violated clearly established law. Judgment is therefore rendered in Deputy Fleming's favor as he is entitled to qualified immunity on this claim.

.

DC CIRCUIT DECISIONS
The Affirmative Defense of Qualified Immunity for Law Enforcement

No cases were selected for publication.

FIRST CIRCUIT DECISIONS

The Affirmative Defense of Qualified Immunity for Law Enforcement

917 F.3d 1 (2019)

Judith GRAY, Plaintiff, Appellant,

v.

Thomas A. CUMMINGS; Town of Athol, Massachusetts, Defendants, Appellees.

No. 18-1303.

United States Court of Appeals, First Circuit.

February 22, 2019.

Gray v. Cummings, 917 F. 3d 1 (1st Cir. 2019)

Appeal from the United States District Court for the District of Massachusetts, [Hon. Timothy S. Hillman, *U.S. District Judge*], [Hon. David H. Hennessy, *U.S. Magistrate Judge*].

Matthew R. Segal, with whom Ruth A. Bourquin, American Civil Liberties Union Foundation of Massachusetts, Inc., Claudia Center, American Civil Liberties Union Foundation, Richard L. Neumeier, and p.5 Morrison Mahoney LLP, were on brief, for appellant.

David W. Ogden, Daniel S. Volchok, Alexandra Stewart, Wilmer Cutler Pickering Hale and Dorr LLP, Aaron M. Panner, Kellogg, Hansen, Todd, Figel & Frederick, P.L.L.C., Nathalie F. P. Gilfoyle, Deanne M. Ottaviano, and Jennifer Mathis on brief for American Psychiatric Association, American Psychological Association, and Judge David L. Bazelon Center for Mental Health Law, amici curiae (in support of neither party).

Thomas R. Donohue, with whom Deidre Brennan Regan, Leonard H. Kesten, and Brody, Hardoon, Perkins & Kesten, LLP, were on brief, for appellees.

Eric R. Atstupenas, Christopher J. Petrini, Peter L. Mello, and Petrini & Associates, P.C. on brief for International Municipal Lawyers Association and Massachusetts Chiefs of Police Association, Inc., amici curiae (in support of affirmance).

Pamela B. Petersen on brief for Axon Enterprise, Inc., amicus curiae (in support of affirmance).

Before KAYATTA, Circuit Judge, SOUTER,[*] Associate Justice, and SELYA, Circuit Judge.

p.4 SELYA, Circuit Judge.

This appeal arises at the intersection of constitutional law and disability-rights law. It touches upon a plethora of important issues. Some of these issues relate to the appropriateness of a police officer's use of a Taser in attempting to regain custody of a mentally ill person who, after being involuntarily committed, absconded from a hospital. Others relate to the applicability vel non of Title II of the Americans with Disabilities Act (ADA), 42 U.S.C. §§ 12131-65, to ad hoc police encounters. In the end, we decide the case on the narrowest available grounds and affirm the entry of summary judgment for the defendants.

I. BACKGROUND

This case has its genesis in an on-the-street encounter between plaintiff-appellant Judith Gray (who suffers from bipolar disorder) and Thomas Cummings, a police officer in Athol, Massachusetts (the Town). Because the case was decided below at the summary judgment stage, we must take the facts in the light most hospitable to the non-moving party (here, Gray), consistent with record support. See Houlton Citizens' Coal. v. Town of Houlton, 175 F.3d 178, 184 (1st Cir. 1999). We caution, though, that we are not obliged to credit "conclusory allegations, improbable inferences, acrimonious invective, or rank speculation." Ahern v. Shinseki, 629 F.3d 49, 54 (1st Cir. 2010).

Here, the raw facts are largely undisputed. In her deposition, Gray testified that she "really [didn't] know what happened" during the incident because she "was in a full-blown manic phase." She added that she "wouldn't know Officer Cummings if [she] fell over him" and that she had reviewed the police report prepared by Cummings and did not know whether or not it accurately described the events that had transpired. Nor did she present any other evidence contradicting Cummings's version of the relevant events. Although we recognize that juries have some leeway to "reject uncontradicted, unimpeached testimony when it is improbable, inherently contradictory, riddled with p.6 omissions, or delivered in a manner giving rise to doubts," Quintana-Ruiz v. Hyundai Motor Corp., 303 F.3d 62, 76 (1st Cir. 2002), that principle has no application here. Accordingly, we elicit many of the facts from Cummings's account. See Harriman v. Hancock County, 627 F.3d 22, 34 (1st Cir. 2010) (finding no material factual dispute when plaintiff "had no memory of being beaten by anyone at anytime relevant to this case"); see also Wertish v. Krueger, 433 F.3d 1062, 1065 (8th Cir. 2006) (deeming police officer's version of events "unrefuted" when plaintiff testified that he had very little memory of relevant events). Even so, we draw all reasonable inferences from those facts in Gray's favor.

On May 2, 2013, Gray — who was then fifty-seven years old — experienced a manic episode and called 911. Athol police officers arrived at Gray's home and transported her to Athol Memorial Hospital. She was admitted to the hospital at around 4:00 a.m., pursuant to Mass. Gen. Laws ch. 123, § 12 (authorizing involuntary "[e]mergency restraint and hospitalization of persons posing risk of serious harm by reason of mental illness"). Approximately six hours later, Gray absconded from the hospital on foot. Hospital staff called the Athol Police Department, asking that Gray — "a section 12 patient" — be "picked up and brought back."

Cummings responded to the call and quickly located Gray, walking barefoot along the sidewalk less than a quarter-mile from the hospital. Cummings got out of his police cruiser. Gray swore at him, and Cummings told her that she "ha[d] to go back to the hospital." Gray again used profanity, declared that she was not going back, and continued to walk away. In response, Cummings radioed for backup and followed Gray on foot. He repeatedly implored Gray to return to the hospital, but his importunings were greeted only by more profanity.

Initially, Cummings followed Gray at a distance of roughly one hundred feet. Within twenty-five to thirty seconds, he closed to within five feet. At that point, Gray stopped, turned around, "clenched her fists, clenched her teeth, flexed her body and stared at [Cummings] as if she was looking right through [him]." She again swore at Cummings and started walking toward him. Cummings grabbed Gray's shirt but he could feel Gray moving her body forward, so he "took her to the ground." It is undisputed that Cummings had a distinct height and weight advantage: he was six feet, three inches tall and weighed 215 pounds, whereas Gray was five feet, ten inches tall and weighed 140 pounds.

Cummings testified that once on the ground, he repeatedly instructed Gray to place her hands behind her back. She did not comply. Instead, she "tucked her arms underneath her chest and flex[ed] tightly," swearing all the while. Cummings warned Gray that she was "going to get ta[s]ed" if she did not place her hands behind her back.[1] Gray did not heed this warning but, rather, swore at Cummings again and told him to "do it." Cummings made "one last final demand [for Gray] to stop resisting" and when "Gray refused to listen," he removed the cartridge from his Taser, placed p.7 it in drive-stun mode,[2] and tased Gray's back for four to six seconds. Gray then allowed him to handcuff her.

Cummings helped Gray to her feet and called an ambulance, which transported Gray to the hospital. According to Gray, she felt "pain all over" at the moment she was tased, but she "must have passed out because [she] woke up in Emergency." Charges were subsequently filed against Gray for assault on a police officer, resisting arrest, disturbing the peace, and disorderly conduct, but were eventually dropped.

In due season, Gray sued Cummings and the Town in the federal district court. She invoked federal question jurisdiction, see 28 U.S.C. § 1331, and asserted causes of action under 42 U.S.C. § 1983 and Title II of the ADA, along with supplemental state-law claims for assault and battery, malicious prosecution, and violations of the Massachusetts Civil Rights Act (MCRA), Mass. Gen. Laws ch. 12, §§ 11H-11I. After the completion of pretrial discovery, the defendants moved for summary judgment. See Fed. R. Civ. P. 56(a). The district court referred the opposed motion to a magistrate judge. See 28 U.S.C. § 636(b)(1)(B); Fed. R. Civ. P. 72(b). Following a hearing, the magistrate judge issued a report and recommendation, suggesting that the motion be granted. Specifically, the magistrate judge found no violation of the Fourth Amendment under section 1983 on the part of either Cummings or the Town and no viable state-law claims. As to Cummings, the magistrate judge added that, in any event, he was entitled to qualified immunity. The magistrate judge further concluded that there had been no abridgement of the ADA because, regardless of Gray's disability, Cummings was entitled to employ an "appropriate level of force in response to an ongoing threat."

Gray objected to the magistrate judge's report and recommendation. See 28 U.S.C. § 636(b)(1)(C); Fed. R. Civ. P. 72(b). On de novo review, see Mercy Hosp., Inc. v. Mass. Nurses Ass'n, 429 F.3d 338, 343 (1st Cir. 2005), the district court entered a two-sentence text order adopting the magistrate judge's report and recommendation in substantial part. Because the court agreed that Cummings was entitled to qualified immunity, it declined to express any opinion on the magistrate judge's determination that "Cummings employed reasonable force under all of the circumstances."

This timely appeal followed. In addition to the parties' briefs and oral argument, we have had the benefit of able briefing by several amici.

II. ANALYSIS

We review an order granting summary judgment de novo. See Houlton Citizens' Coal., 175 F.3d at 184. "We will affirm only if the record reveals 'that there is no genuine dispute as to any material fact and the movant is entitled to judgment as a matter of law.'" Avery v. Hughes, 661 F.3d 690, 693 (1st Cir. 2011) (quoting Fed. R. Civ. P. 56(a)). Against this backdrop, we proceed to Gray's claims.

A. The Section 1983 Claims.

Section 1983 supplies a private right of action against a person who, under color of state law, deprives another of "any rights, privileges, or immunities secured by the Constitution and [federal] laws." 42 p.8 U.S.C. § 1983. To maintain a cause of action under section 1983, "the plaintiff must show a deprivation of a federally secured right." Harrington v. City of Nashua, 610 F.3d 24, 28 (1st Cir. 2010). Gray has advanced separate section 1983 claims against Cummings and the Town. We address these claims sequentially.

1. Cummings. Gray's section 1983 claim against Cummings is premised on the notion that Cummings used excessive force in effecting her arrest and, thus, violated her Fourth Amendment rights. To prevail on such a claim, "a plaintiff must show that the defendant employed force that was unreasonable under all the circumstances." Morelli v. Webster, 552 F.3d 12, 23 (1st Cir. 2009) (citing Graham v. Connor, 490 U.S. 386, 396, 109 S.Ct. 1865, 104 L.Ed.2d 443 (1989)). The degree of force to be used in any given situation is most often a judgment call, which sometimes must be made in a split second by a police officer confronted with rapidly evolving circumstances. Determining whether a particular use of force is reasonable requires consideration of the totality of the circumstances. See Graham, 490 U.S. at 396, 109 S.Ct. 1865. This consideration entails the weighing of a myriad of factors such as "the severity of the crime at issue, whether the suspect pose[d] an immediate threat to the safety of the officers or others, and whether [the suspect was] actively resisting arrest or attempting to evade arrest by flight." Id.

Our starting point is the question of whether a reasonable jury could find that Cummings violated Gray's Fourth Amendment rights through the use of excessive force. The magistrate judge answered this question in the negative, concluding that, as a matter of law, "the single deployment of a taser in drive stun mode" in these particular circumstances was reasonable. Viewing the record most hospitably to Gray and drawing all reasonable inferences to her behoof, we think that a reasonable jury could find that the force employed by Cummings violated the Fourth Amendment. We explain briefly.

The Town's policies describe a Taser in drive-stun mode as a "pain compliance tool."[3] Thus, the question reduces to whether the circumstances surrounding the confrontation between Gray and Cummings, interpreted in the light most favorable to Gray, justified Cummings's use of such a tool.

The magistrate judge analyzed this question in accordance with the Graham factors. In his view, the first factor — "the severity of the crime at issue," id. — favored Cummings because "Ms. Gray assaulted [him]." At summary judgment, though, this assessment is insupportable: it fails to view the facts in the light most favorable to Gray.

In this regard, we think it important that Cummings was not called to the scene to investigate a crime; he was there to return a person suffering from mental illness to the hospital. When the subject of a seizure has not committed any crime, the first Graham factor ordinarily cuts in the subject's favor. See Estate of Armstrong ex rel. Armstrong v. Village of Pinehurst, 810 F.3d 892, 899 (4th Cir. 2016). To be sure, Gray did not submit to Cummings's orders. Withal, this failure to obey was at most a minor crime, not one that would tip the first Graham factor in Cummings's favor. See id. at 899-900.

p.9 Nor does the alleged assault tilt the scales. In Cummings's view, the assault occurred when, after Gray walked toward him, he grabbed her shirt and she "continued pushing against [his] arm." In the circumstances of this case, we think that a reasonable jury could find that the facts did not support the characterization of Gray's actions as an "assault."

The same kind of defect mars the magistrate judge's determination that the second Graham factor — "whether the suspect poses an immediate threat to the safety of the officers or others," 490 U.S. at 396, 109 S.Ct. 1865 — favored Cummings. It is true that Gray was a section 12 patient, that is, an individual who has been involuntarily committed to a hospital pursuant to Mass. Gen. Laws ch. 123, § 12, based on a determination by a qualified medical professional (or, in emergency situations, a police officer) that "failure to hospitalize [her] would create a likelihood of serious harm by reason of mental illness." Id. § 12(a). It is also true that Cummings knew as much. Although a jury could supportably find on these facts that Cummings reasonably believed that Gray posed a danger to him, it could supportably find instead that Gray — who was shuffling down the sidewalk barefoot and unarmed — only posed a danger to herself (especially given Cummings's distinct height and weight advantage). So, too, a jury could supportably find that, at the time of the tasing, Gray had been subdued to a point at which she no longer posed a threat.

The magistrate judge concluded that the final Graham factor — whether Gray was "actively resisting arrest," 490 U.S. at 396, 109 S.Ct. 1865 — favored Cummings. This conclusion seems unimpugnable given Cummings's testimony that he asked Gray several times to put her hands behind her back, but that she would not do so.

The short of it is that the Graham factors point in conflicting directions. Seen through the prism of the totality of the circumstances, the evidence is subject to interpretation and can support plausible though inconsistent inferences. Drawing those inferences beneficially to Gray and aware that Cummings not only had her down on the ground but also outweighed her by some seventy-five pounds, a reasonable jury could find that Gray had committed no crime and that she posed no threat to Cummings when he tased her. When all is said and done, we think that Gray has presented sufficient evidence to make out a jury question as to whether Cummings used excessive force. See, e.g., Morelli, 552 F.3d at 23 (finding triable excessive force claim when officer slammed plaintiff, who "at worst, was suspected of being a petty thief," against wall); Alexis v. McDonald's Rests. of Mass., Inc., 67

F.3d 341, 353 (1st Cir. 1995) (concluding that jury could find excessive force when officer seized and dragged plaintiff to effectuate arrest for crime of trespassing in public restaurant); see also Estate of Armstrong, 810 F.3d at 906 (finding excessive force when officer tased "mentally ill man being seized for his own protection, [who] was seated on the ground, was hugging a post to ensure his immobility, ... and had failed to submit to a lawful seizure for only 30 seconds").

This conclusion does not end our inquiry. Cummings has invoked the defense of qualified immunity. Qualified immunity is a doctrine aimed at providing government officials (including police officers) a modicum of protection from civil damages liability for actions taken under color of state law. See Harlow v. Fitzgerald, 457 U.S. 800, 818, 102 S.Ct. 2727, 73 L.Ed.2d 396 (1982); McKenney v. Mangino, 873 F.3d 75, 80 (1st Cir. 2017), cert. denied, ___ U.S. ___, 138 S.Ct. 1311, 200 L.Ed.2d 475 (2018). This p.10 protection attaches "to all but the plainly incompetent or those who knowingly violate the law." Malley v. Briggs, 475 U.S. 335, 341, 106 S.Ct. 1092, 89 L.Ed.2d 271 (1986). Thus, a government official may invoke the defense of qualified immunity when his actions, though causing injury, did "not violate clearly established statutory or constitutional rights of which a reasonable person would have known." Conlogue v. Hamilton, 906 F.3d 150, 154 (1st Cir. 2018) (quoting Harlow, 457 U.S. at 818, 102 S.Ct. 2727).

The qualified immunity analysis has two facets: "[t]he court must determine whether the defendant violated the plaintiff's constitutional rights" and then must determine "whether the allegedly abridged right was 'clearly established' at the time of the defendant's claimed misconduct." Id. at 155 (quoting McKenney, 873 F.3d at 81). In this instance, we already have decided that a jury could find that Cummings violated Gray's Fourth Amendment rights. We must now determine whether the alleged right was clearly established at the time of Cummings's violation. See id. Specifically, we must ask whether, given the circumstances at hand, Gray's right to be free from the degree of force that Cummings used — particularly, the Taser — was clearly established.

This question, too, has two facets. First, the plaintiff must "identify either 'controlling authority' or a 'consensus of cases of persuasive authority' sufficient to send a clear signal to a reasonable official that certain conduct falls short of the constitutional norm." Alfano v. Lynch, 847 F.3d 71, 75 (1st Cir. 2017) (quoting Wilson v. Layne, 526 U.S. 603, 617, 119 S.Ct. 1692, 143 L.Ed.2d 818 (1999)). Second, the plaintiff must demonstrate that "an objectively reasonable official in the defendant's position would have known that his conduct violated that rule of law." Id. This latter step is designed to achieve a prophylactic purpose: it affords "some breathing room for a police officer even if he has made a mistake (albeit a reasonable one) about the lawfulness of his conduct." Conlogue, 906 F.3d at 155. Taken together, these steps normally require that, to defeat a police officer's qualified immunity defense, a plaintiff must "identify a case where an officer acting under similar circumstances was held to have violated the Fourth Amendment." City of Escondido v. Emmons, ___ U.S. ___, 139 S.Ct. 500, 504, 202 L.Ed.2d 455 (2019) (per curiam) (quoting District of Columbia v. Wesby, ___ U.S. ___, 138 S.Ct. 577, 590, 199 L.Ed.2d 453 (2018)); see Anderson v. Creighton, 483 U.S. 635, 639-40, 107 S.Ct. 3034, 97 L.Ed.2d 523 (1987). Although such a case need not arise on identical facts, it must be sufficiently analogous to make pellucid to an objectively reasonable officer the unlawfulness of his actions.[4] See City of Escondido, 139 S.Ct. at 504; Ashcroft v. al-Kidd, 563 U.S. 731, 741, 131 S.Ct. 2074, 179 L.Ed.2d 1149 (2011).

The district court determined that "the right not to be tased while offering non-violent stationary, resistance to a lawful seizure was not clearly established at the time of the confrontation between Ms. Gray and Officer Cummings" and, therefore, ruled that Cummings was entitled to qualified immunity. We examine the foundation on which this ruling rests.

p.11 We begin with Estate of Armstrong, in which the Fourth Circuit conducted a similar qualified immunity analysis. Specifically, the court considered whether the "right not to be subjected to tasing while offering stationary and non-violent resistance to a lawful seizure" was clearly established. 810 F.3d at 907. Armstrong, who suffered from bipolar disorder and paranoid schizophrenia, had absconded from the hospital to which he had been committed. See id. at 896. The police were called and located Armstrong near the hospital's main entrance. See id. Three police officers approached Armstrong, who responded by "wrapping himself around a four-by-four post that was supporting a nearby stop sign." Id. The officers attempted to pry Armstrong's arms and legs loose but were unsuccessful. See id. One of the officers then warned Armstrong that he would be tased if he did not let go of the post. See id. at 897. Armstrong did not comply, and the officer proceeded to tase him five times in drive-stun mode, over a span of approximately two minutes. See id. Even though Armstrong continued resisting, he was pried loose from the post. See id. A struggle ensued, resulting in Armstrong's demise. See id. at 897-98.

Although the court found that a jury could find the officers had used excessive force, see id. at 906, it nonetheless affirmed summary judgment in favor of the defendants. The court reasoned that even though its finding that the officers had violated Armstrong's Fourth Amendment rights was supported by precedent, the law "was not so settled [as of April 2011] such that 'every reasonable official would have understood that' tasing Armstrong was unconstitutional" under the circumstances. Id. at 908 (quoting Mullenix v. Luna, ___ U.S. ___, 136 S.Ct. 305, 308, 193 L.Ed.2d 255 (2015) (per curiam)).[5]

The Fourth Circuit's conclusion in Estate of Armstrong — that the use of a Taser in drive-stun mode against a noncompliant and resisting individual was not clearly unconstitutional as of 2011 — is not an outlier. Prior to Cummings's encounter with Gray, several other courts of appeals had found the use of a Taser reasonable in situations involving subjects who acted with a level of resistance analogous to that displayed by Gray. See, e.g., Hagans v. Franklin Cty. Sheriff's Office, 695 F.3d 505, 507 (6th Cir. 2012) (granting qualified immunity for use of Taser in drive-stun mode in 2007 when plaintiff "refused to be handcuffed," "lay down on the pavement and locked his arms tightly under his body, kicking his feet and continuing to scream"); Draper v. Reynolds, 369 F.3d 1270, 1278 (11th Cir. 2004) (finding single use of Taser in 2001 reasonable when plaintiff "used profanity, moved around and paced in agitation," and "repeatedly refused to comply with [the officer]'s verbal commands" during traffic stop). Thus, an objectively reasonable officer in Cummings's place and stead could reasonably have believed, in 2013, that the use of a Taser was generally permissible when a subject refuses to be handcuffed.

Even so, the level of force that is constitutionally permissible in dealing with a mentally ill person "differs both in degree and in kind from the use of force that would be justified against a person who has committed a crime or who poses a threat to the community." Bryan v. MacPherson, 630 F.3d 805, 829 (9th Cir. 2010). Consequently, a subject's mental illness is a factor that a police officer must take into account in determining what degree of force, if any, is appropriate. See Estate p.12 of Armstrong, 810 F.3d at 900; Champion v. Outlook Nashville, Inc., 380 F.3d 893, 904 (6th Cir. 2004). Here, however, the only thing that Cummings knew about Gray's mental health was that she had been involuntarily committed under section 12; he did not know whether Gray had been deemed a danger to others or only to herself. Given the skimpiness of this information, we think that an objectively reasonable police officer, standing in Cummings's shoes, would have had to be prepared for the worst.

Based on the body of available case law, we hold that an objectively reasonable police officer in May of 2013 could have concluded that a single use of the Taser in drive-stun mode to quell a nonviolent, mentally ill individual who was resisting arrest, did not violate the Fourth Amendment. Even if such a conclusion was constitutionally mistaken — as a jury could find on the facts of this case — Cummings is shielded by qualified immunity.

Gray demurs. She identifies two of our precedents and posits that — whether viewed singly or in combination — they evince the clearly established nature of her right to be free from tasing. Both precedents are inapposite.

The case on which Gray relies most heavily is Parker v. Gerrish, 547 F.3d 1 (1st Cir. 2008). There, the plaintiff had been stopped on suspicion of driving while intoxicated. After the plaintiff failed several sobriety tests, the officer tried to arrest him. See id. at 3-4. When the plaintiff resisted, the officer drew his Taser and ordered the plaintiff to turn around and place his hands behind his back. See id. at 4. The plaintiff complied but clasped his right wrist with his left hand. See id. Another officer approached and cuffed the plaintiff's left wrist. See id. There was substantial dispute about what happened next, but according to the plaintiff's account (to which the court was required to defer in the posture of the case), he released his right wrist, yet was tased anyway. See id. at 4-5. On these facts, we held that the police officer could be found to have violated the Fourth Amendment by tasing an unarmed suspect who, in the course of an arrest, "present[ed] no significant 'active resistance' or threat"[6] at the time of the tasing. Id. at 10-11.

The case at hand is a horse of a quite different hue. There is no indication here that Gray, despite ample opportunity to do so, ever complied with Cummings's command to put her hands behind her back. Even when Cummings warned her that she would be tased, she did not comply but, rather, continued cursing and told him to "do it."

The second case upon which Gray relies is Ciolino v. Gikas, 861 F.3d 296 (1st Cir. 2017), which involved events occurring in 2013. There, a police officer grabbed the plaintiff in a crowded street and forced him to the ground without giving him any warning. See id. at 299-300. We held that the jury could find that although the plaintiff had "disobeyed a police order," he "was not given a chance to submit peacefully to arrest before significant force was used to subdue him" and, therefore, "an 'objectively reasonable police officer' would have taken a more measured approach." Id. at 304 (quoting Raiche v. Pietroski, 623 F.3d 30, 39 (1st Cir. 2010)).

Once again, the case at hand is readily distinguishable. Cummings repeatedly told Gray that she needed to return to the hospital, and she adamantly refused to obey. What is more, he warned her that he would use his Taser if she remained intransigent, p.13 yet she defied the warning. Thus — unlike the plaintiff in Ciolino — Gray was afforded an adequate opportunity to submit to Cummings's authority before she was tased.

Gray cites a number of other cases in support of her argument that her resistance was "passive" rather than "active" and, thus, did not justify the use of the Taser. This argument is deeply flawed. Labels such as "passive" and "active" are generalizations and cannot serve as substitutes for a careful analysis of the facts of a particular case. In point of fact, the Supreme Court — in an excessive force case — recently cautioned against "defin[ing] the clearly established right at a high level of generality." City of Escondido, 139 S.Ct. at 503. There, the Court reversed a denial of qualified immunity sought by an officer who had tackled a man after he had closed the door to a dwelling despite being instructed not to do so and "tried to brush past" the officer. Id. at 502. The Court criticized the Ninth Circuit for relying on "case law [that] involved police force against individuals engaged in passive resistance" without making any "effort to explain how that case law prohibited [the officer]'s actions in this case." Id. at 503-04 (emphasis in original). And in all events, respectable authority suggests that refusing to be handcuffed constitutes active resistance and may justify the use of a Taser. See Hagans, 695 F.3d at 509 (collecting cases).

We add, moreover, that several of the cases cited by Gray involve deployment of a Taser subsequent to an initial Taser shock. See, e.g., Meyers v. Baltimore County, 713 F.3d 723, 733-34 (4th Cir. 2013); Cyrus v. Town of Mukwonago, 624 F.3d 856, 859-63 (7th Cir. 2010). Nothing of that sort happened here.[7]

In the last analysis, Gray does not cite any case, decided before her encounter with Cummings, that arose out of the use of a Taser on facts fairly comparable to the facts at hand. In the absence of either controlling authority or a consensus of persuasive authority to the contrary, we conclude that Cummings was entitled to qualified immunity.

As a fallback, Gray argues that the doctrine of qualified immunity, as expounded by the Supreme Court, should be modified or overruled. Gray did not raise this argument in the district court and, thus, cannot advance it here. See Teamsters Union, Local No. 59 v. Superline Transp. Co., 953 F.2d 17, 21 (1st Cir. 1992) ("If any principle is settled in this circuit, it is that, absent the most extraordinary circumstances, legal theories not raised squarely in the lower court cannot be broached for the first time on appeal.").

2. Town of Athol. In addition to her section 1983 claim against Cummings, Gray makes a section 1983 failure-to-train claim against the Town. She alleges that her Fourth Amendment rights were violated by the Town's deficient training of its police officers (including Cummings) with p.14 respect to proper protocols for interacting with persons suffering from mental illness. Gray's evidence, though, falls well short of making out a failure-to-train claim against the Town.

We cut directly to the chase. "Triggering municipal liability on a claim of failure to train requires a showing that municipal decisionmakers either knew or should have known that training was inadequate but nonetheless exhibited deliberate indifference to the unconstitutional effects of those inadequacies." Haley v. City of Boston, 657 F.3d 39, 52 (1st Cir. 2011). A plaintiff typically must show a "pattern of similar constitutional violations by untrained employees ... to demonstrate deliberate indifference for purposes of failure to train." Connick v. Thompson, 563 U.S. 51, 62, 131 S.Ct. 1350, 179 L.Ed.2d 417 (2011) (citing Bd. of Cty. Comm'rs of Bryan Cty. v. Brown, 520 U.S. 397, 409, 117 S.Ct. 1382, 137 L.Ed.2d 626 (1997)). Here, however, Gray has made no such showing.

In an effort to close this gap, Gray offers expert testimony about appropriate police practices for interacting with persons with disabilities. Building on this foundation, she insists that "coupled with the facts of the encounter," such evidence "create[s] questions of material fact as to whether the Town failed to properly train Cummings." In our view, these assertions are insufficient to support a failure-to-train claim. It is not enough to show that the Town's training regimen was faulty; Gray must also show that the Town knew or had reason to believe that such a regimen had unconstitutional effects. Gray has tendered no evidence of past violations sufficient to put the Town on notice of such effects. Given this yawning gap in her proof, Gray has not made out a genuine issue of material fact as to whether the Town was deliberately indifferent to the risk of the alleged constitutional violation. Consequently, her failure-to-train claim founders. See id. at 72, 131 S.Ct. 1350; Hill v. Walsh, 884 F.3d 16, 24 (1st Cir. 2018).

B. The State-Law Claims.

Gray's supplemental state-law claims need not detain us. Gray concedes that the assault and battery and MCRA claims "rise and fall with ... [her] § 1983 claim." This concession, coupled with Gray's failure to offer any developed argumentation with respect to these claims, ends our inquiry. See Torres-Arroyo v. Rullán, 436 F.3d 1, 7 (1st Cir. 2006) ("Gauzy generalizations are manifestly insufficient to preserve an issue for appellate review."). We deem waived any claim of error related to the disposition of Gray's assault and battery and MCRA claims.

The magistrate judge also granted summary judgment on Gray's malicious prosecution claim. On appeal, Gray does not challenge this ruling. Consequently, we deem the malicious prosecution claim abandoned. See United States v. Zannino, 895 F.2d 1, 17 (1st Cir. 1990) (explaining that "issues adverted to in a perfunctory manner, unaccompanied by some effort at developed argumentation, are deemed waived").

C. The ADA Claim.

There is one last hill to climb: Gray's claim against the Town under the ADA. Some background is helpful.

Congress enacted the ADA "to provide a clear and comprehensive national mandate for the elimination of discrimination against individuals with disabilities." 42 U.S.C. § 12101(b)(1). Title I proscribes disability-related discrimination in employment, see id. § 12112, and Title III proscribes disability-related discrimination in the provision of public accommodations (such as hotels, restaurants, and theaters), p.15 see id. §§ 12182, 12184. Neither of these titles is implicated here.

Title II broadly provides that "no qualified individual with a disability shall, by reason of such disability, be excluded from participation in or be denied the benefits of the services, programs, or activities of a public entity, or be subjected to discrimination by any such entity." Id. § 12132. Gray's ADA claim against the Town is rooted in this Title.

To establish a violation of Title II, a plaintiff must show:

> (1) that [s]he is a qualified individual with a disability; (2) that [s]he was either excluded from participation in or denied the benefits of some public entity's services, programs, or activities or was otherwise discriminated against; and (3) that such exclusion, denial of benefits, or discrimination was by reason of the plaintiff's disability.

Buchanan v. Maine, 469 F.3d 158, 170-71 (1st Cir. 2006) (quoting Parker v. Universidad de Puerto Rico, 225 F.3d 1, 5 (1st Cir. 2000)). A "qualified individual with a disability" is

> an individual with a disability who, with or without reasonable modifications to rules, policies, or practices, the removal of architectural, communication, or transportation barriers, or the provision of auxiliary aids and services, meets the essential eligibility requirements for the receipt of services or the participation in programs or activities provided by a public entity.

42 U.S.C. § 12131(2). In turn, the term "public entity" includes "any State or local government" as well as "any department, agency, special purpose district, or other instrumentality of a State or States or local government." Id. § 12131(1).

The Town does not gainsay either that Gray is a qualified person with a disability or that the Town is a public entity. Thus, the focal point of our inquiry is whether, during Gray's encounter with Cummings, she was "denied the benefits of [the Town's] services, programs, or activities or was otherwise discriminated against ... by reason of [her] disability." Buchanan, 469 F.3d at 170-71.

Courts have identified two general theories describing ways in which a police officer may violate the ADA in executing an arrest. The first such theory (which we shall call the "effects" theory) holds that a violation may be found when "police wrongly arrested someone with a disability because they misperceived the effects of that disability as criminal activity." Gohier v. Enright, 186 F.3d 1216, 1220 (10th Cir. 1999). The second such theory (which we shall call the "accommodation" theory) holds that a violation may be found when police officers "properly investigated and arrested a person with a disability for a crime unrelated to that disability, [but] they failed to reasonably accommodate the person's disability in the course of investigation or arrest, causing the person to suffer greater injury or indignity in that process than other arrestees." Id. at 1220-21. Before us, Gray advances arguments under both theories.[8] With respect to the "effects" theory, Gray argues that the criminal charges filed against her are an p.16 indication that Cummings misperceived her failure to follow his commands as a crime rather than a symptom of her disability. With respect to the "accommodation" theory, Gray argues that Cummings should have accommodated her disability by "employ[ing] ... time, patience, non-threatening communication, monitoring from a distance, and contacting and waiting for assistance such as an ambulance or a mental health care professional."

In mounting our inquiry, we start with the uncontroversial premise that the services, programs, and activities of a municipal police department are generally subject to the provisions of Title II of the ADA. See, e.g., Haberle v. Troxell, 885 F.3d 170, 179-80 (3d Cir. 2018); Gorman v. Bartch, 152 F.3d 907, 912 (8th Cir. 1998). Yet, three questions loom that are matters of first impression in this circuit:

- Does Title II apply to ad hoc police encounters with members of the public during investigations and arrests, and if so, to what extent?
- Assuming that Title II applies to the encounter that occurred here, may a public entity be held liable under Title II for a line employee's actions[9] on a theory of respondeat superior?
- Is proof of a defendant's deliberate indifference (as opposed to discriminatory animus) sufficient to support a plaintiff's claim for damages under Title II?

We are reluctant to plunge headlong into these murky waters. As we explain below, the answers to these questions are less than certain, and adjudicating Gray's ADA claim against the Town does not require us to run this gauntlet.

The first question asks whether and to what extent Title II of the ADA applies to ad hoc police encounters. The Fifth Circuit has held that "Title II does not apply to an officer's on-the-street responses to reported disturbances or other similar incidents, whether or not those calls involve subjects with mental disabilities, prior to the officer's securing the scene and ensuring that there is no threat to human life." Hainze v. Richards, 207 F.3d 795, 801 (5th Cir. 2000). Other circuits, though, have charted a different course, holding that Title II applies without exception to ad hoc police encounters. See, e.g., Haberle, 885 F.3d at 180 (concluding that "police officers may violate the ADA when making an arrest by failing to provide reasonable accommodations for a qualified arrestee's disability"); Bircoll v. Miami-Dade County, 480 F.3d 1072, 1085 (11th Cir. 2007) (explaining that "Title II prohibits discrimination by a public entity by reason of [plaintiff]'s disability" during investigations and arrests); see also Gohier, 186 F.3d at 1221 (stating that "a broad rule categorically excluding arrests from the scope of Title II ... is not the law"). Under this approach, exigent circumstances attendant to a police officer's decisions during an ad hoc encounter simply weigh in the balance when evaluating the reasonableness of a prospective ADA accommodation. See Haberle, 885 F.3d at 181 n.11; Bircoll, 480 F.3d at 1085-86.[10] While no circuit has found Title II of the ADA wholly inapplicable to ad hoc p.17 police encounters, the differences in approach indicate to us that we should tread cautiously. For present purposes, it is sufficient for us to assume, favorably to Gray, that Title II of the ADA applies to ad hoc police encounters (such as the encounter here) and that exigent circumstances may shed light on the reasonableness of an officer's actions.

The second question asks whether a public entity can be vicariously liable for money damages under Title II of the ADA based on the conduct of a line employee. This question arises because, in Gebser v. Lago Vista Independent School District, 524 U.S. 274, 118 S.Ct. 1989, 141 L.Ed.2d 277 (1998), the Supreme Court held that a school district could not be held liable under Title IX of the Education Amendments of 1972 "unless an official who at a minimum has authority to address the alleged discrimination and to institute corrective measures on the [district]'s behalf has actual knowledge of discrimination." Id. at 290, 118 S.Ct. 1989. Whether the rationale of Gebser should be extended to insulate public entities from liability under Title II of the ADA on a theory of respondeat superior is an open question. Compare, e.g., Duvall v. County of Kitsap, 260 F.3d 1124, 1141 (9th Cir. 2001) (stating that "public entity is liable for the vicarious acts of its employees" under Title II), with, e.g., Liese v. Indian River Cty. Hosp. Dist., 701 F.3d 334, 348-49 (11th Cir. 2012) (finding no respondeat superior liability under section 504 of Rehabilitation Act in light of Gebser).[11] For present purposes, it is sufficient for us to assume, favorably to Gray, that the Town could be held vicariously liable under Title II for Cummings's actions.

The third question asks whether a showing of deliberate indifference is enough to support recovery of money damages under Title II. Since a plaintiff must show "intentional discrimination" on the part of the public entity to be eligible for damages on a Title II claim, Nieves-Márquez v. Puerto Rico, 353 F.3d 108, 126 (1st Cir. 2003), some uncertainty exists as to whether "deliberate indifference" is the functional equivalent of "intentional discrimination." Several of our sister circuits have held that a showing of deliberate indifference may suffice to prove this element. See, e.g., Haberle, 885 F.3d at 181; Duvall, 260 F.3d at 1138. But the question is open in this circuit, and we have stated that, "under Title II, non-economic damages are only available when there is evidence 'of economic harm or animus toward the disabled.'" Carmona-Rivera v. Puerto Rico, 464 F.3d 14, 17 (1st Cir. 2006) (quoting Nieves-Márquez, 353 F.3d at 126-27). This case does not require us to parse whether our use of the word "animus" demands more than a showing of deliberate indifference, cf. S.H. ex. rel. Durrell v. Lower Merion Sch. Dist., 729 F.3d 248, 263 (3d Cir. 2013) (interpreting Nieves-Márquez as requiring "a higher showing of intentional discrimination than deliberate indifference"), particularly since the Town has not advanced such an argument. For present purposes, it is sufficient for us to assume, favorably to Gray, that deliberate indifference is the appropriate standard.

Adjudicating Grays's ADA claim against the Town does not require us to run the gauntlet of these questions. After all, we have admonished before — and today reaffirm p.18 — that "courts should not rush to decide unsettled legal issues that can easily be avoided." United States v. Gonzalez, 736 F.3d 40, 40 (1st Cir. 2013). Consistent with this prudential principle, we decline to answer any of the three questions identified above. No matter how the loaf is sliced, Gray was obliged at a bare minimum to make out a genuine issue of material fact as to Cummings's deliberate indifference to the risk of an ADA violation.

In this context, such a showing requires proof that the defendant knew that an ADA-protected right was likely to be abridged, yet neglected to take available preventative action notwithstanding such knowledge. See Haberle, 885 F.3d at 181; Duvall, 260 F.3d at 1139-40. In other words, to hold the Town vicariously liable under Title II based on Cummings's deliberate indifference, Gray would have to show that Cummings knew that Gray had a disability that required him to act differently than he would otherwise have acted, yet failed to adjust his behavior accordingly. See, e.g., Crane v. Lifemark Hosps., Inc., 898 F.3d 1130, 1136 (11th Cir. 2018); Duvall, 260 F.3d at 1140. Thus, to prevail on her version of the "effects" theory, Gray would at least have to show that Cummings knew that her failure to follow his orders was a symptom of her mental illness rather than deliberate disobedience (warranting criminal charges). Similarly, to prevail on her version of the "accommodation" theory, Gray would at least have to show that Cummings knew that there was a reasonable accommodation, which he was required to provide. Gray has not made either such showing.

To be sure, it is undisputed that Cummings knew that Gray was a section 12 patient and, thus, had a disability (specifically, that she suffered from an unspecified mental illness). See Mass. Gen. Laws ch. 123, § 12. But Gray has not shown that Cummings had any particularized knowledge about the nature or degree of Gray's disability. As we have explained, see supra Part II.A, the fact that Gray was a section 12 patient served only to put Cummings on notice that she had been deemed a danger to herself or to others. There is insufficient evidence to suggest that Cummings knew either that Gray suffered from bipolar disorder or that she was experiencing a manic episode. Without such particularized knowledge, Cummings had no way of gauging whether the conduct that appeared unlawful to him was likely to be a manifestation of the symptoms of Gray's mental illness. So, too, without such particularized knowledge, Cummings had no way of gauging what specific accommodation, if any, might have been reasonable under the circumstances.

Of course, Gray has adduced evidence that national police standards provide protocols for dealing with individuals suffering from any type of mental illness. Critically, though, Gray has not adduced any evidence showing that Cummings knew of the existence of such standards.[12] Consequently, Cummings had no way of knowing that an ADA-protected right was likely to be jeopardized by his actions.

p.19 Nor were Cummings's actions so plainly antithetic to the ADA as to obviate the knowledge requirement. See Haberle, 885 F.3d at 182. The record makes manifest that Cummings tried to talk to Gray before physically engaging with her, telling her repeatedly that she needed to return to the hospital. He followed her from a distance and did not make physical contact with her until she reversed direction and moved toward him. And in the ensuing encounter, he warned her that she would be tased if she did not put her hands behind her back and gave her several chances to comply before using the Taser (in the least intrusive mode available).

Gray has also offered evidence that in failing to wait for backup or to call an ambulance prior to approaching her, Cummings fell short of nationally recognized police standards. But as we have said, she has not shown that Cummings knew of such standards; and in all events, "falling below national standards does not, in and of itself, make the risk of an ADA violation" so obvious as to eliminate the knowledge requirement. Id.

By the same token, Gray has not offered evidence sufficient to sustain a claim of direct liability against the Town. To make out such a claim, Gray could show that the Town's "existing policies caused a failure to 'adequately respond to a pattern of past occurrences of injuries like [hers].'" Id. at 181 (quoting Beers-Capitol v. Whetzel, 256 F.3d 120, 136 (3d Cir. 2001)). Or she could show "that the risk of... cognizable harm was 'so great and so obvious'" as to override the requirement of demonstrating a pattern. Id. (quoting Beers-Capitol, 256 F.3d at 136-37). Gray has not made either showing: she has proffered no evidence of a pattern, nor has she shown an obvious risk of harm. At most, she has put forth evidence that the Town's policies failed to comply with national standards. But such a failure — without more — does not render the risk of harm so great and obvious as to excuse a failure to satisfy the pattern requirement. See id. at 182.

To this point, we have explained why Gray's claim for money damages is impuissant. But Gray's amended complaint also prays for injunctive relief. This form of redress, too, is beyond Gray's reach. Past injury, in and of itself, "is an insufficient predicate for equitable relief." Am. Postal Workers Union v. Frank, 968 F.2d 1373, 1376 (1st Cir. 1992). To have standing to pursue injunctive relief, a plaintiff must "establish a real and immediate threat" resulting in "a sufficient likelihood that [s]he will again be wronged in a similar way." Id. (quoting Los Angeles v. Lyons, 461 U.S. 95, 109, 111, 103 S.Ct. 1660, 75 L.Ed.2d 675 (1983)); see Updike v. Multnomah County, 870 F.3d 939, 948 (9th Cir. 2017), cert. denied sub nom. Multnomah County v. Updike, ___ U.S. ___, 139 S.Ct. 55, 202 L.Ed.2d 19 (2018) (finding that ADA plaintiff "lack[ed] standing to pursue his claims for injunctive relief"); Dudley v. Hannaford Bros. Co., 333 F.3d 299, 306 (1st Cir. 2003) (requiring "real and immediate threat of ongoing harm" for injunctive relief in ADA case). Gray cannot clear this hurdle. When all is said and done, it is not enough for Gray to show that because she has bipolar disorder, she is likely to encounter the police again. She must show that she is likely to be tased once more, see Lyons, 461 U.S. at 105-06, 103 S.Ct. 1660, and she has not managed any such showing.

Because there is no remedy available to Gray under Title II of the ADA, it follows that the district court did not err in entering summary judgment for the Town on Gray's ADA claim. See Carmona-Rivera, 464 F.3d at 18 (affirming summary judgment for defendants where no remedy was available to plaintiff on ADA claim).

p.20 III. CONCLUSION

We need go no further. We add only that this is a hard case — a case that is made all the more difficult because of two competing concerns: our concern for the rights of the disabled and our concern that the police not be unduly hampered in the performance of their important duties. In the end, though, we think that the protections provided by Title II of the ADA can be harmonized with the doctrines of excessive force and qualified immunity, as explicated by the Supreme Court, to achieve a result that gives each of these competing concerns their due. We think that our ruling today — which establishes in this circuit that a jury could supportably find the use of a Taser to quell a nonviolent, mentally ill person who is resisting arrest to be excessive force — satisfies this exacting standard.

Affirmed.

[*] Hon. David H. Souter, Associate Justice (Ret.) of the Supreme Court of the United States, sitting by designation.

[1] Gray testified she was told that she would be tased if she stood up. She also testified that at some point she was ordered to get to her knees, but that, due to prior injuries, she was unable to obey this order. Given Gray's repeated statements that she could not recall the details of the encounter and that she could not identify any factual inaccuracies in Cummings's police report, we find these assertions insufficient to refute Cummings's account. See Wertish, 433 F.3d at 1065.

[2] Drive-stun mode is the least intrusive setting for a Taser: it delivers only a localized impact to the target. This contrasts with probe-deployment mode, which disrupts the target's entire nervous system.

[3] This description is consistent with the descriptions found in the case law. See, e.g., Crowell v. Kirkpatrick, 400 F. App'x 592, 595 (2d Cir. 2010) (explaining that drive-stun mode "typically causes temporary, if significant, pain and no permanent injury").

[4] Sometimes, however, this requirement is relaxed. In circumstances in which a violation of rights is apparent, a plaintiff may thwart a qualified immunity defense simply by demonstrating that "the unlawfulness of the officer's conduct is sufficiently clear even though existing precedent does not address similar circumstances." City of Escondido, 139 S.Ct. at 504 (quoting Wesby, 138 S.Ct. at 590). This is not such a case.

[5] We note that Estate of Armstrong was decided in 2016 and, thus, Cummings did not have the benefit of the Fourth Circuit's decision at the time of the incident sub judice.

[6] We had no occasion in Parker to mull the implications of a qualified immunity defense. There, the officer waived any such defense. See 547 F.3d at 13.

[7] In furtherance of her argument that an objectively reasonable officer standing in Cummings's shoes would have known that the degree of force used was unreasonable, Gray argues in her reply brief that the Town has a policy against tasing someone "known to be suffering from severe mental illness." This argument is doubly waived: first, it was not advanced in the district court, see McCoy v. Mass. Inst. of Tech., 950 F.2d 13, 22 (1st Cir. 1991) ("It is hornbook law that theories not raised squarely in the district court cannot be surfaced for the first time on appeal."); and second, it was not advanced in Gray's opening brief in this court, see Sandstrom v. ChemLawn Corp., 904 F.2d 83, 86 (1st Cir. 1990) ("[B]ecause the argument ... surfac[ed] only in [appellant's] reply brief, it has been waived.").

[8] The magistrate judge concluded that "Gray's complaint very clearly proceeds solely on the basis of the second theory of liability — that is, an alleged failure to reasonably accommodate." This conclusion seems to overlook the allegation in Gray's amended complaint that the Town "brought criminal charges against [Gray] without taking her mental illness into account." Even so, any error was harmless: the magistrate judge prudently considered the merits of Gray's arguments under both the "effects" theory and the "accommodation" theory.

[9] We use the term "line employee" to describe an employee who is not involved in policymaking.

[10] The Ninth Circuit reached the same conclusion in Sheehan v. City & County of San Francisco, 743 F.3d 1211, 1232 (9th Cir. 2014). The Supreme Court granted certiorari in Sheehan in order to resolve whether Title II of the ADA "requires law enforcement officers to provide accommodations to an armed, violent, and mentally ill suspect in the course of bringing the suspect into custody." City & County of San Francisco v. Sheehan, ___ U.S. ___, 135 S.Ct. 1765, 1772, 191 L.Ed.2d 856 (2015). The Court later concluded that certiorari on this question had been improvidently granted. See id. at 1774. The Court took pains to note, though, that whether Title II "applies to arrests is an important question." Id. at 1773.

[11] As a general matter, Title II of the ADA "is to be interpreted consistently with" section 504 of the Rehabilitation Act, which prohibits disability discrimination

by entities receiving federal financial assistance. Theriault v. Flynn, 162 F.3d 46, 48 n.3 (1st Cir. 1998).

[12] For the sake of completeness, we again note that the Town has a policy, which states that Tasers should not be used against "[t]hose known to be suffering from severe mental illness." Based on this policy, it might be argued that refraining from using a Taser against Gray would have been a reasonable accommodation for her disability. It might also be argued that, in tasing Gray in contravention of the policy, Cummings exhibited deliberate indifference. The rub, though, is that Gray has not advanced any such argument either below or in her appellate briefing. "In the absence of extraordinary circumstances, none of which are apparent here, we have regularly declined to consider points which were not seasonably advanced below." Clauson v. Smith, 823 F.2d 660, 666 (1st Cir. 1987).

873 F.3d 75 (2017)

Vicki McKENNEY, individually and as next friend of Stephen McKenney, and as personal representative of the estate of Stephen McKenney, Plaintiff, Appellee,

v.

Nicholas MANGINO, Defendant, Appellant, Cumberland County et al., Defendants.

No. 17-1378.

United States Court of Appeals, First Circuit.

October 6, 2017.

McKenney v. Mangino, 873 F. 3d 75 (1st Cir. 2017)

Appeal from the United States District Court for the District of Maine, [Hon. Jon D. Levy, *U.S. District Judge*].

Peter T. Marchesi, with whom Cassandra S. Shaffer and Wheeler & Arey, P.A. were on brief, for appellant.

Jamesa J. Drake, with whom Drake Law, LLC, Amber L. Tucker, and The Law Office of Amber L. Tucker, LLC were on brief, for appellee.

Before HOWARD, Chief Judge, SELYA and LIPEZ, Circuit Judges.

p.77 SELYA, Circuit Judge.

This is a tragic case in which a man died at the hands of a police officer who was trying to do his job. The underlying suit alleges, in relevant part, that the officer violated 42 U.S.C. § 1983 through the precipitous use of deadly force. In a pretrial p.78 ruling, the district court held that the officer was not entitled to qualified immunity at the summary judgment stage. See McKenney v. Mangino, No. 2:15-cv-00073, 2017 WL 1365959, at *13 (D. Me. Apr. 12, 2017). The officer challenges that ruling. After careful consideration, we dismiss portions of this interlocutory appeal for want of appellate jurisdiction and otherwise affirm.

I. BACKGROUND

Because we are tasked with reviewing a summary judgment ruling, we rehearse the facts in the light most hospitable to the nonmovant, consistent with record support. See Foote v. Town of Bedford, 642 F.3d 80, 82 (1st Cir. 2011).

On April 12, 2014, a clear, sunny day in Windham, Maine, plaintiff-appellee Vicki McKenney called 911 at 6:14 a.m. to report that her husband, 66-year-old Stephen McKenney, was threatening suicide and had been "aggressive" and "physical" with her. She told the dispatcher that her home contained firearms. Within a matter of minutes, Windham police officers James Cook and Seth Fournier arrived at the McKenney residence and met Mrs. McKenney (who was standing outside). She explained that her husband had been experiencing severe back pain and had "snapped" that morning. Almost immediately thereafter, a Cumberland County deputy sheriff, defendant-appellant Nicholas Mangino, drove up in his cruiser to serve as backup.

The three officers entered the front room of the house at 6:22 a.m. and encountered McKenney, who appeared to have a gun in his hand. When asked what he was holding, McKenney replied ".357 Magnum." Although the officers twice directed McKenney to put the gun down, McKenney did not comply. Still, he never pointed his weapon at any of them inside the dwelling, nor did he utter anything resembling a threat.

The officers retreated outdoors, leaving McKenney inside the house. Officer Fournier placed Mrs. McKenney in his patrol car, which he then drove to a cul-de-sac at the end of the street a few hundred yards away. He maintained a clear line of sight, though, to the garage and driveway of the McKenney home. Meanwhile, the defendant, armed with his AR-15 rifle, his Taser, and pepper spray, took cover behind his cruiser (which was parked roughly 100 feet from the McKenneys' garage).[1]

The defendant peeked over his car from time to time to observe the garage and driveway, while simultaneously receiving updates about McKenney's movements from Officer Fournier. Between 6:24 a.m. and 6:31 a.m., McKenney ambled nonchalantly around and about his open garage, driveway, and house. He entered and exited the dwelling around six times during that seven-minute span. At about 6:26 a.m., McKenney left the house with his gun dangling from his hand. The defendant yelled at him three times to "drop the gun." A few seconds later, McKenney — who was approximately 100 feet away from the defendant — raised the gun over his head.[2] By all accounts, McKenney had a p.79 vacant stare and appeared "not at home" mentally. In short order, he lowered the gun without firing it and continued to weave haphazardly into and out of his house between 6:26 a.m. and 6:31 a.m.

At approximately 6:31 a.m., Officer Fournier radioed to the defendant that McKenney, who was still dangling his firearm and walking leisurely, was in front of the garage. Fournier stated: "I can't tell, but he might be pointing that, so be careful." Within seconds, McKenney began walking (still in his driveway) in the direction of the defendant's parked cruiser. He was not making any sudden or evasive movements and was not pointing his gun at anyone. Officer Fournier alerted the defendant that McKenney was "walking toward your car right now." When McKenney had reached a point 69 feet away from the cruiser, the defendant fired an errant shot at McKenney's central mass. Seconds later, he fired a second shot at McKenney's head, which struck and killed McKenney. None of the officers had warned McKenney that they would use deadly force if he refused to drop his weapon.

We fast-forward to February of 2015, when Mrs. McKenney, qua plaintiff, suing individually and as the personal representative of McKenney's estate, brought a civil action in a Maine state court against the defendant and several other persons and entities.[3] As relevant here, the plaintiff sued the defendant under 42 U.S.C. § 1983, which authorizes suit against any person who, while acting under color of state law, violates another person's federally assured constitutional or statutory rights. See Kalina v. Fletcher, 522 U.S. 118, 123, 118 S.Ct. 502, 139 L.Ed.2d 471 (1997). Specifically, the plaintiff's complaint alleged that the defendant's use of deadly force transgressed McKenney's Fourth Amendment right to be free from unreasonable seizures.

The action was seasonably removed to the federal district court. See 28 U.S.C. §§ 1331, 1441(a). Following pretrial discovery, the defendant sought summary judgment on, inter alia, qualified immunity grounds. See Fed. R. Civ. P. 56(a).

The district court denied the motion. Construing the record in the light most favorable to the plaintiff, the court ruled that a rational jury could find that it was unreasonable for the defendant to believe that McKenney "posed an immediate threat to the safety of the [defendant] or others at the time he was shot." McKenney, 2017 WL 1365959, at *12. In explaining this ruling, the court noted that at the time of the shooting, McKenney was ambulating nonchalantly around his driveway with his gun dangling by his side and was nearly 70 feet away from the defendant's cruiser. See id. By the time the defendant pulled the trigger, it had been approximately six minutes since the defendant thought he had seen McKenney pointing the gun at him. See id. Viewing the facts in the requisite light, the court concluded that a rational jury could find that the defendant "had ample opportunity to observe [McKenney's] actions and movements over the course of several minutes, and acted with knowledge of all of the relevant circumstances." Id. Other facts, such as McKenney's suicidality, the fact p.80 that the last order directing him to drop his weapon had come approximately six minutes earlier, and the fact that no one had ever warned McKenney that deadly force would be used if he failed to comply with the officers' orders, "militate[d] against the reasonableness" of the defendant's use of deadly force. Id. In a nutshell, the court below held that on the plaintiff's supportable version of the facts, an objectively reasonable police officer would have understood, at the moment the shot was fired, that employing deadly force against McKenney would contravene clearly established law. See id. at *12-13.

This appeal ensued. Notwithstanding the general prohibition against interlocutory appeals, see 28 U.S.C. § 1291, the defendant asserts that we have jurisdiction because his appeal rests on a denial of qualified immunity and his arguments are purely legal. See Johnson v. Jones, 515 U.S. 304, 319-20, 115 S.Ct. 2151, 132 L.Ed.2d 238 (1995); Camilo-Robles v. Hoyos, 151 F.3d 1, 8 (1st Cir. 1998).

II. ANALYSIS

A district court may only grant summary judgment when the record, construed in the light most congenial to the nonmovant, presents no genuine issue as to any material fact and reflects the movant's entitlement to judgment as a matter of law. See Fed. R. Civ. P. 56(a); Schiffmann v. United States, 811 F.3d 519, 524 (1st Cir. 2016). We review rulings granting or denying summary judgment de novo. See DePoutot v. Raffaelly, 424 F.3d 112, 117 (1st Cir. 2005).

Subject to only a handful of carefully circumscribed exceptions, our appellate jurisdiction is restricted to review of final orders and judgments. See Johnson, 515 U.S. at 309-10, 115 S.Ct. 2151. Consequently, an interlocutory order denying summary judgment is typically not appealable when first entered. See 28 U.S.C. § 1291; Plumhoff v. Rickard, ___ U.S. ___, 134 S.Ct. 2012, 2018, 188 L.Ed.2d 1056 (2014).

But an exception to the general requirement of finality is potentially applicable here. Qualified immunity is a doctrine that shelters government officials from civil damages liability "insofar as their conduct does not violate clearly established statutory or constitutional rights of which a reasonable person would have known." Harlow v. Fitzgerald, 457 U.S. 800, 818, 102 S.Ct. 2727, 73 L.Ed.2d 396 (1982). Courts long have recognized that qualified immunity consists of both an immunity from suit and an immunity from damages. See Mitchell v. Forsyth, 472 U.S. 511, 526, 105 S.Ct. 2806, 86 L.Ed.2d 411 (1985). Thus, claims of qualified immunity ought to be resolved at the earliest practicable time. See Anderson v. Creighton, 483 U.S. 635, 646 n.6, 107 S.Ct. 3034, 97 L.Ed.2d 523 (1987). Consistent with this principle, we have held that, notwithstanding the absence of a final judgment, we have jurisdiction to review interlocutory rulings implicating qualified immunity as long as those rulings are purely legal in nature (say, a ruling that a given body of facts will support a claimed violation of clearly established law). See Stella v. Kelley, 63 F.3d 71, 74 (1st Cir. 1995) (citing Johnson, 515 U.S. at 316-17, 115 S.Ct. 2151). But we may not review, on interlocutory appeal, an order denying qualified immunity "to the extent that [the order] turns on either an issue of fact or an issue perceived by the trial court to be an issue of fact." Id. By virtue of this prohibition, we lack jurisdiction to consider a defendant's argument "that the facts asserted by the plaintiffs are untrue, unproven, warrant a different spin, tell only a small part of the story, and are presented out of p.81 context." Díaz v. Martínez, 112 F.3d 1, 5 (1st Cir. 1997).

It follows that defendants who invoke our limited power of interlocutory review to redress denials of qualified immunity must be prepared to accept the facts in the light most favorable to the plaintiff and "develop the argument that, even drawing all the inferences as the district court concluded a jury permissibly could, they are entitled to judgment as a matter of law." Cady v. Walsh, 753 F.3d 348, 359-60 (1st Cir. 2014). In other words, an appellant must explain why he is entitled to qualified immunity even if one assumes that the district court properly analyzed the facts.[4] See id. at 361; see also Morse v. Cloutier, 869 F.3d 16, 25 (1st Cir. 2017).

Having erected this jurisdictional framework, we turn next to the qualified immunity standard. When a defendant invokes qualified immunity, an inquiring court typically engages in a "two-step pavane." Alfano v. Lynch, 847 F.3d 71, 75 (1st Cir. 2017). First, the court must determine "whether the plaintiff's version of the facts makes out a violation of a protected right." Id. Second, the court must determine "whether the right at issue was 'clearly established' at the time of defendant's alleged misconduct." Id. (quoting Matalon v. Hynnes, 806 F.3d 627, 633 (1st Cir. 2015)). This second step is itself divisible into two components. To begin, the plaintiff must point to "'controlling authority' or a 'consensus of cases of persuasive authority'" that broadcasts "a clear signal to a reasonable official that certain conduct falls short of the constitutional norm." Id. at 76 (quoting Wilson v. Layne, 526 U.S. 603, 617, 119 S.Ct. 1692, 143 L.Ed.2d 818 (1999)). Then, the court must evaluate "whether an objectively reasonable official in the defendant's position would have known that his conduct violated that rule of law." Id. These inquiries are carried out with the understanding that qualified immunity is meant to shield "all but the plainly incompetent or those who knowingly violate the law." White v. Pauly, ___ U.S. ___, 137 S.Ct. 548, 551, 196 L.Ed.2d 463 (2017) (per curiam) (quoting Mullenix v. Luna, ___ U.S. ___, 136 S.Ct. 305, 308, 193 L.Ed.2d 255 (2015) (per curiam)).

Before proceeding further, we lay the relevant constitutional foundation. Here, the background law is supplied by the Fourth Amendment, which guarantees "[t]he right of the people to be secure in their persons, houses, papers, and effects, against unreasonable searches and seizures." U.S. Const. amend. IV. A police officer's use of deadly force is deemed a seizure under the Fourth Amendment, and such an extreme action is reasonable (and, therefore, constitutional) only when "at a minimum, a suspect poses an immediate threat to police officers or civilians." Jarrett v. Town of Yarmouth, 331 F.3d 140, 149 (1st Cir. 2003) (per curiam) (citing Tennessee v. Garner, 471 U.S. 1, 11, 105 S.Ct. 1694, 85 L.Ed.2d 1 (1985)).

Timing is critically important in assessing the reasonableness of an officer's decision to use lethal force. Our case law is "comparatively generous" to officers facing "potential danger, emergency conditions or other exigent circumstances," and p.82 we have fashioned "a fairly wide zone of protection" for the police in borderline cases. Roy v. Inhabitants of City of Lewiston, 42 F.3d 691, 695 (1st Cir. 1994) (citing Graham v. Connor, 490 U.S. 386, 396-97, 109 S.Ct. 1865, 104 L.Ed.2d 443 (1989)); see Berube v. Conley, 506 F.3d 79, 85 (1st Cir. 2007). But that zone of protection has shifting boundaries. Everything depends on context, and the use of deadly force, even if "reasonable at one moment," may "become unreasonable in the next if the justification for the use of force has ceased." Lytle v. Bexar Cty., 560 F.3d 404, 413 (5th Cir. 2009). Put another way, "[a] passing risk to a police officer is not an ongoing license to kill an otherwise unthreatening suspect." Abraham v. Raso, 183 F.3d 279, 294 (3d Cir. 1999).

Among other things, a suspect's physical proximity and the speed of his movements are highly relevant to this inquiry. See Kirby v. Duva, 530 F.3d 475, 482-83 (6th Cir. 2008); Walker v. City of Orem, 451 F.3d 1139, 1160-61 (10th Cir. 2006). When feasible, a police officer must give some sort of warning before employing deadly force. See Garner, 471 U.S. at 11-12, 105 S.Ct. 1694; see also Young v. City of Providence ex rel. Napolitano, 404 F.3d 4, 23 (1st Cir. 2005) (concluding that officer violated Fourth Amendment by firing "extraordinarily quickly" and without "adequate warning" at armed man whose gun was "pointed downwards"). Moreover, federal courts have afforded a special solicitude to suicidal individuals in lethal force cases when those individuals have resisted police commands to drop weapons but pose no real security risk to anyone other than themselves. See Weinmann v. McClone, 787 F.3d 444, 450 (7th Cir. 2015) (collecting appellate precedents holding that, as of 2007, clearly established law prevented police officers from employing "deadly force against suicidal people unless they threaten harm to others"); Mercado v. City of Orlando, 407 F.3d 1152, 1160-61 (11th Cir. 2005) (similar).

Here, the defendant concentrates on the second step of the qualified immunity paradigm and faults the district court for failing to identify a sufficiently similar case that would have served to place him on notice that his use of deadly force violated clearly established Fourth Amendment law.[5] In his view, the contours of the relevant Fourth Amendment law were so blurred at the time that he shot McKenney that he is deserving of qualified immunity. We have jurisdiction to consider this purely legal asseveration. See Johnson, 515 U.S. at 316-17, 115 S.Ct. 2151; Morse, 869 F.3d at 24.

Jurisdiction notwithstanding, this argument lacks force. Although the district court frankly acknowledged that it could not find "[a] case presenting a nearly identical alignment of facts," McKenney, 2017 WL 1365959, at *9, such an exacting degree of precision is not required to thwart a qualified immunity defense.

To be sure, "the clearly established law" employed in a qualified immunity analysis "must be particularized to the facts of the case." White, 137 S.Ct. at 552 (internal quotation marks omitted). This instruction fits hand in glove with the Supreme Court's warning that, when dealing with qualified immunity, we should not over-rely on precedents that are "cast at a high level of generality." Brosseau v. Haugen, 543 U.S. 194, 199, 125 S.Ct. 596, 160 L.Ed.2d 583 (2004) (per curiam). Even so, there need not be "a case directly on point" to satisfy the second step of the p.83 qualified immunity paradigm. Ashcroft v. al-Kidd, 563 U.S. 731, 741, 131 S.Ct. 2074, 179 L.Ed.2d 1149 (2011); see Anderson, 483 U.S. at 640, 107 S.Ct. 3034; Limone v. Condon, 372 F.3d 39, 48 (1st Cir. 2004). The test is whether existing case law has "placed the statutory or constitutional question beyond debate." al-Kidd, 563 U.S. at 741, 131 S.Ct. 2074. In some cases, "a general constitutional rule already identified in the decisional law may apply with obvious clarity to the specific conduct in question." United States v. Lanier, 520 U.S. 259, 271, 117 S.Ct. 1219, 137 L.Ed.2d 432 (1997). What counts is whether precedents existing at the time of the incident "establish the applicable legal rule with sufficient clarity and specificity to put the official on notice that his contemplated course of conduct will violate that rule." Alfano, 847 F.3d at 76; see Tolan v. Cotton, ___ U.S. ___, 134 S.Ct. 1861, 1866, 188 L.Ed.2d 895 (2014) (per curiam); Hope v. Pelzer, 536 U.S. 730, 741, 122 S.Ct. 2508, 153 L.Ed.2d 666 (2002).

The Court's landmark decisions in Graham and Garner, which articulate generalized standards for excessive force liability under the Fourth Amendment, "do not by themselves create clearly established law outside an obvious case." White, 137 S.Ct. at 552 (internal quotation marks omitted). But taking the facts and the reasonable inferences therefrom in the light most favorable to the plaintiff, the threat presented lacked immediacy and alternatives short of lethal force remained open. Seen in that light, this was a case in which the feasibility of a more measured approach was apparent. Moreover, the district court did precisely what the Supreme Court has instructed courts to do: it focused on "the specific context of the case." Brosseau, 543 U.S. at 198, 125 S.Ct. 596 (internal quotation marks omitted). With that context in mind, it relied on well-settled precedents addressing the lawfulness of using deadly force against an individual who was suicidal, armed, slow in gait, some distance away from the officer, and had received no commands or warnings for several minutes. See McKenney, 2017 WL 1365959, at *9-11. We conclude, without serious question, that the precedents identified by the district court and those discussed supra gave the defendant fair warning that, if the facts were as the plaintiff claimed them to be, his use of deadly force against McKenney offended clearly established Fourth Amendment law — and an objectively reasonable officer would have realized as much. Therefore, the district court properly concluded that the absence of a precedent on all fours was not dispositive.

In an effort to dull the force of this reasoning, the defendant makes a series of factbound arguments. Most notably, the defendant repeatedly insists — contrary to the inferences drawn by the district court — that he reasonably perceived McKenney as an imminent danger at the time of the shooting, such that he was left with no real choice but to fire his weapon. In turn, he urges reversal in light of evidence that he maintains the district court either overlooked or insufficiently considered. These facts include data points such as that McKenney had ignored police commands to drop his loaded weapon, had at one time raised his gun, and was approaching the defendant (and the unarmed civilian in the defendant's cruiser) at the time he was shot.

But there is a rub: the defendant's characterization of the summary judgment record collides head-on with the district court's synthesis of the facts. The defendant either ignores or gives unduly short shrift to evidence that was central to the district court's conclusion that, on the version of the facts most hospitable to the plaintiff, the defendant had "ample opportunity p.84 to observe [McKenney's] actions and movements" before pulling the trigger and that the defendant's decision to shoot McKenney was "unreasonably precipitous." McKenney, 2017 WL 1365959, at *12-13. These facts include McKenney's suicidality, the slowness of his gait, the clear visibility, the fact that six minutes had elapsed since any officer had last ordered McKenney to drop his weapon, the fact that nobody had warned McKenney that deadly force would be used if he failed to follow police commands, and the six-minute gap between when McKenney raised his gun skywards and when the defendant pulled the trigger. Rather than accept arguendo that McKenney never came close to pointing his gun in the defendant's direction, the defendant devotes much sound and fury to the proposition that he reasonably perceived McKenney to be aiming his weapon at him. In short, the defendant has woven factbound arguments regarding both the immediacy of the threat posed by McKenney and the feasibility of less drastic action into the warp and woof of his challenge to the district court's qualified immunity analysis. Such an intertwining of disputed issues of fact and cherry-picked inferences, on the one hand, with principles of law, on the other hand, places these arguments beyond our jurisdictional reach on interlocutory appeal. See Cady, 753 F.3d at 359-60; cf. Whitfield v. Meléndez-Rivera, 431 F.3d 1, 8 (1st Cir. 2005) (concluding that the question of whether a suspect appeared threatening before officer employed lethal force was properly resolved by the jury).

To sum up, the precedents make pellucid that the most relevant factors in a lethal force case like this one are the immediacy of the danger posed by the decedent and the feasibility of remedial action. See Garner, 471 U.S. at 11-12, 105 S.Ct. 1694; Whitfield, 431 F.3d at 8; Young, 404 F.3d at 23. Taking the facts in the light most amiable to the plaintiff (as the law required it to do), the district court concluded that a rational jury could reasonably infer both that McKenney did not pose an imminent threat and that viable remedial measures had not been exhausted. The court also concluded that these facts should have been obvious to an objectively reasonable officer in the defendant's position. Although the defendant invites us to adopt a spin on the summary judgment record different from that taken by the district court, we lack jurisdiction to accept that invitation under Johnson and its progeny. See Goguen v. Allen, 780 F.3d 437, 455-56 (1st Cir. 2015) (dismissing appeal for lack of jurisdiction when "defendants repeatedly ignore[d] evidence, and reasonable inferences therefrom" on which the court below premised its interlocutory denial of qualified immunity); Penn v. Escorsio, 764 F.3d 102, 110 (1st Cir. 2014) (dismissing appeal from interlocutory denial of qualified immunity after "peel[ing] away the facade by which" defendants portrayed "purely factual disputes" as legal arguments); Cady, 753 F.3d at 361 (concluding similarly when defendant failed to concede arguendo that the court below "was correct in its determinations regarding what inferences were permissible on the summary judgment record"); Díaz, 112 F.3d at 5 (dismissing appeal for lack of jurisdiction when defendant merely attempted to take "a different spin" on the facts). Accordingly, we dismiss the defendant's factbound challenges to the district court's order for lack of jurisdiction.

III. CONCLUSION

We need go no further. For the reasons elucidated above, we dismiss the appeal in part for want of appellate jurisdiction and otherwise affirm the district court's denial of summary judgment. Costs shall be taxed in favor of the plaintiff.

p.85 Of course, our words here are not the end of the matter. The pretrial denial of qualified immunity is but "a way station in the travel of a case." Camilo-Robles, 151 F.3d at 9. Depending on the facts proven at trial and the inferences drawn by the jury, the defendant may or may not ultimately prevail on his qualified immunity defense.[6] We hold today simply that the defendant's purely legal challenge is devoid of merit and that his factbound arguments are inappropriate for interlocutory appeal.

So Ordered.

[1] For the sake of completeness, we note that Zachary Welch, a civilian who had been invited by the defendant as a ride-along, was crouched in the defendant's parked cruiser.

[2] At his deposition, the defendant testified that he believed that McKenney was pointing the weapon in his direction. Because we are reviewing a summary judgment ruling, however, we recount the facts in the light most favorable to the nonmovant (here, the plaintiff). See Foote, 642 F.3d at 82. The district court seems to have assumed the truth of the fact that the defendant "reasonably believed" that McKenney "had pointed his gun at him." McKenney, 2017 WL 1365959, at *12. Any such assumption was, of course, made only for the sake of argument; otherwise, it would have been unwarranted. The court was obliged to view the summary judgment record in the light most hospitable to the plaintiff. See Foote, 642 F.3d at 82.

[3] Given the narrowly circumscribed scope of this interlocutory appeal, it would serve no useful purpose to enumerate the other parties and causes of actions limned in the complaint.

[4] The Supreme Court has carved out an isthmian exception to this rule, instructing courts to disregard the nonmovant's version of the facts if that version is "blatantly contradicted by the record." Scott v. Harris, 550 U.S. 372, 380, 127 S.Ct. 1769, 167 L.Ed.2d 686 (2007); see Penn v. Escorsio, 764 F.3d 102, 105 n.2 (1st Cir. 2014). Here, however, the defendant does not argue that this exception applies and, in all events, the record belies its applicability.

[5] In this appeal, the defendant does not challenge the district court's finding of a constitutional violation at step one of the qualified immunity paradigm.

[6] We recognize that the defendant faced a challenging situation. On this scumbled record, though, it is for the jury to decide whether McKenney presented a sufficiently serious and imminent threat, such that the defendant's ultimate decision to use lethal force was objectively reasonable or, at least, belongs within the "zone of protection" afforded to police officers in borderline cases. Roy, 42 F.3d at 695.

SECOND CIRCUIT DECISIONS
The Affirmative Defense of Qualified Immunity for Law Enforcement

921 F.3d 48 (2019)

John MARA, Plaintiff-Appellee,
v.
Stephen RILLING, Edward Nook, Frederick Hine, Defendants-Appellants,
Gary MacNamara, Michael Gagner, Antonio Granata, Jason Takacs, Town of Fairfield, Fairfield University, Patrick Cleary, Defendants.[*]

No. 17-3326-cv August Term 2018.

United States Court of Appeals, Second Circuit.

Argued: September 5, 2018.

Decided: April 9, 2019.

Mara v. Rilling, 921 F. 3d 48 (2nd Cir. 2019)

On Appeal from the United States District Court for the District of Connecticut.

On interlocutory appeal from an order denying summary judgment entered in the United States District Court for the District of Connecticut (Chatigny, J.), defendants contend that they are entitled to qualified immunity from plaintiff's suit charging them with violating the United States Constitution and Connecticut state law in investigating and arresting plaintiff for assaulting a guest at a college New Year's Eve party. Defendants prevail because (1) plaintiff was not under arrest when interviewed by police on January 2, 2013, and, thus, police did then not need probable cause to question him; (2) probable cause for plaintiff's February 22, 2013 arrest warrant was established by a non-defective eyewitness identification without regard to plaintiff's allegedly coerced statements; (3) plaintiff's statements not being necessary to establish probable cause, he cannot claim their use in violation of the Fifth Amendment; and (4) the police procedures used at plaintiff's interview were not so egregious or shocking as to violate Fourteenth Amendment due process or to support a state claim for intentional infliction of emotional distress.

REVERSED.

Thomas Gerarde, Esq., Howd & Ludorf, LLC, Hartford, Connecticut, for Defendants-Appellants.

Andrew Bruce Bowman, Esq., Westport, Connecticut, for Plaintiff-Appellee.

Before: Sack, Raggi, and Chin, Circuit Judges.

p.55 Reena Raggi, Circuit Judge:

Plaintiff John Mara ("Mara") sued Fairfield, Connecticut police officials Stephen Rilling, Edward Nook, and Frederick Hine (appellants here) as well as other members of that police department and the Fairfield University Security Office, for alleged violations of the Constitution and state law in connection with a 2013 investigation that led to Mara being criminally charged with assault and disturbing the peace, charges that were eventually dismissed. Specifically, Mara sued defendants for false arrest, coercive interrogation, and malicious prosecution in violation of the Fourth, Fifth, and Fourteenth Amendments, *see* 42 U.S.C. § 1983, as well as for parallel state law claims of false arrest, false imprisonment, malicious prosecution, and intentional infliction of emotional distress. Defendants Rilling, Nook, and Hine here appeal from that part of an order entered in the United States District Court for the District of Connecticut (Robert Chatigny, *Judge*) on September 30, 2017, which denied them summary judgment based on p.56 qualified immunity. *See Mara v. MacNamara,* No. 14-cv-1095, 2017 WL 4368612 (D. Conn. Sept. 30, 2017).[1]

For the reasons stated herein, we conclude that the record, viewed most favorably to Mara, demonstrates defendants' entitlement to qualified immunity as a matter of law because (1) Mara was not under arrest when initially interviewed by the police on January 2, 2013, and, thus, police did not then require probable cause to question him; (2) probable cause for the February 22, 2013 warrant authorizing Mara's arrest was established by a non-defective eyewitness identification without regard to Mara's allegedly coerced statements; (3) Mara's statements not being necessary to establish probable cause, he cannot claim their use in violation of the Fifth Amendment; and (4) the police procedures employed during Mara's interview were not so egregious or shocking as to violate Fourteenth Amendment due process or to support a claim for intentional infliction of emotional distress. Accordingly, we reverse the challenged order, and direct the entry of judgment in favor of defendants.

BACKGROUND

Because Mara claims that police acted unlawfully—even shockingly—in conducting the investigation leading to his arrest and prosecution, we discuss that conduct in some detail preliminary to explaining why Mara's claims fail. The following facts are undisputed or viewed in the light most favorable to Mara.

I. The Blackman Assault and Initial Investigation

In the course of a 2012 New Year's Eve party held at a private home in Fairfield, Connecticut, and attended mostly by vacationing college students, someone hit Philip Blackman in the head with a large bottle, fracturing his skull and causing a severe brain hemorrhage.

While Blackman was undergoing surgery on the morning of January 1, 2013, his father reported the attack to Fairfield police, prompting defendants Rilling and Nook to respond to St. Vincent Hospital. The detectives there spoke with three of Blackman's friends—Dennis DePalmer, Dan Langlais, and James Hansen—who stated that, at about 12:30 a.m., they had seen unknown persons shoving Blackman out of the house where the party was being held. Langlais went to his friend's aid, but when the fracas ended, Blackman was lying on the ground unconscious. None of the three friends had direct knowledge of how Blackman was injured. They could report only that they had heard "[s]omeone" at the party state that Blackman had been hit over the head with a bottle by "Jack Mara," the plaintiff, who was then a senior at Fairfield University. App'x 404-05.

Rilling and Nook then proceeded to 1027 Fairfield Beach Rd., the site of the party, and spoke with its host, Rachel Chase. Chase told the detectives that various uninvited persons had arrived during the party and that things had gotten out of hand, with someone whom she did not know being hit over the head with a bottle.

p.57 At the Chase residence, the detectives also spoke with David O'Brien. He reported attending the prior night's party with his brother Darren. Darren had recovered the black Freixenet champagne bottle used to hit Blackman, which David O'Brien produced for the police later that day. Meanwhile, David O'Brien stated that another party guest, Luke Kazmierczak, had actually witnessed the Blackman assault.

Later on January 1, Darren O'Brien went to the Fairfield police station where he told Rilling that, at the prior night's party, shortly after midnight, he observed an altercation among people he did not know. At some point, he saw a champagne bottle roll on the ground and heard people yelling that someone had been hit with the bottle. Seeing Blackman, a friend of his brother David's, lying on the ground, Darren O'Brien grabbed the bottle and gave it to his brother for safe keeping. Darren O'Brien told Rilling that his friend, Luke Kazmierczak, had witnessed Blackman's assault and that Kazmierczak and the O'Brien brothers had given chase when the assailant started running from the party down Fairfield Beach Rd. On that road, the O'Briens and Kazmierczak encountered a group of men walking toward the party. One man was shirtless, and Kazmierczak identified him to the O'Briens as the person who had hit Blackman with a bottle.

On January 1, Kazmierczak, a student at the University of Wisconsin, came to the Fairfield police station and confirmed that he had seen the prior night's assault on Blackman. He described the assailant as a white male in his 20s, with short, dark hair, who ran east on Fairfield Beach Rd. towards Reef Rd. As Kazmierczak and the O'Brien brothers gave chase, they saw persons walking toward the party. Kazmierczak recognized one of the men—who was shirtless, highly intoxicated, and acting out of control—as Blackman's assailant. Shown a six-photo array that included Mara's four-year old freshman photograph, Kazmierczak identified another individual as Blackman's assailant, reporting 70% certainty. Police contacted that person and determined that he was not at the Chase party.

II. Mara's Police Interview

On the evening of January 1, Mara's mother called the Fairfield police to report that her son was receiving threatening text messages from Blackman's friends, accusing him of committing the New Year's Eve assault. Mara then also spoke with Rilling, and the two agreed to meet at the Fairfield police station the next day at 5:00 p.m. Prior to the meeting, William Heller, an attorney for Mara's father, called Rilling. Rilling told Heller that the police viewed Mara as a witness, not a target, and that Mara did not need an attorney at the meeting. Heller told Rilling that Mara's father would likely accompany his son to the meeting.

On January 2, rather than wait for Mara to come to the police station, Rilling, Nook, and their supervisor, defendant Sergeant Hine, went to Fairfield University at approximately 4:00 p.m., deciding it would be to their advantage to interview Mara there. The officers were dressed in plain clothes and, although armed, none ever displayed a weapon in dealing with Mara that day. As Mara emerged from class, he saw police cars parked behind his own vehicle. Defendants, along with University Safety Officer Patrick Cleary, approached Mara and asked if they could speak with him on campus rather than later at the police station. Mara agreed, traveling to the university's Public Safety Office in p.58 Cleary's vehicle.[2] Defendants told Cleary not to let Mara use his cell phone en route.[3]

At the Public Safety Office, Mara was interviewed in a small room, with Rilling and Nook at a table and Mara seated in a corner. Hine observed the interview on a computer in an adjacent room. The entire exchange lasted approximately one hour and twenty minutes and was videotaped. The tape shows that Mara was never restrained or subjected to any physical force during the interview and that he and the officers maintained calm demeanors throughout.

At the outset, defendants obtained basic pedigree information and photographed Mara—explaining that "so many people" were at the New Year's Eve party under investigation that "we're just taking a picture of everybody." App'x 353.[4] Rilling then advised Mara that he did not have to talk with the officers and could leave at any time.[5] Mara indicated that he understood. At no time thereafter did Mara decline to answer questions or seek to leave.

Asked to recount what he had heard about the events of New Year's Eve, Mara stated that he had "heard that a kid got knocked out, with maybe a beer bottle," but professed not to know much about the assault except that the victim's friends "were really upset that night [be]cause they thought that I [*i.e.,* Mara] did it." *Id.* at 354-55. Mara said that why they thought he did it "is beyond me." *Id.*

Mara told police that he first learned that he was the suspected assailant when he was leaving the party, at which time other partygoers came up to Mara, his older brother Sean, and three friends, "[g]etting in our face, saying that I did it" and was "dead." *Id.* at 355-56.[6] Sean Mara tried to defuse the situation, assuring the accusers that his brother "had nothing to do with" the assault. *Id.* Mara acknowledged that he was himself "yelling back" at the crowd, which got his brother "really... upset." *Id.* at 355. Eventually, Mara and his friends walked away, going to a friend's house.

Mara told defendants that he, his brother, and their friends had arrived at the party around 1:00 a.m., and remained only about twenty minutes. Mara stated that he had already had "a lot" to drink at an earlier party and at a local bar. *Id.* at 357. He had no recollection of seeing an argument at the party, explaining that "[e]ven when my brother said that to me. I um, I don't know, I don't remember it.... I don't know if it's because I drank so much, but I just don't remember it." *Id.* at 358. Mara stated that it was only the next day, p.59 in speaking with his roommate, that he learned that "this kid Phil," whom Mara had met "once or twice," had been hit with a bottle, and that Phil's friends, who thought Mara had done it, were asking for his cell phone number and the kind of car he drove in order to "vandalize" it. *Id.* at 359. Mara insisted he had "no idea" how he came to be suspected of the assault, *id.* at 363, a position he maintained throughout the interview. Specifically, he did not know "how someone could think that it was me if the kid was knocked out before I even got to that house. How my name was brought into it with all these kids there, I don't know." *Id.* at 362.

At about that time—some twenty minutes into the interview—Rilling told Mara that, although the police were "not accusing [him] of anything," he needed to understand that the interview was "the only opportunity" he had to volunteer an account of the prior night's events. *Id.* at 363. Thereafter, police would examine evidence, including any videotapes of the party and any fingerprints on the bottle used in the attack, and if it incriminated Mara, he could be arrested.[7] Rilling then went further and stated that witnesses had already identified Mara as Blackman's assailant: "Do you realize that there's people that don't even know you that picked you out of a lineup?" *Id.* at 365. That was not the case. Indeed, defendants knew that the only then-known eyewitness to the assault, Luke Kazmierczak, had *not* identified Mara when shown his photograph in an array.

Defendants then asked Mara about the threatening calls he had received. He reported that when one caller told him "you['re] dead," Mara stated: "I don't know why you guys think that I hit your friend but I didn't do that," to which the caller replied, "we have witnesses" and threatened Mara with a beating "real soon" before hanging up. *Id.*

Rilling reiterated that the interview was Mara's opportunity to "wipe the slate clean" and to admit "'I got into a fight and hit him [*i.e.,* Blackman] with a bottle.'" *Id.* at 366. Rilling explained why it was important that Mara "be truthful" now: "[I]f for some reason this did happen, it just looks better to say 'you know what, ... I did this thing [*i.e.,* hit Blackman with a bottle]; I don't act this way when I'm [not] drunk'"; it would "look[]" a lot worse" if "it took 5 times" before Mara "came clean" because that would suggest he had "no remorse." *Id.*

Rilling then suggested that Mara might not remember everything that happened the night before because he had been drinking—a point Mara himself had made earlier. *See supra* at 58-59. Mara agreed that sometimes he did not have a full memory of times when he was drinking, but he rejected Rilling's suggestion that he might be an angry drunk, saying, "I just have a lot of fun when I drink." *Id.* at 366-67.

Rilling told Mara that "everything" police had so far was "pointing to" him as Blackman's assailant, and if Mara "just [kept] saying 'I didn't do it, I didn't do it, I didn't do it,' it's not going to look good." *Id.* at 367. What would "look good" would be if Mara said, "you know what, you're right, I f___ed up, I can't believe that it happened." *Id.* Rilling suggested that Mara might simply have been trying to help out a friend who was caught up in a fight where things got out of control. He told Mara, "I think you kinda know a little p.60 bit more than you're saying, and I want you to understand why we're trying to talk to you here and why we're spending the time." *Id.*

Mara replied that he "respect[ed] that but—," whereupon Rilling changed course and asked Mara about his clothing on New Year's Eve. *Id.* Mara described khaki pants and a gray-striped black shirt, but stated that he was bare-chested walking to the party because his shirt was wet from a spilled drink.[8]

After the detectives asked, and Mara responded to, more questions about the party and its aftermath, Nook again told Mara that police would be checking area surveillance cameras for depictions of the Blackman assault, and reiterated the importance of Mara not waiting until the police developed evidence to arrest him before providing a truthful account of the night's events. Nook indicated (1) that it would hardly be unusual for a young man who was drinking to get into a fight, (2) that judges presented with such a situation would take into account that the young man was a college student with a great career ahead of him, and (3) that police would "go to bat" for someone who was "a man" and "owned up" to what he did. *Id.* at 372. On the other hand, if Mara, with "a straight face" and no show of emotion, simply insisted over and over again that he had no role in the fight, it would look like he was "a sociopath," who had acted with "an evil mind." *Id.*[9]

Rilling then observed that if Mara were arrested, he would face felony charges because a bottle used to hit someone over the head would be considered a deadly weapon. That would mean Mara's "career here at school is over" and "probably, actually, not probably," he would serve jail time. *Id.* Rilling stated that "[n]o one wants to see this happen." *Id.* He suggested that might be avoided if Mara were to admit, "'I was a little bit inebriated and I f___ed up [and] I'm sorry'"; Rilling said he could "take that to [Blackman's] family and they'd be happy about that." *Id.*

Nook then had Mara repeat that accusers were telling him they had "witnesses" to Mara assaulting Blackman. *Id.* at 373. Rilling told Mara that was his problem: witnesses had implicated him in the assault, p.61 and "not just one-sided witnesses"; neutral witnesses were "saying 'it was John, it was John, it was John.'" *Id.* As earlier noted, the police then had only hearsay reports of Mara assaulting Blackman; eyewitness Kazmierczak had not identified Mara from a photo array. Nevertheless, Rilling told Mara, "We have one side. We need two sides." *Id.* Mara replied, "I'm telling you what I know," and indicated he would like to talk to some people about the prior night's events, and then contact police later in the day. *Id.* Rilling told Mara it was "absolutely fine" for him to speak with other persons, but he could not promise a second interview opportunity because the police were "under a time constraint." *Id.* at 373-74. Rilling suggested that, as things stood, Mara was "holding all the weight" for the prior night's event. *Id.* at 374 ("Everybody else pretty much ... is walking away."). Telling Mara, "That's what we don't want," Rilling hypothesized that Mara might have hit Blackman in response to being punched himself by some other person. *Id.*

Rilling then asked Mara if he "fe[lt] comfortable enough to talk to us about this." *Id.* Mara replied, "I think I'd like to talk to some other people first and then—" *Id.* Asked with whom he would like to talk, Mara replied, "my father, possibly a lawyer." *Id.* Rilling asked if Mara was "saying you want to talk to a lawyer right now." *Id.* Mara immediately replied, "No, no," explaining that his particular interest was in speaking with his brother and friends. *Id.*

Rilling then reiterated that he could not promise Mara another interview opportunity because the police were going to be turning their attention to other aspects of the investigation. Mara responded, "Well, I told you everything I have now, um, to my fullest." *Id.* at 375. Rilling told Mara that the police "know a lot more than you think we do," and suggested that perhaps "[t]here are things that happened that night that you don't want to talk about." *Id.* Mara asked if Rilling was referring to "my friend's girlfriend getting hit in the face" at the party. *Id.* Rilling and Nook urged Mara to tell them about that, which he did, with the detectives' encouragement.[10] But as it became apparent that Mara was not suggesting that the girlfriend incident had triggered the Blackman assault, Rilling asked why Mara was even bringing it up, and challenged him yet again to explain why people were "picking you out of a lineup saying that you did this." *Id.* at 378. Mara maintained, "I don't know." *Id.*

At that point—about an hour into the interview—Rilling told Mara that not only was it likely that he would be arrested but also that he would face harsh jail conditions:

You are going to have to ... go to court, you [are] going to have to go [to] Bridgeport. It's not like you're going to somewhere nice.... You're going to Bridgeport court and you're going to have to hang out with all the people that are drug addicts, that commit crimes and all that. There's a good chance that you are going to get locked up for a little bit. You're going to end up with some guy that killed somebody, that p.62 robbed somebody, that likes to smoke crack, that likes to do drugs and does cocaine, whatever.

Id.

Rilling told Mara that he did not belong in that scenario: "That's not you." *Id.* But to avoid those consequences, Mara needed "to make a decision right now of how we're leaving this." *Id.* Rilling then stated that he was "getting aggravated" because Mara was "closed off" and "not wanting to tell" the police what he knew. *Id.* Mara repeated that he had told the police "everything I know." *Id.* As for people identifying him, Mara reiterated that he was "not sure" why they would do so, and stated, "I would love to find out if I actually did it." *Id.*

This prompted Rilling to pose a series of "possibility" questions to Mara, such as, "[I]s there a good chance you might have done it and you don't know[?]" Mara replied, "that could have happened ... [b]ecause I was really drunk" and "there's a shot that I wouldn't remember but—" *Id.* at 378-79. Asked if he was "saying that you were that drunk that you could have picked up a bottle or had a bottle and hit somebody over the head with it," Mara replied, "I was drunk and I don't remember some, like a lot of, the night so there's a chance it could have happened." *Id.* at 379. These responses are the focus of Mara's coercion challenge.

Rilling then pressed Mara as to how he could clearly remember other events of the evening—*e.g.,* arguing with his brother, taking off his shirt—but not remember hitting someone over the head. Mara stated, "I don't remember doing that," *i.e.,* hitting someone over the head. *Id.* Both detectives assured Mara that he would "feel so much better if everything comes out." *Id.* Mara replied, "Yea, if I knew that I did it, I would be a man and say so [and] apologize to the kid.... I would love to do that if I 100 percent kn[e]w I did it." *Id.* at 380. Mara told the officers that if they had "a video o[r] anything" indicating that he was Blackman's assailant, he would apologize, but, as for what he recalled, he "just c[ould]n't say I did anything." *Id.* at 382. The detectives told Mara that they didn't want him "found guilty"; what they wanted was for him "to be a man and be truthful." *Id.* They told him the idea that he "could have done it" but not remembered "is just not going to work." *Id.* Mara responded, "Then that's all I have to say. Because that's honestly all I know." *Id.*

Rilling repeated that "impartial people" had inculpated Mara, that the police were going to get an "arrest warrant" for him, and that a judge would hear that he had shown "no remorse," which could result in his being sentenced to "2 years in jail." *Id.* Mara repeated that if he "100 percent knew he did it," he would say so. *Id.* at 383. Nook asked if Mara "50 percent" knew that he did it. *Id.* Mara replied, "I don't know," stating that "[f]rom what I've been told, I had nothing to do with it[, b]ut if the people telling me that are telling me that to look out for me, then that's wrong." *Id.* He again stated, "if I did it and I knew that I did it, I need to apologize and man up about it." *Id.* at 384. And again, he asked if the police could tell him if they in fact knew that he did it. Rather than directly answer the question, Nook stated, "we're here for a reason.... And we'll leave it at that." *Id.*

Nook then raised the possibility that the "evidence" might have pointed police in the wrong direction, and that Mara's brother might be responsible for the assault, at least in part:

> [I]f the evidence for some reason, for some small reason has pointed us in the wrong direction, people really need to man up because you certainly don't need to carry the weight if for some reason p.63 this evidence isn't correct. And it's not a perfect science but this is where we're at. If for some reason your brother has a part in it, I don't think he would be comfortable with you taking the fall for something that maybe he's a part of.

Id. at 385. Mara replied, "Right, Yea. I would just love to find out from him if he knows for sure because if I did do this I would be ashamed of myself." *Id.*

The interview concluded with the detectives —in contrast to their earlier statements about a single interview opportunity —urging Mara to call them at any time if, upon speaking to other people, he got some "lightning information." *Id.* at 387. As everyone shook hands, Nook urged Mara to "[d]o the right thing," observing, "I see you with a great future." *Id.* Mara responded, "I'd love to." *Id.*

III. The Second Photo Array

On meeting Mara, defendants concluded that his present appearance was significantly different from that depicted in his freshman identification photograph. Accordingly, on January 3, they arranged for Kazmierczak to view a second six-photo array, this one containing Mara's January 2 interview photograph, instead of his freshman-year photograph. Kazmierczak immediately identified Mara as Blackman's assailant, this time professing 100% certainty. On January 4, Kazmierczak signed a sworn statement that he had seen Mara come up behind Blackman and hit him over the head with a dark colored bottle.

Defendants also showed the new photo array to David O'Brien, who immediately identified Mara as the person whom Kazmierczak had identified on January 1 as Blackman's assailant. On January 4, O'Brien signed a sworn statement to that effect, adding that he took a cell-phone photograph of Mara on January 1 because Kazmierczak had said he was positive that was who had hit Blackman. David O'Brien sent Rilling this photograph, which bore a date stamp of January 1, 2013, at 1:13 a.m. It depicted Mara, wearing a dark shirt with light stripes.

IV. Further Police Interviews

Over the next two weeks, defendants interviewed other party guests. On January 3, Jack Hansen, whom police had first encountered at St. Vincent Hospital, gave a sworn statement that, in the course of an altercation at the party, he saw a 6-foot tall white male, wearing a dark shirt, hit Blackman from behind with a large champagne bottle and then run down Fairfield Beach Rd. Later that night, Hansen and his friends would encounter the man, who would be identified by his brother as "Jack Mara." *Id.* at 410.

That same day, defendants interviewed Mara's roommate Thomas Freda, who told of how his girlfriend had been hit in the eye at the party by an extremely intoxicated male who was running through the crowd with his elbows flared out. Freda confronted the male, but relented when Rachel Chase said she would ask the man to leave. Five or ten minutes later, at approximately 12:45 a.m., Freda saw the man lying on the ground—presumably Philip Blackman. After leaving the party, Freda encountered John and Sean Mara and their friends on Fairfield Beach Rd. Freda told Mara about his girlfriend getting hit, whereupon Freda and his girlfriend went home and the Mara group continued toward the party. Freda reported that Mara was then "pretty drunk," and acknowledged that Mara had a tendency to go overboard when in that condition. *Id.* at 411.

On January 7, Mara's friend Kyle Cullam told defendants that he was with Mara and others when, at approximately 12:45 a.m. on January 1, they left a bar and p.64 walked to the party at 1027 Fairfield Beach Rd. Mara, having spilled a drink on himself, removed his wet shirt even though it was freezing outside. En route, the group encountered Tom Freda, who told about his girlfriend getting hit at the party, but who said, "It's okay, it's taken care of." *Id.* Upon arriving at the party, Cullam saw people standing around an unknown male lying in the front yard. Cullam and his friends did not stop but proceeded toward the house, where someone bumped Mara, prompting Mara to start yelling. Cullam and Sean Mara tried to calm Mara and told him to put his shirt on, which he did before entering the house. There, a group of men accused Mara of hitting their friend with a bottle. Cullam told the group that Mara had nothing to do with that. The Mara brothers and two of their friends left the party soon after, but Cullam remained. Cullam told police he was positive Mara did not hit anyone with a bottle.

Two other Mara friends interviewed by the police, John Bradley and Matthew Kennedy, effectively corroborated Cullam's account of the evening.

On January 8, defendants interviewed Daniel Langlais, whom they had first spoken to at St. Vincent Hospital on January 1. Langlais told police that while Blackman was lying on the ground injured, he heard someone yell his name, "Dan," and saw that the person who did so was Mara, who was "jumping around crazy" with no shirt on. *Id.* at 412. Langlais, however, could not say whether Mara had been at the party before Blackman was hit.

On January 14, defendants interviewed Philip Blackman. He stated that he had arrived at 1027 Fairfield Beach Rd. at approximately 11:45 p.m. on New Year's Eve. He described a large party with people everywhere. At about midnight, Blackman went inside the house to watch the New Year's ball drop on television, and the next thing he remembered was waking up in the hospital. He had no personal recollection of any altercation. Rather, friends later told him that "kids were trying to kick us out of the party" because Blackman had bumped into a girl by accident. *Id.* Blackman had no recollection of seeing Mara at the party, but stated that his roommate (who was not at the party) told him that Darren O'Brien had said that it was Mara who struck Blackman. Blackman said he was "surprised" because he had met Mara only a couple of times and had "a fine relationship with him." *Id.* at 413. Nevertheless, Blackman said that Mara had a reputation for being a "hot mess." *Id.*

On January 18, defendants interviewed Sean Mara, who told them that he had been with his brother and two friends at a bar from approximately 11:00 p.m. on New Year's Eve until 12:30 a.m., after which they all went to a party at 1027 Fairfield Beach Rd. At the time, his brother was "[p]retty drunk, ... drunker than the rest of us and being an idiot," taking his shirt off, and refusing to put it back on when told to do so. *Id.* As the group walked to the party, they saw Tom Freda, who reported that his girlfriend had been hit at the party, which got John Mara "riled up," but Freda said, "'Don't worry, it's taken care of.'" *Id.*

Sean Mara told police that, as the group continued to walk toward the party, an unknown male came up from behind them saying that "some kid [at the party] got knocked out, he got hit in the head with a bottle." *Id.* When the group arrived at the party, they saw people holding up someone who was passed out, but they just kept walking toward the house. There, John Mara got into an altercation with someone after they bumped into each other. Sean Mara intervened to calm the situation, and had his brother put his shirt back on before p.65 they entered the house. Because it was crowded inside, they did not stay long, leaving at approximately 1:30 a.m.

Sean Mara reported that, as the group was walking home on Fairfield Beach Rd., some unknown males approached John Mara and began taking his photograph on their cell phones. Mara started yelling like a "maniac" and, when more unknown men approached accusing Mara of hitting their friend over the head with a bottle, Mara started cursing at them, requiring Sean Mara to put his brother in a "choke hold" to get him to stop. *Id.* at 414. The accusers kept following the Mara brothers and their friends, saying things like, "your brother is dead bro!" *Id.* Meanwhile, Mara repeatedly accused his brother and friends of not defending him against the accusers, making Sean Mara so angry that he punched his brother "just to shut him up." *Id.* Mara then ran away, with his accusers yelling: "Why is he running away? Because he hit our friend?" *Id.* Sean Mara denied that he, or his brother, had any involvement in hitting anyone with a bottle.

V. Arrest Warrant

On January 21, 2013, Rilling applied for a warrant to arrest Mara on charges of first-degree assault, *see* Conn. Gen. St. 53a-59 (1999), and second-degree breach of the peace, *see id.* 53a-181 (2002). In support, Rilling submitted a thirteen-page affidavit, which had been reviewed and approved by both a supervising officer, Lieutenant Gagner, and by Assistant State Attorney John Smriga. The affidavit detailed the police investigation from the time of Blackman's father's January 1 call through the almost twenty police interviews already detailed. Among other things, the affidavit made clear that numerous persons reported hearing that John Mara was the person who assaulted Blackman, but that only Luke Kazmierczak and James Hansen professed directly to have witnessed the incident. It stated that Kazmierczak failed to identify Mara from a photo array containing Mara's freshman photograph, and in fact had identified another person with 70% certainty. Nevertheless, Kazmierczak subsequently identified Mara with reported 100% certainty from a second photo array containing the January 2 Mara photograph taken by the police.

The affidavit also stated that Kazmierczak and David O'Brien each told police that Kazmierczak had identified Mara as Blackman's assailant when they encountered him on Fairfield Beach Rd. on January 1, and that O'Brien both selected Mara from the second photo array as the person Kazmierczak so identified and provided police with a contemporaneous cell-phone photograph that he had taken of that person, which depicted Mara. As for Hansen, the affidavit reported that, after witnessing the assault, he encountered the assailant later that night in the company of the assailant's brother, who identified the man as Jack Mara.[11]

As for Mara's interview, the affidavit reported Mara's acknowledgment that he "could" have hit Blackman but might not remember doing so because he was drunk. App'x 408 (quoting Mara as saying, "I'm not sure, if I actually did do it, I would love to find out"; "It could have happened because I was very drunk and there's a shot I didn't remember"; "I don't remember, I was drunk and don't remember parts of the night.").[12]

p.66 At the same time, the affidavit reported statements by various persons indicating that Mara had not assaulted Blackman and could not have done so because that event occurred before Mara and his friends arrived at the party. *See, e.g., id.* at 410 (reporting Freda statement that he saw man lying on ground with people standing around him before he left the party); *id.* at 411 (reporting Cullam statement that unknown male was already lying on ground with people standing around him as he and Mara arrived at party); *id.* at 413 (reporting Sean Mara statement that group was still walking to party when unknown male said "some kid" at party had been "knocked out" when "he got hit in the head with a bottle," and, when they arrived at party, they saw someone holding up person who had "passed out").

On February 22, 2013, Connecticut Judge Robert Devlin issued the requested warrant for Mara's arrest. It appears that the warrant was never formally executed. Rather, Mara voluntarily surrendered to the Fairfield Police Department and, after police processing and arraignment in court, he was released on a $100,000 bond.

VI. Dismissal of the Charges Against Mara

Sometime after the arrest warrant issued, Rilling received an anonymous call from a woman who stated that police had "the wrong person" for the Blackman assault. *Id.* at 129. Two weeks later, Rilling received another call from the woman, who continued to remain anonymous. She stated that her son—whom she refused to identify—had spent New Year's Eve with John Cordone, and it was two of Cordone's friends who were responsible for the Blackman assault. Rilling reported the call to State Attorney Smriga, who was handling the Mara prosecution.

Rilling contacted Cordone, then a student at Fairfield University, who admitted hearing about the Blackman assault, but initially denied any knowledge of how the incident occurred or who might be involved. Rilling told Cordone that the police already knew he had been with friends on New Year's Eve who had gotten into a fight. At that point, Cordone "just opened up," identifying the friends as Corey Martin and Michael Arrone. *Id.* at 134. Cordone told Rilling that Arrone had been walking around with a black champagne bottle all evening—which Rilling knew fit the description of the Freixenet bottle used to hit Blackman. Cordone said that when he left the party with his girlfriend, Martin and Arrone stayed behind. An hour or two later, they appeared at Cordone's home, Martin with no shirt on, and Arrone with blood on him. They told Cordone that they had gotten into a fight and "had to hit somebody over the head with a bottle to escape." *Id.* Cordone stated that Martin and Arrone were hoping that the incident would just "go away" and "definitely would have come forward if they knew Mara was going to be convicted." *Id.* at 483. Rilling reported Cordone's account of events to State Attorney Smriga and had Cordone memorialize it in a sworn statement dated March 21, 2013.

A few weeks later, Rilling interviewed Corey Martin who provided a sworn statement dated April 11, 2013, in which he reported that at a New Year's Eve party on Fairfield Beach Rd., he and Michael Arrone had gotten into a fight instigated by three or four men. As the two friends fled the scene, Arrone said that when he saw the men hitting Martin, he (Arrone) "swung a bottle and hit one of the males." *Id.* at 484. Rilling advised Smriga of this account.

p.67 Smriga conveyed the new information to Mara's attorney who, by letter dated May 17, 2013, requested that Smriga drop the charges against his client. In his response, Smriga acknowledged that the Cordone and Martin statements exculpated Mara, but concluded that they were not dispositive. He reported that the authorities hoped to resolve the matter soon but had been impeded by their inability to interview certain witnesses. In fact, Arrone refused to be interviewed on advice of counsel, and Kazmierczak, who had identified Mara as Blackman's assailant, had ceased cooperating with the authorities. The record reveals no other police investigation of the matter between May and October of 2013.

By the fall of 2013, Smriga had concluded that he could neither successfully prosecute Mara for the Blackman assault nor arrest anyone else for that crime. Accordingly, on October 3, 2013, the state charges against Mara were dismissed.

VII. District Court Proceedings

On July 30, 2014, Mara filed the instant action. On July 15, 2016, the Fairfield Police defendants invoked qualified immunity to move for summary judgment, which the district court granted in part, but denied as to defendants Rilling, Nook, Hine, and the Town of Fairfield (sued derivatively under a state indemnification statute). *See Mara v. MacNamara*, 2017 WL 4368612, at *7-8.

In denying defendants' motion, the district court concluded with respect to Mara's Fifth Amendment coerced self-incrimination claim, that defendants' actions, first on campus and then during the interview, raised "a genuine dispute of fact as to whether [Mara's] will was overborne resulting in an inculpatory statement that was used against him." *Id.* at *5.[13] As to Mara's Fourteenth Amendment substantive due process claim, the district court identified a genuine factual dispute as to whether defendants' conduct shocked civilized sensibilities, which also allowed Mara to pursue a state claim for intentional infliction of emotional distress. *See id.* at *7.

In denying defendants' motion with respect to Mara's Fourth Amendment and state law claims for false arrest and malicious prosecution, the district court concluded that Mara had two plausible arrest claims. The first was based on his being unexpectedly confronted on campus by defendants who were armed and had used their cars to block Mara's vehicle; the second based on a deficient warrant. *See id.* at *6. The district court concluded that, at the time of the campus encounter, defendants could not claim even arguable probable cause for an arrest because they then had "no concrete evidence" linking Mara to the Blackman assault. *Id.* As to the warrant, the district court concluded that it would lack probable cause if it depended on (1) statements coerced from Mara, and (2) a photo identification by Kazmierczak tainted by suggestive procedures, both of which presented genuine factual disputes. *See id.* at *5-6.

Defendants timely appealed.

DISCUSSION

I. Jurisdiction

Because the denial of a motion for summary judgment is not a final judgment, p.68 it is generally not immediately appealable. *See, e.g., Jones v. Parmley,* 465 F.3d 46, 54 (2d Cir. 2006). An exception obtains, however, when the denied motion was based on a claim of qualified immunity, at least to the extent the immunity claim presents a "purely legal question." *Mitchell v. Forsyth,* 472 U.S. 511, 530, 105 S.Ct. 2806, 86 L.Ed.2d 411 (1985); *see O'Bert ex rel. Estate of O'Bert v. Vargo,* 331 F.3d 29, 38 (2d Cir. 2003). This is because qualified immunity affords no mere defense to liability but, rather, immunity from suit, which would effectively be lost if a defendant is erroneously required to defend against a case at trial. *See White v. Pauly,* ___ U.S. ___, 137 S.Ct. 548, 551, 196 L.Ed.2d 463 (2017); *Pearson v. Callahan,* 555 U.S. 223, 231, 129 S.Ct. 808, 172 L.Ed.2d 565 (2009); *Saucier v. Katz,* 533 U.S. 194, 199, 121 S.Ct. 2151, 150 L.Ed.2d 272 (2001).

Mara argues that this court lacks jurisdiction to review defendants' qualified immunity claim because it does not present a purely legal question in light of the material disputes of fact identified by the district court. *See Mara v. MacNamara,* 2017 WL 4368612, at *5-7. He is wrong. Even in such circumstances, we have jurisdiction to review a qualified immunity claim if that review is limited to undisputed facts and plaintiff's version of any disputed facts, which are accepted for purposes of the appeal. *See In re World Trade Center Disaster Site Litig.,* 521 F.3d 169, 180 (2d Cir. 2008); *Cowan ex rel. Estate of Cooper v. Breen,* 352 F.3d 756, 761 (2d Cir. 2003). Because we so limit our review here, Mara's jurisdictional challenge fails.

II. Qualified Immunity

This court reviews *de novo* a denial of summary judgment to parties asserting qualified immunity. *See, e.g., Walczyk v. Rio,* 496 F.3d 139, 153 (2d Cir. 2007). Qualified immunity shields government officials from claims for money damages unless a plaintiff adduces facts showing that "(1) the official violated a statutory or constitutional right, and (2) the right was 'clearly established' at the time of the challenged conduct." *Ashcroft v. al-Kidd,* 563 U.S. 731, 735, 131 S.Ct. 2074, 179 L.Ed.2d 1149 (2011) (quoting *Harlow v. Fitzgerald,* 457 U.S. 800, 818, 102 S.Ct. 2727, 73 L.Ed.2d 396 (1982)); *accord Zalaski v. City of Hartford,* 723 F.3d 382, 388 (2d Cir. 2013).

If the answer to the first question is no, "there is no necessity for further inquiries concerning qualified immunity." *Saucier v. Katz,* 533 U.S. at 201, 121 S.Ct. 2151. That is because a defendant has no need for an immunity shield where there is no viable constitutional claim. *See Zalaski v. City of Hartford,* 723 F.3d at 388; *Holcomb v. Lykens,* 337 F.3d 217, 223-25 (2d Cir. 2003). But even if the answer is yes, or not definitively no, a defendant may still be entitled to qualified immunity if the right was not clearly established at the time of his challenged actions. Indeed, a court that decides this second question in a defendant's favor may award qualified immunity without conclusively answering the first. *See Ashcroft v. al-Kidd,* 563 U.S. at 735, 131 S.Ct. 2074 (reaffirming lower courts' discretion to decide order in which to address two prongs of qualified-immunity analysis).

For law to be clearly established, it is not necessary to identify a case directly on point. But precedent must have spoken with sufficient clarity to have placed the constitutional question at issue beyond debate. *See id.* at 741, 131 S.Ct. 2074. Specifically, the law must be so clearly established with respect to the *"particular* conduct" and the "specific context" at issue that "every reasonable official would have understood that his conduct p.69 was unlawful." *Mullenix v. Luna,* ___ U.S. ___, 136 S.Ct. 305, 308, 193 L.Ed.2d 255 (2015) (emphasis in original) (internal quotation marks omitted). If the illegality of the challenged conduct would not be so apparent, officers are entitled to qualified immunity. *See Zalaski v. City of Hartford,* 723 F.3d at 389. "In short, if at least some reasonable officers in the defendant's position 'could have believed that the challenged conduct was within the bounds of appropriate police responses,' the defendant officer is entitled to qualified immunity." *Id.* (quoting *Saucier v. Katz,* 533 U.S. at 208, 121 S.Ct. 2151) (alterations omitted).

This standard is deliberately "forgiving," *Amore v. Novarro,* 624 F.3d 522, 530 (2d Cir. 2010), to give public officials "breathing room to make reasonable but mistaken judgments" without fear of disabling liability, *Messerschmidt v. Millender,* 565 U.S. 535, 546, 132 S.Ct. 1235, 182 L.Ed.2d 47 (2012) (internal quotation marks omitted). Indeed, the Supreme Court has repeatedly observed that qualified immunity protects "'all but the plainly incompetent or those who knowingly violate the law.'" *Ashcroft v. al-Kidd,* 563 U.S. at 743, 131 S.Ct. 2074 (quoting *Malley v. Briggs,* 475 U.S. 335, 341, 106 S.Ct. 1092, 89 L.Ed.2d 271 (1986)).

III. Arrest Claims

The Fourth Amendment protects against "unreasonable ... seizures" of persons. U.S. Const. amend. IV. For a seizure to be reasonable, it must generally be supported by probable cause. *See generally National Treasury Emps. Union v. Von Raab,* 489 U.S. 656, 665, 109 S.Ct. 1384, 103 L.Ed.2d 685 (1989) (stating general principle while acknowledging that neither warrant nor probable cause is indispensable component of reasonableness). Under both federal and Connecticut law, "probable cause to arrest exists when police officers have knowledge or reasonably trustworthy information of facts and circumstances that are sufficient to warrant a person of reasonable caution in the belief that the person to be arrested has committed or is committing a crime." *Walczyk v. Rio,* 496 F.3d at 156 (internal quotation marks omitted); *see State v. James,* 261 Conn. 395, 415, 802 A.2d 820, 835 (2002). Probable cause does not demand that an officer's good-faith belief that a person has committed a crime be "correct or more likely true than false." *Texas v. Brown,* 460 U.S. 730, 742, 103 S.Ct. 1535, 75 L.Ed.2d 502 (1983). "It requires only facts sufficient to establish the sort of fair probability on which reasonable and prudent people, not legal technicians, act." *Zalaski v. City of Hartford,* 723 F.3d at 390 (internal quotation marks and brackets omitted).

A. The Claimed January 2, 2013 Arrest

Applying these principles to Mara's federal and state claims of unlawful arrest on January 2, 2013, we conclude that defendants are entitled to qualified immunity.

Defendants do not here challenge the district court's determination that they lacked probable cause, or even arguable probable cause, to arrest Mara on January 2, 2013. Rather, they claim qualified immunity on the ground that they did not, in fact, arrest Mara on that date and, thus, did not require probable cause lawfully to engage him in a voluntary interview. *See Florida v. Royer,* 460 U.S. 491, 497, 103 S.Ct. 1319, 75 L.Ed.2d 229 (1983) (holding that police do not violate Fourth Amendment by engaging person in voluntary conversation, and "[i]f there is no detention— no seizure within the meaning of the Fourth Amendment—then no constitutional rights have been infringed"); *Rivera v. Double A Transp., Inc.,* 248 Conn. 21, 31, 727 A.2d 204, 209 (1999) (identifying unlawful p.70 restraint as element of false imprisonment). Moreover, they argue that, even when the facts are viewed most favorably to Mara, clearly established law would not have compelled "every reasonable officer" to have concluded that Mara was under arrest. *Mullenix v. Luna,* 136 S.Ct. at 308. We agree.

A person is seized within the meaning of the Fourth Amendment if, under the totality of circumstances, a reasonable person would have believed that he was not free to leave. *See Michigan v. Chesternut,* 486 U.S. 567, 573, 108 S.Ct. 1975, 100 L.Ed.2d 565 (1988) (citing approvingly to test for seizure articulated in *United States v. Mendenhall,* 446 U.S. 544, 554, 100 S.Ct. 1870, 64 L.Ed.2d 497 (1980) (opinion of Stewart, *J.,* joined by Rehnquist, *J.*) (noting that Fourth Amendment "seizure" occurs "only if, in view of all the circumstances ..., a reasonable person would have believed that he was not free to leave")); *accord Kaupp v. Texas,* 538 U.S. 626, 629, 123 S.Ct. 1843, 155 L.Ed.2d 814 (2003) (holding Fourth Amendment seizure occurs when, "taking into account all of the circumstances surrounding the encounter, the police conduct would have communicated to a reasonable person that he was not at liberty to ignore the police presence and go about his business" (internal quotation marks omitted)); *State v. Mangual,* 311 Conn. 182, 197, 85 A.3d 627, 641 (2014) ("The ultimate inquiry [in determining whether plaintiff has been seized is whether] a reasonable person in [plaintiff's] position would believe that he or she was in police custody of the degree associated with a formal arrest."). The standard is objective, looking not to what a particular defendant may have thought, but to what "the typical reasonable person [would] have understood." *Florida v. Jimeno,* 500 U.S. 248, 251, 111 S.Ct. 1801, 114 L.Ed.2d 297 (1991); *United States v. Newton,* 369 F.3d 659, 671 (2d Cir. 2004).

In applying this standard to a claim of qualified immunity, a court necessarily engages in a two-part objective inquiry, asking not only what a reasonable person would have understood about his ability to leave—which determines whether there was a constitutional violation—but also what every reasonable police officer would have understood from established precedent—which determines whether the right was clearly established.

The district court addressed only the first question and concluded that a person in Mara's situation could reasonably have thought he was under arrest on January 2, 2013, because Mara was surprised to be confronted by police on campus, and the police were then "armed and had used their vehicles to block his car, preventing him from leaving." *Mara v. MacNamara,* 2017 WL 4368612, at *6. In fact, when these circumstances are viewed in context, they do not admit an objectively reasonable belief that Mara was under arrest.

First, Mara had voluntarily agreed to meet with the police on January 2. That meeting was initiated by Mara, or at least by Mara's mother, who sought police help in response to threats her son was receiving from persons who blamed him for the Blackman assault. In these circumstances, even if Mara was surprised that police came to his campus at 4:00 p.m. when their agreed-upon meeting was scheduled for the police station at 5:00 p.m., that hardly supports an objectively reasonable belief that the police were then placing Mara under arrest. *See Oregon v. Mathiason,* 429 U.S. 492, 495, 97 S.Ct. 711, 50 L.Ed.2d 714 (1977) (holding that defendant who voluntarily went to police station and was informed he was not under arrest was not
p.71 in custody)[14]; *United States v. Jones,* 818 F.2d 1119, 1125 (4th Cir. 1987) (holding defendants not in custody when they voluntarily went to police station).

Second, police had already told a Mara family lawyer that they would be speaking to Mara as a witness rather than a target, and that he did not need an attorney at the interview. Even if we assume for purposes of this appeal that the statement was somehow misleading, a person provided with such an assurance would have no objectively reasonable basis to conclude that a police request to change the time and place of the agreed-upon meeting meant that he was being arrested.

Third, the proposed change in venue was from the Fairfield police station to a security office at Mara's own university. Such a change, from a potentially more intimidating location to a lesser one, would not support an objectively reasonable belief that one was being arrested. *See United States v. Hughes,* 640 F.3d 428, 435 (1st Cir. 2011) (explaining that interview in "less intimidating atmosphere than ... a police station," did not support an objectively reasonable belief of custodial situation); *see also United States v. Courtney,* 463 F.3d 333, 337 (5th Cir. 2006) (holding that non-threatening location of interviews —one at public restaurant, another at defendant's place of employment—would not support objectively reasonable belief that one was being arrested). Nor is a different conclusion warranted because defendants thought the change might work to their advantage. That fact was not communicated to Mara and, thus, could not inform an objectively reasonable understanding of the circumstances by someone in his position. *See Whren v. United States,* 517 U.S. 806, 813, 116 S.Ct. 1769, 135 L.Ed.2d 89 (1996) (holding that officers' "[s]ubjective intentions play no role in ... Fourth Amendment analysis"). Further, insofar as Mara expected his father to join him for the interview at the police station, nothing in the record indicates that Mara ever asked to wait for his father before the on-campus interview or that he had a reasonable basis to think that such a request would be denied.

Fourth, while defendants were armed on January 2, it is undisputed that they never brandished, or even displayed, their weapons. Thus, a person in Mara's position, who had sought police help and agreed to a police interview, would have no objectively reasonable basis to think that he was under arrest because the officers who came to conduct the interview were routinely armed with holstered handguns. *See United States v. Drayton,* 536 U.S. 194, 205, 122 S.Ct. 2105, 153 L.Ed.2d 242 (2002) (stating that public knows most law enforcement officers are armed; thus, "holstered firearm ... is unlikely to contribute to the coerciveness of the encounter absent active brandishing of the weapon"); *United States v. Thompson*, 546 F.3d 1223, 1227 (10th Cir. 2008) (same); *United States v. Gaynor*, 262 F. App'x 341, 342 (2d Cir. 2008) (summary order) (same).

Fifth, the import of defendants and a campus security officer having parked their cars behind Mara's vehicle is at best ambiguous. Police frequently stop their vehicles in ways that impede the normal flow of traffic—much to the frustration of ordinary motorists. While in some circumstances, using police cars to box in a private vehicle might lead its driver to conclude that he is not free to leave, that conclusion would not reasonably obtain here, where the vehicle owner was not in the car or attempting to drive it at the time in question and had solicited a p.72 meeting with police. *Cf. United States v. Stover*, 808 F.3d 991, 997 (4th Cir. 2015) (holding that reasonable person would not feel free to leave when police officers blocked vehicle, flashed police emergency lights, drew weapons, and trained spotlight on blocked vehicle). Thus, although Mara professes subjectively to have concluded from the way police cars were parked that he could not have refused to go with defendants to the campus security office, the totality of circumstances would not make such a belief objectively reasonable.[15]

In any event, a sixth factor convincingly dispels any arrest concern. The video recorded interview shows that defendants expressly told Mara—who was at no time physically restrained—that he was always free to get up and leave the interview and did not have to answer any questions. *See supra* at 58, n.5 (quoting police statement). Such a statement to an unrestrained person, viewed in light of the totality of circumstances just detailed, would preclude an objectively reasonable belief that one is under arrest. *See Oregon v. Mathiason*, 429 U.S. at 495, 97 S.Ct. 711; *United States v. Haak*, 884 F.3d 400, 415 (2d Cir. 2018) (holding that defendant who "voluntarily came to the police station," was interviewed in "standard interview room" for "not unduly lengthy" period, and who "knew from the outset that he did not have to speak with the police but, rather, could stop the interview at any time," was not in custody); *cf. United States v. Newton*, 369 F.3d at 670 (concluding that disavowal of arrest carries less weight when said to person placed in handcuffs).

Even if the facts admitted any ambiguity as to Mara's arrest status on January 2, 2013, which we conclude they do not, police officers aware of the totality of circumstances just detailed—particularly, Mara's agreement to a police meeting and the officers' express statement to Mara that he was always free to leave the interview—could reasonably have believed that Mara would *not* have understood himself to be under arrest at the interview and, therefore, that probable cause was not required to speak with him. Certainly no clearly established law would have compelled "every reasonable officer" to have concluded otherwise in the context described. *Messerschmidt v. Millender*, 565 U.S. at 546, 132 S.Ct. 1235. Accordingly, as a matter of law, defendants are entitled to qualified immunity on Mara's federal and state claims of unlawful arrest on January 2, 2013.

B. The Second Arrest

Mara maintains that he was also unlawfully arrested following issuance of a February 22, 2013 warrant for his arrest. As earlier noted, it is not evident from the record that Mara ever was formally arrested. Rather, it appears that he (or his attorney) was told that an arrest warrant had issued, whereupon Mara voluntarily surrendered to the authorities for processing and arraignment. In general, damages for unlawful arrest cover from "the time of detention up until issuance of process or arraignment, but no more. From that point on, any damages recoverable must be based on a malicious prosecution claim." *Wallace v. Kato,* 549 U.S. 384, 390, 127 S.Ct. 1091, 166 L.Ed.2d 973 (2007); *see Hygh v. Jacobs,* 961 F.2d 359, 366 (2d Cir. 1992) (holding false arrest claim cognizable from period of arrest p.73 through arraignment). We recognize that the Seventh Circuit has held that a person who is not formally arrested, but who voluntarily surrenders upon learning of a warrant for his arrest, has a "plausible claim for false arrest" because "it is enough that he was booked; that was a seizure of his person within the meaning of the Fourth Amendment." *Albright v. Oliver,* 975 F.2d 343, 344-45 (7th Cir. 1992). We need not here decide whether we agree. The parties have not raised or briefed the issue. We conclude simply that, whether Mara properly sues for unlawful arrest or malicious prosecution in connection with the February 2013 initiation of charges against him, defendants are entitled to qualified immunity because probable cause is a complete defense to either charge, *see Singer v. Fulton Cty. Sheriff,* 63 F.3d 110, 118 (2d Cir. 1995); *McHale v. W.B.S. Corp.,* 187 Conn. 444, 447, 446 A.2d 815, 817 (1982), and the Rilling affidavit establishes probable cause.

An arrest authorized by a judicial warrant is generally "presumed" to be supported by probable cause. *Walczyk v. Rio,* 496 F.3d at 156 (observing that "such warrants may issue only upon a showing of probable cause"). Even where a supporting affidavit is found to be deficient in stating probable cause, "the fact that a neutral magistrate ... issued a warrant is the clearest indication that the officers acted in an objectively reasonable manner," so as to merit qualified immunity. *Messerschmidt v. Millender,* 565 U.S. at 546, 132 S.Ct. 1235. To urge otherwise, a plaintiff must show (1) that supporting warrant affidavits "on their face, fail to demonstrate probable cause"; or (2) that defendants misled a judicial officer into finding probable cause by knowingly or recklessly including material misstatements in, or omitting material information from, the warrant affidavits. *Walczyk v. Rio,* 496 F.3d at 156.

Mara argues that this is such a case because defendants obtained a warrant for his arrest through unconstitutionally obtained evidence, specifically, (1) Mara's coerced statements of January 2, 2013, and (2) Kazmierczak's photo identification of the next day. The district court concluded that both these evidentiary challenges raised disputes of fact. *See Mara v. MacNamara,* 2017 WL 4368612, at *4-5. Then, assuming resolution of the disputes in Mara's favor, the district court determined that probable cause had to be assessed by reference to a "corrected" affidavit deleting the challenged evidence. *See Ganek v. Leibowitz,* 874 F.3d 73, 82 (2d Cir. 2017) (explaining that court assessing warrant application based on challenged information may "consider a hypothetical corrected affidavit" to determine if it satisfies probable cause). Identifying a "genuine dispute" as to whether such a corrected affidavit would here demonstrate even "arguable probable cause," the district court denied defendants qualified immunity. *Mara v. MacNamara,* 2017 WL 4368612, at *6.[16]

We cannot sustain this conclusion. There is no basis in law for deleting the Kazmierczak photo identification from the Rilling affidavit and, with that eyewitness identification restored to the affidavit, probable cause is plainly established even without Mara's challenged statements. *See, e.g., Stansbury v. Wertman,* 721 F.3d 84, p.74

98 (2d Cir. 2013) (stating that, absent indicia of unreliability, victim's identification is typically sufficient to provide probable cause); *United States v. Canfield,* 212 F.3d 713, 719 (2d Cir. 2000) (same re: eyewitness testimony); *United States v. Wagner,* 989 F.2d 69, 73 (2d Cir. 1993) (same re: confidential informant with respect to personally witnessed criminal activity); *Singer v. Fulton Cty. Sheriff,* 63 F.3d 110, 119 (2d Cir. 1995) (same re: sworn victim complaint); *cf. Florida v. J.L.,* 529 U.S. 266, 120 S.Ct. 1375, 146 L.Ed.2d 254 (2000) (holding anonymous tip insufficient).[17]

First, to the extent Mara complains that it was unduly suggestive for only his photographs to be included in both arrays shown to Kazmierczak, clearly established law is to the contrary. "[T]he fact that a suspect's picture was placed in a second array after a witness has failed to select anyone from the first array [does not] automatically make the second array unduly suggestive." *United States v. Concepcion,* 983 F.2d 369, 379 (2d Cir. 1992). The district court acknowledged this precedent, but thought that a case-specific review might nevertheless admit a reasonable finding of suggestivity. *See Mara v. MacNamara,* 2017 WL 4368612, at *5. It did not, however, identify what facts would distinguish this case from *Concepcion* in ways that might admit such a finding. Nor can we. Mara does not—and could not— argue that either of the photo arrays shown to Kazmierczak, which are part of the record, are themselves suggestive. Each array depicts six young, white men with short, dark hair—consistent with the description Kazmierczak gave of Blackman's assailant. In neither array does Mara's photograph "so st[an]d out from all of the other photographs as to suggest to an identifying witness that [Mara] was more likely to be the culprit." *United States v. Thai,* 29 F.3d 785, 808 (2d Cir. 1994) (internal quotation marks omitted).

The lack of suggestivity here is only reinforced by the fact that the two photos of Mara used in the arrays—the first taken in his freshman year, the second taken in his senior year—are markedly different. Nor does anything in the record indicate that the manner of display was suggestive. Quite the contrary: as to both displays, Kazmierczak was cautioned that it was as important to clear the innocent as to identify the guilty. In sum, Mara's suggestivity argument rests solely on the fact that he was the only person depicted in both arrays. But if, as this court has ruled, showing a witness the *same* photograph of a suspect in two different arrays is not unduly suggestive where police do not otherwise urge the photo's identification, *see id.* at 809, it necessarily follows that showing a witness markedly *different* photographs of a suspect, without doing or saying anything to urge identification, is not unduly suggestive, *see Gregory-Bey v. Hanks,* 332 F.3d 1036, 1052 (7th Cir. 2003) (concluding "distinctly unique and different" photographs not unduly suggestive). We thus conclude that no suggestivity concern warrants deletion of Kazmierczak's photo-identification from Rilling's affidavit.

Second, even if the facts could admit a finding of suggestive procedures— which they cannot—that conclusion does p.75 not mean that Kazmierczak's identification cannot inform probable cause determinations. Indeed, this court expressly rejected that conclusion in *Stansbury v. Wertman,* which holds that "'[e]vidence need not be admissible at trial in order to support a finding of probable cause.'" 721 F.3d at 91 n.7 (quoting *Phillips v. Allen,* 668 F.3d 912, 915 (7th Cir. 2012) (interpreting *Illinois v. Gates,* 462 U.S. 213, 103 S.Ct. 2317, 76 L.Ed.2d 527 (1983))). State law agrees. *See State v. Higgins,* 201 Conn. 462, 467, 518 A.2d 631, 634 (1986) ("The fact that [a] confession would not have been admissible at a trial does not preclude its use ... in ascertaining probable cause."). As *Stansbury* explains, the due process limits that *Neil v. Biggers,* 409 U.S. 188, 93 S.Ct. 375, 34 L.Ed.2d 401 (1972), mandates for the use of identifications tainted by suggestive procedures "concern[] the admissibility of identifications at criminal trials, not whether an identification can support probable cause to arrest" a suspect. *Stansbury v. Wertman,* 721 F.3d at 91 n.7; *see Phillips v. Allen,* 668 F.3d at 915 (stating that "*Biggers* and similar decisions ... concern the admissibility of [identification] evidence at criminal trials, not claims for damages against arresting officers"). Thus, *Stansbury* instructs that the critical question for "determining whether an identification can support probable cause," is not whether the identification procedure was suggestive, but whether it was "so defective" that, as a matter of law, "'probable cause could not reasonably be based on it.'" *Stansbury v. Wertman,* 721 F.3d at 91 n.7 (quoting *Jenkins v. City of New York,* 478 F.3d 76, 93 (2d Cir. 2007)).

The one-photo displays in *Stansbury* were undoubtedly suggestive, making identifications therefrom inadmissible at trial. *See id.* at 91. But that did not render them "so defective" that they "could not contribute to a finding of probable cause." *Id.* at 91 n.7. By contrast, telling a witness he "had to pick someone" from a photo array would make the ensuing identification both inadmissible at trial and too defective to support probable cause. *See id.* (deriving scenario from *Jenkins v. City of New York,* 478 F.3d at 93). *Stansbury* explained the distinction: procedures that simply "increase the odds" that a witness will identify the defendant are not so defective as to preclude reliance for probable cause, while procedures that force the witness to make an identification do rise to that level. *See id.*

The arrays here are a far cry from the single-photo displays that *Stansbury* held suggestive—but, nevertheless, not so defective that they could not support probable cause. *See id.* at 91. Mara's photographs were included in multi-photo arrays, his two photographs were significantly different, and nothing about how the photos were presented to Kazmierczak urged an identification of Mara, much less left Kazmierczak with no option but to make such an identification. Moreover, as in *Stansbury,* Kazmierczak confirmed his identification of Mara in a sworn statement, and the police had no reason to question his honesty. Thus, on the *Stansbury* standard that properly applies here, there is no reason for the Kazmierczak photo-identification to be deleted from the Rilling affidavit. *See id.*

Third, and in any event, when applying the *Stansbury* standard in the context of a qualified immunity claim, the determinative question is not whether the challenged identification procedure could be found "so defective" that probable cause could not be based on it, but whether clearly established precedent would compel every reasonable officer to recognize as much. *See Phillips v. Allen,* 668 F.3d at 917. It would not do so here. As already noted, *United States v. Concepcion,* p.76 983 F.2d at 379, and *United States v. Thai,* 29 F.3d at 808, instruct that showing the same subject's photograph in two photo arrays is not necessarily suggestive, and Mara points to no authoritative decision warranting a different conclusion in the particular circumstances of this case, much less a conclusion that the procedure was "so defective" that it could not inform probable cause under *Stansbury v. Wertman,* 721 F.3d at 91. *See Phillips v. Allen,* 668 F.3d at 917.

Indeed, such a conclusion is particularly inapt here for two further reasons. First, when Rilling applied for a warrant to arrest Mara, defendants knew that Kazmierczak had an independent basis for identifying Mara that made it particularly unlikely that viewing a second photograph of him would be unduly suggestive. *See Neil v. Biggers,* 409 U.S. at 199-200, 93 S.Ct. 375 (outlining factors for determining independent reliability of identification); *United States v. Tortora,* 30 F.3d 334, 338 (2d Cir. 1994) (applying *Biggers* factors to find identification independently reliable). Specifically, on the night of the assault— and before any contact with the police— Kazmierczak had identified Mara as Blackman's assailant to the O'Brien brothers from among a group of young men encountered on Fairfield Beach Rd. David O'Brien confirmed that Kazmierczak made such an identification, providing police not only with a sworn statement but also with the cell-phone photograph of Mara that he took at the time of the identification.

Second, Rilling disclosed all circumstances pertinent to Kazmierczak's photo identification in his affidavit in support of an arrest warrant—specifically, the display of two photo arrays, each containing a photograph of Mara; Kazmierczak's failure to identify Mara from a freshman photograph in the first array (and 70%-certain identification of another person), and his 100%-certain identification of Mara from a more recent photograph in the second array; Kazmierczak's January 1 in-person identification of Mara to the O'Brien brothers; and David O'Brien's contemporaneous cell-phone photograph of the person Kazmierczak so identified, which depicts Mara.[18] In short, as to the Kazmierczak photo identification, defendants cannot be charged with misstating or omitting material information. Thus, with a fully informed judge raising no concern about the display of two Mara photographs to Kazmierczak; with defendants' knowledge that Kazmierczak had already made an in-person identification of Mara to friends shortly after the Blackman assault; and in light of the decisions in *Concepcion* and *Thai,* it cannot be said that every reasonable officer would be compelled to conclude that Kazmierczak's photo-identification of Mara was "so defective" that it could not reasonably inform probable cause. *See Stansbury v. Wertman,* 721 F.3d at 91 n.7; *see also Messerschmidt v. Millender,* 565 U.S. at 546, 132 S.Ct. 1235.

Accordingly, we conclude that defendants are entitled to qualified immunity on Mara's federal and state claims of unlawful arrest and/or malicious prosecution stemming from the February 2013 arrest warrant because (1) the Kazmierczak photo identification was not, in fact, so defective as to require deletion from a corrected Rilling affidavit; (2) with that eyewitness p.77 identification included, the affidavit clearly states probable cause to arrest Mara for the Blackman assault, even if Mara's statements are deleted; and (3) with probable cause thus established, it cannot be said that every reasonable officer would conclude that Mara could not lawfully be arrested or prosecuted as a result of the February 2013 arrest warrant.[19]

IV. Statement Claims

Mara claims that defendants violated his Fifth Amendment right against self-incrimination and his Fourteenth Amendment right to substantive due process by coercing him to make inculpatory statements at the January 2 interview. He further claims that defendants' conduct violated state law prohibiting the intentional infliction of emotional distress.

In denying defendants qualified immunity on these claims, the district court concluded that the record, viewed most favorably to Mara, raised genuine disputes of fact as to whether Mara's will was overborne when he made the statements at issue, and whether police conduct was so extreme and outrageous as to go beyond the bounds of human decency. *See Mara v. MacNamara,* 2017 WL 4368612, at *5, *7. Even if we were to agree with this conclusion —which we do not for reasons detailed below—it addresses only the first qualified immunity inquiry, *i.e.,* whether a constitutional violation could be found. The district court still needed to address the second qualified immunity inquiry, *i.e.,* whether the rights at issue were clearly established in the context presented, such that every reasonable officer would have recognized that the challenged conduct was unlawful. That is not this case.

A. Coercion Claim

The Fifth Amendment states that no person "shall be compelled in any case to be a witness against himself." U.S. Const. amend. V. The Fourteenth Amendment extends this prohibition to the states. *See Malloy v. Hogan,* 378 U.S. 1, 6, 84 S.Ct. 1489, 12 L.Ed.2d 653 (1964). The right bars police from coercing involuntary statements from individuals, *see Chambers v. Florida,* 309 U.S. 227, 239, 60 S.Ct. 472, 84 L.Ed. 716 (1940), and applies without regard to whether the person is in custody when statements are so coerced. Thus, the right extends more broadly than the prophylactic procedures mandated in *Miranda v. Arizona,* 384 U.S. 436, 86 S.Ct. 1602, 16 L.Ed.2d 694 (1966), which apply only to persons in custody to "secure the privilege against self-incrimination" in that particular context. *Colorado v. Spring,* 479 U.S. 564, 572, 107 S.Ct. 851, 93 L.Ed.2d 954 (1987) (internal quotation marks omitted).

An actual violation of the right against self-incrimination occurs, however, only when a coerced statement is used against a person "at trial." *United States v. Verdugo-Urquidez,* 494 U.S. 259, 264, 110 S.Ct. 1056, 108 L.Ed.2d 222 (1990); *accord United States v. Allen,* 864 F.3d 63, p.78 82 (2d Cir. 2017) (observing that violation of Fifth Amendment right against self-incrimination "'occurs *only at trial,*' even if 'conduct by law enforcement officials prior to trial may ultimately impair that right'" (quoting *Verdugo-Urquidez,* 494 U.S. at 264, 110 S.Ct. 1056 (emphasis in original))). Because Mara's case was dismissed, no challenged statements were ever used against him at trial.

To the extent he complains that his statements were used to support an arrest warrant that would otherwise have lacked probable cause, his claim would appear to invoke the Fourth Amendment right against unreasonable seizures. We need not pursue the question of how the Fourth and Fifth Amendments might interact in such circumstances. *See, e.g., Michaels v. New Jersey,* 222 F.3d 118, 123 (3d Cir. 2000) (concluding that constitutional guards against coerced confessions only apply when statements are used at trial, not in arrest warrant). For reasons discussed in the immediately preceding point of this opinion, we conclude that, even when Mara's statements are deleted from the warrant application, the remaining facts, specifically, eyewitness Kazmierczak's identification of Mara as Blackman's assailant, convincingly established probable cause for his arrest. Thus, because Mara can demonstrate no Fourth or Fifth Amendment injury from the use of his statements in a warrant affidavit otherwise supported by probable cause, defendants are entitled to qualified immunity on his coerced self-incrimination claim.

B. Substantive Due Process Claim

Mara nevertheless claims that, whether or not his statements were used against him, defendants' tactics in procuring them violated his right to substantive due process. *See Chavez v. Martinez,* 538 U.S. 760, 773, 123 S.Ct. 1994, 155 L.Ed.2d 984 (2003) (Thomas, J.) (plurality opinion) (observing that "Fourteenth Amendment's Due Process Clause, rather than the Fifth Amendment's Self-Incrimination Clause, would govern" such a claim). To maintain that claim, Mara must show more than official misconduct, or even coercion. He must show that defendants' conduct in questioning him was "so egregious, so out-rageous that it may fairly be said to shock the contemporary conscience." *County of Sacramento v. Lewis,* 523 U.S. 833, 847 n.8, 118 S.Ct. 1708, 140 L.Ed.2d 1043 (1998); *see Rochin v. California,* 342 U.S. 165, 172, 72 S.Ct. 205, 96 L.Ed. 183 (1952); *accord Lombardi v. Whitman,* 485 F.3d 73, 79 (2d Cir. 2007).

The Supreme Court identified such conduct in *Rochin,* where police broke into a defendant's home, attempted forcibly to pull drug capsules from his throat and, finally, pumped his stomach to retrieve the capsules. *See Rochin v. California,* 342 U.S. at 166, 72 S.Ct. 205. As the Court explained, such conduct was "too close to the rack and the screw to permit of constitutional differentiation." *Id.* at 210, 72 S.Ct. 205. Not so, however, the conduct in *Chavez v. Martinez,* 538 U.S. at 774, 123 S.Ct. 1994 (holding that questioning defendant then being treated for multiple gunshot wounds did not shock the conscience), or *County of Sacramento v. Lewis,* 523 U.S. at 854, 118 S.Ct. 1708 (holding officer's high-speed pursuit of suspect, even if undertaken imprudently and with deliberate indifference to human life lost in ensuing collision, did not shock the conscience). Nor the conduct in *Lombardi v. Whitman,* 485 F.3d at 81-85 (holding that officials' allegedly false reassurances as to air safety in lower Manhattan after 9/11 attack did not shock the conscience). In short, to shock the conscience and trigger a violation of substantive due process, official conduct must not only be wrong; it must p.79 be extremely so, "truly brutal and offensive to human dignity." *Id.* at 81 (internal quotation marks omitted).

A Connecticut claim for intentional infliction of emotional distress similarly requires conduct that is "extreme and out-rageous." *Petyan v. Ellis,* 200 Conn. 243, 253, 510 A.2d 1337, 1342 (1986) (instructing that claim requires showing "(1) that the actor intended to inflict emotional distress; or that he knew or should have known that emotional distress was a likely result of his conduct; (2) that the conduct was extreme and outrageous; (3) that the defendant's conduct was the cause of the plaintiff's distress; and (4) that the emotional distress sustained by the plaintiff was severe"); *accord Carrol v. Allstate Ins. Co.,* 262 Conn. 433, 443, 815 A.2d 119, 126 (2003) (holding that claim can be maintained "only where the conduct has been so outrageous in character, and so extreme in degree, as to go beyond all possible bounds of decency, and to be regarded as atrocious, and utterly intolerable in a civilized community").

Applying these standards here, we conclude that defendants' conduct during Mara's non-custodial interview—which we have described in detail and which is all video-recorded and undisputed—cannot be characterized as so brutal and offensive, or so outrageous and intolerable, much less so extreme, as to recall the rack and screw or other unjustifiable intrusions on "bodily integrity." *Washington v. Glucksberg,* 521 U.S. 702, 720, 117 S.Ct. 2258, 138 L.Ed.2d 772 (1997) (characterizing *Rochin* as delineating the right "to bodily integrity"); *see also United States v. Haak,* 884 F.3d 400, 409 (2d Cir. 2018) (observing that legal significance of video-recorded—and, therefore, undisputed—interview conduct is properly decided *de novo* on appellate review).

The video-recording shows that Mara's interview, while sometimes tense— as might be expected when criminal conduct is being discussed—was conducted calmly by officers in plain clothes who did not raise their voices, display weapons, or physically restrain Mara. At the start of the interview, Mara was told he did not have to answer any questions and could leave at any time. Mara confirmed his understanding of these ground rules. When, later in the interview, Mara suggested that he might want to speak with a lawyer, questioning stopped until Mara clarified that he was not requesting to speak to a lawyer at that time. Such circumstances, which have informed our decisions granting qualified immunity on coerced-confession claims, *see, e.g., United States v. Haak,* 884 F.3d at 415; *Parsad v. Greiner,* 337 F.3d 175, 184 (2d Cir. 2003); *United States v. Ruggles,* 70 F.3d 262, 265 (2d Cir. 1995), are hardly indicative of police conduct so brutal or extreme as to shock the conscience.

The same conclusion obtains with respect to both the place of the interview, an office at Mara's college, which was certainly less intimidating than the police station where he had earlier agreed to be interviewed, *see United States v. Courtney,* 463 F.3d at 337; and its hour and a half duration, *see Rajah v. Mukasey,* 544 F.3d 427, 445-46 (2d Cir. 2008) (holding seven hours of questioning, with two stints in jail cell, was "long and tiresome" but not shocking). Nor is a different conclusion warranted if, as Mara contends, defendants changed the time and site of the interview to avoid his father's attendance. As earlier noted, Mara does not state that he asked to delay the interview until his father arrived. *See supra* at 71-72. In any event, Mara was 21 years old, college educated, and, as the video-recording shows, well-spoken and self-possessed. Questioning an adult in the absence of a parent is not so brutal, intolerable, p.80 or shocking as to violate due process or intentionally inflict emotional distress. *Cf. Deshawn E. by Charlotte E. v. Safir,* 156 F.3d 340, 348 (2d Cir. 1998) (rejecting due process challenge to short detention, even of minor).

Insofar as defendants, in the course of the interview, told Mara that it would be to his benefit to cooperate and that, otherwise, he would be prosecuted to the full extent of the law, such statements are not even coercive, let alone conscious-shocking. *See United States v. Haak,* 884 F.3d at 412 ("[T]here is nothing improper in police truthfully telling a [suspect] that he will be prosecuted to the full extent of the law if he chooses not to cooperate."); *United States v. Ruggles,* 70 F.3d at 265 (holding statements conveying benefits of cooperation are "not improperly coercive" but, rather, "common sense factual observations"). To the extent defendants went further, implying that cooperation might prompt the Blackman family to forego pressing charges, while prosecution would put Mara in jail with killers, robbers, and drug addicts, such tactics may inform the voluntariness of a defendant's ensuing statements and, therefore, their admissibility. But no clearly established precedent holds such conduct conscious-shocking or intolerable as required to demonstrate a violation of due process or intentional infliction of emotional distress. *See, e.g., Rochin v. California,* 342 U.S. at 171, 72 S.Ct. 205; *Huguez v. United States,* 406 F.2d 366, 381-82 (9th Cir. 1968) (concluding that officers' forcible removal of drugs from rectum of handcuffed defendant held spread-eagled on table constitutes conscious-shocking conduct); *cf. Green v. Scully,* 850 F.2d 894, 903 (2d Cir. 1988) (observing, in case where one officer improperly referenced electric chair while other officer said case was not about electric chair, that other evidence showed ensuing admissions were not coerced).

The same conclusion obtains with respect to defendants' misrepresentations about the strength of the evidence against Mara, specifically, the insinuation that the police already had eyewitness identifications of Mara as Blackman's assailant when, in fact, the only eyewitness then known to the police, Kazmierczak, had failed to identify Mara in the first photo array shown to him. This conduct, too, is relevant to voluntariness. *See, e.g., Frazier v. Cupp,* 394 U.S. 731, 739, 89 S.Ct. 1420, 22 L.Ed.2d 684 (1969) (holding that officer's false statement, although relevant to voluntariness, did not render particular confession inadmissible); *United States v. Anderson,* 929 F.2d 96, 99 (2d Cir. 1991) (holding that even if agent's statements were "false, misleading, or intended to trick and cajole" defendant into confessing, suppression was warranted only if totality of circumstances showed defendant's will was overborne by agent's conduct); *Green v. Scully,* 850 F.2d at 903 (stating that officer's false representation of fingerprint match "makes the issue of voluntariness in this case such a close one" but, nevertheless, finding confession voluntary). Nevertheless, it is not so outrageous or conscience-shocking as to violate due process.

This is not to condone all police deceit or trickery, which can, after all, take various forms, from undercover operations, *see Hoffa v. United States,* 385 U.S. 293, 87 S.Ct. 408, 17 L.Ed.2d 374 (1966) (identifying no coercion in such circumstances), to threats to child welfare, *see Lynumn v. Illinois,* 372 U.S. 528, 534-35, 83 S.Ct. 917, 9 L.Ed.2d 922 (1963) (holding coercive repeated police misrepresentations that suspect would be deprived of financial aid for dependent child). It is simply to note that government misrepresentations about the strength of its evidence may inform voluntariness; p.81 but such conduct here is not so outrageous or inhumane as to violate due process or Connecticut law.

Nor is a different conclusion warranted by the district court's observation that defendants "did not relent" until they got Mara to say that "their version [of events] might be true," *i.e.,* that Mara "could" have hit Blackman and not remembered because of how drunk he was on New Year's Eve. *Mara v. MacNamara,* 2017 WL 4368612, at *5. Like the other conduct discussed, persistent questioning may raise voluntariness concerns, but it does not violate substantive due process. *See Chavez v. Martinez,* 538 U.S. at 775-76, 123 S.Ct. 1994 (holding that even if persistent questioning implicates liberty interest, it is not conscious-shocking). Indeed, Mara himself appears to have sown the seed for the challenged police query about what he could have done without remembering. Early in the interview, Mara volunteered that it was only after the fact that he learned of an argument at the party where "Phil" was hit with a bottle. App'x 359. He himself did not "remember" these occurrences, explaining, "I don't know if it's because I drank so much, but I just don't remember it." *Id.* In these circumstances, it was not shocking or brutal for police to have pressed him as to whether he might also fail to remember being the person who hit Blackman.

In sum, because Mara's interrogation cannot be characterized as brutal or extreme, he cannot show a violation of substantive due process or state tort law, much less show that established precedent would have required every reasonable officer to have recognized such violations. Accordingly, defendants are entitled to qualified immunity on these claims.

CONCLUSION

To summarize, we conclude that qualified immunity entitles defendants Rilling, Nook, and Hine to summary judgment on all Mara's constitutional and state law claims.

1. As to Mara's false arrest and malicious prosecution claims:

a. The record cannot support an objectively reasonable belief that Mara was under arrest on January 2, 2013, and thus, every reasonable police officer would not have been compelled to conclude that probable cause was required to interview Mara on that date;

b. The February 2013 warrant for Mara's arrest was supported by probable cause, specifically, Kazmierczak's January 3, 2013 photo-array identification of Mara as Blackman's assailant. Precedent would not compel every reasonable officer to conclude that the circumstances of that identification —inclusion of a different photograph of Mara than that used in the first array—were unduly suggestive, much less so defective as to preclude the identification from informing a probable cause determination. Thus, Mara's second arrest claim fails without regard to whether allegedly coerced statements are deleted from the warrant affidavit. The same probable cause conclusion defeats Mara's claim of a maliciously initiated prosecution.

2. Because Mara's allegedly coerced statements were not necessary to establish probable cause for an arrest warrant—their only use—he cannot maintain a coercion claim under the Fifth (or Fourth) Amendment or state law.

3. The procedures used to interrogate Mara, including deceit and fear, p.82 were nevertheless not so shocking, brutal, and inhumane that every reasonable police officer would be compelled to recognize that they violated substantive due process.

Accordingly, the order denying qualified immunity is REVERSED and we direct the entry of judgment in favor of defendants Rilling, Nook and Hine on all outstanding claims.

[*] The Clerk of Court is directed to amend the caption as set forth above.

[1] The district court granted summary judgment to Fairfield Police Chief Gary MacNamara, Lieutenant Michael Gagner, Sergeant Anthony Granata, and Detective Jason Takacs. *See Mara v. MacNamara,* 2017 WL 4368612, at *7-8. Plaintiff does not challenge that decision here and, thus, we have no occasion to review it now. The remaining defendants, Fairfield University and its employee Patrick Cleary, were earlier dismissed by stipulation on February 11, 2016. Accordingly, this opinion hereafter uses "defendants" to reference only appellants Rilling, Nook, and Hine.

[2] Detective Rilling testified at his deposition that he offered Mara the choice of driving himself to the Public Safety Office or having School Officer Cleary drive him, and that Mara chose the latter. Because it is not clear from the record whether this fact is disputed, we accord it no weight in viewing the facts most favorably to Mara.

[3] Although Sergeant Hine disputes such an order, in viewing the facts most favorably to Mara, we assume it was given. We note only that nothing in the record indicates whether Mara ever sought to use his cell phone when with the police on January 2.

[4] In some instances, what can clearly be heard on the videotape differs from the transcript provided to the court. The discrepancies are of no import to this decision. Except as otherwise noted all quotations in this opinion derive from the videotape itself.

[5] Specifically, Rilling told Mara: "You know that you can get up any time to leave. You don't have to talk to us. You can just say 'I don't want to talk to you anymore,' get up and leave and no matter what." App'x 354.

[6] Mara subsequently provided defendants with the name of these friends, who were interviewed by the police.

[7] As Rilling's affidavit in support of Mara's arrest warrant would subsequently report, no fingerprints were recovered from the bottle.

[8] This comported with Kazmierczak's report of a shirtless assailant.

[9] Nook's statement reads in pertinent part as follows:

I have to go back, go to the house and look at the surveillance.... So ... this is the chance to say—everyone at a certain point in time that's probably a young man drinks and gets into fisticuffs. You know sometimes it just ends up a little sh____er than others and it's New Year's Eve and there is this bull___t fight; whatever, let's move on. What are you going to do—apologize to the kid[?] What are you going to do— write him a love letter? [You want to say] "Let's move on; I want to finish school and we'll be done with this and no one is harassing me and my friends anymore." Because we [*i.e.,* the police] called everyone and they don't want to be harassed either. So, you know, it just looks that you're deviant. People make a decision as a human being; they're not computers. Judges are human beings and they take into consideration [the fact that] these are college kids who are doing well, have a great career and life and [admitted] "I got drunk. I got into a fight. I got my ass kicked over there." But if we go back and she contradicts everything, it just looks like an evil mindset. Like, "[C]atch me if you can and I'm going to do it again." It's all I'm saying, that we will go to bat for you and say: "F___ it, he's a man. He owned up." Our reports are pretty valuable, and you know, [] if she contradicts you and makes you look bad, we write it up and say, you know, the kid [is] obviously a sociopath, and he['s] sitting there with a straight face, he doesn't look emotional, he just told me, "no, no, no," but evidence showed otherwise. So, I just want to put that out there.

App'x 371-72.

[10] *See* App'x 375 ("You're going down the right path now. You're telling us more stuff. Go ahead."); *id.* at 376 ("Do you feel a weight coming off your shoulders? In the beginning you were carrying the entire world. This is ridiculous that you are going to ... carry weight [you] should be shedding off your shoulder right now. Tell us

everything else."); *id.* at 377 ("I like where you're going with this because you're doing the right thing. You're showing that Phil was not in the right state of mind, ... was drunk. He's as much to blame as anybody in this party.").

[11] The affidavit does not indicate whether Hansen was shown a photo array.

[12] We here quote Mara's statements as reported in Rilling's affidavit. Any differences between these quotes and what can be heard in the record, *see supra* at 58 n.4, are immaterial.

[13] The district court specifically highlighted Mara's age (21); his limited experience with police interrogations; his expectation that he would be going to the police station with his father simply to clear up confusion about the Blackman assault; defendants' surprising Mara on campus, blocking his car, and intimating that he had to talk to them right away; the length of Mara's interrogation (1½ hours); and defendants' telling Mara that he would be put in prison with dangerous persons, and that if he did not confess he would be considered a sociopath. *See Mara v. MacNamara,* 2017 WL 4368612, at *5.

[14] Mara was so informed at the start of the police interview. *See infra* at 72.

[15] As noted *supra* at 58 n.2, on reviewing the record in the light most favorable to Mara, we do not consider police deposition testimony that Mara was offered the choice of driving himself to the university security office or accompanying Security Officer Cleary, and that he voluntarily chose the latter.

[16] As this court has recognized, "arguable probable cause" exists "if either (a) it was objectively reasonable for the officer to believe that probable cause existed, or (b) officers of reasonable competence could disagree on whether the probable cause test was met." *Escalera v. Lunn,* 361 F.3d 737, 742 (2d Cir. 2004); *accord Gonzalez v. City of Schenectady,* 728 F.3d 149, 157 (2d Cir. 2013).

[17] Because we conclude that probable cause is established without Mara's own statements, his coercion challenge to those statements is immaterial to his Fourth Amendment and state law claims of unlawful arrest. Moreover, we need not decide whether the record, viewed most favorably to Mara, admits a finding of coercion because, as explained *infra* at Part IV.A., he cannot show that the statements were used against him as necessary to claim a Fifth Amendment violation.

[18] Even if Kazmierczak's photo identification of Mara were properly deleted from a corrected affidavit, his January 1 identification, and David O'Brien's documented corroboration of that identification, would remain. The district court did not discuss why this evidence would not be sufficient to establish probable cause. We do not pursue the point because we conclude that there is no need to correct the affidavit in support of Mara's arrest to delete Kazmierczak's photo identification.

[19] Insofar as Mara's malicious prosecution claim appears to challenge the maintenance of an action against him after evidence implicating another person came to light, that decision was the prosecutor's rather than defendants and, thus, cannot be maintained against them. *See Wilson v. City of New York,* 480 F. App'x 592, 595 (2d Cir. 2012) (summary order) (holding that "decision to continue prosecution after the new evidence came to light was made by the assistant district attorney and the court, not by" officers, and thus, no reasonable jury could find officers liable); *see also Jones v. City of Chicago,* 856 F.2d 985, 994 (7th Cir. 1988) (concluding that officers can only

be liable for malicious prosecution action where they "have been instrumental in the plaintiff's continued confinement or prosecution").

919 F.3d 161 (2019)

John DETTELIS, Plaintiff-Appellant,

v.

Michael R. SHARBAUGH, Cattaraugus County Department of Probation Supervisor, Denise Longarvsky, Cattaraugus County Department of Probation Officer, Gerald Zimmerman, Cattaraugus County Department of Probation Director, Defendants-Appellees.

Docket No. 17-4150-cv August Term, 2018.

United States Court of Appeals, Second Circuit.

Argued: November 8, 2018.

Decided: March 20, 2019.

Dettelis v. Sharbaugh, 919 F. 3d 161 (2nd Cir. 2019)

Appeal from the United States District Court for the Western District of New York, No.17-cv-407, Geraci, *Chief Judge.*

Plaintiff-Appellant John Dettelis appeals the district court's dismissal of his 42 U.S.C. § 1983 complaint. Dettelis claimed malicious prosecution, alleging that Appellees falsely charged him with violating a condition of his probation. The district court concluded that Dettelis's conviction for that violation, though overturned on appeal, still gave rise to a presumption of probable cause that Dettelis failed to overcome. We refrain from deciding whether that presumption applies and, instead, conclude that Appellees were entitled to qualified immunity.

AFFIRMED.

Matthew A. Albert, Law Offices of Matthew Albert, Buffalo, NY, for Plaintiff-Appellant.

Sean W. Costello, Rupp Baase Pfalzgraf Cunningham LLC, Buffalo, NY, for Defendants-Appellees.

Before: Raggi, Hall, and Sullivan, Circuit Judges.

p.162 Per Curiam.

Plaintiff-Appellant John Dettelis appeals from a judgment of dismissal entered, pursuant to Federal Rule of Civil Procedure 12(b)(6), on November 30, 2017, in the United States District Court for the Western District of New York (Geraci, *C.J.*). Dettelis was serving a term of probation, a condition of which required him to report certain police contact. When he failed to report an incident with a police officer, he was charged with violating the terms of his probation. His resulting conviction was overturned on appeal, and Dettelis then brought this 42 U.S.C. § 1983 suit against County Probation Director Gerald Zimmerman, Probation Supervisor Michael Sharbaugh, and Probation Officer Denise Lengvarsky ("Appellees"), claiming malicious prosecution. The district court granted Appellees' motion to dismiss, concluding in part that Dettelis failed to overcome a presumption of probable cause that arose from the facts underlying his subsequently vacated conviction. This appeal follows.

We affirm the challenged dismissal without delineating the contours of a presumption of probable cause here because we p.163 conclude that Appellees are, in any event, entitled to qualified immunity.

I.

In April 2011, Dettelis was convicted by state court of driving while intoxicated and sentenced to three years' probation.[1] A condition of his probation required him to contact his probation officer "upon arrest or questioning" by law enforcement officials. App. 15, ¶ 54. In November 2012, Dettelis went to the town courthouse in Yorkshire, New York, demanding unrelated records but was asked to leave when he became loud and unruly. At the request of the court clerk, a state police officer went to Dettelis's home and told him not to go to the court for the records but instead to have his lawyer collect those documents.

In December 2013, Dettelis became aware of a Violation of Probation ("VOP") report charging him with having violated the terms of his probation by not reporting the November 2012 police contact. Although the report was dated and notarized in November 2012, Dettelis believed that it had been fabricated by Appellees at the behest of the district attorney. This was done, Dettelis alleged, because county personnel wanted to "imprison [him] by any means possible." App. 17, ¶ 65. The county court nevertheless determined by a preponderance of the evidence that Dettelis had violated his probation and sentenced him to 90 days in jail. The Fourth Department reversed, concluding that "the evidence at the hearing [did] not establish that the interaction between defendant and the police officer amounted to defendant being 'questioned,' which would have triggered his obligation to notify a probation officer." *People v. Dettelis,* 28 N.Y.S.3d 216, 137 A.D.3d 1722, 1723 (4th Dep't 2016).

II.

"We review *de novo* the grant of a Rule 12(b)(6) motion to dismiss for failure to state a claim, accepting all factual allegations as true and drawing all reasonable inferences in favor of the plaintiff." *Trs. of Upstate N.Y. Eng'rs Pension Fund v. Ivy Asset Mgmt.,* 843 F.3d 561, 566 (2d Cir. 2016). To survive a 12(b)(6) motion, the complaint must contain sufficient factual matter, accepted as true, plausibly to give rise to an entitlement to relief. *Crawford v. Cuomo,* 796 F.3d 252, 256 (2d Cir. 2015). Although a complaint "does not need detailed factual allegations," *see Bell Atl. Corp. v. Twombly,* 550 U.S. 544, 555, 127 S.Ct. 1955, 167 L.Ed.2d 929 (2007), Rule 8 of the Federal Rules of Civil Procedure "demands more than an unadorned, the-defendant-unlawfully-harmed-me accusation," *see Ashcroft v. Iqbal,* 556 U.S. 662, 678, 129 S.Ct. 1937, 173 L.Ed.2d 868 (2009). We may affirm on any ground that finds support in the record. *See, e.g., Wells Fargo Advisors, LLC v. Sappington,* 884 F.3d 392, 396 (2d Cir. 2018).

III.

To state a 42 U.S.C. § 1983 claim for malicious prosecution, a plaintiff must plead both "a violation of his rights under the Fourth Amendment" and "the elements of a malicious prosecution claim under state law." *See Manganiello v. City of New York,* 612 F.3d 149, 160-61 (2d Cir. 2010). Under New York law, a malicious-prosecution claim requires a plaintiff to show "(1) the initiation or continuation of a criminal proceeding against plaintiff; (2) termination of the proceeding in plaintiff's p.164 favor; (3) lack of probable cause for commencing the proceeding; and (4) actual malice as a motivation for the defendant's actions." *Murphy v. Lynn,* 118 F.3d 938, 947 (2d Cir. 1997) (internal quotation marks omitted).

Relying in part on a presumption of probable cause arising from Dettelis's violation determination, despite the fact that the violation was overturned on appeal, the district court concluded that Dettelis's pleadings established probable cause for Appellees to bring and prosecute the VOP charge, and, therefore, precluded a plausible malicious prosecution claim. *See Savino v. City of New York,* 331 F.3d 63, 72 (2d Cir. 2003) ("[T]he existence of probable cause is a complete defense to a claim of malicious prosecution in New York."); *see also Mitchell v. Victoria Home,* 434 F.Supp.2d 219, 228 (S.D.N.Y. 2006) (observing that a "conviction establishes the existence of probable cause which, even when the conviction is reversed on appeal, becomes a rebuttable presumption" (internal quotation marks omitted)). In challenging this ruling, Dettelis questions the applicability of a probable cause presumption to probation violations, noting that guilt of such a violation need be proved by only a preponderance of the evidence. We need not here delineate the precise contours of the probable cause presumption or conclusively decide its application to probation violations. Instead, we conclude that qualified immunity bars Dettelis's claim.

As a general matter, probation officers are entitled to immunity in the performance of their duties, but the type of immunity afforded depends on whether "the duties of the defendants were judicial or prosecutorial, which entitles them to absolute immunity, or administrative, which may entitle them to qualified immunity." *King v. Simpson,* 189 F.3d 284, 288 (2d Cir. 1999) (internal quotation marks omitted). Thus, probation officers are entitled to absolute immunity from suit in connection with their "preparing and furnishing presentence reports to the court." *Dorman v. Higgins,* 821 F.2d 133, 137 (2d Cir. 1987); *accord Peay v. Ajello,* 470 F.3d 65, 69 (2d Cir. 2006) (concluding that Connecticut probation officers are "entitled to absolute immunity in suits for damages arising out of their preparation and submission of presentence reports"). They are also entitled to absolute immunity in "initiating parole revocation proceedings and in presenting the case for revocation to hearing officers." *Scotto v. Almenas,* 143 F.3d 105, 112 (2d Cir. 1998); *accord Victory v. Pataki,* 814 F.3d 47, 65 (2d Cir. 2016), *as amended* (Feb. 24, 2016). By contrast, in performing investigatory duties, for example, the filing of a violation report or recommending the issuance of an arrest warrant, a parole officer is entitled only to qualified immunity. *See Scotto,* 143 F.3d at 111; *see also Roberts ex rel. Estate of Roberts v. Lapp,* 297 F. App'x 67, 69 (2d Cir. 2008) (summary order) (holding state parole officer entitled to qualified immunity in recommending that parole warrant issue); *Malik v. Mackey,* 268 F. App'x 83, 84 (2d

Cir. 2008) (holding state parole officer entitled to qualified immunity in filing parole violation charges).

Here, it could be argued that certain Appellees are entitled to absolute immunity for prosecuting a violation of probation, notwithstanding Dettelis's allegation that they did so maliciously. *See Dorman,* 821 F.2d at 139 ("[A]bsolute immunity spares the official any scrutiny of his motives," including "an allegation that [an act] was done in bad faith or with malice."). But we need not resolve which immunity applies here because the allegations in Dettelis's complaint and the documents attached thereto plainly demonstrate that Appellees are entitled at least p.165 to qualified immunity since they had "arguable probable cause" to bring the VOP charge. *See Jenkins v. City of New York,* 478 F.3d 76, 87 (2d Cir. 2007) ("An officer's determination is objectively reasonable if there was arguable probable cause at the time of arrest— that is, if officers of reasonable competence could disagree on whether the probable cause test was met." (internal quotation marks omitted)). True, the Fourth Department ultimately concluded that Dettelis's November 2012 interaction with police did not amount to "questioning" under the terms of his probation —an interpretation of state law that we are bound to accept. *Dettelis,* 137 A.D.3d at 1723; *see Licci ex rel. Licci v. Lebanese Canadian Bank, SAL,* 739 F.3d 45, 48 (2d Cir. 2013). But prior to the Fourth Department so ruling, Appellees' determination that Dettelis's interaction with a law enforcement officer was reportable, such that his failure to report violated a condition of his probation, was objectively reasonable, not having been clearly established as incorrect in state law by the identification of a stricter questioning requirement. *See Betts v. Shearman,* 751 F.3d 78, 82-83 (2d Cir. 2014) (holding officer entitled to qualified immunity where "it was objectively reasonable for [the officer] to believe that [his] actions were lawful at the time of the challenged act" (internal quotation marks omitted)); *see also Figueroa v. Mazza,* 825 F.3d 89, 100 (2d Cir. 2016) (The qualified-immunity inquiry asks "whether *any* reasonable officer, out of the wide range of reasonable people who enforce the laws in this country, *could have* determined that the challenged action was lawful."). Because it was objectively reasonable for the Appellees to believe that there was probable cause that Dettelis violated the conditions of his probation, Appellees were entitled to qualified immunity.

IV.

We have considered Dettelis's remaining arguments and find them without merit. For the reasons stated above, we AFFIRM the judgment of the district court.

[1] The facts as set forth are taken from the allegations in Dettelis's complaint, which we accept here as true, and from the documents attached to the complaint. *See DiFolco v. MSNBC Cable L.L.C.,* 622 F.3d 104, 111 (2d Cir. 2010).

884 F.3d 351 (2018)

Tylon C. OUTLAW, Plaintiff-Appellant-Cross-Appellee,

v.

CITY OF HARTFORD, Defendant-Appellee,

Officer Michael Allen, in his individual capacity, Defendant-Cross-Appellant,

Detective Troy Gordon, in his individual capacity, Defendant.[*]

Docket No. 16-480(L), 16-635(XAP) August Term, 2016.

United States Court of Appeals, Second Circuit.

Argued: January 17, 2017.

Decided: March 7, 2018.

Outlaw v. City of Hartford, 884 F. 3d 351 (2nd Cir. 2018)

Appeal by plaintiff from so much of a judgment of the United States District Court for the District of Connecticut, Geoffrey W. Crawford, *Judge,* as granted summary judgment dismissing his claims against defendant City of Hartford (the "City"), brought principally under 42 U.S.C. § 1983, for failing to supervise its police officers with respect to appropriate use of force; cross-appeal by defendant police officer Michael Allen from so much of the judgment as orders him to pay plaintiff $454,197 in damages following (a) express jury findings that Allen injured plaintiff by intentionally or recklessly using excessive force, in violation of the United States Constitution and the Constitution of the State of Connecticut, and (b) the court's ruling that Allen is not entitled to qualified immunity. Plaintiff contends principally that the district court erred in granting summary judgment in favor of the City, given evidence he proffered to show deliberate indifference by the City to numerous civilian complaints of excessive force by its police officers. Defendant Allen contends principally that he is entitled to qualified immunity on the constitutional claims because of the jury's verdict in his favor on plaintiff's claim against him for assault and battery in violation of state law, and that factual findings by the district court— which the parties had agreed should resolve all aspects of his qualified immunity defense—should be set aside as inconsistent with factual findings he imputes to the jury.

On the appeal, we conclude that the district court did not err in granting summary judgment in favor of the City on plaintiff's municipal liability claims on the ground that the evidence proffered by plaintiff was insufficient to permit an inference of deliberate indifference. We conclude that the cross-appeal is without merit given that as to an affirmative defense of qualified immunity, the burden is on the defendant to prove the necessary factual predicates by a preponderance of the evidence; that in order to avoid having the court instruct the jury that he had that burden, Allen chose not to have submitted to the jury the fact questions as to which he now wants favorable answers presumed; and that the pertinent factual findings made by the district court are not inconsistent with the jury's answers to the questions that were posed.

Affirmed.

RAYMOND J. RIGAT, Clinton, Connecticut, for Plaintiff-Appellant-Cross-Appellee.

NATHALIE FEOLA-GUERRIERI, Senior Assistant Corporation Counsel, Hartford, Connecticut, for Defendant-Appellee.

WILLIAM J. MELLEY III, Hartford, Connecticut, for Defendant-Cross-Appellant.

Before: KATZMANN, Chief Judge, KEARSE and LIVINGSTON, Circuit Judges.

p.355 KEARSE, Circuit Judge:

Plaintiff Tylon C. Outlaw appeals from so much of a judgment of the United States District Court for the District of Connecticut, Geoffrey W. Crawford, *Judge*[**], as summarily dismissed his claims against defendant City of Hartford (the "City"), brought principally under 42 U.S.C. § 1983, alleging deliberate indifference in the supervision of police officers with respect to appropriate use of force, and seeking to hold the City responsible for the use by defendant Michael Allen, an p.356 officer in the Hartford Police Department ("HPD"), of excessive force to arrest Outlaw, in violation of his rights under the Fourth Amendment to the United States Constitution and under the Constitution of the State of Connecticut. The district court granted summary judgment to the City, dismissing those claims on the ground that Outlaw proffered insufficient evidence to permit an inference that the City had a policy or custom of failing to supervise its police officers in the use of force or that the City's customs or policies caused Outlaw's injuries. *See Outlaw v. City of Hartford,* No. 3:07-cv-01769, 2015 WL 1538230, at *6-*12 (D.Conn. Apr. 6, 2015) ("*Outlaw I*"). Outlaw contends that summary judgment was inappropriate, given the evidence he proffered to show that the City had exhibited deliberate indifference to numerous civilian complaints of excessive force by its police officers.

Allen cross-appeals from so much of the district court's judgment as orders him to pay Outlaw $454,197 in damages following express jury findings that Allen injured Outlaw by intentionally or recklessly using excessive force, in violation of the United States and Connecticut Constitutions. Allen contends that he is entitled to qualified immunity on those claims in light of the jury's verdict against Outlaw on Outlaw's claim for assault and battery in violation of state law, and that posttrial factual findings by the district court, made in ruling that Allen is not entitled to qualified immunity for the constitutional violations, *see Outlaw v. City of Hartford,* No. 3:07-cv-01769, 2016 WL 591753 (D. Conn. Feb. 12, 2016) ("*Outlaw II*"), should be set aside as inconsistent with findings that Allen imputes to the jury.

On the appeal, we conclude that the district court did not err in ruling that the evidence proffered by Outlaw in support of his municipal liability claims was insufficient to permit an inference of deliberate indifference on the part of the City to the use of excessive force by HPD officers. On the cross-appeal, we conclude that Allen's contentions are without merit given that, as qualified immunity is an affirmative defense, the burden was on Allen to prove by a preponderance of the evidence any factual predicates necessary to establish that defense; that in order to avoid having the court instruct the jury that he had that burden, Allen chose not to have submitted to the jury the fact questions as to which he now wants favorable answers presumed; that the jury's answers to the interrogatories accompanying its verdict did not imply the factual findings that Allen imputes to the jury; and that the pertinent factual findings by the district court are not inconsistent with the jury's answers to questions that were posed.

I. BACKGROUND

On the night of December 17, 2004, Allen and HPD Detective Troy Gordon confronted and arrested 30-year-old Tylon Outlaw on a downtown street in Hartford, Connecticut. Outlaw was charged with breach of peace, being intoxicated in the roadway, threatening a police officer, and assault on a police officer. The charges were resolved in 2005 by Outlaw's entry of an *Alford* plea to the offense of creating a public disturbance, *see North Carolina v. Alford,* 400 U.S. 25, 91 S.Ct. 160, 27 L.Ed.2d 162 (1970), which is "'simply a guilty plea, with evidence in the record of guilt, typically accompanied by the defendant's protestation of innocence and his or her unequivocal desire to enter the plea,'" *Outlaw I,* 2015 WL 1538230, at *2 n.1 (quoting *Abimbola v. Ashcroft,* 378 F.3d 173, 181 (2d Cir. 2004) (other internal quotation marks omitted)). The arrest occurred after Allen had repeatedly struck Outlaw with a police baton, bloodying his p.357 head in several places and breaking his knee.

Outlaw brought the present § 1983 action in 2007 against Allen, Gordon, and the City, alleging principally that Allen and Gordon had caused his injuries by using excessive force in violation of the Fourth Amendment, and that the City was liable for their conduct because it had a policy or custom of deliberate indifference in failing to train and supervise its police officers as to appropriate use of force during an arrest. Outlaw also asserted claims under the Connecticut Constitution and Connecticut common law.

A. Pretrial Rulings

Following years of discovery, defendants moved for summary judgment dismissing the complaint. In *Outlaw I,* the district court granted the motion to dismiss the Fourth Amendment claim and similar state-law claims against the City, ruling, to the extent pertinent to Outlaw's appeal, that the evidence Outlaw proffered was insufficient to establish that the City had a policy or custom of indifference that caused Outlaw's injuries (*see* Part III below).

The district court denied the individual defendants' motions for summary judgment dismissing the Fourth Amendment and Connecticut constitutional claims of excessive force and the state-law claims of intentional infliction of emotional distress, ruling that there were genuine issues of material fact to be tried. *See Outlaw I,* 2015 WL 1538230, at *3-*6, *12-*14. The court granted the motions to dismiss Outlaw's other constitutional and state-law claims; however, following a motion by Outlaw for reconsideration, it reinstated the state-law claims against Gordon and Allen for assault and battery.

B. The Trial

In 2016, Outlaw's surviving constitutional and common-law tort claims against Allen and Gordon were tried to a jury, which heard two versions of the December 2004 incident: one from Outlaw and several bystanders, the other from Allen and Gordon.

1. Outlaw's Testimony

Outlaw testified that on the night of December 17, 2004, he drove to downtown Hartford to meet his friend Nick Sackandy at a restaurant on Union Place (the "Restaurant") to discuss a proposed business venture. Outlaw arrived around 10 p.m., drank most of one beer, and left around 11:00 or 11:15. As he was returning to his car, walking south on Union Place toward its intersection with Allyn Street, Outlaw heard his name being called from a double-parked taxi; the driver was his high school friend Anthony Carroll. While Outlaw was crossing the street toward the taxi, a Ford Taurus was inching north on Union Place toward the taxi, and the Taurus's driver — who Outlaw later learned was Detective Gordon — shouted at Outlaw, "hey, mother fucker" (Trial Transcript January 4, 2016 ("Jan. 4 Tr."), at 27). Thinking the driver might be an acquaintance, Outlaw returned the greetings (characterized at trial as "inner city" "pleasantries" (Trial Transcript January 5, 2016 ("Jan. 5 Tr."), at 50; Jan. 4 Tr. 54)), then walked around to the driver side of the taxi. As Outlaw was speaking with the rear-seat passengers, who were also friends of his, the Taurus, which bore no markings to indicate that it was a police vehicle, pulled up behind the taxi; Gordon, who had not identified himself as a police officer, summoned Outlaw to the Taurus. Outlaw waved him off. The Taurus then slowly moved past the taxi and stopped two or three car lengths ahead.

p.358 Gordon, dressed in plain clothes, jumped out of his car and approached Outlaw "aggressively" (Jan. 5. Tr. 59), carrying a black object that Outlaw thought was a gun. Gordon kicked Outlaw in the stomach, which did not hurt him but sent him stumbling backward. (*See id.* at 63; Jan. 4 Tr. 36-37.) Gordon kicked again toward Outlaw, but Outlaw blocked that kick with his hands; however, at almost the same instant Outlaw was struck on the back of his head with "a bat-like object" (Jan. 4 Tr. 37), which he eventually learned was a police baton wielded by Allen.

Outlaw fell to the ground, yelling for help. While on the ground on his back or curled into a fetal position, he was repeatedly struck in the head, arms, and legs with a baton and was kicked in the back and stomach. Outlaw had not said anything to Gordon after their initial exchange of "pleasantries" (Jan 5. Tr. 56-57); he had never moved in Gordon's direction, never raised his hand, and never attempted to punch or kick Gordon; Outlaw's only attempt to defend himself was to curl up and try to cover targeted areas of his body. He testified that while he was down, Gordon kicked him in the face; and when Outlaw tried to cover his face and head, Allen hit him in the right knee with the baton, breaking the kneecap, leaving Outlaw unable to move his leg, and causing him the most pain that he (a former high school, college, and professional football player) had ever experienced.

Outlaw testified that Gordon never displayed a badge; and during the incident, neither Gordon nor Allen ever identified himself as a police officer. Outlaw had the impression that there were people other than Allen and Gordon hitting and kicking him while he was on the ground (in his deposition, Outlaw had said that Gordon, after initially kicking him in the stomach, had not kicked or punched him again (*see* Jan. 5 Tr. 69)). Outlaw testified that none of the people hitting or kicking him identified themselves as police officers.

Eventually Allen placed Outlaw face down on the pavement and cuffed his hands behind his back. He then grabbed Outlaw by the collar, dragged him for 60-odd feet, and threw him to the pavement between parked cars, where Outlaw landed on his face. While they awaited the arrival of an ambulance, blood was dripping from Outlaw's head and face.

At the hospital, Outlaw received stitches to his eyebrow and staples in three other places on his head. Surgery was performed on his broken kneecap; a metal strip was installed in the knee to cover the kneecap, held in place with metal screws. After the knee surgery, the police shackled Outlaw's legs to his bed. Outlaw endured a lengthy convalescence. He needed crutches or a cane for six months and had two additional operations on his knee.

2. Testimony by Onlookers

Rachel Killian-Lallier ("Killian") was a passenger in Carroll's taxi on the night in question. She testified that she and her then-boyfriend, in the back seats, and Carroll and his uncle, in the front seats, were chatting with Outlaw, who was standing on the driver side of the taxi, when a car came along and parked about a car length away. A man — undisputedly Gordon — got out of the car; he was not wearing any kind of police uniform, and Killian never saw a badge on him or heard him indicate to anyone that he was a police officer. Gordon appeared to be "very angry" and "walk[ed] very aggressively towards" Outlaw, as if he were on a mission (Jan 5. Tr. 103, 113); he kicked Outlaw, apparently in the abdomen. Soon a number of other people, including police officers, arrived and piled onto Outlaw, who was on the ground, and began punching him.

p.359 Killian testified that Outlaw had never moved toward Gordon, and that she never heard Gordon or the others who piled onto Outlaw identify themselves as police officers.

Carroll, the taxi's driver, similarly described Gordon as "angry" and "raged." (Jan 5. Tr. 142.) He testified that he saw Gordon rush from his vehicle and kick Outlaw and that he saw several other people, some in police uniforms, rush in to punch Outlaw and pile on him on the ground. Carroll never heard Gordon identify himself as a police officer; it was only when Carroll left his taxi to check on Outlaw at the bottom of the pile of people hitting him that Carroll saw Gordon remove a badge from under his shirt.

Sackandy testified that in the meeting at the Restaurant, Outlaw had drunk one beer and no other alcohol. Outlaw had left after about an hour. Sackandy testified that not long after Outlaw left, John Stengel, a friend of Sackandy, arrived, excitedly saying that Hartford policemen were "beating the shit out of some guy outside." (Jan. 5 Tr. 126, 129.)

Stengel, who on December 17, 2004, had never met Outlaw and had not socialized with him since, testified that he had been walking north on Union Place that night toward the Restaurant when he saw a "pretty brutal" interaction involving five or six people, some in police uniform, "beating somebody up pretty badly, kicking, throwing punches." (*Id.* at 170, 172.) Stengel saw no resistance by the person who was on the ground being beaten.

3. The Testimony of Gordon

Gordon testified that on the night of December 17, 2004, before his encounter with Outlaw, he had responded to a reported assault on Allyn Street. At Allyn Street, he did not see a fight, and it was decided that there was nothing for the police to do. Gordon then drove to the end of Allyn and turned right onto Union Place, a one-way street. Gordon saw cars parked along both sides of Union Place and saw a double-parked vehicle on the left, with a man — Outlaw, whom Gordon did not know — standing at the front passenger-side window.

Gordon testified that he asked Outlaw to please move out of the roadway. Gordon was driving a Ford Taurus with no visible police indicia, was dressed in plain clothes, and did not identify himself as a police officer. Gordon testified that Outlaw responded, "why don't you shut the F[uck] up." (Trial Transcript January 6, 2016 ("Jan. 6 Tr."), at 87). Gordon repeated his request, to which Outlaw responded, "why don't you get out of the car and see what happens." (*Id.* at 89.) Gordon began driving away; but when he heard Outlaw say, "if you get out of that car I'm going to kick your A[ss]" (*id.,*) he interpreted that as a threat and decided to arrest Outlaw. He parked his car some two car lengths ahead of the double-parked car — where Outlaw, Gordon testified, was still on the passenger side — and moved his badge from under his shirt to the surface of his clothing to make it visible.

With his radio in hand, Gordon exited his car and approached Outlaw. He testified that Outlaw moved toward him and threw a punch, striking him in the upper chest; Gordon leaned back and defensively kicked Outlaw in the shin. After that kick, he never touched Outlaw again. Gordon testified that he never announced that he was a police officer "because [he] did not have time." (Jan. 6 Tr. 137.) Other officers appeared suddenly and subdued Outlaw, taking him to the ground. Gordon never heard anyone identify himself as a police officer.

p.360 *4.* The Testimony of Allen

Allen testified that on the night of December 17, 2004, he was on patrol in uniform and driving a police cruiser; he was dispatched to Allyn Street to deal with a report of a serious assault. Gordon also arrived at the scene in response to the report. When the officers did not find there either a suspect or a victim, they left Allyn Street. Gordon, in his unmarked car, turned right onto Union Place; Allen, in his cruiser, followed.

Allen testified that on Union Place, he saw an individual — eventually identified as Outlaw — standing at the passenger side of a taxi and that Outlaw was "block[ing] the flow of the northbound traffic that could have gone around the taxicab" (Jan. 6 Tr. 160). Allen stopped his cruiser after Gordon had stopped his unmarked car and exited, blocking traffic.

Allen had not seen or heard any conversation between Gordon and Outlaw. He testified that he saw Gordon approach Outlaw and then saw Outlaw "lunge" toward Gordon and throw "several punches to [Gordon's] face and chest area." (*Id.* at 163.) Allen testified that he exited his cruiser, "hollered," and "identified" himself as a police officer. (*Id.* at 165.) He testified that Outlaw had grabbed Gordon's clothing, and as Outlaw cocked his right arm to deliver another blow, Allen struck Outlaw's right biceps with his baton. Outlaw did not react, but cocked his arm to hit Gordon again. Allen, attempting to protect Gordon from serious injury, swung at Outlaw's arm a second time.

Allen described Outlaw as dropping to the ground "on his butt and elbows" and assaulting Allen with his legs, "violently struggling with [Allen] resisting arrest." (*Id.* at 166-67.) Other officers came to Allen's assistance in making the arrest. Allen testified that he had used only necessary force, that there were no unnecessary blows. Allen swung his baton at Outlaw's thigh and calf; he testified that he did not hit Outlaw's knee.

Allen testified that when he "was escorting Mr. Outlaw to the cruiser," he "noticed there was some blood on [Outlaw's] scalp." (Jan. 6 Tr. 166.) He said he "assumed" that he had hit Outlaw's head with his nightstick. (*Id.*) He acknowledged that he had testified in deposition that his second swing had struck Outlaw in the head.

5. The Verdicts

After being instructed as to the law governing Outlaw's claims of excessive force in violation of the United States Constitution and the Connecticut Constitution (*see* Part II.B. below) and his state-law claims of assault and battery (*see* Part II.C. below) and intentional infliction of emotional distress (or "IIED"), the jury was given a Verdict Form containing interrogatories asking whether Outlaw had proven those claims and had proven that either defendant's conduct caused him injury. Each set of questions dealt separately with Allen or Gordon.

The jury found that Outlaw had not proven any of his claims against Gordon. It answered "No" to the questions whether Gordon had used excessive force, or had applied force or violence in an unlawful manner, or had acted in a manner intended to subject Outlaw to emotional distress. (*See* Verdict Form questions 1, 7, 13, 17.)

As to Allen, the jury found that Outlaw had proven that Allen used excessive force, had done so intentionally or recklessly, and had thereby caused Outlaw injury. The questions and answers were:

> II. FEDERAL CIVIL RIGHTS CLAIM AGAINST DEFENDANT ALLEN
>
> p.361 4. Did defendant Michael Allen employ excessive force against plaintiff on December 17, 2004? *YES.*
>
> 5. Did defendant Michael Allen act intentionally or recklessly in employing excessive force against plaintiff on December 17, 2004? *YES.*
>
> 6. Did the use of excessive force by defendant Michael Allen cause plaintiff to suffer injury? *YES.*

(Verdict Form questions 4-6.)

> IV.   CONNECTICUT   CONSTITUTIONAL   CLAIMS   AGAINST DEFENDANT ALLEN

10. Did defendant Michael Allen violate the plaintiff's civil rights under the Connecticut Constitution by employing excessive force against plaintiff [o]n December 17, 2004? *YES.*

11. Did defendant Michael Allen act intentionally or recklessly in employing excessive force against plaintiff on December 17, 2004? *YES.*

12. Did the use of excessive force by defendant Michael Allen cause plaintiff to suffer injury? *YES.*

(Verdict Form questions 10-12.) The jury found, however, that Outlaw had not proven his state-law claims against Allen for assault and battery or IIED:

VI. ASSAULT and BATTERY CLAIM AGAINST DEFENDANT ALLEN

15. Do you find that defendant Michael Allen applied force or violence to plaintiff's body in an unlawful manner? *NO.*

. . . .

VIII. INTENTIONAL INFLICTION OF EMOTIONAL DISTRESS CLAIM AGAINST DEFENDANT ALLEN

20. Did defendant Michael Allen act towards plaintiff in a manner intended to inflict emotional distress or which he should have known would cause emotional distress? *NO.*

(Verdict Form questions 15, 20.)

The Verdict Form instructed the jury that if it answered "Yes" to any set of questions against either defendant, it should determine the damages Outlaw should recover for the injuries proven. Having found against Allen on the excessive force claims, the jury awarded Outlaw $408,197 for pain, suffering, emotional distress, and loss of enjoyment of life. (*See* Verdict Form Part IX.) Although the jury awarded Outlaw $111,803 for past and future medical expenses, the parties stipulated that that sum should be reduced to $46,000.

C. The Court's Rulings on Allen's Defense of Qualified Immunity

No questions had been submitted to the jury as to facts for predicates of the individual defendants' defense of qualified immunity. In the conference discussing the instructions to be given to the jury, the court had stated that if it posed such questions, it would instruct the jury that as to those factual issues, the burden of proof is on the defendants. (*See* Charge Conference January 6, 2016 ("Conf. Tr."), at 11-12 ("[T]he burden of proof is different.... So if they are going to be making factual determinations ... they have to be applying the right burden of proof. And it's different [as to] qualified immunity because it's on ... the defense as opposed to on the plaintiff that carries it for everything else.... I'm not going to do it unless I can explain to them what questions they are answering ... and who['s] got the burden of proof.").)

p.362 Counsel for Allen and Gordon responded that that would be "very confusing" (*id.* at 12) and ultimately asked that no questions be put to the jury as to facts on which the qualified immunity defense would be predicated (*see id.* at 36-39, 40, 42). The parties agreed that any necessary factual findings would be made by the court. Defense counsel said, "Your Honor has that on your lap, period." (*Id.* at 37.)

Following the jury's verdict against Allen on the excessive force claims, Allen and Outlaw submitted briefs with regard to the defense of qualified immunity. Allen argued principally that

> by finding Detective Gordon not responsible for any tort, the jury rejected the majority of the plaintiff's claims. The issue of *the conduct of the plaintiff was found to necessitate the actions of Detective Gordon.* The movement of the plaintiff, his language, his aggressive action, his failure to stop and his general demeanor, all as described by Detective Gordon, *were found* to be contrary to the statements of the plaintiff.

(Defendant Michael Allen's Brief Regarding Qualified Immunity ("Allen's QI Mem.") at 2 (emphases added); *see also id.* at 4 ("The jury believed Detective Gordon's testimony that the Plaintiff hit, or was attempting to hit, him.").)

Allen also argued that because the jury found against Outlaw on his claim of assault, it "had to have found that *[Allen's] actions* were justified under state law." (*Id.* at 4 (emphasis added); *see id.* at 6 ("The court had charged the jury on the justification for force which *presumably* the jury found. Because the *jury of necessity found* that the application of *the* force was not unlawful, Officer Allen is entitled to qualified immunity for his actions." (emphases added))). He noted that the court had instructed in part as follows:

> "Under Connecticut law, a police officer is justified in using physical force upon another person when and to the extent he or she reasonably believes such to be necessary to effect an arrest or to defend himself or herself or a third party from the use or imminent use of physical force while effecting or attempting to effect an arrest....
>
> In determining whether a defendant reasonably believed that the use of physical force was necessary to arrest plaintiff or to prevent him from harming the officers or others, you should take into account all of the circumstances of the incident. You should consider this instruction in deciding whether the defendants violated the Connecticut Constitution or committed an assault and battery upon the plaintiff."

(*Id.* at 7 (quoting Jury Instructions and Trial Transcript January 7, 2016 ("Instr./Tr. Tr."), at 24-25) (emphasis omitted).) Allen argued that in light of this charge, the jury's verdict in his favor on assault and battery "*represents specific findings*" that he "*reasonably could have* believed," and did "*reasonabl[y] believe[]*" that "the force he used was reasonable and necessary to effectuate [Outlaw's] arrest." (Allen's QI Mem. at 7-8 (emphases added).)

Allen also argued that he was "entitled to qualified immunity because his actions did not violate any clearly established statutory or constitutional right concerning the use of batons *where a fellow officer was being assaulted.*" (*Id.* at 4 (emphasis added).) He argued that "[t]he United States Supreme Court has not addressed the use of batons in the context of excessive force claims," and that a district court case had held it "not [to be] excessive force for an officer to use his baton against three *men who were approaching him threateningly,* at least one of whom had p.363 been drinking." (*Id.* at 3, 4 (emphasis added).)

In *Outlaw II,* the district court rejected Allen's contentions and made findings of specific facts as to which the jury had been asked no questions. As to Outlaw's state of sobriety, the court found that Outlaw "had consumed a beer" at the Restaurant but "was not intoxicated." *Outlaw II*, 2016 WL 591753, at *1. As to the interactions between Outlaw and Gordon, the court's findings included the following:

> From his unmarked car, Detective Gordon called out to Plaintiff and ordered him out of the road. The accounts differ on whether he delivered a civil and professional request or whether he used profane language. *It is undisputed that he did not identify himself as a police officer.* With his back turned to the road, Plaintiff made a dismissive "brush off' gesture. He ignored Detective Gordon and continued his conversation with the occupants of the cab. *Plaintiff had no idea that a police officer had directed him to leave the road.*
>
> Detective Gordon pulled past the taxi cab, parked, and moved quickly on foot towards Plaintiff. *He did not identify himself as a police officer.* He carried an unlit flashlight [*sic*] in his right hand. He wore a badge around his neck, which he had pulled out of his shirt. He also wore a winter jacket. *The badge was not visible to Plaintiff who still had no idea that the man who had spoken to him from his car and was now moving towards him was a police officer*[.] Rather[,] Plaintiff saw a stranger approaching him on an unlit street *carrying an object that he feared was a gun....*
>
>> Detective Gordon kicked Plaintiff in the chest as soon as he reached him.... Officer Allen, who had witnessed these events, got out of his cruiser and pulled out his baton. *He came up behind Plaintiff and struck him repeatedly on the head, cutting his scalp each time. The photographs admitted into evidence show three distinct scalp lacerations. Officer Allen also did not identify himself as a police officer before hitting Plaintiff.*
>
> Plaintiff fell to the ground and curled up in a fetal position with his hands seeking to protect his head. *As Plaintiff lay on the ground, Officer Allen struck him again on the right knee with the baton.* Several other Hartford police officers not named in this lawsuit arrived and joined in beating Plaintiff while he lay on the ground....
>
> . . . .
>
>> At trial, each side blamed the other for causing the altercation. *The court finds that Plaintiff's version of the events is more credible.*

Id. at *2 (emphases added).

The court addressed the specific circumstances of the encounter, making findings as to, *inter alia,* whether Outlaw had attempted to fight with either Gordon or Allen. As to Gordon, the court found that

> *the testimony by Detective Gordon that Plaintiff struck him or, as Officer Allen testified, that Plaintiff grabbed the detective by the coat, pulled him towards him, and punched him, is not credible* and not true. Plaintiff is more credible when he testified that he was accosted by an unknown man on a dark street whom he feared was holding a gun. Without warning, he was kicked in the midsection by Detective Gordon and then struck from behind by Officer Allen. This testimony is corroborated by the testimony of witnesses in the cab, as well as the undisputed testimony that it was Detective Gordon who got out of his car and approached Plaintiff without identifying himself as a police officer.

p.364 *Outlaw II,* 2016 WL 591753, at *3 (emphasis added). As to Allen, the court also found that

> *Officer Al[l]en's testimony that Plaintiff fought with Detective Gordon and then continued to try to kick Officer Allen after being knocked to the ground by a blow to the head is not credible.* Officer Allen struck Plaintiff at least four times with a police baton-drawing blood with the blows to the head and later breaking Plaintiff's knee. *Plaintiff's version that he was struck from behind by Officer Allen, fell to the ground, attempted to protect his head where he had already been hit, and was then struck on the knee is more credible than Officer Allen's version of the events.*

Id. (emphases added).

The court also found that Allen hit Outlaw hard enough to break Outlaw's kneecap: "[T]he treating physician testified on cross-examination that ... he believes the patella was broken by a blow from the baton"; "[t]here was no testimony that Plaintiff struck the pavement with his kneecap or that his fall was actually the cause of the fracture"; and "[t]he jury resolved this issue in Plaintiff's favor when it determined that Officer Allen's conduct was a proximate cause of injury to Plaintiff...." *Id.*

The court rejected Allen's contention that the verdict in his favor on the assault claim meant that the jury found that Outlaw was the aggressor against Gordon and that Allen believed that force was necessary for reasons of safety. The court observed that the elements of the assault and excessive force claims differ and that the different verdicts on those two categories of claims were not necessarily inconsistent. *See id.* at *4.

The court also rejected Allen's contention that the law was not sufficiently clear to alert him that the force he was using against Outlaw was excessive:

> *That the law prohibits excessive force when using force to make an arrest is neither a recent nor surprising development.* Within the District of Connecticut, there are literally hundreds of decisions that articulate this constitutional rule in cases involving police officers. *Many of these decisions issued prior to December 2004 when the incident at issue occurred....*

Outlaw II, 2016 WL 591753, at *5 (citing cases) (emphases added).

> As these cases demonstrate, it was clearly established by December 2004 that the use of excessive force in the course of an arrest is unlawful. Prior to 2004, Hartford police officers had been sued repeatedly on these grounds and, in each case, the courts consistently articulated the legal standard expressed at the national level in [*Tennessee v. Garner,* 471 U.S. 1, 105 S.Ct. 1694, 85 L.Ed.2d 1 (1985)] and *Graham*[*v. Connor,* 490 U.S. 386, 109 S.Ct. 1865, 104 L.Ed.2d 443 (1989)]: that the force applied by the police must be reasonable in light of the requirements of the situation.

Id. Accordingly, the court found in the present case that

> *[a] reasonable officer* in the position of Officer Allen.... *would see that the original offense committed by Plaintiff was a minor pedestrian violation — in effect, a jaywalking incident.* He would see that Plaintiff was facing away from Detective Gordon's car and ignoring him. *He would neither see nor hear threats or serious misconduct on the part of Plaintiff. He would see no signs of resistance or aggression by Plaintiff when Detective Gordon confronted Plaintiff.*

> He would not see Plaintiff *p.365* strike Detective Gordon or pose a threat to Detective Gordon's safety.

Id. (emphases added). Outlaw was "on the ground, unresisting and protecting his head with his hands," and Allen "continu[ed] to strike Plaintiff with his baton with enough force to fracture Plaintiff's knee cap." *Id.*

> The court is aware that Officer Allen describes the incident differently and alleges that Plaintiff violently attacked Detective Gordon with his fist. For purposes of the qualified immunity issue, *the court does not believe Officer Allen's version of the events.* Instead, *the court has found that Plaintiff never fought with either officer. The court does not believe Officer Allen's description that Plaintiff continued to struggle and kick at the officers once on the ground.* As the factual findings show, *it is more likely that Plaintiff's account of curling up and seeking to protect his head is the accurate one.*

Id. at *6 (emphases added). The court added:

> It is obvious from this description of events that *a reasonable officer, armed with the same information as Officer Allen, would have little doubt about the unlawfulness of repeatedly striking an unresisting man with his baton. See Belanger v. City of Hartford,* 578 F.Supp.2d 360, 366 (D. Conn. 2008) ("A reasonable police officer should know that swinging a baton at an individual's face while they are facing away from the officer without prior warning would constitute a violation of that individual's right to be free from excessive force" [discussing events that occurred on December 23, 2004]).

Outlaw II, 2016 WL 591753, at *6 (emphasis added).

> *A reasonable officer* in Officer Allen's position would have seen that Plaintiff had not committed a violent or serious crime. *He would have seen that Plaintiff had not attempted to flee or resist.* He would have seen Detective Gordon push Plaintiff backwards with a kick. He neither identified himself as a police officer nor heard Detective Gordon do so. *Under these facts, and given that Plaintiff posed no threat to the officers or the public safety, striking Plaintiff from behind with a baton and then continuing to strike him as he lay on the ground must be viewed as a clear violation of Plaintiff's Fourth Amendment rights under the law in effect at the time.*

Id. (emphases added). The court "conclude[d] that qualified immunity is not available to Officer Allen in light of the facts of this case." *Id.*

Judgment was entered in Outlaw's favor against Allen on the claims of excessive force in violation of the federal and state constitutions in the amount of $454,197.

II. ALLEN'S CHALLENGES TO THE JUDGMENT AGAINST HIM

In his cross-appeal, Allen does not challenge the jury's findings that in connection with arresting Outlaw he caused Outlaw injury by intentionally or recklessly using excessive force. Nor, he professes, does he contend that there was any inconsistency in the jury's verdict (*see* Allen reply brief on appeal at 4 ("The jury's finding that Officer Allen used excessive force is not inconsistent with its finding that Officer Allen was not liable for assault and battery."); *id.* at 9 ("there is no disagreement in that both parties are claiming the jury's findings on excessive force and assault are not inconsistent and both parties appear to be saying that the jury finding of no assault is explained in light of the instruction that *some* force can be a defense in a claim of assault" (emphasis added))).

p.366 Rather, Allen states that "the only ruling presented for review [on his cross-appeal] is the [posttrial] decision by [the district judge] that Officer Michael Allen is not entitled to qualified immunity for his actions...." (Allen brief on appeal at 10.) In support of his challenge to the court's rejection of his claim of entitlement to immunity, Allen pursues the posttrial arguments he made in the district court, contending that there were exonerative facts that the jury "found" (*e.g.,* Allen brief on appeal at 21), or "had to have" found (*e.g., id.* at 20, 29), or "necessarily found" (*e.g., id.* at 11, 19, 25; Allen reply brief on appeal at 2, 4, 6, 10). He argues that the district court's decision in *Outlaw II* impermissibly made factual findings that were inconsistent with findings that Allen imputes to the jury, such as that Allen "saw the plaintiff acting aggressively towards Detective Gordon" (Allen brief on appeal at 20) and that Allen "believed that he, Detective Gordon, or a third person was in danger" (*id.* at 29).

Although the purely legal proposition — *i.e.,* that, with respect to any factual issues as to which the parties have a Seventh Amendment right to trial by jury, the court may not properly make factual findings that are contrary to findings made by the jury — is eminently sound, *see, e.g., Curtis v. Loether,* 415 U.S. 189, 196 n.11, 94 S.Ct. 1005, 39 L.Ed.2d 260 (1974); *Dairy Queen, Inc. v. Wood,* 369 U.S. 469, 470-73, 82 S.Ct. 894, 8 L.Ed.2d 44 (1962); *LeBlanc-Sternberg v. Fletcher,* 67 F.3d 412, 431-32 (2d Cir. 1995), *cert. denied,* 518 U.S. 1017, 116 S.Ct. 2546, 135 L.Ed.2d 1067 (1996), Allen's contention that the jury necessarily made his hypothesized favorable findings is frivolous. We reach this conclusion based on well-established principles of law and the record in this case.

A. Excessive Force, Qualified Immunity, and Trial Procedure

"The Fourth Amendment prohibits the use of excessive force in making an arrest, and whether the force used is excessive is to be analyzed under that Amendment's 'reasonableness standard.'" *Brown v. City of New York,* 798 F.3d 94, 100 (2d Cir. 2015) (quoting *Graham v. Connor,* 490 U.S. 386, 395, 109 S.Ct. 1865, 104 L.Ed.2d 443 (1989) (other internal quotation marks omitted)). The "proper application" of this standard "requires careful attention to the facts and circumstances of each particular case, including the severity of the crime at issue, whether the suspect poses an immediate threat to the safety of the officers or others, and whether he is actively resisting arrest or attempting to evade arrest by flight." *Graham,* 490 U.S. at 396, 109 S.Ct. 1865. Even where an officer is found to have used excessive force, however, the doctrine of qualified immunity will shield that officer from liability for damages if his "conduct d[id] not violate clearly established statutory or constitutional rights of which a reasonable person would have known." *Mullenix v. Luna,* ___ U.S. ___, 136 S.Ct. 305, 308, 193 L.Ed.2d 255 (2015) (internal quotation marks omitted); *see, e.g., Anderson v. Creighton,* 483 U.S. 635, 639, 107 S.Ct. 3034, 97 L.Ed.2d 523 (1987). Whether the law was sufficiently clearly established is itself an issue of law that we consider *de novo*. *See, e.g., Elder v. Holloway,* 510 U.S. 510, 516, 114 S.Ct. 1019, 127 L.Ed.2d 344 (1994).

Allen contends that in December 2004, the law governing his conduct was not sufficiently clearly established because "it was not clearly established that an officer going to the aid of another law enforcement officer should not use a baton on an individual apparently resisting arrest." (*See* Allen brief on appeal at 27.) We reject p.367 the factual premises underlying Allen's contention for the reasons set out in Part II.C. below. We disagree with his invocation of the "clearly established" standard because its applicability "depends substantially upon the level of generality at which the relevant 'legal rule' is to be identified," *Anderson v. Creighton,* 483 U.S. at 639, 107 S.Ct. 3034: "The contours of the right must be sufficiently clear that a reasonable official would understand that what he is doing violates that right." *Id.* at 640, 107 S.Ct. 3034. "This is not to say," however, "that an official action is protected by qualified immunity unless the very action in question has previously been held unlawful...." *Id.*

> The unconstitutionality of outrageous conduct obviously will be unconstitutional, this being the reason, as Judge Posner has said, that "[t]he easiest cases don't even arise." *K.H. v. Morgan,* 914 F.2d 846, 851 (C.A.7 1990).

Safford Unified School District No. 1 v. Redding, 557 U.S. 364, 377, 129 S.Ct. 2633, 174 L.Ed.2d 354 (2009) (other internal quotation marks omitted). The constitutional prohibition against use of excessive force in making an arrest had been established long before December 2004; no competent police officer could have failed to comprehend that that principle would encompass repeatedly beating an unresisting, supine, jaywalking suspect with a stick.

The qualified immunity standard is an objective standard, asking not whether the defendant officer acted in good faith or what he himself knew or believed, but rather what would have been known to or believed by a reasonable officer in the defendant's position. *See, e.g., Anderson v. Creighton,* 483 U.S. at 640-41, 107 S.Ct. 3034. Where the right at issue in the circumstances confronting police officers was clearly established but was violated, the officer will still be entitled to qualified immunity if it was objectively reasonable for him to believe that his acts did not violate those rights. *See, e.g., id.* at 639-40, 107 S.Ct. 3034; *Rogoz v. City of Hartford,* 796 F.3d 236, 247 (2d Cir. 2015); *Kerman v. City of New York,* 374 F.3d 93, 108 (2d Cir. 2004) ("*Kerman*"). "[T]he matter of whether a defendant official's conduct was objectively reasonable, *i.e.,* whether a reasonable official [in the defendant's position] would reasonably believe his conduct did not violate a clearly established right, is a mixed question of law and fact." *Id.* at 109. If there is a "dispute as to the material historical facts, ... 'the factual question[s] must be resolved by the factfinder.'" *Zellner v. Summerlin,* 494 F.3d 344, 368 (2d Cir. 2007) (quoting *Kerman,* 374 F.3d at 109). After the factfinder's "'*deci[sion as to] what the facts were* that the officer faced or perceived,' the court then may 'make the ultimate legal determination of whether qualified immunity attaches *on those facts.*'" *Kerman,* 374 F.3d at 109 (quoting *Stephenson v. Doe,* 332 F.3d 68, 81 (2d Cir. 2003) (other internal quotation marks omitted) (emphases in *Kerman*)); *see, e.g., Zellner v. Summerlin,* 494 F.3d at 368 ("Once the [factfinder] has resolved any disputed facts that are material to the qualified immunity issue, the ultimate determination of whether the officer's conduct was objectively reasonable is to be made by the court.").

Qualified immunity is an affirmative defense on which the defendant has the burden of proof. *See, e.g., Gomez v. Toledo,* 446 U.S. 635, 640, 100 S.Ct. 1920, 64

L.Ed.2d 572 (1980); *Rogoz v. City of Hartford,* 796 F.3d at 247. "To the extent that a particular finding of fact [i]s essential to an affirmative defense, ... it [i]s incumbent on [the defendant] to request that the [factfinder] be asked the pertinent question." *Kerman,* 374 F.3d at 120.

p.368 Usually, if a jury trial has been properly demanded, the factfinder for such questions will be a jury, *see* Fed. R. Civ. P. 38(a) ("The right of trial by jury as declared by the Seventh Amendment to the Constitution — or as provided by a federal statute — is preserved to the parties inviolate."). The jury may be asked to make its findings by answering special interrogatories. *See, e.g., Kerman,* 374 F.3d at 109. When such interrogatories are used, of course, the court will need to give the jury proper "instructions and explanations," Fed. R. Civ. P. 49(a)(2), 49(b)(1), to enable the jury to make its findings in accordance with, *inter alia,* the proper allocation of the burden of proof.

However, the parties may agree to forgo their Seventh Amendment rights, either entirely or with respect to specified issues. *See generally* Fed. R. Civ. P. 38(c) ("In its demand" for a jury trial, "a party may specify the issues that it wishes to have tried by a jury"; but if another party wishes to have additional issues decided by the jury, it may so ensure by serving a timely "demand for jury trial on any other or all factual issues triable by a jury"). Rule 38 also provides that "[a] proper [jury trial] demand may be withdrawn ... if the parties consent." *Id.* Rule 38(d). Rule 39 similarly allows a nonjury trial on issues for which a jury trial was properly demanded under Rule 38 if "the parties or their attorneys file a stipulation to a nonjury trial or so stipulate on the record...." Fed. R. Civ. P. 39(a)(1). These rules mean that the parties, directly or through their attorneys, are allowed to agree to forgo their Seventh Amendment rights on specified factual questions and have those questions decided by the court.

B. The Jury Instructions on Outlaw's Excessive-Force Claims

In the present case, the district court properly, and without objection, charged the jury as to, *inter alia,* what it must find Outlaw had proven by a preponderance of the evidence in order to return verdicts in his favor on his claims of excessive force in violation of the federal and state constitutions. It instructed that "a police officer may only use such force as is[] objectively reasonable, under all the circumstances" (Instr./Tr. Tr. 17-18); that "[t]he right to make any arrest or to protect the public or another police officer necessarily carries with it the right to use *some* degree of physical coercion or threat thereof to effect the arrest or to protect" (*id.* at 18 (emphasis added)); that "[a] police officer is *not justified* in using physical force which *exceeds the amount reasonably required* under the conditions of the case" (*id.* (emphases added)); and that "[i]n general, a seizure or arrest of a person *is unreasonable* ... if a police officer uses *excessive* force" (*id.* at 17 (emphases added)). The court instructed the jury that, under Connecticut law, neither assault nor excessive force in violation of the Connecticut Constitution is proven if the officer's use of force was justified. (*See id.* at 24.)

The court instructed that the jury could "consider all of the circumstances known to the officers on the scene, including" the severity of Outlaw's alleged crime, whether Outlaw posed an immediate threat to the safety of the officers or others, and whether Outlaw was actively resisting arrest or attempting to flee. (*See id.* at 18-

19.) It also told the jury that it was free to draw such reasonable inferences as it felt justified in light of the evidence and that it should not abandon common sense. (*See id.* at 6-7, 12.)

We presume, absent any indication to the contrary, that the jury followed the court's instructions, and that the jury, having found that Allen intentionally or recklessly subjected Outlaw to force that p.369 was "excessive," did not then conclude that so much of the force as was excessive was justified.

C. The Supposed "Necessary Findings" as to Questions Not Asked

Allen argues that the jury must have found justification for the total amount of force he used because, he says, "[t]he *only* reasonable interpretation of the jury finding Officer Allen liable for excessive force and at the same time not liable for assault is that Officer Allen reasonably believed *the* force was *necessary to protect* himself, Detective Gordon, or third parties *from the Plaintiff's use or imminent use of force*" (Allen brief on appeal at 23 (emphases added)), and that it was "very wrong" for "the District Court [to] ma[k]e findings of fact in contravention of the *jury's finding* that Officer *Allen believed* force was necessary *to prevent harm to himself, another officer, or a third party*" (Allen reply brief on appeal at 3 (emphases added)). This argument is factually, doctrinally, and logically flawed.

The factual flaw is, of course, that there were no jury findings as to Outlaw's conduct or Allen's beliefs. The jury was not asked whether Outlaw used force, or threatened force, or appeared to do so. The jury was not asked what Allen saw or believed.

The doctrinal flaw is that what Allen himself "believed" is not a consideration in determining qualified immunity for a federal constitutional violation but rather is an element only in the state-law concept of justification, *see, e.g.,* Conn. Gen. Stat. § 53a-22(a) (physical force in making an arrest may be justified if based on certain "believed facts"); *cf. Jones v. Marshall,* 528 F.2d 132, 135 (2d Cir. 1975) (in Connecticut, "use of force likely to cause death ... is privileged only if," *inter alia,* "*the force used was actually* and reasonably *believed* by [the officer] *in good faith* to be necessary to effect the arrest. *See Martyn v. Donlin,* ... 151 Conn. [402,] 411-12, 198 A.2d [700,] 705-06 [(1964)]" (emphases added)). As discussed above, the federal standard for qualified immunity is what a reasonable officer in Allen's position would have believed, not what Allen himself believed. *See, e.g., Anderson v. Creighton,* 483 U.S. at 641, 107 S.Ct. 3034 (the defendant officer's "subjective beliefs about the [circumstances] are irrelevant").

Finally, there are several flaws to Allen's logic, stemming from (1) the instructions given as to different permissible motivations for the use of force, (2) the instructions that permitted the jury to differentiate between amounts of force used, and (3) the different allocations of the burden of proof where, as here, the proper quantum of proof is a preponderance of the evidence. First, in arguing that the jury found justification negating the claim of assault, Allen assumes that the jury "had to have made" the "finding[]" that Allen "believed that he, Detective Gordon, or a third person was in danger." (Allen brief on appeal at 29; *see id.* at 21, 23-24; Allen reply brief on appeal at 6 (calling such a finding "crucial"); *id.* at 3, 4, 5, 7, 8; *see also* Allen brief on appeal at 20 ("The jury ... had to have credited Officer Allen's testimony that he saw the plaintiff acting aggressively towards Detective Gordon.")). But this assumption ignores the court's instruction that the jury could find a use of force justified if it found either that there was an objectively reasonable concern for safety or that force was objectively reasonably believed necessary to effect an arrest (*see* Instr./Tr. Tr. 24 (force in connection with an arrest is justified "when and to the extent [the officer] reasonably believes such to be *necessary to effect an* p.370 *arrest or* to defend himself or herself or a third party" (emphases added)); *see also id.* at 17 ("a police officer may only use such force as is[] objectively reasonable")).

It is undisputed that Outlaw was, at least at some point, standing on the passenger side of the taxi that was double-parked on the left side of Union Place, thereby perhaps constricting the traffic lanes; and Outlaw eventually pleaded guilty to creating a public disturbance. The jury, in finding that Outlaw had not proven his claim against Allen for assault, could well have based that finding on an inference that a certain amount of force was reasonably used merely to effect Outlaw's arrest. There is no necessary inference that the jury found — either also or instead — that Allen was apprehensive for his own safety or anyone else's safety.

Second, the jury was instructed in a way that allowed it to conclude that some portion, but not all, of the force used by Allen may have been justifiable. In response to a question from the jury, the court stated, in a supplemental instruction endorsed by the parties, that the standard for force that is excessive "does not apply to the assault and battery claim." (Trial Transcript January 8, 2016, at 6.) Thus, the jury was informed both that

> *[a]ny* harmful or offensive physical contact is sufficient to support a claim of assault and battery unless you find that the use of force was justified for the reasons set out in the [main] jury instructions

(*id.* (emphasis added)), and, in the main instructions, that

> *some* degree of physical coercion [is permissible] to effect the arrest ...

(Instr./Tr. Tr. 18 (emphasis added)). Thus, as Allen himself puts it, "the jury finding of no assault is explained in light of the instruction that *some* force can be a defense in a claim of assault." (Allen reply brief on appeal at 9 (emphasis added).)

But while the jury apparently found that the minimal amount of physical contact that would ordinarily constitute an assault did not violate state law here because "some" degree of force could objectively reasonably have been believed necessary to effect Outlaw's arrest, its verdict against Allen on the claim of excessive force in violation of the Connecticut Constitution negates any possible inference that it found the entire amount of force he used to be justified: The jury had been instructed (*see* Instr./Tr. Tr. 24-25) that under Connecticut law a finding of justification would also mean that a plaintiff had not proven excessive force in violation of the Connecticut Constitution. Accordingly, we infer that the jury rejected Outlaw's assault claim because it found that some force was reasonably believed warranted in order to move Outlaw out of the roadway and effect his arrest, but that it also found that the total amount of force used against him was excessive and was not reasonably believed to be necessary.

A third logical flaw inheres in Allen's total disregard of the principle that, as to the facts necessary to establish his entitlement to qualified immunity, he had the burden of proof. In finding against Outlaw on his claim for assault, the jury indisputably concluded that Outlaw had not proven assault in violation of Connecticut law by a preponderance of the evidence. But, as informed by the court's instructions, the jury could have so concluded if it simply viewed the evidence as to Outlaw's claim as being in equipoise (*see* Instr./Tr. Tr. 13 ("If ... you find the evidence to be in balance or equally probable, ... then the plaintiff has failed to sustain his burden and you must find for the defendants.")). The jury's finding that Outlaw did not carry his burden of proving assault by a p.371 preponderance of the evidence thus did not mean that it found that Allen carried his own burden of establishing the factual predicates on which his claim of entitlement to qualified immunity is based, for example, that Outlaw was hitting Gordon, or attempting to hit Gordon, or acting threateningly or aggressively.

Allen does not suggest that he made any principled attempt to have questions as to facts that could show his entitlement to qualified immunity submitted to the jury. To the contrary, although the transcript of the charge conference indicates that defendants initially wanted to have the jury asked some questions of that nature, the transcript also makes clear, as indicated in Part I.C. above, that defense counsel made a strategic choice to forgo submission of such questions to the jury. The apparent reason was that the district court stated — properly — that as to any such questions the court would have to instruct the jury that the burden of proof as to those matters was on the defendants, and that defense counsel preferred not to have the jury so instructed. Since the court insisted that the jury be instructed properly, defense counsel proposed that no such questions be submitted to the jury and that all of the requisite factual determinations be made by the court. Outlaw, who bore no responsibility for seeing that a sufficient record was created for an affirmative defense, expressly consented. Thus, as defendants wished, questions with regard to "qualified immunity for federal claims" and "qualified immunity for state law claims" were deleted (Conf. Tr. 40); all mentions of the concept of a qualified immunity defense were deleted (*see id.* at 38-40, 42); and an explanation that as to some issues in the case the plaintiff does not have the burden of proof was deleted (*see id.* at 39). As to the entirety of the qualified immunity defense, defense counsel said, "Your Honor has that on your lap, period" (Conf. Tr. 37), and the court accordingly made findings as to facts about which the jury was deliberately not asked. We cannot allow Allen now to put words in the jury's mouth.

While Allen argues that, in asking the court to make factual findings, he did not consent to have the court make findings inconsistent with those made by the jury, that argument is inconsequential. The jury made none of the factual findings he wishes to impute to it.

Finally, we note that Allen makes no attempt to argue that the evidence at trial was insufficient to support the district court's factual findings. Ironically, he argues that "there was no finding by the jury that it necessarily believed" the various witnesses' "testimony concerning [Outlaw's] version of the facts" (Allen reply brief on appeal at 1 (emphasis omitted)). However, in contrast to the lack of any instructions to the jury on defendants' qualified immunity defense, the jury was instructed that "[i]n order for the *plaintiff* to establish [that he was deprived of a constitutional right], *he must show* ... by a preponderance of the evidence," *inter alia,* "*that the defendants committed the acts alleged by the plaintiff.*" (Instr./Tr. Tr. 16-17 (emphases added).) The jury so found with respect to Outlaw's constitutional claims.

In sum, we conclude that Allen's arguments that the jury necessarily made factual findings that (a) would entitle him to qualified immunity, and (b) were contrary to the posttrial factual findings made by the court, are meritless. The jury made no findings, express or implicit, as to whether Allen carried his burden of establishing any factual predicate for his defense. The court, having been asked by the parties to make findings of fact with respect to the qualified immunity defense, had the authority p.372 to make credibility assessments and draw such inferences as it believed appropriate. Its findings of fact, described in Part I.C. above, are amply supported by the trial record. We affirm so much of the judgment as awarded Outlaw damages against Allen.

III. OUTLAW'S APPEAL FROM THE SUMMARY DISMISSAL OF HIS CLAIMS AGAINST THE CITY

In his appeal, Outlaw challenges the district court's grant of summary judgment in favor of the City, dismissing his § 1983 claim and similar state-law claims that the City is liable for the injuries inflicted on him by Allen. His complaint alleged that the City "ha[d] systematically failed to adequately hire, train, supervise, discipline, monitor, counsel, otherwise control and oversee its Police Officers to prevent the kinds of" excessive force inflicted on him. (Complaint ¶ 13.) It alleged that the City and HPD "were on notice of the violent natures and tendencies of its police officer[s]" including Allen, and had "failed to take corrective action to prevent" such conduct. (*Id.* ¶ 14.)

Summary judgment is appropriate only where there are no genuine issues of material fact that preclude judgment for the moving party as a matter of law. See Fed. R. Civ. P. 56(a). We review the grant of a motion for summary judgment *de novo;* we resolve all factual ambiguities in favor of the party against whom summary judgment was sought. *See, e.g., Amnesty America v. Town of West Hartford,* 361 F.3d 113, 122 (2d Cir. 2004) ("*Amnesty America*"); *Weyant v. Okst,* 101 F.3d 845, 854 (2d Cir. 1996).

A. Principles Governing Municipal Liability Under § 1983

It is well established that "under § 1983, local governments are responsible only for 'their *own* illegal acts.'.... They are not vicariously liable under § 1983 for their employees' actions." *Connick v. Thompson,* 563 U.S. 51, 60, 131 S.Ct. 1350, 179 L.Ed.2d 417 (2011) (quoting *Pembaur v. Cincinnati,* 475 U.S. 469, 479, 106 S.Ct. 1292, 89 L.Ed.2d 452 (1986) (emphasis in *Pembaur*)); *see, e.g., Board of County Commissioners v. Brown,* 520 U.S. 397, 403, 117 S.Ct. 1382, 137 L.Ed.2d 626 (1997) ("We have consistently refused to hold municipalities liable under a theory of *respondeat superior.*"); *City of Canton v. Harris,* 489 U.S. 378, 392, 109 S.Ct. 1197, 103 L.Ed.2d 412 (1989); *Monell v. Department of Social Services of the City of New York,* 436 U.S. 658, 665-83, 691, 98 S.Ct. 2018, 56 L.Ed.2d 611 (1978). Plaintiffs who seek to impose liability on local governments under § 1983 must prove, *inter alia,* that the individuals who violated their federal rights took "'action pursuant to official municipal policy.'" *Connick v. Thompson,* 563 U.S. at 60, 131 S.Ct. 1350 (quoting *Monell,* 436 U.S. at 691, 98 S.Ct. 2018).

"Official municipal policy includes" not only "the decisions of a government's lawmakers," but also "the acts of its policymaking officials, and *practices* so persistent and widespread as to practically have the force of law.... These are 'action[s] for which the municipality is actually responsible.'" *Connick v. Thompson*, 563 U.S. at 61, 131 S.Ct. 1350 (quoting *Pembaur,* 475 U.S. at 479-80, 106 S.Ct. 1292 (emphasis ours)). Thus, a § 1983 plaintiff need not prove that his injury was caused by an explicitly stated municipal rule or regulation. Further, a municipality may be liable even for its inaction if, in its failure to act, it "'exhibit[ed] deliberate indifference to constitutional deprivations caused by subordinates.'" *Cash v. County of Erie,* 654 F.3d 324, 334 (2d Cir. 2011) (quoting *Amnesty America,* 361 F.3d at p.373 126), *cert. denied,* 565 U.S. 1259, 132 S.Ct. 1741, 182 L.Ed.2d 528 (2012); *see generally City of Canton,* 489 U.S. at 388-92, 109 S.Ct. 1197.

"[D]eliberate indifference is a stringent standard of fault." *Connick v. Thompson,* 563 U.S. at 61, 131 S.Ct. 1350 (internal quotation marks omitted).

> [Q]uite apart from the state of mind required to establish the underlying constitutional violation ..., a plaintiff seeking to establish municipal liability on the theory that a facially lawful municipal action has led an employee to violate a plaintiff's rights must demonstrate that the municipal action was taken with deliberate indifference as to its known or obvious consequences.... A showing of simple or even heightened negligence will not suffice.

Board of County Commissioners, 520 U.S. at 407, 117 S.Ct. 1382 (internal quotation marks omitted); *see, e.g., Amnesty America,* 361 F.3d at 128 ("The operative inquiry is whether the facts suggest that the policymaker's inaction was the result of a 'conscious choice' rather than mere negligence." (quoting *City of Canton,* 489 U.S. at 389, 109 S.Ct. 1197)).

Thus, to proceed on a deliberate-indifference theory, a plaintiff must first establish "that 'the need for more or better supervision to protect against constitutional violations was obvious.'" *Amnesty America,* 361 F.3d at 127 (quoting *Vann v. City of New York,* 72 F.3d 1040, 1049 (2d Cir. 1995)). This "obvious need may be demonstrated through," for example, "proof of repeated complaints of civil rights violations." *Vann v. City of New York,* 72 F.3d at 1049; *see, e.g., Connick v. Thompson,* 563 U.S. at 61-62, 131 S.Ct. 1350 ("[A] city's 'policy of inaction' in light of notice that its program will cause constitutional violations 'is the functional equivalent of a decision by the city itself to violate the Constitution.'" (quoting *City of Canton,* 489 U.S. at 395, 109 S.Ct. 1197 (opinion of O'Connor, *J.,* concurring in part and dissenting in part))); *Fiacco v. City of Rensselaer,* 783 F.2d 319, 327 (2d Cir. 1986) (a municipality "should not take a laissez-faire attitude toward the violation by its peace officers of the very rights they are supposed to prevent others from violating"), *cert. denied,* 480 U.S. 922, 107 S.Ct. 1384, 94 L.Ed.2d 698 (1987); *Ricciuti v. New York City Transit Authority,* 941 F.2d 119, 123 (2d Cir. 1991) ("The inference that a [municipal] policy existed may... be drawn from circumstantial proof, such as ... evidence that the municipality had notice of but repeatedly failed to make any meaningful investigation into charges that police officers had used excessive force in violation of the complainants' civil rights.").

Finally, inherent in the principle that "a municipality can be liable under § 1983 only where its policies are the 'moving force [behind] the constitutional violation,'" *City of Canton,* 489 U.S. at 389, 109 S.Ct. 1197 (quoting *Monell,* 436 U.S. at 694, 98

S.Ct. 2018), is the concept that the plaintiff must show "a direct causal link between a municipal policy or custom and the alleged constitutional deprivation," *City of Canton,* 489 U.S. at 385, 109 S.Ct. 1197; *see, e.g., Cash v. County of Erie,* 654 F.3d at 333 ("to establish municipal liability under § 1983, a plaintiff must prove that 'action pursuant to official municipal policy' caused the alleged constitutional injury" (quoting *Connick v. Thompson,* 563 U.S. at 60, 131 S.Ct. 1350)).

B. The City's Motion for Summary Judgment

Following discovery, the City moved for summary judgment dismissing the claims against it on the ground that Outlaw could p.374 not show that his injuries resulted from a municipal custom or policy. The City submitted an affidavit stating that Gordon and Allen had undergone background checks before being hired by HPD; describing training that Gordon, Allen, and other HPD officers received pursuant to HPD's policies and procedures; and stating that in the years since they began service with HPD both Gordon and Allen had received additional training. (*See* Affidavit of Ursula Wiebusch dated November 23, 2010, ¶¶ 5-9.) The affidavit attached the training records of Gordon and Allen. It also attached pertinent provisions of the City Code of Ordinances that set out the municipal procedure for citizen review of complaints of excessive force or other civil rights violations by HPD officers. The affidavit stated that Gordon and Allen had received supervision as to the proper use of force. (*Id.* ¶ 10.)

In its accompanying memorandum, the City stated that "there [we]re no founded complaints against" Gordon or Allen for use of excessive force. (City's Memorandum of Law in Support of [its] Motion for Summary Judgment ("City's SJ Mem.") at 18.) The City also attached the deposition testimony of Outlaw's police-practices expert, David Stothers (Deposition of David E. Stothers ("Stothers Dep.")). The City noted that Stothers himself thought the City's training practices were adequate. (*See* City's SJ Mem. at 17; Stothers Dep. at 126 (testifying that Stothers was "no[t]" opining "that the City failed to train" its officers, and that he thought "their training was probably adequate").)

Stothers had, however, written a letter opining that the City was lax in supervising its officers (*see* Stothers Letter dated February 5, 2010 ("Stothers Opinion Letter")), in light of its handling of an incident that occurred in November 2004 (described in Part III.C.3. below). The City pointed out that Stothers testified in his deposition that his opinion as to laxity was based only on HPD's investigation of that November 2004 incident. (*See* City's SJ Mem. at 18; Stothers Dep. 128 ("Q.... Other than that one particular incident, do you have any support for an opinion that the City failed to take corrective action to prevent use of force on the citizens in general? A. Not based upon things I've read, no.").) The City argued that such a single incident does not suffice to support an inference of a municipal custom or policy. (*See* City's SJ Mem. at 14 (citing *Oklahoma City v. Tuttle,* 471 U.S. 808, 823-24, 105 S.Ct. 2427, 85 L.Ed.2d 791 (1985)).)

C. Outlaw's Submissions in Opposition to Summary Judgment

In response to the City's motion, Outlaw did not pursue the complaint's theory of deficient training but argued only that the City failed to conduct proper supervision.

He principally cited (1) the 1994 annual report of the City's Civilian Police Review Board; (2) lists, produced by the City, of lawsuits and nonlawsuit claims filed against the City and/or HPD officers from 1998 through 2005; (3) a list of use-of-force reports filed by Allen, along with two citizen complaints filed against Allen; (4) documents filed in other litigation against City officials, principally *Cintron v. Vaughn,* No. 3:69-cv-13578, 2007 WL 4240856 (D. Conn) (or "*Cintron*"); and (5) Stothers's opinion, *inter alia,* that there was "substantial evidence that the HPD has had a custom or practice that amounts to a deliberate indifference to the constitutional rights of persons with whom the agency has come in contact" (Stothers Opinion Letter at 15). Information in these documents included the following.

1. The Civilian Police Review Board's Annual Report for 1994

The City's Civilian Police Review Board (the "Review Board" or the "Board") was p.375 established in 1992 to review investigations by HPD's Internal Affairs Division ("IAD") of civilian complaints against HPD officers. The Board was required to prepare an annual report detailing, *inter alia,* the type and number of complaints filed against individual officers and the dispositions of the complaints. Outlaw had asked the City to produce the Board's annual reports for 1994 and 2000 to 2005. The City produced only the report for 1994 (the "1994 Report"); the record suggests that annual reports were not prepared for the other years.

According to the 1994 Report, the Review Board's early meetings were met with "mass protest by the police union"; officers "jeered and insulted both the Board and complainants" and threatened some with "bodily harm." (1994 Report 2, 12-13.) The Board also reported difficulties in carrying out its duties, since "[r]epeated requests to the Chief of Police regarding ordinance-mandated data ha[d] been met with marked, delayed responses ... or no response at all"; and the data that were received were "woefully incomplete." (*Id.* at 4.) The 1994 Report stated that the IAD seemed unable "to complete investigations in a timely manner," as a result of which a "public perception that officers w[ould] not be appropriately disciplined [wa]s reinforced." (*Id.* at 7-8.) And the IAD investigation files often gave the impression "that the complainant rather than the officer ... [wa]s being investigated by IAD." (*Id.* at 7.)

In its first 17 months, the Board reviewed 26 cases, 18 of which involved complaints of excessive force. Of the 18 excessive-force complaints, the Board sustained 14; IAD had sustained only two.

2. The Lists of Excessive Force Claims

Outlaw submitted and emphasized two lists, produced by the City, of civilian complaints against the City and/or HPD officers from 1998 through 2005: One listed 66 lawsuits; the other listed 87 claims on which suit had not been brought but which were submitted to the City's insurer. The City stated that it had identified the claims on these two lists as "possibly" containing allegations of excessive force. (Letter from John P. Shea, Jr. to Diane Polan, Esq., dated May 30, 2007, at 1 ("Shea Ltr.").)

The list of 66 lawsuits showed that one suit ended in a judgment against the City. Of the rest, 40 were settled; 17 were described as having resulted in either a dismissal or a judgment in favor of the City; and eight were still pending when the list was produced. The list of 87 claims submitted to the City's insurer showed that 19 claims had been settled; 26 remained pending; 28 had been denied; seven were closed or inactive; six bore the notation "STATUTE OF LIMITATIONS"; and one was described simply as "OTHER."

3. HPD Use-of-Force-Report Procedure and Allen's Uses of Force

During the relevant period, HPD had a procedure requiring officers to file a use-of-non-lethal-force report, known as a "Form 60" — each of which would be assigned a unique number — in any situation in which the officer used "Less Lethal Force," defined as "[a]ny force not reasonably expected to cause death or serious physical injury." HPD General Order 7-27. That regulation required supervisors to forward all Form 60's and related incident reports to an on-duty commander, who was required to review these documents before forwarding them to the Crime Analysis Unit, which in turn was required to forward them to the IAD commander. The HPD Chief of Operations and the Commanders of IAD and Inspections were required to review all use-of-force reporting.

p.376 A list produced by the City indicated that from June 2003 through November 2004, Allen filed 11 Form 60's. Except for the incident involving Outlaw himself, the Form 60's themselves were not produced. As to Allen's Form 60 report with regard to the arrest of Outlaw, the reviewing officer concluded that

> [b]ased on information provided by Det Gordon and Ofc Allen regarding Accused's behavior, Officer Allen's Actions are in compliance with HPD Policy/Procedure and CT General Statutes regarding USE of Force.

(Supervisory Use of Force Review, dated Dec. 22, 2004, of Allen's Form 60, dated Dec. 18, 2004, at 3.) Outlaw did not file a complaint with HPD.

The City produced two citizen complaints that had been filed against Allen, one for an incident that occurred in 2006, principally involving illegal entry into a building, for which he subsequently received remedial training, and the other filed in February 2005 by Clement Nurse with respect to an incident that occurred in November 2004 (the "Nurse Incident"). In the Nurse Incident, Allen, in hitting Nurse on the head, broke his baton. Outlaw cited the depositions of Stothers, a 31-year veteran of the Los Angeles County Sheriff's Department, and Patrick J. Harnett, HPD Chief from 2004 to 2006, who testified that, in their respective several-decades-long careers, they had never heard of an officer striking anyone hard enough to break his baton. (*See* Stothers Dep. 127; Deposition of Patrick J. Harnett at 47.) When HPD investigated Nurse's complaint, three reviewers, including Harnett, sequentially concluded that Allen had used "necessary/reasonable" force against Nurse, in that "the blow to the head [was] inadvertent and [was] caused primarily by the suspect[']s noncompliance." (HPD Internal Investigation Case Review dated 7/13/05, 7/14/05, 8/5/05.) The record does not reveal details of the investigation.

4. *The* Cintron v. Vaughn *Litigation*

Outlaw contended that the City's deliberate indifference to the use by HPD officers of excessive force was proven in other litigation against City officials, particularly *Cintron*. That case had been commenced in 1969 as a class action against the City Manager, the Chief of HPD, and five other officers of HPD — but not against the City itself — alleging a systematic pattern of police misconduct and discrimination toward members of racial minority groups. In 1973, agreement was reached that HPD would, *inter alia*, adopt procedures for internal review of citizen complaints; regulate the use of mace, tear gas, and firearms; and ensure the use of reasonable force during arrests, including by providing training aimed at "eliminat[ing] racial bias and violent reactions to personal conduct." *Cintron v. Vaughn*, No. 3:69-cv-13578, Dkt. No. 107-2, at 2-4, 9, 2007 WL 4240856 (D. Conn., Consent Decree, June 21, 1973).

As described by the *Cintron* court in 2007, the case lay mostly dormant until 1999, when the plaintiffs moved to have the defendants held in contempt for disregard of the obligations to which they had agreed in 1973. *See Cintron v. Vaughn*, No. 3:69-cv-13578, 2007 WL 4240856, at *2 (D. Conn. Nov. 29, 2007). In 2004, the parties reached a new agreement, entered as an Order of the Court ("2004 Order"), creating a Citizen Complaint Procedure designed to improve HPD's investigation of citizen complaints alleging police misconduct. *See id.* In 2005, the plaintiffs moved to have the defendants held in contempt for noncompliance with the 2004 Order. The *Cintron* court found that the defendants were in contempt of certain provisions by, *inter alia*, failing to comply p.377 with the requirement that IAD conclude its investigation within 30 days of receiving a complaint — resulting from HPD's assignment of too few investigators to IAD; failing to notify successful complainants, within 15 days, of the results of disciplinary proceedings; and, when notifying unsuccessful complainants that their complaints were not sustained, failing to send specified explanatory materials. *See id.* at *7-*8.

The City's summary judgment motion included documentation showing that in 2010, *Cintron* had been settled, *see Cintron v. Vaughn*, No. 3:69-cv-13578, Dkt. No. 232, 2007 WL 4240856 (D. Conn., Order Administratively Closing File, February 23, 2010), and the *Cintron* court had "vacated" the contempt "rulings and findings contained in [its] ... November 29, 2007 [Order]," *id.* Dkt. No. 230 (D. Conn, Ruling, February 19, 2010).

5. Stothers's Opinion

Outlaw also pointed to the Stothers Opinion Letter, which focused in part on HPD's failure to implement an early warning system as recommended by a City consultant in 1999 for systematic tracking of officers' uses of force, HPD's failure to have any other procedures in place for critical review of Form 60's, and HPD's failure to timely investigate complaints. Stothers opined that these failures "sen[t] a strong message to police officers" that it was not concerned about citizen complaints. (Stothers Opinion Letter at 16-17.) He also opined that Allen himself had a relatively high number of use-of-force incidents — 11 in 18 months — in the period leading up to the Outlaw incident.

D. The District Court's *Outlaw I* Decision

The district court, after discussing the principles governing municipal liability in an action brought under § 1983 (*see* Part III.A. above), concluded that the evidence pointed to by Outlaw was insufficient to support an inference that the City was deliberately indifferent to HPD officers' use of excessive force. At the outset, the court had noted that "[t]he facts advanced by the City are either admitted by plaintiff or, more frequently, met with a statement that plaintiff lacks information concerning their truth." *Outlaw I,* 2015 WL 1538230, at *2.

The court concluded that the 1994 Review Board Annual Report was too remote in time to be probative of HPD custom, policy, or practice at the time of Outlaw's arrest in 2004. *See id.* at *8. While the court noted that the City consultant's 1999 recommendation for an early warning system was based on a study that perceived flaws closer to the time relevant to Outlaw, it also observed that that study

> makes no reference to complaints of unconstitutional conduct or the department's handling of such complaints. Construed most favorably to plaintiff, the Study suggests that there were deficiencies in the citizen complaint process and a perceived lack of discipline. A general policy of lax discipline, assuming it could be proven, does not demonstrate deliberate indifference to serious misconduct rising to the level of unconstitutional acts.

Id.

The court concluded that Outlaw's reliance on the proceedings and rulings in *Cintron* was misplaced in light of the nature of the claims there asserted. The plaintiffs in that case complained of mistreatment reflecting a systematic pattern of racial discrimination. The court also noted that the backlog of IAD complaints, criticized in *Cintron,* had eventually been eliminated. Although resolutions had not been achieved at an ideal pace, "the fact that there were delays in addressing citizen p.378 complaints against the HPD is insufficient to establish that the City had a policy or custom of failing to supervise its officers in the use of force that caused the alleged constitutional violation in this case." *Id.* at *9.

As to Outlaw's contention that the sheer number of excessive-force complaints filed (87) and lawsuits commenced (66) against HPD officers in 1998-2005, as shown on the lists produced by the City, raised an inference that the City exhibited deliberate indifference to the need to supervise the officers, the district court found the record materially lacking in detail:

> Plaintiff has also provided evidence that from 1998 to 2005, there were eighty-eight [*sic*] complaints of excessive force by Hartford police officers filed with the City, and sixty-five [*sic*] lawsuits involving claims of excessive force. *There is no evidence of the facts of these cases, the outcome in each case, or whether and how thoroughly the complaints were investigated by the City.* Nor is there evidence that these complaints involved the officers in this case. Absent such evidence, *the numbers alone have minimal probative value.*

Id. at *10 (emphases added).

The court also noted that the record contained evidence of very few incidents involving Gordon or Allen and that each incident had been investigated by the City. There was no evidence "that the investigations were superficial or that the City and its police chief 'simply did not care what a thorough investigation would reveal.'" *Id.* (quoting *Fiacco v. City of Rensselaer,* 783 F.2d at 331).

As to Stothers's emphasis on the list of use-of-force reports filed by Allen, the court found that reliance on the mere number of such reports was as flawed as Outlaw's reliance on the mere number of excessive-force claims against the City:

> Stothers states that Officer Allen had eleven use-of-force incidents in the eighteen months leading up to plaintiff's case, "something of which HPD senior management should have been aware." ([Stothers Opinion Letter at 17.]) Again, *no details of these incidents are provided and the statistics alone are meaningless without context. He also opines that the incident in which Officer Al[l]en broke a baton over a suspect's head "should have raised a red-flag to HPD management." (Id.) As noted above, this incident was investigated and Allen was ultimately exonerated. Stothers admitted that he did not see the entire investigation.* ([Stothers Dep. 128.]) The fact that Stothers disagrees with the outcome of the investigation is insufficient to prove that the City was deliberately indifferent to the use of force therein.

Outlaw I, 2015 WL 1538230, at *11 (emphases added).

The court also noted that Stothers's opinion "that the senior management of the HPD has *failed to* meaningfully *review* use-of-force cases" lacked a sound legal foundation because

> Stothers admitted that other than the incident in which Officer Allen broke his baton, Stothers had no support for his opinion that the City failed to take corrective action to prevent use of force on citizens in general.

Id. at *10 (emphases added). Further, Stothers's negative opinion of the way in which HPD reviews excessive force complaints was based only on the method the supervisor had used in Outlaw's case. The court noted that a

> plaintiff's *"personal experience, without more, is insufficient to prove 'deliberate indifference' on the part of the City." Jenkins v. City of New York,* 478 F.3d 76, 95 (2d Cir. 2007); *Hernandez v. Connecticut* p.379 *Court Support Servs. Div.,* 726 F.Supp.2d 153, 157 (D.Conn.2009) (holding that poor investigation of plaintiff's case was insufficient to prove City of Hartford had custom of inadequate training and supervision of police officers that caused constitutional violations).

Outlaw I, 2015 WL 1538230, at *10 (emphasis added).

Accordingly, the court granted the City's motion to dismiss Outlaw's deliberate indifference claim, concluding that

> [t]he evidence provided by plaintiff is insufficient to establish that the City had a policy or custom of failing to supervise its police officers in the use of force that actually caused the alleged constitutional violation in his case.

Id. at *12.

E. The Gaps in the Evidence Relied on by Outlaw

We see no error in the district court's conclusion that Outlaw failed to proffer sufficient evidence to defeat the City's motion for summary judgment. Outlaw's reliance on the proceedings in the *Cintron* litigation is misplaced because the settlement agreements, orders, and findings of contempt in that case must be considered in light of the charges at issue there. The focus of that litigation was not a pervasive use of excessive force; rather, the complaint alleged a systematic pattern of misconduct and discrimination toward members of racial minorities. The *Cintron* proceedings had minimal value to prove the proposition that the City was generally indifferent to HPD officers' use of excessive force.

Nor did the district court err in concluding that there was insufficient probative evidence in the record to support the proposition that the December 2004 injuries to Outlaw were proximately caused by a municipal disregard of the need for better supervision of Allen himself. In response to a discovery request by Outlaw, the City identified only two instances in which excessive-force complaints had been filed against Allen. One, which centered on Allen's improper entry into a building, was filed in 2006. Whatever HPD's response to that incident (which resulted in a requirement of additional search-and-seizure training for Allen) — and whether or not there was an alleged use of excessive force — HPD's handling of it could not have been a proximate cause of the injuries that Outlaw had suffered more than a year earlier.

The other complaint against Allen concerned the Nurse Incident, and although Allen's breaking his baton on Nurse's head occurred in the month before the December 2004 incident with Outlaw, Nurse did not file a complaint with HPD until February 2005. While Stothers suggested that the Nurse Incident "should have raised a red-flag to HPD management," he also opined that "HPD senior management was apparently unaware of" the Nurse Incident "at the time." (Stothers Opinion Letter at 17.) The Nurse Incident was eventually investigated by HPD, and Outlaw's reliance on that event is flawed due to the absence of any evidence that HPD management had deliberately ignored it prior to December 17, 2004. As discussed in Part III.A. above, a § 1983 claim for deliberate indifference by a municipality is not sustainable where its failure is attributable to mere negligence rather than to conscious choice.

The lists of the lawsuits filed and the claims sent to the City's insurer might have led to evidence from which an inference of deliberate indifference to excessive force could properly be drawn, but as noted by the district court, there was no evidence as to the facts underlying those p.380 claims or how thoroughly they were investigated by the City. The simple fact that claims were made and that some of them were settled would not permit an inference that the City was deliberately indifferent in the supervision of HPD officers with respect to the use of excessive force. Indeed, it is not even clear that all of the entries on the lists involved claims of excessive force, as the City stated that they were lists of claims that "the City ha[d] previously identified as *possibly* containing allegations of excessive force" (Shea Ltr. at 1 (emphasis added)). And it noted that "many of" the officers whose names appeared on either list had not necessarily been accused of using "excessive force" (*id.* at 1-2); in the lawsuit list, the City had provided the names of all officers whose names were mentioned anywhere "in the litigation file as having some involvement in the matter," which could have been "their position in the chain of command or *their involvement in any pertinent investigations*" (*id.* at 1 (emphasis added)). That description itself suggests that there had been investigations; but the record provides no information as to the scope of any investigations or any outcomes such as disciplinary actions or remedial training.

The list of the 11 Form 60's filed by Allen indicating his uses of nonlethal force to effect arrests from June 2003 through November 2004 was similarly lacking in sufficient detail. From this list, only the Form 60 with regard to Outlaw is in the record. The record does not show any specifics as to the circumstances of, or the amounts of force used in, the other incidents. And although Stothers opined that 11 was a relatively high number of use-of-force reports for an 18-month period, the record does not indicate his basis for that comparative assessment.

As indicated in Part III.A. above, a municipal policy of deliberate indifference to the use of excessive force by police officers may be shown by evidence that the municipality had notice of complaints of the use of such force but repeatedly failed to make any meaningful investigation into such charges, *see, e.g., Ricciuti v. New York City Transit Authority*, 941 F.2d at 123; *Fiacco v. City of Rensselaer*, 783 F.2d at 326. Thus, *Monell* liability, by its nature, will often turn on evidence concerning victims other than the plaintiffs and alleged misfeasors other than the individual defendants. In addition, a given officer's disciplinary history may be probative of whether it was foreseeable to the municipality that the officer would engage in misconduct yet again. *See, e.g., Vann v. City of New York*, 72 F.3d at 1050-51. To be sure, the right to probative evidence in *Monell* and other actions is "not absolute" and will be "frequently qualified in the interest of protecting legitimate interests." *SEC v. Rajaratnam*, 622 F.3d 159, 181, 182 (2d Cir. 2010). For example, "[a] district court must ... limit 'the frequency or extent of discovery' if it determines that ... 'the burden or expense of the proposed discovery outweighs its likely benefit,'" *id.* at 181 (quoting Fed. R. Civ. P. 26(b)(2)(C) and Fed. R. Civ. P. 26(b)(1)), "[a]nd a district court may issue protective orders 'for good cause ... to protect a party or person from annoyance, embarrassment, oppression, or undue burden or expense,'" *id.* (quoting Fed. R. Civ. P. 26(c)(1)). But objections based on facile claims of undue burden, overbreadth, and lack of relevancy do not take account of these principles.

The record before us does not show that Outlaw made requests for information as to the City's "investigations" of excessive-force complaints; but it does show that he had sought the foundational information as to the existence of such complaints. His effort to obtain that basic preliminary information p.381 was largely resisted by the City. For example, during the discovery period, Outlaw had requested production by the City of, *inter alia*, all excessive-force complaints against HPD officers from 1994 to 2004, and all of Allen's HPD disciplinary records (*see* Outlaw's document request to the City, Nos. 4, 6). Aside from identifying one complaint against Gordon and two against Allen, the City refused production of such complaints, objecting that the request was "overly broad, vague and unduly burdensome" and that as the request covered "a period of nine [*sic*] (9) [*sic*] years prior to the date of the [Outlaw] incident," it was "unlikely to lead to the discovery of admissible evidence" (City's Objection to Outlaw's document request No. 4). Moreover, in response to Outlaw's far more limited request for disciplinary records of just the officers other than Gordon and Allen who were "*involved in the incident/arrest of the Plaintiff referenced in the Complaint*," the City objected that the request was "overly broad, vague, and unduly burdensome" on the specious ground that the "interrogatory *seeks information from the entire Harford [sic] Police Department* based on the term 'involved'" (City's objection to Outlaw's document request No. 3 (emphases added)). And the City declined to disclose Allen's disciplinary records on the ground, *inter alia*, that the request "constitutes an invasion of [Allen's] personal privacy." (City's Objection to Outlaw's document request No. 6.) Allen himself, in response to an interrogatory asking whether he had "ever been accused of violating anyone's civil rights" (Outlaw's Interrogatory No. 1 to Allen), similarly objected to the question as an invasion of his privacy.

The City on appeal criticizes Outlaw for failing to cite any "evidence of any citizen complaint that was filed and was not investigated" (City brief on appeal at 9). Yet the City had objected to the interrogatories that sought to identify all filed complaints — even those limited to the officers who, in addition to Gordon and Allen, had been involved in the arrest of Outlaw.

However, the record does not show any determined effort by Outlaw to obtain the potentially probative information that defendants declined to provide. Following the discovery responses described above, Outlaw moved for an order compelling the City to produce the information he had requested. But he then withdrew his motion. And the record does not reveal any further motion to compel. Some of the City's objections to some Outlaw requests may have been appropriate. But it was incumbent on Outlaw, who of course had the burden of proving the claims he asserted, to utilize procedures provided by the Federal Rules of Civil Procedure to compel responses to his requests that sought necessary information and that were appropriate. Having withdrawn his motion to compel, Outlaw's reliance on the lists of lawsuits and claims filed against the City — one ending in a judgment against the City, dozens being settled, and some perhaps not even involving complaints of excessive force — is flawed by the lack of detailed information he chose not to pursue.

Finally, we see no error in the district court's conclusion that the circumstances described in the Civilian Police Review Board's Annual Report for 1994 described events too remote in time to be probative of HPD's supervision policies in 2004 — especially given that the evidence of more recent events was so lacking in material detail.

CONCLUSION

We have considered all of the arguments by the parties in support of their respective appeals and, for the reasons stated above, have found them to be without merit. p.382 The judgment of the district court is affirmed.

[*] The Clerk of Court is directed to amend the official caption to conform with the above.

[**] Judge Geoffrey W. Crawford, of the United States District Court for the District of Vermont, sitting by designation.

892 F.3d 525 (2018)

Anika **EDREI**, Shay Horse, James Craven, Keegan Stephan, Michael Nusbaum, and Alexander Appel, Plaintiffs-Appellees,

v.

Lieutenant John **MAGUIRE**, individually and in his official capacity, Officer Mike Poletto, individually and in his official capacity, Shield No. 3762. Defendants-Appellants,

William Joseph Bratton, New York Police Department (NYPD) Commissioner, City of New York. Defendants.[*]

Docket No. 17-2065 August Term, 2017.

United States Court of Appeals, Second Circuit.

Argued: March 27, 2018.

Decided: June 13, 2018.

Edrei v. Maguire, 892 F. 3d 525 (2nd Cir. 2018)

Plaintiffs, six individuals who participated in and observed protests in Manhattan on the night of December 4-5, 2014, sued Lieutenant John Maguire and Officer Mike Poletto ("defendants") of the New York Police Department under 42 U.S.C. § 1983. The complaint alleges, among other things, that defendants violated plaintiffs' Fourteenth Amendment right against excessive force when they used a long-range acoustic device ("LRAD"), also known as a "sound gun," to disperse non-violent protesters, resulting in significant injuries, including hearing loss. Defendants moved to dismiss, arguing, in part, that they were entitled to qualified immunity because the complaint neither stated a Fourteenth Amendment claim nor alleged a violation of clearly established law. The district court rejected both arguments, reasoning that LRADs, which can cause injuries comparable to those caused by other tools that are capable of excessive force, fit within the scope of existing precedents. We AFFIRM.

p.528 GIDEON O. OLIVER (Michael Decker and Elena L. Cohen, on the brief), Law Offices of Gideon Orion Oliver, New York, NY, for Plaintiffs-Appellees.

INGRID R. GUSTAFSON (Richard Dearing and Devin Slack, on the brief), for Zachary W. Carter, Corporation Counsel of the City of New York, New York, NY, for Defendants-Appellants.

p.529 Before: KATZMANN, Chief Judge, WALKER, and POOLER, Circuit Judges.

KATZMANN, Chief Judge:

This appeal arises out of the New York Police Department's ("NYPD" or "Department") response to a December 2014 protest in Manhattan. The six individual plaintiffs allege that Lieutenant John Maguire and Officer Mike Poletto ("defendants") violated their Fourteenth Amendment rights by using a long-range acoustic device ("LRAD"), also known as a "sound gun," to compel them and other non-violent protesters to exit the street. The district court held that the plaintiffs adequately alleged an excessive force violation and, accepting the allegations as true, that the defendants were not entitled to qualified immunity. This case comes to us on an interlocutory appeal from that order.

We, like the district court, consider only the factual allegations in the complaint and the videos it incorporates. With this limitation, we are compelled to affirm the denial of qualified immunity. In a narrow ruling, we hold that purposefully using a LRAD in a manner capable of causing serious injury to move non-violent protesters to the sidewalks violates the Fourteenth Amendment under clearly established law. At the same time, recognizing that the complaint before us provides only the vantage point of the plaintiffs, we caution that once both sides present evidence—especially about what the officers observed and knew—the defendants may yet be entitled to qualified immunity.

BACKGROUND

I. Factual History

On an interlocutory appeal from the denial of qualified immunity, our jurisdiction is limited to deciding whether, based on facts alleged by the plaintiffs or stipulated to by the parties, "the immunity defense is established as a matter of law." *Salim v. Proulx,* 93 F.3d 86, 90 (2d Cir. 1996). For purposes of this appeal, the defendants accept as true the allegations set forth in this factual history.

A. LRAD Technology and the NYPD

LRADs are acoustic weapons developed for the U.S. military in the wake of the deadly terrorist attack on the USS *Cole* in 2000. "If mounted aboard a Navy ship, the device's loudspeaker could be used to 'warn off' boats that came too close. If those warnings are ignored, the device could be used to send out sound at a dangerously high level ... to cause pain/hearing damage to try to repel the attack." First Amended Complaint ("FAC") ¶ 11. This technique, known as "area denial," has been used in both military and crowd control settings. *Id.*

An LRAD can produce louder sound than a traditional amplification device, such as a megaphone, and can project over much greater distances. To achieve this effect, LRADs concentrate sound into a 30- to 45-degree cone-shaped beam. They also reshape acoustic energy to produce flatter sound waves that (1) reduce dampening as the wave travels and (2) interact with the air to create additional frequencies within the wave. Alex Pasternack, *The New Sound of Crowd Control,* Motherboard (Dec. 17, 2014), https://motherboard. vice.com/en_us/article/qkve7q/the-new-sound-of-crowd-control (last accessed Mar. 11, 2018). This can produce volumes of up to 146 decibels. For context, the threshold for human discomfort begins between 120 and 140 decibels and the National Institute of Health cautions that hearing loss can result from short exposure to sounds at or above 110 to 120 decibels.

The New York Police Department purchased two Model 3300 LRADs before the p.530 2004 Republican National Convention in New York City. Like other LRADs, the Model 3300 has two functions. One, it can serve as a "loudspeaker" to broadcast police commands over vast distances. And, two, the "area denial" function can "propel piercing sound at higher levels ... than are considered safe to human ears." App. at 85. According to a Department representative speaking at the time of the

Convention, the LRADs were purchased to direct crowds to safety in the event of a calamity.

Following the convention, the NYPD used its LRADs sporadically and, then, mainly as loudspeakers. In 2010, the NYPD's Disorder Control Unit tested the Model 3300 at an empty parking lot in the Bronx. Measured from 320 feet away, the spoken voice commands registered at 102 decibels and the area denial mode at 110 decibels. The Department did not take readings within the 320-foot range, which it described as a "potential danger area." A report analyzing the test results observed that, in the "dangerous range (above 120 decibels), this device can cause damage to someone's hearing and may be painful." FAC ¶ 11.

Shortly thereafter, the NYPD purchased the more portable Model 100X, which also has loudspeaker and area denial functions. The 100X's product sheet boasts that it has a maximum volume of 136 decibels at one meter and the manufacturer guidelines caution not to use it within 10 to 20 meters of people. A diagram on the 100X's control panel shows a red beam emanating from the front of the device and instructs: "DO NOT ENTER WITHIN 10 METERS DURING CONTINUOUS OPERATION." *Id.* ¶ 25.

B. The Protest

On December 3, 2014, a Staten Island grand jury declined to indict the NYPD officer who placed Eric Garner, an unarmed black man, in a fatal chokehold. The next day, protests arose across the nation. In Manhattan, hundreds took to the streets to denounce police brutality. The plaintiffs, many of whom are activists and journalists, participated in and documented the protest. Over the course of the evening and into the pre-dawn hours, the demonstrators marched across the city, escorted by NYPD officers.

Sometime after 1:00 a.m., as the protest crossed through the intersection of 57th Street and Madison Avenue, officers made several arrests. Videos of the scene (which are incorporated into the complaint) show a crowd—cordoned off from the arrests by a chain of officers—gathered in a semicircle to observe. Unable to proceed through the intersection, cars idled in the street as protesters streamed past. Meanwhile, many onlookers inched closer to take photographs only to be waved off by officers or told to "get back." Although some demonstrators demanded that the officers "let [the arrestees] go," none interfered with the arrests. Several plaintiffs reported hearing what sounded like a glass bottle breaking, but it did not appear to strike or injure anyone.

Then, with no warning, NYPD officers discharged pepper spray. Several plaintiffs who had been watching the arrests began to flee. Seconds later the wail of a high-pitched alarm began pulsing though the streets. The defendants had activated the LRAD's area denial function. According to plaintiffs, they had not been ordered to disperse and no such order is audible on the video.

After several bursts from the alarm tone, Lieutenant Maguire and Officer Poletto, both members of the Disorder Control Unit, began broadcasting commands. One officer held the briefcase-sized device in front of him while the other trailed p.531 behind and spoke into a corded microphone. "[T]his is the New York City Police

Department. You must not interfere with vehicular traffic. You must remain on the sidewalk. If you do interfere with vehicular traffic, you will be placed into custody." Video 1 at 3:23-3:41. Variants of this refrain, punctuated by alarm tones, were repeated for about three minutes as the officers walked the length of 57th Street between Madison and Park Avenues. Although many people in the LRAD's path "were already fleeing on the sidewalks," the officers followed close on their heels, sometimes from fewer than ten feet. FAC ¶ 124. Plaintiffs maintain that the defendants "knew or should have known that the use of the LRAD could cause permanent hearing damage and other injury." *Id.* ¶ 130.

In the days and weeks following the protest, each plaintiff reported physical injuries. Many claimed that they experienced significant ear pain, prolonged migraines, vertigo, and ringing in the ears. Most sought medical treatment. One plaintiff "had extreme difficulty with his hearing." *Id.* ¶ 370. His doctor explained that "the pressure of the extreme level of the noise from the LRAD had pushed a bone in his ear inwards, impacting and damaging a nerve in his ear." *Id.* ¶ 372. His hearing improved after a course of steroidal medication. Several plaintiffs allege that they are now afraid to attend protests, which, for some, has harmed their professional opportunities as journalists.

II. Procedural History

In March 2016, the six plaintiffs sued Lieutenant Maguire and Officer Poletto, as well as then-NYPD Commissioner William Bratton and the City of New York. They asserted claims under 42 U.S.C. § 1983 premised on violations of the First, Fourth, and Fourteenth Amendments, as well as related municipal liability and New York state law claims. Defendants moved to dismiss the amended complaint, arguing that plaintiffs had failed to state a claim and that the officers were entitled to qualified immunity.

The motion was granted in part and denied in part. The district court found that plaintiffs had adequately pleaded excessive force in violation of the Fourteenth Amendment (as well as the related municipal liability claim) and denied defendants qualified immunity. It also permitted the state-law assault and battery claims to proceed, including the claims against the City under a theory of *respondeat superior*. The district court dismissed the other claims, including all claims against Commissioner Bratton.

On the Fourteenth Amendment claim, the district court reasoned that "[t]he use of the [Model 100X] as a projector of powerfully amplified sound is no different than other tools in law enforcement's arsenal that have the potential to be used either safely or harmfully," such as stun grenades. Special App. at 16. As to qualified immunity, the district court rejected defendants' argument that amplified noise did not constitute unconstitutional force under existing precedent. "[T]here is much case law discussing the need for careful, vicinity-specific considerations when using tools like distraction devices," the court explained, and, if the circumstances were as plaintiffs allege, these analogous cases would have informed the officers of the illegality of their actions. *Id.* at 21.

Lieutenant Maguire and Officer Poletto timely filed this interlocutory appeal.

DISCUSSION

I. Appellate Jurisdiction and Standard of Review

The sole issue on appeal is whether defendants are entitled to qualified p.532 immunity on the Fourteenth Amendment claim. Ordinarily a district court order denying a motion to dismiss is not appealable. *See* 28 U.S.C. § 1291. Yet the Supreme Court has "repeatedly ... stressed the importance of resolving immunity questions at the earliest possible stage in litigation." *Hunter v. Bryant,* 502 U.S. 224, 227, 112 S.Ct. 534, 116 L.Ed.2d 589 (1991) (per curiam). This is because qualified immunity represents not simply a bar on liability but also an "entitlement not to stand trial or face the burdens of litigation." *Mitchell v. Forsyth,* 472 U.S. 511, 526, 105 S.Ct. 2806, 86 L.Ed.2d 411 (1985). Accordingly, denying qualified immunity "conclusively determines that the defendant[s] must bear the burdens of discovery; is conceptually distinct from the merits of the plaintiff[s'] claim; and would prove effectively unreviewable on an appeal from a final judgment." *Ashcroft v. Iqbal,* 556 U.S. 662, 672, 129 S.Ct. 1937, 173 L.Ed.2d 868 (2009) (internal quotation marks and brackets omitted). It follows that, "[p]rovided it turns on an issue of law," the district court's denial of qualified immunity is a final reviewable order. *Id.* (internal quotation marks omitted).

"Of course, [by] presenting [their] immunity defense on a Rule 12(b)(6) motion instead of a motion for summary judgment[, the defendants] must accept the more stringent standard applicable to this procedural route." *McKenna v. Wright,* 386 F.3d 432, 436 (2d Cir. 2004). Briefly summarized, we accept the complaint's factual allegations as true and draw all reasonable inferences in the plaintiffs' favor, including both those that support the claim and "those that defeat the immunity defense." *Id.* This standard represents a "formidable hurdle." *Id.* at 434. Because the facts are undisputed, our review is *de novo. Johnson v. Newburgh Enlarged Sch. Dist.,* 239 F.3d 246, 250 (2d Cir. 2001).

II. Qualified Immunity

Assured of our jurisdiction, we turn to the merits. Section 1983 establishes a private right of action for money damages against state officials, acting "under color" of law, who violate a constitutional or statutory right. 42 U.S.C. § 1983. This "deter[s] governmental abuse and remed[ies] unlawful governmental transgressions." *Newburgh,* 239 F.3d at 250. At the same time, "permitting damages suits against government officials can entail substantial social costs, including the risk that fear of personal monetary liability and harassing litigation will unduly inhibit officials in the discharge of their duties." *Anderson v. Creighton,* 483 U.S. 635, 638, 107 S.Ct. 3034, 97 L.Ed.2d 523 (1987). To balance the need for accountability and the potential chilling effect, "the Supreme Court established qualified immunity as an affirmative defense to § 1983 claims." *Newburgh,* 239 F.3d at 250. This defense is designed to "reduce[] the general costs of subjecting officials to the risks of trial" by immunizing them from monetary liability "based on unsettled rights." *Connell v. Signoracci,* 153 F.3d 74, 79 (2d Cir. 1998) (internal quotation marks omitted).

Officers are entitled to qualified immunity "unless a plaintiff pleads facts showing (1) that the official violated a statutory or constitutional right, and (2) that the right was 'clearly established' at the time of the challenged conduct." *Ashcroft v. al-Kidd,* 563 U.S. 731, 735, 131 S.Ct. 2074, 179 L.Ed.2d 1149 (2011) (quoting *Harlow v. Fitzgerald,* 457 U.S. 800, 818, 102 S.Ct. 2727, 73 L.Ed.2d 396 (1982)). Failure to establish either prong would resolve this case and we may "exercise [our] sound discretion in deciding which... should be addressed first." *Pearson v.* p.533 *Callahan,* 555 U.S. 223, 236, 129 S.Ct. 808, 172 L.Ed.2d 565 (2009). Like the district court, we begin with the first prong.

A. Fourteenth Amendment Violation

The right not to be subject to excessive force, perhaps most commonly associated with the Fourth and Eighth Amendments, can also arise under the Fourteenth. *See Graham v. Connor,* 490 U.S. 386, 394, 109 S.Ct. 1865, 104 L.Ed.2d 443 (1989); *Hemphill v. Schott,* 141 F.3d 412, 418 (2d Cir. 1998). This is because "[t]he touchstone of due process," which "is protection of the individual against arbitrary action of government," *Wolff v. McDonnell,* 418 U.S. 539, 558, 94 S.Ct. 2963, 41 L.Ed.2d 935 (1974), bars "the exercise of power without any reasonable justification in the service of a legitimate governmental objective," *Cty. of Sacramento v. Lewis,* 523 U.S. 833, 846, 118 S.Ct. 1708, 140 L.Ed.2d 1043 (1998). When the government action is executive, rather than legislative, the Supreme Court has cautioned that "only the most egregious official conduct can be said to be arbitrary in the constitutional sense." *Lewis,* 523 U.S. at 846, 118 S.Ct. 1708 (internal quotation marks omitted). This standard is most readily satisfied when conduct is "intended to injure in some way unjustifiable by any government interest." *Id.* at 849, 118 S.Ct. 1708.

While the parties agree that the Fourteenth Amendment establishes a right against excessive force, they disagree about the relevant test. Defendants maintain that the proper inquiry is whether the conduct shocks the conscience. Appellants' Reply Br. at 11. They argue that this standard includes a subjective element— whether the officers behaved "maliciously and sadistically for the very purpose of causing harm." Appellants' Br. at 33 (quoting *Tierney v. Davidson,* 133 F.3d 189, 196 (2d Cir. 1998)). According to defendants, this standard is "distinct from, and more stringent than, objective reasonableness." Appellants' Reply Br. at 11. Plaintiffs counter that conduct shocks the conscience when the use of force was both "objectively unreasonable" and "intentional, as opposed to negligent." Appellees' Br. at 33. In addressing this disagreement, we apply the law as it exists at the time of decision. *See Whitney v. Empire Blue Cross & Blue Shield,* 106 F.3d 475, 477 (2d Cir. 1997) (per curiam).

Defendants are correct that many cases describe the test for excessive force under the Fourteenth Amendment with the shorthand "shocks the conscience." *See, e.g., Rochin v. California,* 342 U.S. 165, 172, 72 S.Ct. 205, 96 L.Ed. 183 (1952). For many years, courts have understood this standard to be distinct from the Fourth Amendment's prohibition against "unreasonable" government action. *See Lewis,* 523 U.S. at 842-43, 118 S.Ct. 1708. As recognized in *Graham,* this distinction reflects the varied sources of excessive force claims. 490 U.S. at 393-94, 109 S.Ct. 1865. Arrestees may invoke the Fourth Amendment's prohibition against "unreasonable" seizures. U.S. Const. amend. IV. Those incarcerated for a criminal conviction draw on the

Eighth Amendment's ban on "cruel and unusual punishments." U.S. Const. amend. VIII. Meanwhile, pretrial detainees and non-incarcerated persons rely on the constitutional guarantee of "due process." U.S. Const. amends. V, XIV.

In *Johnson v. Glick,* this Court identified four illustrative factors for assessing whether conduct, in the words of *Rochin,* "shocks the conscience." 481 F.2d 1028, 1033 (2d Cir. 1973) (Friendly, J.) (quoting *Rochin,* 342 U.S. at 172, 72 S.Ct. 205). The factors are: "the need for the application of force, the relationship between the need and the amount of force that was used, the p.534 extent of the injury inflicted, and whether the force was ... [inflicted] maliciously or sadistically." *Id.* In the decades since *Glick* was decided, these factors have continued to guide our Fourteenth Amendment excessive force analysis. *See, e.g., Tierney,* 133 F.3d at 199. But they have never been exhaustive, nor is each factor necessary. *See Glick,* 481 F.2d at 1033 (stating only that "a court must look to such factors as..."). In particular, we have never treated malice or sadism as a requirement for stating (or proving) an excessive force claim under a due process theory. Where officials lacked "any legitimate government objective and [caused] substantial injury," we have treated malicious or sadistic conduct as presumptively unconstitutional. *Newburgh,* 239 F.3d at 252. But we have also found excessive force under the Fourteenth Amendment without ever examining an officer's subjective intent. *See, e.g., Robison v. Via,* 821 F.2d 913, 924 (2d Cir. 1987); *Bellows v. Dainack,* 555 F.2d 1105, 1106 & n.1 (2d Cir. 1977).

In 2015 (after the events at issue in this case) the Supreme Court revisited the Fourteenth Amendment standard in *Kingsley v. Hendrickson,* ___ U.S. ___, 135 S.Ct. 2466, 192 L.Ed.2d 416 (2015). The question there was whether a pretrial detainee alleging a Fourteenth Amendment violation must prove that the officers were subjectively aware that the force was excessive, as in the Eighth Amendment context, or merely that the force was objectively excessive. 135 S.Ct. at 2470. In resolving this question, the Court began by clarifying that excessive force claims involve "two separate state-of-mind questions." *Id.* at 2472. The first concerns the official's "state of mind with respect to his physical acts." *Id.* Drawing on its decision in *Lewis,* the Court explained that accidental or negligent acts are not subject to Fourteenth Amendment liability while those committed purposefully, knowingly, or (perhaps) recklessly are. *Id.*

The second mental state, and the one at issue in *Kingsley,* "concerns the defendant's state of mind with respect to whether his use of force was 'excessive.'" *Id.* On this score, the Supreme Court held that, unlike in the Eighth Amendment context, the standard for a pretrial detainee suing under the Fourteenth Amendment is "objective" and merely requires showing that "the force purposely or knowingly used against him was objectively unreasonable." *Id.* at 2472-73. This objective showing can be established through contextual factors and the Court identified six non-exhaustive "considerations." *Id.* at 2473. These factors included proportionality or, as the Court described it, "the relationship between the need for the use of force and the amount of force used." *Id.* They also included related indicia such as "the extent of the plaintiff's injury; any effort made by the officer to temper or to limit the amount of force; the severity of the security problem at issue; the threat reasonably perceived by the officer; and whether the plaintiff was actively resisting." *Id.*

Viewed against the backdrop of this circuit's Fourteenth Amendment jurisprudence, *Kingsley* offers two important insights. First, the objective standard it announced confirms that the subjective mental state referenced in *Glick* and some of this Court's other precedents is not a necessary showing. Second, and more significantly, *Kingsley* used modified terminology to describe the Fourteenth Amendment standard. Although prior excessive force cases spoke of whether the official's conduct "shocks the conscience," *Lewis,* 523 U.S. at 846-47, 118 S.Ct. 1708 (collecting cases), *Kingsley* asked whether the force was "objectively unreasonable," 135 S.Ct. at 2473. More on this later.

p.535 Returning to the case at hand, defendants protest that, contrary to plaintiffs' assertion, *Kingsley* is not the appropriate touchstone for assessing the alleged Fourteenth Amendment violation. On defendants' reading, *Kingsley*'s holding is doubly inapposite because it is limited to pretrial detainees and did not abdicate the traditional "shocks the conscience" standard. Both arguments are unpersuasive.

Defendants' first—and principal—argument is based on a misinterpretation of this Court's earlier statement that *Kingsley* "addressed only the legally requisite state of mind required for a pretrial detainee's excessive force claims." *Dancy v. McGinley,* 843 F.3d 93, 117 (2d Cir. 2016). Defendants understand this language as limiting *Kingsley* to pretrial detainees only. But this ignores the context. *Dancy* involved a Fourth Amendment excessive force claim and this Court was distinguishing between principles that applied under the Fourteenth Amendment and those that governed under the Fourth. *See id.* It follows that *Dancy* had no reason to address *Kingsley*'s applicability to non-detainees bringing claims under the Fourteenth Amendment.

Moreover, we have not treated the precise factual context at issue in *Kingsley*—a pretrial detainee claiming excessive force—as a limitation on the Fourteenth Amendment standard announced therein. In our one case to engage closely with *Kingsley,* we held that its standard applied not just to excessive force claims, but also to those alleging deliberate indifference toward pretrial detainees. *Darnell v. Pineiro,* 849 F.3d 17, 33-34 (2d Cir. 2017). In reaching this conclusion, the *Darnell* Court did not apply *Kingsley*'s language mechanically. Instead it looked to the sweep and substance of the Supreme Court's reasoning. We do the same.

To begin where *Kingsley* did, "a pretrial detainee can prevail" by alleging "that the challenged governmental action is not rationally related to a legitimate governmental objective or that it is excessive in relation to that purpose." 135 S.Ct. at 2473-74. As discussed above, this standard is the essence of all Fourteenth Amendment claims, not merely those brought by pretrial detainees. In *Lewis,* a case that involved a non-detainee, the Supreme Court grounded its analysis in the same principle: "the touchstone of due process" is protection from "the exercise of power without any reasonable justification in the service of a legitimate governmental objective." 523 U.S. at 845-46, 118 S.Ct. 1708 (brackets omitted). What's more, *Kingsley*'s reliance on *Lewis* as the source of the Fourteenth Amendment standard belies defendants' suggestion that claims by non-detainees are subject to a distinct test. *See Kingsley,* 135 S.Ct. at 2472-73.[1]

The distinction *Kingsley* drew was not between pretrial detainees and non-detainees. Instead, it was between claims brought under the Eighth Amendment's Cruel and Unusual Punishment Clause and those brought under the Fourteenth Amendment's Due Process Clause. 135 S.Ct. at 2475. As the Court observed, not only do the two clauses use distinct language, but, "most importantly, pretrial detainees (unlike convicted prisoners) cannot be punished *at all.*" *Id.* (emphasis added). The same is true of non-detainees, except more so. After all, with a non-detainee the government has not even shown probable p.536 cause of criminal activity, much less a public safety (or flight) risk warranting detention. For this reason, it would be extraordinary to conclude that "pretrial detainees... cannot be punished at all, much less 'maliciously and sadistically,'" *id.,* while requiring non-detainees to prove malice and sadism.

Defendants offer no principled justifications to buttress such an implausible standard, nor could they. Their argument is contrary to this Court's entire body of non-detainee cases, which have long applied the standard announced in *Glick,* a pretrial detainee case. *See, e.g., Newburgh,* 239 F.3d at 251-52; *Tierney,* 133 F.3d at 199. And yet, although defendants acknowledge that *Kingsley* represents a new gloss on the pretrial detainee standard, they would hold the non-detained plaintiffs to this Court's prior articulation of the pretrial detainee standard. To state the argument is to reveal its untenability.[2]

Shifting gears, defendants contend that *Kingsley* did not formally overrule the "shocks the conscience" standard. That may be true, but we think it is beside the point. This is because defendants' focus on phrasing reflects an overly formalistic view of Fourteenth Amendment law. To repeat, the central inquiry has always been whether the government action was rationally related to a legitimate government objective. *Lewis,* 523 U.S. at 846, 118 S.Ct. 1708. Although the Supreme Court has "spoken of the cognizable level of executive abuse of power as that which shocks the conscience," this merely showed that the "due process guarantee does not ... impos[e] liability whenever someone cloaked with state authority causes harm." *Id.* at 846, 848, 118 S.Ct. 1708. Instead, "the Due Process Clause is violated by executive action only when it can properly be characterized as arbitrary, or conscience shocking, in a constitutional sense." *Id.* at 847, 118 S.Ct. 1708 (internal quotation marks omitted).

As the Supreme Court has observed, "the measure of what is conscience shocking is no calibrated yard stick"; it merely "point[s] the way." *Id.* (internal quotation marks omitted). Mindful of this indefiniteness, *Kingsley* is best read as elaborating on this standard, not abandoning it. *Kingsley* held that excessiveness is measured objectively and then identified various considerations that inform the ultimate Fourteenth Amendment inquiry: whether the governmental action was rationally related to a legitimate governmental objective. 135 S.Ct. at 2473 (considering such things as the "relationship between the need for the use of force and the amount of force used").[3] To put a finer point on it, *Kingsley* teaches that purposeful, knowing or (perhaps) reckless action that uses an objectively unreasonable degree of force *is* conscience shocking.[4]

p.537 Although we now hold that *Kingsley* provides the appropriate standard for all excessive force claims brought under the Fourteenth Amendment, it bears emphasizing that this new formulation is but a modest refinement of *Glick*'s four-factor test, on which this Court has long relied. The first three factors identified in *Glick*—the need for force, the relationship between the need and the degree of force used, and the extent of the injury, 481 F.2d at 1033—parallel the six non-exhaustive factors identified in *Kingsley.* Consider *Glick*'s first factor, the need to use force. *Kingsley* effectively disaggregates this into three considerations that all bear on whether force was necessary. 135 S.Ct. at 2473 (encouraging courts to consider "the severity of the security problem," the threat perceived, and "whether the plaintiff was actively resisting"). As for *Glick*'s next two factors—"the relationship between the need and the amount of force that was used" and "the extent of injury inflicted,"481 F.2d at 1033—these are explicitly incorporated into *Kingsley. See* 135 S.Ct. at 2473 (highlighting "the relationship between the need for the use of force and the amount of force used" and "the extent of the plaintiff's injury").

Turning to the fourth *Glick* factor, whether the force was applied "maliciously and sadistically for the very purpose of causing harm," 481 F.2d at 1033, *Kingsley* explained that this is not a "necessary condition for liability," 135 S.Ct. at 2476 (emphasis omitted). Instead it is simply one consideration "that *might* help show that the use of force was excessive." *Id.* (emphasis added). This interpretation is consistent with our own precedents, which have repeatedly assessed excessive force claims without looking to subjective intent. *See, e.g., Robison,* 821 F.2d at 924 (holding that the assertion that officers "yanked [a woman] out [of her car], threw her up against the fender, and twisted her arm behind her back" was enough to prevent summary dismissal of an excessive force claim (internal quotation marks omitted)); *Bellows,* 555 F.2d at 1106 & n.1 (concluding that plaintiff stated an excessive force claim based solely on the injuries and absence of a legitimate government interest).

Applying *Kingsley*'s analysis to the allegations at hand, we conclude that the plaintiffs' complaint states a Fourteenth Amendment violation. First, consider the need for force. Under plaintiffs' account, which we must accept as true, the security threat posed by the protest was low. The video footage confirms that the demonstrators were non-violent and there was a robust police presence monitoring the crowd. Although someone may have thrown a glass bottle, this appears to have been an isolated and victimless incident. None of the onlookers filming and photographing the arrests interfered and additional officers were on scene to keep protesters at bay. The most significant problem confronting law enforcement appears to have been traffic disruption caused by protesters walking in the street. However, while mixing cars and pedestrians might have presented a hazard, this is the sort of public safety risk common to large public demonstrations, not necessarily an imminent threat warranting a significant use of force. In short, on the facts alleged, the "severity of the security problem" was minimal and the "threat reasonably perceived by the officers" was negligible. *Kingsley,* 135 S.Ct. at 2473.

In addition, there is no indication that plaintiffs were "actively resisting." *Id.* Quite the opposite: the complaint alleges that once the police began ordering people p.538 to move to the sidewalks the plaintiffs promptly complied. (One plaintiff admits that he briefly stepped off the curb while yelling a critical comment at the police. But this was, as most, *de minimis* resistance.)

Turning to proportionality, the disparity between the threat posed by the protest and the degree of force is stark. The Department's 2010 report describes the purpose of an earlier LRAD model's area denial function as "send[ing] out sound at a *dangerously high* level [to cause] attackers to turn away, or at least, to *cause pain/hearing damage* to try to repel [an] attack." App. at 85 (emphases added). The control panel on the Model 100X that was used here warned operators in capital letters that entering within 10 meters of the device during operation was dangerous. *See* FAC ¶ 25. The device's product sheet likewise listed the LRAD's maximum volume as 136 decibels at one meter, well above the 120 decibels threshold where pain begins and just short of the 140 decibels at which the report advised that "[s]hort term exposure can cause permanent damage." App. at 86. Exposure to this dangerous volume (which we must assume from the pleadings) is a severe consequence for blocking traffic.

The injuries alleged by the plaintiffs (another *Kingsley* consideration, *see* 135 S.Ct. at 2473) are consistent with the report's projections. They endured auditory pain, migraines, tinnitus, and hearing loss, of varying degrees and duration. Several plaintiffs claimed that they still had periodic tinnitus as of the complaint's filing (a year and a half after the protest) and at least one plaintiff said that he experienced constant ringing. Another suffered nerve damage and hearing loss that required medical treatment. These impairments fit comfortably on the spectrum of injuries that this Court has found sufficient to state a Fourteenth Amendment violation. *See, e.g., Newburgh,* 239 F.3d at 252 (holding that "head trauma, lacerations, and bruising" constitute a "substantial physical injury"); *Robison,* 821 F.2d at 924 (denying qualified immunity for a Fourteenth Amendment violation when officers caused bruises that lasted "a couple weeks").

Kingsley also asks whether the officers tried to "temper or to limit the amount of force." 135 S.Ct. at 2473. Nothing in the complaint suggests that they did. There was no audible dispersal warning before the defendants activated the area denial function, nor any other visible attempt to move protesters out of the street. Looking at the force itself, the plaintiffs allege that the officers used the LRAD at close range while "pointing it" at the demonstrators. FAC ¶ 229. In addition, the alleged injuries support an inference that the LRAD was set to an extremely high decibel-level.

Pulling these threads together, plaintiffs' allegations indicate that the officers' use of the LRAD's area denial function was disproportionate to the limited security risk posed by the non-violent protest and caused substantial physical injuries. Or, stated somewhat differently, the defendants' use of a device capable of causing pain and hearing loss was an "exercise of power without any reasonable justification in the service of a legitimate government objective." *Lewis,* 523 U.S. at 846, 118 S.Ct. 1708. Because defendants have chosen to appeal the denial of a motion to dismiss, we are compelled to accept the allegations as true and must therefore conclude that the complaint adequately states a Fourteenth Amendment claim.

B. Clearly Established Law

The remaining question is whether the constitutional right at issue was "clearly established at the time of the challenged conduct." *al-Kidd,* 563 U.S. at p.539 735, 131 S.Ct. 2074 (internal quotation marks omitted). This inquiry "ensure[s] that the official being sued had fair warning that his or her actions were unlawful." *Terebesi v. Torreso,* 764 F.3d 217, 230 (2d Cir. 2014) (internal quotation marks omitted). And, because officers cannot have fair warning of rights that are not yet established, we look to precedent in existence at the time of the events. *See Anderson,* 483 U.S. at 639, 107 S.Ct. 3034. Here, this means that, for purposes of "clearly established law," we apply the Fourteenth Amendment analysis from *Glick,* not the Supreme Court's 2015 decision in *Kingsley.*

We begin with the delicate task of defining the right at issue. In doing so, we must be mindful that, on the one hand, "[c]haracterizing the right too narrowly to the facts of the case might permit government actors to escape personal liability." *Newburgh,* 239 F.3d at 251. On the other hand, defining clearly established law at too high a level of generality "avoids the crucial question whether the official acted reasonably in the particular circumstances that he or she faced." *Plumhoff v. Rickard,* ___ U.S. ___, 134 S.Ct. 2012, 2023, 188 L.Ed.2d 1056 (2014).

Here, defendants' frame the question as "whether the officers violated the Fourteenth Amendment by using the LRAD 100X to aid in moving protesters to the sidewalks after the protest became obstructive and potentially violent." Appellants' Br. at 28. This framing puts not one but two thumbs on the scale in favor of defendants. First, it focuses on the officers' professed objective—moving protesters onto the sidewalk—while ignoring the degree of force that the officers allegedly used. Second, it recasts the protest as "violent," a characterization that, based on plaintiffs' allegations and the scene captured in the videos, is at best arguable. *See, e.g., id.* at 34 (describing a "large crowd of hostile demonstrators—who greatly outnumbered and had surrounded the officers, were becoming violent, and were obstructing traffic"). Perhaps this is an inference that a factfinder might ultimately make, but at this stage we must draw all inferences in favor of the plaintiffs, not the defendants.

Defining the Fourteenth Amendment right according to the "particular circumstances" requires attention to the precipitating events, the government interest at issue, the degree of force used, and the reasonably anticipated consequences of the government action. To illustrate, consider the Supreme Court's analysis in *Plumhoff.* The Court began with the context, a "lengthy, high-speed pursuit" that "posed a danger both to the officers involved and to any civilians who happened to be nearby." 134 S.Ct. at 2023. The officers' objective was to "protect those whom [the suspect's] flight might endanger." *Id.* After the suspect crashed and then tried to speed away, several officers fired a collective 15 shots. *Id.* at 2024. It was undisputed that this was "deadly force." *Id.* at 2021, 2022, 2024. Weaving all these circumstances together, the Court addressed whether it was clearly established in 2004 that a suspect who leads a long and dangerous car chase has a right not to be subjected to deadly force used to protect public safety. *Id.* at 2023-24. The Court held that he did not. *Id.* Following this template, and accepting the facts alleged by the plaintiffs, the question here is whether, in 2014, non-violent protesters and onlookers, who officers had not ordered to disperse, had a right not to be subjected to pain and serious injury that was inflicted to move them onto the sidewalks.

Preliminarily, we address whether this conduct alleges a Fourteenth Amendment p.540 violation under the legal standard applicable in 2014. Although our earlier discussion drew on *Kingsley,* the result is the same under *Glick*'s parallel factors. To repeat, this Court's longstanding test for excessive force claims teaches that force must be necessary and proportionate to the circumstances. *See Glick,* 481 F.2d at 1033; *see also Newburgh,* 239 F.3d at 253 ("[W]hether force is excessive depends as much upon the need for force as the amount of force used."). Here, on the allegations that we must accept as true, the problem posed by protesters in the street did not justify the use of force, much less force capable of causing serious injury, such as hearing loss.

The most significant difference between the *Kingsley* factors applied above and *Glick* is, of course, the latter's inquiry into "whether force was applied in a good faith effort to maintain or restore discipline or maliciously and sadistically for the very purpose of causing harm." *Glick,* 481 F.2d at 1033. But, as our prior cases show, this evidence has never been necessary for a Fourteenth Amendment excessive force claim. *See, e.g., Robison,* 821 F.2d at 924; *Bellows,* 555 F.2d at 1106 & n.1. And, when parties choose to present evidence on this point, they can establish subjective intent through circumstantial evidence. *See Blue v. Koren,* 72 F.3d 1075, 1084 (2d Cir. 1995). Although the plaintiffs need not allege facts showing that defendants subjectively intended to use excessive force, we conclude that, given the gross disparity between the need for force and the level of pain and injury inflicted, the plaintiffs have sufficiently alleged that the officers behaved "maliciously and sadistically." *See Newburgh,* 239 F.3d at 252 (concluding that the fourth *Glick* factor was satisfied where the force used "far surpassed anything that could reasonably be characterized as serving legitimate government ends").

The remaining question is whether the right was clearly established. Would reasonable officers have known that subjecting non-violent protesters to pain and serious injury simply to move them onto the sidewalks violated the Fourteenth Amendment? Defendants insist that the circumstances before them were too dissimilar from then-existing precedents to provide this notice. They raise two principal arguments. Neither withstands scrutiny.

First, the defendants deny that it was clearly established in December 2014 that using force in a crowd control context violates due process. In their view, because this Court has not applied "substantive due process principles to crowd control," the officers lacked notice that the right against excessive force applies to non-violent protesters. Appellants' Br. at 37. But that is like saying police officers who run over people crossing the street illegally can claim immunity simply because we have never addressed a Fourteenth Amendment claim involving jaywalkers. This would convert the fair notice requirement into a presumption against the existence of basic constitutional rights. Qualified immunity doctrine is not so stingy. In fact, we rebuffed a nearly identical argument in *Newburgh.* There, a teacher who brutally assaulted a student insisted that he was entitled to qualified immunity because the right to be free from excessive force had not been "applied to the educational setting." 239 F.3d at 253. Unpersuaded, we declined to adopt such a piecemeal view of Fourteenth Amendment protections. *Id.* We see no reason to take a different tack here.

Were this not enough, a wealth of cases inform government officials that protesters enjoy robust constitutional protections. "[O]ur constitutional command of p.541 free speech and assembly is basic and fundamental and encompasses peaceful social protest, so important to the preservation of the freedoms treasured in a democratic society." *Cox v. Louisiana,* 379 U.S. 559, 574, 85 S.Ct. 476, 13 L.Ed.2d 487 (1965); *see also Jones v. Parmley,* 465 F.3d 46, 56 (2d Cir. 2006) ("[T]he First Amendment protects political demonstrations and protests ...."); *Belknap v. Leary,* 427 F.2d 496, 499 (2d Cir. 1970) (Friendly, *J.*) (recognizing a "First Amendment right[] to protest peaceably against the war—or anything else"). Against this backdrop, it would be passing strange to presume that protesters exercising a foundational constitutional right have weaker substantive due process rights than citizens in other contexts.

To be sure, government officials may stop or disperse a protest when faced with an "immediate threat to public safety, peace, or order," including "interference with traffic upon the public streets." *Parmley*, 465 F.3d at 57 (quoting *Cantwell v. Connecticut*, 310 U.S. 296, 308, 60 S.Ct. 900, 84 L.Ed. 1213 (1940)). But this authority is not without limits. Among other things, officials have an obligation, "absent imminent harm," to inform demonstrators that they must disperse, *id.* at 60, and may not use unreasonable force, *id.* at 63. In short, our cases amply establish that protesters enjoy robust constitutional protection, protection of which reasonable law enforcement officers are well aware.

In spite of this precedent, defendants, drawing on distinguishable out-of-circuit authority, would have us believe that courts generally conclude that "use of force in a crowd control context [does] not violate substantive due process." Appellants' Br. at 37 n.12. Hardly. Our sister circuits and district courts in this Circuit have routinely applied excessive force principles to crowd control situations. *See, e.g., Nelson v. City of Davis*, 685 F.3d 867, 882-83 (9th Cir. 2012); *Buck v. City of Albuquerque*, 549 F.3d 1269, 1289-90 (10th Cir. 2008); *Asociacion de Periodistas de Puerto Rico v. Mueller*, 529 F.3d 52, 59-62 (1st Cir. 2008); *Darrah v. City of Oak Park*, 255 F.3d 301, 306-08 (6th Cir. 2001); *Duran v. Sirgedas*, 240 Fed.Appx. 104, 112-13 (7th Cir. 2007) (summary order); *Piper v. City of Elmira*, 12 F.Supp.3d 577, 589-96 (W.D.N.Y. 2014). Training our focus on controlling authority, we see that this Court has repeatedly emphasized that officers engaging with protesters must comply with the same principles of proportionality attendant to any other use of force. *See Parmley*, 465 F.3d at 53, 63; *Amnesty Am. v. Town of W. Hartford*, 361 F.3d 113, 119, 123-24 (2d Cir. 2004). A brief summary of these cases is instructive.

In *Parmley* we refused to condone officers' assault on protesters who distributed flyers on a public highway. *See* 465 F.3d at 52. The record showed that several dozen protesters had gathered on private property for a lawful demonstration. *Id.* At some point, a contingent walked to a nearby highway to distribute fliers to passing cars. *Id.* After the protesters left the highway, a large group of officers stormed onto the private property without "order[ing] the protesters to disperse or provid[ing] them with any warning or justification for their actions." *Id.* at 53. They went on to assault non-violent, compliant protesters, "beating them with ... riot batons, dragging them by their hair and kicking them." *Id.* Failing to discern a legitimate justification for this violent response, we readily concluded that that the officers' motion for summary judgment based on qualified immunity was properly denied. *Id.* at 63.

We have also warned officers against gratuitously employing "pain compliance techniques," such as bending protesters' wrists, thumbs, and fingers backwards. p.542 *Amnesty Am.*, 361 F.3d at 119, 123-24. Reasoning that the pain associated with these techniques was "comparable [to] amounts of force" that we considered unreasonable when "used during the arrest of a nonviolent suspect," we concluded that a reasonable factfinder could decide that the force was excessive. *Id.* at 124. We elaborated that liability would turn on whether a jury found either that such techniques were a proportionate response to protesters purposefully making themselves difficult to arrest or that "the officers gratuitously inflicted pain in a manner that was not a reasonable response to the circumstances." *Id.* Gratuitous infliction of a pain compliance technique—the strategy behind the LRAD's area denial function— is exactly what the current plaintiffs allege.

Both *Parmley* and *Amnesty America* gave the defendants fair warning that the prohibition on excessive force applies to protesters. This is true even though both those cases arose under the Fourth Amendment. *See Poe v. Leonard,* 282 F.3d 123, 137 (2d Cir. 2002) ("Although the Fourth Amendment cases are not on all fours with [plaintiff's] claim under the Fourteenth Amendment, they are instructive....").[5] After all, there is no intuitive reason to think a recalcitrant protester who is being arrested has more robust rights than a compliant protester who is not. Thus, we see no merit in defendants' argument that they lacked notice of the substantive due process rights of protesters.

Shifting attention from the protesters to the technology at issue, defendants' second argument is that, at the time of the events, the Fourteenth Amendment did not apply to LRADs. This argument has two parts: First, defendants contend that the officers cannot be liable because no decision from this Court or the Supreme Court "held or clearly foreshadowed that it would be unconstitutional to use an acoustic device under any circumstances," much less "under circumstances like those faced by the officers." Appellants' Br. at 19, 36-37 (emphasis omitted). Second, defendants insist that, because LRADs "function[] solely by sound," which is not an "instrument[] of force," a reasonable officer would not think that the Fourteenth Amendment applied. *Id.* at 23; *see also id.* at 35. We disagree on both fronts.

Defendants' first argument echoes a common refrain in qualified immunity cases—"pointing to the absence of prior case law concerning the precise weapon, method, or technology employed by the police." *Terebesi,* 764 F.3d at 237 n.20. But novel technology, without more, does not entitle an officer to qualified immunity. *See Hope v. Pelzer,* 536 U.S. 730, 731, 122 S.Ct. 2508, 153 L.Ed.2d 666 (2002) ("[O]fficials can be on notice that their conduct violates established law even in novel factual situations."). In our first encounter with stun grenades, we concluded that, although neither this Court nor the Supreme Court had addressed that particular technology, "the Fourth Amendment principles governing police use of force apply with obvious p.543 clarity[] to the unreasonable deployment of an explosive device in the home." *Terebesi,* 764 F.3d at 237 (internal quotation marks and citation omitted). Drawing on a decision from the Ninth Circuit, we declared, "[a]n officer is not entitled to qualified immunity" for lack of notice "every time a novel method is used to inflict injury." *Id.* (quoting *Mendoza v. Block,* 27 F.3d 1357, 1362 (9th Cir. 1994)). Instead, we instructed that "[s]ome measure of abstraction and common sense is required with respect to police methods and weapons." *Id.* at 237 n.20. To drive the point home, we listed a series of innovative non-lethal weapons to which officers should apply common sense, including "sound guns" or "acoustical weaponry." *Id.* Given our call for common sense in the face of new technology, defendants cannot credibly complain they lacked notice that the proscription on excessive force applied to acoustic devices.

As to whether LRADs are instruments of force, defendants go astray by focusing on the mode of delivery rather than the physical effect. Under this Court's precedent, a device that has "incapacitating and painful effects" when used on a person is considered an instrument of force. *Tracy v. Freshwater,* 623 F.3d 90, 98 (2d Cir. 2010). Applying this standard, we have held that pepper spray, which employs chemical reactions rather than kinetic energy, "constitutes a significant degree of force." *Id.*[6] Drawing on well-established principles, we added that because "gratuitous force is unreasonable and therefore excessive[,]... we presume that no reasonable officer could have believed that he was entitled to use pepper spray gratuitously against a restrained and unresisting arrestee." *Id.* at 99 n.5. In support, we relied on a First Circuit case concluding that unprovoked use of pepper spray against members of a nonthreatening crowd was excessive, an indication that this sort of gratuitous force against crowds is verboten. *Id.* (citing *Asociacion de Periodistas,* 529 F.3d at 60-62).

In *Terebesi,* to add just one more example, we followed the same approach. There, the officers urged that they were immune because no precedent established that the right against excessive force applied to stun grenades. 764 F.3d at 236. But we rejected that argument. Emphasizing the dangerous effects of these devices, which "cause[] fires, burns, and other injuries," we held that "a reasonable officer would [not] think it was constitutional to use these devices in routine searches." *Id.* at 236, 238.

We reach the same conclusion here. Even though sound waves are a novel method for deploying force, the effect of an LRAD's area denial function is familiar: pain and incapacitation. *See Tracy,* 623 F.3d at 98. In fact, this is what the LRAD was designed for. As explained in the NYPD's own report, the purpose of the area denial function is to "cause pain/hearing damage" that repels those in its path. App. at 85. Using common sense, any reasonable officer with knowledge of the LRAD's operations would understand that the area denial function represents a "significant degree of force." *See Tracy,* 623 F.3d at 98.

p.544 To recap, assuming the truthfulness of the allegations in the complaint, and drawing all reasonable inferences in plaintiffs' favor, the defendants knew or should have known that the area denial function could cause serious injury. When engaging with non-violent protesters who had not been ordered to disperse, no reasonable officer would have believed that the use of such dangerous force was a permissible means of moving protesters to the sidewalks. Whatever legitimate interest the officers had in clearing the street, the use of sound capable of causing pain and hearing loss in the manner alleged in the complaint was not rationally related to this end. We therefore conclude that the district court properly denied the defendants' motion to dismiss based on qualified immunity.

* * *

Our decision regarding the defendants' use of the LRAD is a narrow one. We do not hold that the Fourteenth Amendment bars law enforcement from using LRADs. To the contrary, we are confident that, in appropriate circumstances, following careful study and proper training, LRADs can be a valuable tool for law enforcement. Their usefulness as a long-range communications device is plain. We also think that, under certain conditions, an LRAD that is properly calibrated might be a lawful means of ordering (or perhaps even compelling) protesters to disperse. We merely hold (1) that, on the allegations before us, which we must accept as true, the plaintiffs have stated a Fourteenth Amendment excessive force claim and (2) that purposefully using the LRAD in a manner capable of causing serious injury to move non-violent protesters to the sidewalks violated law that was clearly established as of 2014.

We are also mindful that the complaint before us is just one side of the story, told from the perspective of the plaintiffs. But courts and juries must assess excessive force claims from "the perspective of a reasonable officer on the scene, including what the officer knew at the time, not with the 20/20 vision of hindsight." *Kingsley,* 135 S.Ct. at 2473. It follows that, once the allegations are tested by evidence, particularly evidence about what the officers saw and knew, the defendants may yet be entitled to qualified immunity.

We can envision various factual showings that would change the calculus. One key variable is the state of unrest at the protest. The evidence may show that the defendants observed a more violent scene than is portrayed in the complaint and incorporated videos. Another key consideration is how the LRAD was used, most notably the volume of the device and its proximity to protesters and passersby. And, third, as *Kingsley* acknowledges, much hinges on what the defendants knew. Perhaps the defendants had not seen the report on the Model 3300 and lacked knowledge of the LRAD's harmful effects. The complaint alleges that the NYPD "has not properly trained its officers" on LRAD use and acknowledges that Department's use of force protocols "do not account for LRAD use." FAC ¶¶ 98, 412. So perhaps the defendants had received training but reasonably believed that they were not using the device in an unsafe or gratuitous manner. Any one of these non-exhaustive factors could warrant a reappraisal of qualified immunity.

Finally, we emphasize that when viewing the evidence from the perspective of a reasonable officer a factfinder must afford "ample room for mistaken judgments." *Malley v. Briggs,* 475 U.S. 335, 343, 106 S.Ct. 1092, 89 L.Ed.2d 271 (1986). This is particularly true where officers "have obligations that tend to tug against each other." *Lewis,* 523 U.S. at 853, 118 S.Ct. 1708.

> Their duty is to restore and maintain lawful order, while not exacerbating disorder p.545 more than necessary to do their jobs. They are supposed to act decisively and to show restraint at the same moment, and their decisions have to be made in haste, under pressure, and frequently without the luxury of a second chance.

Id. (internal quotation marks omitted). It follows that a jury or a court viewing events from the defendants' perspective must consider not just what the officers saw and knew, but also the rapidly evolving, uncertain, and tense circumstances in which they acted. We trust that discovery will provide fuller insight into this perspective.

CONCLUSION

For the foregoing reasons, we AFFIRM the district court's order insofar as it denied defendants qualified immunity for the Fourteenth Amendment claim. This case is REMANDED for further proceedings.

[*] The Clerk of Court is directed to amend the official caption to conform to the above.

[1] Additionally, when the *Kingsley* defendants argued that *Lewis* supported a subjective intent standard, the Court had an opportunity to distinguish its earlier decision as a case limited to non-detainees. But the Court did no such thing. Instead, it explained why that argument misread *Lewis*'s holding. 135 S.Ct. at 2475.

[2] Defendants, moreover, point to no case in our Circuit dealing with non-detainees—before or after *Kingsley*—that treated proof of subjective intent as a necessary precondition for a successful Fourteenth Amendment excessive force

claim. Thus, even if they could convince us that *Kingsley* should be cabined to pretrial detainees (which they cannot), this would not require us to dismiss an excessive force claim absent an allegation of malice or sadism. *Kingsley* made explicit what we have long taken for granted: a government actor's use of force violates due process when it is objectively excessive.

[3] Framed in these terms, defendants cannot seriously dispute *Kingsley*'s logic. After all, their own brief acknowledges that, "[i]t is where officials take injurious action with *no apparent government interest* that this Court has found their conduct conscience-shocking." Appellant's Br. at 39 (emphasis added).

[4] One might argue that this conclusion is in tension with *Dancy*'s observation that "Fourth Amendment claims are tied to reasonableness, which is considerably less demanding" than the Due Process Clause. 843 F.3d at 117. But, once again, because *Dancy* focused on the intent standard under the Fourth Amendment, it did not purport to address how *Kingsley* affected cases brought under the Due Process Clause.

[5] Defendants' reply brief argues that Fourth Amendment cases "cannot establish the law for Fourteenth Amendment purposes." Appellants' Reply Br. at 22. This argument is inconsistent with the practice of the Supreme Court and this Circuit, both of which cross-pollinate between Fourth, Eighth, and Fourteenth Amendment contexts. *See, e.g., Graham,* 490 U.S. at 396, 109 S.Ct. 1865 (relying on language from *Glick,* a Fourteenth Amendment case, to explain Fourth Amendment constraints); *Hudson v. McMillian,* 503 U.S. 1, 9, 112 S.Ct. 995, 117 L.Ed.2d 156 (1992) (drawing on *Glick* in the Eighth Amendment context); *Medeiros v. O'Connell,* 150 F.3d 164, 170 (2d Cir. 1998) (analyzing Eighth Amendment case law to define a Fourteenth Amendment right).

[6] Defendants claim that an LRAD differs from pepper spray because "it includes a highly effective loudspeaker mode that can help *avoid* the need for measures historically regarded as force." Appellants' Br. at 23. This is effectively an argument that LRAD's are dual-use devices capable of both exerting dangerous force and serving valuable, non-forceful functions. But the same is true of a riot stick, which can both bludgeon and direct traffic. Rather than absolving the riot stick from scrutiny, this dual functionality is all the more reason to focus on the particular action and ensuing effect, not the device itself.

864 F.3d 200 (2017)

Stephen L. KASS, Plaintiff-Appellee,

v.

CITY OF NEW YORK, Michael Alfieri, NYPD Officer; Shield #800, K. Ernst, New York City Police ("NYPD") Officer, Defendants-Appellants, NYPD Officer Jane Beggin, NYPD Officer John Doe, NYPD Officer Meredith Biggin, Defendants.[*]

No. 15-2053-cv August Term, 2016.

United States Court of Appeals, Second Circuit.

Argued: August 23, 2016.

Decided: July 24, 2017.

Kass v. City of New York, 864 F. 3d 200 (2nd Cir. 2017)

Appeal from the United States District Court, for the Southern District of New York. No. 14 Civ. 7505 — Andrew L. Carter, Jr., Judge.

MELANIE T. WEST (Deborah A. Brenner, on the brief), on behalf of Zachary W. Carter, Corporation Counsel of the City of New York, New York, NY, for Defendants-Appellants.

ANDREW G. CELLI, JR. (Alison Frick, on the brief) Emery Celli Brinckerhoff & Abady LLP, New York, NY for Plaintiff-Appellee.

Before: WALKER, CHIN, and LOHIER, Circuit Judges.

p.203 JOHN M. WALKER, JR., Circuit Judge:

Defendants-appellants the City of New York ("the City") and certain New York City Police Department ("NYPD") officers bring this interlocutory appeal from an order of the United States District Court for the Southern District of New York (Andrew L. Carter, Jr., J.) denying their motion for judgment on the pleadings. We consider in this appeal (1) whether the NYPD officers are entitled to qualified immunity from plaintiff-appellee Stephen L. Kass's federal false arrest and imprisonment claim under 42 U.S.C. § 1983 and (2) whether we should exercise pendent jurisdiction over Kass's state law claims against these officers and the City.

We hold that, because the officers had arguable probable cause to arrest Kass for obstructing governmental administration, N.Y. Penal Law § 195.05, and refusing to comply with a lawful order to disperse, N.Y. Penal Law § 240.20(6), they are entitled to qualified immunity. We therefore REVERSE the district court's denial of the defendants-appellants' motion with respect to Kass's federal and state false arrest and imprisonment claims. We DISMISS the remainder of the appeal for lack of appellate jurisdiction.

p.204 BACKGROUND

On September 17, 2013, protestors gathered in Zuccotti Park in New York City to commemorate the second anniversary of the Occupy Wall Street movement. The NYPD placed barricades around the perimeter of the park to cordon off the area where the protestors were gathered and to separate the protestors, who were inside the park, from the pedestrians who were on the adjacent sidewalk along lower Broadway. NYPD Sergeant Michael Alfieri, Officer Karen Ernst, and Officer Meredith Biggin were stationed on the sidewalk near the barricades.

At around 4:40 p.m., Stephen L. Kass, then a 73-year-old attorney, was walking north on Broadway when he noticed the crowd of people in Zuccotti Park. Kass approached the barricades and, while standing on the sidewalk, engaged in a non-confrontational conversation with several protestors. Kass did not impede pedestrian or vehicular traffic during this conversation. After Kass had spoken with the protestors for a minute or two, Ernst approached Kass and instructed him to "keep walking." Joint App'x at 16. Kass replied that he wanted to hear the protestors' views, he was not blocking pedestrian traffic, and he had a right to remain on the sidewalk. Ernst repeated that Kass had to move away from the barricade. When Kass continued to refuse to comply, Ernst called over Alfieri.

At this point, one of the protestors began recording a video of the interaction, the authenticity and accuracy of which is not in dispute. As can be seen on the video, Ernst and Alfieri instructed Kass several times to continue walking. Kass repeated that he wanted to talk to the protestors, that he was not blocking pedestrian traffic, and that he would not move. Alfieri then directed Kass to follow him and placed his hand on Kass's elbow, attempting to guide him away from the barricades. Kass pulled away, telling Alfieri to take his hands off of him and that he was talking to the protestors. Ernst then suggested that Kass could go inside the park to continue his conversation with the protestors.

After Kass continued to refuse to comply, Alfieri grabbed Kass's right arm and pulled him toward the middle of the sidewalk, away from the barricade and protestors. Kass immediately objected, saying "get your hands off of me, how dare you, get your hands off me." A third unidentified officer then grabbed Kass's other arm, and the officers handcuffed Kass. Kass was brought to the precinct and issued a summons for disorderly conduct under New York Penal Law § 240.20(5). This charge was ultimately dismissed for failure to prosecute.

On September 16, 2014, Kass filed the instant action against the City and NYPD officers Ernst and Alfieri. Kass also named as a defendant an NYPD officer who was later identified as Meredith Biggin and who was served with the complaint on May 13, 2015. Kass alleged that the officers did not have probable cause to arrest him and that the City was liable for the actions of its employees under the doctrine of *respondeat superior*. Kass asserted federal claims against the officers for false arrest and imprisonment as well as malicious prosecution, and New York state law claims against all of the defendants for false arrest and imprisonment, malicious prosecution, and assault and battery.

On March 16, 2015, before Biggin was served with the complaint, the City, Ernst, and Alfieri moved for judgment on the pleadings pursuant to Federal Rule of Civil Procedure 12(c). Ernst and Alfieri argued that they were entitled to qualified immunity because there was probable cause or, at least, arguable probable cause to support Kass's arrest. The City, Ernst, p.205 and Alfieri also sought dismissal of the state law claims against them. While this motion was pending, Kass withdrew his federal malicious prosecution claim.

On June 8, 2015, the district court dismissed Kass's withdrawn claim, but otherwise denied the defendants-appellants' motion. The district court did not explain its basis for rejecting the officers' qualified immunity defense. On June 24, 2015, the City, Ernst, Alfieri, and Biggin timely filed an interlocutory appeal.

DISCUSSION

As an initial matter, we address whether defendant Biggin is properly included as an appellant in this action. Kass argues that because Biggin was not a party to the Rule 12(c) motion, she should not be permitted to appeal the district court's denial of that motion. Although Kass only cursorily raises this issue and the defendants do not present any arguments in response, we must address whether Biggin has standing to pursue this appeal before we turn to the merits of her arguments. *See Official Comm. of Unsecured Creditors of WorldCom, Inc. v. SEC*, 467 F.3d 73, 77 (2d Cir. 2006) (noting "[s]tanding to appeal is an essential component of our appellate jurisdiction"); *see also Tachiona v. United States*, 386 F.3d 205, 210-11 (2d Cir. 2004).

In order to have standing on appeal, "a party must be aggrieved by the judicial action from which it appeals." *Swatch Grp. Mgmt. Servs. Ltd. v. Bloomberg L.P.*, 756 F.3d 73, 92 (2d Cir. 2014) (citation omitted). A party that is "not bound by a [district court order] will, in the usual case, have difficulty showing that it meets the Article III standing requirement" that it has suffered such an injury. *Tachiona*, 386 F.3d at 211; *see, e.g., Arizonans for Official English v. Arizona*, 520 U.S. 43, 66, 117 S.Ct. 1055, 137 L.Ed.2d 170 (1997) (noting "grave doubts" as to whether parties who "were not bound by the judgment" of the district court had Article III standing to appeal).

Here, defendant Biggin was not a party to the relevant Rule 12(c) motion, she is not bound by the district court's order denying that motion, and the defendants have failed to argue on appeal that she has sustained any legal injury as a result of this order. We therefore agree with Kass that she is not properly an appellant before this Court. Thus, our decision concerns only Kass's claims against the City, Ernst, and Alfieri, the defendants-appellants.

I. Federal False Arrest and Imprisonment Claim

On appeal, the defendants-appellants argue first that Kass's federal false arrest and imprisonment claim should be dismissed against Officers Ernst and Alfieri because the district court incorrectly rejected their qualified immunity defense. Although generally an appeal must await a final dispositive judgment in the district court, we have jurisdiction over an interlocutory appeal from a denial of qualified immunity when, as is the case here, the matter can be decided as a matter of law. *See DiStiso v. Cook*, 691 F.3d 226, 239 (2d Cir. 2012). That is because an individual who is entitled to qualified immunity is immune not only from liability, but also from further legal proceedings, and should receive such immunity at "the earliest possible stage of the litigation." *Wood v. Moss,* ___ U.S. ___, 134 (S.Ct. 2056, 2065 n.4, 188 L.Ed.2d 1039 2014) (citation and brackets omitted).

We review *de novo* a district court's denial of a motion for judgment on the pleadings based on qualified immunity. *See Anderson v. Recore,* 317 F.3d 194, 197 p.206 (2d Cir. 2003); *Garcia v. Does,* 779 F.3d 84, 91 (2d Cir. 2015). We apply the same standard as that applicable to a motion under Rule 12(b)(6), accepting the allegations contained in the complaint as true and drawing all reasonable inferences in favor of the nonmoving party. *Anderson,* 317 F.3d at 197. However, when the record includes a video that the parties concede is authentic and accurate, as is the case here, we view the allegations of the complaint as true only "to the extent that they are not contradicted by video evidence." *See Garcia,* 779 F.3d at 88.

The burden is on the defendants to demonstrate that qualified immunity applies and that their motion for judgment on the pleadings should be granted. *McKenna v. Wright,* 386 F.3d 432, 436 (2d Cir. 2004). The defendants therefore must show that, construing all reasonable inferences in the plaintiff's favor, "the facts supporting the [immunity] defense appear on the face of the complaint" and that "it appears beyond doubt that the plaintiff can prove no set of facts in support of his claim that would entitle him to relief." *Id.* (citation omitted).

An officer is entitled to qualified immunity from a federal false arrest and imprisonment claim if he had arguable probable cause to arrest the plaintiff for any offense, regardless of the offense with which the plaintiff was actually charged. *Betts v. Shearman,* 751 F.3d 78, 82-83 (2d Cir. 2014); *Myers v. Patterson,* 819 F.3d 625, 632-33 (2d Cir. 2016); *Zalaski v. City of Hartford,* 723 F.3d 382, 390 n.4 (2d Cir. 2013). Probable cause exists when "the facts and circumstances within ... the officers' knowledge and of which they had reasonably trustworthy information are sufficient in themselves to warrant a man of reasonable caution in the belief that an offense has been or is being committed by the person to be arrested." *Marcavage v. City of N.Y.,* 689 F.3d 98, 109 (2d Cir. 2012) (citation omitted). Arguable probable cause exists when "it was objectively reasonable for the officer to believe that probable cause existed, or ... officers of reasonable competence could disagree on whether the probable cause test was met." *Myers,* 819 F.3d at 633 (citation omitted). In other words, an officer is entitled to qualified immunity unless "no officer of reasonable competence could have made the same choice in similar circumstances." *Id.* (citation omitted). The qualified immunity defense, thus, is a broad shield that protects "all but the plainly incompetent or those who knowingly violate the law." *Zalaski,* 723 F.3d at 389 (citation omitted).

Here, the officers assert that they are entitled to qualified immunity because they had probable cause or, at least, arguable probable cause to arrest Kass for two separate offenses: obstructing governmental administration, N.Y. Penal Law § 195.05, and refusing to comply with a lawful order to disperse, N.Y. Penal Law § 240.20(6). We agree that the officers are shielded by qualified immunity, and we reverse the district court's denial of the officers' motion for judgment on the pleadings with respect to Kass's federal false arrest and imprisonment claim.

i. Obstruction of Governmental Administration

We first address whether the officers had arguable probable cause to arrest Kass for obstructing governmental administration. New York Penal Law § 195.05 provides that,

> A person is guilty of obstructing governmental administration when he intentionally obstructs, impairs or perverts the administration of law or other governmental function or prevents or attempts to prevent a public servant from p.207 performing an official function, by means of intimidation, physical force or interference, or by means of any independently unlawful act.

An individual, therefore, may be convicted under this statute when (1) a public servant is performing an official function; (2) the individual prevents or attempts to prevent the performance of that function by interfering with it; and (3) the individual does so intentionally. *See* N.Y. Penal Law § 195.05. For the following reasons, we think that it was at least debatable and reasonable officers could disagree as to whether all three of these elements were met in the instant case.

a. Official Function

The first element is that the public servant must be performing an official function that is "authorized by law." *In re Verna C.,* 143 A.D.2d 94, 531 N.Y.S.2d 344, 345 (2d Dep't 1988). The defendants argue that, in ordering Kass to move, the officers were lawfully regulating pedestrian traffic and addressing any congestion or security issues relating to the protest. Kass responds that it was not objectively reasonable for the officers to believe that he had committed a crime and thus that they had the authority to arrest him for standing on a public sidewalk and refusing to move.

Kass's argument misses the point. An officer does not need to believe that an individual has committed a crime before he or she may lawfully direct the individual to move from where he is standing. *See, e.g., Marcavage,* 689 F.3d at 110 (concluding that officers lawfully directed protestors to move because protestors were standing in a designated no-demonstration zone). And, contrary to Kass's assertion, the officers did not direct Kass to move simply because he was standing on a sidewalk or, as we will discuss below, arrest him because he refused to obey an arbitrary order to move. Kass's argument ignores the context in which the officers' orders occurred: on a sidewalk in the heart of downtown Manhattan, shortly before 5 p.m., and near a public protest that the officers were attempting to maintain within a confined area to ensure crowd control and security. We think that, under such circumstances, it was objectively reasonable for the officers to believe that they had the authority to order Kass, who was engaging with protestors while standing on a sidewalk adjacent to the protest, either to "keep walking" or enter the park to continue speaking with the protestors.

Kass also argues that these orders were unconstitutional under the First Amendment because they "arbitrarily and forcibly remove[d] a passer-by from a public sidewalk" and prevented him from hearing the protestors' message. Appellee Br. at 17. The First Amendment, which applies to the states through the Fourteenth Amendment, guarantees freedom of speech. U.S. CONST. amend. I; *see Thornhill v. Alabama,* 310 U.S. 88, 95, 60 S.Ct. 736, 84 L.Ed. 1093 (1940). This guarantee extends not only to the right to speak, but also to the right to listen and receive information. *See Va. State Bd. of Pharmacy v. Va. Citizens Consumer Council, Inc.,* 425 U.S. 748, 756, 96 S.Ct. 1817, 48 L.Ed.2d 346 (1976) ("[W]here a speaker exists, as is the case here, the protection afforded is to the communication, to its source and to its recipients both." (footnote omitted)); *Conant v. Walters,* 309 F.3d 629, 643 (9th Cir. 2002) ("[T]he right to hear and the right to speak are flip sides of the same coin.").

The First Amendment, however, "does not guarantee the right to communicate... at all times and places or in any manner that may be desired." *Heffron v. Int'l Soc'y for Krishna Consciousness, Inc.,* 452 U.S. 640, 647, 101 S.Ct. 2559, 69 L.Ed.2d 298 (1981). The extent to which p.208 the government may permissibly restrict such communications depends in part upon the circumstances under which those communications and the receipt of those communications occur. *Zalaski v. City of Bridgeport Police Dep't,* 613 F.3d 336, 341 (2d Cir. 2010) (per curiam). Traditional public fora, such as sidewalks and parks, are afforded the broadest protections for free expression. *Id.; see also McCullen v. Coakley,* ___ U.S. ___, 134 S.Ct. 2518, 2536, 189 L.Ed.2d 502 (2014) ("[N]ormal conversation ... on a public sidewalk ... [is a form of expression that has] historically been more closely associated with the transmission of ideas than others."). In such public fora, the government may apply content-neutral time, place, and manner restrictions only if they are "narrowly tailored to serve a significant government interest" and if "ample alternative channels of communication" are available. *Zalaski,* 613 F.3d at 341 (citation omitted).[1]

At issue here is the balance between an individual's First Amendment right to engage in a conversation on a public sidewalk with protestors and the government's interest in maintaining public safety and order. Although sidewalks are generally open to the public, including for "expressive activities," we have recognized that the government "certainly has a significant interest in keeping its public spaces safe and free of congestion." *Marcavage,* 689 F.3d at 104 (citations omitted); *see also Mastrovincenzo v. City of New York,* 435 F.3d 78, 100 (2d Cir. 2006) ("[R]educing sidewalk and street congestion in a city with eight million inhabitants[] constitute[s] [a] 'significant governmental interest[]'."). Here, as we have noted, Kass was standing on a sidewalk in downtown Manhattan that was adjacent to the protest and that was being used by pedestrians. We agree with the officers that the government had a significant interest in ensuring that the protest remained within the park and that pedestrian traffic on this sidewalk was not impeded.

The officers' orders also were narrowly tailored to achieve this significant government interest. *See Zalaski,* 613 F.3d at 341. A restriction on free speech is narrowly tailored if it does not "burden substantially more speech than is necessary to further the government's legitimate interests." *McCullen,* 134 S.Ct. at 2535 (citation omitted); *see also Frisby v. Schultz,* 487 U.S. 474, 485, 108 S.Ct. 2495, 101 L.Ed.2d 420 (1988) ("A statute is narrowly tailored if it targets and eliminates no more than the exact source of the 'evil' it seeks to remedy." (citation omitted)). The restriction, however, need not be "the least restrictive or least intrusive means of [achieving those interests]." *Mastrovincenzo,* 435 F.3d at 98 (citation omitted). In *Marcavage v. City of New York,* for example, we held that police officers, who were regulating pedestrian traffic during the 2004 Republican National Convention and who instructed protestors to leave an area that had been designated as a no-demonstration zone, were performing a lawful governmental function that did not violate the protestors' First Amendment rights. 689 F.3d at 109. We determined that, because there were crowds of protestors and pedestrians associated with the convention and the non-protest areas were limited to a two-block stretch during the convention, these restrictions were sufficiently tailored to achieve the government's significant interest in keeping such public spaces safe and free of congestion. *Id.* at 106-07.

p.209 Here, the officers ordered Kass, after he had conversed with the protestors for a minute or two while standing outside of the designated protest area, to either keep walking or enter the park to continue his conversation. The officers' orders targeted and sought to eliminate the risk that the protest might expand beyond the barricades and that individuals who were not within the park, such as Kass, might cause congestion or a security issue by interacting with protestors on the sidewalk outside of the protest area. We acknowledge that, when the officers ordered Kass to move, he was the only individual speaking with the two protestors and he was not then impeding pedestrian or vehicular traffic. Whether the officers' orders were justified under these circumstances, however, "should not be measured by the disorder that would result from granting an exemption solely to [one individual] because if [he] were allowed a dispensation, so too must other groups, which would then create a much larger threat to the [City's] interest in crowd control and security." *See id.* at 107 (citation omitted). Further, we do not think that to avoid liability the officers needed to refrain from intervening until Kass actually impeded pedestrian traffic or caused a security issue. *See id.* (rejecting plaintiffs' argument that, because they were two protestors who were "standing out of the way," the congestion and security risks justifying a no-demonstration zone did not apply to them). We also note that once Alfieri tried to move Kass away from the barricades, Kass became agitated and hostile, thereby further increasing the risk that he would impede traffic or pose a security threat. Under such circumstances, the officers' repeated orders that Kass either "keep walking" or enter the protest area to continue his conversation were narrowly tailored to maintain crowd control and security.

Finally, the officers' orders did not foreclose ample, alternative channels of communication. Such channels need not "be perfect substitutes for those ... denied to [the plaintiff] by the regulation at hand." *Mastrovincenzo,* 435 F.3d at 101; *see also Connection Distrib. Co. v. Reno,* 154 F.3d 281, 293 (6th Cir. 1998) ("[T]he requirement that ample alternative channels be left available does not mean that there must be a channel where [plaintiffs] can express themselves in precisely the same manner."). Here, the officers suggested a reasonable alternative: Kass could continue his conversation with the protestors if he simply entered the park. Kass does not advance any argument on appeal as to why this would not have been an adequate, alternative forum for his conversation.

Thus, because the officers' orders were content neutral, narrowly tailored, and allowed an adequate, alternative channel of communication, they were a permissible time, place, and manner restriction on speech and did not violate the First Amendment.

b. Interference with the Official Function

The second element is that an individual must prevent or attempt to prevent a public official from performing a lawful official function by interfering with that function. *See* N.Y. Penal Law § 195.05. Although the interference must at least in part be "physical" and cannot consist solely of verbal statements, *People v. Case,* 42 N.Y.2d 98, 101-02, 396 N.Y.S.2d 841, 365 N.E.2d 872 (1977), an officer may consider both words and deeds in determining whether the individual's conduct is sufficiently obstructive to justify an arrest, *In re Davan L.,* 91 N.Y.2d 88, 91-92, 666 N.Y.S.2d 1015, 689 N.E.2d 909 (1997). Such interference can consist of "inappropriate and disruptive conduct at the scene p.210 of the performance of an official function even if there is no physical force involved." *People v. Romeo,* 9 A.D.3d 744, 779 N.Y.S.2d 860, 861-62 (3d Dep't 2004) (internal citations omitted). This element of the statute is satisfied when an individual "intrude[s] himself into, or get[s] in the way of, an ongoing police activity." *In re Kendell R.,* 71 A.D.3d 553, 897 N.Y.S.2d 83, 84 (1st Dep't 2010); *see also Davan L.,* 91 N.Y.2d at 91, 666 N.Y.S.2d 1015, 689 N.E.2d 909 ("[C]riminal responsibility should attach to minimal interference set in motion to frustrate police activity.").

Here, Kass physically interfered with the officers' efforts to confine the protest to the park and keep the sidewalk clear for pedestrians. Kass refused to obey the officers' repeated orders to move along and, after Alfieri placed his hand on Kass's elbow to guide Kass away from the barricades, Kass instructed Alfieri to "get [his] hands off" of him and pulled away. A reasonable officer could conclude under these circumstances that Kass had physically "[gotten] in the way of" and had frustrated the officers' efforts to contain the protest and prevent sidewalk congestion. *See Kendell R.,* 897 N.Y.S.2d at 84; *see also Marcavage,* 689 F.3d at 110 (probable cause to arrest protestors for refusing to leave the no-demonstration zone despite officers' repeated requests); *Romeo,* 779 N.Y.S.2d at 861 (probable cause to arrest individual who was "belligerent, uncooperative and refused several direct requests that he keep away from the officers as they attempted to subdue his girlfriend").

c. Intent to Prevent Performance of Official Function

Finally, the third element is that an individual who interferes with an official function must intend to prevent the officers from performing that function. *See* N.Y. Penal Law § 195.05. However, because "the practical restraints on police in the field are greater with respect to ascertaining intent ..., the latitude accorded to officers considering the probable cause issue in the context of mens rea crimes must be correspondingly great." *Zalaski,* 723 F.3d at 393 (citation omitted); *see also Conner v. Heiman,* 672 F.3d 1126, 1132 (9th Cir. 2012) (whether inference of innocent intent "was also reasonable ... does not matter so long as the [officer's] conclusion [that there was culpable intent] was itself reasonable").

Here, as we have described, the officers were stationed on the public sidewalk and in close proximity to the protest in order to maintain crowd control and security. The officers informed Kass that he needed to move in order to keep the sidewalk clear for pedestrian traffic. Kass, however, verbally and physically refused to obey the officers' orders either to "keep walking" or join the protestors inside of the park. We think that it was reasonable for the officers to infer that, based on Kass's repeated refusals to move, he intended to interfere with their efforts to confine the protest in the designated area and prevent sidewalk congestion. *See Marcavage,* 689 F.3d at 110 (probable cause to arrest protestors who were "hostile and noncompliant" when officers ordered them to move); *Davan I.,* 91 N.Y.2d at 91-92, 666 N.Y.S.2d 1015, 689 N.E.2d 909 (probable cause to arrest individual who rode bicycle into "confined and defined" police activity area, despite being "put on specific direct notice" not to do so).

In sum, because reasonable officers could at least debate whether there was probable cause to arrest Kass for obstructing governmental administration in violation of New York Penal Law § 195.05, we hold that the officers are entitled to qualified immunity for Kass's federal false arrest and imprisonment claim.

p.211 ii. Refusal to Comply with a Lawful Order to Disperse

Although we must reverse the district court's ruling if the officers had arguable probable cause to arrest Kass for any offense, we think the officers also had arguable probable cause to arrest Kass for disorderly conduct. Pursuant to New York Penal Law § 240.20(6), "a person is guilty of disorderly conduct when, with intent to cause public inconvenience, annoyance or alarm, or recklessly creating a risk thereof... [h]e congregates with other persons in a public place and refuses to comply with a lawful order of the police to disperse." This offense consists of the following elements: the individual (1) congregated with other persons in a public place; (2) was given a lawful order of the police to disperse; (3) refused to comply with that order; and (4) acted with intent to cause or recklessly created a risk of public inconvenience, annoyance or alarm. *Id.*

a. Congregating with Others in a Public Place

First, it was objectively reasonable for the officers to determine that Kass was "congregat[ing] with other persons in a public place." *See* N.Y. Penal Law § 240.20(6). New York courts have defined this term as a gathering of "at the very least three persons ... at a given time and place," including the individual who was arrested. *People v. Carcel,* 3 N.Y.2d 327, 333, 165 N.Y.S.2d 113, 144 N.E.2d 81 (1957); *see also United States v. Nelson,* 500 Fed.Appx. 90, 92 (2d Cir. 2012) (summary order). Kass argues on appeal that he approached only one protestor. He alleged in his complaint, however, that he was "arrested while speaking with *protestors*" and that he "engaged in a brief discussion with a protestor who was holding [a] sign and with another protestor standing nearby." Joint App'x at 13, 16 (emphasis added). Based on Kass's own allegations, therefore, he was speaking with at least two protestors.

Kass also argues that he did not "congregate" with these protestors because he refused to cross the barricades to join the protest. In support of this argument, he cites two cases in which New York state courts determined that the individual at issue was not physically close enough to other demonstrators to satisfy this element of the statute. In *People v. Millhollen,* the court found that a woman who was protesting while perched in a tree was not "congregating with others" because, although she had supporters who were standing on the ground, there was no one else in the tree who was protesting with her. 5 Misc.3d 810, 786 N.Y.S.2d 703, 708 (Ithaca City Ct. 2004). Similarly, in *People v. Carcel,* the court determined that two individuals — one who was walking outside of the United Nations' headquarters and the other who was standing "quite some distance apart" handing out leaflets — were not congregating with one another because they were "not even standing together" and were "only two in number." 3 N.Y.2d at 331, 333, 165 N.Y.S.2d 113, 144 N.E.2d 81.

In the instant case, it was objectively reasonable for the officers to conclude that Kass had gathered with the two protestors, even though there was a barricade between them. Kass does not dispute that he was standing in close proximity to the protestors while he was conversing with them. Further, although this conversation lasted only for a short period before the officers ordered that Kass move along, the officers did not have any basis to believe that Kass was pausing only momentarily on the sidewalk. Indeed, when they instructed Kass to leave, he refused to do so and stated that he wanted to continue talking with the protestors.

p.212 *b.* **Lawful Order to Disperse**

Second, the officers lawfully ordered Kass to disperse. As an initial matter, Kass disputes that the officers directed him to leave the area where he was standing and argues that they made a "series of confusing and contradictory statements." Appellee Br. at 34. The video clearly contradicts this assertion. The officers ordered Kass to "keep walking" and to "move on" several times. Joint App'x at 16-17, 120. Although Ernst suggested that Kass could join the protestors in the park, the unavoidable implication was that he could no longer stand on the sidewalk near the barricades while speaking with the protestors. Moreover, Kass responded that he would not move from where he was standing, thereby indicating that he heard and understood the officers' orders.

Further, New York courts have held that "a refusal to obey such an order [to move] can be justified only where the circumstances show conclusively that the police officer's direction was purely arbitrary and was not calculated in any way to promote the public order." *People v. Todaro,* 26 N.Y.2d 325, 328-29, 310 N.Y.S.2d 303, 258 N.E.2d 711 (1970) (quoting *People v. Galpern,* 259 N.Y. 279, 284-85, 181 N.E. 572 (1932)); *Crenshaw v. City of Mount Vernon,* 372 Fed.Appx. 202, 206 (2d Cir. 2010) (summary order) (same). As we have described earlier, the officers lawfully ordered Kass to move in furtherance of a legitimate public purpose — to maintain crowd control and security — and thus their orders were not "purely arbitrary." *See Todaro,* 26 N.Y.2d at 328-29, 310 N.Y.S.2d 303, 258 N.E.2d 711.

c. **Refusal to Obey the Order to Disperse**

Third, Kass explicitly refused to obey the officers' orders. In response to Ernst's repeated requests that he "keep walking," he stated that he "was not part of the protest," that "he was a citizen who wanted to hear what the protestor was saying," and that "he had a right to do so." Joint App'x at 16-17. Alfieri then approached Kass and instructed him to leave the area, to which Kass responded that he would not move because he was "talking to these people." Alfieri took hold of Kass's elbow to guide Kass away from the barricades, and Kass instructed Alfieri to "get [his] hands off" of him and pulled away from Alfieri.

Based on this conduct, a reasonable officer could infer that Kass was refusing to obey the officers' orders to disperse. *See Shamir v. City of N.Y.,* 804 F.3d 553, 557 (2d Cir. 2015) (noting where plaintiff initially obeyed officer's order to move and then went back to the officer and called him a thug, plaintiff's "approach to the officer [after he was told to move] is the antithesis of complying with an order to disperse"); *see also Rivera v. City of N.Y.,* 40 A.D.3d 334, 836 N.Y.S.2d 108, 112 (1st Dep't 2007) (failure of protestors to disperse after lawful order to do so, even when protestors asserted right to remain, supported probable cause for arrest).

d. Recklessly Creating Risk of Causing Public Inconvenience, Annoyance or Alarm

Finally, fourth, reasonable officers could disagree about whether Kass's continued refusal to leave the area where he was standing "recklessly creat[ed] a risk" of "caus[ing] public inconvenience, annoyance or alarm." *See* N.Y. Penal Law § 240.20(6). Although "the risk of public disorder does not have to be realized[,] the circumstances must be such that defendant's intent to create such a threat (or reckless disregard thereof) can be readily inferred." *People v. Baker,* 20 N.Y.3d 354, 360, 960 N.Y.S.2d 704, 984 N.E.2d 902 p.213 (2013) (citation omitted). In determining whether this element is satisfied, New York courts consider "the time and place of the episode under scrutiny; the nature and character of the conduct; the number of other people in the vicinity; whether they are drawn to the disturbance and, if so, the nature and number of those attracted; and any other relevant circumstances." *Id.* (citation omitted).

Here, as we have noted, Kass was standing on a sidewalk in the heart of downtown Manhattan shortly before 5 p.m. and in close proximity to a public protest. It is not clear based on the video whether protestors or pedestrians were drawn to Kass's interaction with the police. After Kass initially refused the officers' orders to "keep walking," however, at least one unidentified individual interjected by responding to the officers that Kass was not blocking the sidewalk. Further, as can be seen on the video, once Alfieri placed his hand on Kass to guide him away from the barricades, Kass became increasingly agitated. A third officer eventually needed to intervene in order to help Alfieri physically move Kass, who was resisting Alfieri's attempts to pull him away from the barricades.

Given the context in which Kass repeatedly refused to comply with the officers' orders — on a public sidewalk where pedestrians were passing, at a time of day when the sidewalks might shortly become more congested, and in close proximity to a public protest — and because Kass became increasingly hostile and resistant toward the officers, it was objectively reasonable for the officers to infer that Kass's continued defiance of their orders recklessly created a risk that he would "cause public inconvenience, annoyance or alarm," including a public disturbance. *See* N.Y. Penal Law § 240.20(6). At the very least, competent police officers could reasonably disagree as to whether, by remaining on the sidewalk despite numerous requests to move on, Kass recklessly created such a risk.

In sum, we conclude that Ernst and Alfieri had arguable probable cause to arrest Kass for violating both New York Penal Law § 195.05 and § 240.20(6) and are entitled to qualified immunity for Kass's federal false arrest and imprisonment claim. Any other conclusion, in our view, would not appropriately confine the denial of qualified immunity to officers who are "plainly incompetent" or "knowingly violate the law." *See Zalaski,* 723 F.3d at 389.

II. State Law Claims

The defendants also request that this Court dismiss Kass's state law claims against the officers and the City. In exercising jurisdiction over an immediate appeal from the denial of qualified immunity, we may consider issues that are "inextricably intertwined" with the qualified immunity question, such that "no additional inquiry or analysis is necessary" once the question of qualified immunity has been resolved. *Skehan v. Vill. of Mamaroneck,* 465 F.3d 96, 105 (2d Cir. 2006) (citations omitted), *overruled on other grounds by Appel v. Spiridon,* 531 F.3d 138, 139-40 (2d Cir. 2008).

Because the officers are immune from suit with respect to Kass's federal false arrest claim, we dismiss Kass's state law false arrest claim against the officers. *See Jenkins v. City of N.Y.,* 478 F.3d 76, 86-87 (2d Cir. 2007) ("If the ... defendants [are] entitled to qualified immunity under federal law, ... judgment [is] similarly appropriate on [plaintiff's] state law false arrest claim."). We also dismiss Kass's state law false arrest claim against the City, which is based solely on his allegation that the City is responsible for any false arrest that was p.214 committed by the officers. *See Demoret v. Zegarelli,* 451 F.3d 140, 152-53 (2d Cir. 2006). Kass's remaining state law claims for malicious prosecution and assault and battery, however, require additional analysis and we therefore lack appellate jurisdiction over those claims. *See Skehan,* 465 F.3d at 105; *Toussie v. Powell,* 323 F.3d 178, 184-85 (2d Cir. 2003).

CONCLUSION

For the foregoing reasons, we REVERSE the district court's denial of the defendants-appellants' motion for judgment on the pleadings with respect to Kass's federal and state false arrest and imprisonment claims and DISMISS the remainder of the appeal.

[*] The Clerk of Court is directed to amend the caption as set forth above.

[1] There is no claim here that the officers were responding based on the content of the protestors' or Kass's speech.

873 F.3d 162 (2017)

Gregory A. GRICE, III, Plaintiff-Cross Defendant-Appellee,

v.

**Anthony McVEIGH, Frank Farina, Individually, Defendants-Appellants,
Derek Hosein, Individually, Michael Alfalla, Individually, Kenneth Stewart,
Individually, Donald Heagle, Individually, Kevin Maddine, Individually, Jonathan
Piscatelli, Individually, Michael Sachar, Individually, Mark Delia, Individually,
Herman Killebrew, Individually, Robert Barnett, Individually, Thomas McCormack,
Individually, Joseph Horesky, Individually, Kathleen Cristiano, Individually, Brian
Scott, Individually, and James Luciano, Individually, Defendants,
Town of North Castle, New York, Defendant-Cross Claimant-Cross Defendant,**

p.163

**Westchester County, John Hosein, John and Jane Doe 1-15, and Town of
Greenburgh, New York, Defendants-Cross Defendants,
Metropolitan Transit Authority, Defendant-Cross Claimant.**

Docket No. 15-4124-cv August Term, 2016.

United States Court of Appeals, Second Circuit.

Argued: April 4, 2017.

Decided: September 29, 2017.

Grice v. McVeigh, 873 F. 3d 162 (2nd Cir. 2017)

Plaintiff-Appellee Gregory A. Grice, III, a teenaged train enthusiast, was stopped and handcuffed after police received a report that someone holding an electronic device was bending down by the tracks at a rail crossing. The United States District Court for the Southern District of New York (Román, J.), denied a motion by the police seeking qualified immunity. We reverse.

Thomas J. Troetti, White Plains, New York, for Appellants Anthony McVeigh and Frank Farina.

Brett H. Klein, (Lissa Green-Stark, on the brief) New York, New York for Appellee Gregory A. Grice, III.

Before: WALKER, JACOBS, and PARKER, Circuit Judges.

p.164 DENNIS JACOBS, Circuit Judge:

Plaintiff-Appellee Gregory A. Grice, III, a 16 year old train enthusiast, was stopped and handcuffed after the Greenburgh Police Department received a 911 report that someone holding an electronic device was p.165 bending down by the tracks at a rail crossing. After a search of the tracks by the Metropolitan Transit Authority ("MTA"), the Greenburgh officers turned Grice over to the MTA officers, who detained him and charged him with trespass.

When the trespass charge was dismissed, Grice sued all concerned. The only remaining defendants are Sergeant Anthony McVeigh and Lieutenant Frank Farina of the Greenburgh police. Grice alleges false arrest, failure to intervene, and failure to supervise. The United States District Court for the Southern District of New York (Román, J.) denied their motion for qualified immunity. On this interlocutory appeal, we reverse. It cannot be said that every reasonable officer in their circumstances would know that the conduct complained of violated clearly established law.

I

The facts are undisputed for the purpose of this appeal. Grice's cellphone (set to record the trains) taped audio of his encounter with the police, and the two officers have (necessarily) agreed to accept Grice's version of the facts. "Once a defendant asserting qualified immunity has agreed to be bound by the plaintiff's version of the facts, the issues become purely legal and we have jurisdiction over an interlocutory appeal from a denial of immunity." Loria v. Gorman, 306 F.3d 1271, 1280 (2d Cir. 2002). Defendants may try to "evade their agreement by spinning the facts in their favor"; but we simply ignore any factual contentions that contradict the plaintiff's version of the facts. Id.

In the evening on June 6, 2011, Grice was lawfully watching trains at the Virginia Road railroad crossing in Greenburgh, New York. He was seen by a passing driver, Mary Andrachik, who told a 911 dispatcher that someone with a red shirt "was actually on the train tracks" and was holding "a little controller." Joint App'x at 521-22. She said his behavior seemed "suspicious" and "bizarre." Id. at 521. The dispatcher directed police units to investigate "a male white, wearing a red shirt bending down by the tracks with a remote control object in his hands" at "Virginia Road, by the train tracks crossing." Id. at 524.

Sergeant Anthony McVeigh of the Greenburgh police arrived at the scene first, alone. A police officer since 1995, he was commander for some years of Greenburgh's Special Operations Unit, which includes the SWAT team. Over the course of a year, he had received several briefings and bulletins about the possibility that terrorists would attempt to sabotage railroad tracks; about a month before the encounter with Grice, McVeigh received a circular on attempted rail sabotage in a nearby town.

When McVeigh arrived at the crossing, Grice was wearing a red shirt, was holding a camera, and was standing approximately 12-15 feet from the tracks, next to a barricade. A backpack was on the ground, and two electronic devices — one with an antenna — were next to him on top of the barricade. One device was a cell phone; the other, a radio scanner. The only deviation from the radioed description of Grice was his race: the dispatcher said he was white, while Grice is African-American.

McVeigh asked Grice what he was doing, and seemed puzzled when Grice said he was taking pictures of the trains and listening to Metro North broadcasts. Grice told McVeigh that he had a letter from the MTA explaining that what he was doing was "okay." Id. at 558. Grice then suggested that he or McVeigh could retrieve that letter from his backpack. But McVeigh was concerned that there might be a sabotage p.166 device that could be activated remotely; so he told Grice a few minutes into their conversation, "Right now I'm going to cuff you for my safety and your safety... Until I find out what's going on here." Id. at 559.

Lieutenant Frank Farina and several other Greenburgh police officers arrived shortly after. Grice explained to them that he was a "rail fan" who had watched the trains at Virginia Road several times. McVeigh responded:

We don't know what you're doing out here. It's very unusual to do what you're doing. We don't get complaints like this... You're the first guy in my career that's ever been sitting next to a train with a radio looking at trains and taking pictures[.]

Id. at 566-67.

MTA officers arrived approximately 15 minutes after McVeigh cuffed Grice. They began questioning Grice anew, and the tracks were searched for a bomb by officers and a dog. When the search turned up nothing, McVeigh asked the MTA officers if he could switch out his handcuffs with the MTA's, and an MTA officer agreed. Grice was in McVeigh's handcuffs for about 33 minutes.[1] When the involvement of McVeigh and Farina ended at this point, MTA officers took Grice to an MTA facility, placed him in a cell, interrogated him, and gave him a summons for trespass. The trespass charge was ultimately dropped.

Grice sued several police officers and government entities, including the MTA, seeking damages for his handcuffing, arrest, and prosecution. He settled his claims against most of the defendants for a total of $24,000. Remaining are claims for false arrest, failure to intercede, and supervisory liability against (variously) McVeigh and Farina. The district court denied the officers' motion for summary judgment, and they appeal, arguing that they are entitled to qualified immunity.

II

"Qualified immunity protects officials from liability for civil damages as long as their conduct does not violate clearly established statutory or constitutional rights of which a reasonable person would have known." Taravella v. Town of Wolcott, 599 F.3d 129, 133 (2d Cir. 2010) (internal quotation marks omitted). Rights must be clearly established in a "particularized" sense, rather than at a high level of generality; and such rights are only clearly established if a court can "identify a case where an officer acting under similar circumstances" was held to have acted unconstitutionally. White v. Pauly, ___ U.S. ___, 137 S.Ct. 548, 552, 196 L.Ed.2d 463 (2017). The qualified immunity standard is "forgiving" and "protects all but the plainly incompetent or those who knowingly violate the law." Amore v. Novarro, 624 F.3d 522, 530 (2d Cir. 2010) (internal citations omitted).

A. The Unlawful Arrest Claim Against McVeigh

Grice's unlawful arrest claim fails because his handcuffing was an "investigatory detention" (otherwise known as a "Terry stop") that never ripened into an arrest and was supported by reasonable suspicion. Police stops fall into two categories: p.167 arrests and Terry stops. Arrests require probable cause, while a police officer may make a Terry stop "as long as the officer has reasonable suspicion that the person to be detained is committing or has committed a criminal offense." United States v. Compton, 830 F.3d 55, 61 (2d Cir. 2016). The standard for reasonable suspicion is "not high," and is less than what probable cause requires. United States v. Bailey, 743 F.3d 322, 332 (2d Cir. 2014) (internal citation omitted). Whether an officer's suspicion is "reasonable" is an objective inquiry based on the totality of the circumstances as they would appear through the eyes of a reasonable and cautious police officer, guided by his experience and training. United States v. Singletary, 798 F.3d 55, 60 (2d Cir. 2015).

McVeigh had reasonable suspicion to stop Grice, either for unlawful interference with a train or for trespass. N.Y. R.R. Law § 53-e; N.Y. Penal Law § 140.05. McVeigh had been ordered to look out for sabotage on the railroad. Less than a month earlier, he had received a training circular advising that someone had attempted to sabotage a railroad in nearby Patterson, New York, using "a homemade device, wrapped in black tape with a radio-control antenna affixed." Joint App'x at 101. The dispatcher called in a tip from an observer that someone was "bending down by the tracks with a remote control object in his hands," id. at 524, and McVeigh saw someone matching the observer's description with various electronic devices, some more familiar than others.

McVeigh was unaware of any plausible innocent reason that could explain why someone would be taking photos of trains and listening to the railroad's radio broadcasts. Grice told McVeigh he was a train buff and that he had received permission from the MTA to take photographs as long as he was not on MTA property, but McVeigh had never heard of trainspotting until the encounter at the railroad crossing. He was not required to credit an innocent explanation that seemed implausible given his knowledge at the time. "Suspicious circumstances may have innocent explanations; but the availability of an innocent explanation does not create an issue of fact as to the reasonableness of the suspicion." Holeman v. City of New London, 425 F.3d 184, 191 (2d Cir. 2005). McVeigh's suspicion that Grice may have committed a crime was reasonable, and he was entitled to stop him to investigate.

A Terry stop is limited to the degree of intrusion necessary to confirm or dispel the reasonable suspicion that justifies the stop in the first place. Compton, 830 F.3d at 64; United States v. Perea, 986 F.2d 633, 644 (2d Cir. 1993). In general, to determine whether a Terry stop is so intrusive as to become an arrest, we look to:

> the amount of force used by police, the need for such force, and the extent to which the individual's freedom of movement was restrained, and in particular such factors as the number of agents involved, whether the target of the stop was suspected of being armed, the duration of the stop, and the physical treatment of the suspect, including whether or not handcuffs were used.

Id. at 645 (internal punctuation and citations omitted).

Handcuffing is ordinarily not incident to a Terry stop, and tends to show that a stop has ripened into an arrest. But a police officer, "faced with the possibility of danger, has a right to take reasonable steps to protect himself and an obligation to ensure the safety of innocent bystanders, regardless of whether probable cause to arrest exists." United States v. Alexander, 907 F.2d 269, 272 (2d Cir. 1990). In p.168 certain unusual circumstances, we have therefore held that handcuffing a suspect to investigate a reasonable suspicion does not transform a Terry stop into an arrest. See, e.g., United States v. Newton, 369 F.3d 659, 675 (2d Cir. 2004) (handcuffing a potentially armed suspect to search him for a firearm was not an arrest); United States v. Vargas, 369 F.3d 98, 102 (2d Cir. 2004) ("[A]lthough under ordinary circumstances, drawing weapons and using handcuffs are not part of a Terry stop, intrusive and aggressive police conduct is not an arrest when it is a reasonable response to legitimate safety concerns on the part of the investigating officers." (internal punctuation omitted)). We ask if "police have a reasonable basis to think that the person detained poses a present physical threat and handcuffing is the least intrusive means to protect against that threat." Bailey, 743 F.3d at 340.

These circumstances can easily be classified as unusual. McVeigh was on the lookout for railroad sabotage, received a report by police radio of an individual matching Grice's description bending down by the tracks with a remote control device, and was unaware of a pastime that could explain the behavior that was observed. He therefore had reason to believe, suspect, and fear that Grice might use an electronic device to set off an explosive on the tracks. It was not unreasonable for a lone officer to handcuff Grice in order to ensure that Grice could not press a detonator button on any electronic device until the tracks could be searched.

McVeigh's intent to handcuff Grice for protection rather than pursuant to arrest is clear: he never administered a Miranda warning, and he explained to Grice that he was handcuffing him "for my safety and your safety ... [u]ntil I find out what's going on." Joint App'x at 559. McVeigh released Grice from his handcuffs after the MTA finished its investigation of the tracks; and thirty-three minutes was not an unreasonable interval to keep the handcuffs on while officers and a dog searched the tracks for a potential bomb. United States v. Tehrani, 49 F.3d 54, 61 (2d Cir. 1995) ("We decline to hold that a thirty minute detention based on reasonable suspicion is, per se, too long."); see also United States v. Vega, 72 F.3d 507, 516 (7th Cir. 1995) (concluding that a Terry stop lasting 62 minutes was not a de facto arrest because "part of that 62 minutes consisted of waiting for the narcotics sniffing dog to arrive."); United States v. Sharpe, 470 U.S. 675, 687 n.5, 105 (S.Ct. 1568, 84 L.Ed.2d 60)5 1985 (finding it reasonable for state patrolman to detain plaintiff pending federal agent's arrival because "as a highway patrolman, he lacked [the agent's] training and experience in dealing with narcotics investigations."). Because McVeigh had an objectively reasonable suspicion to detain Grice, and because McVeigh's detention of Grice did not ripen into an arrest, McVeigh is entitled to qualified immunity on the false arrest claim.

According to the dissent, it was obvious to the police that Grice was engaged in an innocent pastime: Grice's explanation that he was "just taking pictures" was "a fact easily corroborated by the fact that Grice had a camera rather than a 'remote control' device ... or a bomb." Dissent at 2. But Grice also had an electronic device with an antenna sitting on the barricade (which turned out to be a police scanner) as well as a cell phone. True, the use of a cell phone as a remote control detonator is not a feature promoted by manufacturers; at the same time, remote detonation of a bomb or improvised explosive device by cell phone is a standard technique for terrorists, p.169 as demonstrated in the margin.[2]

B. The Failure to Intercede Claim Against McVeigh and Farina

Grice argues that the defendants are liable for their failure to intervene with the MTA police officers to prevent Grice's continued handcuffing. McVeigh and Farina, as officers of the Town of Greenburgh, had no evident authority over officers of the MTA, who serve in a separate hierarchy in a separate jurisdiction with particular responsibility for security of the railroad. In any event, MTA officers did not seem to be mistreating Grice, and could reasonably decide to interview Grice at the MTA facility. If McVeigh and Farina had a duty to intervene in those circumstances, that duty was not clearly established, and the defendants therefore enjoy qualified immunity on that claim. See Pauly, 137 S.Ct. at 552 (holding that law is clearly established only when a court can "identify a case where an officer acting under similar circumstances" was held to have acted unconstitutionally).

C. The Supervisory Liability Claim Against Farina

Defendants are entitled to qualified immunity on a supervisory liability claim unless the actions of the supervisor *and* the subordinate both violate clearly established law. Poe v. Leonard, 282 F.3d 123, 140 (2d Cir. 2002). Since, as we have already ruled, McVeigh did not violate clearly established law, Farina is entitled to qualified immunity as well.

CONCLUSION

For the foregoing reasons, the order of the district court is reversed.

BARRINGTON D. PARKER, Circuit Judge, dissenting:

The majority, by granting qualified immunity to Sergeant Anthony McVeigh and Officer Frank Farina of the Greenburgh, New York police department, absolves them of the arrest of Gregory Grice. Grice was an indisputably innocent 16-year old young man who was arrested while standing at a location where he had every right to be and doing what he had every right to do. The majority mischaracterizes Grice's detention as a *Terry* stop. It was no such thing: it was an arrest and the facts that we are obligated to accept for purposes of this appeal establish that there was no probable cause for the arrest. Because McVeigh and Farina are not entitled to qualified immunity, I respectfully dissent.

I

Those facts establish the following. Grice is a train buff just like many others. As an aspiring engineer, he has an extensive knowledge of trains, attends public hearings of New York's Metropolitan Transportation Authority ("MTA"), volunteers on Saturdays at a railway museum in Danbury, CT, and enjoys taking photographs p.170 of passing MTA trains. This hobby led to his arrest.

On June 6, 2011, Grice left school and headed for a section of MTA train tracks, arriving around 4:30 p.m. at a train crossing in Greenburgh. He was familiar with the MTA's rules and, as was his habit, diligently followed them on that day. He had done this precise activity many times before. He had with him an MTA rule book as well as a letter from the MTA permitting him to take the photographs that led to his arrest. MTA personnel were quite familiar with him and were well aware of his penchant for photographing trains.

However, a passing motorist saw Grice, and, at 5:54 p.m., called the Greenburgh Police Department ("GPD") to report a "suspicious" "mix race" male near the tracks.

Joint App'x ("JA") 521-24. At 5:57 p.m., the GPD dispatcher radioed out an (incorrect) description of the individual seen by the motorist: "a male white, wearing a red shirt bending down by the tracks with a remote control object in his hands." JA 524. McVeigh heard that dispatch and, minutes later, at 6:03 p.m., arrived at Grice's location. What he witnessed differed from the dispatcher's report. Grice is black, not white, had no "remote control," and was not trespassing but was well back from the tracks.

McVeigh, in order to determine what was occurring, engaged Grice, who immediately informed McVeigh that he was "just taking pictures," a fact easily corroborated by the fact that Grice had a camera rather than a "remote control" device the dispatch reported or a bomb. JA 555. Grice's statements to McVeigh further corroborated the innocent nature of Grice's presence near the tracks: "I'm a rail fan like everybody else," and "I always keep myself at a safe distance." JA 558. Moreover, contrary to the majority's view, Op. at 175, McVeigh need not have taken Grice at his word; Grice offered McVeigh evidence establishing that his acts were innocent. Grice promptly told McVeigh: "I have a letter I e-mailed the MTA and they said [what I am doing] is okay. I can show you the letter. It's in my bag." JA 558. Grice even told McVeigh he could "take [the letter] out of my bag." JA 558. For whatever reason, McVeigh chose not to retrieve or review the e-mail, even though officers who had stopped Grice in the past had any suspicions they may have had alleviated by reviewing that letter. JA 565, 578-79.

About two minutes later, without any meaningful inquiry and having seen nothing illegal or suspicious,[1] McVeigh handcuffed Grice, ostensibly for "my safety and your safety." JA 559. It is clear that handcuffing in these circumstances constituted an arrest. The law of our Circuit is that "handcuffs are generally recognized as a p.171 hallmark of a formal arrest." *U.S. v. Bailey,* 743 F.3d 322, 340 (2d Cir. 2014). McVeigh then required that Grice sit on the ground and proceeded to question him extensively and aggressively.[2] It is not possible rationally to conclude that these circumstances constituted anything other than an arrest. After all, Grice was under the most complete measure and method of restraint that McVeigh had available to him and no one could believe that Grice was free to leave. No opinion of our Court has ever held that handcuffing for the period of time experienced by Grice and behaving in the way he behaved was not an arrest.

Other GPD officers shortly came on scene, including Officer Frank Farina. They were followed by officers of the MTA, who arrived shortly thereafter and immediately recognized Grice as the hobbyist with whom they were familiar. *See* JA 597 (MTA Officer Hosein, for example, stated that he had "seen [Grice] around a million times before"). Nevertheless, the MTA officers investigated the scene and determined that Grice posed no threat. JA 334-35. McVeigh and Farina acknowledge that while Grice was detained, it became clear to them that Grice posed no threat of violence or train interference. JA 470, 477, 502.

Although McVeigh initially told Grice he was being detained for his protection, after it became clear that Grice posed no threat, McVeigh and Farina changed their story. McVeigh subsequently justified the detention exclusively on the basis that he suspected that Grice had trespassed on the tracks, JA 470, and Farina joined McVeigh's new version. Farina responded to Grice's inquiry about what he did wrong not by mentioning anything of safety, but by saying, "[y]ou're trespassing." JA 5.

However, McVeigh and Farina had no first-hand basis to conclude that Grice trespassed. McVeigh and Farina's suspicion of trespass was based only on the unverified and unsworn report of an absent 911 caller (which was clearly insufficient to establish probable cause for trespass).

The majority ignores this changing rationale for Grice's detention. Specifically, the majority asserts that "McVeigh released Grice from his handcuffs as soon as the MTA finished its investigation of the tracks." Op. at 168; *see also* Op. at 166 (McVeigh released Grice "[w]hen the search [for a bomb] turned up nothing"). However, McVeigh's testimony and Farina's statement to Grice belie that assertion. *See* JA 470, 573.

In contrast to the majority's view, it was not until well after McVeigh and Farina were aware that Grice posed no threat to the tracks that McVeigh removed his handcuffs from Grice. Yet, rather than release Grice, McVeigh handed over custody of Grice to MTA officers based on McVeigh's newly minted trespass theory. p.172 To justify doing this, McVeigh told the MTA that when he arrived he personally saw Grice standing on the tracks. JA 471. This version sharply contrasts with that of Grice who asserts that he was never on the tracks and never closer than 12 to 15 feet from them. Accepting those facts as true and drawing every inference in Grice's favor, as we must, requires us to assume for qualified immunity purposes that McVeigh's statement to the MTA police about Grice's location on the tracks was not true. McVeigh's fabrication is significant because the record makes clear that the sole basis for the MTA's decision to keep Grice in custody and charge him with suspicion of trespass was McVeigh's report. *See* JA 520. Unsurprisingly, the trespass charge was later dropped, given there was no credible evidence to conclude Grice ever trespassed.

Having been cleared of all wrongdoing, Grice sued all involved. Most defendants settled. McVeigh and Farina did not. After extensive discovery, and despite McVeigh and Farina's objections that they were protected by qualified immunity, the district court denied summary judgment on the ground that there were factual disputes requiring a trial. The majority reverses that decision. I would not.

II

I begin by noting that today's decision oversteps our jurisdiction. No final decision was entered below, a fact which would ordinarily preclude our review. *See* 28 U.S.C. § 1291. However, under certain conditions we may review the denial of a summary judgment motion when that motion was based on a claim of qualified immunity. *See Plumhoff v. Rickard,* ___ U.S. ___, 134 S.Ct. 2012, 2019, 188 L.Ed.2d 1056 (2014). In determining whether we may assert jurisdiction in such a case, the "critical issue is whether the interlocutory appeal raises purely legal questions." *Loria v. Gorman,* 306 F.3d 1271, 1280 (2d Cir. 2002). And, generally, "an order denying summary judgment based on a determination of 'evidence sufficiency' does not present a legal question." *Plumhoff,* 134 S.Ct. at 2019 (citing *Johnson v. Jones,* 515 U.S. 304, 314, 115 S.Ct. 2151, 132 L.Ed.2d 238 (1995)).

McVeigh and Farina invoke a narrow exception to this rule in which "a defendant asserting qualified immunity has agreed to be bound by the plaintiff's version of the facts [and] the issues [therefore] become purely legal." *Loria,* 306 F.3d at 1280. It is well settled that this avenue is available only where appellants are "willing to accept plaintiff's version of the facts for purposes of the appeal." *Savino v. City of New York,* 331 F.3d 63, 72 (2d Cir. 2003); *see also Loria,* 306 F.3d at 1280. In addition, we must "disregard so much of [defendant's] version as is contrary to plaintiff's version." *O'Bert v. Vargo,* 331 F.3d 29, 39 (2d Cir. 2003). Neither McVeigh or Farina nor the majority accept Grice's version.[3]

p.173 Once we assume for purposes of this appeal Grice's version of the facts, we are dealing with a record that establishes the following. (i) Grice was at all times where he had every right to be and was doing what he had every right to do; (ii) Grice had evidence, previously accepted by the police, which established his innocence and that evidence was made available to McVeigh at the outset of the encounter; (iii) Grice never engaged in any threatening, unsafe, or suspicious behavior, and was at all times calm and cooperative; (iv) Grice never trespassed, nor did McVeigh or Farina have any first-hand basis to conclude that he did; (iv) yet, once it became clear that Grice posed no terrorist threat, McVeigh told the MTA police that he saw Grice trespassing. The majority in large part ignores these elements of Grice's story, and turns instead to the contradictory version presented on appeal by McVeigh and Farina. The majority, without discussion, condones this bait-and-switch. I would not.

III

Turning to the merits, I agree that McVeigh had sufficient suspicion for a *Terry* stop and, indeed, he would have been derelict had he not inquired as to what Grice may have been doing. But Grice's detention was not a *Terry* stop, but an arrest. A *Terry* stop consists of a police officer's brief detention of an individual for questioning when that officer has "a reasonable suspicion that the individual is, has been, or is about to be engaged in criminal activity." *U.S. v. Padilla,* 548 F.3d 179, 186 (2d Cir. 2008) (internal quotation marks omitted). In comparison to an arrest, a *Terry* stop "is an intermediate response allowing police to pursue a limited investigation when they lack the precise level of information necessary for probable cause to arrest." *Id.* (internal quotation marks omitted). A *Terry* stop must be as minimally intrusive as possible, bearing in mind the circumstances that gave rise to the suspicion. *U.S. v. Tehrani,* 49 F.3d 54, 58 (2d Cir. 1995).

In certain situations, a *Terry* stop ripens into an arrest. Under the law of this Circuit, the following factors determine whether that occurs:

> the amount of force used by the police, the need for such, and the extent to which an individual's freedom of movement was restrained, and in particular such factors as the number of agents involved, whether the target of the stop was suspected of being armed, the duration of the stop, and the physical treatment of the suspect, including whether or not handcuffs were used.

U.S. v. Vargas, 369 F.3d 98, 101 (2d Cir. 2004). Handcuffing is especially important. It is well settled that handcuffs are a hallmark of a formal arrest. *New York v. Quarles,* 467 U.S. 649, 655, 104 S.Ct. 2626, 81 L.Ed.2d 550 (1984); *U.S. v. Newton,* 369 F.3d 659, 676 (2d Cir. 2004); *see also U.S. v. Polanco,* 2011 WL 240140, at *7 (S.D.N.Y. Jan. 19, 2011) (handcuffing is "a maximal intrusion under the Fourth Amendment" (citing *U.S. v. Ceballos,* 654 F.2d 177, 180-81, 184 (2d Cir. 1981)).) Because every one of these factors points to an arrest and not to a *Terry* stop, I easily conclude that Grice was arrested.

p.174 The cases on which the majority relies to establish that Grice's detention was a simple *Terry* stop, rather than an arrest, despite his lengthy handcuffing are far off point. In *Newton,* a Fifth Amendment case, police officers responded to a specific "report that Newton illegally possessed a firearm and had recently threatened to kill his mother and her husband." 369 F.3d at 675. Given "such a volatile situation," we held that a "certainly brief" handcuffing that "last[ed] only the few minutes it took the officers to locate the sought-for firearm" did not constitute an arrest. *Id. Vargas* is similar. There, police officers responded to a report that Vargas was carrying a gun in his waistband. When the officers arrived on the scene and identified themselves, Vargas "immediately turned and fled." 369 F.3d at 100. The officers gave chase, and "[a]fter a brief struggle, [Vargas] was placed on the ground, handcuffed and patted down," a pat down which resulted in the officers quickly finding a loaded gun. *Id.* On appeal, we rejected Vargas' fanciful argument that he was under arrest during the "very brief" period between the placing of the handcuffs and the discovery of the weapon. Contrary to the majority's intimation, neither *Newton* nor *Vargas* stand for a broad exception that removes this case from our general rule that "handcuffs are generally recognized as a hallmark of a formal arrest." *Bailey,* 743 F.3d at 340.

The majority's reliance on *Tehrani, Newton* and *Vargas* to highlight that the length of the arrest was reasonable is similarly irrelevant to this case. After all, in determining the permissible time frame for a *Terry* stop, the Supreme Court has explained that "we consider it appropriate to examine whether the police diligently pursued a means of investigation that was likely to confirm or dispel their suspicions quickly." *U.S. v. Sharpe,* 470 U.S. 675, 686, 105 S.Ct. 1568, 84 L.Ed.2d 605 (1985); *accord U.S. v. Glover,* 957 F.2d 1004, 1011 (2d Cir. 1992); *see also U.S. v. McCargo,* 464 F.3d 192, 198-99 (2d Cir. 2006). Thus, where there has been "delay unnecessary to the legitimate investigation of the law enforcement officers" then the detention cannot be justified under *Terry* and becomes a *de facto* arrest. *Sharpe,* 470 U.S. at 687, 105 S.Ct. 1568. In the three cases cited above, the police had no alternate means of dispelling their suspicions without a lengthy detention. In contrast, here, had the officers simply agreed to look at the letter in Grice's bag after handcuffing him, their suspicions would have been dispelled almost immediately.

In the teeth of the myriad facts establishing that Grice was arrested, the majority maintains that it was a *Terry* stop. After acknowledging that "[h]andcuffing is ordinarily not incident to a Terry stop, and tends to show that a stop has ripened into an arrest," Op. at 167, the majority concludes that generalized terror concerns permit it to ignore the constitutionally grounded distinction between a *Terry* stop and an arrest. After all, the majority says, terrorists can "press a detonator button on any electronic device." Op. at 168.

The majority then proceeds to riff on this observation, listing instances of the use of cell phones by terrorists. *See* Op. at 169 n. 2. But if a generalized fear of terrorism coupled with the possession of a cell phone is sufficient to justify an arrest, then our Fourth Amendment is in real jeopardy. Practically every American now has a cell phone. As of 2017, there are more cell phones in America than Americans. Specifically, in a population of 326,776,164 there are 396,000,000 cell phones in use today or roughly 1.2 devices for p.175 every person in the country.[4] Our government is not entitled to use vague, unsubstantiated reports of disorder or terror to justify an arrest. That is why we have a Fourth Amendment.

In any event, the fact that some terrorists use cell phones is beside the point. McVeigh should have easily and quickly determined that Grice was a train buff, not a terrorist. As we have seen, Grice had on his person correspondence with the police corroborating his explanation of what he was doing.

Notwithstanding our law that handcuffing is the "hallmark of an arrest," the majority concludes that Grice's handcuffing did not constitute an arrest because "McVeigh's intent [was] to handcuff Grice for protection rather than pursuant to arrest." Op. at 168. None of this is correct. Because McVeigh lacked probable cause to arrest Grice, he had no legal right in these circumstances to handcuff Grice for Grice's protection. And because McVeigh had no basis whatever to believe that Grice was either armed or dangerous, he had no right to handcuff Grice for McVeigh's protection. Handcuffs are not a tool that police officers can casually use whenever they choose. Their use is not justified because it is a easy or convenient way for the police to go about their business. As our case law makes clear, handcuffing is a significant intrusion on a citizen's dignity and liberty.

The majority's reliance on "McVeigh's intent" is misplaced. Intent is irrelevant. Whether one is arrested is "an objective inquiry [that] pointedly eschews consideration of intent." *Gilles v. Repicky,* 511 F.3d 239, 245 (2d Cir. 2007) (internal quotation marks omitted). Accordingly, McVeigh's "subjective intent does not calculate into the analysis of when [Grice was] arrested." *Vargas,* 369 F.3d at 101. Rather, "[t]he intent that counts under the Fourth Amendment is the intent that has been conveyed to the person confronted." *Brendlin v. California,* 551 U.S. 249, 260-61, 127 S.Ct. 2400, 168 L.Ed.2d 132 (2007); *see also Yarborough v. Alvarado,* 541 U.S. 652, 662, 124 S.Ct. 2140, 158 L.Ed.2d 938 (2004). Consequently, we do not ask on what subjective basis McVeigh actually handcuffed Grice, we ask whether there was an objectively "reasonable basis to think that [Grice] pose[d] a physical threat and that handcuffing [was] the least intrusive means to protect against that threat." *Bailey,* 743 F.3d at 340. The answer is, of course, no.

Nevertheless, the majority both improperly credits McVeigh and Farina's contention that they subjectively intended only to detain Grice for his protection and that they had an objectively reasonable concern for safety. McVeigh and Farina acknowledge that they detained Grice at least in part because they suspected he committed a crime, a fact *told to Grice* while he was handcuffed. As discussed, McVeigh testified that while Grice was handcuffed he became convinced that Grice posed no threat, but that he did not release him because he suspected Grice committed an unlawful trespass. Specifically, McVeigh was asked at deposition "why wasn't [Grice] let go ... [a]t the point you determined he didn't do anything harmful[?]." JA 470. McVeigh responded: "We have him for criminal trespass." JA 470. Likewise, when Grice stated to Farina that he had done nothing wrong, Farina responded, "[y]ou're trespassing." JA 573. Thus it was *expressly* conveyed to Grice that he was being detained on suspected criminality, p.176 not for protection. The majority ignores this point entirely, yet it conclusively shows that, at the very least, Grice was under arrest (for trespass) at the point at which McVeigh had cleared Grice as any sort of danger to "my safety and your safety." JA 559. We should take McVeigh and Farina at their word: their basis for handcuffing Grice was not, as the majority asserts, for protection, but incident to Grice's arrest for trespassing.

More fundamentally, the facts we are obligated to accept demonstrate that there was never an objectively reasonable basis to view Grice as any sort of threat. This is especially so given the credible and quickly and easily verifiable explanation Grice provided for his presence and his conduct. In other words, McVeigh and Farina's highly generalized terrorism fear is a completely insufficient basis for dispensing with a showing of probable cause.

IV

The majority rests its opinion entirely on its conclusion that Grice was the subject of a valid *Terry* stop supported by reasonable suspicion. Because it concluded Grice was not arrested — a necessary element of Grice's claims for false arrest, failure to intervene, and supervisory liability — it felt no need to assess whether McVeigh and Farina had probable cause, the other core question underlying Grice's claims. I need engage no prolonged discussion on this question because my views make clear that I would easily conclude that McVeigh and Farina lacked probable cause to arrest Grice. I would therefore send each of Grice's claims to a jury.

Grice's false arrest claim should survive because there was no probable cause to arrest Grice in relation to supposed train interference. And, even if there were, the claim would still lie because McVeigh and Farina continued their detention of Grice after they cleared him of any threat to the tracks. We have made clear that probable cause "dissipates" where "a police officer's awareness of the facts supporting a defense... eliminate[s] probable cause." *Jocks v. Tavernier,* 316 F.3d 128, 135, 137-38 (2d Cir. 2003); *see also Gilles,* 511 F.3d at 247. Here, any justification for Grice's arrest was dissipated by the information provided McVeigh by the other officers.

I would also hold McVeigh and Farina to account for their role in the MTA's detention of Grice. I would do so for two reasons: (i) a police officer is liable for false arrest where, as here, it was reasonably foreseeable that his misconduct (*i.e.,* McVeigh's false report to the MTA) would "contribute to an 'independent' decision that results in a deprivation of liberty," *Higazy v. Templeton,* 505 F.3d 161, 177 (2d Cir. 2007); *Kerman v. City of N.Y.,* 374 F.3d 93, 126-27 (2d Cir. 2004); and (ii) a failure to intervene claim lies where a "police officer has an affirmative duty to intercede on the behalf of a citizen whose constitutional rights are being violated in his presence by other officers," *Ricciuti v. N.Y.C. Trans. Auth.,* 124 F.3d 123, 129 (2d Cir. 1997) (internal quotation marks omitted). Finally, I would conclude that a triable question of fact remains as to whether Farina should be liable on a supervisory liability claim.

At a trial, McVeigh and Farina could well be exonerated by a jury that has been presented with the relevant facts. A jury could conclude that, given the circumstances the officers faced, they acted appropriately. Juries very frequently reach just this result. But where, as here, the record is pock-marked with contradictions, whether the officers are entitled to exoneration should be determined by a jury selected from the community the officers are committed to serve and not by judges dealing with a record such as this one.

p.177 For these reasons, I would affirm the district court.

[1] The dissent argues that McVeigh advanced contradictory explanations for the handcuffs. First, he told Grice he was being handcuffed for safety, and then, after no bomb was found, kept him cuffed for trespassing. But McVeigh and Farina both made clear from the onset of their interaction with Grice that they believed that Grice had been on the MTA railroad tracks. So the two explanations do not contradict: if a bomb had been found, the trespass would not have been worth mentioning.

[2] A cell phone has been used as a detonator in virtually every recent attempted or actual bombing in the U.S. In New York, Ahmad Rahimi detonated multiple bombs in Manhattan and on the Jersey Shore using cell phones. See Compl. at 4, U.S. v. Rahimi, No. 16-cr-760 (S.D.N.Y. Sep. 20, 2016), ECF No. 1; see also Compl. at 20, U.S. v. Nafis, No. 12-cr-720 (E.D.N.Y. Oct. 17, 2012), ECF No. 1 (convicted terrorist attempted to bomb the Federal Reserve Bank in Manhattan using a cell phone as the detonator). Other relatively recent examples include the Boston Marathon Bombing and attempts in Washington, D.C., Dallas, Florida, and outside Chicago. About a month ago, the FBI arrested a man in Oklahoma City who attempted to blow up a vehicle containing a 1,000-pound ammonium nitrate bomb using a cell phone as the detonating device. See Compl. at 17, U.S. v. Varnell, No. 17-mj-368 (W.D. Okla. Aug. 13, 2017), ECF No. 1.

[1] The majority summarily states that "McVeigh was unaware of any plausible innocent reason that could explain why someone would be taking photos of trains and listening to the railroad's radio broadcasts." Op. at 167. It is unclear to me how the majority can make this statement when we are to assume the truth of Grice's story, which is that there are "thousands" of rail fans just like him. JA 566; *see also* JA 558 (Grice telling McVeigh that he is "a rail fan *like everybody else*"). The necessary inference from that record evidence is that taking photos of trains is fairly common and that therefore McVeigh did in fact have reason to understand what Grice was doing. Moreover, any pre-handcuffing lack of awareness of the innocence of Grice's behavior is of McVeigh's own making. He for some reason chose not to review the MTA's letter giving Grice express permission to do what he was doing. Had McVeigh reviewed that letter — which, in my view, any reasonable officer would have done — he would have been quite aware of a "plausible innocent reason" that Grice was by the tracks.

[2] McVeigh contends that his treatment of Grice was warranted because he believed Grice might have been a terrorist. McVeigh contends that "[s]ince 9/11 terrorism is a big concern in mass transit." JA 215. McVeigh and Farina introduced six documents (totaling 11 pages) received by the GPD supporting the existence of terrorist threats. Three describe highly general nation-wide threats posed by al-Qaida. JA 96-100. Another is a brief description of an incident that occurred at a railroad crossing nearly 50-miles away in which a "homemade device" was found on the tracks that had no "impact to rail operations" other than causing an electrical circuit to break. JA 101. The report does not indicate what the device was or whether it was put on the tracks intentionally. Nothing in the record connects the device to any terrorist activity. Finally, the last two are MTA police department alerts which are irrelevant because they are dated well *after* the incident with Grice. JA 102-04.

[3] The fact that we do not accept appellants' representation as to what facts they agree to is especially important here. Although McVeigh and Farina purport to accept

Grice's facts in order to get before this court, they in fact do not do so. In their reply brief, McVeigh and Farina concede that Grice "was detained for 45-50 minutes, in handcuffs, even though he was no closer than 12-15 feet from the train tracks." Reply Br. of Appellants at 1-2. Despite this purported concession, appellants presented numerous other disputed facts. For example, the briefs differ on whether Grice had a scanner in-hand on McVeigh's arrival on scene. *Compare* Br. of Appellants at 9 n.4 *with* Br. of Appellee at 7. McVeigh and Farina's counsel also offered disputed highly relevant facts at oral argument. Specifically, he adamantly argued that the decision by the MTA to charge Grice with trespass was motivated by the motorist's report, rather than information from McVeigh. *See* Oral Arg. Recording at 32:15. This assertion directly contradicts Grice's version of the facts, namely, that the MTA "issued the summons based on information provided ... by McVeigh." Br. of Appellee at 11. Counsel's contradiction of this point is especially striking given that Grice's view is readily supported by the record. MTA Sergeant Heagle testified that he would not have made the arrest had "McVeigh originally saw [Grice] in a non-trespassing area." JA 520.

[4] CT IA-T he Wireless Association, Everything Wireless, *Wireless Snapshot 2017* (2017), https://www.ctia.org/docs/default-source/default-document-library/ctia-wireless-snapshot.pdf.

811 F.3d 569 (2016)

Todd LYNCH, Plaintiff-Appellee,
v.
Margaret ACKLEY, Defendant-Appellant,
City of New London, Defendant.

Docket No. 14-3751-cv.

United States Court of Appeals, Second Circuit.
Argued: May 8, 2015.
Decided: January 28, 2016.

Lynch v. Ackley, 811 F. 3d 569 (2nd Cir. 2016)

p.573 Defendant Margaret Ackley, Police Chief of New London, Connecticut, appeals from the order of the United States District Court for the District of Connecticut (Shea, *J.*) denying her motion for summary judgment to have the suit dismissed by reason of her qualified immunity. The suit, brought by a police officer under 42 U.S.C. § 1983, claims unconstitutional retaliation for his criticisms of the defendant's performance as chief. *Held,* the district court erred in denying qualified immunity because there was no clearly established precedent at the time of the defendant's conduct that her conduct violated constitutional norms. REVERSED and REMANDED.

Michael J. Rose, Rose Kallor, LLP, Hartford, CT (Allison L. Pannozzo, on the brief), for Defendant-Appellant.

Christine S. Synodi, Synodi & Videll, LLC, Waterford, CT, for Plaintiff-Appellee.

Before: LEVAL, LOHIER, and DRONEY, Circuit Judges.

LEVAL, Circuit Judge:

Defendant Margaret Ackley, Chief of the New London Police Department ("NLPD"), appeals from the order of the United States District Court for the District of Connecticut (Shea, *J.*) denying her motion for summary judgment on the ground of qualified immunity. The plaintiff, Todd Lynch, a police officer and a member and officer of the police union, alleges under 42 U.S.C. § 1983 (as well as making claims based on Connecticut law) that Ackley violated his First Amendment rights by retaliating against him for various episodes of speech critical of Ackley's performance as Chief. Ackley moved for summary judgment dismissing the § 1983 claims by reason of qualified immunity. The district court concluded that Lynch made a *prima facie* case for unconstitutional retaliation and that factual issues in dispute prevented the court from ruling on whether Ackley was entitled to qualified immunity under *Pickering v. Board of Education,* 391 U.S. 563, 88 S.Ct. 1731, 20 L.Ed.2d 811 (1968). The court therefore reserved decision on Ackley's qualified immunity defense until a jury could resolve the factual issues at trial.

The court did not correctly apply the law for determining whether a state actor is entitled by reason of qualified immunity to dismissal of a suit charging her under § 1983 with unconstitutional conduct. The defendant was entitled to have the court construe disputed facts in the light most favorable to the plaintiff and dismiss the claim if, at the time of the defendant's conduct, the law was unclear whether the facts, so construed, constituted a violation of the plaintiff's constitutional rights. We conclude that Ackley established her entitlement to summary judgment on Lynch's § 1983 claims by reason of her qualified immunity.

BACKGROUND

I. Factual Background

Plaintiff Lynch has been a New London patrolman and canine handler (K-9) since 2007, having previously served in the Connecticut State Police. In March 2011, he became Vice President of the New London Police Union, AFSCME Local 724 (the "Union"), and became President in November 2011. Defendant Ackley has been p.574 Chief of the NLPD since June 2009. Lynch submitted evidence showing that over a period of roughly three years beginning in August 2010, he spoke on eight occasions, either publicly or in union meetings, criticizing Ackley's performance of her responsibilities, and evidence sufficient for a factfinder to find that Ackley retaliated. Those episodes of speech and associations by Lynch and Ackley's alleged retaliatory actions were as follows.[1]

(1) In August 2010, Lynch advocated among the union membership that the Union assert a grievance protesting Ackley's uninvited presence at a union meeting convened to discuss the NLPD's flex-time policy. Lynch asserts that, as retaliation, the department, claiming to be acting in compliance with the terms of the Union's collective bargaining agreement (the "CBA"), revoked compensation time accrued by him and by two other K-9 officers.

(2) At a September 2010 union meeting, Lynch asked that the Union consider a no-confidence vote against Ackley, expressing lack of confidence in her leadership. Later that month, Lynch was denied paid leave to attend the funeral of a former state police classmate, and was not allowed to attend a K-9 conference. He was also advised in October that he would not receive a $500 insurance stipend because he had not properly opted out of his insurance plan during the open enrollment period.

(3) In June 2011, the Union, with Lynch now serving as Vice President, endorsed the mayoral candidacy of City Councilor Michael Buscetto, who was an openly avowed critic of Ackley. In August and September 2011, in alleged retaliation Ackley sent emails to Kathleen Mitchell, a local political commentator, suggesting that Mitchell submit Freedom of Information requests to obtain civilian complaints filed against Lynch and the NLPD's K-9 unit.[2]

(4) In September 2011, the Union sponsored a paid advertisement in *The Day*, a New London newspaper, titled "Open Letter to the Citizens of New London," which questioned Ackley's leadership and asserted that her lack of judgment was negatively affecting police operations and public safety. The following day, Ackley sent Mitchell an email suggesting that she investigate Lynch's time sheets from the time of his service in the Connecticut State Police. In October, Ackley eliminated the day shift to which Lynch was assigned.[3] Ackley later ordered Deputy Chief Marshall Segar to investigate Lynch's use of union-business leave.

(5) In February 2012, Lynch wrote to the mayor accusing Ackley of violating New London Executive Order No. 004, which prohibits officers from inquiring about an individual's immigration status p.575 unless it directly pertains to a criminal investigation. The letter noted that, in view of a police officer's duty to inform the chain of command of violations of the law, Lynch was obligated to bring Ackley's violation of law to the mayor's attention, as the mayor was at the top of the chain of command. Ackley, allegedly in retaliation, then ordered that a sergeant be present for all K-9 training, urged the mayor and city council to reduce the K-9 unit's budget, and, in response to the mayor's request, sent him statistical information reflecting a racial disparity in bites by K-9 dogs.

(6) In September 2012, Lynch wrote to the mayor on behalf of the Union, expressing the Union's concern that the NLPD's depleted officer ranks were jeopardizing public safety, and later, at the city council's request, Lynch participated in an October 2012 public safety committee ("PSC") meeting discussing the issues raised in Lynch's letter. Ackley then denied Lynch overtime pay for attending the PSC meeting, and in November removed certain K-9 unit records from his control.

(7) In May 2013, Lynch spoke at a PSC meeting on whether civilian complaints against officers should be discussed in open or executive session. Ackley later revoked Lynch's union business leave and placed him on AWOL status when he did not return to work as ordered after a collective bargaining meeting broke down.

(8) Finally, in June 2013, speaking at another PSC meeting, Lynch spoke of low police department morale and a high turnover rate of officers, and expressed concern that two dogs from the K-9 unit had been forced to retire. Ackley then limited K-9 unit training. In addition, when asked for guidance by a mayoral assistant who had received a Freedom of Information request from a reporter for *The Day,* Ackley advised him to proceed in accordance with City policy. The reporter then published an article discussing racial disparity in bites by K-9 dogs, focusing on an incident involving Lynch and his K-9 dog.

II. Procedural History

On March 15, 2012, Lynch filed a complaint in Connecticut Superior Court alleging, *inter alia,* a claim against Ackley and the City of New London (the "City") under § 1983 for First Amendment retaliation.[4] Defendants removed the action to the federal district court, and Ackley moved under Federal Rule of Civil Procedure 12(b)(6) to dismiss the First Amended Complaint on the basis of qualified immunity. The district court (then Arterton, *J.*) denied the motion.[5] Lynch then filed this Second Amended Complaint, which added allegations that Ackley retaliated against him for two new instances of speech. Ackley renewed her motion, now seeking dismissal of the Second Amended Complaint. p.576 The district court (Shea, *J.*) denied the motion.

At the conclusion of discovery, Ackley moved for summary judgment, arguing, with respect to Lynch's § 1983 claims, that her conduct did not violate the First Amendment and that, in any event, she was entitled to have the case against her dismissed by reason of her qualified immunity. The district court denied Ackley's motion. *Lynch v. Ackley,* No. 3:12-CV-537 (MPS), 2014 WL 4782812 (D.Conn.Sept.

24, 2014). The court ruled that Lynch's speech was protected from retaliation by the First Amendment and that Lynch raised genuine issues of fact as to whether Ackley's conduct amounted to an adverse employment action, whether Ackley had a retaliatory motive for taking those actions, and whether, under the *Pickering* balancing test, Ackley's interests in preventing disruption of the operations of the department clearly outweighed Lynch's interests in speaking on matters of public concern. As the result of these disputed issues of fact, the court reasoned that it could not yet determine whether Ackley violated Lynch's First Amendment rights. With respect to Lynch's claim of qualified immunity, the court similarly ruled that, because there were disputed issues of fact, it could not determine whether Lynch's actions contravened law that was clearly established at the time. The court denied Ackley's motion. Ackley then brought this interlocutory appeal challenging the district court's denial of qualified immunity.

DISCUSSION

I. Appellate Jurisdiction

Before reaching the merits of Ackley's appeal, we must address Lynch's contention that we lack jurisdiction to review the district court's ruling at this stage. Lynch argues that there was no appealable final decision below because the district court rested its denial of qualified immunity on its finding that factual disputes underlying the *Pickering* balancing test precluded it from determining whether there was a constitutional violation as a matter of law. We disagree.

"A district court's denial of a claim of qualified immunity, to the extent that it turns on an issue of law, is deemed an appealable 'final decision' within the meaning of 28 U.S.C. § 1291 notwithstanding the absence of a final judgment." *Mitchell v. Forsyth*, 472 U.S. 511, 530, 105 S.Ct. 2806, 86 L.Ed.2d 411 (1985). This exception is justified by the fact that because qualified immunity is not only a defense to liability, but also provides immunity from suit, an important part of its benefit is effectively lost if a case is erroneously permitted to go to trial; thus, the defendant's entitlement to qualified immunity should be resolved "at the earliest possible stage in litigation." *Pearson v. Callahan*, 555 U.S. 223, 231-32, 129 S.Ct. 808, 172 L.Ed.2d 565 (2009). Whether an asserted constitutional violation was clearly established at the time of the defendant's challenged conduct may be a purely legal question. *Martinez v. Simonetti*, 202 F.3d 625, 632 (2d Cir.2000). "[A]s long as the defendant can support an immunity defense on stipulated facts, facts accepted for purposes of the appeal, or the plaintiff's version of the facts that the district judge deemed available for jury resolution, an interlocutory appeal is available to assert that an immunity defense is established as a matter of law." *Smith v. Edwards*, 175 F.3d 99, 104-05 (2d Cir. 1999) (quotation marks omitted). Adjudication of Ackley's motion for qualified immunity does not need to await jury resolution of disputed factual issues. If on Lynch's version of disputed facts — accepting reasonable inferences most favorable p.577 to him — there was no clear law at the time prohibiting Ackley's conduct, then Ackley is entitled to qualified immunity. Ackley's motion can be adjudicated on this basis as a pure question of law, and this appeal is properly before us.[6]

II. The Law of Unconstitutional Retaliation for Speech

The Supreme Court has long recognized that the First Amendment affords a degree of protection to public employees to exercise the right of free speech without risk of retaliation by the State employer if the employee's speech in question is "on matters of public interest." *See Pickering,* 391 U.S. at 568, 88 S.Ct. 1731. At the same time, however, "the State has interests as an employer in regulating the speech of its employees that differ significantly from those it possesses in connection with regulation of the speech of the citizenry in general." *Id.* Thus, while those who "accept[] public employment... do[] not check all of their First Amendment rights at the door," nonetheless "a citizen, upon entering government service, by necessity must accept certain limitations on his or her freedom." *Jackler v. Byrne,* 658 F.3d 225, 234 (2d Cir. 2011) (internal quotation marks and citations omitted). In adjudicating the rights of public employees to speak without facing retaliation from a government employer, courts attempt "to arrive at a balance between the interests of the [employee], as a citizen, in commenting upon matters of public concern and the interest of the State, as an employer, in promoting the efficiency of the public services it performs through its employees." *Pickering,* 391 U.S. at 568, 88 S.Ct. 1731. Courts must weigh the employee's speech interests against the government's interest in "effective and efficient fulfillment of [its] responsibilities to the public, including promoting efficiency and integrity in the discharge of official duties, and maintain[ing] proper discipline in public service." *Lane v. Franks,* ___ U.S. ___, 134 S.Ct. 2369, 2381, 189 L.Ed.2d 312 (2014) (internal quotation marks and alterations omitted).[7]

The Supreme Court has identified a further limitation on the public employee's First Amendment right to be free of retaliation for speech. In *Garcetti v. Ceballos,* the Court held that "when public employees make statements pursuant to their official duties, the employees are not speaking as citizens for First Amendment purposes, and the Constitution does not insulate their communications from employer discipline." 547 U.S. 410, 421, 126 S.Ct. 1951, 164 L.Ed.2d 689 (2006). "When a public employee speaks pursuant to employment responsibilities, ... there is no p.578 relevant analogue to speech by citizens who are not government employees." *Id.* at 424, 126 S.Ct. 1951. In such circumstances, to require a "delicate balancing of the competing interests surrounding the speech and its consequences" (as required when employees speak as citizens) "would be to demand permanent judicial intervention in the conduct of governmental operations to a degree inconsistent with sound principles of federalism and the separation of powers." *Id.* at 423, 126 S.Ct. 1951.

In pursuit of this balance the Supreme Court has identified three circumstances in which public employee speech is not protected from retaliation by State employers. First, speech about *personal* matters, as opposed to "matters of public concern," is not protected from retaliation. *Connick v. Myers,* 461 U.S. 138, 147, 103 S.Ct. 1684, 75 L.Ed.2d 708 (1983). Second, even speech on matters of public concern is not protected from retaliation unless the employee's First Amendment interests outweigh government employers' legitimate interests in efficient administration. *Pickering,* 391 U.S. at 568, 88 S.Ct. 1731. Third, speech made by employees "pursuant to ... official duties" rather than "as a private citizen" is not protected from retaliation.[8] *See Garcetti,* 547 U.S. at 421-22, 126 S.Ct. 1951.

III. Qualified Immunity

A state actor charged under § 1983 with violating a plaintiff's constitutional rights is entitled to have the action dismissed on the basis of qualified immunity if at the time of the challenged conduct there was no "clearly established law" that such conduct constituted a constitutional violation. *Harlow v. Fitzgerald,* 457 U.S. 800, 818, 102 S.Ct. 2727, 73 L.Ed.2d 396 (1982). This is so even if the court would conclude that, under law at the later time of the court's ruling, the defendant's conduct would be found to violate the Constitution. *Id.* at 818-19, 102 S.Ct. 2727. This rule is based on the proposition that public officers should freely act in pursuance of their duties without fear of being held liable for damages under constitutional standards of which they have no notice because the standards were not yet developed at the time of their conduct. *See Ashcroft v. al-Kidd,* 563 U.S. 731, 131 S.Ct. 2074, 2085, 179 L.Ed.2d 1149 (2011). We have ruled that the need for "clearly established" law is satisfied if the law on the subject was defined at the time with reasonable clarity or clearly foreshadowed in rulings of the Supreme Court or the p.579 Second Circuit,[9] so that the defendant should have understood that her conduct was unlawful. *See Looney v. Black,* 702 F.3d 701, 706 (2d Cir.2012); *Varrone v. Bilotti,* 123 F.3d 75, 79 (2d Cir.1997).

IV. Application of Qualified Immunity to Lynch's First Amendment Claims[10]

Ackley contends she is entitled as a matter of law to dismissal of Lynch's First Amendment claims by reason of qualified immunity. She argues that, construing the facts in the light most favorable to Lynch, her allegedly retaliatory actions did not violate constitutional standards that were clearly established at the time. We agree that there was no clear law at the time of the events establishing that Ackley's conduct constituted a First Amendment violation, and we express no view on whether Ackley's alleged conduct should be found to violate the First Amendment.[11]

With respect to what may be Lynch's strongest claim for protection from retaliation — his claim that Ackley retaliated against him for his perceived role in the Union's endorsement of Buscetto for mayor — there was no clear law as to whether Ackley's alleged retaliatory actions constituted *prohibited* retaliation because Ackley's alleged retaliatory acts were limited to her exercise of her own First Amendment right to defend herself against Lynch's attacks. Her speech in defending herself involved core First Amendment issues of public importance. With respect to Lynch's claim relating to retaliation for a union grievance, the grievance he expressed was not clearly a matter of public p.580 concern under *Pickering.* Finally, with respect to Lynch's remaining claims, we find that because Lynch's speech interfered significantly with Ackley's ability to effectively run the NLPD, she was arguably entitled to retaliate under *Pickering's* balancing test, even under the version of the facts most favorable to Lynch.

A. The Union's Endorsement of Buscetto

Lynch claims that Ackley's retaliation for his perceived role in the Union's endorsement of Councilman Steve Buscetto for Mayor of New London failed to satisfy the three-pronged test described above. The endorsement undoubtedly expressed a matter of public concern. Endorsements of candidates for political office are at the core of First Amendment protected speech. Lynch's role in the Union endorsement constituted speech as a citizen, rather than as an employee speaking pursuant to employment duties, and an employee's First Amendment interest in expressing support for a candidate for election to public office will, in most circumstances,[12] outweigh the employer's interest in the efficient accomplishment of the public responsibilities of the agency.

For his role in the Union's endorsement of Buscetto, Lynch alleges that Ackley encouraged an investigative reporter to seek out and publish derogatory information about Lynch relating to civilian complaints on his conduct as a K-9 officer. This allegedly retaliatory conduct, however, consisted of Ackley's exercise of her own core First Amendment rights in a public forum about a matter of public importance relating to employment to defend herself against Lynch's attacks. It is hard to see why in this context Ackley has any less entitlement to First Amendment protection than Lynch.

To the extent Lynch argues that, notwithstanding his employment in government, he retained free-speech rights guaranteed by the First Amendment, it appears to us that the same argument is available to Ackley. Lynch contends Ackley was forbidden by the First Amendment from taking retaliatory action against him, but it is hardly the conventional role of the First Amendment to bar Ackley from exercising her free-speech rights in defense against Lynch's attacks on her. In any event, we need not decide the issue. It suffices for our purposes that, given the nature of Ackley's allegedly retaliatory speech, there was no clear law or precedent communicating to Ackley that her exercise of free-speech rights about a matter of public importance relating to employment in an effort to defend herself publicly against Lynch's attacks violated Lynch's First Amendment rights. That absence of authority compels the grant of qualified immunity to Ackley on this claim.

We recognize that adverse employment actions may include adverse actions taken outside the employment context as well as harm to the incidents of employment. *See Burlington Northern & Santa Fe Ry. Co. v. White,* 548 U.S. 53, 63, 126 S.Ct. 2405, 165 L.Ed.2d 345 (2006). But it seems highly improbable that the anti-retaliation component of the First Amendment may muzzle an employer's p.581 speech on matters of public concern in this context, preventing her from engaging, or soliciting support, against one who declared himself to be her foe in public debate. In other contexts in which public officials have been sued under 42 U.S.C. § 1983 with allegations that their retaliatory speech unconstitutionally violated the First Amendment rights of plaintiffs, we have ruled that the speech of the defendants was protected by the First Amendment, while noting that such protection was not absolute and that such retaliatory speech might be actionable notwithstanding the First Amendment when it could "reasonably be interpreted as intimating that some form of punishment or adverse regulatory action will follow the [plaintiff's] failure to accede to the official's [desires]." *Hammerhead Enterprises, Inc. v. Brezenoff,* 707 F.2d 33, 39 (2d Cir.1983). And in *X-Men Sec., Inc. v. Pataki,* 196 F.3d 56, 71 (2d Cir.1999), we noted that, notwithstanding First Amendment protection of legislators' "advocacy" and other forms of speech related to affairs of government, protection might not extend to speech inviting "threats, intimidation, or coercion." Another Circuit, in a similar context, noted a "possible exception" to the First Amendment's protection of public officials' retaliatory speech when "the retaliatory disclosure of information relates to those personal rights that can be deemed fundamental or implicit in the concept of ordered liberty," such as when the retaliatory disclosures are "sufficiently embarrassing, humiliating, or emotionally distressful." *Suarez Corp. Indus. v. McGraw,* 202 F.3d 676, 688 (4th Cir.2000) (internal quotation marks omitted).

The few arguably precedential rulings we have found have not tried to specify the limits of the First Amendment's protection of retaliatory speech by public officials, and neither do we. Nonetheless, the fact that Ackley's allegedly retaliatory speech involved efforts to defend herself against the verbal attacks of an employee accusing of her of incompetence and bad administration, and addressed matters of public importance relevant to the attacker's public employment duties, tends to support her entitlement to First Amendment protection. We know of no authority establishing the contrary. We therefore hold, in the absence of any clear authority for Ackley's liability, that Ackley is entitled to qualified immunity as to this claim.

B. Filing of Union Grievances

Lynch also claims that Ackley retaliated against him for various incidents of his union activity, which included his filing a union grievance protesting Ackley's presence at a union meeting discussing the Department's flex-time policy. It is far from clear that this grievance asserted a matter of public concern, rather than a "personal grievance[]." *Ruotolo v. City of N.Y.,* 514 F.3d 184, 189 (2d Cir.2008). Lynch contends his grievance expressed a matter of public concern because management intrusion in union matters can "chill and deter union members from openly discussing their positions." Joint App'x at 169. Labor versus management disputes, needless to say, almost invariably involve a conflict between the labor force and management over an issue that concerns the terms and conditions of employment. Such disputes often have a strong flavor of "personal grievance" notwithstanding that the personal grievance is shared by numerous employees. On the other hand, especially in the case of employment in a public agency, which renders service to the general public, it is rarely difficult for a plaintiff to construct an argument that the dispute is a matter of public concern, either because it relates to the delivery of services to the public, or because it invokes basic aspects of the right to unionization. p.582 Some such arguments might well be persuasive, others not. Suffice it to say about Lynch's argument that it was unclear whether such a grievance should be viewed as a matter of public concern for purposes of *Pickering* analysis.

Lynch's reliance on *Hoyt v. Andreucci,* 433 F.3d 320 (2d Cir.2006), and *Clue v. Johnson,* 179 F.3d 57 (2d Cir.1999), is unavailing. The issue in *Hoyt* was very different from this case. That case involved an employee who alerted the Albany County legislature that one of the county's employees was disciplining corrections officers in an unlawful manner. The court found that "concerns raised to the government about the lawfulness of public officials' actions" were issues of public concern. 433 F.3d at 330. Lynch's grievance against Ackley does not clearly implicate concerns remotely similar to *Hoyt.*

Clue gives Lynch no better support. *Clue* involved a claim of management retaliation against a minority faction of the Transit Workers' Union, which sought to unseat union leadership. The court held that the activity in question did implicate matters of public concern because "[t]he intraunion dispute here did not merely involve internal union affairs," but rather involved "a struggle over the labor policies of the Transit Authority and what role the [union] ought to play in changing those policies." 179 F.3d at 61. The issue in *Clue* was nothing like Lynch's grievance. Though the court said in dicta that "retaliation solely for union activity clearly raises a public concern under *Connick,*" *id.,* it obviously did not mean that all activities undertaken through a union necessarily become matters of public concern merely by virtue of their collateral connection to the union. *Cf. Borough of Duryea v. Guarnieri,* 564 U.S. 379, 428, 131 S.Ct. 2488, 180 L.Ed.2d 408 (2011) ("A petition filed with an employer using an internal grievance procedure in many cases will not seek to communicate to the public or to advance a political or social point of view beyond the employment context."). Indeed, it recognized that some union activity was likely unprotected from retaliation. *Clue,* 179 F.3d at 61.[13]

C. Lynch's Remaining Claims

The remainder of Lynch's claims involve retaliation for communication with town leaders or the public at large concerning Lynch's and the Union's contentions that Ackley was a bad chief, and that her continuing presence in that position endangered p.583 the safety of NLPD officers and the public. We assume — without holding — that each of these instances of speech constituted speech as a citizen on a matter of public concern. Nonetheless we hold that, even given the version of the facts most favorable to Lynch, Ackley's retaliatory actions were not prohibited by clearly established law.

Under *Pickering,* Ackley was permitted to retaliate against Lynch's speech if Lynch's speech interests were out-weighed by the government's interest in "promoting the efficiency of the public services it performs through its employees." *Pickering,* 391 U.S. at 568, 88 S.Ct. 1731. Lynch's speech obviously threatened to disrupt Ackley's ability to administer the NLPD effectively. Indeed, the whole *purpose* of Lynch's speech, as a union officer, was to undermine and impair her authority over the Department. Lynch's opposition to Ackley was hostile and very public, and included his efforts to persuade the executive and legislative authorities of New London to block and countermand her policies. Even construing the evidence in the light most favorably to Lynch, his actions were sufficiently disruptive as to render at least unclear whether his free-speech interest outweighed Ackley's interest in the effective management of the Police Department.

* * *

Because no authority clearly establishes that Lynch's interest in speech as a union officer attacking Ackley's competence as chief outweighed Ackley's governmental interest in effective administration of her department, Ackley is entitled to summary judgment on the ground of qualified immunity.

V. Lynch's Freedom of Association Claim

Lynch also claims unlawful retaliation for his associations with City Councilor Buscetto and the Union. The sole associative activity with Buscetto cited by Lynch to justify his claim is the union's endorsement of Buscetto as a mayoral candidate. This claim based on Lynch's First Amendment association rights is subject to the same analysis as set forth above for Lynch's First Amendment free-speech right based on the same incident.

As for Lynch's claim based on his association with the Union, he has made no showing that Ackley retaliated against him *because of* his union membership, particularly as he has presented no evidence that she retaliated against any other police officer for membership or for holding office in the Union. We recognize that Lynch's evidence was sufficient to show that Ackley retaliated against him for the *things he said* in the framework of the Union. There was no showing, however, that she retaliated because of his association with the Union.[14] Ackley was entitled to summary judgment on this claim whether on the theory of qualified immunity or on the merits.[15]

CONCLUSION

For the foregoing reasons, the district court's ruling denying Ackley's motion to p.584 dismiss by reason of qualified immunity is REVERSED.

[1] At various times in the proceedings below, Lynch raised three additional instances of speech, including his speech at a March 2011 city council committee meeting, his September 2011 call for a no-confidence vote, and his speech during union negotiations in June 2013. The district court ruled that Lynch either waived his arguments with respect to these instances or failed to present sufficient evidence on them. Because Lynch provides no basis for showing that the district court erred in that reasoning, we do not address those instances.

[2] Lynch also alleges that Ackley prevented him from securing locations and equipment for K-9 training and deprived him of control over K-9 records and the NLPD's drug safe. However, these events allegedly took place before the union's endorsement in June 2011, and seem to relate only to Lynch's claims of retaliation for Lynch's March 2011 ascendancy to vice presidency of the union — claims that Lynch does not press on appeal.

[3] Lynch does not dispute that his request to be placed on another squad's day shift was subsequently granted.

[4] The complaint also included claims for libel *per se* and under Conn. Gen.Stat. § 31-51q, which imposes liability on public employers who discipline or discharge an employee on account of the employee's exercise of speech rights protected by the United States Constitution or the Connecticut Constitution. Those claims are not at issue in this appeal, and we leave it to the district court to consider what impact, if any, our ruling has on Lynch's § 31-51q claims on remand.

[5] At oral argument of this appeal, Lynch argued that Judge Arterton's denial of Defendants' motion to dismiss the First Amended Complaint created "law of the case" on the issue whether Lynch's speech was made as a citizen on a matter of public

concern. We reject that argument. Judge Arterton ruled only that the court was unable to make a determination *at the pleading stage. See Lynch v. Ackley,* No. 3:12-CV-537 (JBA), 2012 WL 6553649, at *4-6 (D.Conn. Dec. 14, 2012).

[6] *Locurto v. Safir,* 264 F.3d 154 (2d Cir.2001), cited by Lynch, does not conflict with our acceptance of jurisdiction. In that case, the defendants appealed the district court's denial of qualified immunity at summary judgment only on the ground that their assessment of the disruption caused by the plaintiffs' speech was objectively reasonable under *Pickering. Id.* at 168. We dismissed the portion of the appeal challenging that ruling because the defendants' subjective intent was a factual issue that precluded resolution on the *Pickering* test as a matter of law. *Id.* at 169-70. Here, in contrast, the basis for Ackley's appeal is that, on Lynch's version of the facts, Lynch did not establish a violation of a federally protected right and that any such violation was not based on clearly established law. Both are issues that are capable of resolution as a matter of law.

[7] *Lane* was decided after the events in question in this case, and does not bear on the court's analysis of qualified immunity. We quote it here for its helpful explanation of the law established by *Pickering, Garcetti v. Ceballos,* 547 U.S. 410, 126 S.Ct. 1951, 164 L.Ed.2d 689 (2006), and their progeny.

[8] To prevail on a claim, the employee must also prove that she has suffered an adverse employment action, for which the speech was a motivating factor. *See Cobb v. Pozzi,* 363 F.3d 89, 102 (2d Cir.2003). Moreover, as a prerequisite to this whole analysis, the speech must come within the protection of the First Amendment to begin with. *See Anemone v. Metro. Transp. Auth.,* 629 F.3d 97, 114 (2d Cir.2011). This element is rarely in dispute, as practically all speech enjoys some First Amendment protection — with rare exceptions for such things as obscenity, fighting words, and yelling "fire" in a movie theater. *See Chaplinsky v. New Hampshire,* 315 U.S. 568, 571-72, 62 S.Ct. 766, 86 L.Ed. 1031 (1942). And perhaps because it is hardly ever in dispute, it is generally assumed, rather than explicitly stated, that this is an essential element of the claim. A semantic confusion does, however, often arise in the explanation of a ruling on a State employee's claim of unconstitutional retaliation for speech. Courts sometimes characterize the determinative question in § 1983 First Amendment retaliation suits as whether the employee speech at issue was "constitutionally protected." In most cases, such words seem intended as shorthand for whether the speech was constitutionally protected *from employer retaliation.* The test for establishing unconstitutional retaliation for an employee's speech is far more stringent than the test for establishing that speech enjoys protection under the First Amendment.

[9] In some circumstances, decisions of other circuits can "clearly establish" law for this circuit. *See Terebesi v. Torreso,* 764 F.3d 217, 231 (2d Cir.2014).

[10] We review de novo a district court's denial of qualified immunity. *Clubside, Inc. v. Valentin,* 468 F.3d 144, 152 (2d Cir.2006). Because Ackley's motion was for summary judgment, we construe the evidence in the light most favorable to Lynch. *See id.* Summary judgment may be granted only if "there is no genuine dispute as to any material fact and the movant is entitled to judgment as a matter of law." Fed.R.Civ.P. 56(a).

[11] Prior to the Supreme Court's decision in *Pearson v. Callahan,* 555 U.S. 223, 129 S.Ct. 808, 172 L.Ed.2d 565 (2009), under the rule of *Saucier v. Katz,* 533 U.S. 194, 121 S.Ct. 2151, 150 L.Ed.2d 272 (2001), an inferior federal court was obligated to give an advisory ruling whether the challenged conduct amounted to a constitutional violation before considering whether the defendant was entitled to qualified immunity because of the absence of clearly settled law to that effect at the time of the conduct. *Id.* at 201, 121 S.Ct. 2151. In *Pearson,* however, the Supreme Court rescinded that requirement, giving courts discretion whether to follow the *Saucier* formula or go directly to the question whether the law was clearly established at the time. *Pearson,* 555 U.S. at 236, 129 S.Ct. 808. The Supreme Court's reason for originally adopting the *Saucier* rule was to avoid having unconstitutional conduct go repeatedly unremedied if courts could repeatedly rule that the defendant's qualified immunity made it unnecessary to reach the question whether the defendant's conduct in fact violated the Constitution. *See id.* at 232, 129 S.Ct. 808 (citing *Saucier,* 533 U.S. at 201, 121 S.Ct. 2151). In this case, however, there is little likelihood that frequently repeated instances of questionable conduct would repeatedly escape review. Qualified immunity applies only to a plaintiff's claim against an individual state actor for damages. It has no application when the suit is brought against a municipality, nor when the suit seeks injunctive relief. *See Owen v. City of Independence,* 445 U.S. 622, 637-38, 100 S.Ct. 1398, 63 L.Ed.2d 673 (1980). Accordingly, if other plaintiffs brought allegations similar to Lynch's, qualified immunity would not be available in the very likely event that those plaintiffs sought damages against the municipality or injunctive relief. It appears there is little likelihood of the circumstance *Saucier* was designed to prevent.

[12] We do not mean to suggest that a public employee's endorsement of a candidate for public office would *always* be protected from employer retaliation. If, for example, a governor's speechwriter or an elected district attorney's chief aide publicly endorsed the candidate opposing her boss's campaign for election, there would no doubt be a strong argument that such an affront sufficiently risked impairing the supervising official's performance of her public duties as to justify the aide's demotion or dismissal without offending the standards of the First Amendment.

[13] A further question is where, as the law stood at the time of Ackley's actions, Lynch's union activities would have fallen under *Garcetti's* classifications. *Garcetti* essentially divided all speech by employees into two categories — speech "pursuant to ... official duties," which is ineligible for protection from retaliation, and speech "as a citizen," which is eligible and is protected from retaliation if the requirements of *Pickering* are met. 547 U.S. at 421-22, 126 S.Ct. 1951. It is not clear that speech by employees in the role of union officers, involving advocacy as to the *terms and conditions of employment,* fits comfortably into either category. While such speech is not made pursuant to duties *imposed by the employer,* such speech *is* made pursuant to duties that arise from the employment relationship between management and the union membership — the duty of union officers is to represent the membership in advocacy and negotiation as to the terms and conditions of employment. Whether such speech belonged in the category of citizen speech, eligible for protection from retaliation, seems to us to have been unclear at the time of Ackley's actions.

The Supreme Court's later ruling in *Lane v. Franks* arguably narrowed the scope of ineligible employee speech. But *Lane* was decided subsequent to Ackley's conduct. It therefore had no bearing on the crucial issue for purposes of qualified immunity — whether the law at the time of Ackley's conduct gave her clear notice that her conduct violated Lynch's rights under the First Amendment.

[14] Lynch's claim differs substantially from the union-based association claim at issue in *State Emp. Bargaining Agent Coalition v. Rowland,* 718 F.3d 126 (2d Cir.2013), in which plaintiffs claimed that the state employer terminated approximately 2,800 unionized state employees, but no non-union workers. *See id.* at 130.

[15] We note, furthermore, that it is unclear whether, and if so, how, *Garcetti* applies to claims of retaliation against protected association.

825 F.3d 89 (2016)

Eli Samuel FIGUEROA, a/k/a Eli Samuel, Plaintiff-Appellant,

v.

Donna Marie MAZZA, individually and as a Detective with the New York City Police Department, Christopher Karolkowski, individually and as a Detective with the New York City Police Department, Todd Nagrowski, individually and as a Detective with the New York City Police Department, Joseph Failla, individually and as a Detective with the New York City Police Department, and Detective Dennis Chan, individually and as a Detective with the New York City Police Department, Defendants-Appellees.[*]

No. 14-4116-cv August Term 2015.

United States Court of Appeals, Second Circuit.

Argued: October 22, 2015.

Decided and Amended: June 3, 2016.

Figueroa v. Mazza, 825 F. 3d 89 (2nd Cir. 2016)

p.92 Appeal from the United States District Court for the Eastern District of New York

We consider here whether defendants-appellees are, as the District Court determined, entitled to judgment as a matter of law on plaintiff-appellant's claims for false arrest, excessive force, assault, failure to intervene, and unlawful entry. We conclude that defendants-appellees are entitled to the protection of qualified immunity with respect to the false arrest claims and that they did not use excessive force or commit an assault in arresting plaintiff-appellant. We also conclude, however, that the claims of failure to intervene and unlawful entry present issues of fact that must be resolved by a jury.

Plaintiff-appellant Eli Samuel Figueroa appeals a September 30, 2014 judgment of the United States District Court for the Eastern District of New York (Jack B. Weinstein, *Judge*) entering judgment as a matter of law in favor of defendants-appellees Donna Marie Mazza, Christopher Karolkowski, Todd Nagrowski, Joseph Failla, and Dennis Chan, each a detective with the New York City Police Department.

In the proceeding below, plaintiff asserted claims under 42 U.S.C. § 1983 and state law for false arrest, excessive force, assault, failure to intervene, and unlawful entry, all arising out of his arrest on June 30, 2010. The District Court granted summary judgment as to the claims of unlawful entry. The other claims were tried to a jury. Following a verdict in plaintiff's favor on the counts of false arrest, excessive force, and assault, and a mistrial on the count of failure to intervene, the District Court granted judgment to defendants under Federal Rule of Civil Procedure 50(b). Plaintiff appeals the judgment as to each claim and further asserts that the District Court "abused its discretion" in dismissing unnamed defendants from the case and closing discovery.

We agree with the District Court's disposition of plaintiff's false arrest claims. The trial record establishes that a reasonable law enforcement officer could have concluded that there existed probable cause to arrest plaintiff on the evening of June 30, 2010; accordingly, defendants can claim the protection of qualified immunity. We also conclude, as did the District Court, that the force used in effecting plaintiff's arrest was reasonable as a matter of law, and we find no error in the District Court's dismissal of unnamed defendants or discovery rulings. We thus AFFIRM the judgment insofar as it disposed of plaintiff's claims for false arrest, excessive force, and assault, dismissed unnamed defendants, and refused to permit further discovery.

We do not agree, however, with the District Court's disposition of plaintiff's claims for failure to intervene and unlawful entry. The District Court erred in concluding, as a matter of law, that defendants had no realistic opportunity to intervene in an alleged assault on plaintiff by an unidentified police officer and that plaintiff lacked a legitimate expectation of privacy in his mother's apartment. Accordingly, we VACATE so much of the judgment as rejected plaintiff's failure-to-intervene and unlawful-entry claims as a matter of law and REMAND for such further pretrial proceedings as may be appropriate in the circumstances, or for trial.

Judge KEARSE concurs in part and dissents in part in a separate opinion.

ROBERT MILTON RAMBADADT (Rosa Barreca, on the brief), The Rambadadt Law Office, New York, NY, for Plaintiff-Appellant.

ELIZABETH S. NATRELLA (Pamela Seider Dolgow, on the brief), for Zachary W. Carter, Corporation Counsel of the City of New York, New York, NY, for Defendants-Appellees.

Before: KEARSE, WALKER, and CABRANES, Circuit Judges.

Judge KEARSE concurs in part and dissents in part in a separate opinion.

p.93 JOSÉ A. CABRANES, Circuit Judge:

We consider here whether defendants-appellees are, as the District Court determined, entitled to judgment as a matter of law on plaintiff-appellant's claims for false arrest, excessive force, assault, failure to intervene, and unlawful entry. We conclude that defendants-appellees are entitled to the protection of qualified immunity with respect to the false arrest claims and that they did not use excessive force or commit an assault in arresting plaintiff-appellant. p.94 We also conclude, however, that the claims of failure to intervene and unlawful entry present issues of fact that must be resolved by a jury.

Plaintiff-appellant Eli Samuel Figueroa ("Samuel") appeals a September 30, 2014 judgment of the United States District Court for the Eastern District of New York (Jack B. Weinstein, *Judge*) entering judgment as a matter of law in favor of defendants-appellees Donna Marie Mazza ("Mazza"), Christopher Karolkowski ("Karolkowski"), Todd Nagrowski ("Nagrowski"), Joseph Failla ("Failla"), and Dennis Chan ("Chan") (jointly, "defendants"), each a detective with the New York City Police Department.

In the proceeding below, Samuel asserted claims under 42 U.S.C. § 1983 and state law for false arrest, excessive force, assault, failure to intervene, and unlawful entry, all arising out of his arrest on June 30, 2010. The District Court granted summary judgment as to the claims of unlawful entry. The other claims were tried to a jury. Following a verdict in Samuel's favor on the counts of false arrest, excessive force, and assault, and a mistrial on the count of failure to intervene, the District Court granted judgment to defendants under Federal Rule of Civil Procedure 50(b). Samuel appeals the judgment as to each claim and further asserts that the District Court "abused its discretion" in dismissing unnamed defendants from the case and closing discovery.

We agree with the District Court's disposition of Samuel's false arrest claims. The trial record establishes that a reasonable law enforcement officer could have concluded that there existed probable cause to arrest Samuel on the evening of June 30, 2010; accordingly, defendants can claim the protection of qualified immunity. We also conclude, as did the District Court, that the force used in effecting Samuel's arrest was reasonable as a matter of law, and we find no error in the District Court's dismissal of unnamed defendants or discovery rulings. We thus AFFIRM the judgment insofar as it disposed of Samuel's claims for false arrest, excessive force, and assault, dismissed unnamed defendants, and refused to permit further discovery.

We do not agree, however, with the District Court's disposition of Samuel's claims for failure to intervene and unlawful entry. The District Court erred in concluding, as a matter of law, that defendants had no realistic opportunity to intervene in an alleged assault on Samuel by an unidentified police officer and that Samuel lacked a legitimate expectation of privacy in his mother's apartment. Accordingly, we VACATE so much of the judgment as granted judgment to defendants on Samuel's failure-to-intervene and unlawful-entry claims and REMAND for such further pretrial proceedings as may be appropriate in the circumstances, or for trial.

BACKGROUND

I. The Facts[1]

On June 29, 2010, a Duane Reade pharmacy in Brooklyn received eleven phone calls from an unidentified woman. App. 222, 679-81; SPA 8.[2] The calls, which were fielded by an employee named Esteban Arias, concerned an order for photographs that had been placed at the pharmacy. App. 222, 230-33. The caller "plead[ed]" that Arias locate the order in Duane p.95 Reade's system and delete it without developing the photos. App. 222.

Arias tracked down the photos, which apparently had already been developed. He intended to throw them away, as the caller had directed, but hesitated when he discerned their subject matter. App. 232. The photos appeared to have been taken in a public restroom. They depicted a young boy, perhaps two years old, naked and apparently distressed. Some showed close-up images of the boy's genitals and anus. App. 124-30, 222, 1040-57. In each, a date-stamped money order and a copy of the June 25, 2010 *New York Daily News* appeared in the background. App. 124-25, 222.

Arias called the police. Officers responded and viewed the photos themselves. Some, noting the presence of the date-stamped money order and newspaper, suspected that they were so-called "proof-of-life" photos — that is, photos taken to establish that a missing child is still alive, with the aim of securing a ransom. App. 510. Others thought that the photos might be related to sex trafficking, App. 261, or child pornography, App. 222. Concluding that "urgent[ ]" action was needed to locate the child and ensure his safety, App. 260-61, 275, a number of officers (including the five named defendants) from numerous divisions began investigating. By the next day police had viewed security footage from the pharmacy showing that a young woman had ordered the photos on June 26, 2010.[3] App. 244-45.

In the meantime, other officers tried to determine who owned the phone that had been used to call the pharmacy. They learned that on June 28, 2010, a complaint had been lodged with the department under the same phone number. App. 271, 303, 620. The complainant had identified himself as "Eli Samuel."

Samuel had filed the complaint on behalf of a woman named Shirley Saenz ("Saenz") on the ground that Saenz had recently reported to the police suspected child abuse, but her claim had not been taken seriously. App. 595-96. More particularly, Saenz had told police that she thought her son's father was abusing the boy during weekend visits. App. 105, 111-12. Suspecting abuse, she had documented her son's pre-visitation physical condition by taking photos of him while he was unclothed.[4] App. 104. But the police had been of little help, prompting Samuel — a rabbi and spiritual advisor who was providing financial aid and guidance to Saenz, App. 102-03, 536-40 — to complain. Samuel's complaint also accused Saenz's mother, Beatrice Saenz ("Beatrice"), of harassment.[5] App. 304, 596.

Although this information might have suggested that the Duane Reade photos had not been taken for a nefarious purpose, police continued to investigate the case as a potential kidnapping. App. 416. Detective Nagrowski used the information p.96 in Samuel's complaint to locate Beatrice.[6] Along with six members of the Brooklyn South Homicide Task Force (the "Task Force"), he interviewed her at her residence around 8:00 p.m. on June 30, 2010. App. 270-71, 311. Beatrice told Nagrowski that Saenz was her daughter and, having been shown the photos from Duane Reade, that the child was her grandson. App. 272-74. She went on to say that she had recently kicked Saenz out of her home and that Saenz had joined a cult led by someone named "Eli Samuel." App. 274. According to Beatrice, she had noticed one day that her daughter had sustained a number of bruises. Confronted about her injuries, Saenz had said that Samuel had inflicted them while exorcising demons from her. *Id.* Beatrice also informed Nagrowski that she and Saenz were engaged in a legal battle for visitation rights concerning her grandson, App. 307, and that Saenz was currently living with a friend named Isabel Romero, App. 311-12.

Nagrowski and the other officers proceeded to Romero's apartment. There they found Romero, who told them that Saenz and her child had been in the apartment that morning; at the time, however, she did not know where they were. App. 280, 999.

While Nagrowski and the members of the Task Force were interviewing Beatrice and Romero, other officers were trying to locate Samuel. They tracked the location of his phone to an apartment in Manhattan (which turned out to be Samuel's mother's). App. 417, 619. Officers headed to the apartment around 10:00 p.m. At the same time — having not yet discounted the possibility that Saenz's child had been kidnapped — a hostage negotiator called Samuel's phone. App. 416-18, 620-22.

Samuel answered, and the negotiator asked him about the complaint he had filed with the department. Samuel stated, as he had in the complaint, that Saenz's child was being abused and the police were failing to appropriately respond. App. 621. The negotiator told Samuel that Saenz and her child had been kidnapped and asked him to come to the 72nd Precinct; Samuel responded that they had not been kidnapped and that he would not come to the precinct willingly. He then hung up. App. 621-24.

A short time later, officers knocked on the door of Samuel's mother's apartment. According to Samuel, his mother opened the door a foot or two; Samuel, seeing Detectives Karolkowski and Failla, stepped in front of her and tried to shut it, but Karolkowski forced it open. App. 627-28. According to defendants, Samuel invited them in. App. 428.

Karolkowski and Failla, along with Detective Mazza, entered the apartment, and Karolkowski and Failla approached Samuel. App. 629. Karolkowski "gripped" Samuel's shoulder. *Id.* Without placing him in handcuffs, officers led Samuel out of the apartment and down a flight of stairs to the street. App. 636. Samuel did not fight back, but by his own admission he "resist[ed]," App. 640, by stiffening his legs as the officers "pushed" him along, App. 633. This use of light force caused Samuel no injury. App. 726.

Once outside, the officers placed Samuel in the backseat of an unmarked police car. Failla and Detective Chan were sitting in front. App. 640-41. According to Samuel's trial testimony, an unidentified officer suddenly opened the cruiser's back door, grabbed Samuel, and punched him a number p.97 of times. App. 643-44. Samuel reenacted this event during trial. Based on his demonstration, Judge Weinstein stated on the record that the assault lasted between ten and twenty seconds, nearer to ten than twenty. App. 931. But another witness testified that the assault lasted at least one minute and as many as two. App. 562. Neither Failla nor Chan, sitting in front, tried to intercede. App. 643-44.

Shortly after Samuel's arrest, police located the child in the Duane Reade photos. He had not been kidnapped or, indeed, harmed at all; he had been with his mother. The two were found safe late at night on June 30, 2010. App. 505-06. The lone charge against Samuel — endangering the welfare of a child, in violation of N.Y. Penal Law § 260.10 — was eventually dropped. *Figueroa v. Mazza,* 59 F.Supp.3d 481, 485 (E.D.N.Y. 2014); Pl.'s Br. 19.

II. The District Court Proceeding

Samuel filed suit against the City of New York and a number of individual officers, bringing claims under 42 U.S.C. § 1983 and New York law for Fourth Amendment and state-law violations.[7] As relevant here, he sought relief on four theories: that (1) Mazza, Nagrowski, Karolkowski, Failla, and Chan arrested him without probable cause; (2) Karolkowski and Failla used excessive force (and committed an assault under state law) while arresting him; (3) Failla and Chan failed to intervene when an unidentified officer assaulted him following his arrest; and (4) Mazza, Karolkowski, Failla, and Chan unlawfully entered his mother's apartment without a warrant. *See Figueroa,* 59 F.Supp.3d at 485; Third Am. Compl. at 22-25, Figueroa v. Mazza, No. 11 Civ. 3160 (JBW) (E.D.N.Y. Apr. 25, 2014), ECF No. 107.

Defendants moved for summary judgment. *See* Mem. Supp. Mot. Summ. J., *Figueroa v. Mazza,* No. 11 Civ. 3160 (JBW) (E.D.N.Y. July 31, 2014), ECF No. 146. The District Court granted their motions as to the § 1983 unlawful-entry claims on the ground that Samuel did not reside in his mother's apartment and consequently lacked a reasonable expectation of privacy in the property. Tr. Oral Ruling at 9, Figueroa v. Mazza, No. 11 Civ. 3160 (JBW) (E.D.N.Y. Aug. 21, 2014), ECF No. 220. The remaining claims were tried to a jury, which returned verdicts against all defendants on the § 1983 false arrest claims and against Karolkowski and Failla on the § 1983 excessive force and state-law assault claims. *Figueroa,* 59 F.Supp.3d at 487. The jury failed to reach a verdict on the § 1983 failure-to-intervene claims against Failla and Chan, and a mistrial was declared with respect to those claims only. *Id.*

Following the verdict, defendants moved for relief under Federal Rule of Civil Procedure 50(b). Concluding that the evidence submitted to the jury was insufficient to support a verdict as to any of the claims, including the failure-to-intervene claims on which the jury could not reach a verdict, p.98 the District Court granted defendants' motions and entered judgment in their favor.

III. Samuel's Appeal

Samuel timely appealed the District Court's September 30, 2014 judgment. He contends that the District Court erred in entering judgment as a matter of law in favor of defendants on his claims for (1) false arrest, (2) excessive force and assault, (3) failure to intervene, and (4) unlawful entry. He also challenges a May 1, 2014 order of the District Court denying his request for further discovery.

We find no error in the District Court's decision to deny Samuel further discovery, and we agree with the District Court that defendants were entitled to judgment as a matter of law on Samuel's false arrest, excessive force, and assault claims. We conclude, however, that the District Court erred in (1) granting summary judgment in defendants' favor on Samuel's unlawful-entry claims, and (2) granting Rule 50(b) relief in defendants' favor on Samuel's failure-to-intervene claims. As to these claims, we vacate the judgment and remand for further proceedings.

DISCUSSION

We review *de novo* both the District Court's grant of summary judgment and its grant of relief under Rule 50(b), "construing all facts in favor of the non-moving party." *Runner v. N.Y. Stock Exch., Inc.,* 568 F.3d 383, 386 (2d Cir. 2009). Summary judgment may be granted only "if the movant shows that there is no genuine dispute as to any material fact and the movant is entitled to judgment as a matter of law." Fed. R. Civ. P. 56(a). A "material" fact is one capable of influencing the case's outcome under governing substantive law, and a "genuine" dispute is one as to which the evidence would permit a reasonable juror to find for the party opposing the motion. *Anderson v. Liberty Lobby, Inc.,* 477 U.S. 242, 248, 106 S.Ct. 2505, 91 L.Ed.2d 202 (1986). "The standard for post-verdict judgment as a matter of law is the same as for summary judgment under Fed. R. Civ. P. 56."[8] *Runner,* 568 p.99 F.3d at 386 (internal quotation marks omitted); *see* Fed. R. Civ. P. 50(a)-(b).

The District Court's discovery order is reviewed with a lighter touch. District courts have "wide latitude to determine the scope of discovery"; a discovery ruling will warrant relief on appeal only if it constitutes an "abuse of discretion." *In re "Agent Orange" Prod. Liab. Litig.,* 517 F.3d 76, 103 (2d Cir. 2008).

I. False Arrest

The District Court granted Rule 50(b) relief on Samuel's false arrest claims on the ground that defendants had probable cause to arrest him. We need not determine whether probable cause was indeed present. *See Sudler v. City of New York,* 689 F.3d 159, 168 (2d Cir. 2012) ("We may affirm on any ground supported by the record."). Even if it was not, defendants are entitled to judgment as a matter of law on the basis of qualified immunity because, in light of the facts known to police at the time of Samuel's arrest, an officer "of reasonable competence" could have concluded that the arrest was justified by probable cause. *See Malley v. Briggs,* 475 U.S. 335, 341, 106 S.Ct. 1092, 89 L.Ed.2d 271 (1986).

The existence of probable cause to arrest — even for a crime other than the one identified by the arresting officer — will defeat a claim of false arrest under the Fourth Amendment. *Devenpeck v. Alford,* 543 U.S. 146, 152-54, 125 S.Ct. 588, 160 L.Ed.2d 537 (2004). "Probable cause to arrest exists when the arresting officer has knowledge or reasonably trustworthy information of facts and circumstances that are sufficient to warrant a person of reasonable caution in the belief that the person to be arrested has committed or is committing a crime." *Escalera v. Lunn,* 361 F.3d 737, 743 (2d Cir. 2004) (internal quotation marks omitted). Probable cause is a "fluid" standard that "does not demand hard certainties or mechanistic inquiries"; nor does it "demand that an officer's good-faith belief that a suspect has committed or is committing a crime be correct or more likely true than false." *Zalaski v. City of Hartford,* 723 F.3d 382, 389, 390 (2d Cir. 2013) (citations and internal quotation marks omitted). Rather, it requires only facts establishing "the kind of fair probability" on which a "reasonable and prudent" person, as opposed to a "legal technician[ ]," would rely. *Florida v. Harris,* ___ U.S. ___, 133 S.Ct. 1050, 1055, 185 L.Ed.2d 61 (2013) (internal quotation marks omitted).

Even if we determine that an officer made an arrest without probable cause, our inquiry concerning that officer's individual liability is not at an end. The defense of qualified immunity "shields law enforcement officers from § 1983 claims for money damages provided that their conduct does not violate clearly established constitutional rights of which a reasonable person would have been aware." *Zalaski,* 723 F.3d at 388. The doctrine aims to give officials room to act with confidence in gray areas by absolving from personal liability "all but the plainly incompetent or those who knowingly violate the law." p.100 *Mullenix v. Luna,* ___ U.S. ___, 136 S.Ct. 305, 308, 193 L.Ed.2d 255 (2015) (quoting *Malley,* 475 U.S. at 341, 106 S.Ct. 1092).

In the context of § 1983 actions predicated on allegations of false arrest, we have held that an arresting officer is entitled to qualified immunity so long as "arguable probable cause" was present when the arrest was made. *Zalaski,* 723 F.3d at 390 (internal quotation marks omitted). A police officer has arguable probable cause "if either (a) it was objectively reasonable for the officer to believe that probable cause existed, or (b) officers of reasonable competence could disagree on whether the probable cause test was met." *Id.* (internal quotation marks omitted). Put another way, an arresting officer will find protection under the defense of qualified immunity unless "no reasonably competent officer" could have concluded, based on the facts known at the time of arrest, that probable cause existed. *See Malley,* 475 U.S. at 341, 106 S.Ct. 1092.

This point merits emphasis. When a plaintiff alleges that a law enforcement officer's official conduct renders him personally liable in damages, our inquiry is not whether the officer *should have* acted as he did. Nor is it whether a singular, hypothetical entity exemplifying the "reasonable officer" — a creature akin to the "reasonable man" of the law of torts, *see* Restatement (Second) of Torts § 283 cmt. c (Am. Law Inst. 1975) — *would have* acted in the same way. It is instead whether *any* reasonable officer, out of the wide range of reasonable people who enforce the laws in this country, *could have* determined that the challenged action was lawful. *See Malley,* 475 U.S. at 341, 106 S.Ct. 1092; *compare Walczyk v. Rio,* 496 F.3d 139, 154 n. 16 (2d Cir. 2007), *with id.* at 169-70 (Sotomayor, J., concurring).

Applying this standard, we hold that defendants are entitled to qualified immunity on Samuel's claims of false arrest. We address, first, why it was reasonable for the arresting officers to have concluded that a crime had been committed; and, second, why it was reasonable for them to have concluded that Samuel committed it.

A. Defendants' Belief that a Crime Had Been Committed

Samuel does not appear to contest — and at all events, we have no trouble concluding — that, early in their investigation, defendants developed evidence sufficient to warrant a reasonable officer in the belief that the child in the Duane Reade photos had been the victim of a crime. Karolkowski testified that he had believed the pictures to be proof-of-life photos — that is, photos taken to establish that a kidnapped person is still alive and can be saved through payment of a ransom. *See* App. 510. Absent some competing explanation for the presence of the newspaper and date-stamped money order — and taking into account the photos' disturbing content — the officers had probable cause to believe that the boy had been kidnapped. We do not understand Samuel to argue otherwise.

Other officers, in the early going, formed the conclusion that the Duane Reade photos were examples of child pornography. *See* App. 222-23. That view was also justified. Though Samuel does not appear to argue to the contrary, we pause to explain why.

Under New York law in effect at the time of the arrest, a person would commit the offense of "promoting a sexual performance by a child" if, "knowing the character and content thereof, he produces, directs or promotes any performance which includes sexual conduct by a child less than seventeen years of age," N.Y. Penal Law § 263.15 (McKinney 2001); a p.101 person would commit the offense of "possessing a sexual performance by a child" if, "knowing the character and content thereof, he knowingly has in his possession or control any performance which includes sexual conduct by a child less than sixteen years of age," *id.* § 263.16 (McKinney 1996). As used in each statute, the term "performance" includes photographs, *id.* § 263.00(4) (McKinney 2003), and the term "sexual conduct" includes "lewd exhibition of the genitals," *id.* § 263.00(3). The statute does not define "lewd exhibition of the genitals," but the New York courts have used a six-factor test to determine whether a given exhibition qualifies as "lewd":

> (1) whether the focal point of the visual depiction is on the child's genitalia or pubic area;
>
> (2) whether the setting of the visual depiction is sexually suggestive, i.e., in a place or a pose generally associated with sexual activity;
>
> (3) whether the child is depicted in an unnatural pose, or in inappropriate attire, considering the age of the child;
>
> (4) whether the child is fully or partially clothed, or nude;
>
> (5) whether the visual depiction suggests sexual coyness or a willingness to engage in sexual activity; [and]
>
> (6) whether the visual depiction is intended or designed to elicit a sexual response in the viewer.

People v. Horner, 300 A.D.2d 841, 752 N.Y.S.2d 147, 149-50 (3d Dep't 2002) (quoting *United States v. Dost,* 636 F.Supp. 828, 832 (S.D. Cal. 1986), *aff'd sub nom. United States v. Wiegand,* 812 F.2d 1239 (9th Cir. 1987)). Not all of the elements described in the foregoing factors need be present for a depiction to qualify. *Id.* at 150. A court must consider "the combined effect of the setting, attire, pose and emphasis on the genitals and whether it is designed to elicit a sexual response in the viewer, albeit perhaps not the average viewer, but perhaps in the pedophile viewer." *Id.* (internal quotation marks omitted).

Applying this standard to the Duane Reade photos, we conclude that the officers who viewed them at the outset of the investigation had probable cause to believe that they constituted child pornography (or, in the language of the New York statute, a "sexual performance by a child"). In a number of the photos, the child's genitals are the primary object of focus; indeed, some photos show nothing else save the child's lower torso and upper thighs. *See, e.g.,* App. 1039, 1047; *cf. United States v. Rivera,* 546 F.3d 245, 249-50 (2d Cir. 2008) (applying the *Dost* factors and observing that the photographic subject was depicted with "his genitals prominent at or about the center of the frame"). In some, the child appears to be unnaturally posed and the shot taken to capture only his genitalia, perineum, and anus. *See* App. 1048-50; *cf. People v. Bimonte,* 187 Misc.2d 677, 726 N.Y.S.2d 830, 836 (N.Y. Crim. Ct. 2001). In each photo, the child is nude. The suggestion *vel non* of sexual "coyness" is, of course, inapplicable in the case of a subject so young, *see Wiegand,* 812 F.2d at 1244 ("The district court noted the unlikelihood of the 10-year-old girl intending any sexual invitation by her pose."), and though officers had no direct way to divine whether the photographer intended the photos to elicit a sexual response in the viewer, the photos' content permitted an inference of such intent.

Thus, when officers first viewed the Duane Reade photos, they were justified in concluding that the photos qualified as unlawful child pornography and that a violation of § 263.15, § 263.16, or both had been committed. Moreover, the determination that an unknown person had produced child pornography would easily have supported a reasonable conclusion that that p.102 person had committed a separate offense, that of endangering the welfare of a child, by "knowingly act[ing] in a manner likely to be injurious to the physical, mental or welfare of" the boy in the photographs. N.Y. Penal Law § 260.10(1); *see People v. Pinkoski,* 300 A.D.2d 834, 752 N.Y.S.2d 421, 425 (3d Dep't 2002).

Samuel's principal argument is that, irrespective of what defendants might reasonably have thought at the beginning of their investigation, they had, by the time of his arrest, uncovered new information that vitiated probable cause. More particularly, Samuel argues that when the officers learned from Isabel Romero that Saenz and her child had been together at Romero's apartment on the morning of June 30, it fatally undermined the hypothesis that the child had been kidnapped (and proof-of-life photos taken) days earlier. He also argues that, when officers came to realize that Saenz had taken similar photos in the past for the avowed purpose of demonstrating that the child's father was abusing him, it should have negated any reasonable belief that the images were pornographic. *See* Pl.'s Br. 26-27.

Samuel is correct in noting that an officer making a probable-cause determination is not at liberty to ignore evidence tending to exculpate the suspect, *see Panetta v. Crowley,* 460 F.3d 388, 395 (2d Cir. 2006), and that the officers were accordingly not entitled to disregard the information from Romero or their knowledge of Saenz's earlier photos. But we nevertheless conclude that, even after learning that Saenz had recently told police that she took nude photos of her son to show that the boy's father was abusing him, officers of reasonable competence could have (1) disbelieved Saenz's explanation and concluded that there was probable cause to think that the photos constituted child pornography, or (2) accepted Saenz's explanation but nevertheless concluded that those responsible for the photos had endangered the welfare of a child.[9]

We turn first to whether the officers who arrested Samuel could reasonably have doubted the truth of Saenz's description of the photos' purpose. Her explanation plainly bears to some degree on the reasonableness of the conclusion that the photos were pornographic in nature. The question is whether that explanation so thoroughly and reliably accounted for the officers' earlier suspicions that it negated any reasonable belief that probable cause existed.

We conclude that it did not. Probable cause does not necessarily disappear simply because "an innocent explanation may be consistent with" facts that an officer views as suspicious.[10] *Panetta,* 460 F.3d at 395. The officers were not required to accept Saenz's account on faith. Rather, they were entitled to weigh her explanation (along with its context: that Saenz included it in a report to police doubtless lent it some credibility) against the facts on the other side of the ledger.

Those facts were unsettling. As discussed above, the photos, considered by themselves, appeared to be examples of child pornography. A person had called Duane Reade — eleven times — "pleading" p.103 that the photographic order be deleted and the photos not developed. SPA 8. From this, a police officer could have inferred that the caller was desperate to ensure that nobody viewed the photos — an inference consistent with the hypothesis that they were contraband.

Of course, such agitation might also have resulted from Saenz's fear that the explicit photos of her son would not remain private, and to that extent her calls to the pharmacy arguably comported with her explanation of the photos' purpose. But other facts known to the officers did not. An officer might have questioned, for instance, why a person legitimately concerned with the child's welfare would have forced him to submit to a series of elaborately staged nude photos when the child was obviously in some distress. *See* App. 1036-57. So too might an officer have asked why a person looking after the child's interests would have stripped him naked in the restroom of a McDonald's, of all places, to participate in the photo session. *See* App. 264-65. Indeed, an officer might well have hesitated to believe that a concerned mother would have delivered such explicit photos of her child to be developed at a pharmacy, where they were likely to be viewed by third parties during processing. All in all, the photos of the child were so disturbing, and the circumstances so bizarre, that it cannot be said that *no* reasonable officer could have rejected Saenz's explanation notwithstanding its arguable consistency with the known facts.

Furthermore, even if defendants had been constrained to accept Saenz's account of the photos' purpose — and thus could not have concluded that they constituted child pornography[11] — a reasonable officer could nonetheless have determined that those responsible for the photos had endangered the child's welfare in violation of § 260.10(1). Viewed without knowledge of the circumstances surrounding their creation, the photos appear to be examples of child pornography. Even if Saenz's subjective intent in creating the photos took them outside the ambit of New York's child pornography statutes (and any and all reasonable officers would have to so conclude), the fact remains that Saenz not only produced, but took to a pharmacy for development, photos of her child that were by all appearances pornographic.

An officer could have concluded that in so doing, Saenz (along with anyone who had aided her) created a serious risk to the child's welfare in violation of § 260.10(1) — even if she did not intend to do so, *see People v. Fernandez,* 126 A.D.3d 639, 5 N.Y.S.3d 436, 436 (1st Dep't 2015) (specific intent to cause injury is not an element of endangering the welfare of a child); *People v. Vega,* 185 Misc.2d 73, 712 N.Y.S.2d 283, 286 n. 3 (N.Y. Crim. Ct. 2000) (same), and even if the risk did not materialize into actual harm, *People v. Simmons,* 92 N.Y.2d 829, 677 N.Y.S.2d 58, 699 N.E.2d 417, 418 (1998) ("Actual harm to the child need not result for liability under [§ 260.10(1)] to attach...."). It should have been clear to Saenz that Duane Reade employees would likely see the photos in the normal course of developing them and that, in taking the photos to the p.104 pharmacy, she was sharing with perfect strangers a series of images of her son that bore the objective indicia of child pornography. We cannot say that *no* reasonable officer could have concluded that these facts, viewed in the light of governing law, provided probable cause to believe that Saenz had "knowingly act[ed] in a manner likely to be injurious to the physical, mental or moral welfare of" her son. *See* N.Y. Penal Law § 260.10(1); *Pinkoski,* 752 N.Y.S.2d at 422, 425 (reversing trial court's dismissal of indictment and reinstating count of endangering the welfare of a child where the defendant took explicit photographs of her five-year-old daughter and brought them to be developed at a Wal-Mart); *cf. Ashcroft v. Free Speech Coal.,* 535 U.S. 234, 249, 122 S.Ct. 1389, 152 L.Ed.2d 403 (2002) (observing that the circulation of images that constitute child pornography causes continuing harm to the children portrayed).

In sum, we conclude that prior to arresting Samuel, defendants could reasonably have concluded that they possessed probable cause to believe that a crime had been committed.

B. Defendants' Belief That Samuel Committed the Crime

Samuel argues that, even if defendants could reasonably have concluded that Saenz's child had been the victim of a crime, they had no basis on which to conclude that Samuel had committed it. We disagree.

At the time of Samuel's arrest, officers possessed several independent items of evidence linking him to the Duane Reade photos and the suspected crime (or crimes). First, on the morning of June 29, 2010, someone used Samuel's phone to call Duane Reade — eleven times — to request that the photos of Saenz's son be deleted. App. 222, 679-81. It is true, as the District Court noted, that defendants did not know that Samuel was present when these calls were made (although he was). *Figueroa,* 59 F.Supp.3d at 490. But "for the purpose of qualified immunity and probable cause," we do not deny officers the benefit of "reasonable inferences [drawn] from the facts they possess at the time of a seizure." *Cerrone v. Brown,* 246 F.3d 194, 203 (2d Cir. 2001). Defendants, knowing that someone had used Samuel's phone to place a number of calls to the pharmacy, could reasonably have concluded that Samuel was in some way connected with the photos and probably had knowledge of the order the caller was attempting to cancel.

The particulars of Samuel's complaint to the police on June 28, 2010 — particulars which, as he emphasizes, were known to the officers, Pl.'s Br. 14, 24-25 — fortified this conclusion. Samuel had lodged the complaint on behalf of Saenz, the mother of the child in the Duane Reade photos. App. 272-74, 596. Samuel had referred to the police report made by Saenz in which she had disclosed to officers her practice of photographing her son nude; he had also revealed his awareness that explicit photographs of the boy had been taken in the recent past. App. 596-597. This information strengthened the link between Samuel and the photos.

Finally, during an interview with Detective Nagrowski, Saenz's mother Beatrice confirmed the connections between Samuel, Saenz, and the child. Beatrice told Nagrowski that Saenz was the mother of the boy in the photos and that Samuel not only knew Saenz, but was a strong source of malign influence in her life. She claimed that Saenz had become a member of his cult, and Samuel had physically harmed her during the course of an exorcism. App. 272-74. To be sure, defendants were not at liberty to accept these assertions uncritically. Beatrice was, by her own admission, p.105 involved in a custody fight with her daughter, App. 307, and Nagrowski was aware that Samuel had filed a complaint with police concerning Beatrice, App. 998. Accordingly, Beatrice had reason to speak ill of Saenz and Samuel, and a reasonable officer might have recognized that this bore on her credibility. But, at a minimum, Nagrowski's interview with Beatrice provided further confirmation that Samuel was closely linked with Saenz and with the child in the Duane Reade photos.

We need not decide whether this information, taken as a whole, provided probable cause to conclude that Samuel had committed the crimes discussed above by participating in the creation of the photos or the attempt to have them developed. We decide only that, at the time of his arrest, reasonable police officers could have disagreed on the point. In view of Samuel's close association with Saenz, his knowledge of the explicit photos, and the repeated use of his phone in the attempt to cancel the order at Duane Reade, we cannot say that the officers who participated in his arrest were either "plainly incompetent" or "knowingly violat[ing] the law."

Mullenix, 136 S.Ct. at 308 (quoting *Malley,* 475 U.S. at 341, 106 S.Ct. 1092). Those officers are therefore entitled to the protection of qualified immunity.

II. Excessive Force and Assault

The District Court granted Rule 50(b) relief in favor of Karolkowski and Failla on Samuel's excessive force and state-law assault claims,[12] concluding that the force applied by the officers was reasonable as a matter of law.[13] Samuel argues that the Court erred in so concluding. We disagree.

Whether the force used to effect an arrest is "reasonable" or "excessive" turns on "a careful balancing of the nature and quality of the intrusion on the individual's Fourth Amendment interests against the countervailing government interests at stake." *Graham v. Connor,* 490 U.S. 386, 396, 109 S.Ct. 1865, 104 L.Ed.2d 443 (1989) (internal quotation marks omitted). In conducting this balancing, we look to a number of factors, including "the need for the application of force, the relationship between the need and the amount of force that was used, the extent of injury inflicted, and whether force was applied in a good faith effort to maintain or restore discipline or maliciously and sadistically for the very purpose of causing harm." *Johnson v. Newburgh Enlarged Sch. Dist.,* 239 F.3d 246, 251-52 (2d Cir. 2001) (internal quotation marks omitted).

Here, defendants did nothing more than "grip[]" Samuel's shoulders, App. 629, and "push[]" him out of his mother's apartment to the waiting police car, App. 633. The officers had need to push Samuel along because he lightly resisted by stiffening his legs, App. 639-40, and their pushing caused him no injury, App. 726. There is no suggestion in the record that this application of light force was actuated by malice or a desire to cause harm. Accordingly, every factor enumerated in *Johnson* weighs against Samuel, who complains basically of the kind of *de minimis* p.106 physical contact common to virtually every custodial arrest. *See Graham,* 490 U.S. at 396, 109 S.Ct. 1865 ("[T]he right to make an arrest or investigatory stop necessarily carries with it the right to use some degree of physical coercion or threat thereof to effect it."). The District Court did not err in overriding the jury's verdict and entering judgment for defendants on these claims.

III. Failure to Intervene

On Samuel's failure-to-intervene claim, on which the jury failed to reach a verdict, the District Court entered judgment for Failla and Chan. Samuel argues that this was error, and we agree.

A police officer is under a duty to intercede and prevent fellow officers from subjecting a citizen to excessive force, and may be held liable for his failure to do so if he observes the use of force and has sufficient time to act to prevent it. *O'Neill v. Krzeminski,* 839 F.2d 9, 11-12 (2d Cir. 1988). Liability attaches on the theory that the officer, by failing to intervene, becomes a "tacit collaborator" in the illegality. *See id.*

The District Court concluded that, as a matter of law, defendants did not have sufficient time to intercede when an unidentified officer allegedly assaulted Samuel in the back of the police cruiser. In support, it pointed to Samuel's testimony describing the attack. On the stand, Samuel made hand gestures while stating, "boom boom boom boom boom." App. 644. The Court timed this description at roughly ten seconds (perhaps a bit longer, but at all events "well under" twenty seconds). App. 931. When an assault "take[s] place in 'less than thirty seconds,'" wrote the Court, officers who are present lack "sufficient time to intercede in order to prevent the assault." *Figueroa,* 59 F.Supp.3d at 490 (quoting *Sash v. United States,* 674 F.Supp.2d 531, 545 (S.D.N.Y. 2009)).

For three reasons, we conclude that this was error. First, Samuel never claimed that he was reenacting the duration of the attack. He was asked to describe what happened after the officers placed him in a police car. App. 642. In construing the evidence in the light most favorable to Samuel, the District Court should not have interpreted his hand gestures as a formal demonstration or reenactment of the total time frame of the punches.

Second, although Samuel's gestures at trial apparently lasted less than twenty seconds, a separate witness present during the event testified that the assault went on for at least one minute and as many as two. *See* App. 562. Defendants do not argue that Samuel's demonstration qualifies as a judicial admission that conclusively establishes the duration of the alleged assault. *See Hoodho v. Holder,* 558 F.3d 184, 191 (2d Cir. 2009) (defining judicial admissions as "formal concessions in the pleadings in the case or stipulations by a party or counsel that have the effect of withdrawing a fact from issue and dispensing wholly with the need for proof of the fact" (quoting 2 McCormick on Evidence § 254 (6th ed. 2006))). Nor is there any basis for treating it as such. A party that admits on the witness stand a fact damaging to his case is ordinarily free to contradict that fact through the testimony of other witnesses and argue that their testimony should be believed over his own. Such an argument might cut no ice with the finder of fact, but the matter lies squarely in the jury's province. *Lee v. Smith & Wesson Corp.,* 760 F.3d 523, 528 (6th Cir. 2014) (holding that a plaintiff's testimony did not qualify as a judicial admission and observing that a party "should be able to testify honestly to his memory p.107 of what happened and still have his lawyer argue that on the evidence as a whole it is more probable than not that the memory was faulty"); *Keller v. United States,* 58 F.3d 1194, 1198 n. 8 (7th Cir. 1995) ("When a party testifying at trial or during a deposition admits a fact which is adverse to his claim or defense, it is generally preferable to treat that testimony as solely an evidentiary admission [rather than a conclusive judicial admission]."); *cf. Keepers, Inc. v. City of Milford,* 807 F.3d 24, 34-35 (2d Cir. 2015) (stating that deposition testimony given pursuant to Federal Rule of Civil Procedure 30(b)(6) does not "bind a corporate party irrevocably to whatever its designee happens to recollect during her testimony"). Here, in holding Samuel to his own testimony, construing that testimony unfavorably, and disregarding more favorable evidence given by a different witness, the District Court strayed into the realm of improper fact-finding.

The District Court again strayed into that realm when stating that the assault consisted of only five punches. *See Figueroa,* 59 F.Supp.3d at 487. Samuel presented eyewitness testimony at trial that the assault involved between six and twelve punches, App. 555, and that it included not only the period of punching but an additional period during which the unidentified officer screamed obscenities at him, grabbed him by the neck, choked him, and shook him, App. 647. To consider the evidence in the light most favorable to Samuel, the District Court should have analyzed the attack as a one-to-two-minute incident, consisting of as many as twelve punches following a period of choking and shaking.

These conclusions require us to vacate so much of the judgment as dismissed Samuel's failure-to-intervene claims and remand to the District Court.[14] We pause, however, to address a third error in the District Court's analysis, on the theory that it may prove instructive should Samuel's claims be retried.

Having found that the alleged assault on Samuel lasted less than twenty seconds, the District Court granted judgment for Failla and Chan because "[a]ssaults that take place in 'less than thirty seconds' do not offer police officers sufficient time to intercede in order to prevent the assault." *Figueroa,* 59 F.Supp.3d at 490 (quoting *Sash,* 674 F.Supp.2d at 545). We think this bright-line rule unsupportable. Failure-to-intervene claims can arise out of a limitless variety of factual circumstances. In each case, the question whether a defendant had a realistic chance to intercede will turn on such factors as the number of officers present, their relative placement, the environment in which they acted, the nature of the assault, and a dozen other considerations. Among these considerations, of course, the assault's duration will always be relevant and will frequently assume great importance. *See, e.g., O'Neill,* 839 F.2d at 11-12 (holding that the defendant officer lacked time to intervene because a different officer hit the plaintiff three times in "rapid succession"). But this does not permit distillation of a hard-and-fast temporal cutoff of the kind relied on by the District Court. Instead, courts must evaluate each case on its own facts, keeping in mind that circumstances other than an assault's duration might bear significantly on an officer's ability to stop it from happening. The essential inquiry is whether, under the circumstances actually presented, an officer's failure to intervene permits a reasonable conclusion that he became a "tacit collaborator" p.108 in the unlawful conduct of another. *See id.*

Turning to the facts before us, we conclude that Samuel's failure-to-intervene claims — even assuming that the assault lasted less than twenty seconds — were for the jury to decide. Taking into account all the circumstances and viewing them favorably to Samuel, as required in reviewing a trial court's decision to override the role assigned to the jury, we cannot hold that the assault occurred so quickly that the defendant officers lacked time to intercede as a matter of law. Samuel testified that, at the time he was assaulted, he was sitting in the back of a police cruiser and Failla and Chan were sitting in front. App. 643-44. Nothing in the record suggests that they would have for any reason found it difficult to reach into the backseat, exit the vehicle to assist Samuel, or communicate with the officer who committed the assault. Yet — according to Samuel's testimony — both officers sat passively through the entire event. App. 643-44, 931. In light of the officers' placement relative to Samuel, the apparent absence of any obstacles that might have hindered their ability to intercede, and the assault's stated duration, a reasonable juror could infer that defendants became, by their inaction, "tacit collaborator[s]" in the unlawful conduct alleged.

In sum, in entering judgment for defendants on Samuel's failure-to-intervene claims, the District Court erred by engaging in improper fact-finding and by misapplying the relevant legal standard. As to those claims, the judgment will be vacated and the cause remanded.

IV. Unlawful Entry into Samuel's Mother's Apartment

On Samuel's claim of unlawful entry, the District Court granted judgment for defendants on the ground that Samuel lacked a legitimate expectation of privacy in his mother's apartment. We hold that this was error.

A person's ability to assert a claim of unlawful entry under the Fourth Amendment depends on whether he "has a legitimate expectation of privacy in the invaded place." *Rakas v. Illinois,* 439 U.S. 128, 143, 99 S.Ct. 421, 58 L.Ed.2d 387 (1978). Though a person might subjectively expect privacy in a particular location, that "subjective expectation of privacy is legitimate" only "if it is one that society is prepared to recognize as reasonable." *Minnesota v. Olson,* 495 U.S. 91, 95-96, 110 S.Ct. 1684, 109 L.Ed.2d 85 (1990) (internal quotation marks omitted).

The Fourth Amendment specifically provides that "the people" shall be secure against "unreasonable searches" in "their" houses, U.S. Const. amend. IV, but it has long been recognized that a person may claim a legitimate expectation of privacy in a dwelling other than his own. The Supreme Court held in *Minnesota v. Olson,* 495 U.S. at 98, 110 S.Ct. 1684, that an "overnight guest" can legitimately expect privacy in his host's home. The Court has never extended this holding to embrace all social guests, but it is clear that "overnight" status is not a precondition to a guest's ability to contest a search of his host's dwelling. *See Minnesota v. Carter,* 525 U.S. 83, 90, 119 S.Ct. 469, 142 L.Ed.2d 373 (1998) (holding that a guest lacked a legitimate expectation of privacy in his host's apartment because there was nothing "*similar to* the overnight guest relationship in *Olson* to suggest a degree of acceptance into the household" (emphasis supplied)); *United States v. Fields,* 113 F.3d 313, 321 (2d Cir. 1997) ("Although *Olson* establishes that status as an overnight guest *can* give rise to a legitimate expectation of privacy, it does not suggest that such status is required before a guest p.109 can have privacy in the home." (citation omitted)).

In determining whether a guest who is not an "overnight guest" may legitimately expect privacy in his host's home, we look to a number of different factors. In *Minnesota v. Carter,* for example, the Supreme Court focused on whether the guest's visit was social or commercial in nature, the length of time the guest spent on the premises, and the presence or absence of a previous connection between the guest and the householder. 525 U.S. at 90-91, 119 S.Ct. 469. Courts have also considered whether the guest possesses a key to the dwelling, is permitted to make use of the premises in the householder's absence, *Fields,* 113 F.3d at 320, or keeps belongings in the host's home, *see United States v. Rhiger,* 315 F.3d 1283, 1287 (10th Cir. 2003). These and related considerations shed useful light on our ultimate inquiry: whether the host has so liberally shared his own privacy interest with his guest that it shelters the guest against unreasonable government intrusion.

With these principles in mind, we turn to the particulars of Samuel's relationship with his mother's apartment. During his deposition, Samuel stated that he was "visiting" his mother on the evening of June 30, 2010 and did not live in her apartment (or, indeed, in the same borough), but he would not say where he *did* live. Dep. Eli Samuel at 18-20, *Figueroa v. Mazza,* No. 11 Civ. 3160 (JBW) (E.D.N.Y. July 31, 2014), ECF No. 148-1. He also stated that he was about to leave the apartment at the time the officers arrived, but he did not say whether he intended to return that night. *Id.* at 24. After defendants moved for summary judgment, Samuel submitted an affidavit — which the District Court did not exclude — supplementing this information. In the affidavit, he stated that for more than a year prior to his arrest, he had been staying at his mother's apartment three nights a week.[15] Decl. Eli Samuel at 2 ¶ 11, *Figueroa v. Mazza,* No. 11 Civ. 3160 (JBW) (E.D.N.Y. Aug. 18, 2014), ECF No. 157-9.

The District Court concluded that this information, even viewed in the light most favorable to Samuel, did not demonstrate that he possessed a legitimate expectation of privacy in his mother's apartment. In an oral ruling granting defendants' motion for summary judgment, the Court observed that Samuel "was not a resident" of the apartment, "temporarily or any other way," and that "he was about to leave the apartment" at the time of his arrest. Tr. Oral Ruling at 9, *Figueroa v. Mazza,* No. 11 Civ. 3160 (JBW) (E.D.N.Y. Aug. 21, 2014), ECF No. 220. For several reasons, we cannot agree with the District Court's analysis.[16]

First, the Court's emphasis that Samuel did not "reside[]" in his mother's apartment was misplaced. A person need not "reside" in a particular dwelling, in the sense of living primarily at that location, to enjoy a legitimate expectation of privacy when he is on the premises. As we have p.110 already discussed, a social guest can, under some circumstances, legitimately expect privacy in his host's home. *See Olson,* 495 U.S. at 98, 110 S.Ct. 1684.

Second — though the District Court's oral ruling is not perfectly clear on the point — it appears that the Court might have concluded that because Samuel "was about to leave the apartment" when he was arrested, he did not qualify as an "overnight guest" and thus could not claim a legitimate expectation of privacy in the property. Tr. Oral Ruling at 9, *Figueroa v. Mazza,* No. 11 Civ. 3160 (JBW) (E.D.N.Y. Aug. 21, 2014), ECF No. 220. (The Court might have reasoned that if Samuel was leaving the apartment at 10:00 p.m., the time of his arrest, he was not likely to come back that night.) Even if the Court correctly concluded that Samuel was not an "overnight guest" as the case law uses the term — a question we need not decide[17] — it nonetheless erred in determining that, as a matter of law, he did not legitimately expect privacy in his mother's apartment.

The Fourth Amendment looks with favor on "overnight guests" not because there is something talismanic about a person's intent to stay in a dwelling on a particular night, but because a host's willingness to take in a guest to sleep — slumber being a vulnerable state during which privacy is cherished — indicates that the guest has been accepted into the private sphere of the household. *Carter,* 525 U.S. at 90, 119 S.Ct. 469; *Olson,* 495 U.S. at 99-100, 110 S.Ct. 1684. Construing the record in the light most favorable to Samuel, we conclude that ("overnight guest" or not) he enjoyed a degree of acceptance into his mother's home sufficient to trigger Fourth Amendment protection. Indeed, each factor mentioned in *Carter* weighs strongly in Samuel's favor. His visit was social in nature. He had, in the past, spent a great deal of time at the apartment, sleeping there nearly as frequently as he slept at his own dwelling. He had a close relationship — indeed, a familial one — with the apartment's tenant. We have found no case denying Fourth Amendment standing on similar facts, and have found a number of cases finding Fourth Amendment standing on less convincing facts. *See, e.g., Fields,* 113 F.3d at 321 (concluding that the defendant possessed a legitimate expectation of privacy in an apartment to which he was invited by a guest of the tenant, and where he spent "several hours before being interrupted by [a] police intrusion"); *Rhiger,* 315 F.3d at 1285-87 (finding Fourth Amendment standing in the case of a guest p.111 who had known his host for "about two weeks," had slept at the host's home two to four times, and had once entered the home unannounced to take a nap).

Accordingly, we conclude that Samuel's unlawful-entry claims should have survived a motion for summary judgment.[18] We thus vacate so much of the judgment as dismissed those claims and remand to the District Court for such further pretrial proceedings as may be appropriate in the circumstances, or for trial.

V. Dismissing the Unnamed Defendants and Closing Discovery

In an order announced on May 1, 2014, the District Court dismissed from the case all unnamed defendants, reasoning that the case had been pending for several years and that Samuel still had not identified the unnamed individuals. Tr. Proceedings at 46-47, *Figueroa v. Mazza,* No. 11 Civ. 3160 (JBW) (E.D.N.Y. May 1, 2014), ECF No. 119. Samuel states that in this same order, the District Court closed discovery. We are unable to locate any such language in the order, but it is clear that on several occasions the District Court refused Samuel's requests for further discovery of documents. *See, e.g.,* Order at 2, *Figueroa v. Mazza,* No. 11 Civ. 3160 (JBW) (E.D.N.Y. Mar. 3, 2014), ECF No. 87.

Samuel asserts that the District Court erred or "abused its discretion" in entering these orders. He argues that the District Court dismissed the unnamed defendants and closed discovery because counsel for defendants represented that all relevant documents had been produced. *See id.* After the May 1, 2014 order, however, defendants supplemented discovery by producing 200 pages of new documents — most of it in the month before trial. Pl.'s Br. 39. Samuel appears to argue that if he had received these documents earlier, he could have used the information they contained to depose new witnesses and uncover the identity of some unnamed defendants.

This argument is unpersuasive. Samuel does not explain why, in his view, the District Court was wrong to rely on defense counsel's statements that all documents had been turned over. He does not argue, for instance, that at the time it made its rulings the District Court had been made aware of information throwing doubt on the accuracy of counsel's representations.[19] Rather, he appears to suggest that the mere fact of defendants' late production renders the District Court's order infirm. But if the Court had no reason to think that defendants possessed additional documents — and, indeed, had excellent reason (counsel's representations) to think they did not — it cannot now be faulted for closing discovery and moving the case toward a conclusion. Accordingly, we find no error in the District Court's discovery rulings.

CONCLUSION

To summarize, we hold as follows:

p.112 (1) Defendants are entitled to qualified immunity with respect to Samuel's false arrest claims, because we cannot say that, in the circumstances obtaining at the time of Samuel's arrest, no reasonable police officer could have concluded that probable cause existed.

(2) The force employed by Detectives Karolkowski and Failla in effecting Samuel's arrest was reasonable as a matter of law.

(3) On the basis of the evidence presented at trial, a reasonable juror could have determined that Detectives Failla and Chan had a realistic opportunity to intervene in the alleged assault on Samuel but failed to do so.

(4) The facts in the summary-judgment record would have allowed a reasonable juror to conclude that Samuel enjoyed a legitimate expectation of privacy in his mother's apartment.

(5) The District Court did not err or "abuse its discretion" when it entered rulings dismissing unnamed defendants from the case and refusing Samuel's requests for further discovery.

Accordingly, we AFFIRM the District Court's September 30, 2014 judgment insofar as it (1) granted judgment in defendants' favor on Samuel's claims for false arrest, excessive force, and assault, (2) denied further discovery, and (3) dismissed unnamed defendants from the case. We VACATE so much of the judgment as granted judgment in defendants' favor on Samuel's claims for failure to intervene and unlawful entry and REMAND the cause to the District Court for such further pretrial proceedings as may be appropriate in the circumstances, or for trial.

KEARSE, Circuit Judge, dissenting in part:

I respectfully dissent from so much of the majority's opinion as rules that "[t]he trial record establishes" "as a matter of law," Majority Opinion, ante at 94, 99, that the defendant detectives, most of them from the New York City Police Department's 72nd Precinct (or "Precinct"), who arrested plaintiff Eli Samuel Figueroa ("Samuel") on a charge of endangering the welfare of a child, are entitled to qualified immunity with respect to Samuel's false arrest claims, on the basis that a reasonable law enforcement official in their position could have concluded that there existed probable cause to arrest Samuel on the night of June 30, 2010, giving them "arguable" probable cause. My disagreement has several sources, among them the following: First, the record in this case shows that the defendants' relevant knowledge consisted not just of their observations of the Duane Reade photographs of a nude boy on June 29 but rather included repeated complaints about suspected sexual abuse of the boy, complaints made by Samuel and the boy's mother Shirley Saenz ("Saenz") to the police department — beginning at the 72nd Precinct — over the preceding two weeks. Second, the majority opinion does not, although it claims to, "view the facts in the light most favorable to Samuel," id. at 94 n.1, which is required in awarding his opponents judgment as a matter of law. Third, the majority appears to ignore the fact that it is granting judgment as a matter of law on the basis of qualified immunity, an affirmative defense. In taking issue with this dissent, the majority focuses on "Samuel's ... false arrest claims" and the evidence "Samuel ... offered... to support them" and states, "our analysis of Samuel's false arrest claims does not take account of evidence — such as a series of written reports from a Detective Hawkins concerning Saenz's mid-June complaint to police — that was never put before the jury," Majority Opinion at 98 n.8 (emphases added). However, p.113 the proper focus for the majority's decision is not whether Samuel presented sufficient evidence on the elements of his false arrest claims (including the absence of probable cause — an absence that the properly instructed jury presumably found proven in finding defendants liable to Samuel on these claims). For the grant of judgment as a matter of law to these defendants on the basis of qualified immunity, the proper question is whether the evidence compels the conclusion that it was objectively reasonable for a police officer in their position to believe there was probable cause to arrest Samuel — an affirmative defense on which defendants have the burden of proof.

Fourth, in my view, what should properly be considered on the issue of arguable probable cause in the present appeal includes all relevant evidence in the district court's record, not just the evidence admitted at trial. Although the majority states that "[i]n considering defendants' Rule 50 motion as to [Samuel's] claims, the District Court properly confined its review to the trial record, ... and we must do the same in considering the claims on appeal," Majority Opinion at 99 n.8, this position suffers a major flaw: The Rule 50 motion granted by the district court was based on the position that Samuel had failed to prove the absence of probable cause as an element of false arrest, see *Figueroa v. Mazza*, 59 F.Supp.3d 481, 490-91 (E.D.N.Y. 2014); that decision indeed was to be made on the basis of the evidence admitted at trial. But this is not the basis for the majority's grant of judgment as a matter of law. The majority's decision is that defendants are entitled to judgment as a matter of law on the basis of qualified immunity because it views probable cause as "arguable." The qualified immunity defense was never submitted to the jury; there is thus no reason to limit consideration to the evidence that was admitted. Further, the reports by Detective Deborah Hawkins, which the majority chooses not to consider, are in the district court record. (See, e.g., Trial Transcript ("Tr.") 551 (statement of defense counsel to the court: "There are documents that explicitly say — that are listed as plaintiff's exhibits that explicitly say Detective Hawkins looked at the reports from the pediatrician ... and that, in fact, the police department called the pediatrician and said you indicated in this letter that you thought that there might have been some sort of anal penetration. What made you say that? And he said I don't know, it's possible." (emphases added)).) The Detective Hawkins reports were in fact offered in evidence at trial — by each side — but were excluded (erroneously each time, in my view: erroneously when offered by Samuel, since the reports (a) showed that the pediatrician confirmed to Detective Hawkins Saenz's statement that the doctor himself thought "some sort of anal penetration" was "possible," and (b) confirmed that the police department had in its possession a letter from the doctor to that effect; and erroneously when offered by defendants to show that Hawkins had in fact investigated before reaching a different conclusion).

Finally, even if consideration of defendants' entitlement to the defense of qualified immunity as a matter of law is limited to the evidence that was admitted at trial, there was ample evidence that in the two weeks preceding Samuel's arrest Saenz had complained to the police at the 72nd Precinct and to Detective Hawkins of suspected sexual abuse of her son by the boy's father; evidence that the police and Detective Hawkins were well aware of Saenz's attempts to document her suspicion with before-and-after pictures; evidence that Saenz had informed Detective Hawkins that two doctors had opined that such molestation was possible; and, in the p.114 words of defendants' own attorney, evidence "that there are doctor reports that indicate that abuse was happening" (Tr. 550).

There was evidence that Samuel complained to the police department's Internal Affairs Bureau ("IAB") asserting that Detective Hawkins had failed to investigate; in that complaint Samuel detailed Saenz's complaints to the police and her submission to the police of before-and-after pictures; and defendants, prior to arresting Samuel, were indisputably aware of Samuel's IAB complaint. The police department records of these repeated attempts by Samuel and Saenz to get the police to prevent what the boy's mother and doctors thought could be sexual abuse eliminated any objectively reasonable basis for any officer to believe there was probable cause to arrest Samuel for child pornography or child endangerment.

A. The Trial Evidence

It is undisputed that for some two weeks prior to the arrest of Samuel, Shirley Saenz, accompanied by Samuel, had repeatedly complained to the police that, when her son had an overnight visit with his father, the boy was returned to her with bruises and swelling in his anal area and that doctors said it was possible that the boy was being sexually molested. Saenz testified at trial: "[O]n June 5th of 2010, my son came back to me with red anal swelling"; "I took him to Methodist Hospital"; "I showed the doctor, Doctor Farebrothers [sic], and she said it looks like my son was getting molested, so she made a report to the state central registry." (Tr. 58-59; see, e.g., id. at 119 ("the hospital told me on June 5th that it was possible that my son was getting molested").) When her son "continued to come back" from visits with his father "with anal traumas," Saenz complained to the police and began to document the boy's changed condition with pictures of him before and after his visits with his father; she was allowed to take such pictures in the police station. (Tr. 57 ("at the precinct ... the police officer said it was fine to do it like away from the public in the backroom").) Other sets of pictures were taken in the office of the boy's pediatrician; Saenz testified that that doctor too "had told me that it looked like my son was getting possibly anally penetrated and he wrote a letter to the Family Court" (Tr. 58; see also id. at 118-19 ("Doctor Hassan, my son's ped[iatric]ian, said that it was possible my son was getting molested. That's what he said and he wrote it in a letter....")).

On June 15, two weeks before the police department's June 29 receipt of the Duane Reade photos on which they based their arrest of Samuel, Saenz — accompanied by Samuel — had informed police at the 72nd Precinct and Detective Hawkins at the police department's Brooklyn Child Advocacy Center ("Child Advocacy Center") of her suspicion that her son was being molested by his father, and had given them pictures that, like the Duane Reade photos, were before-and-after pictures of the boy's body. (See, e.g., Tr. 64-65 (testimony of Saenz); 533-37, 541-42 (testimony of Samuel).) Saenz testified:

> I went to the 72nd Precinct. I told them that I was taking the photographs on the advise [sic] of my attorney and according to Social Service laws 415, 416, 419, and then I told them that I was concerned that my son could have been getting molested and they didn't let me write a report. They just took a copy of everything that I had, like the hospital record, the photographs and they faxed it over to Brooklyn Child Advocacy Center and they made copies and I spoke

with — spoke with Lieutenant Jaime Ortiz.... And there was like another officer there, and they actually put me p.115 on the phone with Detective Deborah Hawkins....

(Tr. 64-65 (emphases added).) In that telephone conversation, Saenz told Detective Hawkins "I think my son is getting molested, this is what the doctor said...." (Tr. 65; see also id. at 542 (testimony of Samuel that 72nd Precinct officers faxed to Detective Hawkins "[t]he doctor's report — before-and-after doctor's report").)

On June 16, Saenz went to the Child Advocacy Center and met with Detective Hawkins, who had received the materials — including the photos — sent to her by the officers at the 72nd Precinct. Saenz testified that when Detective Hawkins asked "why do you think your son is getting molested. I told her it was based on what my doctor said, based on what the hospital said." (Tr. 66.)

Saenz testified that Detective Hawkins would not allow her to make a formal complaint of child abuse. Saenz complained that the police department and Detective Hawkins, "didn't do anything." (Tr. 59.)

On June 28, Samuel telephoned IAB, identified himself, and complained that Hawkins had not allowed Saenz to file a child-abuse complaint against the boy's father. (See Tr. 544-48.) Samuel's IAB complaint was "[v]ery detailed" (Tr. 547) as to Saenz's efforts, including her showing the police the pictures she had taken to document her concerns. He provided addresses and telephone numbers for the boy's father, as well as for Saenz's mother Beatrice Saenz ("Beatrice"), about whom Samuel also complained.

Defendants plainly were aware of the contents of Samuel's June 28 complaint to IAB: It was only by means of information in that complaint that they located Beatrice, whom they interviewed prior to arresting Samuel. And, as the majority opinion notes, in all other respects "defendants do not contest that all relevant officers had knowledge of Samuel's complaint and Saenz's report at all relevant times," Majority Opinion at 95 n.5 (emphasis added); see id. at 96 n.6.

B. The "Arguable Probable Cause" Standard Is Not Met

When determining whether actual probable cause existed, we "look to the totality of the circumstances" as to what the officers knew at the time of the arrest; we "must consider those facts available to the officer at the time of the arrest and immediately before it," bearing in mind that "an officer may not disregard plainly exculpatory evidence." Fabrikant v. French, 691 F.3d 193, 214 (2d Cir. 2012) (internal quotation marks omitted) (emphases mine); see also Hunter v. Bryant, 502 U.S. 224, 229, 112 S.Ct. 534, 116 L.Ed.2d 589 (1991) (qualified immunity does not protect "the plainly incompetent" (internal quotation marks omitted)). "Review for probable cause should encompass plainly exculpatory evidence alongside inculpatory evidence to ensure the court has a full sense of the evidence that led the officer to believe that there was probable cause to make an arrest." Stansbury v. Wertman, 721 F.3d 84, 93 (2d Cir. 2013) (internal quotation marks omitted) (emphasis mine).

In determining whether there was "arguable" probable cause, for purposes of qualified immunity, our focus is no narrower; "we examine the same evidence under the same circumstances," id. at 89 n.3, for arguable probable cause does not "mean 'almost' probable cause," Jenkins v. City of New York, 478 F.3d 76, 87 (2d Cir. 2007). Rather, the test for arguable probable cause is "whether it was objectively reasonable for the officer to conclude that probable cause existed." Id.

The majority acknowledges that "an officer making a probable-cause determination p.116 is not at liberty to ignore evidence tending to exculpate the suspect ... and that the officers [here] were accordingly not entitled to disregard ... their knowledge of Saenz's earlier photos," Majority Opinion at 102. The majority finds arguable probable cause, however, on the basis that "officers of reasonable competence could have... disbelieved Saenz's explanation" — apparently referring to her reason for taking photos of her unclothed son — and that "[t]he officers were not required to accept Saenz's account on faith," Majority Opinion at 102 (emphases added). This would be far more persuasive if defendants were considering an explanation given after-the-fact and if ample support for Saenz's "account" were not already in police records weeks before receipt of the Duane Reade photos. As the police had no contact with Saenz between their June 29 receipt of the Duane Reade photos and Samuel's June 30 arrest, the reference to a Saenz "explanation" apparently refers to Saenz's proffers of such photographs earlier. But police department records clearly documented that Saenz had submitted such photos to the police in mid-June in an effort to provide evidentiary support for her suspicions of child abuse by the boy's father. And whether or not her suspicions were correct, it is undisputed that Saenz repeatedly told Detective Hawkins that both the boy's pediatrician and Doctor Fairbrother at Methodist Hospital had stated that it was possible that the boy had been subjected to some type of anal penetration.

Officers of course are not required to take a complainant's assertions "on faith," and defendants here certainly were not required to believe that Saenz's son had in fact been abused by his father. But nor were defendants entitled to conclude without any investigation that Saenz's repeated communications of her concerns to the police department were a sham. And the most obvious line of inquiry would have quickly shown that her concern was genuine. As defendants "at all relevant times" "had knowledge of Samuel's complaint and Saenz's report," Majority Opinion at 95-96 n.5, the most obvious course would have been to inquire of Detective Hawkins, who was most sharply criticized in Samuel's complaint to IAB about the handling of Saenz concerns. Had they inquired, defendants would have learned that Detective Hawkins's file included a copy of the letter from the pediatrician indicating that he thought that there might have been some sort of anal penetration (see Tr. 542 (72nd Precinct officers faxed to Detective Hawkins "[t]he doctor's report — before-and-after doctor's report")). Further, if defendants had read Detective Hawkins's reports, they would have seen that the pediatrician reiterated to Detective Hawkins that "it's possible" that "there might have been some sort of anal penetration" (Tr. 551 (statement of defense counsel)).

This record — whether or not Detective Hawkins's reports are considered — does not allow defendants to prevail on a defense of arguable probable cause, for they were not entitled to ignore the record of Saenz's efforts, with Samuel's assistance, to protect her son. Defendants knew of the complaints to — and about — Detective Hawkins. If they asked what was in Detective Hawkins's files or what her investigation had turned up, they could not "disbelieve[]" Saenz's "explanation" except by arbitrarily ignoring this clearly exculpatory evidence that resided in the relevant police records. And if they failed to inquire, their investigation clearly was not competent. Qualified immunity does not protect "the plainly incompetent." Hunter, 502 U.S. at 229, 112 S.Ct. at 537 (internal quotation marks omitted).

The majority's view that a reasonable officer could have concluded that the photos p.117 constituted crimes of child pornography or child endangerment on the theory that Saenz was willing to share nude pictures of the boy "with perfect strangers," to wit, the "Duane Reade employees [who] would likely see the photos in the normal course of developing them," Majority Opinion at 103-04, improperly draws inferences contrary to Samuel and the record. The Duane Reade surveillance tape that police officers reviewed on June 30 showed that Saenz in fact had attempted to have the pictures — taken with a digital camera — printed not by Duane Reade employees but rather by a Duane Reade computerized self-service printer. The photos were eventually retrieved from the printer by a Duane Reade employee only because the self-service system had malfunctioned. Saenz's thwarted attempt to print the pictures herself in no way indicated a willingness to have them seen by strangers.

In my view, in light of these facts that were known to the police, and were known or available to defendants prior to Samuel's arrest, no reasonable officer could have concluded that there was probable cause to believe that the crime of either child pornography or child endangerment had been committed.

I note that the majority does not actually specify the crime as to which it concludes defendants had arguable probable cause to arrest Samuel; if they had arguable probable cause as to any crime, even if there was not agreement among the defendants as to which crime, they were entitled to that defense, cf. Devenpeck v. Alford, 543 U.S. 146, 152-56, 125 S.Ct. 588, 593-95, 160 L.Ed.2d 537 (2004). For the reasons stated above, I see no basis for arguable probable cause as to child pornography or child endangerment. Nor was there a basis to arrest Samuel for kidnaping. Although the majority opinion suggests that defendants, having viewed the June 25 Duane Reade photos, did not know Saenz's son was not being held as a "kidnap[]" victim until "[s]hortly after Samuel's [June 30] arrest," Majority Opinion at 96-97 (emphasis added), they in fact knew he was not being so held before Samuel was arrested. Police records show that at 9 p.m. on June 30, defendant Todd Nagrowski and other officers interviewed Saenz's roommate, who told them, inter alia, that she had left Saenz and the boy asleep in the living room that morning. As the majority concedes, defendants were "not entitled to disregard th[is] information from [Saenz's roommate]," Majority Opinion at 102. Thus, when Nagrowski and others proceeded to arrest Samuel after 10 o'clock that night, defendants had no reason to believe there had been a kidnaping.

Finally, even if there had been arguable probable cause to believe a crime had been committed, there was no evidence to warrant a person of reasonable caution in the belief that the crime had been committed by Samuel. The police had no evidence that Samuel had any role in the taking of the Duane Reade pictures, or was present when they were taken, or participated in the attempt to have them printed. The police reviewed the Duane Reade surveillance tape of the person attempting to have the pictures printed; that person was a woman. The 11 telephone calls to Duane Reade thereafter, asking that the pictures not be printed, were all made by a woman. In addition, the photos included an image of a dated money order, and the police were able to obtain a surveillance picture of its purchase; they saw that the purchaser of the money order was also a woman.

The only objective evidence the police had of any conduct by Samuel in connection with the Duane Reade photos was that he had accompanied Saenz when she gave similar pictures to the police in an effort to prevent further harm to her son, that he p.118 complained to IAB when the police refused to assist Saenz in that effort, and that he apparently loaned the woman who called Duane Reade his phone.

Given the totality of the circumstances, including the documentation in the police files as to Saenz's intense communications with the police about her suspicion that her son was being abused, accompanied by her report of multiple doctors' statements and a copy of least one doctor's written opinion that her suspicion could be correct — all of which defendants knew or should have known — I dissent from so much of the majority opinion as rules that defendants are entitled to qualified immunity on Samuel's false arrest claims as a matter of law.

[*] The Clerk of Court is directed to amend the official caption to conform with the caption above.

[1] We view the facts in the light most favorable to Samuel. *See Runner v. N.Y. Stock Exch., Inc.,* 568 F.3d 383, 386 (2d Cir. 2009).

[2] References to "App." are to plaintiff-appellant's appendix. References to "SPA" are to the special appendix.

[3] Police had also ascertained that the photos had been taken in the restroom of a McDonald's restaurant. App. 264-65.

[4] In April 2010, a judge of the Kings County Family Court, having learned that Saenz was taking explicit photographs of her son for this purpose, had directed that she stop the practice lest she be "prosecuted for child pornography" and lose custody of the child. App. 150-54. But this was not known to the officers at the time of Samuel's arrest and was not relied on by the District Court in ruling on defendants' Rule 50 motion. *Figueroa v. Mazza,* 59 F.Supp.3d 481, 491 (E.D.N.Y. 2014).

[5] With one exception, discussed below in note 6, defendants do not contest that all relevant officers had knowledge of Samuel's complaint and Saenz's report at all relevant times. *See* Defs.' Br. 33.

[6] Though defendants suggest otherwise, *see* Defs.' Br. 15; App. 309, it appears that, at the time Nagrowski interviewed Beatrice, he was aware that Samuel had lodged a complaint against her, *see* App. 998.

[7] Title 42 of the United States Code, section 1983, creates a private right of action for damages against a person who, acting under color of state law, deprives another of a right secured by the laws of the United States. *Rehberg v. Paulk,* ___ U.S. ___, 132 S.Ct. 1497, 1501, 182 L.Ed.2d 593 (2012). It provides, in relevant part:

Every person who, under color of any statute, ordinance, regulation, custom, or usage, of any State or Territory or the District of Columbia, subjects, or causes to be subjected, any citizen of the United States or other person within the jurisdiction thereof to the deprivation of any rights, privileges, or immunities secured by the Constitution and laws, shall be liable to the party injured in an action at law, suit in equity, or other proper proceeding for redress ....

42 U.S.C. § 1983.

[8] We pause to note that, although the standard applied is the same in each case, Rule 50 motions and summary-judgment motions are decided on different evidentiary records. Because "summary judgment motions are usually made before trial," they are "decided on documentary evidence." *Anderson,* 477 U.S. at 251, 106 S.Ct. 2505 (internal quotation marks omitted). It follows from the purpose of the summary-judgment device — to determine whether there exists a genuine issue of material fact for trial — that any evidence considered on summary judgment must be reducible to admissible form. *See* Fed. R. Civ. P. 56(c)(2); *Santos v. Murdock,* 243 F.3d 681, 683 (2d Cir. 2001). By examining such documentary evidence as could be admitted at trial, a court adjudicating a summary-judgment motion determines whether any reasonable juror could, if presented with that evidence at trial, find for the nonmovant.

The Rule 50 inquiry differs. Because "[Rule 50] motions are made at trial," they are decided not on what evidence *could have been* admitted, but on "the evidence that *has been* admitted." *Anderson,* 477 U.S. at 251, 106 S.Ct. 2505 (emphasis supplied) (internal quotation marks omitted); *see Rothstein v. Carriere,* 373 F.3d 275, 284 (2d Cir. 2004) ("[O]nce a trial has occurred, the focus is on the evidence that was actually admitted at trial, not on the earlier summary judgment record."). What we care about at the Rule 50 stage is not whether the nonmovant has managed to collect evidence sufficient to support his cause, but whether he has actually put that evidence before the jury charged with deciding the dispute. Evidence kept hidden under a bushel, never brought out to enlighten the factfinder, does not figure in the calculus.

For that reason, we are unable to endorse our dissenting colleague's view that "[the record that] should properly be considered on the issue of arguable probable cause [as to Samuel's false arrest claims] ... includes all relevant evidence in the district court's record, not just the evidence admitted at trial." Dissenting Op. at 113. Samuel brought his false arrest claims to trial and, at trial, offered evidence to support them. In considering defendants' Rule 50 motion as to those claims, the District Court properly confined its review to the trial record, *see Figueroa,* 59 F.Supp.3d at 486-87, and we must do the same in considering the claims on appeal. Accordingly, our analysis of Samuel's false arrest claims does not take account of evidence — such as a series of written reports from a Detective Hawkins concerning Saenz's mid-June complaint to police — that was never put before the jury, but on which our dissenting colleague thinks it appropriate to rely. *See* Dissenting Op. at 113-14.

[9] In light of these conclusions, we need not determine whether a reasonable officer could have determined that, notwithstanding Romero's statement that she had seen Saenz and her child on June 30, 2010, there was probable cause to believe that the boy had been kidnapped.

[10] We discuss below whether Saenz's explanation was indeed "innocent" or must necessarily have been viewed as such by a reasonable officer.

[11] We will assume that if a reasonable officer were to view these photos knowing why they were produced, he would be forced to conclude that they are not pornographic, *see Horner,* 752 N.Y.S.2d at 149 (reviewing court must consider "whether the visual depiction is intended or designed to elicit a sexual response in the viewer" (internal quotation marks omitted)), and that, accordingly, an officer required to accept Saenz's explanation of the photos' provenance could not reasonably have determined that § 263.15 or § 263.16 had been violated.

[12] These claims pertain to the conduct of defendants in apprehending Samuel within his mother's apartment and escorting him outside. They do not relate to the incident during which Samuel allegedly was punched while sitting in the police cruiser; the officer who is said to have perpetrated that assault has never been identified.

[13] A lawful arrest is not an assault or battery under New York law, provided the force used is reasonable. *See Cunningham v. United States,* 472 F.Supp.2d 366, 381 (E.D.N.Y. 2007) (collecting New York cases).

[14] Failla and Chan do not argue that, if a constitutional violation indeed occurred, they are entitled to qualified immunity.

[15] A party may not create an issue of fact that will defeat summary judgment by submitting an affidavit that contradicts the party's prior deposition testimony, but it is permissible to clarify by affidavit ambiguous or incomplete deposition testimony. *Maxwell v. City of New York,* 380 F.3d 106, 109 (2d Cir. 2004). Nothing in Samuel's affidavit contradicts the testimony he gave at his deposition.

[16] As is true of Samuel's failure-to-intervene claims, defendants do not argue that they are entitled to qualified immunity on the unlawful-entry claims if their conduct violated the Fourth Amendment.

[17] The cases do not define the phrase. In *Olson,* for instance, the defendant had slept in the searched dwelling the night prior to the search (which occurred late in the afternoon). *Olson,* 495 U.S. at 93-94, 97 n. 6, 110 S.Ct. 1684. But for "several days" before that, he had been sleeping someplace else, *id.* at 97 n. 6, 110 S.Ct. 1684, and the Court did not discuss whether he had ever slept in the relevant dwelling before or had planned to sleep there the night after the search occurred. (The facts suggested that the defendant had not planned to sleep in the dwelling a second night: the police had been told that he planned to "leave town." *Id.* at 93, 110 S.Ct. 1684.) The Supreme Court nevertheless characterized the defendant as an "overnight guest" and held that he was entitled to claim the protection of the Fourth Amendment in his hosts' home.

We need not determine what this says about whether Samuel — who often stayed in his mother's apartment, but might not have stayed there the night before his arrest and might not have planned to stay there the night of his arrest — was an "overnight guest." Nor do we think such an exercise would be particularly useful. As discussed below, a person's status as an "overnight guest" matters because sleeping in a dwelling says much about one's connection with the property and one's expectations while present there; the law can take account of these considerations without drawing hard lines concerning what kind of guest counts as an "overnight" one.

[18] Defendants also argue that, even if Samuel enjoyed a legitimate expectation of privacy in his mother's apartment, this portion of the judgment can stand because the trial record shows that Samuel's mother consented to defendants' entry. We disagree. The officers so testified, but Samuel testified that his mother did nothing more than open the door a foot or two before Samuel stepped in front of her. App. 627-28. If Samuel is believed, his mother did not consent to defendants' entering her apartment. *See United States v. Vasquez,* 638 F.2d 507, 527 (2d Cir. 1980) (concluding that merely opening a door when officers knock is not consent).

[19] Samuel does not appear to have sought additional discovery *after* the new documents were produced. *See* Pl.'s Br. 39-40; Pl.'s Reply Br. 47-50.

THIRD CIRCUIT DECISIONS

The Affirmative Defense of Qualified Immunity for Law Enforcement

879 F.3d 504 (2018)

Don KARNS, Appellant

v.

Kathleen SHANAHAN; Sandra McKeon Crowe; New Jersey Transit; John DOE
Supervisors #1-50
Robert Parker, Appellant

v.

Kathleen Shanahan; Sandra McKeon Crowe; New Jersey Transit; John DOE
Supervisors #1-50.

No. 16-2171, No. 16-2172.

United States Court of Appeals, Third Circuit.

Argued: January 26, 2017.

Filed: January 11, 2018.

Karns v. Shanahan, 879 F. 3d 504 (3rd Cir. 2018)

Appeal from the United States District Court for the District of New Jersey, (Nos. 3:14-cv-04429 & 3:14-cv-4104), District Judge: Hon. Mary L. Cooper.

John M. Bloor, Esq. [ARGUED] Drinker Biddle & Reath, 18th and Cherry Streets, One Logan Square, Suite 2000, Philadelphia, PA 19103, F. Michael Daily, Jr., Esq., 216 Haddon Avenue, Sentry Office Plaza, Suite 106, Westmont, NJ 08108, Counsel for Appellants.

Jennifer J. McGruther, Esq. [ARGUED] Stephen R. Tucker, Esq., Benjamin H. Zieman, Esq., Office of Attorney General of New Jersey, Department of Law & Public Safety, Division of Law, Richard J. Hughes Justice Complex, 25 Market Street, P.O. Box 112, Trenton, NJ 08625, Counsel for Appellees.

Before: CHAGARES, RESTREPO, and ROTH, Circuit Judges.

p.510 OPINION

CHAGARES, Circuit Judge.

Don Karns and Robert Parker filed civil rights actions against the New Jersey Transit Corporation ("NJ Transit") and NJ Transit Officers Kathleen Shanahan and Sandra McKeon Crowe in their official and individual capacities, alleging violations of the First, Fourth, and Fourteenth Amendments. Officers Shanahan and Crowe arrested Karns and Parker for defiant trespass and obstruction of justice after Karns and Parker refused to vacate the NJ Transit train platform on which they were preaching without the required permit. The District Court granted the defendants' motion for summary judgment on Eleventh Amendment immunity and qualified immunity grounds. This consolidated appeal followed. For the reasons that follow, we will affirm the District Court's judgment.

I.

Karns and Parker are evangelical Christian ministers who regularly preach the Christian gospel. At around 6:00 a.m. on June 26, 2012, Karns and Parker were loudly preaching on the railway platform at the Princeton Junction station, which is owned by NJ Transit. They also carried signs with Bible verses on them. Parker had previously been informed that a permit was required to preach on NJ Transit property pursuant to N.J. Admin. Code § 16:83-1.1, which provides that persons wishing to engage in non-commercial speech on NJ Transit property are required to obtain a non-commercial certificate of registration.[1] Appendix ("App.") 118. Karns was apparently unaware of this requirement. App. 244-45. Neither Karns nor Parker applied for or obtained such a permit during the period leading up to the incident giving rise to this lawsuit.

p.511 Officers Shanahan and Crowe are law enforcement officers who are NJ Transit employees. NJ Transit maintains a policy that its officers be familiar with and uniformly enforce the permitting regulations, and all NJ Transit officers were instructed on this policy. App. 136; App. 470-71; App. 858. This policy was communicated in an email dated May 6, 2010 from NJ Transit Deputy Chief Joseph Kelly. App. 136. The email instructed that in the event a NJ Transit officer observes an individual engaging in non-commercial speech without a permit, the officer should explain the permitting rules and provide information about the permit application process. App. 136. The email directed that the officer shall take "appropriate enforcement action" if the individual has been made aware of the application process and permit requirement and continues to engage in non-commercial expression. App. 136.

While on patrol on the morning of June 26, 2012, Officers Shanahan and Crowe received a radio dispatch informing them that individuals were preaching loudly on the Princeton Junction station platform. This was not the first incident of loud preaching on NJ Transit property. Rather, there had been several incidents involving "[c]ommuters complaining of loud preaching at different stations" throughout the NJ Transit system. App. 470.

In response to the dispatch call, Officers Shanahan and Crowe approached the Princeton Junction station. The officers were able to hear shouting emanating from the platform from as far as the parking lot beside the station. Once on the train platform, Officers Shanahan and Crowe approached Karns and Parker, noticing that Parker's behavior "was not the normal behavior of a commuter" and that he "was shaking uncontrollably." App. 208. Officer Crowe indicated that she "wasn't paying attention to what [the plaintiffs] were saying" as she approached them. App. 197. Karns and Parker ceased preaching as the officers approached them. Parker took out his cell phone to record the encounter, but Officer Shanahan requested that he put it away. Parker eventually complied. The officers then asked Karns and Parker whether they had a permit to speak at the station. They responded that they did not. Officer Shanahan informed them that a permit was required, but Parker responded that he had been preaching at the station for years without any form of permit.

The officers then asked Parker to provide identification. Parker produced an expired college identification card. Karns refused to provide any form of identification. Believing that Karns and Parker were interfering with their investigation by failing to produce sufficient identification, the officers then arrested Karns and Parker and charged them each with one count of obstruction under N.J. Stat. Ann. § 2C:29-1(a) and one count of obstruction under N.J. Stat. Ann. § 2C:29-1(b). Karns and Parker were also each charged with one count of defiant trespass in violation of N.J. Stat. Ann. § 2C:18-3(b) on the basis of the officers' belief that engaging in non-commercial expression on NJ Transit property without a permit constitutes trespassing.

Karns was ultimately acquitted of all charges. The obstruction of justice charges against Parker were dismissed, but he was convicted of defiant trespass. That charge was ultimately reversed by the New Jersey Superior Court.

On June 26, 2014, Karns and Parker jointly filed a complaint against NJ Transit and Officers Shanahan and Crowe in their official and individual capacities. The District Court ordered Karns to file an amended complaint and Parker to file a separate complaint. On July 14, 2014, p.512 Karns and Parker filed individual complaints, each alleging violations of the First, Fourth, and Fourteenth Amendments. The actions were consolidated for discovery purposes, and NJ Transit and the officers moved for summary judgment. On March 31, 2016, the District Court granted summary judgment in favor of all of the defendants and against Karns and Parker.

Karns and Parker filed this timely appeal.

II.

The District Court had jurisdiction pursuant to 28 U.S.C. § 1331. We have jurisdiction pursuant to 28 U.S.C. § 1291. We exercise plenary review over a grant of summary judgment and apply the same standard as the District Court. Goldenstein v. Repossessors Inc., 815 F.3d 142, 146 (3d Cir. 2016); Beers-Capitol v. Whetzel, 256 F.3d 120, 130 n.6 (3d Cir. 2001). We review de novo the legal grounds underpinning a claim of qualified immunity or sovereign immunity. Halsey v. Pfeiffer, 750 F.3d 273, 287 (3d Cir. 2014); Blanciak v. Allegheny Ludlum Corp., 77 F.3d 690, 694 (3d Cir. 1996).

III.

Karns and Parker first argue that the District Court erred by concluding that NJ Transit was an "arm of the state" entitled to claim immunity from suit in federal court under the Eleventh Amendment. They relatedly argue that NJ Transit is liable for damages under 42 U.S.C. § 1983 for maintaining unconstitutional policies relating to the permitting scheme. We have considered Karns's and Parker's arguments and, for the following reasons, we will affirm the District Court's judgment.

A.

The Eleventh Amendment to the United States Constitution provides: "The Judicial power of the United States shall not be construed to extend to any suit in law or equity, commenced or prosecuted against one of the United States by Citizens of another State, or by Citizens or Subjects of any Foreign State." U.S. Const. amend. XI. The Supreme Court in Hans v. Louisiana, 134 U.S. 1, 10 S.Ct. 504, 33 L.Ed. 842 (1890), "extended the Eleventh Amendment's reach to suits by in-state plaintiffs, thereby barring all private suits against non-consenting States in federal court." Lombardo v. Pa., Dep't of Pub. Welfare, 540 F.3d 190, 194 (3d Cir. 2008) (emphasis omitted). Immunity from suit in federal court under the Eleventh Amendment is designed to preserve the delicate and "proper balance between the supremacy of federal law and the separate sovereignty of the States." Alden v. Maine, 527 U.S. 706, 757, 119 S.Ct. 2240, 144 L.Ed.2d 636 (1999). The Eleventh Amendment serves two fundamental imperatives: safeguarding the dignity of the states and ensuring their financial solvency. See Hess v. Port Auth. Trans-Hudson Corp., 513 U.S. 30, 52, 115 S.Ct. 394, 130 L.Ed.2d 245 (1994) (identifying "States' solvency and dignity" as the concerns underpinning the Eleventh Amendment).

It is "well established that even though a State is not named a party to the action, the suit may nonetheless be barred by the Eleventh Amendment." Edelman v. Jordan, 415 U.S. 651, 663, 94 S.Ct. 1347, 39 L.Ed.2d 662 (1974).[2] The Eleventh Amendment p.513 immunizes from suit in federal court both non-consenting states and those entities that are so intertwined with them as to render them "arms of the state." Bowers v. Nat'l Collegiate Athletic Ass'n, 475 F.3d 524, 545 (3d Cir. 2007), amended on reh'g (Mar. 8, 2007). Eleventh Amendment immunity does not, however, extend to counties and municipalities despite their status as political subdivisions of a state. See Bolden v. Se. Pa. Transp. Auth., 953 F.2d 807, 813 (3d Cir. 1991) (en banc). In determining whether an entity is entitled to immunity, we must consider "the provisions of state law that define the agency's character," but the ultimate question of "whether a particular state agency [is] ... an arm of the State, and therefore 'one of the United States' within the meaning of the Eleventh Amendment, is a question of federal law." Regents of the Univ. of Cal. v. Doe, 519 U.S. 425, 430 n.5, 117 S.Ct. 900, 137 L.Ed.2d 55 (1997).

We apply a fact-intensive three-part test to determine whether an entity is an "arm of the state" for Eleventh Amendment purposes. Fitchik v. N.J. Transit Rail Operations, Inc., 873 F.2d 655, 659 (3d Cir. 1989) (en banc) (citing Urbano v. Bd. of Managers, 415 F.2d 247, 250-51 (3d Cir. 1969)). We examine the following factors: "(1) whether the payment of the judgment would come from the state; (2) what status the entity has under state law; and (3) what degree of autonomy the entity has." Bowers, 475 F.3d at 546. Subsequent to "identifying the direction in which each factor points, we balance them to determine whether an entity amounts to an arm of the State." Maliandi v. Montclair State Univ., 845 F.3d 77, 84 (3d Cir. 2016).

We historically considered the first factor — the state-treasury factor — as "most important." Fitchik, 873 F.2d at 659; see also Bolden, 953 F.2d at 818. Hence, in Fitchik itself, we concluded that because the funding factor disfavored immunity and because the remaining two factors — status under state law and the degree of autonomy — only "slightly" favored a finding of immunity, NJ Transit was not entitled to claim Eleventh Amendment immunity. 873 F.2d at 664. Since our decision in Fitchik, however, we have "recalibrated the factors," Maliandi, 845 F.3d at 84, in light of the Supreme Court's intervening precedent in Regents of the University of California v. Doe. In Regents of the University of California, the Supreme Court recognized that "it is the entity's potential legal liability, rather than its ability or inability to require a third party to reimburse it, or to discharge the liability in the first instance, that is relevant" to the Eleventh Amendment inquiry. 519 U.S. at 431, 117 S.Ct. 900. The Court emphasized that the inquiry into immunity from suit in federal court is not merely "a formalistic question of ultimate financial liability." Id.; see also Cooper v. Se. Pa. Transp. Auth., 548 F.3d 296, 302 (3d Cir. 2008).

The Supreme Court's holding in Regents of the University of California has led us to depart from the analytical framework articulated in Fitchik, and we thus "no longer ascribe primacy to the [state-treasury] factor." Benn v. First Judicial Dist. of Pa., 426 F.3d 233, 239 (3d Cir. 2005). Under this evolved approach, none of the three Fitchik factors is "predominant." Cooper, 548 F.3d at 301. Rather, each of the factors is considered "co-equal," Benn, 426 F.3d at 240, and "on the same terms," Cooper, 548 F.3d at 302. We emphasize that courts should not simply p.514 engage in a formulaic or mechanical counting up of the factors, nor do we do so here. Rather, each case must be considered on its own terms, with courts determining and then weighing the qualitative strength of each individual factor in the unique factual circumstances at issue. See Maliandi, 845 F.3d at 84 (explaining that each cases requires a "fresh analysis" and "'individualized determinations' for each entity claiming Eleventh Amendment immunity" (quoting Bowers v. Nat'l Collegiate Athletic Ass'n, 475 F.3d 524, 546 (3d Cir. 2007))). While the Fitchik Court's analysis of each individual factor "remains instructive," Cooper, 548 F.3d at 302, we consider and weigh each factor on the record before us today.

Notwithstanding this fundamental shift in our approach to Eleventh Amendment immunity analysis, Karns and Parker argue that the balancing analysis we conducted in Fitchik must control the outcome of this case. Karns and Parker specifically maintain that NJ Transit is collaterally estopped[3] from raising an Eleventh Amendment immunity defense because in Fitchik we determined that the three factors, on balance, weighed against affording Eleventh Amendment immunity to NJ Transit. See Karns and Parker Br. 14-15. This argument overlooks the significant evolution of Supreme Court jurisprudence and our own conforming law in this area since Fitchik. Contrary to Karns's and Parker's suggestion, collateral estoppel is not appropriate when the "controlling facts or legal principles have changed significantly since the [prior] judgment." Montana v. United States, 440 U.S. 147, 155, 99 S.Ct. 970, 59 L.Ed.2d 210 (1979); see also Duvall v. Att'y. Gen. of United States, 436 F.3d 382, 391 (3d Cir. 2006) ("[Collateral estoppel] ... will not preclude relitigation of the issue when there is... a material intervening change in governing law."). Collateral estoppel, then, does not preclude us from reconsidering our balancing of the Fitchik factors in light of intervening Supreme Court precedent.

Our Internal Operating Procedures also do not prevent us from revisiting the balancing analysis conducted in Fitchik. Pursuant to those procedures, "the holding of a panel in a precedential opinion is binding on subsequent panels." 3d Cir. I.O.P. 9.1. We are therefore generally obligated to follow our precedent absent en banc reconsideration. United States v. Tann, 577 F.3d 533, 541 (3d Cir. 2009). Nonetheless, a panel may revisit a prior holding of the Court "which conflicts with intervening Supreme Court precedent." In re Krebs, 527 F.3d 82, 84 (3d Cir. 2008); see also Council of Alt. Political Parties v. Hooks, 179 F.3d 64, 69 (3d Cir. 1999) (observing that reconsideration of an issue decided by another panel of our Court in a prior appeal is appropriate when there has been an intervening change in law).

Indeed, we are "compelled p.515 to apply the law announced by the Supreme Court as we find it on the date of our decision." Tann, 577 F.3d at 541 (quoting United States v. City of Philadelphia, 644 F.2d 187, 192 n.3 (3d Cir. 1980)); see also Mennen Co. v. Atl. Mut. Ins. Co., 147 F.3d 287, 294 n.9 (3d Cir. 1998) (observing that our Court's Internal Operating Procedures must "give way when the prior panel's holding is in conflict with Supreme Court precedent"). Our respect for the uniformity of decisions within this Court therefore must succumb when a prior holding of our Court — even an en banc decision — conflicts with a subsequent Supreme Court holding. See United States v. Singletary, 268 F.3d 196, 202 (3d Cir. 2001).

Adherence to our holding in Fitchik here must yield in light of the Supreme Court's Regents of the University of California decision, which unquestionably presents an intervening shift in the applicable Eleventh Amendment immunity analytical framework. Further, a reflexive application of our original Fitchik framework here would be at odds with the analytical approach employed by our esteemed colleagues in many other Eleventh Amendment cases, thus generating a potentially fractured body of jurisprudence. Compare Cooper, 548 F.3d at 301, Febres v. Camden Bd. of Educ., 445 F.3d 227, 235-36 (3d Cir. 2006), and Benn, 426 F.3d at 239, with Fitchik, 873 F.2d at 664. In these circumstances, we are not bound to follow our prior balancing of factors in Fitchik. We must instead examine each of the three Fitchik factors, balancing them equally, to determine whether NJ Transit's relationship with the state entitles it to immunity under the "holistic analysis" compelled by the Regents of the University of California decision, see Benn, 426 F.3d at 241, and to which we have adhered in our subsequent case law.

1.

Turning to the analysis of whether an entity is an arm of the state, we first ask "[w]hether the money that would pay the judgment would come from the state," which includes considering "whether payment will come from the state's treasury, whether the agency has the money to satisfy the judgment, and whether the sovereign has immunized itself from responsibility for the agency's debts." Fitchik, 873 F.2d at 659. Our Court has observed that the "crux of the state-treasury criterion" is not whether the state will be the principal source of any funding, but rather whether the state is "legally responsible for the payment of [the] judgment." Febres, 445 F.3d at 233.

The Fitchik Court concluded that NJ Transit is financially independent from the state. See Fitchik, 873 F.2d at 660-62 (reviewing relevant financial details and observing that NJ Transit's "money does not come predominantly from the state"). The parties have not offered updated financial information to undermine this assessment. NJ Transit instead argues that because it relies on state funds to meet its operating deficit, an adverse judgment would have the practical effect of impacting the state treasury. NJ Transit Br. 27-32. NJ Transit, in support of this position, relies upon two cases in which Courts of Appeals have deemed transit operations arms of the state: Alaska Cargo Transportation, Inc. v. Alaska R.R. Corp., 5 F.3d 378 (9th Cir. 1993) and Morris v. Washington Metropolitan Area Transit Authority, 781 F.2d 218 (D.C. Cir. 1986). In Alaska Cargo Transportation, Inc., the Court of Appeals for the Ninth Circuit afforded Eleventh Amendment immunity to the Alaska Railroad

Corporation. Although the state disclaimed liability for it by statute, Alaska still provided it a "financial safety net of broad dimension," largely because federal p.516 law effectively required Alaska to keep the railroad operational. Alaska Cargo Transp., Inc., 5 F.3d at 381 ("Significantly, federal law further provides that, until 1994, the State of Alaska must continue to provide rail carrier services across its system."). Similarly, in Morris, Eleventh Amendment immunity was afforded to the Washington Metropolitan Area Transit Authority ("WMATA"), an interstate transit system created by a congressional compact whose signatories were Maryland, Virginia, and the District of Columbia. 781 F.2d at 219. The Court of Appeals for the District of Columbia Circuit determined that the practical result of any judgment against WMATA would be against the treasuries of Maryland and Virginia. Id. at 225-26. As in Alaska Cargo Transportation, Inc., the Morris Court's conclusion was premised on the fact that congressional funding for the system was contingent on the states' agreement to meet WMATA's operating deficits. Id. NJ Transit maintains that both cases are applicable here, yielding the conclusion that the state-treasury factor likewise favors immunity for NJ Transit.

We do not agree, and NJ Transit's reliance on both cases is misplaced. We have consistently observed that both Alaska Cargo Transportation and Morris are inapplicable when Congress has not "put a proverbial 'gun to the head' of the State to sustain the entity even without a legal obligation." Maliandi, 845 F.3d at 87 n.7; see also Cooper, 548 F.3d at 305 (discussing but rejecting reliance on both cases because of the lack of congressional coercion); Febres, 445 F.3d at 235 n.9 (distinguishing the cases to the "limited circumstances" under which federal law essentially requires the state to keep afloat the agency claiming immunity). That is plainly not the case here, where the state is under no legal or other obligation to pay NJ Transit's debts or to reimburse NJ Transit for any judgments that it pays. See N.J. Stat. Ann. § 27:25-17. Indeed, this case is much more similar to the Cooper case, where the state treasury factor did not favor immunity because the transportation agency claiming immunity could "satisfy the deficit itself by raising fares, reducing service, and/or laying off employees." Cooper, 548 F.3d at 305. Moreover, New Jersey may choose to appropriate funds to help NJ Transit cover its operating deficit, but it is not obligated to do so. To this end, NJ Transit concedes that it is not entirely reliant on state funds but rather that it receives a "combination of federal, state, and local funds" to balance its budget. NJ Transit Br. 31. We therefore reject NJ Transit's suggestion that the "practical effect" of a judgment would be equivalent to a "legal obligation" sufficient to satisfy the funding factor. See Maliandi, 845 F.3d at 87 n.7. The state-treasury factor, as a result, does not favor a finding of immunity in this case.

2.

We turn next to the second Fitchik factor, which requires consideration of the status of the agency under state law. Considerations include "how state law treats the agency generally, whether the entity is separately incorporated, whether the agency can sue or be sued in its own right, and whether it is immune from state taxation." Fitchik, 873 F.2d at 659. We have also considered "the entity's authority to exercise the power of eminent domain, application of state administrative procedure and civil service laws to the entity, the entity's ability to enter contracts and make purchases on its own behalf, and whether the entity owns its own real estate." Maliandi, 845 F.3d at 91. The Fitchik Court concluded that "[b]ecause [NJ Transit's] status under New p.517 Jersey law is uncertain, the analysis of this factor does not significantly help in determining whether [NJ Transit] is entitled to immunity from suit in federal court." Fitchik, 873 F.2d at 662. In the twenty-eight years since our Court's decision in Fitchik, however, it has become much more apparent that New Jersey law regards NJ Transit as an arm of the state. The state law factor therefore weighs strongly in favor of immunity.

There is considerable indication that New Jersey law considers NJ Transit an arm of the state. First, consistent with the New Jersey Constitution, NJ Transit is "allocated within the Department of Transportation," N.J. Stat. Ann. § 27:25-4, which is a principal department within the Executive Branch of the State of New Jersey, N.J. Stat. Ann. § 27:1A-2. NJ Transit, moreover, is statutorily "constituted as an instrumentality of the State exercising public and essential governmental functions." N.J. Stat. Ann. § 27:25-4. Although NJ Transit can sue and be sued, N.J. Stat. Ann. § 27:25-5, this is not dispositive. Cf. Coll. Sav. Bank v. Fla. Prepaid Postsecondary Educ. Expense Bd., 527 U.S. 666, 676, 119 S.Ct. 2219, 144 L.Ed.2d 605 (1999) (observing that a state does not "consent to suit in federal court merely by stating its intention to 'sue and be sued'"). NJ Transit is also considered state property for tax purposes and is exempt from state taxation. N.J. Stat. Ann. § 27:25-16. These factors favor immunity. See, e.g., Christy v. Pa. Tpk. Comm'n, 54 F.3d 1140, 1148 (3d Cir. 1995) (noting that exemption from state property taxation is an attribute associated with sovereignty); Skehan v. State Sys. of Higher Educ., 815 F.2d 244, 249 (3d Cir. 1987) (concluding that immunity from local taxation of real property favors immunity). NJ Transit also has the power of eminent domain, N.J. Stat. § 27:25-13(a), (c)(1), which likewise favors immunity. See, e.g., Christy, 54 F.3d at 1148 (recognizing that the power of eminent domain is associated with sovereignty). Finally, NJ Transit officers are vested with "general authority, without limitation, to exercise police powers and duties ... in all criminal and traffic matters at all times throughout the State." N.J. Stat. Ann. § 27:25-15.1(a). This fact, too, supports the conclusion that New Jersey law regards NJ Transit as exercising the official police powers of the state.

State case law also regards NJ Transit as an agency of the state. For instance, in Muhammad v. New Jersey Transit, 176 N.J. 185, 821 A.2d 1148 (2003), the New Jersey Supreme Court surveyed its relevant case law and, to "remove any doubt," declared that NJ Transit "is a public entity within the ambit of the [New Jersey Tort Claims Act]." Id. at 1153; see also Cavuoti v. N.J. Transit Corp., 161 N.J. 107, 735 A.2d 548, 563 (1999) (holding that the New Jersey discrimination statute "allows the award of punitive damages against public entities" and affirming an award of punitive damages against NJ Transit); Weiss v. N.J. Transit, 128 N.J. 376, 608 A.2d 254, 258 (1992) (holding that NJ Transit is entitled to legislative immunity as a public entity); Maison v. NJ Transit Corp., No. A-1761-14T2, 2015 WL 4067411, at *3 (N.J. Super. Ct. App. Div. July 6, 2015) (unpublished) ("NJ Transit is a public entity."); Lopez v. N.J. Transit, 295 N.J.Super. 196, 684 A.2d 986, 988 (Ct. App. Div. 1996) ("Plaintiffs' claim [is] against New Jersey Transit, a public entity"). Several other New Jersey cases have also determined that NJ Transit is a surrogate of the state or is a state agency responsible for performing essential governmental functions. See, e.g., Davis v. N.J. Transit, No. A-4901-10T1, 2012 WL 3192716, at *3 (N.J. Super. Ct. App. Div. Aug. 8, 2012) (unpublished) ("[NJ Transit] is a 'surrogate of the State.'" (quoting Geod Corp. v. N.J. Transit p.518 Corp., 678 F.Supp.2d 276, 288 (D.N.J. 2009))); N.J. Transit PBA Local 304 v. N.J. Transit Corp., 290 N.J.Super. 406, 675 A.2d 1180, 1181 (Ct. App. Div. 1996) ("[NJ Transit] is a state agency responsible for operating and improving public transportation in New Jersey."), aff'd, 151 N.J. 531, 701 A.2d 1243 (1997); see also N.J. Transit Corp. v. Mori, 435 N.J.Super. 425,89 A.3d 237, 239-40 (Ct. App. Div. 2014) (holding, in a condemnation action instituted by NJ Transit, that "[b]ecause NJ Transit was a public entity, it was entitled to a discounted 2.3 to 1 ratio of filled wetlands to mitigation credits. A private developer, such as Mori, would have paid a high ratio.").[4] In light of this case law, it is apparent that the second Fitchik factor strongly favors a finding of immunity — a determination that has become that much more apparent since the original Fitchik decision.

3.

Third, we must consider the autonomy of the entity. The Fitchik Court concluded that state's fairly "substantial control" over NJ Transit counseled in favor of according it Eleventh Amendment immunity. Fitchik, 873 F.2d at 664. Our consideration of this factor is largely in accord. NJ Transit is subject to several operational constraints by the New Jersey Legislature and the Governor, who is also responsible for appointing the entire NJ Transit governing board, which is composed of several members of the Executive Branch. N.J. Stat. Ann. § 27:25-4(b); see, e.g., Bowers, 475 F.3d at 548-49 (holding that a governor's appointment of a state university's entire governing board demonstrated a lack of autonomy favoring immunity); see also Irizarry-Mora v. Univ. of P.R., 647 F.3d 9, 15 (1st Cir. 2011) ("In further support of the proposition that the University is an arm of the Commonwealth, we note that ten of the thirteen members of its governing board are appointed by the governor."); Md. Stadium Auth. v. Ellerbe Becket Inc., 407 F.3d 255, 257 (4th Cir. 2005). The Commissioner of Transportation, an Executive Branch official who is the chairman of the NJ Transit governing board, has the power and duty to review NJ Transit's expenditures and budget. N.J. Stat. Ann. § 27:25-20(a). Moreover, NJ Transit must annually report on its condition and its budget to the Governor and the Legislature and is subject to audit at any time. N.J. Stat. Ann. § 27:25-20. The Governor can veto any action taken by NJ Transit's governing board. N.J. Stat. Ann. § 27:25-4(f); see also Fitchik, 873 F.2d at 664 ("[T]he degree of control [of NJ Transit] by the governor is fairly substantial."). Certain of its acquisitions are also subject to legislative veto. See N.J. Stat. Ann. § 27:25-13(h).

All of these facts suggest that NJ Transit is an instrumentality of the state, exercising limited autonomy apart from it. See, e.g., Bowers, 475 F.3d at 548-49. We conclude that the autonomy factor weighs in favor of immunity.

* * * * * *

After giving equal consideration to all three factors, we weigh and balance them. We no longer adhere to the balancing analysis conducted in Fitchik in light of intervening changes in Eleventh Amendment immunity analysis articulated by the Supreme p.519 Court. Applying the revised analysis, we determine that while the state-treasury factor counsels against awarding Eleventh Amendment immunity, the state law and autonomy factors both tilt in favor of immunity. Indeed, in the intervening years since our decision in Fitchik, it has become apparent that the state law factor weighs heavily in favor of a finding of immunity. Weighing and balancing the qualitative strength of each factor in the context of the circumstances presented, we hold that NJ Transit is an arm of the state. We therefore conclude that NJ Transit is entitled to claim the protections of Eleventh Amendment immunity, which in turn functions as an absolute bar to any claims in this case against NJ Transit and the officers in their official capacities.[5]

B.

Karns and Parker argue that NJ Transit is liable for damages under 42 U.S.C. § 1983 for purportedly maintaining an unconstitutional custom of discriminatory enforcement of the permitting requirement. Karns and Parker Br. 24. They also claim that NJ Transit maintained a policy of promoting illegal arrests unsupported by probable cause. Karns and Parker Br. 33-35. Neither claim is viable.

A plaintiff seeking relief under 42 U.S.C. § 1983 must establish that the individual or entity who allegedly committed the constitutional violation is a "person" for the purposes of § 1983. 42 U.S.C. § 1983; see also Indep. Enters. Inc. v. Pittsburgh Water & Sewer Auth., 103 F.3d 1165, 1172 (3d Cir. 1997). "States or governmental entities that are considered 'arms of the State' for Eleventh Amendment purposes" are not "persons" under § 1983. Will v. Mich. Dep't of State Police, 491 U.S. 58, 70, 109 S.Ct. 2304, 105 L.Ed.2d 45 (1989); see also Howlett By & Through Howlett v. Rose, 496 U.S. 356, 365, 110 S.Ct. 2430, 110 L.Ed.2d 332 (1990) ("Will establishes that the State and arms of the State, which have traditionally enjoyed Eleventh Amendment immunity, are not subject to suit under § 1983 in either federal court or state court."). As discussed at length above, see Section III(A), supra, NJ Transit is an arm of the state. The Eleventh Amendment therefore functions as a complete bar, immunizing NJ Transit from any § 1983 liability.[6] Accordingly, the District Court did not err in granting summary judgment in favor of NJ Transit as to the claims that it maintained unconstitutional policies.[7]

IV.

Karns and Parker also brought several claims of constitutional wrongdoing pursuant p.520 to 42 U.S.C. § 1983 against Officers Crowe and Shanahan in their individual capacities. Karns and Parker specifically alleged that the officers violated: (1) the First and Fourteenth Amendments by selectively enforcing N.J. Admin. Code § 16:83-1.4; (2) the First Amendment by arresting them in retaliation for their protected speech; (3) the Fourth Amendment by arresting them without probable cause; and (4) the First Amendment by curtailing their right to record police officers during an investigative detention. The District Court concluded that Crowe and Shanahan were entitled to qualified immunity as to each of these claims. For the following reasons, we agree.

A plaintiff seeking relief under 42 U.S.C. § 1983 must demonstrate "that the defendants, acting under color of law, violated the plaintiff's federal constitutional or statutory rights, and thereby caused the complained of injury." Elmore v. Cleary, 399 F.3d 279, 281 (3d Cir. 2005). The doctrine of qualified immunity, however, insulates government officials from lawsuits, shielding them "from undue interference with their duties and from potentially disabling threats of liability." Wright v. City of Philadelphia, 409 F.3d 595, 599 (3d Cir. 2005) (quoting Elder v. Holloway, 510 U.S. 510, 514, 114 S.Ct. 1019, 127 L.Ed.2d 344 (1994)). In determining the applicability of qualified immunity, courts examine two prongs. First, whether the facts alleged (in the context of a motion to dismiss or for judgment on the pleadings) or shown (in the context of a motion for summary judgment or a trial) "make out a violation of a constitutional right." Pearson v. Callahan, 555 U.S. 223, 232, 129 S.Ct. 808, 172 L.Ed.2d 565 (2009). Second, "whether the right at issue was 'clearly established' at the time of defendants' alleged misconduct." Id. (quoting Saucier v. Katz, 533 U.S. 194, 201, 121 S.Ct. 2151, 150 L.Ed.2d 272 (2001)). A right is "clearly established" when its "contours ... [are] sufficiently clear that a reasonable official would understand that what he is doing violates that right." Wilson v. Layne, 526 U.S. 603, 615, 119 S.Ct. 1692, 143 L.Ed.2d 818 (1999) (quotation marks omitted). Courts need not evaluate the two prongs sequentially, Pearson, 555 U.S. at 236, 129 S.Ct. 808, and the failure of either prong will result in application of qualified immunity, James v. City of Wilkes-Barre, 700 F.3d 675, 679 (3d Cir. 2012).

A.

Karns and Parker first argue that the officers were not entitled to qualified immunity on their selective enforcement claim[8] under the First and Fourteenth Amendments. Upon reviewing the record and considering the evidence in the light most favorable to the plaintiffs, we agree with the District Court that Karns and Parker failed to establish a selective enforcement claim adequate to survive a motion for summary judgment. Saucier, 533 U.S. at 201, 121 S.Ct. 2151 ("If no constitutional right would have been violated were the allegations established, there is no necessity for further inquiries concerning qualified immunity.").

A plaintiff seeking to establish a selective enforcement claim must demonstrate (1) that he was treated differently from other similarly situated individuals;[9] p.521 and (2) that this selective treatment was based on an unjustifiable standard, such as race, religion, some other arbitrary factor or to prevent the exercise of a fundamental right. Dique v. N.J. State Police, 603 F.3d 181, 184 n.5 (3d Cir. 2010); Gov't of V.I. v. Harrigan, 791 F.2d 34, 36 (3d Cir. 1986). Hence, to maintain a selective enforcement claim, a plaintiff must provide "evidence of discriminatory purpose, not mere unequal treatment or adverse effect." Jewish Home of E. Pa. v. Ctrs. for Medicare & Medicaid Servs., 693 F.3d 359, 363 (3d Cir. 2012); see also Zahra v. Town of Southold, 48 F.3d 674, 684 (2d Cir. 1995) (recognizing that the mere fact that similarly situated parties are treated differently does not by itself establish an actionable selective enforcement claim). A federal constitutional violation does not exist merely because of the "exercise of some selectivity in enforcement." Oyler v. Boles, 368 U.S. 448, 456, 82 S.Ct. 501, 7 L.Ed.2d 446 (1962); see also Gardenhire v. Schubert, 205 F.3d 303, 319 (6th Cir. 2000) ("[T]here is a strong presumption that the state actors have properly discharged their official duties, and to overcome that presumption the plaintiff must present clear evidence to the contrary; the standard is a demanding one." (quoting Stemler v. City of Florence, 126 F.3d 856, 873 (6th Cir. 1997))).

Karns and Parker have proffered insufficient evidence to support a cognizable selective enforcement claim as a matter of law. Indeed, apart from their wholly generalized allegation that "selective enforcement of the law by a state officer is a violation of the constitution," Karns and Parker Br. 20, Karns and Parker point to no evidence that Officers Shanahan and Crowe treated similarly situated individuals differently. They do not even identify other individuals who might be similarly situated.[10] Nor have Karns and Parker offered evidence of discriminatory purpose. This lack of record evidence compels us to conclude that the selective enforcement claim lacks merit. See, e.g., Jewish Home of E. Pa., 693 F.3d at 363 (affirming judgment as a matter of law on a selective enforcement claim when the plaintiff failed to show that it was treated differently from other similarly situated entities and did not show discriminatory purpose); Doninger v. Niehoff, 642 F.3d 334, 357 (2d Cir. 2011) (affirming summary judgment for the defendants when the plaintiff failed to produce any comparator evidence); Zahra, 48 F.3d at 684. Even without inquiring as to whether the right Karns and Parker identify here is clearly established, the failure to establish a factual basis for the purported constitutional violation is an independently sufficient ground on which to affirm the grant of summary judgment in favor of the individual officers. See, e.g., Spady v. Bethlehem Area Sch. Dist., 800 F.3d 633, 637 (3d Cir. 2015) (holding that courts may affirm on either prong of the qualified immunity analysis). Accordingly, the officers were entitled to qualified immunity p.522 and summary judgment was properly granted on the selective enforcement claim.

B.

We next address Karns's and Parker's retaliation claim. To establish unlawful retaliation under the First Amendment, a plaintiff must prove: "(1) constitutionally protected conduct, (2) retaliatory action sufficient to deter a person of ordinary firmness from exercising his constitutional rights, and (3) a causal link between the constitutionally protected conduct and the retaliatory action." Thomas v. Indep. Twp., 463 F.3d 285, 296 (3d Cir. 2006) (citing Mitchell v. Horn, 318 F.3d 523, 530 (3d Cir. 2003)). Karns and Parker maintain that there was a genuine factual dispute as to whether their exercise of their First Amendment rights — namely, their protesting of the officers' demands and their attempt to make a video recording of the officers — caused their subsequent arrest, thus precluding the entry of summary judgment. Karns and Parker Br. 19, 23.

Even assuming Karns and Parker could show sufficient facts supporting their retaliation claim, their claim fails on the "clearly established" prong of the qualified immunity analysis. Karns and Parker maintain that the law was clearly established that the First Amendment prohibits government officials from subjecting individuals to retaliation for their protected speech. Karns and Parker Br. 22-23. This articulation of the relevant right, however, "put[s] the question of whether the 'clearly established' standard has been met at much too high a level of abstraction." Zaloga v. Borough of Moosic, 841 F.3d 170, 175 (3d Cir. 2016); see also Wilson, 526 U.S. at 615, 119 S.Ct. 1692; Sharp v. Johnson, 669 F.3d 144, 159 (3d Cir. 2012). The proper inquiry, instead, is whether Karns and Parker had a "more specific right to be free from retaliatory arrest that is otherwise supported by probable cause." Zaloga, 841 F.3d at 175 (quoting Reichle v. Howards, 566 U.S. 658, 665, 132 S.Ct. 2088, 182 L.Ed.2d 985 (2012)).

The Supreme Court's decision in Reichle, which was decided just weeks before Karns's and Parkers' arrests, conclusively disposes of this inquiry. The Court, on the facts of that case, held that "it was not clearly established that an arrest supported by probable cause could give rise to a First Amendment violation." 566 U.S. at 670, 132 S.Ct. 2088. As we discuss in the next section, ample probable cause supported the arrests of Karns and Parker. Given the state of the law at the relevant time period, it was therefore reasonable for the officers to believe that an arrest otherwise supported by probable cause would not violate Karns's and Parker's First Amendment rights. The District Court did not err in concluding that the officers were entitled to qualified immunity on the retaliation claim.

C.

We turn to Karns's and Parker's claim alleging that the officers lacked probable cause to arrest them. As noted, the determination of whether there was sufficient probable cause to support Karns's and Parker's arrests is relevant both to their First Amendment retaliation claim and to their Fourth Amendment claim that the officers lacked a reasonably objective basis for their arrests.

Officers who "reasonably but mistakenly conclude that probable cause is present" are entitled to qualified immunity. Hunter v. Bryant, 502 U.S. 224, 227, 112 S.Ct. 534, 116 L.Ed.2d 589 (1991) (quoting Anderson v. Creighton, 483 U.S. 635, 641, 107 S.Ct. 3034, 97 L.Ed.2d 523 (1987)). We employ an objective test to p.523 determine whether an arrest is without probable cause, looking to "the facts available to the officers at the moment of arrest." Barna v. City of Perth Amboy, 42 F.3d 809, 819 (3d Cir. 1994) (quoting Beck v. Ohio, 379 U.S. 89, 96, 85 S.Ct. 223, 13 L.Ed.2d 142 (1964)). Probable cause exists when "the facts and circumstances within the arresting officer's knowledge are sufficient in themselves to warrant a reasonable person to believe that an offense has been or is being committed by the person to be arrested." United States v. Cruz, 910 F.2d 1072, 1076 (3d Cir. 1990). Although the probable cause inquiry is usually a question for the jury, courts "may conclude in the appropriate case ... that probable cause did exist as a matter of law if the evidence, viewed most favorably to [the p]laintiff, reasonably would not support a contrary factual finding." Sherwood v. Mulvihill, 113 F.3d 396, 401 (3d Cir. 1997).

We look to the elements of the offense to determine whether an arrest was supported by probable cause. See Wright, 409 F.3d at 602. Karns and Parker were first charged with trespass under N.J. Stat. Ann. § 2C:18-3(b). Under that statute, "[a] person commits a petty disorderly persons offense if, knowing that he is not licensed or privileged to do so, he enters or remains in any place as to which notice against trespass is given by ... [a]ctual communication to the actor." N.J. Stat. Ann. § 2C:18-3(b). Generally, there will be "sufficient circumstantial evidence to constitute probable cause" when there is "information supporting a conclusion that the potential defendant in a trespass case was not licensed or privileged and that he was so advised by the custodian of the property." Paff v. Kaltenbach, 204 F.3d 425, 437 (3d Cir. 2000). This will "normally be true even where the potential defendant, upon being confronted by a law enforcement officer, makes a claim of entitlement to be on the premises." Id.

The record in this case indicates that Parker knew that a permit was required to engage in speech at the station. App. 118, 244-45. Moreover, the officers affirmatively informed Karns and Parker of this requirement before requesting that they vacate the platform. Karns and Parker were, thus, well aware that they were not licensed to be on the train platform. Karns and Parker also led the officers to believe that they would remain on the platform despite knowing that they lacked the requisite permit. These facts amply support the officers' determination of probable cause that Karns and Parker were engaged in criminal trespass. See Paff, 204 F.3d at 437.

As a result, Officers Shanahan and Crowe were entitled to qualified immunity on their claim that the officers arrested them without probable cause.[11]

D.

Turning finally to Karns's and Parker's "right to record" claim, it was not clearly established as of the date of Karns's and Parker's arrests that there was a First Amendment right to videotape police officers during an investigative stop. In Kelly v. Borough of Carlisle, 622 F.3d p.524 248 (3d Cir. 2010), we concluded that there was "insufficient case law establishing a right to videotape police officers during a traffic stop to put a reasonably competent officer on 'fair notice' that seizing a camera or arresting an individual for videotaping police during the stop would violate the First Amendment." Id. at 262. In light of this precedent, it was not unreasonable for the officers to regard their conduct as lawful. Moreover, even if the instant case is distinguishable from Kelly on the basis that the encounter here was not a traffic stop, Karns and Parker have not offered a Circuit-level case supporting their position that the right to record was clearly established. See Taylor v. Barkes, ___ U.S. ___, 135 S.Ct. 2042, 2044, 192 L.Ed.2d 78 (2015) ("We do not require a case directly on point, but existing precedent must have placed the statutory or constitutional question beyond debate." (quoting al-Kidd, 563 U.S. at 744, 131 S.Ct. 2074)).[12] The District Court therefore did not err in concluding that the officers were entitled to qualified immunity on the "right to record" claim.

V.

For the foregoing reasons, we will affirm the District Court's entry of summary judgment.

ROTH, Circuit Judge, dissenting.

Were we writing on a blank slate, it would be within the prerogative of the Majority to decide this case as it does. But the slate is not blank. The precise question that we examine here, whether NJ Transit is an "arm of the state" entitled to Eleventh

Amendment sovereign immunity," we have already fully considered and resolved *en banc* in *Fitchik v. N.J. Transit Rail Operations, Inc.*[1] Little has changed since we decided this question. Thus, stare decisis, principles of estoppel, and our own Internal Operating Procedures all require that we decline the invitation to overrule *Fitchik*. For this reason, I respectfully dissent from Part III of the majority opinion.

I.

The doctrine of stare decisis is simple: Like cases should be decided alike. We should not overturn our precedential opinions absent special justification. Adherence to stare decisis thereby "permits society to presume that bedrock principles are founded in the law rather than in the proclivities of individuals[.]"[2] Our effort to maintain a consistent and reliable body of p.525 jurisprudence is memorialized in our Internal Operating Procedures (I.O.P.), which state explicitly that "it is the tradition of this court that the holding of a panel in a precedential opinions is binding on subsequent panels."[3] *En banc* consideration by the full Court is required to overrule a prior precedential opinion.[4]

To be sure, there are exceptions to this rule. As the Majority notes, we may — even without the blessing of an *en banc* majority — depart from a precedential opinion when its holding is in conflict with intervening Supreme Court authority.[5] My colleagues permit New Jersey Transit and the Transit officers to wriggle through this loophole. They suggest that *Fitchik* is no longer binding in light of the Supreme Court's intervening decision in *Regents of the University of California*. The Majority then concludes that changes in the legal underpinnings of *Fitchik* justify overruling it. I disagree with both holdings.

A. Intervening Legal Changes Do Not Require *Fitchik*'s Overruling

Fitchik explains the analytical framework that we use to determine whether a state entity, such as NJ Transit, is "an arm of the state," entitled to Eleventh Amendment immunity. *Fitchik* instructs us to employ a fact-intensive, three-factor balancing test. We consider the funding factor, the status under state law factor, and the autonomy factor.[6] After making an individual determination as to whether each factor supports a finding for or against immunity, we balance them to decide whether an entity is an arm of the state.[7] After a thorough review of the facts as they pertain to each factor, the *Fitchik* Court held that NJ Transit is "not the alter ego of New Jersey [and] is not entitled to eleventh amendment immunity."[8]

Fitchik treats the funding factor as the most important.[9] We recently explained, however, that "[w]hile our jurisprudence had long afforded the first factor — state funding — more weight than the others, we recalibrated the factors in light of the Supreme Court's observation in *Regents of the University of California v. Doe* that an Eleventh Amendment inquiry should not be a 'formalistic question of ultimate financial liability.'"[10] Thus, "[w]e now treat all three *Fitchik* factors as 'co-equals,' with the funding factor breaking the tie in a close case."[11]

Even though *Fitchik* explicitly acknowledges that no single factor is determinative in its evaluation, the Majority believes that its treatment of the funding factor as the most important warrants a complete overruling of the opinion. But in *Fitchik,* we engaged in a qualitative assessment of each factor; we explicitly considered the degree to which each factor counseled in favor of or against immunity. Based on the record that was before us — which is largely unchanged today — we held that NJ Transit is not entitled to immunity because the funding factor "provides extremely strong indication that NJT is not the alter ego of New Jersey" while "[t]he other p.526 factors — NJT's treatment under state law, and its degree of autonomy — provide only weak support for the conclusion that NJT is New Jersey's alter ego."[12] Thus, *Fitchik* established that a showing of one factor can be strong enough to outweigh two factors that make weaker showings for the opposite outcome. Central to this holding was the idea that the strength of each factor must be qualitatively weighed.

Neither the Supreme Court's *Regents of the University of California* decision nor *Benn v. First Judicial Dist. of Pa.*'s pronouncement that the factors are now "coequal"[13] undercuts this aspect of *Fitchik.* The Majority believes that *Regents of the University of California* requires courts to count the factors that favor or disfavor immunity, however slightly, and simply rule on the side of where two of the three factors lie. The "holistic analysis" compelled by *Regents of the University of California* does not require this formalistic approach, and our subsequent cases — including *Benn* — do not either. *Benn,* which explicitly considered *Regents of the University of California,* established only that no single *Fitchik* factor is "predominant" in our analysis.[14] Our cases have since understood that no factor is entitled to presumptive weight, and no factor is independently dispositive. This approach does not preclude *Fitchik*'s qualitative method, and we have not understood it to have done so.

The qualitative strength of each factor has consistently guided our analysis. *Febres v. Camden Board of Education*[15] is demonstrative. There we found that the autonomy factor "*slightly* favor[ed]" immunity while the other two factors — funding and status — counseled against immunity.[16] Ultimately, we declined to recognize any immunity.[17] In *Cooper v. Southeastern Pennsylvania Transit Authority,* we again declined to recognize Eleventh Amendment immunity because, unlike the state status factor — which weighed "slightly" in favor of immunity — the autonomy and state funding factors together weighed "slightly" against a finding of immunity.[18] Our consideration in *Bowers v. National Collegiate Athletic Association* also explicitly considered the qualitative strength of each *Fitchik* factor.[19] There we concluded that the university was an arm of the state because the state-treasury factor weighed only "slightly" against immunity and the status and autonomy factors weighed "heavily" in favor of it.[20] As demonstrated, the cases we have decided after *Regents of the University of California* and *Benn* do not merely rely on a mechanical counting of the factors. Instead, they explicitly assess the degree to which each factor makes a showing. That is because *Fitchik* requires — and *Regents of the University of California* permits — us to do so.

The fact that in cases such as *Febres, Cooper,* and *Bowers,* our assessment of the factors has declined to recognize immunity when at least two *Fitchik* factors have cautioned against such a finding does not change our conclusion. Our post-*Regents of p.527 the University of California* cases have not considered a situation like the one we confronted in *Fitchik* — where one factor provides "extremely strong" support for one conclusion while the other two factors provide only "weak" support for the opposite outcome. Thus, those decisions are distinguishable and do not necessarily conflict with *Fitchik*. As a result, I do not believe that the circumstances here rise to the kind of exceptional circumstances we ordinarily require to warrant a departure from a precedential opinion absent *en banc* consideration. *Fitchik* can and should be read harmoniously with *Regents of the University of California* and our subsequent opinions. Only an *en banc* majority of our Court should decide whether the "strong indication" compelled by New Jersey Transit's funding can be overcome by the "weak support" of the "state law" and "autonomy" factors.

The Majority, however, fears that our continued application of *Fitchik* could generate "a potentially fractured body of jurisprudence."[21] Indeed, when two of our decisions are inconsistent, one of them must yield. But as I have explained, there is no inconsistency here. And even if there were, overruling *Fitchik* would be the improper course. We have "long held that if [this Circuit's] cases conflict, the earlier is the controlling authority and the latter is ineffective as precedents."[22] In light of *Fitchik*'s continuing validity, it remains the opinion that governs because it came first. So, to the extent that our post-*Fitchik* precedents are inconsistent with *Fitchik* in ways not required by *Regents of the University of California,* they are without effect.[23] *Fitchik* remains the controlling authority and, as a result, this panel is foreclosed from reconsidering the question re-presented here.

B. The Circumstances Have Not Changed So Significantly That Our Reexamination Is Required

Our Court has long recognized that principles of estoppel permit a litigant who was not a party to a prior judgment to use that judgment to prevent a defendant from relitigating issues resolved in the earlier proceeding.[24] Relying on this recognition, Karns and Parker argue that NJ Transit is collaterally estopped from claiming that it is an arm of the state because *Fitchik* conclusively rejected that argument. They are right. The Majority, however, believes that our reconsideration is appropriate because legal developments over the past twenty-seven years have changed the weighing of the factors upon which *Fitchik* was based.[25] In its view, a re-balancing of p.528 the factors in light of these alleged new circumstances clearly weighs in favor of sovereign immunity. I disagree because the circumstances have remained largely unchanged.[26]

Fitchik held that the first factor — "whether the judgment would be paid by state funds — provides an extremely strong indication that NJT is not the alter ego of New Jersey."[27] As the Majority observes, NJ Transit has "not offered updated financial information to undermine this assessment."[28] Thus, for the reasons my colleagues note, this factor continues to "provide[] extremely strong indication" that NJ Transit is not the entitled to Eleventh Amendment immunity.[29]

The second *Fitchik* factor requires us to consider "[t]he status of the agency under state law...."[30] In *Fitchik,* we held that this factor "tilt[s] in favor of [the transit authority's] contention that [NJ Transit Rail Operations] is entitled to sovereign immunity, *but only slightly.*"[31] The Majority contends that "in the intervening years since our decision in *Fitchik,* it has become apparent that the state law factor weighs heavily in favor of a finding of immunity."[32] I disagree.

My colleagues conclude that the state law factor now favors a finding of immunity because NJ Transit is statutorily constituted as an instrumentality of the State, constitutionally allocated within the Department of Transportation, vested with the authority to exercise police powers, considered state property under state tax laws, designated as an "alter ego of the State" by a state's trial and intermediate level courts, subject to the Administrative Procedures Act, and has the power of eminent domain.[33] This evidence might be more compelling had our Court not considered it when NJ Transit first raised its immunity defense in *Fitchik*. We explicitly recognized that "[t]here is some indication that New Jersey law considers [NJ Transit] to be an arm of the state,"[34] noting that

> [NJ Transit] is subject to New Jersey Tort Claims Act; is immune from state property tax; has the power of eminent domain; and is subject to the strictures of the state administrative procedure act. Further, the New Jersey Supreme Court has declared [NJ Transit] to be a "public" entity, although not in the context of sovereign immunity.[35]

Thus, NJ Transit's allocation under the state constitution and the fact that it possesses official police powers are the only facts set forth here that we did not explicitly consider in *Fitchik*. I doubt that these facts are so significant that they warrant a new determination by this panel. NJ Transit offers the fact of the constitution's treatment of the transit body to show that New Jersey deems it an instrumentality of the State exercising essential governmental functions. But *Fitchik* fully appreciated that, under state law, NJ Transit seems to p.529 be an arm of the state.[36] That fact, however, was not conclusive.[37] I also doubt that the grant of official police powers to NJ Transit alone requires a change in our *Fitchik* holding.[38] In light of the foregoing, I cannot conclude that NJ Transit has presented new evidence requiring us to hold that the second *Fitchik* factor now "strongly favors a finding of immunity."[39]

Under the third factor, we consider the degree of autonomy the entity has from the State.[40] Weighing the pertinent facts — which have not since changed in any meaningful way — the *Fitchik* Court concluded that although NJ Transit is "significantly autonomous," the final *Fitchik* factor "counsels slightly in favor of according immunity."[41] That is principally because "the degree of control by the governor is fairly substantial...."[42] The Majority's "consideration of this factor is largely in accord," and thus does not suggest that new circumstances with respect to this factor warrant our reexamination.[43]

NJ Transit suggests that there are additional considerations that compel us to conclude that the factor here "weighs heavily in finding immunity."[44] Their argument is based on the fact that (1) NJ Transit's board must present its annual budget to the governor and legislature, (2) the New Jersey governor appoints the entire board, and (3) the transit system's acquisition of privately owned transportation entities are subject to legislative veto. These arguments were all made in *Fitchik*'s dissenting opinion.[45] Because the *Fitchik* majority considered them and remained unpersuaded, we are bound by its conclusion. Accordingly, this factor continues to only "counsel slightly in favor of according immunity to NJT" in light of *Fitchik*.[46]

As demonstrated, NJ Transit's funding scheme, status under state law, and organizational structure have remained largely unchanged over the last twenty-seven years. NJ Transit's arguments here were fully considered and resolved in *Fitchik*; as a result, principles of collateral estoppel preclude NJ Transit from relitigating them here.

II.

In light of the principles underlying the doctrines of stare decisis and collateral estoppel, it has been the tradition of this court to refrain from overturning our precedents "lightly."[47] Today we depart from p.530 that tradition. Because I believe we do so unjustifiably, I respectfully dissent.

[1] Permits are available on a first-come, first-served basis. App. 241. All permits are approved as long as the applicant executes the permit and states his or her understanding of the relevant regulations. App. 243. NJ Transit typically issues ten to twenty permits weekly. App. 243. Indeed, the record shows that between June 2012 and July 2012, NJ Transit received forty-six permit requests, including thirty from religious organizations or entities and fifteen from political campaigns or entities. App. 116; 118-19. Only two of these requests were denied, either because the permit was returned too late or not at all. App. 119-20. Permit holders are required to remain at specific locations within the station as determined by the station manager to ensure the safety of NJ Transit customers and permit holders. App. 241-42.

[2] As we have discussed in other contexts, "the Eleventh Amendment does not define the scope of the States' sovereign immunity; it is but one particular exemplification of that immunity." Lombardo, 540 F.3d at 195 (quoting Fed. Mar. Comm'n v. S.C. State Ports Auth., 535 U.S. 743, 753, 122 S.Ct. 1864, 152 L.Ed.2d 962 (2002)). This case principally concerns only immunity from suit in federal court — Eleventh Amendment immunity — and not immunity from liability, and thus we address only that aspect of sovereign immunity herein.

[3] Collateral estoppel, also known as issue preclusion, prohibits relitigation of an issue that has been fully and fairly litigated previously. The elements for collateral estoppel are satisfied when: "(1) the issue sought to be precluded [is] the same as that involved in the prior action; (2) that issue [was] actually litigated; (3) it [was] determined by a final and valid judgment; and (4) the determination [was] essential to the prior judgment." Nat'l R.R. Passenger Corp. v. Pa. Pub. Util. Comm'n, 342 F.3d 242, 252 (3d Cir. 2003) (alterations in original) (quoting Nat'l R.R. Passenger Corp. v. Pa. Pub. Util. Comm'n, 288 F.3d 519, 524-25 (3d Cir. 2002)). Karns and Parker here invoke a variant of this doctrine, known as offensive non-mutual collateral estoppel, in which "a plaintiff [seeks] to estop a defendant from relitigating the issues which the defendant previously litigated and lost against another plaintiff." Parklane Hosiery Co., Inc. v. Shore, 439 U.S. 322, 329, 99 S.Ct. 645, 58 L.Ed.2d 552 (1979).

[4] Our dissenting colleague does not address these significant changes in New Jersey law, all of which post-dated our Fitchik decision. Even assuming that the factual record has remained largely unchanged since our Court decided Fitchik, we

cannot consider that "status under state law" factor as it was in 1989. Rather, we must contend with relevant legal developments in the twenty-eight years since we first considered the issue.

[5] Defendants sued in their official capacities are entitled to claim the same Eleventh Amendment immunity that the "entity, qua entity, may possess." Kentucky v. Graham, 473 U.S. 159, 167, 105 S.Ct. 3099, 87 L.Ed.2d 114 (1985).

[6] We emphasize that the Eleventh Amendment and § 1983 determinations are "analytically distinct," although sometimes overlapping. Estate of Lagano v. Bergen Cty. Prosecutor's Office, 769 F.3d 850, 857 (3d Cir. 2014); see also Callahan v. City of Philadelphia, 207 F.3d 668, 669 (3d Cir. 2000). Where, as here, the entity claiming immunity is determined to be an arm of the state, however, it is beyond dispute that it is not a "person" for § 1983 purposes. See Will, 491 U.S. at 71, 109 S.Ct. 2304.

[7] NJ Transit additionally argues that summary judgment is appropriate because Karns and Parker have failed to adduce sufficient evidence to support their unconstitutional permitting policy. NJ Transit Br. 50. The District Court did not reach the factual underpinnings of this claim against NJ Transit. We, too, deem it unnecessary to analyze this claim because it is apparent that Karns and Parker cannot overcome the Eleventh Amendment bar in this case.

[8] This claim arises from Karns's and Parker's contention that NJ Transit's permitting policy was selectively enforced against religious speech or speech that the officers deemed "subjectively objectionable." Karns and Parker Br. 19.

[9] "Persons are similarly situated ... when they are alike in 'all relevant aspects.'" Startzell v. City of Philadelphia, 533 F.3d 183, 203 (3d Cir. 2008) (quoting Nordlinger v. Hahn, 505 U.S. 1, 10, 112 S.Ct. 2326, 120 L.Ed.2d 1 (1992)).

[10] The sole evidence that Karns and Parker proffer in support of this claim is the deposition testimony of two NJ Transit employees who are responsible for preparing and approving non-commercial speech permits. App. 559, 628. According to that testimony, political candidates are not required to obtain permits to speak on NJ Transit property. App. 559, 628. Karns and Parker have not, however, offered any factual detail as to the identities of the political candidates against whom the permit requirement was purportedly unenforced. Karns and Parker have also adduced no facts suggesting that Crowe and Shanahan were aware of such a purportedly discriminatory policy, much less involved in executing it with respect to the individual plaintiffs in this case.

[11] We decline to address whether Karns's and Parker's failure to produce valid identification created probable cause for the obstruction offenses, N.J. Stat. Ann. § 2C:29-1(a), (b). The existence of probable cause as to the trespass offense is an independently adequate ground on which to affirm the award of qualified immunity to the officers on the Fourth Amendment claim. See Barna, 42 F.3d at 819 ("[A]s long as the officers had some reasonable basis to believe [the arrestee] had committed a crime, the arrest is justified as being based on probable cause. Probable cause need only exist as to any offense that could be charged under the circumstances." (emphasis added)).

[12] In the intervening period since Karns's and Parker's arrests in 2012, our Court has held that "the First Amendment protects the act of photographing, filming, or otherwise recording police officers conducting their official duties in public." Fields

v. City of Philadelphia, 862 F.3d 353, 356 (3d Cir. 2017). However, as in Fields itself, this right was not clearly established at the time of the challenged conduct. Id. at 362 ("[W]e cannot say that the state of the law at the time of our cases (2012 and 2013) gave fair warning so that every reasonable officer knew that, absent some sort of expressive intent, recording public police activity was constitutionally protected."). Accordingly, although the right identified by Karns and Parker is now clearly established in this Circuit, our qualified immunity analysis in this case remains unchanged. See Brosseau v. Haugen, 543 U.S. 194, 200 n.4, 125 S.Ct. 596, 160 L.Ed.2d 583 (2004) (observing that decisions "that postdate the conduct in question ... are of no use in the clearly established inquiry" (citations omitted)).

[1] 873 F.2d 655 (3d Cir. 1989) (*en banc*).

[2] *United States v. Babich,* 785 F.2d 415, 417 (3d Cir. 1986) (quoting *Vasquez v. Hillery,* 474 U.S. 254, 266, 106 S.Ct. 617, 88 L.Ed.2d 598 (1986)); *see also Payne v. Tennessee,* 501 U.S. 808, 827, 111 S.Ct. 2597, 115 L.Ed.2d 720 (1991) ("Stare decisis is the preferred course because it promotes the evenhanded, predictable, and consistent development of legal principles, fosters reliance on judicial decisions, and contributes to the actual and perceived integrity of the judicial process.").

[3] 3d Cir. I.O.P. 9.1 (2015).

[4] 3d Cir. I.O.P. 9.1.

[5] *See* Maj. Op. 513-14; *Mennen Co. v. Atl. Mut. Ins. Co.,* 147 F.3d 287, 294 n.9 (3d Cir. 1998).

[6] Maliandi v. Montclair State Univ., *845 F.3d 77, 83 (3d Cir. 2016).*

[7] *Id.* at 84 (citing *Fitchik,* 873 F.2d at 664).

[8] *Fitchik,* 873 F.2d at 664.

[9] *Id.* at 659-60.

[10] *Maliandi,* 845 F.3d at 84 (internal citations omitted).

[11] *Id.* (internal citations omitted).

[12] *Fitchik,* 873 F.2d at 664.

[13] Benn v. First Judicial Dist. of Pa., *426 F.3d 233, 240 (3d Cir. 2005).*

[14] *Cooper v. Se. PA Transp. Auth.,* 548 F.3d 296, 301 (3d Cir. 2008) (citing *Benn,* 426 F.3d at 240).

[15] 445 F.3d 227 (3d Cir. 2006).

[16] *Id.* at 232, 237 (emphasis added).

[17] *Id.* at 237.

[18] 548 F.3d 296, 311 (3d Cir. 2008).

[19] 475 F.3d 524, 549-50 (3d Cir. 2007), *amended on reh'g* (Mar. 8, 2007).

[20] *Id.*

[21] Maj. Op. 515.

[22] *Pardini v. Allegheny Intermediate Unit,* 524 F.3d 419, 426 (3d Cir. 2008) (internal quotation marks and citation omitted); *see also United States v. Tann,* 577 F.3d 533, 541 (3d Cir. 2009) ("In the unique circumstance when our panel decisions conflict and our Court has not spoken *en banc,* ... the earlier decision is generally the controlling authority." (citation omitted))

[23] *Holland v. N.J. Dep't of Corrections,* 246 F.3d 267, 278 n.8 (3d Cir. 2001) ("[T]o the extent that [a case within the circuit] is read to be inconsistent with earlier case law, the earlier case law ... controls."); *O. Hommel Co. v. Ferro Corp.,* 659 F.2d 340, 354 (3d Cir.1981) ("[A] panel of this court cannot overrule a prior panel precedent. To the extent that [the later case] is inconsistent with [the earlier case, the later case] must be deemed without effect." (internal citation omitted)).

[24] *Burlington N. R.R. Co. v. Hyundai Merch. Marine Co.,* 63 F.3d 1227, 1232 (3d Cir. 1995) (citation omitted).

[25] Resp't's Br. 19; Maj. Op. 517 (contending that "[i]n the twenty-seven years since our Court's decision in *Fitchik,* ... it has become much more apparent that New Jersey law regards NJ Transit as an arm of the state.").

[26] In addition, as we state in Part A above, the strength of each of the factors found in *Fitchik* was weighed qualitatively, a procedure which is consistent with the approach of the Court in *Regents of the University of California.*

[27] *Fitchik,* 873 F.2d at 664.

[28] Maj. Op. at 515.

[29] *Fitchik,* 873 F.2d at 664.

[30] *Id.* at 663.

[31] *Id.* (emphasis added).

[32] Maj. Op. 519.

[33] Maj. Op. 515-17.

[34] *Fitchik,* 873 F.2d at 662.

[35] *Id.* at 662-663 (citations omitted).

[36] *Id.* at 662 ("There is some indication that New Jersey law considers [NJ Transit] to be an arm of the state.").

[37] *Id.* at 663 ("On the other side of the equation, New Jersey has given power to NJT in two spheres that *Urbano* identified as indicative that an agency is not entitled to sovereign immunity.").

[38] NJ Transit does not suggest that its enforcement officers did not have general police authority at the time *Fitchik* was decided. Indeed, the statutory provision granting New Jersey Transit officers general police powers appears to have been passed in 1989, well before *Fitchik.*

[39] Maj. Op. 518.

[40] *Fitchik,* 873 F.2d at 659.

[41] *Id.* at 664.

[42] *Id.*

[43] Maj. Op. 517.

[44] Resp't's Br. 27.

[45] *Fitchik,* 873 F.2d at 667-68 (Rosenn, J., dissenting).

[46] *Id.* at 664.

[47] Al-Sharif v. U.S. Citizenship & Immigration Servs., *734 F.3d 207, 212 (3d Cir. 2013).*

902 F.3d 185 (2018)

Brandy KANE, Appellant

v.

Shawn BARGER, in his Individual Capacity as a Police Officer for the Borough of Coraopolis.

No. 17-3027.

United States Court of Appeals, Third Circuit.

Submitted Under Third Circuit L.A.R. 34.1(a) June 12, 2018.

Opinion filed: August 22, 2018.

Kane v. Barger, 902 F. 3d 185 (3rd Cir. 2018)

On Appeal from the United States District Court for the Western District of Pennsylvania, (No. 2-15-cv-00846), District Judge: Honorable Mark R. Hornak.

Noah Geary, Esq., Washington Trust Building, Suite 225, Washington, PA 15301, Attorney for Appellant.

Mark R. Lane, Esq., Dell, Moser, Lane & Loughney, LLC, Two Chatham Center, Suite 1500, 112 Washington Place, Pittsburgh, PA 15219, Attorney for Appellee.

Before: CHAGARES, GREENBERG, and FUENTES, Circuit Judges.

p.187 OPINION OF THE COURT

FUENTES, Circuit Judge.

On June 27, 2013, Brandy Kane went to the hospital and reported that she may have been the victim of a sexual assault. That night, Officer Shawn Barger of the Coraopolis Police Department went to the hospital to interview Kane regarding the possible assault. At that time, Kane says Barger told her to bring the clothes she wore during the alleged incident to him at the police station.

p.188 The next day, Kane — accompanied by a friend — brought her clothes to the police station. While there, contrary to department policy, Barger met alone with Kane in a back room of the station. Then, also in violation of department policy, Barger used his personal cell phone to photograph intimate areas of Kane's body.

During this encounter, Barger touched Kane twice. First, rather than relying on Kane to do so, Barger pulled Kane's shorts down to photograph a bruise on her right buttock. At this point, Kane says she "felt something touch her butt crack which caused her to jump."[1] Second, again without asking Kane to do so, Barger pulled Kane's tank top down to expose a bruise on her upper chest.

Kane says that, while photographing her, Barger repeatedly asked about her breasts, vagina, and buttocks. In this regard, Barger persistently inquired if Kane sustained injuries to her vagina. Despite Kane's consistent denials, Barger's relentless questioning led Kane to expose her vagina to him.

After photographing Kane, Officer Barger failed to document the clothing evidence that Kane provided. Moreover, when Kane later reported Barger's actions, he gave inconsistent accounts of his behavior. Indeed, while Barger initially denied photographing Kane at all — let alone with his cell phone — he later admitted he lied because he did not want his girlfriend to be jealous that he photographed Kane.

Against this background, Kane alleges that Barger violated her Fourteenth Amendment right to bodily integrity by — in the course of purportedly interviewing her about her alleged sexual assault — touching her and using his personal cell phone to photograph her intimate areas in violation of department policy. The District Court granted summary judgment in favor of Barger, finding that — even if Barger's conduct was unlawful — he was still immune from suit under the exacting "clearly established" prong of our qualified immunity analysis.

Viewing the record in the light most favorable to Kane, which supports an inference that Barger acted for personal gratification rather than investigative ends, we hold that Barger's conduct shocks the conscience and violated Kane's right to bodily integrity. We further hold that the right at issue was clearly established at the time of Barger's conduct. Accordingly, we will reverse and remand for further proceedings.

I.

A.[2]

In the early morning of June 27, 2013, Kane — then 20 years old — was arrested and charged with disorderly conduct, underage drinking, resisting arrest, and escape. After being released from jail that day, Kane — who had "blacked out" from alcohol consumption — grew concerned that she may have been sexually assaulted because she was not wearing pants when she was arrested, she had a large amount of vaginal discharge, and she could not recall what happened. Because of these concerns, Kane went to the hospital that night for both a psychiatric evaluation and a rape kit examination. As part of the rape kit examination, a doctor photographed injuries to Kane's arms, shoulders, knees, and legs.

p.189 That evening, Officer Barger — then 40 years old — went to the hospital to collect the rape kit. Barger also interviewed Kane in the presence her mother and a victim advocate. The parties dispute what occurred next. While Kane maintains that Barger told her to bring the clothes she wore during the purported assault to him at the police station the following day, Barger contends that Kane came to the station to get her cell phone. In any event, the next day, Kane — and her friend, Cayla Combs — went to the Coraopolis Police Station with the clothes she wore during the alleged incident.

At the station, Kane and Combs both met separately with Barger. Contrary to department policy, Kane and Barger met alone in a back room of the station. Kane asserts that Barger closed the hallway door. However, while Barger admits that he directed Kane to the back room, he says that the door to the hallway was open. During this meeting, in further violation of department policy, Barger used his personal cell phone to photograph Kane's intimate areas, including her breasts and buttocks.

At the outset, Barger asked Kane if she had bruising on or around her intimate areas. Kane told Barger that the hospital photographed all of her injuries except for a bruise on her right buttock. Barger then asked Kane if he could photograph the bruise on her right buttock. In so doing, Barger said he had a special application on his personal cell phone for taking photographs.[3] Kane agreed.

Before Barger photographed Kane's right buttock, Kane pulled down her gym shorts to expose that area. Thereafter, without asking Kane to do so, Barger pulled Kane's shorts down further to more fully expose the bruise on her right buttock so he could photograph it.[4] At this point, Kane "felt something touch her butt crack which caused her to jump."[5] Barger denies touching Kane's buttocks and maintains that he only moved the tag on the back of Kane's shorts.

Kane says that Barger repeatedly asked about her breasts, vagina, and buttocks while holding his personal cell phone and photographing her. Because Barger kept asking about her buttocks, Kane asked if he wanted to photograph her other injuries. Barger answered in the affirmative. Altogether, Kane believes Barger photographed her between four and eight times. Nevertheless, Kane does not know for sure because she did not see any photographs or hear a camera "click." Barger admits that he attempted to photograph Kane between five and seven times.

During that first round of photographing, Barger twice asked Kane if she had injuries to her vagina. She responded in the negative both times. Barger later told Kane that the photographs did not save and asked her if he could retake them. Kane agreed. Kane contends that, during this second round of photographing, Barger again asked her if she had injuries to her vagina. Kane again responded in the negative. However, despite her repeated denials, at some point Kane exposed her p.190 vagina to Barger. Kane also asserts that Barger looked at her vagina. While Kane is unsure whether Barger photographed her vagina, she asserts he made her "feel like he did" because "he kept asking about it."[6]

At one point, after Barger asked about a bruise on Kane's chest, he — again without having Kane do so — pulled her tank top down to expose her upper chest area. After Barger did so, Kane held her tank top where Barger positioned it so he could photograph the bruise on her upper chest area. While Kane's breasts were not fully exposed, her upper chest was. Kane contends that Barger also had her sit on a table so he could photograph her inner thighs. Barger denies this and says that Kane merely stood on the opposite side of the desk. Kane further maintains that Barger instructed her to pull her shorts up to her bikini line so he could photograph her inner thighs.

After photographing Kane, Barger said he would continue his investigation. Kane then left the police station. Barger later interviewed a number of possible witnesses to Kane's sexual assault. However, Barger failed to document the clothing evidence that Kane brought to him at the station. While Barger asserts that Kane's clothing was given to an "evidence officer to take custody of," he claims he does not know what happened to those items.[7]

Kane's mother later reported Barger's conduct to the Allegheny County Police Department. Then, on July 9, Kane met with Allegheny County Detective Michael Kuma to discuss the photographs that Barger had taken. After meeting with Kane, Kuma began investigating Barger. During Kuma's first interview with Barger, Barger denied photographing Kane at all in the back room of the station, let alone with his personal cell phone. Nevertheless, during a follow-up interview with Kuma, Barger admitted that he photographed Kane using his personal cell phone.

According to Kuma's official report, Barger explained that he lied about photographing Kane because he was worried that his girlfriend might become jealous upon learning he had done so. Kuma further reported that Barger said he took six or seven photographs of Kane's upper chest, buttocks, inner thighs, and the front and back of her legs. Kuma also said that Barger told him he deleted the photos. Barger concedes that he lied in his initial meeting with Kuma. However, Barger maintains that — while he attempted to photograph Kane — he did not delete photographs of Kane because his phone never saved them in the first place.[8]

Ultimately, Barger consented to disciplinary action for "serious violations of departmental policy," including using his cell phone — instead of department equipment — to photograph Kane, interviewing and photographing a female without a fellow officer or witness present, and failing to initially provide a full disclosure of the p.191 underlying incident.[9] Barger was also removed from the investigation into Kane's alleged sexual assault and suspended for two weeks without pay.

B.

Subsequently, Kane filed this civil rights action under 42 U.S.C. § 1983 alleging that Barger violated her Fourteenth Amendment right to bodily integrity during his investigation into whether she was the victim of a sexual assault. Barger moved for summary judgment on two grounds. First, he argued that his conduct — even when viewed in the light most favorable to Kane — did not violate Kane's right to bodily integrity. Second, he asserted that — even if he violated Kane's right to bodily integrity — he was entitled to qualified immunity.

The District Court granted summary judgment for Barger on qualified immunity grounds. Two aspects of the decision below warrant mention here.

On one hand, the District Court stated that, "although it did not involve direct sexual contact, Officer Barger's conduct in the course of his duties, considered as a whole," could be "sufficiently appalling in terms of violating Kane's bodily integrity to be considered conscious-shocking [sic] for purposes of the constitutional tort that Kane advances in this case."[10] On this point, the District Court observed that "[t]here is little question that the record here would amply support a finding that the conduct to which Officer Barger has admitted was improper and highly inappropriate."[11]

However, the District Court did not ultimately decide whether Barger violated Kane's right to bodily integrity. Rather, the District Court found that, even if Barger violated Kane's rights, her claim would still fail under "the exacting standard of the 'clearly established' prong of the qualified immunity analysis."[12] In so holding, the District Court noted that — in light of the law at the time of Barger's conduct — it could not conclude that "every reasonable police officer in Officer Barger's position would have known that his particular conduct in photographing or attempting to photograph Kane in what is alleged to be a sexually-gratifying manner and in violation of [] professional and Departmental standards during an investigation into her possible sexual assault deprived Kane" of her right to bodily integrity.[13] This appeal followed.[14]

II.

"Qualified immunity shields government officials from civil damages liability unless the official violated a statutory or constitutional right that was clearly established at the time of the challenged conduct."[15] We conduct a two-step inquiry to determine whether a government official is entitled to qualified immunity. "First, we ask whether the facts — taken in the light most favorable to the nonmoving party — show that a government official violated a p.192 constitutional right."[16] "Second, we ask whether that right was clearly established at the time of the official's actions."[17]

A.

Kane argues that Barger violated her substantive due process right to bodily integrity by touching her and using his personal cell phone to photograph her intimate areas in violation of department policy while supposedly interviewing her about her alleged sexual assault. To demonstrate that her substantive due process rights were violated, Kane must establish that "the particular interest at issue is protected by the substantive due process clause," and that "the government's deprivation of that protected interest shocks the conscience."[18] We address each element in turn.

With regard to the first element, we have recognized that "[i]ndividuals have a constitutional liberty interest in personal bodily integrity that is protected by the Due Process Clause of the Fourteenth Amendment."[19] The Supreme Court has also specifically observed that "the 'liberty' specially protected by the Due Process Clause includes the right[] ... to bodily integrity."[20] With this context, as the District Court rightly observed, "Kane had a right to not have her bodily integrity violated by a police officer investigating her potential sexual assault."[21]

Accordingly, we must proceed to the second element of our substantive due process inquiry: specifically, whether Barger's conduct shocks the conscience. While "only the most egregious official conduct" can shock the conscience,[22] "[t]he level of culpability required for behavior to shock the conscience largely depends on the context in which the action takes place."[23] In this regard, we have observed that "[i]n a hyperpressurized environment, such as a high-speed police chase, intent to harm is required."[24] However, "where deliberation is possible and officials have the time to make unhurried judgments, deliberate indifference is sufficient."[25] Here, there is no indication that Barger faced circumstances calling for quick decision-making while photographing Kane. To the contrary, Barger had time for "actual deliberation."[26] Accordingly, the standard here is deliberate indifference, which requires "a conscious disregard of a substantial risk of serious harm."[27]

p.193 Against this background, Barger contends that Kane's substantive due process claim fails because he did not "commit[] a serious battery that shocks the conscience."[28] In support, Barger relies on out-of-circuit cases in which conduct he describes as "well beyond anything alleged against [him]" was found to not be conscience-shocking.[29] For example, Barger cites the Eighth Circuit's decision in *Hawkins v. Holloway*.[30] In *Hawkins,* male police officers alleged that their sheriff violated their substantive due process rights by groping them and making lewd comments.[31] In rejecting the officers' argument, the Court explained that, while the sheriff's conduct was "perverted," the officers' "allegations of inappropriate sexual contact on the sheriff's part [] fall into the category of misconduct for which no constitutional remedy is available."[32]

Barger also cites two unpublished district court cases from the Seventh Circuit, *Nagle v. McKernan,*[33] and *Decker v. Tinnel*.[34] In *Nagle,* the plaintiff alleged that a fire marshal violated her right to bodily integrity while inspecting her place of employment by cornering her in her office, leaning against her body, and breathing on her while intimately pressing his face against the back of her head and neck.[35] The Northern District of Illinois disagreed, concluding that — while his behavior was "strange and inappropriate" — the fire marshal's conduct did not shock the conscience.[36]

Likewise, in *Decker,* the plaintiff — an 18-year-old woman — alleged that a police officer violated her right to bodily integrity during a police ride-along by touching her breasts and thighs, kissing her, and repeatedly making sexually suggestive comments.[37] While the Northern District of Indiana characterized the officer's conduct as "improper and reprehensible," it nevertheless held that it "d[id] not rise to the level of a constitutional violation" that shocked the conscience.[38]

We are not persuaded. As explained, wholly contrary to department policy, Barger met with Kane — then considered a possible sexual assault victim — alone in the back room of the police station. During that encounter, Barger charted a course that, viewed in the light most favorable to Kane, violated her right to bodily integrity and shocks the conscience. In the back room, in further violation of department policy, Barger photographed intimate areas of Kane's body with his personal cell phone. In the course of taking the photos, Barger personally pulled Kane's shorts and tank top down to expose her right buttock and upper chest, rather than having Kane do so herself. Moreover, when Barger tugged her shorts, Kane "felt something touch her butt crack which caused her to jump."[39] Further, while Kane repeatedly said her vagina was not injured, Barger's incessant questioning about her vagina ultimately caused Kane to expose her vagina to him.

p.194 Barger's conduct after his encounter with Kane only underscores a conscience-shocking disregard for Kane's right to bodily integrity. Indeed, after photographing Kane, Barger failed to document the clothing evidence that Kane provided. That evidence remains unaccounted for. Moreover, after Kane reported Barger's conduct, Barger initially lied to outside investigators and said he never photographed Kane, let alone with his personal cell phone. On this point, after Barger came clean with investigators, he said he lied because he did not want his girlfriend to be jealous of the fact that he photographed Kane.

Altogether, the record — again, viewed in the light most favorable to Kane — supports the inference that Barger acted for his own personal gratification, rather than investigative ends, in both touching Kane and photographing her intimate bodily areas with his personal cell phone in violation of department policy. That is conscience-shocking behavior. Thus, Barger violated Kane's right to bodily integrity.[40]

B.

Having found Kane's right to bodily integrity was violated, we now ask if that right was clearly established at the time of Barger's conduct.[41]

"A clearly established right is one that is sufficiently clear that every reasonable official would have understood that what he is doing violates that right."[42] "We do not require a case directly on point" to find that a right was clearly established.[43] Rather, "[t]o be clearly established," a right need only have "a sufficiently clear foundation in then-existing precedent."[44] In this inquiry, "[w]e look first to applicable Supreme Court precedent."[45] However, "[e]ven if none exists, it may be possible that a robust consensus of cases of persuasive authority in the Courts of Appeals could clearly establish a right for purposes of qualified immunity."[46]

"Defining the right at issue is critical to this inquiry," and "[w]e must frame the right in light of the specific context of the case, not as a broad general proposition."[47] This does not mean that "an official action is protected by qualified immunity unless the very action in question has previously been held unlawful."[48] Accordingly, "it need not be the case that the p.195 exact conduct has previously been held unlawful so long as the contours of the right are sufficiently clear."[49] Said another way, we do not require a case "directly mirror[ing] the facts" at hand, so long as "there are sufficiently analogous cases that should have placed a reasonable official... on notice that his actions were unlawful."[50] As such, "officials can still be on notice that their conduct violates established law even in novel factual circumstances."[51]

Here, the right at issue is an individual's right not to be sexually fondled and illicitly photographed by a police officer investigating his or her case, for the officer's own gratification. Thus, based on the above, "[t]he ultimate question is whether the state of the law when the offense occurred" gave Barger "fair warning" that his conduct violated this right.[52] We conclude that it did.

Intuitively, it seems absurd to analyze whether the right to be free from an officer's sexual assault was clearly established by case law at the time of Barger's conduct. This is because, given the egregiousness of Barger's violation of Kane's personal security and bodily integrity, the right here is so "obvious" that it could be deemed clearly established even without materially similar cases.[53] Indeed, while Barger has not been convicted of a crime, his actions — viewed in the light most favorable to Kane — resemble the crime of indecent assault in Pennsylvania, where Barger's conduct occurred.[54] Under Pennsylvania law, "indecent contact" is defined as "[a]ny touching of the sexual or other intimate parts of the person for the purpose of arousing or gratifying sexual desire, in any person."[55] By touching Kane's intimate areas for his own personal gratification, that is effectively what Barger did here.[56]

Further, at the time of Barger's conduct, both our case law and that of other circuits placed Barger on notice that he acted unconstitutionally. In this regard, our decision in *Doe v. Luzerne Cty.*[57] is illustrative. In *Doe,* we held that male police officers violated a female colleague's Fourteenth Amendment right to privacy by videotaping her partially unclothed p.196 body without her consent in a showering area.[58] While *Doe* did not involve the specific right to bodily integrity, *Doe* and the present matter both involved male police officers who deceptively used recording devices to capture images of the intimate bodily areas of vulnerable females. Without doubt, Barger's "specific conduct" is "sufficiently factually similar" to our decision in *Doe* to have placed him on notice that his conduct was unconstitutional.[59] Thus, in light of these factual similarities, *Doe* announced a "sufficiently clear" right to personal bodily security that "applie[d] with obvious clarity" at the time Barger acted.[60]

Analogous cases from other circuits underscore that the right here was clearly established. For example, in *Haberthur v. City of Raymore,* the Eighth Circuit reversed the dismissal of a plaintiff's substantive due process claim based on an officer's sexual misconduct.[61] There, the plaintiff alleged that the officer reached under her shirt, fondled her chest, and caressed her body while making sexually suggestive remarks.[62] In finding that the plaintiff stated a claim, the Court characterized the officer's conduct as "intrusive, demeaning, and violative of [the plaintiff's] personal integrity."[63]

Similarly, in *Fontana v. Haskin,* the Ninth Circuit analyzed a highway patrol officer's conduct toward a plaintiff who was handcuffed and detained in the back of a patrol car.[64] On the way to the police station, the defendant officer sat next to the plaintiff in the back seat while his partner drove.[65] At that time, the officer inappropriately put his arm around the plaintiff and massaged her shoulders.[66] The officer also made sexually suggestive statements concerning the plaintiff's appearance and relationship status.[67] While the case was decided on Fourth Amendment grounds because the plaintiff was handcuffed during the encounter, the Court held — in the alternative — that the officer's sexual predation "was egregious and outrageous and shocks the conscience as a matter of law" under the Fourteenth Amendment.[68]

With this context, it is clear that — at the time Barger acted — the law provided fair warning that his sexual misconduct toward Kane was unlawful. As such, the right was clearly established for purposes of qualified immunity.

III.

For the foregoing reasons, we reverse the District Court's grant of summary judgment and remand for further proceedings consistent with this opinion.

[1] App. 173.

[2] Because we are reviewing a claim of qualified immunity, we recount the facts in the light most favorable to Kane. *Karns v. Shanahan,* 879 F.3d 504, 520 (3d Cir. 2018).

[3] Barger says, and his official report reflects, that the department's digital camera was inoperative. However, his report also failed to mention that he photographed Kane using his personal cell phone.

[4] In his deposition, Barger described his attempt as "unsuccessful" because the application would "freeze" when he "would take a photograph." App. 212. Nevertheless, in a request for admission, Barger agreed that he "took photographs

of Brandy Kane in the Coraopolis Borough Police Station." App. 252. In any event, Barger concedes that he intended to photograph Kane.

[5] App. 173.

[6] App. 174.

[7] App. 210.

[8] Kuma later used an extraction device to review approximately thirteen thousand photographs on Barger's personal cell phone. During his review, Kuma could not conclusively identify any photographs of Kane. However, Kuma did find a photograph of an unidentifiable woman — who could have been Kane — whose pants were pulled down to expose her buttocks. While Kuma maintains that the device should have recovered any photographs of Kane that Barger deleted, he explained that "[i]n [his] experience using the [extraction] device, there is no hard and fast rule that it downloads everything." SA 464.

[9] App. 245.

[10] App. 29.

[11] App. 22.

[12] App. 29.

[13] App. 31.

[14] The District Court had jurisdiction under 28 U.S.C. § 1331. We have jurisdiction under 28 U.S.C. § 1291. We exercise plenary review over the District Court's grant of summary judgment. *Curley v. Klem,* 298 F.3d 271, 276 (3d Cir. 2002).

[15] *Reichle v. Howards,* 566 U.S. 658, 664, 132 S.Ct. 2088, 182 L.Ed.2d 985 (2012).

[16] *Santini v. Fuentes,* 795 F.3d 410, 417 (3d Cir. 2015).

[17] *Id.*

[18] *Chainey v. Street,* 523 F.3d 200, 219 (3d Cir. 2008).

[19] *Phillips v. Cty. of Allegheny,* 515 F.3d 224, 235 (3d Cir. 2008); *see also Black by Black v. Ind. Area Sch. Dist.,* 985 F.2d 707, 709 n.1 (3d Cir. 1993) (noting that the Fourteenth Amendment protects a liberty interest in bodily integrity).

[20] *Washington v. Glucksberg,* 521 U.S. 702, 720, 117 S.Ct. 2258, 138 L.Ed.2d 772 (1997) (citation omitted).

[21] App. 31.

[22] *Chainey,* 523 F.3d at 219 (citation and quotation marks omitted).

[23] *L.R. v. Sch. Dist. of Philadelphia,* 836 F.3d 235, 246 (3d Cir. 2016); *see also Cty. of Sacramento v. Lewis,* 523 U.S. 833, 847, 118 S.Ct. 1708, 140 L.Ed.2d 1043 (1998) (noting that the "measure of what is conscience shocking is no calibrated yard stick").

[24] *L.R.,* 836 F.3d at 246 (citation and quotation marks omitted).

[25] *Id.* (citation and quotation marks omitted).

[26] *Lewis,* 523 U.S. at 851, 118 S.Ct. 1708.

[27] *L.R.,* 836 F.3d at 246 (citation and quotation marks omitted).

[28] Appellee's Br. at 16.

[29] Appellee's Br. at 21.

[30] 316 F.3d 777 (8th Cir. 2003).

[31] *Id.* at 784-85.

[32] *Id.* at 785.

[33] No. 07 C 680, 2007 WL 2903179 (N.D. Ill. Sept. 28, 2007).

[34] No. 2:04-CV-227, 2005 WL 3501705 (N.D. Ind. Dec. 20, 2005).

[35] *Nagle,* 2007 WL 2903179 at *1.

[36] *Id.* at *2.

[37] *Decker,* 2005 WL 3501705 at *1-2.

[38] *Id.* at *9.

[39] App. 173.

[40] To be clear, today's holding is limited to the facts of this case and by no means suggests that photographing and/or touching a possible sexual assault victim during an investigation is a *de facto* violation of the right to bodily integrity. Indeed, we can conceive of many legitimate investigative reasons for engaging in such conduct. Here, however, by acting in a manner that could be interpreted as prioritizing his personal gratification over his investigative duties, Barger fell on the wrong side of the line.

[41] *See Fields v. City of Philadelphia,* 862 F.3d 353, 361 (3d Cir. 2017) (noting that "we look at the state of the law" when the underlying conduct occurred "[t]o determine whether the right [was] clearly established").

[42] *Mullenix v. Luna,* ___ U.S. ___, 136 S.Ct. 305, 308, 193 L.Ed.2d 255 (2015) (citation and quotation marks omitted).

[43] *Ashcroft v. al-Kidd,* 563 U.S. 731, 741, 131 S.Ct. 2074, 179 L.Ed.2d 1149 (2011).

[44] *District of Columbia v. Wesby,* ___ U.S. ___, 138 S.Ct. 577, 589, 199 L.Ed.2d 453 (2018).

[45] *L.R.,* 836 F.3d at 247-48.

[46] *Id.* at 248 (alteration, citation, and quotation marks omitted).

[47] *Id.* (citation and quotation marks omitted).

[48] *Anderson v. Creighton,* 483 U.S. 635, 640, 107 S.Ct. 3034, 97 L.Ed.2d 523 (1987); *see also Hope v. Pelzer,* 536 U.S. 730, 741, 122 S.Ct. 2508, 153 L.Ed.2d 666 (2002) (explaining that "[a]lthough earlier cases involving 'fundamentally similar' facts can provide especially strong support for a conclusion that the law is clearly established, they are not necessary to such a finding").

[49] *Kedra v. Schroeter,* 876 F.3d 424, 450 (3d Cir. 2017) (citation and quotation marks omitted); *see also id.* at 451-52 (admonishing against defining a right in a narrow and fact-bound way for purposes of qualified immunity).

[50] *L.R.,* 836 F.3d at 249.

[51] *Hope,* 536 U.S. at 741, 122 S.Ct. 2508.

[52] *L.R.,* 836 F.3d at 247 (citation and quotation marks omitted).

[53] *Hope,* 536 U.S. at 741, 122 S.Ct. 2508; *see also White v. Pauly,* ___ U.S. ___, 137 S.Ct. 548, 552, 196 L.Ed.2d 463 (2017) (per curiam) (noting, in the Fourth Amendment context, that "general statements of the law are not inherently incapable of giving fair and clear warning to officers" in "an obvious case" (citations and quotation marks omitted)).

[54] *See* 18 Pa. Cons. Stat. § 3126(a)(1) (providing that "[a] person is guilty of indecent assault if the person has indecent contact with the complainant ... for the

purpose of arousing sexual desire in the person ... without the complainant's consent").

[55] *Id.* § 3101.

[56] *See Malley v. Briggs,* 475 U.S. 335, 341, 106 S.Ct. 1092, 89 L.Ed.2d 271 (1986) (explaining that qualified immunity does not protect "those who knowingly violate the law").

[57] 660 F.3d 169 (3d Cir. 2011).

[58] *Id.* at 175-78.

[59] *Kedra,* 876 F.3d at 449 n.19 (citation and quotation marks omitted).

[60] *Id.* at 450 (citation and quotation marks omitted); *see also Brown v. Muhlenberg Twp.,* 269 F.3d 205, 211 n.4 (3d Cir. 2001) ("If the unlawfulness of the defendant's conduct would have been apparent to a reasonable official based on the current state of the law, it is not necessary that there be binding precedent from this circuit so advising.").

[61] 119 F.3d 720, 724 (8th Cir. 1997).

[62] *Id.* at 721, 724.

[63] *Id.* at 724.

[64] 262 F.3d 871, 875 (9th Cir. 2001).

[65] *Id.*

[66] *Id.*

[67] *Id.*

[68] *Id.* at 882 n.7.

905 F.3d 711 (2018)

Michael SAUERS, Individually and as Administrator of the Estate of Carola R. Sauers, deceased

v.

BOROUGH OF NESQUEHONING; Chief of Police Sean Smith; Officer Stephen Homanko Officer Stephen Homanko, Appellant.

No. 17-1591.

United States Court of Appeals, Third Circuit.

Argued June 4, 2018.

Opinion Filed: October 2, 2018.

Sauers v. Borough of Nesquehoning, 905 F. 3d 711 (3rd Cir. 2018)

On Appeal from the United States District Court for the Middle District of Pennsylvania, (D.C. No. 3-16-cv-00811), District Judge: Hon. James M. Munley.

Joshua M. Autry [ARGUED], Frank J. Lavery, Jr., Lavery Faherty Patterson, 225 Market Street, Suite 304, P.O. Box 1245, Harrisburg, PA 17108, Counsel for Appellant.

Michael B. Kaspszyk [ARGUED], Merwine Hanyon & Kaspszyk, 2642 Route 940, Pocono Summit, PA 18346, Counsel for Appellee.

Before: AMBRO, JORDAN, and VANASKIE, Circuit Judges.

p.715 OPINION OF THE COURT

JORDAN, Circuit Judge.

This case arises out of a tragic car accident that injured Michael Sauers and killed his wife. The crash resulted from the criminally reckless driving of police officer Stephen Homanko. Sauers later brought this suit against Homanko and others pursuant to 42 U.S.C. § 1983 and state law for, among other things, violating his and his wife's Fourteenth Amendment substantive due process rights. Homanko moved to dismiss the § 1983 claim for failure to state a claim and, in the alternative, he sought qualified immunity. The District Court denied the motion and Homanko appealed. Because we conclude that it was not clearly established at the time of the crash that Homanko's conduct, as alleged in the complaint, could give rise to constitutional liability under the Fourteenth Amendment, we will vacate the District Court's denial of qualified immunity. We hope, however, to establish the law clearly now.

I. Background[1]

On May 12, 2014, Sauers and his wife were driving southbound on Route 209 in the Borough of Nesquehoning, Pennsylvania. At the same time, Homanko was on patrol on Route 209 and traveling in the same direction when he observed the driver of a yellow Dodge Neon commit a summary traffic offense in the northbound lane.

Based on that observation alone, he turned around and began to pursue the Dodge. At some point he took the time to radio ahead to the police in the neighboring borough to request that officers there pull the Dodge over when it reached their jurisdiction.[2]

Homanko then decided that catching the Dodge himself was important enough to warrant a chase at speeds of over 100 miles-per-hour. Several members of the public observed him driving recklessly. During the pursuit, Homanko lost control of his police car while going around a curve. His car began to spin, crossed the center line into southbound traffic, and crashed into Sauers's car. The accident seriously injured Sauers and killed his wife. Homanko was subsequently charged and pled guilty to vehicular homicide, which requires proof beyond a reasonable doubt of reckless or grossly negligent driving, and reckless endangerment.[3]

The criminal case was not the end of Homanko's legal trouble. Sauers — individually and as the administrator of his wife's estate — initiated the present lawsuit against him, setting forth federal and state law causes of action, including a claim under § 1983.[4] Sauers premised his § 1983 claim on a "state-created danger" theory of liability. Homanko moved to dismiss only that claim. He argued that the complaint p.716 did not plausibly allege a state-created danger claim and, in the alternative, that he was entitled to qualified immunity because it was not clearly established in May 2014 that negligent or reckless police driving could give rise to a constitutional cause of action. The District Court denied Homanko's motion as to both liability and qualified immunity.

As to liability, the Court determined that the complaint adequately pled a state-created danger claim, a determination that Homanko does not now appeal. The Court further concluded that the law was clearly established in May 2014 that "any reasonable officer would have known that pursuing a potential traffic offender in excess of 100 miles-per-hour under the[] circumstances [alleged in the complaint] gives rise to a state-created danger claim." (App. at 21.) That determination is the subject of this appeal.

II. Discussion[5]

Qualified immunity protects government officials from civil damages for conduct that "does not violate clearly established statutory or constitutional rights of which a reasonable person would have known." *Pearson v. Callahan,* 555 U.S. 223, 231, 129 S.Ct. 808, 172 L.Ed.2d 565 (2009) (citation omitted). Thus, courts assessing a claim of qualified immunity must answer two questions. One is whether the defendant's conduct violated a statutory or constitutional right. The other is whether the right at issue was clearly established when the conduct took place. We have discretion to address either inquiry first. *Id.* at 236, 129 S.Ct. 808.

In its recent decisions addressing qualified immunity, the Supreme Court has "repeatedly told courts ... not to define clearly established law at a high level of generality." *Kisela v. Hughes,* ___ U.S. ___, 138 S.Ct. 1148, 1152, 200 L.Ed.2d 449 (2018) (citation omitted). The question in this case therefore cannot be framed simply in terms of recklessness generally. Homanko's request for qualified immunity must be assessed within the context of the case law that has developed from accidents caused by high-speed police pursuits that injure third parties.

A. Sauers's Complaint Pleads a Plausible State-Created Danger Claim.

Homanko has not appealed the District Court's determination that the complaint adequately describes a constitutional violation, and for good reason. The pleadings describe a police officer driving at speeds over 100 miles-per-hour on a two-way, undivided road to catch someone who had committed a minor traffic infraction. There was no emergency at all, and Homanko likely did the most that was warranted when he radioed the police in a neighboring jurisdiction to stop the offender. His hyper-aggressive decision to chase the Dodge cannot be justified. Nonetheless, to determine whether his conduct violated a clearly established constitutional right, we must take the time to define that right and explain why the conduct violated it.

Defining a right at the appropriate level of specificity is often the most critical aspect of a qualified immunity analysis. In undertaking that task, we are guided by the Supreme Court's repeated instructions p.717 to do so in light of the particular facts of the case at hand. *See Kisela,* 138 S.Ct. at 1152; *White v. Pauly,* ___ U.S. ___, 137 S.Ct. 548, 552, 196 L.Ed.2d 463 (2017); *Mullenix v. Luna,* ___ U.S. ___, 136 S.Ct. 305, 308, 193 L.Ed.2d 255 (2015). We accordingly define the right at issue here as one not to be injured or killed as a result of a police officer's reckless pursuit of an individual suspected of a summary traffic offense when there is no pending emergency and when the suspect is not actively fleeing the police.

As earlier noted, Sauers's complaint relies on the state-created danger theory of liability to establish his right to be free from what Homanko did. That doctrine embodies the principle that the government has an obligation under the Fourteenth Amendment's Due Process Clause "to protect individuals against dangers that the government itself creates." *Haberle v. Troxell,* 885 F.3d 170, 176 (3d Cir. 2018). Establishing a claim under that doctrine requires a plaintiff to plead four elements:

> (1) [t]he harm ultimately caused was foreseeable and fairly direct;
>
> (2) a state actor acted with a degree of culpability that shocks the conscience;
>
> (3) a relationship between the state and the plaintiff existed such that the plaintiff was a foreseeable victim of the defendant's acts, or a member of a discrete class of persons subjected to the potential harm brought about by the state's actions, as opposed to a member of the public in general; and
>
> (4) a state actor affirmatively used his or her authority in a way that created a danger to the citizen or that rendered the citizen more vulnerable to danger than had the state not acted at all.

Id. at 176-77 (citation omitted). It is clear, we think, that the complaint adequately alleges elements one, three, and four. Whether Homanko's alleged conduct shocks the conscience is a closer call.

The level of culpability required "to shock the contemporary conscience" falls along a spectrum dictated by the circumstances of each case. *County of Sacramento v. Lewis,* 523 U.S. 833, 847-49 & n.8, 118 S.Ct. 1708, 140 L.Ed.2d 1043 (1998). Our case law establishes three distinct categories of culpability depending on how much time a police officer has to make a decision. *Haberle,* 885 F.3d at 177. In one category are actions taken in a "hyperpressurized environment[.]" *Id.* (citation omitted). They will not be held to shock the conscience unless the officer has "an intent to cause harm." *Id.* (citation omitted). Next are actions taken within a time frame that allows an officer to engage in "hurried deliberation." *Id.* (citation omitted). When those actions "reveal a conscious disregard of a great risk of serious harm" they will be sufficient to shock the conscience.[6] *Id.* (quotation marks and citation omitted). Finally, actions undertaken with "unhurried judgments," with time for "careful deliberation," will be held to shock the conscience if they are "done with deliberate indifference." *Id.* (citation omitted). Our case law is clear that this "shocks the conscience" framework for analysis applies p.718 to police-pursuit cases. *Brown v. Pa. Dep't of Health & Emergency Med. Servs. Training Inst.,* 318 F.3d 473, 480 (3d Cir. 2003); *cf. Kedra v. Schroeter,* 876 F.3d 424, 432, 448 (3d Cir. 2017) (relying on pre-2014 case law to conclude that the state-created danger doctrine was a clearly established theory of liability in September 2014).

The District Court rightly interpreted the complaint to allege that Homanko "had at least some time to deliberate" before deciding whether and how to pursue the traffic offender. (App. at 16.) That places the fact-pattern in the second category of culpability, requiring inferences or allegations of a conscious disregard of a great risk of serious harm. That conclusion is supported by the allegation that Homanko, at some point, had time to call the neighboring police department as he was contemplating his actions. It is further supported by an obvious inference from the nature of the Dodge driver's mild provocation: there was no emergency arising from a simple traffic violation. The liability question thus becomes whether deciding to pursue a potential summary traffic offender at speeds of over 100 miles-per-hour, after radioing for assistance from the neighboring jurisdiction where the potential offender was headed, demonstrates a conscious disregard of a great risk of serious harm. We have no difficulty in concluding that it does.

Engaging in a high-speed pursuit on public roadways at speeds of over 100 miles-per-hour threatens "all those within... range [of the pursuit], be they suspects, their passengers, other drivers, or bystanders." *Lewis,* 523 U.S. at 853, 118 S.Ct. 1708. Every police officer understands that risk. That is why we expect our law enforcement personnel to engage in such pursuits only when "reasonable justification" exists. *Id.* at 846, 118 S.Ct. 1708. Responding to a true emergency may be a reasonable justification. Pursuing an actively fleeing suspect who is endangering the public welfare may also be a reasonable justification. But attempting to catch someone who has committed a minor traffic offense, especially when other law enforcement officials have been alerted to stop the offender, is not a reasonable justification for driving "careless[ly]" and at "speed[s] in excess of 100 mph." (App. at 31-32.) Homanko did not have to make a split-second decision "in haste" and "under pressure." *Lewis,* 523 U.S. at 853, 118 S.Ct. 1708 (citation omitted). He could have let the officers in the neighboring jurisdiction handle the routine traffic stop as, in fact, they did. Instead, he chose to engage in a reckless and unjustifiable pursuit, with tragic consequences.

In sum, Sauers adequately pled that Homanko's conduct was conscience-shocking under our state-created danger framework. The complaint therefore contains a plausible claim that Homanko violated Sauers's and his wife's Fourteenth Amendment substantive due process rights.

B. The Right at Issue Was Not Clearly Established In May 2014.

The existence of a substantive due process claim having been established, we now turn to the central issue of this appeal, namely whether Homanko had fair warning that he could be subject to constitutional liability for actions taken in conscious disregard of a great risk of harm during the course of a police pursuit. We conclude that he did not. At the time of the crash in May 2014, the state of the law was such that police officers may have understood they could be exposed to constitutional liability for actions taken during a police pursuit only when they had an intent to harm. Thus, it was not at that time clearly established that Homanko's actions p.719 could violate the substantive due process rights of Sauers and his wife.

A right is clearly established when the law is "sufficiently clear that every reasonable official would have understood that what he is doing violates that right." *Reichle v. Howards,* 566 U.S. 658, 664, 132 S.Ct. 2088, 182 L.Ed.2d 985 (2012) (internal quotation marks, citation, and alteration omitted). That does not require a prior precedent with indistinguishable facts, "but existing precedent must have placed the statutory or constitutional question beyond debate." *Ashcroft v. al-Kidd,* 563 U.S. 731, 741, 131 S.Ct. 2074, 179 L.Ed.2d 1149 (2011). Existing precedent is sufficient to place a constitutional question beyond debate and to defeat qualified immunity only if it is "controlling authority in [the relevant] jurisdiction," *Wilson v. Layne,* 526 U.S. 603, 617, 119 S.Ct. 1692, 143 L.Ed.2d 818 (1999), or if "a 'robust consensus of cases of persuasive authority' in the Court of Appeals" has settled the question, *Mammaro v. N.J. Div. of Child Prot. & Permanency,* 814 F.3d 164, 169 (3d Cir. 2016) (quoting *Taylor v. Barkes,* ___ U.S. ___, 135 S.Ct. 2042, 2044, 192 L.Ed.2d 78 (2015)).

When qualified immunity is at issue, context matters. The "inquiry 'must be undertaken in light of the specific context of the case, not as a broad general proposition.'" *Mullenix,* 136 S.Ct. at 308 (quoting *Brosseau v. Haugen,* 543 U.S. 194, 198, 125 S.Ct. 596, 160 L.Ed.2d 583 (2004) (per curiam)). When courts fail to take into consideration the "particularized" facts of a case, they permit plaintiffs "to convert the rule of qualified immunity ... into a rule of virtually unqualified liability simply by alleging violation of extremely abstract rights." *White,* 137 S.Ct. at 552 (alteration in original) (quoting *Anderson v. Creighton,* 483 U.S. 635, 639-40, 107 S.Ct. 3034, 97 L.Ed.2d 523 (1987)).

There is, moreover, an important distinction between assessing whether a plaintiff has pled a "clearly established theory of liability" and the question of whether that theory is fairly applied to a government official in light of the facts in a given case. *See Kedra,* 876 F.3d at 435 (explaining that a particular right is only clearly established when the state of the law gave the relevant official "fair warning that his actions were unconstitutional in the particular factual scenario he confronted" (internal quotation marks, citation, and editorial marks omitted)). It is only when both the theory of liability and its application to the established facts are sufficiently plain that the legal question of liability is beyond legitimate debate and a plaintiff can defeat a qualified immunity defense. *Id.* at 435-36. In this instance, as discussed above, Sauers's complaint relies on the clearly established state-created danger theory of liability. The particular factual allegations, meanwhile, involve a police pursuit of a non-fleeing summary traffic offender.

Accordingly, to assess whether the right to be free of the risk associated with a non-emergency but reckless police pursuit was clearly established in May 2014, we must ask whether Supreme Court precedent, our own precedent, or a consensus of authority among the courts of appeals placed that right beyond debate. *See al-Kidd,* 563 U.S. at 741-42, 131 S.Ct. 2074; *Kedra,* 876 F.3d at 450. Qualified immunity, after all, protects even those officials who exercise extraordinarily poor judgment. *al-Kidd,* 563 U.S. at 743, 131 S.Ct. 2074. Law enforcement officials do not get stripped of qualified immunity every time a judge, with the clarity afforded by hindsight, believes that an official has committed a wrong. Otherwise, the very purpose of qualified immunity — to give law enforcement p.720 officials the benefit of all reasonable doubt in the exercise of their professional duties — would be undermined. If any uncertainty existed in the law in May 2014 as to whether reckless police driving could give rise to constitutional liability in circumstances such as those alleged here, then we must afford Homanko the protections of qualified immunity. Our survey of the relevant cases reveals that the law was not so clear as to be "beyond debate." *Id.* at 741, 131 S.Ct. 2074.

An officer on patrol in May 2014 could have reasonably understood, based on prevailing law, that he could pursue a potential traffic offender, even recklessly, without being subjected to constitutional liability. The Supreme Court, in *County of Sacramento v. Lewis,* 523 U.S. 833, 118 S.Ct. 1708, 140 L.Ed.2d 1043 (1998), had adopted an intent-to-harm standard in a police pursuit case involving a high-speed chase of dangerously fleeing suspects. *Id.* at 854, 118 S.Ct. 1708. In the years between that decision and the events at issue here, the courts of appeals were inconsistent in whether to apply the intent-to-harm standard in police-pursuit cases only when an exigency necessitated a chase, or whether to apply that standard in all police-pursuit cases, regardless of any exigencies.

Lewis involved a police officer who was pursuing two suspects actively fleeing the police in a dangerous manner. *Id.* at 836, 118 S.Ct. 1708. The suspects, riding together on a motorcycle, were weaving in and out of traffic at high speeds. *Id.* After the driver of the motorcycle lost control and crashed, the pursuing officer accidentally struck and killed one of the suspects. *Id.* at 837, 118 S.Ct. 1708. The Court characterized the situation as involving an officer who had to make an "instantaneous" reaction to the fleeing suspects' "outrageous behavior[.]" *Id.* at 855, 118 S.Ct. 1708. It held that, in such circumstances, a police pursuit will not give rise to a substantive due process violation absent a specific intent to harm. *Id.* at 854, 118 S.Ct. 1708. In reaching that conclusion, the Court noted that conduct intended to cause harm was "most likely to rise to the conscience-shocking level" and that negligent conduct was never sufficient for a substantive due process claim. *Id.* at 849, 118 S.Ct. 1708. It also explained, however, that conduct falling between intentional conduct and negligent conduct was "a matter for closer calls" that could, given the right circumstances, be actionable under the Fourteenth Amendment. *Id.*

Lewis, then, clearly established that an officer can be liable for a substantive due process violation resulting from a high-speed pursuit of a dangerously fleeing suspect only if the officer intended to cause harm. But it left open the possibility that a lower level of culpability could suffice in the right circumstances. In May 2014, the courts of appeals had not coalesced around what those circumstances might be in the police-pursuit context. The Tenth Circuit, in *Green v. Post,* addressed a police officer's request for qualified immunity in a case analogous to ours and explained that

> there are many permutations on the theme of police pursuits; while most involve high speeds, there are many variables, including whether the officer is responding to an emergency or not, whether he or she is directly pursuing a fleeing suspect or not, and, significantly under *Lewis* and cases interpreting it, whether the officer has time for actual deliberation.

574 F.3d 1294, 1309 (10th Cir. 2009).

In *Green,* an innocent driver was killed after a police officer crashed into the victim's car as the officer "was simply trying to catch up to [a] suspected violator of the law[.]" *Id.* at 1297. The suspect had allegedly p.721 filled his car up with approximately $30 worth of gas without paying for it. *Id.* at 1296. The crash occurred as the officer "was traveling straight through [an] intersection at a high rate of speed and without his vehicle's siren or lights on[.]" *Id.* The officer admitted "that he was not responding to an emergency situation" and that the suspect was not actively fleeing him. *Id.* at 1297.

The court identified the officer's actions as falling "in the middle range of the culpability spectrum" identified by *Lewis* — more than negligent but not quite intentional — that could potentially give rise to a substantive due process violation. *Id.* at 1302 (citation omitted). It thus applied the "deliberate indifference" standard when assessing the officer's conduct. *Id.* at 1302-03. Although it concluded that the conduct was not sufficiently conscience-shocking to violate the Fourteenth Amendment, the court nonetheless proceeded to analyze whether the law on police pursuits was clearly established. *Id.* at 1303-04.

It noted that at least two of our sister circuits — the Eighth and Ninth Circuits — have adopted an "intent to harm" standard for all police pursuit cases, whether or not an emergency existed at the time of pursuit. *Id.* at 1308-09 (citing *Bingue v. Prunchak,* 512 F.3d 1169, 1177 (9th Cir. 2008); *Helseth v. Burch,* 258 F.3d 867, 871 (8th Cir. 2001) (en banc)). The Ninth Circuit, for its part, held "that the *Lewis* standard of 'intent to harm' applies to all high-speed police chases," and it refused to "draw a distinction between 'emergency' and 'non-emergency' situations" involving an officer's attempt to apprehend a suspect.[7] *Bingue,* 512 F.3d at 1177. Similarly, the Eighth Circuit interpreted *Lewis* as meaning "that the intent-to-harm standard, rather than the deliberate indifference standard, applies to *all* high-speed police pursuits aimed at apprehending suspected offenders." *Helseth,* 258 F.3d at 871. After surveying the state of the law after *Lewis,* the Tenth Circuit concluded that "it was not clearly established [in June 2006] what specific standard [of culpability] applied to ... [an] officer ... engaged in a high-speed non-emergency response to a call to locate and arrest a suspected gas thief." *Id.* at 1304.

The Eighth Circuit has since reemphasized its interpretation of *Lewis.* In *Sitzes v. City of West Memphis,* it was faced with circumstances in which a police officer responded to a 911 report of a robbery in a Wal-Mart parking lot involving $55 and an alleged assault. 606 F.3d 461, 464 (8th Cir. 2010). Despite the fact that the crime was not reported to be ongoing, and that other officers were already en route to the scene, the defendant-officer decided to drive between 80 and 90 miles-per-hour on a 30 mile-per-hour two-way street without turning on his sirens or emergency lights. *Id.* In racing to the parking lot, the officer crossed over into opposing traffic, ultimately crashing into a bystander's car at an intersection and killing one of the occupants. *Id.* The court nevertheless upheld the application of an intent-to-harm standard because the defendant-officer had testified that he "subjectively" believed that he was responding to an emergency. p.722 *Id.* at 468. The court explained that that standard was appropriate even though the facts "might not qualify as an 'emergency' under" police department policies. *Id.* And, importantly, it held that it did "not 'reject intent-to-harm as the governing standard whenever a judge or a jury could say, with the wisdom of hindsight, that an officer engaged in a high-speed pursuit had ample time to deliberate.'" *Id.* (citation omitted). According to that court, "the amount of time [an officer has] to deliberate on his actions is not, by itself, sufficient to render the intent-to-harm standard inapplicable." *Id.*

Given those decisions by the Eighth, Ninth, and Tenth Circuits, we cannot conclude that case law by May of 2014 had clearly established that an officer's decision to engage in a high speed pursuit of a suspected traffic offender could, in the absence of an intent to harm, give rise to constitutional liability.[8] A police officer could have understood that, as long as he believed a pursuit was justified, constitutional liability would not follow based on recklessness alone.

Our dissenting colleague disagrees, concluding that it was obvious in May 2014 that Homanko's conduct violated the Constitution. Concur./Dissent at 727-28. To the dissent, it is of high importance that the Tenth Circuit in *Green* applied a deliberate difference standard to a police driving case that, as here, involved neither an emergency nor an actively fleeing suspect. But the dissent discounts the fact that no court of appeals (until now) has joined the Tenth Circuit in distinguishing between those police pursuit cases in which a true exigency exists and those in which less is at stake. As we have described above, at least two courts of appeals have explicitly questioned the sort of distinction drawn by the Tenth Circuit.[9]

We agree with the Tenth Circuit's application of a culpability standard below that of "intent to harm" in a non-emergency police pursuit case — indeed the entire panel here is in accord on that point. Where we part company with our dissenting colleague is at his rejection of the rest of the Tenth Circuit's decision. That court acknowledged that the law was not yet clearly established. We accept the accuracy of that assessment then and believe the law as of May 2014 still remained unsettled; our dissenting colleague disagrees. While he evidently views the legal conclusion about constitutional liability as obvious, we do not. Nor can we say that the Tenth Circuit's decision in *Green* alone amounts to the "'robust consensus of cases of persuasive authority' in the Court of Appeals" that we have held necessary to clearly establish a right in the absence of controlling precedent. *Mammaro,* 814 F.3d p.723 at 169 (quoting *Taylor,* 135 S.Ct. at 2044). That is especially so in light of the Eighth Circuit's post-*Green* decision in *Sitzes.*

The dissent also suggests that Homanko's guilty plea to vehicular homicide and reckless endangerment supports the conclusion that he violated a clearly established constitutional right. Concur./Dissent at 728 n.3. Assuming that a guilty plea to a state criminal statute is important in deciding whether the culpable conduct violated a clearly established right guaranteed by the United States Constitution, *see Kane v. Barger,* 902 F.3d 185, 194-96 (3d Cir. 2018) (suggesting, though not holding, that conduct meeting a state criminal statute is more likely to violate a clearly established constitutional right),[10] a conviction for reckless behavior does not help answer the issue in this appeal: namely, was the law settled in May 2014 that, absent a specific intent to harm, constitutional liability could be imposed on a police officer engaged in a police pursuit. We think it was not, and the sympathy we have for the victims of Officer Homanko's serious error does not change that.

Consequently, although Homanko's judgment was bad to the point of recklessness, he is entitled to qualified immunity on Sauers's § 1983 state-created danger claim.[11]

C. Establishing the Law in the Third Circuit.

Although the state of the law in May 2014 was unsettled as to whether police officers engaged in a police pursuit could be subject to constitutional liability for a level of culpability less than an intent to harm, our opinion today should resolve any ambiguity in that regard within this Circuit. Police officers now have fair warning that their conduct when engaged in a high-speed pursuit will be subject to the full body of our state-created danger case law. That law clearly establishes that the level of culpability required to shock the conscience exists on a spectrum tied to the amount of time a government official has to act. In the police pursuit context, it is also necessary to take into consideration the officer's justification for engaging in the pursuit. We recognize that most high-speed police pursuits arise when officers are responding to emergencies or when they must make split-second decisions to pursue fleeing suspects. Our holding today does nothing to alter the longstanding principle that, in such cases, constitutional liability cannot exist absent an intent to harm. But when there is no compelling justification for an officer to engage in a high-speed pursuit and an officer has time to consider whether to engage in such inherently risky behavior, constitutional liability can arise when the officer proceeds to operate his vehicle in a manner that demonstrates a conscious disregard of a great risk of serious harm.

III. Conclusion

For the foregoing reasons, we will vacate the District Court's denial of Homanko's request for qualified immunity.

p.724VANASKIE, Circuit Judge, concurring in part and dissenting in part.

I agree with my colleagues that under our state-created danger framework, the facts alleged by Appellee Michael Sauers readily establish that Officer Homanko's conduct was conscience-shocking. I also agree that, going forward, "[p]olice officers now have fair warning that their conduct when engaged in a high-speed pursuit will be subject to the full body of our state-created danger case law." Maj. Op. at 723. I therefore join parts II.A and II.C of the majority's decision in full. However, because I believe that a reasonable officer in Homanko's position would have known on May 12, 2014, that the outrageous conduct alleged in this case was unconstitutional, I respectfully dissent from the majority's finding that Homanko is entitled to qualified immunity.

I.

Under the second prong of the qualified immunity analysis, we must ask "the objective (albeit fact-specific) question whether a reasonable officer could have believed [Homanko's conduct] to be lawful, in light of clearly established law and the information [he] possessed." *Anderson v. Creighton,* 483 U.S. 635, 641, 107 S.Ct. 3034, 97 L.Ed.2d 523 (1987). In undertaking this analysis, the "key issue" is whether a reasonable police officer in Homanko's position could have believed that driving a police cruiser at speeds in excess of 100 miles-per-hour to catch up to an unsuspecting motorist, who allegedly committed a minor traffic infraction, "comported with established legal standards" as they existed on the date of the accident. *Beers-Capitol v. Whetzel,* 256 F.3d 120, 142 n.15 (3d Cir. 2001) (citation omitted). Critically, "it need not be the case that the exact conduct has previously been held unlawful so long as the 'contours of the right' are sufficiently clear such that a 'general constitutional rule already identified in the decisional law' applies with 'obvious clarity'" to the established facts. *Kedra v. Schroeter,* 876 F.3d 424, 450 (3d Cir. 2017) (internal citations omitted) (quoting *Anderson,* 483 U.S. at 640, 107 S.Ct. 3034; *Hope v. Pelzer,* 536 U.S. 730, 741, 122 S.Ct. 2508, 153 L.Ed.2d 666 (2002)). This principle holds true "'even in novel factual circumstances,' because the relevant question is whether the state of the law at the time of the events gave the officer 'fair warning.'" *Id.* (quoting *Hope,* 536 U.S. at 741, 122 S.Ct. 2508).

Here, I agree with the majority that, as of May 2014, it was "clear" that Homanko's conduct would be evaluated pursuant to our Court's sliding scale of culpability.[1] Maj. Op. at 717. I also agree with the majority that our Court has "been clear in recent years that the level of culpability required to shock the conscience when an officer has time for hurried deliberation is a conscious disregard of a great risk of serious harm." *Id.* at 717 n.6 (alterations and citations omitted). And, like the majority, I too "have no difficulty in concluding" that an officer who exhibits deplorable judgment and "unjustifiabl[y]" pursues "a potential summary traffic offender at speeds of over 100 miles-per-hour, after radioing for assistance from the neighboring jurisdiction where the potential offender was headed, demonstrates a conscious p.725 disregard of a great risk of serious harm." *Id.* at 718. Applying these mutually held premises to the question of whether the Sauers' due process rights were clearly established on the date in question, it would appear, therefore, that the majority and I are in agreement that "the contours of the right are sufficiently clear[] such that a general constitutional rule already identified in the decisional law applies with obvious clarity" to the established facts. *Kedra,* 876 F.3d at 450 (internal citations omitted).

Yet despite our conspicuous agreements on the pertinent legal principles and their application to the facts at hand, the majority has concluded that Homanko is entitled to qualified immunity on the ground that the law was not "settled in May 2014 that, absent a specific intent to harm, constitutional liability could be imposed on a police officer engaged in a police pursuit." Maj. Op. at 723 (emphasis added). Justification for such a finding eludes me. To endorse the majority's conclusion, one must accept the proposition that on May 12, 2014, a reasonable police officer — fully informed of the legal principles recited above — would not have considered it conscience-shocking to (1) execute a U-turn into oncoming traffic for the sole purpose of catching a potential traffic offender, and then (2) proceed in breakneck fashion to pursue the unmindful offender at speeds over 100 miles-per-hour, all while being fully aware that there are officers ahead better positioned to execute a stop.

Our case law does not compel such an implausible conclusion. On the date in question here, a reasonable officer undertaking a non-emergency, high-speed pursuit would have known that in police pursuit cases brought under 42 U.S.C. § 1983, we assess whether an officer's conduct "shocks the conscience" by gauging how much time the officer had to deliberate before deciding to give chase. Maj. Op. at 727 (citing, *inter alia, Brown v. Pa. Dep't of Health & Emergency Med. Servs. Training Inst.,* 318 F.3d 473, 480 (3d Cir. 2003)). Indeed, five years prior to the date in question, the Tenth Circuit held in *Green v. Post,* 574 F.3d 1294, 1302-03 (10th Cir. 2009), that *Lewis*'s intent-to-harm standard does not apply if — as here — an officer is not engaged in a hot pursuit of a fleeing suspect, but rather is engaged in a non-emergency, high-speed, unilateral pursuit of a suspected offender who is unaware that she is being chased. In such circumstances, the officer's conduct is evaluated under a "middle level [standard] of culpability" that looks to whether the officer acted with "conscious, deliberate indifference to an extreme risk of very serious harm to the plaintiff." *Id.* at 1303. The "middle level standard" applied in *Green* mirrors the "mid-level standard" that we formally adopted in *Sanford v. Stiles,* 456 F.3d 298, 307 (3d Cir. 2006), and that the majority applied here. *See* Maj. Op. at 717 n.6.

In my view, qualified immunity should not be granted here simply because there is little case law imposing liability on a police officer who drives his cruiser at speeds in excess of 100 miles per hour in a non-emergency situation. Neither the Supreme Court nor our Court has ever adopted a liability-based litmus test for determining whether a right was clearly established on the date in question. *See Kedra,* 876 F.3d at 450 ("[I]t need not be the case that the exact conduct *has previously been held unlawful* so long as the 'contours of the right' are sufficiently clear....") (quoting *Anderson,* 483 U.S. at 640, 107 S.Ct. 3034) (emphasis added); *see also Brown v. Muhlenberg Twp.,* 269 F.3d 205, 211 n.4 (3d Cir. 2001) ("If the unlawfulness of the defendant's conduct would have been apparent to a reasonable official based on the current state of the p.726 law, it is not necessary that there be binding precedent from this circuit so advising."). Instead the touchstone of our analysis is reasonableness: "Qualified immunity gives government officials breathing room to make reasonable but mistaken judgments about open legal questions." *Ashcroft v. al-Kidd,* 563 U.S. 731, 743, 131 S.Ct. 2074, 179 L.Ed.2d 1149 (2011). And based on the state of the law on May 12, 2014, it is readily apparent to me that a reasonable officer would have known — based on the general constitutional principles delineated in our case law and *Green*'s pronouncement that *Lewis* does not apply to unilateral, non-emergency pursuits of a non-fleeing suspect — that the type of conduct exhibited by Officer Homanko was unconstitutional.

The three cases cited by the majority — two of which pre-date *Green* by several years — do not, in my opinion, alter this conclusion. When seeking guidance from our sister courts, "[t]he dispositive question is whether the violative nature of *particular* conduct is clearly established." *L.R. v. Sch. Dist. of Philadelphia,* 836 F.3d 235, 248 (3d Cir. 2016) (quoting *Mullenix v. Luna,* ___ U.S. ___, 136 S.Ct. 305, 308, 193 L.Ed.2d 255 (2015) (per curiam) (emphasis in original)). And the *particular* conduct at issue here is not found in either *Bingue v. Prunchak,* 512 F.3d 1169 (9th Cir. 2008), or *Helseth v. Burch,* 258 F.3d 867 (8th Cir. 2001) (en banc), as both of those cases centered on conduct that took place during the hot pursuit of a "fleeing" suspect and, as such, were clearly governed by *Lewis. See Bingue,* 512 F.3d at 1177 ("We conclude that high-speed police chases, by their very nature, do not give the officers involved adequate time to deliberate in either deciding to join the chase or how to drive while in pursuit of the *fleeing* suspect.") (emphasis added); *see also Helseth,* 258 F.3d at 872 ("[The suspect] was a *fleeing* criminal, whose irresponsible high-speed driving endangered countless citizens and ultimately killed one innocent bystander and maimed another....") (emphasis added).

Nor did *Sitzes v. City of West Memphis,* 606 F.3d 461 (8th Cir. 2010), involve the particular conduct at issue here. *Sitzes* involved an accident in February of 2007 when an officer responding to a reported robbery and assault drove his vehicle at speeds between 80 and 90 m.p.h. and collided in an intersection with another car, killing the innocent driver and injuring a passenger. The majority in *Sitzes* relied upon the fact that the officer in question subjectively believed that he was responding to an emergency in holding that the "intent to harm" standard, and not a "deliberate indifference" or "conscious disregard of a great risk of serious harm" standard, applied to the officer's conduct. Significantly, the majority plainly indicated that the "intent to harm" standard would *not* control where the officer did not subjectively believe that the situation presented a real emergency, stating:

> Although we are deeply troubled by Officer Wright's actions, we cannot say that the district court erred in applying the intent-to-harm standard in this case. First, we must reject plaintiffs' primary argument, which bases liability on the situation ... not being a "true" emergency. *Terrell [v. Larson],* forecloses inquiry into the objective nature of the emergency, as substantive due process liability turns on the intent of the government actor. 396 F.3d [975], 980 [(8th Cir. 2005)]. Thus, the fact that the situation... was not as serious as those presented in *Helseth* or *Terrell,* or that it might not qualify as an "emergency" under the [police department] Policy and Procedure manual, is not determinative of the appropriate level of scrutiny. Neither is the fact, emphasized by the dissent, p.727 that Officer McDougal and others testified that they would never have driven in the manner that Officer Wright did, or that Officer McDougal responded to the situation ... differently than Officer Wright. This would all be more relevant if our question was whether the situation was an objectively "true" emergency. However, it bears little relevance to the question of what Officer Wright subjectively believed....
>
> We agree with the dissent that our opinion should not be read to establish a rule that an officer can insulate himself from substantive due process liability, no matter the circumstances, by simply averring that he subjectively believed the situation to which he was responding was an emergency. *See Terrell,* 396 F.3d at 980 n. 2. This could lead to the absurd results forecasted by the dissent. For example, the dissent fears that this case could be used to insulate from substantive due process liability an officer who drove "100 miles per hour through a children's playground during recess time," or an officer who drove "the wrong way down an interstate highway... when responding to something as routine as a reported accident requiring traffic control[,]" as long as the officer stated that he believed the situation to be an emergency. First, such cases

are far beyond the factual scenarios of *Lewis, Helseth,* and *Terrell,* which involved officers using conventional emergency driving techniques to respond to perceived emergencies. Nothing in our opinion would countenance granting summary judgment in either of the two situations presented by the dissent. Second, we think it very likely that an officer who intentionally drove through a playground or the wrong way on an interstate highway could be held liable even under the intent-to-harm standard, regardless of the officer's avowed belief, at least absent some compelling exigency not described in the hypotheticals. In sum, we do not understand this case to establish a per se rule that an officer's self-serving affidavit will always insulate that officer from substantive due process liability. Instead, we simply hold that the plaintiffs have failed to create a genuine issue of fact as to Officer Wright's subjective belief and that this belief is not so preposterous as to reflect bad faith on the part of Officer Wright.

Id. at 468, 469-70. Thus, far from rejecting application of a conscious disregard standard to police conduct that did not concern an emergency situation, *Sitzes* actually suggests that such a standard does apply when it is clear that the officer was not confronted with an emergency situation. And in our case, we are in full agreement that "[t]here was no emergency at all, and Homanko likely did the most that was warranted when he radioed the police in a neighboring jurisdiction to stop the offender." Maj. Op. at 716. The reliance in *Sitzes* on the officer's belief in that case that he faced an emergency situation can be read as providing notice to law enforcement officers that they are not insulated from liability for engaging in egregiously reckless criminal conduct in a non-emergency context.[2]

p.728 *Green* on the other hand — as the majority plainly recognized — "arose in a non-emergency setting and did not involve a suspect fleeing the police in a dangerous manner." Maj. Op. at 720. Those facts — again as the majority recognized — are akin "to the allegations in this case...." *Id.* The majority is correct in its assertions that "[w]hen qualified immunity it at issue, context matters" and that courts must "take into account the 'particularized' facts of a case." Maj. Op. at 718. *Green,* therefore, is the only case that addresses the context and *particularized* conduct at issue here. And when read in conjunction with the "general constitutional rule already identified in the decisional law," it is evident — indeed, "obvious" — that a reasonable officer would have known on May 12, 2014, that Officer Homanko's admittedly criminal conduct was unconstitutional.[3] *Kedra,* 876 F.3d at 450 (citation omitted).

Our decision in *Kedra* supports this conclusion. There, the mother of a Pennsylvania State Trooper brought a § 1983 claim against a police instructor who accidentally shot a loaded handgun into the trooper's chest during a routine training session, killing him. *Kedra,* 876 F.3d at 432. The complaint alleged that the officer's conduct was conscience shocking because he "bypassed all of the safety checks [and] failed to physically or visually inspect the gun to ensure it was unloaded" before pulling the trigger. *Id.* at 433. Like the majority here, we concluded in *Kedra* that the allegations gave rise to the inference that the officer "acted with actual knowledge of a substantial risk of lethal harm" so as to shock the conscience under a then-clearly established theory of deliberate indifference. *Id.* at 448 (citations omitted). We then turned to the question of whether the right at issue — *i.e.,* "an individual's right not to be subjected, defenseless, to a police officer's demonstration of the use of deadly force in a manner contrary to all applicable safety protocols" — was clearly established on the date in question. *Id.* at 449 (footnote omitted). After reciting the general constitutional rules identified in our decisional law and analyzing the facts of a "closely analogous case from the First Circuit," we concluded that a reasonable officer would have had fair warning that the conduct at issue p.729 was constitutionally prohibited on the date in question. *Id.* at 450-52 (citation omitted).

The same conclusion applies here. The general constitutional principles are clear. *Green* applied those principles to an analogous set of facts. The unconstitutional nature of Homanko's actions, placing at substantial risk those traveling a two-lane, undivided highway in recklessly criminal pursuit of an unsuspecting motorist for a minor traffic infraction, was clearly established when he slammed into the Sauers' vehicle, mortally injuring Mrs. Sauer and severely injuring her husband.

I respectfully dissent.

[1] When reviewing an appeal from a district court's ruling on a motion to dismiss, we accept allegations in the complaint as true and draw all plausible inferences from those allegations in favor of the plaintiff. *Kedra v. Schroeter,* 876 F.3d 424, 432, 434 (3d Cir. 2017).

[2] When the car arrived in the neighboring jurisdiction, the officers stopped it as requested but did not charge the driver with a traffic violation or any other crime.

[3] As recounted in his briefing, Homanko additionally pled guilty to a number of minor traffic offenses.

[4] Sauers also sued the Borough of Nesquehoning and the Nesquehoning Police Chief. Those parties filed a motion to dismiss the complaint, separately from Homanko. The District Court granted the motion as to the police chief and granted it in part and denied it in part as to the Borough. Those rulings have not been appealed. Accordingly, this appeal addresses only the District Court's denial of Homanko's request for qualified immunity.

[5] The District Court had jurisdiction under 28 U.S.C. §§ 1331, 1343, and 1367. We have jurisdiction pursuant to 28 U.S.C. § 1291 over interlocutory appeals raising a purely legal challenge to a denial of qualified immunity. *Mirabella v. Villard,* 853 F.3d 641, 648 (3d Cir. 2017). Because this appeal raises only a question of law, we have jurisdiction and our review is plenary. *Id.*

[6] The District Court identified "gross negligence or arbitrariness" as the level of culpability required to shock the conscience when an officer has time only for hurried deliberation. (App. at 11-12.) We have described the "gross negligence or arbitrariness" standard, however, as one "that provides little guidance." *Sanford v. Stiles,* 456 F.3d 298, 310 (3d Cir. 2006). We have been clear in recent years that the level of culpability required to shock the conscience when an officer has time for hurried deliberation is "a conscious disregard of 'a great risk of serious harm[.]'" *Haberle,* 885 F.3d at 177 (quoting *Sanford,* 456 F.3d at 310); *accord Kedra,* 876 F.3d at 437.

[7] Although the Ninth Circuit appears to have limited its application of *Lewis's* intent-to-harm standard to "situations involving high-speed chases aimed at apprehending a fleeing suspect," any such limitation does not undermine that court's

explicit refusal to distinguish between "'emergency' and 'non-emergency' situations." *Bingue,* 512 F.3d at 1177. It also leaves open the question of whether a suspect leaving the scene of a crime, who does not know that the police are pursuing him, should be considered a "fleeing suspect." It is far from certain, therefore, what standard of culpability the Ninth Circuit would apply to the facts at issue here.

[8] Our own precedents do not provide any added clarity regarding the proper standard by which to judge whether an officer's conduct shocks the conscience in police pursuits that involve neither an emergency nor a fleeing suspect. Although we have indicated that the "shocks the conscience" standard applies to police pursuit cases, *see Brown,* 318 F.3d at 480 ("[T]he 'shocks the conscience' standard should apply in all substantive due process cases if the state actor had to act with urgency[, including] police pursuit cases[.]"), our cases do not give fair warning that, absent an intent to harm, police could face constitutional liability based on a high-speed pursuit, *see, e.g., Davis v. Twp. of Hillside,* 190 F.3d 167, 171 (3d Cir. 1999) (applying *Lewis* intent to harm standard to injury of bystander who was injured as a result of a high-speed pursuit of a fleeing suspect).

[9] The dissent minimizes the import of *Bingue* and *Helseth* because those cases involved conduct differing from the conduct alleged here. But those differences do not alter those courts' explicit holdings that the intent-to-harm standard should apply to police pursuits whether or not the officer is responding to a pending emergency.

[10] We note that *Kane*'s ultimate rejection of qualified immunity rested on the fact that our own precedent contained factually and legally analogous case law to put the defendant "on notice that he acted unconstitutionally." *Kane,* 902 F.3d at 195. No such case law existed in our Circuit in May 2014 that would have given Homanko fair warning that he could be subject to constitutional liability for actions during a police pursuit that were not taken with an intent to harm.

[11] We emphasize that our decision on qualified immunity does not mean that Homanko is immune from any suit arising from his conduct; he is only immune to a suit alleging the federal constitutional claims made here. He remains exposed to state law tort claims that can, and have been, brought against him, so Sauers is not without a remedy.

[1] The Supreme Court in *County of Sacramento v. Lewis,* 523 U.S. 833, 118 S.Ct. 1708, 140 L.Ed.2d 1043 (1998), indicated that a sliding scale of culpable conduct applied to determine whether a law enforcement officer's actions were sufficiently conscienceshocking to impose liability, stating that the deliberate indifference "standard is sensibly employed only when actual deliberation is practical." *Id.* at 851, 118 S.Ct. 1708. There is no dispute here that "actual deliberation" by Homanko was practical.

[2] Contrary to the majority's assertion, we do not minimize the import of the Ninth Circuit's holding in *Bingue* or the Eighth Circuit's holding in *Helseth.* Instead, we rely upon the Eighth Circuit's post-*Helseth* and post-*Bingue* careful delineation between emergency and non-emergency situations articulated in *Sitzes.* We also rely and on the Tenth Circuit's holding in *Green* that the intent to harm standard does not apply in the non-emergency context to conclude that a reasonable police officer would know in May of 2014 that the type of conduct engaged in by Homanko was conscience-shocking such that liability could be imposed.

[3] It bears reiterating that Officer Homanko pled guilty to vehicular homicide and reckless endangerment. A reasonable officer engaged in criminal conduct that resulted in the loss of life and severe personal injuries in a violent collision surely would understand that his conduct would be regarded as sufficiently conscienceshocking so as to preclude the defense of qualified immunity. Indeed, it would appear that his guilty plea would defeat the defense of official immunity under Pennsylvania tort law that would otherwise be available to Officer Homanko for engaging in conduct that fell within the scope of his duties. *See* 42 Pa.C.S.A. § 8550 (application of official immunity otherwise available under 42 Pa. C.S.A. § 8446(2) is foreclosed where "it is judicially determined that the act of the employee caused the injury and that such act constituted a crime, actual fraud, actual malice or willful misconduct."). This reinforces the conclusion that a reasonable law enforcement officer would understand that he could not take another person's life through criminal conduct and yet retain qualified immunity. Notably, in *Kane v. Barger,* 902 F.3d 185, 195 (3d Cir. 2018), we held that a law enforcement officer's conduct that merely "resemble[d] the crime of indecent assault" — the officer had touched the plaintiff's intimate parts for his own gratification — was such that "given the egregiousness of [defendant's] violation of [plaintiff's] personal security and bodily integrity, the right here is so 'obvious' that it could be deemed clearly established even without materially similar cases." So, too, here the obviousness of Officer Homanko's violation of the plaintiffs' rights to life and bodily integrity defeats the defense of qualified immunity even in the absence of materially similar cases.

900 F.3d 77 (2018)

Corey BLAND; Virginia Bland

v.

CITY OF NEWARK; City of Newark Police Department; New Jersey Division of State Police; State of New Jersey; Sergeant James Thompson; Sergeant Brian Murphy; Trooper II Thomas Espinoza; Trooper II William Legg; Trooper Miguel Holguin; Trooper Anthony Sardanopoli; Trooper John Oliveira; Trooper Stephen Riefler; Detective Thomas Del Mauro; Detective Brian Costa; Detective David Martinez; Sergeant Thomas Roe; Officer Danny Costa; John Does (1-100); ABC Entities (1-100), A Series of Fictitious Names,
New Jersey State Police, State of New Jersey, Anthony Sardanopoli, James Thompson, Brian Murphy, Thomas Espinoza, William Legg, Miguel Holguin, John Oliveira and Stephen Riefler, Appellants in No. 17-2228,
Thomas Delmauro, David Martinez and Ruben Torres, Appellants in No. 17-2229.

Nos. 17-2228 17-2229.

United States Court of Appeals, Third Circuit.

Argued March 22, 2018.

Filed: August 15, 2018.

Bland v. City of Newark, 900 F. 3d 77 (3rd Cir. 2018)

On Appeal from the United States District Court for the District of New Jersey, (D.C. No. 2-13-cv-02985), District Judge: Honorable Katharine S. Hayden.

Pamela L. Brause, Peter Ventrice [Argued], Brause Brause & Ventrice, 276 Main Street, P.O. Box 232, Metuchen, NJ 08840, Lucas E. Phillips, Jr. [Argued], 134 Evergreen Place, Suite 301, P.O. Box 2487, East Orange, NJ 07019, Attorneys for Appellees.

Michael C. Walters [Argued], Office of Attorney General of New Jersey, Division of Law, Richard J. Hughes Justice Complex, 25 Market Street, P.O. Box 112, Trenton, NJ 08625, Attorney for All Appellants.

Gary S. Lipshutz [Argued], City of Newark Department of Law, 920 Broad Street, Room 316, Newark, NJ 07102, Attorney for Appellants Thomas Del Mauro, David Martinez, and Ruben Torres.

Michael H. Freeman, Greenberg Dauber Epstein & Tucker, One Gateway Center, p.80 Suite 600, Newark, NJ 07102, Matthew J. Lynch, Office of Attorney General of New Jersey, Division of Law, Richard J. Hughes Justice Complex, 25 Market Street, Trenton, NJ 08625, Attorneys for Appellants State of New Jersey, New Jersey State Police, James Thompson, Brian Murphy, Thomas Espinoza, William Legg, Miguel Holguin, Anthony Sardanopoli, John Oliveira and Stephen Riefler.

Before: SMITH, Chief Judge, HARDIMAN, and BIBAS, Circuit Judges.

p.79 OPINION OF THE COURT

HARDIMAN, Circuit Judge.

This interlocutory appeal was filed by several law enforcement officers who were involved to varying degrees in a prolonged pursuit of a fleeing motorist, Corey Bland. The pursuit involved the use of lethal force against Bland, who sustained severe injuries after he was shot between 16 and 18 times. The question presented is whether the District Court committed legal error when it denied the officers summary judgment on qualified immunity grounds. Because the officers' conduct was within the bounds of the Supreme Court's relevant decisions regarding the use of lethal force, we will reverse.

I

A. Initial Pursuit

In the early evening of December 26, 2011, Newark Police received a report that a black Audi bearing Pennsylvania license plate number PZK821C had been carjacked at gunpoint. Approximately three hours later, New Jersey State Troopers James Thompson and Brian Murphy spotted the carjacked vehicle in Newark. Appellee Corey Bland was behind the wheel. The troopers activated their police lights, but Bland failed to stop. Instead, he accelerated and began to drive recklessly, running red lights and shutting off his headlights as he went. The troopers lost sight of the Audi, but an officer from the Summit Police Department began following it shortly thereafter. Bland nearly struck that officer's vehicle and collided with an embankment, but he continued driving. He reached speeds exceeding 100 miles per hour, weaving in and out of light traffic.

State Trooper John Oliveira joined the chase in his marked police car after receiving reports that units from the State Police and Summit Police Departments were pursuing a carjacked vehicle. State Trooper Miguel Holguin,[1] driving an unmarked Chrysler 300 accompanied by State Troopers Anthony Sardanopoli and Stephen Riefler, got involved after hearing a radio broadcast by Thompson and Murphy containing details about the carjacked vehicle. Bland continued to drive recklessly, frequently changing lanes, disregarding traffic lights, turning his lights off, accelerating to more than 80 miles an hour in an area with a 25-mile-per-hour speed limit, and driving over a curb in an empty parking lot, which caused the Audi to begin to smoke. Despite all this, the Audi was not disabled, and Bland continued to evade police.

B. Lincoln Park Events

Eventually, Bland began driving the wrong way down Lincoln Park, a one-way street. While doing so, he collided both with Thompson and Murphy in their marked state police car and an occupied Newark Police vehicle. When Bland hit the p.81 Newark police car, he was travelling approximately 25 to 35 miles per hour, and the impact caused the police car to strike an unoccupied parked car. As a result, the Audi, the police car, and the unoccupied car became entangled. State Trooper Thomas Espinoza, who had received a radio transmission about an ongoing pursuit involving a vehicle carjacked at gunpoint, arrived on the scene shortly after these collisions.

Numerous officers surrounded the Audi, including Murphy, Thompson, Oliveira, Sardanopoli, Espinoza, and State Trooper William Legg.[2] Many of the officers ordered Bland to surrender, and one officer attempted to break the Audi's window by striking it. During this encounter, the six state troopers fired a total of 28 shots, none of which hit Bland. Newark Police Officer Thomas Del Mauro was present at Lincoln Park, but he did not discharge his weapon.

There is no evidence in the record that Bland attempted to surrender at this time. Instead, he revved the Audi's engine, spun its tires, and tried to get the vehicle to accelerate. Bland ultimately freed the Audi from the Newark police car by reversing and striking the now-unoccupied state police car a second time.[3] He then drove over a curb and through a public park.

Upon exiting the park, Bland continued to speed through Newark with his lights off, at times on roads populated with vehicular and pedestrian traffic. Officers and state troopers continued to pursue Bland, but Thompson and Murphy were no longer involved because their vehicle was disabled when it was struck by the Audi at Lincoln Park. During this portion of the chase, a state police car struck an occupied civilian vehicle. Bland eventually drove to the intersection of 18th Avenue and Livingston Street, where the most vigorously disputed series of events took place.

C. The Terminus of the Chase

At the intersection of 18th and Livingston, the unmarked Chrysler 300 driven by Holguin allegedly rammed the Audi, sending the Audi into scaffolding that surrounded a school. State Troopers Holguin, Sardanopoli, and Riefler exited the Chrysler 300 and moved toward the Audi, which remained entangled in the scaffolding. Holguin approached the driver's side with Riefler standing behind him, while Sardanopoli moved to the Audi's passenger side.

All three troopers began firing their weapons at the Audi. Holguin and Riefler testified that they initially discharged their weapons because Bland refused to comply with their orders to show his hands and to stop moving and because he repeatedly threatened to kill the officers. Sardanopoli stated that he fired his weapon after he saw Holguin firing. Legg — also on the scene — asserted that he fired because he could see Bland moving around in the Audi as Holguin and Riefler discharged their weapons. Bland, for his part, denied that the troopers shouted any verbal commands or that he made evasive movements, but he conceded that nothing in the record contradicts the officers' allegations that he threatened to kill them.

After the first volley of shots, Riefler approached the driver's side of the Audi, whereupon Riefler testified that Bland attempted p.82 to climb through the window while again threatening to kill him. In response, Riefler fired his weapon again. Espinoza also discharged his weapon, as did Newark Officers Del Mauro, Reuben Torres, and David Martinez, who had heard about the carjacking at roll call earlier that evening. The Newark officers stated that they fired their weapons because they saw the Audi moving or heard it revving, indicating that it was still capable of flight.

Bland disputed this assertion, arguing instead that the Audi became inoperable once it crashed into the scaffolding. Oliveira, though present, did not discharge his weapon at the terminus.

The shooting finally ceased once Riefler observed Bland slumped over, and a Newark sergeant called for the officers to hold their fire. Bland was shot between 16 and 18 times, including in the face, chest, and abdomen. He suffered numerous injuries, including a traumatic brain injury, respiratory failure, vision loss, and multiple facial fractures. No gun was recovered from the scene, and no officer observed Bland with a weapon during the course of the pursuit.

II

Bland and his wife Virginia filed a complaint in the Superior Court of New Jersey Law Division alleging (among other things) that Defendants violated Bland's Fourth Amendment rights. *See* 42 U.S.C. § 1983; N.J. Stat. Ann. § 10:6-2(c). Defendants removed the case to federal court and sought summary judgment, claiming qualified immunity.

After oral argument, the District Court concluded that it was "not in a position to grant or deny qualified immunity." App. 78. Instead, it held that a jury must first decide two issues of material fact: (1) whether the Audi's engine was revving (and thus whether the car was capable of moving) after it crashed into the scaffolding; and (2) whether the officers could see Bland's movements inside the vehicle. The District Court opined that the Supreme Court's decision in *Plumhoff v. Rickard,* 572 U.S. 765, 134 S.Ct. 2012, 188 L.Ed.2d 1056 (2014), issued three years *after* the car chase, may decide the "central" question of "whether or not Corey Bland was an active threat to the officers at the terminus so as to justify their actions in using deadly force to end that risk." App. 73. Accordingly, it denied Defendants' motion, including with respect to the three officers who were neither present nor discharged their weapons at the terminus of the chase. Defendants moved for a stay of trial, which the District Court denied. We entered an order staying the district court proceedings pending the resolution of this timely interlocutory appeal.

III

A

The District Court had jurisdiction under 28 U.S.C. §§ 1331 and 1367. We have jurisdiction under 28 U.S.C. § 1291 pursuant to the collateral order doctrine. *Dougherty v. Sch. Dist. of Phila.,* 772 F.3d 979, 986 (3d Cir. 2014) (citation omitted). Our jurisdiction lies "only to the extent that the order turns on an issue of law." *Id.* (internal quotation marks, citation, and alteration omitted). We "possess jurisdiction to review whether the set of facts identified by the district court is sufficient to establish a violation of a clearly established constitutional right," but "we lack jurisdiction to consider whether the district court correctly identified the set of facts that the summary judgment record is sufficient to prove."[4] *Id.* (quoting *Ziccardi* p.83

v. City of Philadelphia, 288 F.3d 57, 61 (3d Cir. 2002)). "To the extent we have jurisdiction, this Court exercises plenary review." *Id.*

Summary judgment is proper only when the record "shows that there is no genuine dispute as to any material fact and the movant is entitled to judgment as a matter of law." Fed. R. Civ. P. 56(a). A fact is material if it "affect[s] the outcome of the suit under the governing law." *Anderson v. Liberty Lobby, Inc.,* 477 U.S. 242, 248, 106 S.Ct. 2505, 91 L.Ed.2d 202 (1986). In determining whether a genuine dispute of material fact exists, we view the underlying facts and draw all reasonable inferences in favor of the party opposing the motion. *Dougherty,* 772 F.3d at 986.

B

"The doctrine of qualified immunity shields officials from civil liability so long as their conduct 'does not violate clearly established statutory or constitutional rights of which a reasonable person would have known.'" *Mullenix v. Luna,* ___ U.S. ___, 136 S.Ct. 305, 308, 193 L.Ed.2d 255 (2015) (per curiam) (quoting *Pearson v. Callahan,* 555 U.S. 223, 231, 129 S.Ct. 808, 172 L.Ed.2d 565 (2009)). In resolving questions of qualified immunity, "courts engage in a two-pronged inquiry: (1) whether the plaintiff sufficiently alleged the violation of a constitutional right, and (2) whether the right was 'clearly established' at the time of the official's conduct." *L.R. v. Sch. Dist. of Phila.,* 836 F.3d 235, 241 (3d Cir. 2016). We may tackle these steps "in the order we deem most appropriate for the particular case before us." *Santini v. Fuentes,* 795 F.3d 410, 418 (3d Cir. 2015) (citation omitted).

Just two terms ago, the Supreme Court reiterated the "longstanding principle that clearly established law should not be defined at a high level of generality," but must instead "be particularized to the facts of the case." *White v. Pauly,* ___ U.S. ___, 137 S.Ct. 548, 552, 196 L.Ed.2d 463 (2017) (per curiam) (internal quotation marks omitted); *see also L.R.,* 836 F.3d at 248. Moreover, at the time the action is taken, the "legal principle [must] clearly prohibit the officer's conduct in the particular circumstances before him. The rule's contours must be so well defined that it is clear to a reasonable officer that his conduct was unlawful in the situation he confronted." *District of Columbia v. Wesby,* ___ U.S. ___, 138 S.Ct. 577, 590, 199 L.Ed.2d 453 (2018) (internal quotation marks and citation omitted). Thus, "qualified immunity protects 'all but the plainly incompetent or those who knowingly violate the law.'" *Mullenix,* 136 S.Ct. at 308 (quoting *Malley v. Briggs,* 475 U.S. 335, 341, 106 S.Ct. 1092, 89 L.Ed.2d 271 (1986)).

C

The District Court focused its analysis on the events that occurred at the terminus of the reckless flight that ensued after Bland failed to comply with the traffic stop initiated by the New Jersey State Police. We begin by discussing the deadly force used by six of the state troopers at Lincoln Park, and we conclude that they are all entitled to qualified immunity.

The Supreme Court has consistently held that officers either did not violate the p.84 Fourth Amendment or were entitled to qualified immunity when they used deadly force during car chases similar to the one at issue here. In *Brosseau v. Haugen,* 543 U.S. 194, 125 S.Ct. 596, 160 L.Ed.2d 583 (2004) (per curiam), the Court held that an officer was entitled to qualified immunity after she shot "a disturbed felon, set on avoiding capture through vehicular flight, when persons in the immediate area [were] at risk from that flight." *Id.* at 200, 125 S.Ct. 596. In *Scott v. Harris,* 550 U.S. 372, 127 S.Ct. 1769, 167 L.Ed.2d 686 (2007), the Court concluded that an officer did not violate the Fourth Amendment when he "terminate[d] the car chase by ramming his bumper" into the car of a fugitive whose reckless driving "posed an actual and imminent threat to the lives of any pedestrians who might have been present, to other civilian motorists, and to the officers involved in the chase." *Id.* at 381, 384, 127 S.Ct. 1769. This was so even though the officer ran the motorist off the road instead of employing the standard "PIT maneuver"[5] to get the fleeing vehicle to stop, and this decision caused the vehicle to run down an embankment and overturn, rendering the plaintiff a quadriplegic. *Id.* at 375, 127 S.Ct. 1769.

In *Plumhoff v. Rickard,* 572 U.S. 765, 134 S.Ct. 2012, 188 L.Ed.2d 1056 (2014), decided after the events giving rise to this suit, the Court held that officers did not violate the Fourth Amendment and alternatively were entitled to qualified immunity when they fatally shot a fugitive whom the officers reasonably believed was "intent on resuming" a chase that "pose[d] a deadly threat for others on the road." *Id.* at 2022. A year later, in *Mullenix v. Luna,* ___ U.S. ___, 136 S.Ct. 305, 193 L.Ed.2d 255 (2015), the Court concluded that an officer who shot and killed a motorist during a high-speed pursuit in which the fugitive threatened to kill police officers was entitled to qualified immunity, even though the officer's decision to shoot defied his supervisor's orders. *Id.* at 306-07, 312.

Like the cases just mentioned, Bland's behavior threatened the safety of the officers, as well as the public at large. Before shots were fired at Lincoln Park, Bland drove at high speeds, disregarded traffic signals, drove the wrong way down a one-way street, collided with two occupied police vehicles, and failed to comply with orders to surrender. As the gunfire erupted, he repeatedly attempted to flee from police and state troopers, including by trying to drive with officers standing in close proximity to the Audi. And he engaged in all of this behavior in a vehicle that had been reportedly taken at gunpoint a few hours earlier. Bland does not direct us to any caselaw indicating that, especially in light of the precedent just discussed, "only someone plainly incompetent or who knowingly violates the law would have perceived a sufficient threat and acted as [the state troopers] did" in this situation. *Mullenix,* 136 S.Ct. at 310 (internal quotation marks and alteration omitted); *see also Fields v. City of Philadelphia,* 862 F.3d 353, 361 (3d Cir. 2017) (noting that clearly established rights are derived either from binding Supreme Court and Third Circuit precedent or from a "robust consensus of cases of persuasive authority in the Courts of Appeals" (citation omitted)). Given the troopers' reasonable belief that Bland was armed, and the mortal threat that his conduct posed to those around him, the troopers who discharged their weapons at Lincoln Park did not violate Bland's clearly established constitutional rights. And because p.85 Thompson, Murphy, and Oliveira fired their weapons only at this location, they are plainly entitled to qualified immunity.

D

The events at the terminus of the car chase present a more complicated picture, but we reach the same conclusion because Bland identifies no caselaw indicating that the officers violated clearly established law extant in 2011. *See Anderson v. Creighton,* 483 U.S. 635, 639, 107 S.Ct. 3034, 97 L.Ed.2d 523 (1987). He instead states in conclusory fashion that "every ... reasonable member of law enforcement should be aware that [the officers'] conduct would constitute excessive force." Bland Br. 36. In support, Bland argues that the officers were not in a position to see whether he made threatening movements inside the vehicle, and that the Audi's impact with the scaffolding rendered it inoperable, bringing the car chase to an end.[6] As a result, Bland contends that *Brosseau* and *Scott* no longer control, and we should instead look to *Tennessee v. Garner* for guidance. In *Garner,* the Supreme Court held that "if the suspect threatens the officer with a weapon or there is probable cause to believe that he has committed a crime involving the infliction or threatened infliction of serious physical harm, deadly force may be used if necessary to prevent escape, and if, where feasible, some warning has been given." *Tennessee v. Garner,* 471 U.S. 1, 11-12, 105 S.Ct. 1694, 85 L.Ed.2d 1 (1985). Applying that standard, the Court concluded that an officer violated the Fourth Amendment by shooting an "unarmed, nondangerous" suspect in the back of the head as he attempted to flee the scene of a burglary. *Id.* at 11, 105 S.Ct. 1694.

Bland's reliance on *Garner* is misplaced. The Supreme Court has noted that *Garner* "lay[s] out excessive-force principles at only a general level" and "do[es] not by [itself] create clearly established law outside an obvious case." *White,* 137 S.Ct. at 552 (internal quotation marks omitted); *see also Scott,* 550 U.S. at 382, 127 S.Ct. 1769 (noting that "*Garner* did not establish a magical on/off switch that triggers rigid preconditions whenever an officer's actions constitute 'deadly force'").

The officers here confronted a scenario quite different from the one presented in *Garner,* where the officer pursued and shot a nondangerous suspect in the back of the head, even though the officer was "reasonably sure" the suspect was unarmed. 471 U.S. at 3-4, 105 S.Ct. 1694; *see also Brosseau,* 543 U.S. at 201, 125 S.Ct. 596 (noting that analysis of qualified immunity "depends very much on the facts of each case"). This becomes especially clear once we consider the officers' actions "in light of the specific context of the case," as we are required to do. *Fields,* 862 F.3d at 361. The state troopers and Officer Del Mauro — all of whom were present at Lincoln Park — continued to pursue a fugitive who once again disobeyed traffic p.86 lights, drove at excessive speeds, and put pedestrians and motorists at great risk. Under Bland's version of events, at least one innocent civilian suffered harm by his flight when a state police car struck an occupied vehicle during the final leg of the pursuit. *See Scott,* 550 U.S. at 379-80, 127 S.Ct. 1769 (noting that the police were "forced to engage in the same hazardous maneuvers just to keep up" with the plaintiff). After the crash, Bland threatened to kill the officers, and the record provides no evidence that he attempted to surrender at any time. Though the Audi remained pinned against the scaffolding, the officers had previously seen Bland successfully free the car and continue to flee after the crash at Lincoln Park. And although the officers did not see a weapon, the police reports of an armed carjacking gave them reason to believe Bland was armed. *See Pearson,* 555 U.S. at 244, 129 S.Ct. 808 (noting that qualified immunity "turns on the objective legal reasonableness of the action" (internal quotation marks and citation omitted)). This was the situation the officers confronted at the terminus of the chase when they discharged their weapons. Bland identifies no cases with similar facts that, in 2011, would have "put every reasonable offic[er] on notice" that using deadly force in such a situation violated clearly established constitutional rights. *Fields,* 862 F.3d at 361 (internal quotation marks omitted). Therefore, accepting (as we must) the truth of Bland's assertions regarding the Audi's immobility and the officers' ability to see Bland's hands, our conclusion remains the same: the actions taken by the State Troopers and Officer Del Mauro are protected by qualified immunity.

But what about Newark Officers Torres and Martinez, who, according to Bland, "arrived on the scene[and] joined in the shooting without knowing whether Mr. Bland was firing at them, and without ever first observing Mr. Bland to be in possession of any firearm"? Bland Br. 5. The Newark officers contend that video footage refutes this allegation, but we need not resolve that dispute.[7] Here again, Bland has presented no caselaw demonstrating that the officers, who reasonably believed that Bland was armed, violated a clearly established right by joining in the chaotic scene and discharging their weapons.

A recent Supreme Court decision demonstrates that Torres's and Martinez's actions did not violate clearly established rights. In *White v. Pauly,* the Court granted qualified immunity to an officer who arrived late to an armed confrontation between multiple officers and individuals. 137 S.Ct. at 549, 551. After seeing one of the civilians fire shots, the defendant officer, without giving a warning, shot and killed another individual who pointed a weapon at the officers surrounding the house. *Id.* at 550. The plaintiffs argued that the other officers had not adequately alerted the occupants to the fact that they were officers, and that White, although late to the scene, should have been aware that "corrective p.87 action was necessary." *Id.* at 552. In reversing the denial of qualified immunity, the Court stated that "[c]learly established federal law does not prohibit a reasonable officer who arrives late to an ongoing police action in circumstances like this from assuming that proper procedures ... have already been followed," and that "[n]o settled Fourth Amendment principle requires that officer to second-guess the earlier steps already taken by his or her fellow officers." *Id.* So too here. In the absence of any controlling law to the contrary, Newark Officers Martinez and Torres likewise are entitled to qualified immunity.[8]

IV

Because Defendants did not violate any of Bland's clearly established constitutional rights, we will reverse the order of the District Court so summary judgment may be entered for Defendants.

[1] Discrepancies exist about the spelling of this trooper's name. We adopt the spelling provided by the trooper in his deposition.

[2] Bland does not identify any actions taken by Riefler or Holguin at Lincoln Park.

[3] Both the Newark officers and the state troopers contend that Bland drove aggressively at the officers as he attempted to flee, but Bland disputes this characterization. That dispute is immaterial, however, because all parties agree that officers were standing less than 10 feet from the Audi as Bland extricated it from the two vehicles.

[4] The Newark officers argue that the District Court erred by considering Bland's expert testimony, which purported to establish that the Audi was incapable of moving once it crashed into the scaffolding. We do not have jurisdiction to review this ruling. *See Blaylock v. City of Philadelphia,* 504 F.3d 405, 409 (3d Cir. 2007) (noting that, in appeals from denials of qualified immunity, "we lack jurisdiction to review questions of 'evidence sufficiency'" and must instead confine ourselves to "pure questions of law").

[5] In a Pursuit Intervention Technique maneuver, the pursuing vehicle applies pressure to the rear of the fleeing vehicle, causing the fleeing vehicle to turn abruptly and come to a stop.

[6] After the parties submitted their summary judgment papers, Bland received a report from an automotive expert concerning whether the Audi could have moved after it collided with the scaffolding. The report contained pictures taken after the incident, including one that purportedly showed the driver's side tinted window in one piece on the ground. At oral argument, Bland contended that this photograph demonstrated that the window was up during the final moments of the chase, meaning that the officers could neither have seen what Bland was doing inside the Audi nor heard his death threats. We need not decide whether the District Court properly considered this evidence because, even assuming that its decision to do so was correct, Bland has failed to show that the officers violated clearly established law.

[7] Though we need not look to the video for guidance, we take this opportunity to remind district courts of their obligation to do so when necessary to identify disputed issues of material fact. At oral argument, the Newark officers requested that the District Court consider video footage they proffered to counter Bland's version of events. The Court declined this invitation, stating that it did not think it was "particularly smart" to "hav[e] judges review individual tapes and say, hey, I'm satisfied." App. 27. Notwithstanding the District Court's independent assessment of the wisdom of this approach, the Supreme Court has instructed courts to consider video evidence in the record and to "view[] the facts in the light depicted by the videotape," especially when it "blatantly contradict[s]" the nonmovant's narrative. *Scott,* 550 U.S. at 380-81, 127 S.Ct. 1769.

[8] Because Defendants are entitled to qualified immunity, we need not reach the underlying Fourth Amendment questions. *Pearson,* 555 U.S. at 236, 129 S.Ct. 808. Nothing in this opinion should be read to suggest that law enforcement officers violate the Fourth Amendment where, as here, they employ lethal force to neutralize a carjacking suspect reasonably perceived to be armed, dangerous, and unwilling to peacefully surrender.

876 F.3d 424 (2017)

Joan KEDRA, in her own right and as personal representative of the estate of David Kedra, Appellant

v.

Richard SCHROETER.

No. 16-1417.

United States Court of Appeals, Third Circuit.

Argued December 5, 2016.

(Filed: November 28, 2017).

Kedra v. Schroeter, 876 F. 3d 424 (3rd Cir. 2017)

On Appeal from the United States District Court for the Eastern District of Pennsylvania, (E.D. Pa. No. 2-15-cv-05223), District Judge: Honorable Eduardo C. Robreno.

Michael J. Quirk, Esq. (Argued), Gerald J. Williams, Esq., Williams Cuker & Berezofsky, 1515 Market Street, Suite 1300, Philadelphia, PA 19102, Counsel for Appellant

Kevin R. Bradford, Esq., Stephen R. Kovatis, Esq., Claudia M. Tesoro, Esq. (Argued), Office of Attorney General of Pennsylvania, 21 South 12th Street, Philadelphia, PA 19107, Counsel for Appellee

Before: FISHER,[*] KRAUSE, and MELLOY,[**] Circuit Judges.

p.431 OPINION OF THE COURT

KRAUSE, Circuit Judge.

This case arises from the grievous death of State Trooper David Kedra, who was shot and killed by his instructor, then-Corporal p.432 Richard Schroeter, during a routine firearms training. Although a longterm veteran of the police force and specifically certified in the safe use of firearms, Schroeter allegedly disregarded each of the steps that he previously acknowledged in writing were required to safely perform a live demonstration of a firearm — skipping over both his own safety check and an independent check by a second person, treating the gun as if it were unloaded instead of loaded, pointing it at a person instead of a safe target, bypassing the required visual and physical inspection before a "trigger pull," and then pulling the trigger with the gun aimed at Kedra's chest. JA 31.

Appellant brought a civil rights complaint under 42 U.S.C. § 1983 alleging that Schroeter's conduct had subjected her deceased son to a state-created danger in violation of his Fourteenth Amendment substantive due process rights. But because the complaint did not allege that Schroeter had actual knowledge that there was a bullet in the gun when he fired it at Kedra, the District Court held that Schroeter was entitled to qualified immunity and dismissed the complaint with prejudice. Its reasoning was that the complaint pleaded only an objective theory of deliberate indifference, i.e., what a reasonable official should have known because the risk was so obvious, which was not then-clearly established, and was insufficient to plead the clearly established subjective theory of deliberate indifference, i.e., that Schroeter was actually aware that his conduct carried a substantial risk of serious harm. We agree with the District Court that the objective theory of deliberate indifference was not clearly established at the time of the shooting. However, because obviousness of risk is relevant to proving actual knowledge and the allegations of the complaint here are more than sufficient to support a reasonable inference that Schroeter had such knowledge, we conclude the complaint adequately pleads a state-created danger claim under a then-clearly established theory of liability. We therefore will reverse the District Court's grant of qualified immunity and remand for further proceedings.

I. Background

As this is an appeal from a grant of a motion to dismiss, the factual allegations are taken from the complaint and are accepted as true.[1] *See Bridge v. Phoenix Bond & Indem. Co.,* 553 U.S. 639, 642 n.1, 128 S.Ct. 2131, 170 L.Ed.2d 1012 (2008). David Kedra was a twenty-six-year-old Pennsylvania State Trooper stationed in Montgomery County, Pennsylvania. In September 2014, Kedra was ordered to attend a routine firearm safety training, which included a demonstration of the features and operation of the new model of a State Police-issued handgun. The training was led by then-Corporal Schroeter, a trained firearms instructor who had been a police officer for about twenty years.

Before the training, Schroeter acknowledged in writing a list of firearms safety rules for instructors, including that he must always perform a safety check of a gun before using it for training; that he must implement a second check on whether it is loaded by, e.g., having a second person check the gun; that he must treat all guns as if they are loaded; that he must never point the muzzle of a gun at another person; that he must keep his finger off the trigger, unless he opens the gun to verify it is unloaded before pointing it at a p.433 safe target and pulling the trigger; and that he must open the gun to visually and physically determine that it is unloaded before ever pulling the trigger. At the training itself, however, Schroeter violated each of these rules when, in the course of explaining the "trigger reset" function on an operational handgun, he bypassed all of the safety checks, failed to physically or visually inspect the gun to ensure it was unloaded, raised the gun to chest level, pointed it directly at Kedra, and pulled the trigger. JA 32. The gun, in fact, was loaded, and it fired a bullet into Kedra's abdomen at close range, causing Kedra's death several hours later.

Criminal charges were filed by state authorities, eventually resulting in Schroeter's guilty plea in Pennsylvania state court to five counts of reckless endangerment of another person and his retirement from the State Police. In addition, Kedra's mother, as the representative of her son's estate, filed a one-count civil complaint against Schroeter in the U.S. District Court for the Eastern District of Pennsylvania, claiming a violation of Kedra's substantive due process rights to life and liberty under the Fourteenth Amendment, and making the above-referenced factual allegations, including as to Schroeter's training and experience, his written acknowledgement of the risks and attendant safety protocols, and his guilty plea.

Schroeter moved to dismiss the complaint under Federal Rule of Civil Procedure 12(b)(6), claiming he was entitled to qualified immunity because "[t]he gravamen of

[p]laintiff's [c]omplaint is that ... Schroeter should have known that his firearm posed a substantial risk to those attending his class, not that ... Schroeter actually did know that there was such a risk." Memorandum of Law in Support of Defendant's Motion to Dismiss Complaint at 9-10, *Kedra v. Schroeter,* No. 15-5223 (E.D. Pa. Jan. 6, 2016), ECF No. 5-1. That theory of liability, Schroeter argued, was not then-clearly established and, hence, he was entitled to qualified immunity. Schroeter relied in particular on *Sanford v. Stiles,* 456 F.3d 298, 310 n.13 (3d Cir. 2006) (per curiam), in which we identified as an open question whether "deliberate indifference" — the mental state required for a state-created danger claim like this one — could be demonstrated using an objective test (i.e., merely by pointing to a substantial risk of serious harm that is so obvious that it should have been known), or whether, instead, a plaintiff must show the defendant had actual, subjective knowledge of the risk.

The District Court accepted both Schroeter's premise and conclusion, ruling, first, that Appellant's complaint did not plead deliberate indifference based on actual knowledge because Appellant conceded she "could not and would not plead that [Schroeter] knew there was a bullet in the gun," *Kedra v. Schroeter,* 161 F.Supp.3d 359, 363 (E.D. Pa. 2016), and, second, that in view of *Sanford,* it was not clearly established that deliberate indifference could exist based only on the risk being "so obvious that it should be known," *id.* at 364-65 (quoting *Sanford,* 456 F.3d at 309). The District Court acknowledged Appellant's argument that, by alleging Schroeter had pleaded guilty to reckless endangerment, Appellant had necessarily pleaded actual knowledge because the mens rea for this offense under Pennsylvania law is "conscious disregard of a known risk of death or great bodily injury to another person." *Kedra,* 161 F.Supp.3d at 364 n.5 (quoting *Commonwealth v. Klein,* 795 A.2d 424, 428 (Pa. Super. Ct. 2002)). However, the District Court deemed Schroeter's guilty plea irrelevant on the ground that it would not satisfy the criteria for non-mutual offensive collateral estoppel.[2] p.434 *Id.* Accordingly, the District Court viewed this case as "present[ing] the scenario anticipated but left unresolved by *Sanford:* a state actor proceeding despite a patently obvious risk that the actor should have recognized, but without actual knowledge that the risk existed," and, thus, a theory of deliberate indifference that was not clearly established as required to defeat qualified immunity. *Id.* at 364-66. On that basis, the District Court dismissed the complaint with prejudice,[3] *Kedra,* 161 F.Supp.3d at 365-66, and this timely appeal followed.

II. Jurisdiction and Standard of Review

The District Court had federal question jurisdiction under 28 U.S.C. § 1331, and we have jurisdiction under 28 U.S.C. § 1291. We exercise plenary review over both a District Court's dismissal under Federal Rule of Civil Procedure 12(b)(6) and its grant of qualified immunity. *Morrow v. Balaski,* 719 F.3d 160, 165 (3d Cir. 2013); *McLaughlin v. Watson,* 271 F.3d 566, 570 (3d Cir. 2001). In reviewing an order of dismissal under Federal Rule of Civil Procedure 12(b)(6), we, like the District Court, must "accept as true all factual allegations in the complaint and draw all inferences from the facts alleged in the light most favorable to [the plaintiff]." *Phillips v. Cty. of Allegheny,* 515 F.3d 224, 228, 230 (3d Cir. 2008).

III. Discussion

The doctrine of qualified immunity shields government officials from civil liability for constitutional violations only if "their actions could reasonably have been thought consistent with the rights they are alleged to have violated." *Anderson v. Creighton,* 483 U.S. 635, 638, 107 S.Ct. 3034, 97 L.Ed.2d 523 (1987). In considering whether qualified immunity attaches, courts perform a two-pronged analysis to determine: (1) "whether the facts that [the] plaintiff has alleged ... make out a violation of a constitutional right," and (2) "whether the right at issue was 'clearly established' at the time of [the] defendant's alleged misconduct." *Pearson v. Callahan,* 555 U.S. 223, 232, 129 S.Ct. 808, 172 L.Ed.2d 565 (2009). Here, the District Court disposed of the complaint at the second prong by concluding that because Appellant had not alleged Schroeter's actual knowledge of a bullet in the chamber, her theory of deliberate indifference was based solely on the objective test we had p.435 identified in *Sanford* as unresolved, so that "the violative nature of Defendant's alleged conduct ha[d] not been clearly established." *Kedra,* 161 F.Supp.3d at 364-66.

As a preliminary matter that will inform the scope of our review, we note that by taking this approach, the District Court addressed the "clearly established" inquiry only in part. For the question posed by the District Court — whether it was then-clearly established that obviousness of risk untethered from actual knowledge could prove deliberate indifference — goes to whether the plaintiff sufficiently pleaded the elements of a state-created danger claim, as then defined. *See Phillips,* 515 F.3d at 235, 240-42. In contrast, the clearly established inquiry at the second prong, as we have described it, goes not to whether a plaintiff sufficiently pleaded a constitutional violation (the question answered at the first prong), but to whether the right allegedly violated — defined in terms of the "particularized" factual context of that case, *Anderson,* 483 U.S. at 639-40, 107 S.Ct. 3034 — was a "clearly established statutory or constitutional right[] of which a reasonable [officer] would have known," *Beers-Capitol v. Whetzel,* 256 F.3d 120, 142 n.15 (3d Cir. 2001) (quoting *Harlow v. Fitzgerald,* 457 U.S. 800, 818, 102 S.Ct. 2727, 73 L.Ed.2d 396 (1982)).[4]

Granted, the contours of a given right are necessarily co-extensive with the scope of conduct that violates that right, so that where it would not be clear to "a reasonable official ... that what he is doing violates [a] right," *Anderson,* 483 U.S. at 640, 107 S.Ct. 3034, the second prong of qualified immunity would not be satisfied regardless of whether the lack of clarity arose from an uncertain theory of liability or from the application of a clearly established theory of liability to a set of facts so novel as to deprive an actor of fair notice of the violative nature of his actions. But where a defendant contends that neither the theory of liability nor the right at issue is clearly established, the reviewing court may need to analyze both to determine conclusively whether the defendant is entitled to qualified immunity. *See, e.g., Beers-Capitol,* 256 F.3d at 142 n.15 (observing, on the one hand, that the constitutional right as defined by the factual context of that case was clearly established and, on the other hand, that the "doctrine of deliberate indifference was also clearly established at the relevant time").

Here, the District Court addressed the "clearly established" inquiry only in the first sense, determining that the theory of p.436 liability was not clearly established. Because we conclude this was error, we also address the inquiry in the second sense, assessing whether, under the facts of this case, the specific right at issue was clearly established.[5] Thus, first we will undertake a review of relevant substantive due process principles. *See infra* Section III.A. Second, we will examine whether the complaint sufficiently pleads a violation of Kedra's substantive due process rights under a theory of deliberate indifference that was clearly established. *See infra* Section III.B. And third, we will consider whether the particular right at issue was clearly established at the relevant time, *see infra* Section III.C, i.e., "whether the law, as it existed [at the time of the shooting], gave [Schroeter] 'fair warning' that [his] actions were unconstitutional" in the particular factual scenario he confronted. *Estate of Smith v. Marasco*, 430 F.3d 140, 154 (3d Cir. 2005).

A. Applicable Legal Principles

In asserting her claim under 42 U.S.C. § 1983 for a deprivation of Kedra's rights to life and liberty, Appellant invokes the Due Process Clause, which at its core protects individuals against arbitrary government action. *See Cty. of Sacramento v. Lewis*, 523 U.S. 833, 845-46, 118 S.Ct. 1708, 140 L.Ed.2d 1043 (1998). While "the Due Process Clause does not impose an affirmative obligation on the state to protect its citizens," there is an exception to this general rule that nevertheless holds an officer liable if his conduct exposes an individual to a "state-created danger."[6] *Phillips*, 515 F.3d at 235. Such a claim requires proof of four elements: (1) the harm caused was foreseeable and fairly direct; (2) the state official "acted with a degree of culpability that shocks the conscience"; (3) the state and the plaintiff had a relationship such that "the plaintiff was a foreseeable victim of the defendant's acts"; and (4) the official affirmatively used his authority "in a way that created a danger to the citizen or that rendered the citizen more vulnerable to danger" than had he never acted. *Bright v. Westmoreland Cty.*, 443 F.3d 276, 281 (3d Cir. 2006).

Here, the District Court focused, as do the parties on appeal, on the second element of a state-created danger claim.[7] p.437 *See Kedra*, 161 F.Supp.3d at 363. That is, because "[l]iability for negligently inflicted harm is categorically beneath the threshold of constitutional due process," *Lewis*, 523 U.S. at 849, 118 S.Ct. 1708, government action rises to the level of an actionable constitutional violation only when it is "so egregious, so outrageous, that it may fairly be said to shock the contemporary conscience," *id.* at 847, 118 S.Ct. 1708 n.8. The exact level of culpability required to shock the conscience, however, depends on the circumstances of each case, and the threshold for liability varies with the state actor's opportunity to deliberate before taking action. *Phillips*, 515 F.3d at 240-41; *see also Lewis*, 523 U.S. at 848-54, 118 S.Ct. 1708.

We have identified three potential levels of culpability. In "hyperpressurized environment[s] requiring a snap judgment," an official must actually intend to cause harm in order to be liable. *Vargas v. City of Philadelphia*, 783 F.3d 962, 973 (3d Cir. 2015) (internal quotation marks omitted). In situations in which the state actor is required to act "in a matter of hours or minutes," we require that the state actor "disregard a great risk of serious harm." *Sanford*, 456 F.3d at 310. And where the actor has time to make an "unhurried judgment[]," a plaintiff need only allege facts supporting an inference that the official acted with a mental state of "deliberate indifference." *Id.* at 309.

As the District Court correctly recognized, *see Kedra,* 161 F.Supp.3d at 363, because Appellant here alleged that Schroeter had the opportunity to exercise "unhurried judgment[]," she was required to plead facts in her complaint supporting the inference that Schroeter acted with "deliberate indifference," which we have described variously as a "conscious disregard of a substantial risk of serious harm," *Vargas,* 783 F.3d at 973-74 (brackets and internal quotation marks omitted), or "willful disregard" demonstrated by actions that "evince a willingness to ignore a foreseeable danger or risk," *Morse v. Lower Merion Sch. Dist.,* 132 F.3d 902, 910 (3d Cir. 1997). While categorically different from "intent to cause harm," which is the threshold mental state reserved for officials in "hyperpressurized" situations where "snap judgment[s]" may be required, *Vargas,* 783 F.3d at 973, deliberate indifference "has an elusive quality to it," *Sanford,* 456 F.3d at 301, "fall[ing] somewhere between intent, which 'includes proceeding with knowledge that the harm is substantially certain to occur' and negligence, which involves 'the mere unreasonable risk of harm to another,'" *Morse,* 132 F.3d at 910 n.10.

Here the District Court examined one of the elusive aspects of deliberate indifference with which we and other Courts of Appeals have wrestled over time: whether deliberate indifference in the substantive due process context — as opposed to the Eighth Amendment context — may be satisfied using an objective test or only a subjective "actual knowledge" test. *See Kedra,* 161 F.Supp.3d at 364-65 (citing *Sanford,* 456 F.3d at 309 & n.13). In the Eighth Amendment context, p.438 the Supreme Court has rejected an objective standard for "deliberate indifference," i.e., a standard where liability may be premised on an official's objective "failure to alleviate a significant risk that he should have perceived but did not," *Farmer v. Brennan,* 511 U.S. 825, 838, 114 S.Ct. 1970, 128 L.Ed.2d 811 (1994), and the Court has instead explicitly required a showing of "subjective culpability," *id.* at 843 n.8, 114 S.Ct. 1970, i.e., a showing that "the official kn[ew] of and disregard[ed] an excessive risk," *id.* at 837, 114 S.Ct. 1970. But uncertainty about whether this "subjective culpability" requirement carried over to pretrial detainees and other plaintiffs asserting substantive due process claims produced a split among the Courts of Appeals.[8] That split led us in *Sanford* to note, in the substantive due process context, "the possibility that deliberate indifference might exist without actual knowledge of a risk of harm when the risk is so obvious that it should be known," 456 F.3d at 309, and to acknowledge shortly thereafter that we "ha[d] not yet definitively answered the question of whether the appropriate standard in a non-Eighth Amendment substantive due process case is subjective or objective," *Kaucher v. Cty. of Bucks,* 455 F.3d 418, 430-31 (3d Cir. 2006).

More recently, both the Supreme Court and this Court have spoken to the issue. In *Kingsley v. Hendrickson,* ___ U.S. ___, 135 S.Ct. 2466, 192 L.Ed.2d 416 (2015), distinguishing between the different language of the Eighth Amendment and the Due Process Clause and the different nature of those claims, the Supreme Court held that a pretrial detainee claiming a substantive due process violation based on excessive force "must show ... only that the officers' use of that force was *objectively* unreasonable" and not "that the officers were *subjectively* aware that their use of force was unreasonable." *Id.* at 2470, 2475. While the Court acknowledged that "the defendant must possess a purposeful, a knowing, or possibly a reckless state of mind" because "liability for negligently inflicted harm is categorically beneath the threshold of constitutional due process," it clarified that this subjective requirement pertained only to "the defendant's state of mind with respect to his physical acts" — in other words, his actions themselves needed to be deliberate and not "accidental[]" or "negligent[]" — but did not pertain to whether the actions the defendant deliberately took were "unreasonable" or "excessive in relation to [a legitimate] purpose." *Id.* at 2472-73 (emphasis omitted). Rejecting the arguments that an objective test would devolve into a negligence standard, *id.* at 2474, was not "workable," *id.,* or would lead to a "flood of claims," *id.* at 2476, the Court held that "the defendant's state of mind with respect to the proper *interpretation*" of his physical acts should be assessed by an "objective standard," depending on "the perspective of a reasonable officer on the scene."[9] *Id.* at 2472-73.

p.439 Consistent with this approach, we too recently embraced an objective standard in the context of a substantive due process claim — in particular, for a claim of state-created danger. In *L.R. v. School District of Philadelphia,* we denied qualified immunity to a teacher who released a kindergartener to a stranger who then abused the child. 836 F.3d 235 (3d Cir. 2016). After reiterating our observation in *Sanford* that "deliberate indifference might exist without actual knowledge of a risk of harm when the risk is so obvious that it should be known," *id.* at 246, we held this standard was met by the allegations in that complaint. Specifically, we held the risk of harm from the teacher's conduct was "'so obvious' as to rise to the level of deliberate indifference," *id.,* and that L.R. had sufficiently pleaded as "a matter of common sense" that the teacher "knew, *or should have known,* about the risk of his actions," *id.* at 245 (emphasis added). Although we indicated that the plaintiff's allegations also satisfied the subjective standard, *id.* at 246 ("What is more,... the fact that [the teacher] asked [the stranger] for her identification illustrates that [the teacher] himself was indeed aware of the risk of harm[.]"), we concluded that "[e]xposing a young child to an obvious danger is the quintessential example of when qualified immunity should not shield a public official from suit," *id.* at 250.[10]

p.440 Seeking to benefit from the trajectory of this case law,[11] Appellant would have us rely on *L.R.* to conclude an objective standard of deliberate indifference was clearly established at the time Schroeter shot Kedra and to reverse the District Court on that basis. We reject that invitation, however, because we assess qualified immunity based on the law that was "clearly established at the time an action occurred," *Harlow,* 457 U.S. at 818, 102 S.Ct. 2727, while *L.R.* was not decided until nearly two years after the action at issue in this case. That is, regardless of what may be deemed "clearly established" in the wake of *Kingsley* and *L.R.,* we must look to the state of the law at the time of shooting. And at that point, as the District Court correctly recognized, it was not yet clearly established whether deliberate indifference in the substantive due process context was governed by an objective or subjective standard. *See Kedra,* 161 F.Supp.3d at 364-65 (citing *Sanford,* 456 F.3d at 309 & n.13). The question to which we therefore turn is whether Appellant pleaded deliberate indifference under the subjective test, which was then-clearly established, or under an objective test, which then was not.

B. Whether Appellant Pleaded Her Claim Under A Clearly Established Theory of Deliberate Indifference

Given the historical ambiguity in our case law, we agree with the District Court that Schroeter's arguments might have traction if Appellant had pleaded deliberate indifference based merely on what Schroeter *should have known* in view of the obviousness of a particular risk. But there's the rub: That is not what Appellant pleaded. Contrary to the way that Schroeter and the District Court characterize it, the complaint here clearly and unmistakably alleges facts that support an inference of actual, subjective knowledge of a substantial risk of lethal harm, and neither the Supreme Court nor we have wavered from the well-established principle that a plaintiff may plead and prove deliberate indifference in the substantive due process context using this subjective test.

In the discussion to follow, we first address whether the complaint pleads deliberate indifference under the clearly established subjective test and then turn to the District Court's misunderstanding of that test in requiring Appellant to plead knowledge of the certainty of harm instead of knowledge of the substantial risk of harm.

1. Application of the Deliberate Indifference Standard

At the pleading stage, courts must "accept all factual allegations as true, construe the complaint in the light most favorable to the plaintiff, and determine whether, under any reasonable reading of the complaint, the plaintiff may be entitled p.441 to relief." *Phillips,* 515 F.3d at 233. Although "[f]actual allegations must be enough to raise a right to relief above the speculative level," *Bell Atl. Corp. v. Twombly,* 550 U.S. 544, 555, 127 S.Ct. 1955, 167 L.Ed.2d 929 (2007), we demand "only enough facts to state a claim to relief that is plausible on its face" and "do not require heightened fact pleading of specifics," *id.* at 570, 127 S.Ct. 1955. Determining whether the facts pleaded have "nudged" the claim "across the line from conceivable to plausible" is "a context-specific task that requires the reviewing court to draw on its judicial experience and common sense." *Ashcroft v. Iqbal,* 556 U.S. 662, 679-80, 129 S.Ct. 1937, 173 L.Ed.2d 868 (2009).

To make this assessment on a Rule 12(b)(6) motion, "courts must consider the complaint in its entirety," *Tellabs, Inc. v. Makor Issues & Rights, Ltd.,* 551 U.S. 308, 322, 127 S.Ct. 2499, 168 L.Ed.2d 179 (2007), and "determine whether the complaint as a whole contains sufficient factual matter to state a facially plausible claim," *Argueta v. U.S. Immig. & Customs Enf't,* 643 F.3d 60, 74 (3d Cir. 2011). "The inquiry, as several Courts of Appeals have recognized, is whether *all* of the facts alleged, taken collectively, give rise to a strong inference of scienter, not whether any individual allegation, scrutinized in isolation, meets that standard." *Tellabs,* 551 U.S. at 322-23, 127 S.Ct. 2499.

Here, then, the relevant question is whether the complaint, considering all the allegations, pleads sufficient facts to support the inference that when Schroeter pointed his gun at Kedra at close range and deliberately pulled the trigger without even once checking whether the gun was loaded, he acted with subjective deliberate indifference, i.e., actual awareness of a substantial risk of serious harm, lying "somewhere between intent ... and negligence." *Morse,* 132 F.3d at 910 n.10. A plaintiff can plead deliberate indifference by reference to circumstantial and direct evidence. *See Farmer,* 511 U.S. at 842, 114 S.Ct. 1970. Three broad categories of circumstantial evidence are alleged in the complaint, and we have deemed each probative of deliberate indifference in the past: (1) evidence that the risk was obvious or a matter of common sense, (2) evidence that the actor had particular professional training or expertise, and (3) evidence that the actor was expressly advised of the risk of harm and the procedures designed to prevent that harm and proceeded to violate those procedures.

First, the complaint points to the obvious risk of harm in pointing the muzzle of a gun at another person and pulling the trigger, while skipping any kind of safety check. Perhaps because it concluded that Appellant pleaded deliberate indifference by relying on only the objective obviousness of risk, the District Court did not acknowledge or discuss the relevance of obviousness of risk to proving actual knowledge of risk. *See Kedra,* 161 F.Supp.3d at 362-66. But the Supreme Court has long recognized that, even under a subjective test, "the fact that the risk of harm is obvious" is relevant, among other pieces of evidence, to "infer the existence of this subjective state of mind." *Hope v. Pelzer,* 536 U.S. 730, 738, 122 S.Ct. 2508, 153 L.Ed.2d 666 (2002). We, too, have observed that "subjective knowledge on the part of the official can be proved by circumstantial evidence to the effect that the excessive risk was so obvious that the official must have known of the risk."[12] *Beers-Capitol,* 256 F.3d at 133.

p.442 For that reason, we have regularly relied on the obviousness of risk as a permissible and highly relevant basis from which to infer actual knowledge — even directing in our Model Civil Jury Instructions that, in assessing deliberate indifference for state-created danger claims, a jury is "entitled to infer from the obviousness of the risk that [the state actor] knew of the risk." Third Circuit Model Civil Jury Instructions § 4.14 (Mar. 2017). In *Kneipp v. Tedder,* for example, police officers sent a woman home "unescorted in a visibly intoxicated state in cold weather," and we reversed a grant of summary judgment in their favor, citing the foreseeable and obvious risk that the woman would later fall down an embankment and suffer hypothermia. 95 F.3d 1199, 1201-03, 1208-09, 1211 (3d Cir. 1996). In *Phillips v. County of Allegheny,* 911 dispatchers gave confidential information to a distressed and suspended co-worker concerning the whereabouts of his ex-girlfriend, and we likewise reversed the dismissal of a complaint against the dispatchers because they were "aware that [the co-worker] was distraught over his break up" and they could reasonably foresee that some type of serious harm could result from giving him the information; hence, the inferences to be drawn from "ordinary common sense" supported the dispatchers' knowledge of risk. 515 F.3d at 228-29, 241, 246. So too here: The risk of lethal harm when a firearms instructor skips over each of several safety checks designed to ascertain if the gun is unloaded, points the gun at a trainee's chest, and pulls the trigger is glaringly obvious, and this obviousness supports the inference that the instructor had actual knowledge of the risk of serious harm.

Second, the complaint alleges that Schroeter was a specially trained firearms instructor with twenty years of experience. And that training and experience is no less relevant to Schroeter's actual knowledge of the substantial risk of harm here than the "medical training" of which we took note for the emergency medical technicians in *Rivas v. City of Passaic,* 365 F.3d 181, 185, 194-95 (3d Cir. 2004), or the "experience as a teacher in charge of a kindergarten classroom" that we deemed relevant to the teacher's knowledge of risk in releasing the child to a stranger in *L.R.,* 836 F.3d at 245;[13] *see also MBIA Ins. Corp. v. Royal Indem. Co.,* 426 F.3d 204, 217 (3d Cir. 2005) (observing that, even where a risk is "so obvious," an individual's prior "experience and knowledge" makes it more likely that he will "realize[]" that risk). Thus, even if, hypothetically, the obviousness of the risk here would not be sufficient to impute actual knowledge to a layperson, the combination of obviousness with Schroeter's specialized training and expertise in firearms safety is easily sufficient to give rise to an inference of actual knowledge of risk.

p.443 *Third,* the complaint alleges that Schroeter was expressly advised of the lethal risk in handling any operational firearm through the safety rules that he acknowledged in writing and that, as a training instructor, he himself was responsible for teaching to others. Those safety protocols were clear and detailed, requiring that an instructor, prior to demonstrating the use of a firearm, (a) conduct a safety check to ensure the gun was not loaded, (b) implement a second safety check by, e.g., having a second person independently verify the gun is not loaded, (c) always treat the firearm as if it were loaded, (c) point the muzzle only at a safe target, (d) never point the firearm at another person, (e) always keep his finger off the trigger unless firing at a safe target, and (f) before demonstrating a "trigger pull," open the gun to visually and physically confirm it is unloaded. JA 31. The complaint alleges that Schroeter not only ignored these directives but directly contravened each and every one of them. Those allegations — which could be characterized as not merely circumstantial, but even direct, evidence of mens rea — give rise to at least as strong an inference of knowledge of risk as the kindergarten teacher's knowledge and disregard of school policy concerning the release of children in *L.R.,* 836 F.3d at 240 & n.2, 245, and the 911 dispatchers' "unauthorized" disclosure of what they knew constituted "confidential information" in *Phillips,* 515 F.3d at 229, 241.

In addition to these three categories of evidence that support an inference of actual knowledge, the complaint also alleges direct evidence of Schroeter's mental state in the form of his criminal plea to reckless endangerment. That guilty plea required Schroeter, as a matter of Pennsylvania law, to admit that he "recklessly engage[d] in conduct which place[d]... another person in danger of death or serious bodily injury," 18 Pa. Cons. Stat. § 2705, with the mental state of "conscious[] disregard[] [of] a substantial and unjustifiable risk" of serious harm, 18 Pa. Cons. Stat. § 302(b)(3); *see also Klein,* 795 A.2d at 427-28. In other words, even assuming Appellant could not invoke "non-mutual offensive collateral estoppel" to seek a judgment based in part on issue preclusion — which was the ground on which the District Court disregarded the plea,[14] *Kedra,* 161 F.Supp.3d at 364 n.5 — the allegation in the complaint that Schroeter pleaded guilty to these charges reflects a statement by a party-opponent, presumptively admissible at trial, *see* Fed. R. Evid. 801(d)(2), that Schroeter acted with the requisite knowledge of risk.

In sum, this is not a case where Appellant's theory of deliberate indifference devolves to mere negligence or is based only on what Schroeter objectively should have known given the obvious risk. Instead, the obviousness of the risk in p.444 pointing a gun at a defenseless person and pulling the trigger without undertaking any safety check whatsoever only reinforces the many other allegations of the complaint reflecting Schroeter's "conscious disregard of a substantial risk of serious harm." *Vargas,* 783 F.3d at 973 (brackets and internal quotation marks omitted). "[D]raw[ing] all inferences from the facts alleged in the light most favorable to [Appellant]," *Phillips,* 515 F.3d at 228, the allegations in Appellant's complaint are more than sufficient to state a claim for a state-created danger based on actual knowledge of a substantial risk of serious harm — the subjective theory of deliberate indifference that was then-clearly established. *See Sanford,* 456 F.3d at 309-10 & n.13.

2. The District Court's Misapprehension of the Culpability Required for Deliberate Indifference

The District Court reached the opposite conclusion, relying on the premise that Schroeter's conduct could not reflect a "conscious disregard of a substantial risk of serious harm," *Vargas,* 783 F.3d at 973-74 (brackets and internal quotation marks omitted), unless Schroeter actually knew there was a bullet in the chamber, *see Kedra,* 161 F.Supp.3d at 363-66. That approach, however, fundamentally misapprehends (1) the relevance of circumstantial evidence to inferring actual knowledge, (2) the pleading standard applicable at this stage of the case, (3) the culpability required for cases involving "unhurried judgment[]," *Vargas,* 783 F.3d at 973, and (4) the essential purposes of the state-created danger doctrine.

First, by requiring Appellant to plead Schroeter's knowledge of a bullet in the chamber, the District Court in effect required plaintiffs to plead actual knowledge using only direct evidence. But the Supreme Court has instructed that "[w]hether a [state actor] ha[s] the requisite knowledge of a substantial risk is a question of fact subject to demonstration in the usual ways, including inference from circumstantial evidence, and a factfinder may conclude that a prison official knew of a substantial risk from the very fact that the risk was obvious," *Farmer,* 511 U.S. at 842, 114 S.Ct. 1970 (citation omitted); *see also Hope,* 536 U.S. at 738, 122 S.Ct. 2508, and we have likewise stated that "[i]nferring mental state from circumstantial evidence is among the chief tasks of factfinders," *United States v. Wright,* 665 F.3d 560, 569 (3d Cir. 2012); *see also McFadden v. United States,* ___ U.S. ___, 135 S.Ct. 2298, 2304 n.1, 192 L.Ed.2d 260 (2015) ("The Courts of Appeals have held that, as with most *mens rea* requirements, the Government can prove the requisite mental state through either direct evidence or circumstantial evidence.").

Second, in concluding that the allegations of the complaint (other than Schroeter's criminal guilty plea) do not give rise to an inference of actual knowledge of risk, the District Court and our concurring colleague have done the inverse of what we are required to do at the pleading stage: Instead of considering the complaint as a whole, they consider "whether any individual allegation, scrutinized in isolation, meets that standard," *Tellabs,* 551 U.S. at 322-23, 127 S.Ct. 2499, and instead of "draw[ing] all inferences from the facts alleged in the light most favorable to [the plaintiff]," *Phillips,* 515 F.3d at 228, they draw all inferences in the light most favorable to the defendant. For example, while acknowledging that obviousness of risk can support an inference of actual knowledge, the Concurrence posits that obviousness of risk "could also ... support an inference that there was not deliberate indifference." Concurrence at 456. While not disputing p.445 that Schroeter's training and experience are relevant to assessing Schroeter's state of mind, the Concurrence hypothesizes that they make it less plausible, not more plausible, that Schroeter was aware that his conduct carried a substantial risk of lethal harm.[15] And while granting that Schroeter acknowledged in writing the safety protocols he failed to follow, the Concurrence rejects the unavoidable inference that Schroeter therefore knew the risk of harm those protocols were intended to prevent and instead speculates that Schroeter possibly "d[id] not ... remember[]" his training and did not know that "he failed to follow" the rules. Concurrence at 456-57. Only by drawing each inference in favor of the defendant can the District Court and Concurrence conclude that Schroeter was not "aware ... that pulling the trigger carried a deadly risk," *Kedra,* 161 F.Supp.3d at 363-64, or that it is no more than "possibl[e]" or "conceivable" that he knew the gun "might be loaded" when he fired it. Concurrence at 456 (alteration in original).

Although, at trial, Schroeter might offer evidence that he affirmatively believed the gun was unloaded and had some reasonable basis for such a belief, we may not prevent the case from ever reaching trial by positing other possible inferences and "den[ying]" the plaintiff "the inferences to which her complaint is entitled," *Phillips,* 515 F.3d at 237. Instead, we need only ask whether it is "plausible" — given the obviousness of the risk — to believe a trained firearms instructor with twenty years' experience knows that any unchecked gun might be loaded and therefore cannot be fired at another person without substantial risk of serious harm.[16] To state the question p.446 is, as a matter of "common sense," *Iqbal,* 556 U.S. at 679, 129 S.Ct. 1937, to answer it: Appellant's allegations are more than enough to "nudge[]" her claim "across the line from conceivable to plausible." *Twombly,* 556 U.S. at 570, 129 S.Ct. 1849.

Third, by requiring Appellant to plead that Schroeter had actual knowledge of a bullet in the chamber, the District Court imposed a novel and heightened culpability standard on a plaintiff pleading deliberate indifference, elevating knowledge of a "substantial risk" of harm to knowledge of a certainty of harm, confusing the "conscious disregard" standard that applies where an officer can exercise "unhurried judgment" with the far higher standard of "intent to harm" that applies when an officer a state actor must act in a "hyperpressurized environment requiring a snap judgment," *Vargas,* 783 F.3d at 973-74 (brackets and internal quotation marks omitted), and, at bottom, requiring a plaintiff to plead criminal (and here, homicidal) intent to overcome qualified immunity.[17]

"Intent to harm," however, far exceeds what is required to plead deliberate indifference. *Vargas,* 783 F.3d at 973-74. In discussing deliberate indifference in the Eighth Amendment context, the Supreme Court has emphasized that a claimant "need not show that a prison official acted or failed to act believing that harm actually would befall an inmate; it is enough that the official acted or failed to act despite his knowledge of a substantial risk of serious harm." *Farmer,* 511 U.S. at 842, 114 S.Ct. 1970. We too have made this distinction clear in the Fourteenth Amendment context, describing "deliberate indifference" as a "willingness to ignore a foreseeable danger or risk," *Morse,* 132 F.3d at 910, and observing that conscience-shocking behavior for "unhurried" situations, *Vargas,* 783 F.3d at 973, requires "proof of something less than knowledge that the harm was practically certain ... [to] occur," *Ziccardi v. City of Philadelphia,* 288 F.3d 57, 66 (3d Cir. 2002).

The cases in which we have applied this standard also illustrate that the subjective knowledge test requires knowledge p.447 only of the substantial *risk* of serious harm, not of the certainty of that harm. For instance, in *Kneipp,* we held that the plaintiffs could show the defending police officers' mental state of "willful disregard" based on the foreseeable risk that serious harm was likely to befall an unescorted woman whom they had left "in a visibly intoxicated state in cold weather"; we did not require the plaintiffs to allege that the police officers knew with certainty that the woman would fall down an embankment and suffer hypothermia. 95 F.3d at 1208-09. In *Phillips,* we held that the plaintiff adequately alleged deliberate indifference because the complaint had "allege[d] facts [showing] that the defendants ... foresaw the danger of harm their actions presented," even if the complaint did not allege that the defendants knew with certainty that their former co-worker would find and kill his ex-girlfriend, her sister, and her then-boyfriend. 515 F.3d at 228-29, 240-41. And more recently in *L.R.,* we denied qualified immunity to the teacher who released a kindergartener into the custody of a stranger, observing that the teacher was "aware of the risk of harm in releasing [the child] to a stranger, even if he was unaware of [the perpetrator's] specific criminal intent." 836 F.3d at 246.

As these cases make clear, all that is required to satisfy deliberate indifference is "conscious disregard of a substantial risk of serious harm," *Vargas,* 783 F.3d at 973-74 (brackets and internal quotation marks omitted), regardless of whether that harm is either intended or certain to occur, *see Lewis,* 523 U.S. at 852 n.11, 118 S.Ct. 1708; *L.R.,* 836 F.3d at 246; *Phillips,* 515 F.3d at 241; *Kneipp,* 95 F.3d at 1208-09. That is the standard applicable where, as here, an official has time to make "unhurried judgments," *Vargas,* 783 F.3d at 973, and Appellant's factual allegations are more than sufficient to satisfy that standard. *See supra* Section III.B.1. What is *not* required is knowledge of certainty of harm or the intent to harm — the standard expressly adopted by the District Court. *See Kedra,* 161 F.Supp.3d at 363-66.

Lastly, the District Court's approach to deliberate indifference is inconsistent not only with the applicable pleading and culpability standards, but also with the purposes of the state-created danger doctrine. Although the District Court found that Schroeter could not be held liable for deliberate indifference without an allegation of intent to harm, *see Kedra,* 161 F.Supp.3d at 363-66, this approach is mistaken, for requiring criminal or even homicidal intent for liability under the state-created danger doctrine disregards the twin goals of compensation and deterrence underlying the doctrine and, more broadly, ignores the statutory goals that Congress codified in 42 U.S.C. § 1983.

The state-created danger doctrine — rooted in the Fourteenth Amendment's guarantee of due process, which is "designed to ... secure certain individual rights against both State and Federal Government," *Daniels v. Williams,* 474 U.S. 327, 332, 106 S.Ct. 662, 88 L.Ed.2d 662 (1986) — exists to provide plaintiffs with recompense when a state official, who is entrusted with particular responsibilities and duties with respect to a particular person or "class of persons," *Bright,* 443 F.3d at 281 (discussing *DeShaney v. Winnebago Cty. Dep't of Soc. Servs.,* 489 U.S. 189, 201, 109 S.Ct. 998, 103 L.Ed.2d 249 (1989)), acts with at least "conscious disregard of a substantial risk of serious harm," *Vargas,* 783 F.3d at 973-74 (brackets and internal quotation marks omitted), and affirmatively uses his authority "in a way that create[s] a danger to [a] citizen or that render[s] the citizen more vulnerable to danger" than had he not acted at all, *Bright,* 443 F.3d at 281. Because the state-created p.448 danger doctrine applies only where these particular special relationships exist, the victims of the state officials' acts will always be persons who either expected the officials not to injure them or justifiably relied on the officials to protect them from threats to their safety. *See, e.g., L.R.,* 836 F.3d at 239-40, 247; *Phillips,* 515 F.3d at 228-29, 242-43; *Kneipp,* 95 F.3d at 1201-05, 1209 (citing *DeShaney,* 489 U.S. at 199-200, 109 S.Ct. 998). Where such officials in unhurried situations consciously disregard the risk of harm to persons relying on them for safety, even if the officials did not know with certainty that their actions would lead to serious or lethal harm, the victims — or at least their survivors — are entitled to recompense.

What's more, remedies under § 1983, as applied to state-created danger cases, not only seek to "provide relief to victims," but also serve the additional "purpose ... [of] deter[ring] state actors from using the badge of their authority to deprive individuals of their federally guaranteed rights." *Squires v. Bonser,* 54 F.3d 168, 172 (3d Cir. 1995) (quoting *Wyatt v. Cole,* 504 U.S. 158, 161, 112 S.Ct. 1827, 118 L.Ed.2d 504 (1992)). When officers know that they may be held liable under § 1983 for conscience-shocking behavior that endangers persons relying on them, *see Bright,* 443 F.3d at 281, the threat of § 1983 state-created danger suits acts as a deterrent force against individual officers acting with "conscious disregard of a substantial risk of serious harm," *Vargas,* 783 F.3d at 973-74 (brackets and internal quotation marks omitted). This "important public purpose" also helps "protect[] the rights of the public at large," *Livingstone v. N. Belle Vernon Borough,* 91 F.3d 515, 535 (3d Cir. 1996), because, to the extent that municipalities may be held liable for their officers' conduct, *see Monell v. Dep't of Soc. Servs.,* 436 U.S. 658, 694, 98 S.Ct. 2018, 56 L.Ed.2d 611 (1978), and to the extent non-municipal governmental entities are obliged to indemnify officers held liable under § 1983, *see generally, e.g.,* N.J. Stat. Ann. § 59:10A-1, state-created danger suits encourage these entities to implement and provide training on policies that deter such conscience-shocking conduct, *cf. Monell,* 436 U.S. at 694-95, 98 S.Ct. 2018.

In sum, because the allegations in Appellant's complaint collectively give rise to the inference that Schroeter acted with actual knowledge of a substantial risk of lethal harm — that is, knowledge that gives rise to "a degree of culpability that shocks the conscience" under the then-clearly established actual knowledge theory of deliberate indifference, *Bright,* 443 F.3d at 281; *see Farmer,* 511 U.S. at 837-38, 843 n.8, 114 S.Ct. 1970; *Sanford,* 456 F.3d at 309-10 & n.13 — Appellant has adequately pleaded her state-created danger claim.[18]

C. Whether the Right at Issue Was Clearly Established

Having concluded that the facts, as alleged, plead the elements of a substantive due process violation under a clearly established theory of liability, we must still contend with Schroeter's argument that p.449 there was no precedent sufficiently "*factually similar to the plaintiff's allegations*[] to put [him] on notice that his ... conduct [was] constitutionally prohibited." Appellee's Br. 26 (quoting *Mammaro v. N.J. Div. of Child Prot. & Permanency,* 814 F.3d 164, 169 (3d Cir. 2016)). This targets the second prong of the qualified immunity analysis from a different angle and requires us to ask "the objective (albeit fact-specific) question whether a reasonable officer could have believed [Schroeter's conduct] to be lawful, in light of clearly established law and the information [he] possessed." *Anderson,* 483 U.S. at 641, 107 S.Ct. 3034; *see also Beers-Capitol,* 256 F.3d at 142 n.15.

Because the District Court here concluded Appellant's theory of deliberate indifference was not clearly established law, it did not proceed to define the specific right at issue or to address whether that right was itself clearly established at the relevant time. *See Kedra,* 161 F.Supp.3d at 365. However, "[d]efining the right at issue is critical to this inquiry." *L.R.,* 836 F.3d at 248. We must frame the right at issue "in light of the specific context of the case, not as a broad general proposition," *Mullenix v. Luna,* ___ U.S. ___, 136 S.Ct. 305, 308, 193 L.Ed.2d 255 (2015) (per curiam), and so while "[i]ndividuals indeed have a broad substantive due process right to be free from 'unjustified intrusions on personal security,'" *L.R.,* 836 F.3d at 248-49, that defines the right at issue at too high a level of generality.

Here, in view of the allegations of the complaint, we define what is at issue as an individual's right not to be subjected, defenseless, to a police officer's demonstration of the use of deadly force in a manner contrary to all applicable safety protocols.[19] We then must determine whether the contours of that right are sufficiently clear that "a reasonable officer would understand p.450 that what he is doing violates that right." *Rivas,* 365 F.3d at 200. We typically look to Supreme Court precedent or a consensus in the Courts of Appeals to give an officer fair warning that his conduct would be unconstitutional. *Mammaro,* 814 F.3d at 169. However, it need not be the case that the exact conduct has previously been held unlawful so long as the "contours of the right" are sufficiently clear, *Anderson,* 483 U.S. at 640, 107 S.Ct. 3034, such that a "general constitutional rule already identified in the decisional law" applies with "obvious clarity," *Hope,* 536 U.S. at 741, 122 S.Ct. 2508. "If the unlawfulness of the defendant's conduct would have been apparent to a reasonable official based on the current state of the law, it is not necessary that there be binding precedent from this circuit so advising." *Brown v. Muhlenberg Twp.,* 269 F.3d 205, 211 n.4 (3d Cir. 2001). "[O]fficials can still be on notice that their conduct violates established law even in novel factual circumstances," because the relevant question is whether the state of the law at the time of the events gave the officer "fair warning." *Hope,* 536 U.S. at 741, 122 S.Ct. 2508.

We are persuaded that Schroeter had such fair warning at the time of the shooting. This was not merely an accidental discharge of a firearm that happened to be "point[ed] ... at another officer" at the time. Concurrence at 452. Instead, at a training Kedra was required to attend, he was subjected to his training instructor contravening each and every firearm safety protocol by skipping over both required safety checks, treating the firearm as if it were unloaded, pointing the firearm directly at Kedra, and pulling the trigger.

Our case law made it clear at that time that state actors may be liable for affirmatively exposing a plaintiff to a deadly risk of harm through "highly dangerous ... conduct," *Morse,* 132 F.3d at 910 n.10, or through "us[ing] their authority as police officers to create a dangerous situation or to make [the victim] more vulnerable to danger had they not intervened," *Kneipp,* 95 F.3d at 1209, and that officials are expected to use the benefit of their expertise and professional training when confronted with situations in which they are responsible for preventing harm to other individuals, *see Rivas,* 365 F.3d at 194-95. Under that case law, no reasonable officer who was aware of the lethal risk involved in demonstrating the use of deadly force on another person and who proceeded to conduct the demonstration in a manner directly contrary to known safety protocols could think his conduct was lawful. On the contrary, as we observed in *Beers-Capitol,* "a reasonable [state actor] could not believe that h[is] actions comported with clearly established law while also believing that there is an excessive risk to the plaintiff[] and failing to adequately respond to that risk." 256 F.3d at 142 n.15.

In addition to our own case law and that of the Supreme Court, "we routinely consider decisions by other Courts of Appeals as part of our 'clearly established' analysis when we have not yet addressed the specific right asserted by the plaintiff." *Williams v. Bitner,* 455 F.3d 186, 192-93 (3d Cir. 2006) (collecting cases). A closely analogous case from the First Circuit confirms that a reasonable officer would anticipate liability for this conduct. In *Marrero-Rodríguez v. Municipality of San Juan,* that court considered the actions of a police lieutenant who violated numerous safety protocols while engaging in a training session. 677 F.3d 497, 500 (1st Cir. 2012). In participating in the live demonstration exercise there, the officer failed to discharge the bullets from his gun into a sandbox as required when entering the training area, used a real gun p.451 rather than the required "dummy" gun, and shot the gun directly into the back of a trainee — who was not wearing a bulletproof vest — while the trainee was lying face-down on the ground. *Id.* Just as here, there was no allegation that the officer knew his gun was loaded or that he intended to harm his fellow officer. The court nonetheless concluded that "using what was obviously lethal force, entirely disproportionate to any reasonable need, in conducting the lesson" was "shockingly indifferent to the rights" of the trainee.[20] *Id.* at 501-02; *cf. Hawkins v. Holloway,* 316 F.3d 777, 787 (8th Cir. 2003) (holding that "an official's threat to employ deadly force" with a firearm rose to the level of "arbitrary and conscience shocking behavior prohibited by substantive due process"); *Grandstaff v. City of Borger,* 767 F.2d 161, 167-68 (5th Cir. 1985) (holding it was clearly established that the use of "deadly force, in *conscious disregard* of substantial risk of harm to innocent parties" was a constitutional due process violation).[21]

Schroeter, however, relies on *Spady v. Bethlehem Area School District* to argue that the right here should be defined more narrowly and that this right was not clearly established at the time. 800 F.3d 633 (3d Cir. 2015). In *Spady,* a student was briefly submerged in water during a swimming class, exited the pool and complained of some chest pain, returned to the pool as directed for the remainder of the class, and more than an hour later suffered serious distress and death from a rare condition known as "dry drowning." *Id.* at 635-36. In the face of this extremely unusual and "non-apparent condition," we defined the right there as "the right to affirmative intervention by the state actor to minimize the risk of secondary or dry drowning," and held that risk would not have been apparent to a reasonable gym teacher under our state-created danger cases. *Id.* at 638-42. Drawing on that analysis, Schroeter contends that the harm that came to Kedra was also due to a "non-apparent" condition, *id.* at 639, such that the right should be defined as a "right ... in favor of a trainee in a state office which ... requires affirmative compliance with all required safety procedures so as to ... 'minimize the risk' to the trainees during a training session." Oral Arg. at 25:45-27:38 (quoting *Spady,* 800 F.3d at 638).

This argument mischaracterizes the risk of harm presented on the face of Appellant's complaint and misstates our case law. There is nothing "non-apparent,"

Spady, 800 F.3d at 639, in the risk of harm caused by pointing a firearm at an unarmed
p.452 person and pulling the trigger at close range. Quite the opposite: The substantial
risk of lethal harm is glaringly obvious here and bears no resemblance to the obscure
and improbable risk of dry drowning, which we concluded the coach in *Spady* could
not have been reasonably expected to know about or protect against. Indeed, we
expressly distinguished the facts of *Spady* from those of *Kneipp,* pointing out that in
Kneipp, the officers' "act of separating a visibly intoxicated person from her traveling
companion and then forcing her to walk home alone ... necessarily increased the
obvious risk that she would fall and injure herself." *Spady,* 800 F.3d at 639. And at
issue here is not a training instructor's failure to "compl[y] with all required safety
procedures" to minimize the risk to trainees, Oral Arg. at 26:00-26:06; it is a training
instructor's physical demonstration of the use of deadly force on a defenseless subject
while failing to comply with *any* required safety procedure to avoid the risk of death.
Spady is simply inapposite where, as here, the risk was obvious, the risk was actually
known to the state actor, the safety precautions that could have avoided that risk
were the very subject matter of the actor's training and expertise, and those safety
precautions were skipped or directly contravened.

In sum, the right alleged to have been violated was clearly established, and
Appellant's complaint sufficiently pleads a violation of that right. Accordingly,
Schroeter was not entitled to qualified immunity.

IV. Conclusion

For the foregoing reasons, we will reverse and remand for proceedings consistent
with this opinion.

FISHER, Circuit Judge, concurring.

It is undeniable that this tragic death never should have occurred and it is
indisputable that defendant Schroeter should have known better than to point a gun
at another officer without following proper safety precautions. So at first glance, it is
difficult to find fault with the majority's compelling discussion of why Schroeter's
conduct shocks the conscience. Nonetheless, I file this concurrence to explain my
belief that the District Court's judgment should be reversed on narrower grounds
than those on which the majority relies.

I.

"Qualified immunity shields government officials from civil damages liability
unless the official violated a statutory or constitutional right that was clearly
established at the time of the challenged conduct." *Reichle v. Howards,* 566 U.S. 658,
132 S.Ct. 2088, 2093, 182 L.Ed.2d 985 (2012). It involves a two-step process, which
a court may address in either order. *Pearson v. Callahan,* 555 U.S. 223, 236, 129 S.Ct.
808, 172 L.Ed.2d 565 (2009). The first step "asks whether the facts, taken in the light
most favorable to the party asserting the injury, show the officer's conduct violated
a federal right." *Tolan v. Cotton,* ___ U.S. ___, 134 S.Ct. 1861, 1865, 188 L.Ed.2d 895

(2014) (per curiam) (internal quotation marks and alterations omitted). The second step "asks whether the right in question was clearly established at the time of the violation." *Id.* at 1866 (internal quotation marks omitted).

The District Court granted Schroeter qualified immunity under the second prong, concluding that it was not clearly established that he could violate a constitutional right without actual knowledge that his actions posed a substantial risk of harm. The majority reverses, concluding that (1) Kedra has pleaded that Schroeter acted with actual knowledge that his actions posed a substantial risk of harm, and p.453 (2) the right at issue here was clearly established.

The Supreme Court recently noted that it "has issued a number of opinions reversing federal courts in qualified immunity cases" over "the last five years." *White v. Pauly,* ___ U.S. ___, 137 S.Ct. 548, 551, 196 L.Ed.2d 463 (2017) (per curiam). It has expressed "reluctan[ce] to expand the concept of substantive due process because guideposts for responsible decisionmaking in this unchartered area are scarce and open-ended." *Collins v. City of Harker Heights,* 503 U.S. 115, 125, 112 S.Ct. 1061, 117 L.Ed.2d 261 (1992). Mindful of these cautionary words, I would limit this decision to the narrowest possible grounds, and would reverse solely because of the allegation that Schroeter pleaded guilty to recklessly endangering another person in Pennsylvania court. I do not believe that the other allegations on which the majority relies are sufficient — separately or together — to state a claim.

A.

To prove a constitutional violation under the state created danger theory, a plaintiff must establish four elements: that "(1) the harm ultimately caused was foreseeable and fairly direct; (2) a state actor acted with a degree of culpability that shocks the conscience; (3) relationship between the state and the plaintiff existed such that the plaintiff was a foreseeable victim of the defendant's acts ...; and (4) a state actor affirmatively used his or her authority in a way that created a danger to the citizen or that rendered the citizen more vulnerable to danger than had the state not acted at all." *Sanford v. Stiles,* 456 F.3d 298, 304-05 (3d Cir. 2006) (per curiam). In the District Court, the parties agreed that the element at issue is the second one: whether Kedra alleged that Schroeter's conduct shocks the conscience.[1]

The Supreme Court has explained that "negligently inflicted harm is categorically beneath the threshold of constitutional due process," while "conduct intended to injure in some way unjustifiable by any government interest is the sort of official action most likely to rise to the conscience-shocking level." *County of Sacramento v. Lewis,* 523 U.S. 833, 849, 118 S.Ct. 1708, 140 L.Ed.2d 1043 (1998). "Whether the point of the conscience shocking is reached when injuries are produced with culpability falling within the middle range, following from something more than negligence but less than intentional conduct, such as recklessness or gross negligence, is a matter for closer calls." *Id.* (internal quotation marks and citation omitted). This is precisely such a close-call case — which is why we should, as the Supreme Court has advised, be reluctant to expand the concept of substantive due process. *Collins,* 503 U.S. at 125, 112 S.Ct. 1061.

I agree with the majority that here, there was no "hyperpressurized environment" and "unhurried judgments" were possible. Therefore, the level of culpability required to shock the conscience is deliberate indifference. *Sanford,* 456 F.3d at 309. We have defined deliberate indifference as falling in the "middle range" identified by the Supreme Court — "between intent, which includes proceeding with knowledge p.454 that the harm is substantially certain to occur and negligence, which involves the mere unreasonable risk of harm to another." *Morse v. Lower Merion Sch. Dist.,* 132 F.3d 902, 910 n.10 (3d Cir. 1997) (internal quotation marks omitted). Since we first adopted the state created danger theory, we have repeatedly left open whether the appropriate standard for evaluating deliberate indifference in a substantive due process case is subjective or objective. *See, e.g., Kaucher v. Cnty. of Bucks,* 455 F.3d 418, 428 n.5 (3d Cir. 2006); *Sanford,* 456 F.3d at 309 n.13. In many cases, a subjective standard will be more demanding, requiring the plaintiff to allege specific facts that shed light on the defendant's mental state, rather than more general notions of what should have been objectively clear.

The majority acknowledges that the subjective standard applies here, because it was the standard established in our case law at the time of Trooper Kedra's death. Nevertheless, the majority goes on to analyze case law post-dating the conduct at issue: *Kingsley v. Hendrickson,* ___ U.S. ___, 135 S.Ct. 2466, 192 L.Ed.2d 416 (2015), and *L.R. v. School District of Philadelphia,* 836 F.3d 235, 246 (3d Cir. 2016), among others. Maj. Op. at 438-39. This discussion is unnecessary to the resolution of the case, and I would therefore avoid it. Because the majority has spoken, though, I feel compelled to note my disagreement.

The majority definitively states that we settled the question of whether a subjective or objective standard applies when we observed that the risk of harm from the teacher's alleged conduct was "'so obvious' as to rise to the level of deliberate indifference." *L.R.,* 836 F.3d at 246. In *L.R.,* however, we did not explicitly acknowledge the existence of two possible standards — subjective versus objective — or discuss the differences between them. *See id.* We did not indicate that we were adopting the objective standard or provide any reason for doing so, which would be a surprising way of ruling definitively on an issue that has split our sister Circuits. Moreover, the *L.R.* plaintiff made allegations that would be sufficient under the subjective standard: the teacher asked the stranger for identification, illustrating that he was "indeed aware of the risk of harm" in releasing the child to a stranger. *Id.* Therefore, *L.R.*'s less-than-clear allusion to the objective standard was dicta that was unnecessary to our resolution of the appeal.

The majority's other cases are no more persuasive. In *Kingsley,* the Supreme Court held that an objective standard applied to a § 1983 claim alleging a violation of Fourteenth Amendment substantive due process rights. 135 S.Ct. at 2472. But *Kingsley* involved an excessive force claim by a pretrial detainee. 135 S.Ct. at 2470. Although *Kingsley* and this case both involve Fourteenth Amendment claims, I do not see that prisoner cases, which implicate a host of specialized policy concerns, have much bearing on state created danger cases. The Supreme Court's reasons for adopting the objective standard included prior case law analyzing pretrial detainee excessive force claims; the objective standard's congruence with prison guards' training; and the fact that the objective standard incorporates "deference to policies and practices needed to maintain order and institutional security." *Id.* at 2473-75.

None of those reasons apply here. Pretrial detainee cases from our sister Circuits are similarly unpersuasive. *See Darnell v. Pineiro,* 849 F.3d 17, 33 (2d Cir. 2017); *Castro v. Cnty. of Los Angeles,* 833 F.3d 1060, 1069 (9th Cir. 2016). Prisoner claims under the Eighth Amendment are even further afield. *See Palakovic v. Wetzel,* 854 F.3d 209 (3d Cir. 2017).

p.455 The subjective standard is the appropriate test for deliberate indifference in a substantive due process case because the Fourteenth Amendment is not a "font of tort law to be superimposed upon whatever systems may already be administered by the States." *Daniels v. Williams,* 474 U.S. 327, 332, 106 S.Ct. 662, 88 L.Ed.2d 662 (1986) (internal quotation marks omitted). The subjective standard better aligns with the purposes and limits of § 1983. *Kaucher,* 455 F.3d at 428 n.5 (an "objective standard" would "move the concept of deliberate indifference ... closer to the pole of negligence").

Regardless of my disagreement with the majority's reading of cases it acknowledges are unnecessary to its decision here, I agree with the majority that the qualified immunity determination turns on whether Kedra has pleaded facts from which we can infer that Schroeter acted with actual knowledge or "a 'conscious disregard of a substantial risk of serious harm.'" *L.R.,* 836 F.3d at 246 (quoting *Vargas v. City of Phila.,* 783 F.3d 962, 973-74 (3d Cir. 2015)). And while I appreciate that the lines between intentional conduct, negligence, gross negligence, recklessness, and conscious disregard may be difficult to pinpoint, in a case like this they are critical. Because negligence is not enough to shock the conscience but instead denotes "culpable carelessness," *Negligence,* Black's Law Dictionary (10th ed. 2014), Kedra must allege that Schroeter acted with more than culpable carelessness to have violated the Constitution.

Kedra satisfies this burden due to her allegation that Schroeter pleaded guilty in Pennsylvania court to reckless endangerment of another person. As the majority notes, by doing so, Schroeter agreed that he "recklessly engage[d] in conduct which place[d] ... another person in danger of death or serious bodily injury." 18 Pa. Cons. Stat. § 2705. Under Pennsylvania law, "[t]he mens rea for recklessly endangering another person is a conscious disregard of a known risk of death or great bodily harm to another person." *Commonwealth v. Hopkins,* 747 A.2d 910, 916 (Pa. Super. Ct. 2000) (internal quotation marks omitted); *see also Commonwealth v. Rich,* 167 A.3d 157, 162 (Pa. Super. Ct. 2017) (statutory definition provides that "[a] person acts recklessly ... when he consciously disregards a substantial and unjustifiable risk....") (quoting 18 Pa. Cons. Stat. § 302(b)(3)).

That language closely tracks with what is required for conscience-shocking behavior: "a 'conscious disregard of a substantial risk of serious harm.'" *L.R.,* 836 F.3d at 246 (quoting *Vargas,* 783 F.3d at 973-74). Therefore, I agree with the majority that Kedra's allegation that Schroeter pleaded guilty to reckless endangerment sufficiently alleges that he acted in a way that shocks the conscience. I also agree that the District Court missed the mark when it concluded that the guilty plea allegation is relevant "only if non-mutual offensive collateral estoppel is extended here." *Kedra v. Schroeter,* 161 F.Supp.3d 359, 362 n.5 (E.D. Pa. 2016). This case is at the pleading stage, so all that is required is that the guilty plea "nudge[]" Kedra's allegation that Schroeter's behavior shocks the conscience "across the line from conceivable to plausible." *Bell Atl. Corp. v. Twombly,* 550 U.S. 544, 570, 127 S.Ct. 1955, 167 L.Ed.2d

929 (2007). Because the guilty plea does just that, the complaint adequately alleges what is needed for the first prong of the qualified immunity analysis — namely, that Schroeter's "conduct violated a federal right," *Tolan,* 134 S.Ct. at 1865, and "shocks the conscience," *Sanford,* 456 F.3d at 304. In contrast to the majority's treatment of the guilty plea as one more allegation that saves the complaint, p.456 I believe this is where our analysis should end.

B.

Aside from the guilty plea, the majority also relies on what it calls circumstantial evidence of conscience-shocking behavior: (1) the obviousness of the risk of pointing a gun at another person, (2) Schroeter's professional training, and (3) Schroeter's violation of safety protocols. I diverge from the majority in my belief that none of those factors adequately allege conduct that shocks the conscience.

The "obviousness of a risk is not conclusive" as to a defendant's subjective awareness of that risk. *Farmer v. Brennan,* 511 U.S. 825, 843 n.8, 114 S.Ct. 1970, 128 L.Ed.2d 811 (1994).[2] So while we "may infer the existence of this subjective state of mind from the fact that the risk is obvious," *Hope v. Pelzer,* 536 U.S. 730, 738, 122 S.Ct. 2508, 153 L.Ed.2d 666 (2002), the obviousness of a risk could also, in an appropriate case, support an inference that there was not deliberate indifference. If Schroeter knew he failed to follow the safety procedures, he would have had to know that his gun might be loaded when he pointed it at Kedra. In other words, in order for the obviousness of the risk to support an inference of deliberate indifference, we would have to infer that Schroeter deliberately chose not to do what was necessary to determine whether the gun was loaded. That may be "possibl[e]" or "conceivable" (for instance, if Schroeter had a mental illness). But in the absence of the guilty plea — through which Schroeter admitted conscious disregard of a known risk — I would not find it "plausible," as the pleading standard requires. *Iqbal,* 556 U.S. at 679-80, 129 S.Ct. 1937.

Likewise, I do not believe that Schroeter's professional training and violation of safety protocols would adequately allege conscience-shocking behavior in the absence of the guilty plea. To begin with, those allegations have a temporal problem: under a subjective standard, the relevant inquiry is Schroeter's state of mind at the time he acted. The fact that he received training beforehand does not mean he remembered it, let alone that he was aware in the moment that he failed to follow it. Second, a failure to follow police protocol is not itself sufficient to establish a constitutional violation. *Lewis,* 523 U.S. at 855, 118 S.Ct. 1708 ("Regardless whether [the officer's] behavior offended the ... balance struck in law enforcement's own codes of sound practice, it does not shock the conscience...."); *City of San Francisco v. Sheehan,* ___ U.S. ___, 135 S.Ct. 1765, 1777, 191 L.Ed.2d 856 (2015) ("Even if an officer acts contrary to her training ... that does not itself negate qualified immunity where it would otherwise be warranted.").

Most importantly, the majority's ruling could be read, in the future, to significantly expand the circumstances in which a p.457 plaintiff can defeat a claim of qualified immunity. Every public official receives employment-related rules and trainings, but acknowledging those rules does not itself indicate conscious awareness of the risk of harm on a future occasion. Nor does violating an established rule transform negligence into conscience-shocking behavior. However, in seeming to accord equal weight to Schroeter's prior training and his guilty plea, I fear the majority continues a trend of reducing the standard of deliberate indifference too close to negligence while also transforming qualified immunity "from a guarantee of immunity into a rule of pleading." *Anderson v. Creighton,* 483 U.S. 635, 639, 107 S.Ct. 3034, 97 L.Ed.2d 523 (1987). And in transforming qualified immunity into a rule of pleading, our approach risks "destroy[ing] the balance that our cases strike between the interests in vindication of citizens' constitutional rights and in public officials' effective performance of their duties." *Id.* (internal quotation marks omitted).

In short, after scrutinizing the entire complaint, I conclude that aside from Schroeter's guilty plea to reckless endangerment, the remaining allegations in Kedra's complaint make out only a strong case of negligence. I do not believe they would be sufficient, by themselves, to state a claim that Schroeter acted with the deliberate indifference required to shock the conscience.

C.

To summarize, Kedra adequately pleaded deliberate indifference, and therefore she alleged all four required elements of a state created danger claim. *Sanford,* 456 F.3d at 304-05. Having adequately pleaded her constitutional claim, Kedra has met the first requirement of the qualified immunity analysis: conduct by an officer that violates a federal right. *Tolan,* 134 S.Ct. at 1865 (2014). I arrive, then, at the second element that must be shown in order to defeat Schroeter's claim of qualified immunity: that "the right in question was clearly established at the time of the violation." *Id.* at 1866. I agree with the majority's conclusion that the right at issue in this case was clearly established — but again, based on different reasoning.

To be clearly established under qualified immunity's second prong, "a right must be sufficiently clear that every reasonable official would have understood that what he is doing violates that right." *Reichle,* 132 S.Ct. at 2093 (internal quotation marks and alterations omitted). "This is not to say that an official action is protected by qualified immunity unless the very action in question has previously been held unlawful; but it is to say that in the light of pre-existing law the unlawfulness must be apparent." *Anderson,* 483 U.S. at 640, 107 S.Ct. 3034 (internal citation omitted). "[A] case directly on point" is not required, "but existing precedent must have placed the ... constitutional question beyond debate." *Ashcroft v. al-Kidd,* 563 U.S. 731, 741, 131 S.Ct. 2074, 179 L.Ed.2d 1149 (2011); *see also Hope,* 536 U.S. at 741, 122 S.Ct. 2508 ("we [have] expressly rejected a requirement that previous cases be fundamentally similar" or "materially similar") (internal quotation marks and citation omitted). The touchstone is reasonableness: "[q]ualified immunity gives government officials breathing room to make reasonable but mistaken judgments about open legal questions. When properly applied, it protects all but the plainly incompetent or those who knowingly violate the law." *al-Kidd,* 563 U.S. at 743, 131 S.Ct. 2074 (internal quotation marks omitted).

As the Supreme Court has explained, "the operation of this standard" — that is, whether a right is clearly established — "depends substantially upon the level of p.458 generality at which the relevant legal rule is to be identified." *Anderson,* 483 U.S. at 639, 107 S.Ct. 3034 (internal quotation marks omitted). Therefore, the Court has repeatedly instructed us "not to define clearly established law at a high level of generality," that "[t]he dispositive question is whether the violative nature of *particular* conduct is clearly established," and that our inquiry into the clearly established prong "must be undertaken in light of the specific context of the case, not as a broad general proposition." *Mullenix v. Luna,* ___ U.S. ___, 136 S.Ct. 305, 308, 193 L.Ed.2d 255 (2015) (per curiam) (internal quotation marks omitted).

The majority defines the right at issue here as "an individual's right not to be subjected, defenseless, to a police officer's demonstration of the use of deadly force in a manner contrary to all applicable safety protocols." Maj. Op. at 449. I would define the right more narrowly, and in accordance with my analysis of the first qualified immunity prong in Section I.A., as: a police officer's right not to be subjected to a firearms training in which the instructor acts with deliberate indifference, that is, consciously disregards a known risk of death or great bodily harm. Schroeter's admitted deliberate indifference is crucial, in my opinion, to the conclusion at the first step of the analysis that a right was violated. *See supra* Section I.A., B. Therefore, in order to narrowly define the right in light of the particular conduct at issue, *Mullenix,* 136 S.Ct. at 308, I would include deliberate indifference in the definition.

The majority disagrees with this definition of the right, saying that it conflates the first and second elements of the qualified immunity analysis. Maj. Op. at 449 n.19. I am not the first, however, to include a state of mind in the definition of a right. *See Grandstaff v. City of Borger,* 767 F.2d 161, 167-68 (5th Cir. 1985) (holding it was clearly established that the use of "deadly force, in *conscious disregard* of substantial risk of harm to innocent parties," was a constitutional due process violation). Nor is it troublesome, as a general proposition, that one element of a legal test overlaps with another element of the same or a related test. Indeed, the first requirement for defeating qualified immunity is redundant with the four prongs of a state created danger claim, and there is no shortage of other examples.[3]

Given the unique facts of this case — namely, Schroeter's guilty plea — I believe it is appropriate to tether the right in question to the standard of care he admitted he breached. The majority's approach, by contrast, suffers from its focus on the violation of "all applicable safety protocols," which will inevitably lead to disputes over how many safety protocols need to be violated for qualified immunity to be forfeited. And those disputes, I predict, will devolve into a negligence-type analysis, which precedent clearly forbids. The majority's definition of the right could prove fertile ground for future plaintiffs seeking to lower the bar yet further in § 1983 cases.

Turning to whether the right as I define it was clearly established, I conclude that in light of existing case law, a reasonable person could not have believed that it was consistent with Kedra's substantive due process rights to subject him to a firearms p.459 training at which the instructor was deliberately indifferent to his safety. Therefore, the right was clearly established.

Unlike the majority, I do not read existing cases as being "fundamentally" or "materially" similar to this one. *See Hope,* 536 U.S. at 741, 122 S.Ct. 2508. The lack of on-point precedent gives me pause, because a case's "present[ation] [of] a unique set of facts and circumstances" can be "an important indication" that the conduct at issue "did not violate a clearly established right." *White,* 137 S.Ct. at 552 (internal quotation marks omitted). Nonetheless, I feel constrained to conclude that Supreme

Court and Circuit precedents have "clearly established" the "violative nature," *Mullenix,* 136 S.Ct. at 308, of conducting a firearms training with deliberate indifference to a known risk.

To begin with, the deliberate indifference standard was clearly enunciated in the state created danger context more than a decade ago and was clear at the time of Kedra's death in 2014. *Sanford,* 456 F.3d at 309 (ruling that "where deliberation is possible and officials have the time to make unhurried judgments, deliberate indifference is sufficient" to shock the conscience); *see also Phillips v. Cnty. of Allegheny,* 515 F.3d 224, 241 (3d Cir. 2008). While our state created danger cases are not factually similar to this one — they do not involve police officers conducting firearms training — I cannot see how any reasonable official could believe that acting with deliberate indifference in the police firearms training context would be consistent with trainees' constitutional rights. A reasonable officer could not be heard to say that although he knew that 911 employees cannot release information from their database in a deliberately indifferent manner, *id.* at 243, he nevertheless thought it would comport with trainees' substantive due process rights to conduct a firearms training with deliberate indifference.

We have reasoned, in the past, that deliberate indifference is simply inconsistent with objectively reasonable conduct. *Beers-Capitol v. Whetzel,* 256 F.3d 120, 142 n.15 (3d Cir. 2001) (reasonable defendant "could not believe that her actions comported with clearly established law while also believing that there is an excessive risk to the plaintiffs and failing to adequately respond to that risk[;] [c]onduct that is deliberately indifferent to an excessive risk ... cannot be objectively reasonable conduct"); *Carter v. City of Phila.,* 181 F.3d 339, 356 (3d Cir. 1999) ("If Carter succeeds in establishing that the ... defendants acted with deliberate indifference to constitutional rights — as Carter must in order to recover under section 1983 — then *a fortiori* their conduct was not objectively reasonable.").

The majority emphasizes the importance of *Marrero-Rodriguez v. San Juan,* 677 F.3d 497 (1st Cir. 2012), to its conclusion that the right at issue here was clearly established. Maj. Op. at 450-51. *Marrero-Rodriguez* involves a police trainer's deliberate indifference toward a trainee, 677 F.3d at 502, but the case has important distinctions as well. There, "dummy guns" were supposed to be used, *id.* at 500, while here, Schroeter needed to use an actual gun in order to train the other officers on its features. Also in *Marrero-Rodriguez,* what the instructor was supposedly "training" the other officers to do would have itself amounted to a gross violation of the rights of criminal suspects. *Id.* at 502. There are no such allegations here.

The majority dismisses the materially differing facts in *Marrero-Rodriguez* as a distinction without a difference. But the fact that the instructor there brought a real gun to a training meant to involve dummy weapons injected a level of danger p.460 into the training that never would have existed absent that deliberate act. Here, the training required a live weapon, so the inherent risk was of a different order than the risk involved in the *Marrero-Rodriguez* training. Kedra does not allege that Schroeter's conduct was anything other than a mistake, however reckless. The same cannot be said for the instructor in *Marrero-Rodriguez,* and that should make a difference.

Regardless, as I explain above, the Supreme Court's and our court's precedents clearly establish the right in question, even in the absence of directly on-point precedent. It is therefore immaterial whether *Marrero-Rodriguez* may have also put Schroeter on notice that his conduct was violative of that right.

II.

I am concerned by the impact that the breadth of the majority's decision could have on the law of qualified immunity. I am equally troubled by the recent trajectory of this Court's jurisprudence. In my mind, we have gradually expanded substantive due process protections to cases where they should not apply by tortifying the Constitution and chipping away at the standards necessary to show deliberate indifference.

The Due Process Clause of the Fourteenth Amendment provides that "[n]o State shall ... deprive any person of life, liberty, or property without due process of law." U.S. Const. amend. XIV, § 1, cl. 2. Shortly after the Fourteenth Amendment's adoption, the Supreme Court analyzed the meaning of the Due Process Clause and stated that the Clause was "intended to secure the individual from the arbitrary exercise of the powers of government, unrestrained by the established principles of private right and distributive justice." *Hurtado v. California,* 110 U.S. 516, 527, 4 S.Ct. 292, 28 L.Ed. 232 (1884) (quoting *Bank of Columbia v. Okely,* 17 U.S. (4 Wheat.) 235, 244, 4 L.Ed. 559 (1819)). Since then, the Supreme Court has explained that "the Due Process Clause of the Fourteenth Amendment was intended to prevent the government from abusing its power," *DeShaney v. Winnebago Cnty. Dep't of Soc. Servs.,* 489 U.S. 189, 196, 109 S.Ct. 998, 103 L.Ed.2d 249 (1989) (internal quotation marks and alterations omitted), but not to "transform every tort committed by a state actor into a constitutional violation." *Id.* at 202, 109 S.Ct. 998; *see also Lewis,* 523 U.S. at 845, 118 S.Ct. 1708 ("We have emphasized time and again that the touchstone of due process is protection of the individual against arbitrary action of government....") (internal quotation marks omitted). The Supreme Court has accordingly "emphasized that only the most egregious official conduct can be said to be arbitrary in the constitutional sense." *Id.* at 846, 118 S.Ct. 1708 (internal quotation marks omitted).

In assessing what behavior is egregious enough to state a claim under the Due Process Clause, the Supreme Court has "spoken of the cognizable level of executive abuse of power as that which shocks the conscience" or "violates the 'decencies of civilized conduct.'" *Id.* In so doing, it has recognized that the Due Process Clause is "phrased as a limitation on the State's power to act, not as a guarantee of certain minimal levels of safety." *DeShaney,* 489 U.S. at 195, 109 S.Ct. 998. But it has also recognized some limited exception to that rule. In *DeShaney,* the Supreme Court noted that "when the State takes a person into custody and holds him there against his will, the Constitution imposes upon it a corresponding duty to assume some responsibility for his safety and general well-being." *Id.* at 199-200, 109 S.Ct. 998. *DeShaney* also left open the question of p.461 whether a constitutional violation could occur absent a custodial relationship when it stated: "[w]hile the State may have been aware of the dangers that Joshua faced in the free world, it played no part in their creation, nor did it render him any more vulnerable to them." *Id.* at 201, 109 S.Ct. 998.

Relying on that dicta in *DeShaney,* several Circuits recognized a state created danger theory for establishing a constitutional claim under § 1983, and we joined them in

Kneipp v. Tedder, 95 F.3d 1199 (3d Cir. 1996). The Supreme Court has yet to explicitly adopt the now widely-recognized state created danger theory, and the Circuits have yet to enforce a uniform approach to its application. But consistent with the fact that the Due Process Clause was not meant to constitutionalize state tort law, our state created danger theory encompasses four elements that provide some insurance that it protects the individual only from those abuses of power that lie at the heart of the concept of due process. Since "liability for negligently inflicted harm is categorically beneath the threshold of constitutional due process," *Lewis,* 523 U.S. at 849, 118 S.Ct. 1708, the requirement that the government official act with a degree of culpability that shocks the conscience is perhaps the most critical element to providing that insurance. And recognizing the importance of the culpability requirement, our cases have frequently sought to evaluate the degree of culpability required to prevail under our state created danger theory.

Unfortunately, because the rules of substantive due process are not "subject to mechanical application in unfamiliar territory," *id.* at 850, 118 S.Ct. 1708, we have, like the Supreme Court, struggled with how to define culpability falling between the intentional conduct that can sustain a due process violation and the negligent conduct that cannot. In this regard, the Supreme Court has offered that recklessness or gross negligence may be actionable in some cases, but the only case the *Lewis* court cited as establishing liability in that middle range, *City of Revere v. Massachusetts General Hospital,* 463 U.S. 239, 103 S.Ct. 2979, 77 L.Ed.2d 605 (1983), involved a pre-trial detainee who was in government custody and therefore restrained from acting on his own behalf. Because "when the State takes a person into custody" it renders him unable to exercise ordinary responsibility for his own welfare, such cases implicate a unique context where "the Constitution imposes upon [the State] a ... duty to assume some responsibility for [that person's] safety and general well-being." *Deshaney,* 489 U.S. at 199-200, 109 S.Ct. 998. And consequently, Justices Scalia and Thomas have asserted that the Supreme Court has "expressly left open whether, in a context in which the individual has *not* been deprived of the ability to care for himself in the relevant respect, something less than intentional conduct, such as recklessness or gross negligence, can ever constitute a deprivation under the Due Process Clause." *Lewis,* 523 U.S. at 863, 118 S.Ct. 1708 (Scalia, J., concurring in the judgment) (internal quotation marks omitted).

Despite the fact that the Supreme Court left this question open, we have recognized such liability by defining deliberate indifference as "appear[ing] to fall somewhere between intent, which includes proceeding with knowledge that the harm is substantially certain to occur and negligence, which involves the mere unreasonable risk of harm to another." *Morse,* 132 F.3d at 910 n.10 (internal quotation marks omitted). I question the validity of this definition. Gross negligence and recklessness are cognizable under state tort law, and the Supreme Court has "rejected claims that the Due Process Clause should be p.462 interpreted to impose federal duties that are analogous to those traditionally imposed by state tort law." *Collins,* 503 U.S at 128, 112 S.Ct. 1061; *see also Kingsley v. Hendrickson,* ___ U.S. ___, 135 S.Ct. 2466, 2479, 192 L.Ed.2d 416 (2015) (Scalia, J., dissenting).

In my view, it is troubling how far we have expanded substantive due process, a concept the Supreme Court has been reluctant to expand. *Collins,* 503 U.S. at 125, 112 S.Ct. 1061. Originally, the Due Process Clause prevented only those government actions that violate "those canons of decency and fairness which express the notions of justice of English-speaking peoples." *Rochin v. California,* 342 U.S. 165, 169, 72 S.Ct. 205, 96 L.Ed. 183 (1952) (internal quotation marks omitted). We took a second step by fashioning a state created danger theory. *Kneipp,* 95 F.3d at 1211. We then took a third step, stating that there could be liability in non-custodial situations for gross negligence. *See, e.g., Sanford,* 456 F.3d at 310. The Supreme Court, however, is still at step one. Given that our substantive due process doctrine has gradually lowered the bar for bringing a state created danger claim, it may be time for this full Court to reexamine the doctrine.

III.

Perhaps the full Court will revisit the qualified immunity framework to reexamine whether it is consistent with the history of the Due Process Clause. Perhaps the Supreme Court will clarify the governing law by weighing in on the state created danger theory before we expand this substantive due process doctrine even further. In the meantime, it is worth remembering:

> The people ... may well prefer a system of liability which would place upon the State and its officials the responsibility for failure to act in situations such as the present one. They may create such a system, if they do not have it already, by changing the tort law of the State in accordance with the regular lawmaking process. But they should not have it thrust upon them by this Court's expansion of the Due Process Clause of the Fourteenth Amendment.

DeShaney, 489 U.S. at 203, 109 S.Ct. 998. I offer this concurrence in the hope that it might steer us toward a firmer commitment to this principle.

[*] Honorable D. Michael Fisher, United States Circuit Judge for the Third Circuit, assumed senior status on February 1, 2017.

[**] Honorable Michael J. Melloy, Senior Circuit Judge, United States Court of Appeals for the Eighth Circuit, sitting by designation.

[1] Appellant filed a First Amended Complaint that differed from her original complaint only in listing her title as "personal representative of the Estate." JA 29. As the substance of the complaints is the same, we will simply refer to the relevant document as the "complaint."

[2] Collateral estoppel is a judicial doctrine that precludes relitigation of an issue already decided in a previous proceeding if "(1) the issue decided in the prior adjudication was identical with the one presented in the later action, (2) there was a final judgment on the merits, (3) the party against whom the plea is asserted was a party or in privity with a party to the prior adjudication, and (4) the party against whom it is asserted has had a full and fair opportunity to litigate the issue in question in a prior action." *Dici v. Pennsylvania,* 91 F.3d 542, 547-48 (3d Cir. 1996). The District Court believed this last criterion was not satisfied because Schroeter did not "ha[ve] a 'full and fair opportunity to litigate' the question of his constitutional culpability on the basis of a guilty plea in a state criminal court." *Kedra,* 161 F.Supp.3d at 364 n.5. Although Appellant did not rely on the guilty plea for its preclusive effect, but only

as a basis from which to infer Schroeter's actual knowledge of the risk of harm, the District Court assumed that the requirements for collateral estoppel had to be satisfied for the plea to be considered in any way relevant. *Id.*

[3] Appellant argues before us that the dismissal should have been without prejudice so that she could have an opportunity to supplement her pleading of deliberate indifference in an amended complaint. Because we conclude Appellant already pleaded sufficient facts to sustain her claim, *see infra* Section III.B.1, we need not address whether the District Court erred in denying leave to amend.

[4] In ruling that an objective test was not a clearly established means to plead deliberate indifference, the District Court's approach arguably combined elements of both the first and second prongs of the qualified immunity analysis. Yet, those inquiries diverge in a significant respect with regard to mens rea, for even where an element of a claimed violation includes a subjective test, "the test for qualified immunity is objective.... That is, [an official] is entitled to qualified immunity only if she can show that a reasonable person in her position at the relevant time could have believed, in light of clearly established law, that her conduct comported with established legal standards." *Beers-Capitol,* 256 F.3d at 142 n.15. And for that reason, we have instructed courts to treat the two prongs of qualified immunity as analytically distinct so as to avoid confusing their different mens rea requirements. *Phillips,* 515 F.3d at 242. At the same time, as the Supreme Court has recognized, "whether a particular complaint sufficiently alleges a clearly established violation of law cannot be decided in isolation from the facts pleaded," and "[i]n that sense the sufficiency of [Appellant's] pleadings is both inextricably intertwined with, and directly implicated by, the qualified immunity defense." *Ashcroft v. Iqbal,* 556 U.S. 662, 673, 129 S.Ct. 1937, 173 L.Ed.2d 868 (2009) (citations and internal quotation marks citations omitted); *accord L.R. v. Sch. Dist. of Phila.,* 836 F.3d 235, 241 (3d Cir. 2016).

[5] We undertake this inquiry in the first instance to decide whether we may affirm on this alternative ground, *see MRL Dev. I, LLC v. Whitecap Inv. Corp.,* 823 F.3d 195, 202 (3d Cir. 2016), and because it turns on a purely legal question, our resolution of which will best serve the interests of judicial efficiency on remand, *see Wallach v. Eaton Corp.,* 837 F.3d 356, 374-75 (3d Cir. 2016); *Loretangeli v. Critelli,* 853 F.2d 186, 189 n.5 (3d Cir. 1988).

[6] We are unconvinced by Schroeter's argument that no state-created danger claim is cognizable where, as here, the alleged violation is based on a state actor's endangerment of a fellow government employee. While the Due Process Clause does not guarantee state employees "certain minimal levels of safety and security" in the workplace, *Collins v. City of Harker Heights,* 503 U.S. 115, 126, 112 S.Ct. 1061, 117 L.Ed.2d 261 (1992), we have long held that a government employee may bring a substantive due process claim against his employer if the state compelled the employee to be exposed to a risk of harm not inherent in the workplace, *see Kaucher v. Cty. of Bucks,* 455 F.3d 418, 430-31 (3d Cir. 2006); *Eddy v. V.I. Water & Power Auth.,* 256 F.3d 204, 212-13 (3d Cir. 2001). We have no trouble concluding this standard is met in the context of a mandatory firearms training in which the trainees were required to be physically present without protection and the firearms instructor, instead of following safety protocols and demonstrating the proper use of a firearm, disregarded all protocols and fired directly at a trainee at close range.

[7] Schroeter also appears to contest the fourth element by casting his conduct as an omission to check the gun for a bullet and contending that he may be held liable only for an affirmative act. Yet the complaint alleges Schroeter skipped over required safety checks, picked up a firearm, raised it, pointed it at Kedra, and pulled the trigger. These indisputably affirmative acts "created an opportunity for harm that would not have otherwise existed." *Rivas v. City of Passaic,* 365 F.3d 181, 197 (3d Cir. 2004). Those acts, which directly caused Kedra's death, also set this case apart from those that we have deemed to involve mere omissions. *See, e.g., Bright,* 443 F.3d at 284-85 (state actor not liable for failing to prevent harm inflicted by a third party); *D.R. ex rel. L.R. v. Middle Bucks Area Vocational Tech. Sch.,* 972 F.2d 1364, 1374-76 (3d Cir. 1992) (en banc) (same).

[8] *Compare, e.g., Board v. Farnham,* 394 F.3d 469, 478 (7th Cir. 2005) (noting that the test for deliberate indifference under the Fourteenth Amendment is "closer to tort recklessness" than to the Eighth Amendment's "criminally reckless" standard), *Spencer v. Knapheide Truck Equip. Co.,* 183 F.3d 902, 905-06 (8th Cir. 1999) (suggesting that the purely subjective standard from *Farmer* may be inappropriate for due process claims brought by pretrial detainees), *and Christiansen v. City of Tulsa,* 332 F.3d 1270, 1281 (10th Cir. 2003) (framing the standard in the state-created danger context as whether the risk was "obvious or known"), *with, e.g., Ewolski v. City of Brunswick,* 287 F.3d 492, 513 (6th Cir. 2002) (adopting *Farmer*'s subjective standard for due process claims), *and Hare v. City of Corinth,* 74 F.3d 633, 648 (5th Cir. 1996) (en banc) (same).

[9] Recognizing the significance of *Kingsley,* the Ninth Circuit, sitting en banc, has extended it to failure-to-protect claims, framing the test as whether a "reasonable officer in the circumstances would have appreciated the high degree of risk involved — making the consequences of the defendant's conduct obvious," *Castro v. Cty. of Los Angeles,* 833 F.3d 1060, 1071 (9th Cir. 2016) (en banc), and the Second Circuit has extended it to conditions-of-confinement claims, holding that "deliberate indifference should be defined objectively for a claim of a due process violation" and that the relevant inquiry post-*Kingsley* is what the "defendant-official knew, or should have known," *Darnell v. Pineiro,* 849 F.3d 17, 35-36 (2d Cir. 2017). *Cf. Alderson v. Concordia Parish Corr. Facility,* 848 F.3d 415, 419 n.4 (5th Cir. 2017) (declining to extend *Kingsley* to failure-to-protect claims absent en banc reconsideration of controlling Circuit precedent). Like the Supreme Court, both Circuits explicitly rejected arguments that an objective test would devolve into a negligence standard. *See Darnell,* 849 F.3d at 36 ("[A]ny § 1983 claim for a violation of due process requires proof of a *mens rea* greater than mere negligence."); *Castro,* 833 F.3d at 1071 n.4 (observing that an objective test "prevent[s] 'overinclusiveness' by ensuring that liability will attach only in cases where the defendant's conduct is more egregious than mere negligence").

[10] In his concurrence, Judge Fisher seeks to revisit *L.R.,* positing, despite its terms, that it left *Sanford*'s question unanswered; that its reliance on the objective test was dictum because it also observed the teacher's conduct would meet the subjective test, *but see Woods v. Interstate Realty Co.,* 337 U.S. 535, 537, 69 S.Ct. 1235, 93 L.Ed. 1524 (1949) (discussing the significance of alternative holdings); *Meister v. Comm'r,* 504 F.2d 505, 509 (3d Cir. 1974) (noting that where we give "an alternative basis for our holding" prefaced with language such as "*additionally,*" this does not mean the earlier holding is to be "disregarded" or is any less "critical"); and that an objective

test cannot distinguish between conscience-shocking behavior and mere negligence and thus risks rendering the Fourteenth Amendment a "font of tort law," Concurrence at 454-55; *but see Kingsley,* 135 S.Ct. at 2474; *Palakovic,* 854 F.3d at 231; *Darnell,* 849 F.3d at 35-36; *Castro,* 833 F.3d at 1071. While our concurring colleague may disagree with the evolution of our substantive due process jurisprudence, we generally may not, short of en banc reconsideration, alter our Circuit precedent, *see Bimbo Bakeries USA, Inc. v. Botticella,* 613 F.3d 102, 116 (3d Cir. 2010), and we have no occasion to do so today. Instead, our concern is whether Appellant sufficiently pleaded deliberate indifference under a culpability standard that was then-clearly established. For the reasons we explain below, *see infra* Section III.B.1, Appellant's allegations as to Schroeter's training and experience, to say nothing of his written acknowledgements and admissions in the context of his guilty plea, are more than sufficient to show deliberate indifference under the then-clearly established subjective standard and conduct that was not merely negligent but "shocks the conscience," *Bright,* 443 F.3d at 281.

[11] We also recently resolved what we had identified as an open question after *Farmer, see Woloszyn v. Cty. of Lawrence,* 396 F.3d 314, 321 (3d Cir. 2005), as to whether the "deliberate indifference" standard in the prison suicide context is a subjective or objective one. *Palakovic v. Wetzel,* 854 F.3d 209 (3d Cir. 2017). There too we held the standard was objective and identified the relevant inquiry for both substantive due process claims and Eighth Amendment claims as whether "the prison official knew or *should have known* of the individual's particular vulnerability," *id.* at 224 (emphasis added), explaining that "[i]t is not necessary for the custodian to have a subjective appreciation of the detainee's particular vulnerability. Rather, ... 'reckless or deliberate indifference to that risk' only demands 'something more culpable on the part of the officials than a negligent failure to recognize the high risk of suicide,'" *id.* at 231 (citation omitted).

[12] Our Sister Circuits, with near unanimity, also have recognized the relevance of obviousness of risk to proving actual knowledge. *See, e.g., Miranda-Rivera v. Toledo-Davila,* 813 F.3d 64, 75 (1st Cir. 2016); *Gant ex rel. Gant v. Wallingford Bd. of Educ.,* 195 F.3d 134, 141 n.6 (2d Cir. 1999); *McQueen v. Beecher Cmty. Sch.,* 433 F.3d 460, 469 (6th Cir. 2006); *Farnham,* 394 F.3d at 478; *Ryan v. Armstrong,* 850 F.3d 419, 425 (8th Cir. 2017); *Kennedy v. City of Ridgefield,* 439 F.3d 1055, 1064 (9th Cir. 2006); *Valderrama v. Rousseau,* 780 F.3d 1108, 1116 (11th Cir. 2015).

[13] Schroeter argues that we should disregard *L.R.* entirely because it post-dated the shooting. As the Supreme Court has observed, however, a later-decided case may still be considered when assessing whether a principle was clearly established to the extent the case is merely "illustrative of the proper application" of a previously established constitutional principle. *Wiggins v. Smith,* 539 U.S. 510, 522, 123 S.Ct. 2527, 156 L.Ed.2d 471 (2003) (discussing this meaning of "clearly established" in the habeas context). It is for that limited purpose that we refer to *L.R.* in this part of our discussion.

[14] The question whether a state criminal conviction based on a guilty plea may be preclusive of any claims or issues is a question of the law of the state where the criminal proceeding took place, *see Allen v. McCurry,* 449 U.S. 90, 104-05, 101 S.Ct. 411, 66 L.Ed.2d 308 (1980); *Dici,* 91 F.3d at 547-48, and one we need not answer as Appellant relies on the plea at this stage not to invoke issue preclusion, but only to

argue that her allegations were sufficient to survive Schroeter's motion to dismiss. We note, however, that under Pennsylvania law, a party's "criminal conviction may be used to establish the operative facts in a subsequent civil case based on those same facts, and ... [a] guilty plea constitutes an admission to all the facts averred in the indictment." *Commonwealth, Dep't of Transp. v. Mitchell,* 517 Pa. 203, 535 A.2d 581, 585 (1987) (citation omitted); *see also* Restatement (Second) of Judgments § 85 cmt. c (Am. Law Inst. 1982). Particularly where, as here, a party is not claiming issue preclusion but is relying on a plea only as a factual allegation to support an inference of actual knowledge, the plea is, at least to that extent, relevant.

[15] At oral argument, Schroeter's counsel went even further, stating that "[b]ecause Corporal Schroeter was an experienced person with training experience, in particular, it can't be alleged that he knew he wasn't following [the safety protocols]. He has to have believed he was following ... them or he would not have done what he did." Oral Arg. at 37:43-38:06, *available at* http://www2.ca3.uscourts.gov/oralargument/audio/16-1417Kedrav.Schroeter.mp3. Aside from being entirely circular, Schroeter's reasoning that the more obvious the risk, the weaker the inference of conscious disregard, flies in the face of Supreme Court precedent, which not only treats obviousness of risk as a basis from which to infer actual knowledge of risk, *see, e.g., Hope,* 536 U.S. at 738, 122 S.Ct. 2508; *see also Phillips,* 515 F.3d at 237-39; *Morse,* 132 F.3d at 910 n.10; *Kneipp,* 95 F.3d at 1208-09, but, as discussed above, also instructs us, in reviewing the sufficiency of a complaint, to draw this very reasonable inference in favor of the plaintiff — not, as Schroeter urges, the other way around, *see Iqbal,* 556 U.S. at 678, 129 S.Ct. 1937; *see also Phillips,* 515 F.3d at 231, 233. Counsel's argument points up another reason qualified immunity must be denied in this case: The complaint alleges that Schroeter acted with actual awareness of the risk; Schroeter disputes that allegation. What we have here portends a quintessential disputed issue of material fact, turning on the credibility of witnesses to be assessed by a jury, *see Metzger v. Osbeck,* 841 F.2d 518, 521 (3d Cir. 1988), and certainly not appropriate for resolution on a motion to dismiss, *see Phillips,* 515 F.3d at 234-35.

[16] The Concurrence contends that obviousness of risk could not, in and of itself, be sufficient to plead actual knowledge, excerpting from *Farmer* that "obviousness of a risk is not conclusive." Concurrence at 456 (quoting *Farmer,* 511 U.S. at 843 n.8, 114 S.Ct. 1970). In context, however, that excerpt proves precisely the opposite, for the Supreme Court there explained that, at the summary judgment stage — despite the indisputable inference of actual knowledge raised by obviousness of risk — there may yet be a genuine issue of material fact because "a prison official may show that the obvious escaped him." *Farmer,* 511 U.S. at 843 n.8, 114 S.Ct. 1970. The Court then proceeded to observe that, at trial, obviousness of risk *alone* could support a finding of liability, stating that if "circumstances suggest that the defendant-official being sued had been exposed to information concerning the risk and thus 'must have known' about it, then such evidence could be sufficient to permit a trier of fact to find that the defendant-official had actual knowledge of the risk." *Id.* at 842-43, 114 S.Ct. 1970. In short, *Farmer* recognizes that obviousness of risk alone can be sufficient to survive summary judgment and to establish actual knowledge at trial; *a fortiori,* it is sufficient to give rise to an inference of actual knowledge at the pleading stage.

[17] The District Court also suggested at one point that the complaint was deficient for failure to plead that Schroeter was "consciously aware that he had failed to follow all of the safety rules and proceeded anyway," emphasizing the lack of an allegation that Schroeter "realize[d] in the moment" he was not following the rules. *Kedra,* 161 F.Supp.3d at 363. There is no requirement, however, that a defendant be thinking "in the moment" he causes injury that he is violating relevant safety rules. As Appellant astutely observes, to the extent the District Court acknowledged the allegation that Schroeter knew the gun safety rules and acted in violation of them, but found fault in Appellant's failure to specifically allege that Schroeter "kn[ew] he was acting in violation of them," its parsing of the culpability analysis "seems akin to counting angels dancing on the head of a pin." Appellant's Br. 18. More importantly, however, *Farmer* and our case law have not required a plaintiff to plead and prove conscious disregard of safety rules as an element of a state-created danger claim, but rather "conscious disregard of a substantial risk of serious harm," *Vargas,* 783 F.3d at 973-74 (brackets and internal quotation marks omitted); *see also Farmer,* 511 U.S. at 842, 114 S.Ct. 1970 — a standard that, as discussed *supra* at Section III.B.1, may be supported (as it is here) by a variety of factual allegations, including the state actor's violation of applicable safety protocols before the harm is actually inflicted.

[18] Contrary to our concurring colleague's concerns about what our holding in this case portends for state-created danger cases or the element of deliberate indifference going forward, we do not today "reduc[e] the standard of deliberate indifference" anywhere "close to negligence." Concurrence at 456-57. Instead, we require of Appellant's complaint what we have historically required for liability under the state-created danger doctrine: allegations of conscience-shocking, affirmative behavior from a state official that caused "foreseeable and fairly direct" harm to a person who was a foreseeable victim of that behavior. *Bright,* 443 F.3d at 281.

[19] Our concurring colleague would define the right at issue as "a police officer's right not to be subjected to a firearms training in which the instructor acts with deliberate indifference, that is, consciously disregards a known risk of death or great bodily harm." Concurrence at 458. But that definition is broader, not narrower, than what we articulate because it is susceptible to a wide range of applications and is not, by its terms, anchored in any factual scenario. Moreover, with that definition, it is a foregone conclusion whether the right is "clearly established," because its definition merely repeats the elements of the claim. Both to "give[] government officials breathing room to make reasonable but mistaken judgments," *Messerschmidt v. Millender,* 565 U.S. 535, 546, 132 S.Ct. 1235, 182 L.Ed.2d 47 (2012), and to avoid turning the test for clearly established rights into a mere tautology, *see, e.g., Saucier v. Katz,* 533 U.S. 194, 204, 121 S.Ct. 2151, 150 L.Ed.2d 272 (2001) (rejecting a suggestion to make "excessive force analysis indistinguishable from qualified immunity, rendering the separate immunity inquiry superfluous and inappropriate," and holding that the two "inquiries ... remain distinct"), the Supreme Court has repeatedly admonished courts to define the right "not as a broad general proposition," *Mullenix,* 136 S.Ct. at 308, but in terms "'particularized' to the facts of the case," *White v. Pauly,* ___ U.S. ___, 137 S.Ct. 548, 552, 196 L.Ed.2d 463 (2017) (per curiam). That definition also conflates the first and second prongs of the qualified immunity analysis, for while a plaintiff assuredly must establish the elements of a constitutional violation at the first prong, we do not require those elements to

be restated within the definition of a right at the second prong to assess whether that right was clearly established. Rather, the focus of that assessment is whether the specific conduct at issue is sufficiently "factually similar" to then-existing precedent to put a reasonable officer "on notice that his... conduct [was] constitutionally prohibited," *Mammaro,* 814 F.3d at 169, and the right at the second prong is therefore generally defined by the factual context of the "particular conduct," *Saucier,* 533 U.S. at 201, 121 S.Ct. 2151, not by the legal elements of the claim, *Mullenix,* 136 S.Ct. at 308.

[20] The Concurrence seeks to distinguish *Marrero-Rodríguez* from this case on the ground that there "dummy guns" were to be used, 677 F.3d at 500, whereas here the training involved real firearms. For purposes of deliberate indifference, however, this is a distinction without a difference. In both cases, the officer used a firearm in a way that was not allowed by failing to conduct basic safety checks to determine whether the firearm was loaded prior to firing it. That Schroeter made a "mistake, however reckless," Concurrence at 460, is exactly the point: "[R]eckless[] disregard[]" of a "substantial risk of serious harm" is the very definition of deliberate indifference. *Farmer,* 511 U.S. at 836, 114 S.Ct. 1970.

[21] As Appellant points out, Fourth Amendment excessive force cases like *Baird v. Renbarger,* 576 F.3d 340 (7th Cir. 2009), and *Couden v. Duffy,* 446 F.3d 483 (3d Cir. 2006), which recognize a citizen's clearly established right not to have a police officer "point" a gun at him if he poses "no hint of danger," *Baird,* 576 F.3d at 346-47; *accord Couden,* 446 F.3d at 497-98, also support the notion that the substantive due process right here was clearly established. While we need not rely on those cases given the ample case law supporting the clearly established nature of this right in the substantive due process context itself, those Fourth Amendment cases only reinforce our conclusion here.

[1] The majority notes that on appeal, Schroeter appears to contest the fourth element by arguing that his conduct constituted a failure to act, rather than an "affirmative act," as is required. *Sanford v. Stiles,* 456 F.3d 298, 305 (3d Cir. 2006). The complaint sufficiently alleges that, by not performing safety checks and then raising and firing the gun, Schroeter "created an opportunity for harm that would not have otherwise existed." *Rivas v. City of Passaic,* 365 F.3d 181, 197 (3d Cir. 2004) (combination of acts and omissions satisfied fourth prong of state created danger analysis).

[2] The majority offers an interpretation under which *Farmer,* as applied at the pleading stage, means the opposite of what it says — namely, that the obviousness of a risk is, in fact, conclusive. Maj. Op. at 445-46 n.16. However, that interpretation is built on the premise that *Farmer* holds that the obviousness of risk alone could support liability. *Id.* That is incorrect. *Farmer* posits that liability could be premised on what might be called obviousness-plus: evidence that a "substantial" risk was "longstanding, pervasive, well-documented, or expressly noted by prison officials in the past." 511 U.S. at 842, 114 S.Ct. 1970 (internal quotation marks and citation omitted). Therefore, *Farmer* does not say or signify that obviousness of a risk alone is sufficient to survive a motion to dismiss. In any event, my analysis of *Farmer* is simpler than the majority's; I take it to mean what it says.

[3] *See, e.g., Kosilek v. Spencer,* 774 F.3d 63, 83 (1st Cir. 2014) ("[W]e have recognized that the subjective deliberate indifference inquiry may overlap with the objective

serious medical need determination...."); *Gen. Tel. Co. of Sw. v. Falcon*, 457 U.S. 147, 158 n.13, 102 S.Ct. 2364, 72 L.Ed.2d 740 (1982) ("The commonality and typicality requirements of [Federal Rule of Civil Procedure] 23(a) tend to merge," and both "also tend to merge with the adequacy-of-representation requirement....").

870 F.3d 273 (2017)

Lena DAVENPORT, an adult individual

v.

BOROUGH OF HOMESTEAD, a Municipal corporation; City of Pittsburgh, a Municipal corporation; Ian Strang, individually and in his official capacities as a Police Officer of the Borough of Homestead; James Ilgenfritz, individually and his official capacities as a Police Officer of the Borough of Homestead; Louis Schweitzer, individually and in his official capacities as a Police Officer of the City of Pittsburgh; Stephen Matakovich, individually and in his official capacities as a Police Officer of the City of Pittsburgh; Calvin Kennedy, individually and in his official capacities as a Police Officer of the City of Pittsburgh; Thomas Gorecki, individually and in his official capacities as a Police Officer of the City of Pittsburgh, and; Nathan Harper, Commander, in his official capacity as a Chief of Police of the City of Pittsburgh; Jeffrey Desimone, in his official capacity as Chief of Police of Borough of Homestead, and; Igor Boyko, individually and in his official capacity of a Police Officer of the City of Pittsburgh

Louis Schweitzer; Stephen Matakovich; Calvin Kennedy; Thomas Gorecki, Appellants.

No. 16-3892.

United States Court of Appeals, Third Circuit.

Argued: May 24, 2017.

(Opinion Filed: August 29, 2017).

Davenport v. Borough of Homestead, 870 F. 3d 273 (3rd Cir. 2017)

On Appeal from the United States District Court for the Western District of Pennsylvania, (W.D. Pa. No. 2-13-cv-00250), District Judge: Honorable David S. Cercone.

Bryan Campbell, Law Offices of Bryan Campbell, 310 Grant Street, Suite 2620, Pittsburgh, PA 15219, Allison N. Genard, Marshall Dennehey Warner Coleman & Goggin, 600 Grant Street, 2900 U.S. Steel Tower, Pittsburgh, PA 15219, John J. Hare, Shane Haselbarth [ARGUED], Marshall Dennehey Warner Coleman & Goggin, 2000 Market Street, Suite 2300, Philadelphia, PA 19103, Counsel for Appellants.

J. Kerrington Lewis, Sr. [ARGUED], Lewis Lewis & Reilly, 1040 Fifth Avenue, Pittsburgh, PA 15219, Counsel for Appellee.

Before: HARDIMAN, ROTH, and FISHER, Circuit Judges.

p.276 OPINION OF THE COURT

FISHER, Circuit Judge.

On an early Sunday morning in January 2013, Lena Davenport was riding in the front passenger seat of a vehicle driven by her son Donald Burris, Jr. After running a red light and refusing to pull over, Burris led police officers on a nearly five-mile low speed pursuit into the City of Pittsburgh. As the pursuit entered an area with high pedestrian traffic, City of Pittsburgh Police Officers Louis Schweitzer, Stephen Matakovich, Calvin Kennedy, and Thomas Gorecki each opened fire on Burris's vehicle. Davenport was struck by one of the officers' bullets. She filed this suit under 42 U.S.C. § 1983 against the officers and others alleging, *inter alia,* that the officers used excessive force in violation of both the Fourth Amendment and the Fourteenth Amendment's Due Process Clause. The District Court granted summary judgment on the basis of qualified immunity in favor of many of the defendants but denied it as to Schweitzer, Matakovich, Kennedy, and Gorecki, finding that their alleged conduct violated clearly established law. We will dismiss the appeal in part as to Gorecki and reverse in part as to Schweitzer, Matakovich, and Kennedy.

I

At about 1:38 a.m. on Sunday, January 13, 2013, Donald Burris, Jr. ran a red light in Homestead, Pennsylvania. Burris's mother, Lena Davenport, was the only passenger in his car. When a Homestead police officer attempted to stop the car, Burris did not comply. Instead, a pursuit began, heading into the City of Pittsburgh. As Burris entered Pittsburgh's South Side neighborhood on East Carson Street, several p.277 Pittsburgh police officers joined the pursuit. About 1:42 a.m., as the pursuit reached a busy area, the Sergeant of the Pittsburgh Police Department called it off.

Despite the Sergeant's orders, officers deployed spike-strips near the intersection of East Carson Street and 24th Street. It is undisputed that until reaching the 24th Street intersection, the pursuit did not jeopardize the safety of other motorists or pedestrians. However, in an attempt to avoid the spike-strips, Burris swerved between East Carson Street's inbound and outbound lanes.

As these events transpired, Officers Schweitzer, Matakovich, Kennedy, and Gorecki were working approved off-duty security jobs at bars on East Carson Street. They heard about the pursuit through police radio communications.

Near the 17th Street intersection, Schweitzer was the first to shoot at Burris's car, opening fire after observing the vehicle swerve between lanes of traffic and drive toward him. He fired at the front of the vehicle three times and once more at the vehicle's rear as it passed his position. At some point near this intersection, a bullet grazed a pedestrian's back.

Between the 16th and 15th Street intersections, after attempting to clear the street of pedestrians, Matakovich looked up and saw Burris's car heading toward him from the opposite lane. He shot at the vehicle four times and claims he jumped out of the way to avoid being struck. Kennedy, who was standing near Matakovich, fired once at the vehicle. Burris again swerved between lanes and, upon reaching the 15th Street intersection, side-swiped a parked car.

As the pursuit approached the 14th Street intersection, Burris continued to swerve, hitting a car in the outbound lane and then returning to the inbound lane. Near the 13th Street intersection, at about 1:44 a.m., the pursuit ended when Burris collided with a taxicab. At or around the same time, Gorecki fired two shots directly into the driver compartment of the vehicle. The parties dispute whether Gorecki fired before or after the final collision. The taxicab's dash-camera footage shows Gorecki's conduct, but it is not clear from the video when he actually discharged his firearm. Minutes later, at 1:47 a.m., paramedics arrived. They found Davenport on the floor of the vehicle's passenger compartment, having sustained a single gunshot wound near her right eye. It is unclear which officer's bullet actually struck Davenport.

At no time did the pursuit exceed forty-five miles per hour. Additionally, a forensic expert's evaluation of the vehicle's bullet holes indicates that one bullet was fired directly into the passenger compartment and another was fired after the vehicle's airbags deployed. Importantly, it is unclear whether the airbags deployed before the taxicab collision.

Relevant to this appeal, Davenport brought suit under 42 U.S.C. § 1983 alleging that Schweitzer, Matakovich, Kennedy, and Gorecki violated her Fourth Amendment right to be free from excessive force and her Fourteenth Amendment right to due process. The officers moved for summary judgment on the basis of qualified immunity. The District Court identified two factual disputes that, in its view, required sending the claims against those officers to trial. The first was whether the officers intentionally or indiscriminately fired into the passenger compartment of Burris's vehicle with knowledge of Davenport's presence therein. And the second was whether the officers fired into the vehicle even though it posed little or no danger to themselves or others. A reasonable jury, the court held, could determine p.278 that, on January 13, 2013, the officers violated clearly established law. *Davenport v. Borough of Homestead,* 2016 WL 5661733, at *19-22 (W.D. Pa. Sept. 30, 2016). The four officers appealed.

II

The District Court had jurisdiction under 28 U.S.C. § 1331. The collateral order doctrine provides us with jurisdiction to review the District Court's denial of the officers' claims of qualified immunity under 28 U.S.C. § 1291, but only "to the extent that it turns on an issue of law." *Mitchell v. Forsyth,* 472 U.S. 511, 530, 105 S.Ct. 2806, 86 L.Ed.2d 411 (1985).

Insofar as the District Court's order pertains to Schweitzer, Matakovich, and Kennedy, "we possess jurisdiction to review whether the set of facts identified by the district court is sufficient to establish a violation of a clearly established constitutional right." *Dougherty v. Sch. Dist. of Phila.,* 772 F.3d 979, 986 (3d Cir. 2014) (internal quotation marks omitted). However, we lack jurisdiction to review the order insofar as it pertains to Gorecki because he challenges the District Court's determination that the "pretrial record sets forth a 'genuine' issue of fact" for the jury. *Johnson v. Jones,* 515 U.S. 304, 319-20, 115 S.Ct. 2151, 132 L.Ed.2d 238 (1995); *see also Monteiro v. City of Elizabeth,* 436 F.3d 397, 405 (3d Cir. 2006) ("[W]hen qualified immunity depends on disputed issues of fact, those issues must be determined by the jury."). Relying on the taxicab's dash-camera footage, Gorecki argues that the District Court should have concluded that no reasonable jury could find that he discharged his firearm into Burris's vehicle *after* the pursuit ended. Appellants' Br. 17. And Gorecki's legal challenges assume the absence of this otherwise disputed fact. Because we are unable to address the factual challenge about *when* Gorecki discharged his firearm at Burris's vehicle at this stage of the proceedings, we are precluded from addressing the derivative legal challenges. *See Johnson,* 515 U.S. at 317, 115 S.Ct. 2151 ("[A]n interlocutory appeal concerning this kind of issue in a sense makes unwise use of appellate courts' time, by forcing them to decide in the context of a less developed record, an issue very similar to the one they may well decide anyway later, on a record that will permit a better decision.").

To the extent we have jurisdiction, we exercise plenary review over an appeal from a denial of summary judgment based on a lack of qualified immunity. *Zaloga v. Borough of Moosic,* 841 F.3d 170, 174 n.3 (3d Cir. 2016). We will reverse if "there is no genuine dispute as to any material fact and the movant is entitled to judgment as a matter of law." Fed. R. Civ. P. 56(a). To determine if there is a genuine dispute of material fact, we "view the underlying facts and all reasonable inferences therefrom in the light most favorable to the party opposing the motion[.]" *Dougherty,* 772 F.3d at 986 (internal quotation marks omitted).

III

Before reaching the merits of Schweitzer, Matakovich, and Kennedy's qualified immunity defense, we must first address an error committed by the District Court — the court's independent analysis of Davenport's Fourteenth Amendment claims. *See Davenport,* 2016 WL 5661733, at *14-15. The Supreme Court has instructed that "*all* claims that law enforcement officers have used excessive force — deadly or not — in the course of an arrest, investigatory stop, or other 'seizure' of a free citizen should be analyzed under the Fourth Amendment and its 'reasonableness' standard, rather than under a 'substantive p.279 due process' approach." *Graham v. Connor,* 490 U.S. 386, 395, 109 S.Ct. 1865, 104 L.Ed.2d 443 (1989). Therefore, an independent substantive due process analysis of an excessive force claim is inappropriate where, as here, the plaintiff's claim is covered by the Fourth Amendment. *See County of Sacramento v. Lewis,* 523 U.S. 833, 843, 118 S.Ct. 1708, 140 L.Ed.2d 1043 (1998).

The Supreme Court has "express[ed] no view" on whether a passenger in Davenport's position may recover under a Fourth Amendment theory. *Plumhoff v. Rickard,* ___ U.S. ___, 134 S.Ct. 2012, 2022 n.4, 188 L.Ed.2d 1056 (2014). And the federal appellate courts appear divided on the issue. *Compare, e.g., Lytle v. Bexar Cty.,* 560 F.3d 404, 410 (5th Cir. 2009) (suggesting yes), *Vaughan v. Cox,* 343 F.3d 1323, 1328-29 (11th Cir. 2003) (same), *Fisher v. City of Memphis,* 234 F.3d 312, 318-19 (6th Cir. 2000) (same), *and Pittman v. Nelms,* 87 F.3d 116, 120 (4th Cir. 1996) (same), *with, e.g., Medeiros v. O'Connell,* 150 F.3d 164, 169 (2d Cir. 1998) (suggesting no in the context of a hostage situation), *and Landol-Rivera v. Cruz Cosme,* 906 F.2d 791, 794-96 (1st Cir. 1990) (same). *See also Carabajal v. City of Cheyenne,* 847 F.3d 1203, 1212 (10th Cir. 2017) (declining to address the issue and resolving the case on other grounds). Nevertheless, the majority of circuits have suggested that a passenger in Davenport's position may seek relief under the Fourth Amendment; those circuits that have suggested otherwise reached their decisions on this issue before the Supreme Court decided *Brendlin v. California,* 551 U.S. 249, 127 S.Ct. 2400, 168 L.Ed.2d 132 (2007).

In *Brendlin,* the Supreme Court held that in intentionally stopping a vehicle, an officer subjects not only the driver, but also the vehicle's passengers to a Fourth Amendment seizure. 551 U.S. at 254-56, 127 S.Ct. 2400. It also made clear that an officer's knowledge of a passenger's presence in the vehicle is not dispositive because "an unintended person may be the object of the detention, so long as the detention is willful and not merely the consequence of an unknowing act." *Id.* at 254, 127 S.Ct. 2400 (alterations and internal quotation marks omitted). And in *Brower v. County of Inyo,* the Supreme Court cautioned courts not to "draw too fine a line" in "determining whether the means that terminates the freedom of movement is the very means that the government intended." 489 U.S. 593, 598, 109 S.Ct. 1378, 103 L.Ed.2d 628 (1989). Accordingly, even if the officers' intended application of force would have only incidentally seized Davenport, because her freedom of movement was terminated "by the very instrumentality set in motion or put in place in order to achieve" Burris's and her detention, *id.* at 599, 109 S.Ct. 1378, there is no set of facts that precludes a finding of a Fourth Amendment seizure. Today we join the majority of circuits in holding that a passenger shot by an officer during the course of a vehicular pursuit may seek relief under the Fourth Amendment. Because Davenport may do so, the Fourth Amendment, "not the more generalized notion of 'substantive due process,' must be the guide for analyzing these claims." *Graham,* 490 U.S. at 395, 109 S.Ct. 1865. Consequently, the District Court erred in independently analyzing Davenport's Fourth and Fourteenth Amendment claims.

IV

"The doctrine of qualified immunity shields officials from civil liability so long as their conduct 'does not violate clearly established statutory or constitutional rights of which a reasonable person p.280 would have known.'" *Mullenix v. Luna,* ___ U.S. ___, 136 S.Ct. 305, 308, 193 L.Ed.2d 255 (2015) (per curiam) (quoting *Pearson v. Callahan,* 555 U.S. 223, 231, 129 S.Ct. 808, 172 L.Ed.2d 565 (2009)). In resolving questions of qualified immunity, we conduct a two-part inquiry. First, "[t]aken in the light most favorable to the party asserting the injury, do the facts alleged show the officer's conduct violated a constitutional right?" *Saucier v. Katz,* 533 U.S. 194, 201, 121 S.Ct. 2151, 150 L.Ed.2d 272 (2001). Second, we consider whether, in light of the specific context of the case, "the right was clearly established." *Id.* Although we need not address these prongs in any particular order, *Pearson,* 555 U.S. at 236, 129 S.Ct. 808, we exercise our discretion to address both "[b]ecause we believe this case will clarify and elaborate upon our prior jurisprudence in important and necessary ways." *Williams v. Sec'y Pa. Dep't of Corr.,* 848 F.3d 549, 558 (3d Cir. 2017) (internal quotation marks omitted).

A

We first consider whether Schweitzer, Matakovich, and Kennedy's alleged conduct violated the rights secured to Davenport by the Fourth Amendment. The Fourth Amendment requires that a seizure be objectively reasonable. *Graham,* 490 U.S at 396-97, 109 S.Ct. 1865. Determining objective reasonableness involves "a careful balancing of the nature and quality of the intrusion on the individual's Fourth Amendment interests against the countervailing governmental interests at stake." *Id.* at 396, 109 S.Ct. 1865 (internal quotation marks omitted). The government has an interest in ensuring public safety, and a fleeing vehicle may pose a threat to that interest. *Scott v. Harris,* 550 U.S. 372, 383, 127 S.Ct. 1769, 167 L.Ed.2d 686 (2007). However, because our analysis "requires careful attention to the facts and circumstances of each particular case," *Graham,* 490 U.S. at 396, 109 S.Ct. 1865, the fact that a vehicle is in flight does not necessarily render an officer's use of deadly force objectively reasonable. The question is "whether the totality of the circumstances justified a particular sort of ... seizure." *Tennessee v. Garner,* 471 U.S. 1, 8-9, 105 S.Ct. 1694, 85 L.Ed.2d 1 (1985). We evaluate each officer's conduct "from the perspective of a reasonable officer on the scene, rather than with the 20/20 vision of hindsight," understanding that "officers are often forced to make split-second judgments — in circumstances that are tense, uncertain, and rapidly evolving — about the amount of force that is necessary in a particular situation." *Graham,* 490 U.S. at 396-97, 109 S.Ct. 1865.

Based on Davenport's version of facts, the District Court concluded that a reasonable jury could find that the officers intentionally shot at Davenport and that the pursuit posed no serious threat of immediate harm to others. This was error, as these assertions are "blatantly contradicted by the record." *Scott,* 550 U.S. at 380, 127 S.Ct. 1769. First, video evidence indisputably shows a heavy pedestrian presence during the course of the pursuit. And second, throughout the pursuit Burris continuously swerved between inbound and out-bound lanes, which ultimately led to his colliding with three other vehicles. Considering the serious threat of immediate harm to others, no reasonable jury could conclude that the officers fired at the vehicle for any reason other than to eliminate that threat.

Schweitzer shot at the vehicle with the knowledge that Burris refused to yield to officers' continued pursuit and swerved between lanes in an area with high pedestrian traffic. Matakovich and Kennedy shot at the vehicle with the additional knowledge p.281 that Burris continued the dangerous vehicular pursuit despite sustaining police fire. Given the serious threat of immediate harm to East Carson Street's many pedestrians, even if the officers knew that a passenger was in the vehicle, their conduct was objectively reasonable as a matter of law. *See id.* (In "weighing the perhaps lesser probability of injuring or killing numerous bystanders against the perhaps larger probability of injuring or killing a single person," courts must "take into account... the number of lives at risk."). As such, Schweitzer, Matakovich, and Kennedy are entitled to summary judgment because they did not violate Davenport's Fourth Amendment rights.

B

There is an additional and distinct basis on which we must reverse the District Court's denial of qualified immunity to Schweitzer, Matakovich, and Kennedy — their alleged conduct did not violate clearly established law. The crux of the "clearly established" analysis "is whether officers have 'fair notice' that they are acting unconstitutionally." *Mullenix,* 136 S.Ct. at 314. In other words, an officer is not entitled to qualified immunity if "at the time of the challenged conduct, the contours of [the] right [were] sufficiently clear that every reasonable official would have understood that what he [was] doing violates that right." *Ashcroft v. al-Kidd,* 563 U.S. 731, 741, 131 S.Ct. 2074, 179 L.Ed.2d 1149 (2011) (alteration and internal quotation marks omitted). "We do not require a case directly on point, but existing precedent must have placed the statutory or constitutional question beyond debate." *Id.* "The dispositive question is whether the violative nature of *particular* conduct is clearly established. This inquiry must be undertaken in light of the specific context of the case, not as a broad general proposition." *Mullenix,* 136 S.Ct. at 308 (citation and internal quotation marks omitted). Accordingly, the specific question presented by this case is whether, on January 13, 2013, the law clearly established that an officer who, in an attempt to eliminate the serious threat of immediate harm to others created by a vehicle's flight shoots the vehicle's passenger, violates that passenger's rights under the Fourth Amendment. We hold that it did not.

The District Court concluded that *Tennessee v. Garner* clearly established that the officers' alleged conduct was unlawful. *See Davenport,* 2016 WL 5661733, at *20. *Garner* held that a "police officer may not seize an unarmed, nondangerous suspect by shooting him dead." 471 U.S. at 11, 105 S.Ct. 1694. The Supreme Court, however, has applied *Garner's* "general" test for excessive force in only the "obvious" case. *Brosseau v. Haugen,* 543 U.S. 194, 199, 125 S.Ct. 596, 160 L.Ed.2d 583 (2004) (per curiam). And courts have found "obvious" cases only in the absence of a serious threat of immediate harm to others. *See, e.g., Lytle,* 560 F.3d at 417 (finding an obvious case where an officer shot a passenger in a vehicle without a sufficient threat of harm to others); *Adams v. Speers,* 473 F.3d 989, 991-94 (9th Cir. 2007) (finding same where, without a sufficient threat of harm to others, an officer shot a fleeing suspect on the highway and by using deadly force actually created a serious hazard for himself and the suspect); *Smith v. Cupp,* 430 F.3d 766, 773, 776 (6th Cir. 2005) (finding same where, without a sufficient threat of harm to others, an officer shot an intoxicated suspect who took control of a patrol car in a parking lot); *Vaughan,* 343 F.3d at 1331 (finding same where, without a sufficient threat of harm to others, an officer shot suspects who were merely evading arrest).

In concluding that this was such an "obvious" case, the District Court improperly p.282 ignored the serious threat of immediate harm to others posed by Burris's flight. The District Court justified limiting its analysis to the threat of harm posed by Davenport's conduct by citing *Plumhoff v. Rickard* for the proposition that "Fourth Amendment rights are personal rights that may not be vicariously asserted." *Davenport,* 2016 WL 5661733, at *21. But acknowledging the threat of harm posed by Burris's flight neither enhances nor diminishes Davenport's Fourth Amendment rights. Rather, as discussed above, *see* Part IV-A, *supra,* it is a necessary factor of our "objective reasonableness" analysis. Given the serious threat of immediate harm to others that Schweitzer, Matakovich, and Kennedy sought to eliminate, *Garner* does not clearly establish their alleged conduct violated Davenport's constitutional rights.

The Supreme Court has never addressed the rights of a passenger involved in a dangerous vehicular pursuit. And while, in the absence of applicable Supreme Court precedent, we may consider "a robust consensus of cases of persuasive authority," *al-Kidd,* 563 U.S. at 742, 131 S.Ct. 2074 (internal quotation marks omitted), Davenport cites no precedent from this Circuit, or any other, that is on point. Given this near absence of cases, we cannot conclude that Schweitzer, Matakovich, and Kennedy acted in a plainly incompetent manner when they attempted to address the serious threat of immediate harm to others posed by Burris's flight. *See Ziglar v. Abbasi,* ___ U.S. ___, 137 S.Ct. 1843, 1867, 198 L.Ed.2d 290 (2017) ("[Q]ualified immunity protects all but the plainly incompetent or those who knowingly violate the law." (internal quotation marks omitted)).

* * *

For the reasons stated, the judgment of the District Court will be reversed in part and the case remanded with instructions to enter summary judgment on the basis of qualified immunity in favor of Schweitzer, Matakovich, and Kennedy. The appeal will be dismissed in part for lack of jurisdiction with respect to Gorecki.

862 F.3d 353 (2017)

Richard FIELDS, Appellant

v.

CITY OF PHILADELPHIA; Sisca, Police Officer, Badge No. 9547; Joe Doe, an Unknown Philadelphia Police Officer.

Amanda Geraci, Appellant

v.

City of Philadelphia; Dawn Brown, Police Officer, Badge No. 2454; Terra M. Barrow, Police Officer, Badge No. 1147; Nikki L. Jones, Police Officer, Badge No. 2549; Rhonda Smith, Police Officer, Badge No. 1373.

Nos. 16-1650, 16-1651.

United States Court of Appeals, Third Circuit.

Argued May 9, 2017.

(Opinion filed: July 7, 2017).

Fields v. City of Philadelphia, 862 F. 3d 353 (3rd Cir. 2017)

Appeal from the United States District Court for the Eastern District of Pennsylvania, (D.C. Civil Action Nos. 2-14-cv-04424/05264), District Judge: Honorable Mark A. Kearney.

Jonathan H. Feinberg, Esquire, Kairys Rudovsky Messing & Reinberg, 718 Arch Street, Suite 501 South, Philadelphia, PA 19106, John J. Grogan, Esquire, Peter E. Leckman, Esquire, Langer Grogan & Diver, 1717 Arch Street, Suite 4130, Philadelphia, PA 19103, Seth Kreimer, Esquire, University of Pennsylvania School of Law, 3400 Chestnut Street Philadelphia, PA 19104, Mary Catherine Roper, Esquire, Molly M. Tack-Hopper, Esquire (Argued), American Civil Liberties Union of Pennsylvania, P.O. Box 60173, Philadelphia, PA 19106, Counsel for Appellants.

Craig R. Gottlieb, Esquire (Argued), City of Philadelphia Law Department, 1515 Arch Street, 17th Floor, One Parkway, Philadelphia, PA 19102, Counsel for Appellees.

Dorothy A. Hickok, Esquire, Alfred W. Putnam, Jr., Esquire, Mark D. Taticchi, Esquire, Drinker Biddle & Reath, 18th & Cherry Streets, One Logan Square, Suite 2000, Philadelphia, PA 19103, Ilya Shapiro, Esquire, Cato Institute, 1000 Massachusetts Ave., N.W., Washington, DC 20001, Counsel for Amicus Appellant, Cato Institute.

Eli Segal, Esquire, Pepper Hamilton, 217 Ryers Avenue, Philadelphia, PA 19103, Counsel for Amicus Appellant, Society for Photographic Education.

Sharon M. McGowan, Esquire, April J. Anderson, Esquire, Tovah R. Calderon, Esquire, United States Department of Justice, Civil Rights Division, Appellate Section, RFK 3724, P.O. Box 14403, Ben Franklin Station, Washington, DC 20044, Counsel for Amicus Appellant, United State of America.

Bruce D. Brown, Esquire, Gregg P. Leslie, Esquire, The Reporters Committee for Freedom of the Press, 1156 15th Street, p.355 N.W., Suite 1250, Washington, DC 20005, Counsel for Amicus Appellant, Reporters Committee for Freedom of the Press and 31 Media Organizations.

Sophia S. Cope, Esquire, Adam Schwartz, Esquire, Electronic Frontier Foundation, 815 Eddy Street, San Francisco, CA 94109, Counsel for Amicus Appellant, Electronic Frontier Foundation.

Robert J. LaRocca, Esquire, Kohn Swift & Graf, One South Broad Street, Suite 2100, Philadelphia, PA 19107, Counsel for Amicus Appellant, First Amendment Law Professors.

Patrick G. Geckle, Esquire, 1500 John F. Kennedy Boulevard, Two Penn Center Plaza, Suite 1850, Philadelphia, PA 19102, John Burton, Esquire, The Marine Building, 128 North Fair Oaks Avenue, Pasadena, CA 91103, David Milton, Esquire, Law Offices of Howard Friedman, PC, 90 Canal Street, Fifth Floor, Boston, MA 02114, Counsel for Amicus Appellant, National Police Accountability Project.

Jason P. Gosselin, Esquire, Drinker Biddle & Reath, 18th & Cherry Streets, One Logan Square, Suite 2000, Philadelphia, PA 19103, John W. Whitehead, Esquire, Douglas R. McKusick, Esquire, Christopher F. Moriarty, Esquire, The Rutherford Institute, P.O. Box 7482, Charlottesville, VA 22906, Counsel for Amicus Appellant, Rutherford Institute.

Before: AMBRO, RESTREPO, and NYGAARD, Circuit Judges

p.354 OPINION OF THE COURT

AMBRO, Circuit Judge.

In 1991 George Holliday recorded video of the Los Angeles Police Department officers beating Rodney King and submitted it to the local news. Filming police on the job was rare then but common now. With advances in technology and the widespread ownership of smartphones, "civilian recording of police officers is ubiquitous." Jocelyn Simonson, *Copwatching,* 104 Cal. L. Rev. 391, 408 (2016); *see* Seth F. Kreimer, *Pervasive Image Capture and the First Amendment: Memory, Discourse, and the Right to Record,* 159 U. Pa. L. Rev. 335, 337 (2011). These recordings have both exposed police misconduct and exonerated officers from errant charges. However, despite the growing frequency of private citizens recording police activity and its importance to all involved, some jurisdictions have attempted to regulate the extent of this practice. Individuals making recordings have also faced retaliation by officers, such as arrests on false criminal charges and even violence.

This case involves retaliation. Richard Fields and Amanda Geraci attempted to record Philadelphia police officers carrying out official duties in public and were retaliated against even though the Philadelphia Police Department's official policies recognized that "[p]rivate individuals have a First Amendment right to observe and record police officers engaged in the public discharge of their duties." J.A. 1187. No party contested the existence of the First Amendment right. Yet the District Court concluded that neither Plaintiff had engaged in First Amendment activity because the conduct — the act of recording — was not sufficiently expressive. However, this case is not about whether Plaintiffs expressed themselves through conduct. It is whether they have a First Amendment right of access to information about how our public servants operate in public.

Every Circuit Court of Appeals to address this issue (First, Fifth, Seventh, Ninth, and Eleventh) has held that there is a First Amendment right to record police activity in public. *See Turner v. Lieutenant Driver*, 848 F.3d 678 (5th Cir. 2017); *Gericke v. Begin*, 753 F.3d 1 (1st Cir. p.356 2014); *Am. Civil Liberties Union of Ill. v. Alvarez*, 679 F.3d 583 (7th Cir. 2012); *Glik v. Cunniffe*, 655 F.3d 78 (1st Cir. 2011); *Smith v. City of Cumming*, 212 F.3d 1332 (11th Cir. 2000); *Fordyce v. City of Seattle*, 55 F.3d 436 (9th Cir. 1995). Today we join this growing consensus. Simply put, the First Amendment protects the act of photographing, filming, or otherwise recording police officers conducting their official duties in public.

I. BACKGROUND

In September 2012, Amanda Geraci, a member of the police watchdog group "Up Against the Law," attended an anti-fracking protest at the Philadelphia Convention Center. She carried her camera and wore a pink bandana that identified her as a legal observer. About a half hour into the protest, the police acted to arrest a protestor. Geraci moved to a better vantage point to record the arrest and did so without interfering with the police. An officer abruptly pushed Geraci and pinned her against a pillar for one to three minutes, which prevented her from observing or recording the arrest. Geraci was not arrested or cited.

One evening in September 2013, Richard Fields, a sophomore at Temple University, was on a public sidewalk where he observed a number of police officers breaking up a house party across the street. The nearest officer was 15 feet away from him. Using his iPhone, he took a photograph of the scene. An officer noticed Fields taking the photo and asked him whether he "like[d] taking pictures of grown men" and ordered him to leave. J.A. 8. Fields refused, so the officer arrested him, confiscated his phone, and detained him. The officer searched Fields' phone and opened several videos and other photos. The officer then released Fields and issued him a citation for "Obstructing Highway and Other Public Passages." These charges were withdrawn when the officer did not appear at the court hearing.

Fields and Geraci brought 42 U.S.C. § 1983 claims against the City of Philadelphia and certain police officers. They alleged that the officers illegally retaliated against them for exercising their First Amendment right to record public police activity and violated their Fourth Amendment right to be free from an unreasonable search or seizure.

They also pointed out that the City's Police Department's official policies recognized their First Amendment right. In 2011 the Department published a memorandum advising officers not to interfere with a private citizen's recording of police activity because it was protected by the First Amendment. In 2012 it published an official directive reiterating that this right existed. Both the memorandum and directive were read to police officers during roll call for three straight days. And in 2014, after the events in our case and the occurrence of other similar incidents, the Department instituted a formal training program to ensure that officers ceased retaliating against bystanders who recorded their activities.

The District Court nonetheless granted summary judgment in favor of Defendants on the First Amendment claims. They did not argue against the existence of a First Amendment right, but rather contended that the individual officers were entitled to qualified immunity and that the City could not be vicariously liable for the officers' acts. Yet the District Court on its own decided that Plaintiffs' activities were not protected by the First Amendment because they presented no evidence that their "conduct may be construed as expression of a belief or criticism of police activity." *Fields v. City of Philadelphia,* 166 F.Supp.3d 528, 537 (E.D. Pa. 2016). p.357 When confronted by the police, Plaintiffs did not express their reasons for recording. Their later deposition testimony showed that Geraci simply wanted to observe and Fields wanted to take a picture of an "interesting" and "cool" scene. *Id.* at 539. In addition, neither testified of having an intent to share his or her photos or videos. *Id.* The District Court thus concluded that, "[a]bsent any authority from the Supreme Court or our Court of Appeals, we decline to create a new First Amendment right for citizens to photograph officers when they have no expressive purpose such as challenging police actions." *Id.* at 542.

Because of this ruling, the District Court did not reach the issues of qualified immunity or municipal liability. However, it allowed the Fourth Amendment claims to go to trial. *Id.* ("The citizens are not without remedy because once the police officer takes your phone, alters your technology, arrests you or applies excessive force, we proceed to trial on the Fourth Amendment claims."). By stipulation, Plaintiffs dismissed their Fourth Amendment claims so that they could immediately appeal the First Amendment ruling.

II. JURISDICTION AND STANDARDS

The District Court had subject matter jurisdiction over these federal civil rights claims under 28 U.S.C. §§ 1331 & 1343, and we have jurisdiction under 28 U.S.C. § 1291. We exercise plenary review over the District Court's grant of summary judgment. *Melrose, Inc. v. City of Pittsburgh,* 613 F.3d 380, 387 (3d Cir. 2010). It "is appropriate only where, drawing all reasonable inferences in favor of the non-moving party, there is no genuine issue as to any material fact and ... the moving party is entitled to judgment as a matter of law." *Id.* (alteration in original and citation omitted). Because this is a First Amendment case, we must also "engage in a searching, independent factual review of the full record." *Am. Civil Liberties Union v. Mukasey,* 534 F.3d 181, 186 (3d Cir. 2008) (citations omitted).

III. ORDER OF ANALYSIS

Defendants ask us to avoid ruling on the First Amendment issue. Instead, they want us to hold that, regardless of the right's existence, the officers are entitled to qualified immunity and the City cannot be vicariously liable for the officers' acts. We reject this invitation to take the easy way out. Because this First Amendment issue is of great importance and the recording of police activity is a widespread, common practice, we deal with it before addressing, if needed, defenses to liability.

In *Saucier v. Katz,* the Supreme Court held that courts must determine whether a constitutional right existed before deciding if it had been "clearly established" such that defendants would not be entitled to qualified immunity. 533 U.S. 194, 200-01, 121 S.Ct. 2151, 150 L.Ed.2d 272 (2001). Less than a decade later, however, the Court reversed course in *Pearson v. Callahan,* holding that courts instead have the discretion to choose to address immunity first and bypass the substantive constitutional issue. 555 U.S. 223, 236, 129 S.Ct. 808, 172 L.Ed.2d 565 (2009). We have not ruled on the First Amendment right, instead merely holding that at the time of our rulings the claimed right was not clearly established. *Kelly v. Borough of Carlisle,* 622 F.3d 248 (3d Cir. 2010); *True Blue Auctions v. Foster,* 528 Fed.Appx. 190 (3d Cir. 2013).

In the years since, First Amendment issues from the recording of police activity recur, and they deal directly with constitutional doctrine. With technological progress and the ubiquity of smartphone ownership p.358 — especially in the years since our *Kelly* decision — we are now in an age where the public can record our public officials' conduct and easily distribute that recording widely. This increase in the observation, recording, and sharing of police activity has contributed greatly to our national discussion of proper policing. Consequently, police departments nationwide, often with input from the U.S. Department of Justice, are developing polices addressing precisely these issues, and our opinion can assist in their efforts to comply with the Constitution. Moreover, in the case before us the constitutional question is not "so factbound that [our] decision [will] provide[] little guidance for future cases." *Pearson,* 555 U.S. at 237, 129 S.Ct. 808. All we need to decide is whether the First Amendment protects the act of recording police officers carrying out official duties in public places. We also have excellent briefing on appeal, including counsel for the parties and eight *amici,* including the U.S. Department of Justice, the Cato Institute, well-known First Amendment law professors, and some of the largest news organizations in the country. We therefore address the First Amendment question before moving to the defenses.

IV. THE FIRST AMENDMENT RIGHT TO RECORD

The District Court concluded that Plaintiffs engaged in conduct only (the act of making a recording) as opposed to expressive conduct (using the recording to criticize the police or otherwise comment on officers' actions). It did so by analogy, applying the "expressive conduct" test used to address symbolic speech: "Conduct is protected by the First Amendment when the nature of the activity, combined with the factual context and environment in which it was undertaken, shows that the activity was sufficiently imbued with elements of communication to fall within the First Amendment's scope." *Fields,* 166 F.Supp.3d at 534 & n.34 (quoting *Tenafly Eruv Ass'n, Inc. v. Borough of Tenafly,* 309 F.3d 144, 158 (3d Cir. 2002)).

We disagree on various fronts. Foremost is that the District Court focused on whether Plaintiffs had an expressive intent, such as a desire to disseminate the recordings, or to use them to criticize the police, *at the moment when* they recorded or attempted to record police activity. *See id.* at 534-35. This reasoning ignores that the value of the recordings may not be immediately obvious, and only after review of them does their worth become apparent. The First Amendment protects actual photos, videos, and recordings, *see Brown v. Entm't Merchants Ass'n,* 564 U.S. 786, 790, 131 S.Ct. 2729, 180 L.Ed.2d 708 (2011), and for this protection to have meaning the Amendment must also protect the act of creating that material. There is no practical difference between allowing police to prevent people from taking recordings and actually banning the possession or distribution of them. *See Alvarez,* 679 F.3d at 596 ("Restricting the use of an audio or audiovisual recording device suppresses speech just as effectively as restricting the dissemination of the resulting recording."); *see also* Cato Institute *Amicus* Br. 7 ("[B]oth precedent and first principles demonstrate that the First Amendment protects the process of capturing inputs that may yield expression, not just the final act of expression itself"); Kreimer, 159 U. Pa. L. Rev. at 366 ("[T]he threat of arrest remains a potent deterrent to spontaneous photographers who have no deep commitment to capturing any particular image."). As illustrated here, because the officers stopped Ms. Geraci from recording the arrest of the protestor, she never had the opportunity to decide to put any recording to expressive use.

p.359 Plaintiffs and some *amici* argue that the act of recording is "inherently expressive conduct," like painting, writing a diary, dancing, or marching in a parade. *See, e.g.,* First Amendment Law Professors *Amicus* Br. 8 ("If writing in an undistributed diary is speech, making an undistributed recording can be characterized as speech as well."); Society for Photographic Education *Amicus* Br. 2 ("Making a photograph merits First Amendment protection because it is artistic expression just the same as painting a landscape, sketching a street scene, or sculpting a statue."); *Tenafly Eruv Ass'n,* 309 F.3d at 160 ("'Parades are thus a form of expression, not just motion ....'") (quoting *Hurley v. Irish-American Gay, Lesbian and Bisexual Grp. of Bos.,* 515 U.S. 557, 568, 115 S.Ct. 2338, 132 L.Ed.2d 487 (1995)). Regardless of the merits of these arguments, our case is not about people attempting to create art with police as their subjects. It is about recording police officers performing their official duties.

The First Amendment protects the public's right of access to information about their officials' public activities. It "goes beyond protection of the press and the self-expression of individuals to prohibit government from limiting the stock of information from which members of the public may draw." *First Nat'l. Bank of Bos. v. Bellotti,* 435 U.S. 765, 783, 98 S.Ct. 1407, 55 L.Ed.2d 707 (1978). Access to information regarding public police activity is particularly important because it leads to citizen discourse on public issues, "the highest rung of the hierarchy of First Amendment values, and is entitled to special protection." *Snyder v. Phelps,* 562 U.S. 443, 452, 131 S.Ct. 1207, 179 L.Ed.2d 172 (2011) (quoting *Connick v. Myers,* 461 U.S. 138, 145, 103 S.Ct. 1684, 75 L.Ed.2d 708 (1983)); *Garrison v. Louisiana,* 379 U.S. 64, 77, 85 S.Ct. 209, 13 L.Ed.2d 125 (1964) (recognizing the "paramount public interest in a free flow of information to the people concerning public officials, their servants"). That information is the wellspring of our debates; if the latter are to be "'uninhibited, robust, and wide-open,'" *Snyder,* 562 U.S. at 452, 131 S.Ct. 1207 (quoting *N. Y. Times Co. v. Sullivan,* 376 U.S. 254, 270, 84 S.Ct. 710, 11 L.Ed.2d 686 (1964)), the more credible the information the more credible are the debates.

To record what there is the right for the eye to see or the ear to hear corroborates or lays aside subjective impressions for objective facts. Hence to record is to see and hear more accurately. Recordings also facilitate discussion because of the ease in which they can be widely distributed via different forms of media. Accordingly, recording police activity in public falls squarely within the First Amendment right of access to information. As no doubt the press has this right, so does the public. *See PG Publ'g. Co. v. Aichele,* 705 F.3d 91, 99 (3d Cir. 2013); *Branzburg v. Hayes,* 408 U.S. 665, 684, 92 S.Ct. 2646, 33 L.Ed.2d 626 (1972).

Bystander videos provide different perspectives than police and dashboard cameras, portraying circumstances and surroundings that police videos often do not capture. Civilian video also fills the gaps created when police choose not to record video or withhold their footage from the public. *See* Nat'l Police Accountability Project *Amicus* Br. 7 (noting that "[a] recent survey of 50 major police departments' policies on body cameras revealed that many policies either failed to make clear when officers must turn on their body cameras, gave officers too much discretion when to record, or failed to require explanations when officers did not record") (citation omitted).

The public's creation of this content also complements the role of the news media. p.360 Indeed, citizens' gathering and disseminating "newsworthy information [occur] with an ease that rivals that of the traditional news media." 2012 U.S. D.O.J. Letter to Baltimore Police Department; J.A. 1684. *See also Glik,* 655 F.3d at 78 ("The proliferation of electronic devices with video-recording capability means that many of our images of current events come from bystanders with a ready cell phone or digital camera rather than a traditional film crew, and news stories are now just as likely to be broken by a blogger at her computer as a reporter at a major newspaper."). In addition to complementing the role of the traditional press, private recordings have improved professional reporting, as "video content generated by witnesses and bystanders has become a common component of news programming." The Reporters Committee for Freedom of the Press and 31 Media Organizations *Amicus* Br. 11; *see also id.* at 2 ("Today, the first source of information from the scene of a newsworthy event is frequently an ordinary citizen with a smart phone."). And the inclusion of "bystander video enriches the stories journalists tell, routinely adding a distinct, first-person perspective to news coverage." *Id.* at 12.

Moreover, the proliferation of bystander videos has "spurred action at all levels of government to address police misconduct and to protect civil rights." *See* Nat'l Police Accountability Proj. *Amicus* Br. 1. These videos have helped police departments identify and discipline problem officers. They have also assisted civil rights investigations and aided in the Department of Justice's work with local police departments. And just the act of recording, regardless what is recorded, may improve policing. *See Glik,* 655 F.3d at 82-83. Important to police is that these recordings help them carry out their work. They, every bit as much as we, are concerned with gathering facts that support further investigation or confirm a dead-end. And of particular personal concern to police is that bystander recordings can "exonerate an officer charged with wrongdoing." *Turner,* 848 F.3d at 689.

We do not say that all recording is protected or desirable. The right to record police is not absolute. "[I]t is subject to reasonable time, place, and manner restrictions." *Kelly,* 622 F.3d at 262; *see Whiteland Woods, L.P. v. Twp. of W. Whiteland,* 193 F.3d 177, 183 (3d Cir. 1999). But in public places these restrictions are restrained.

We need not, however, address at length the limits of this constitutional right. Defendants offer nothing to justify their actions. Fields took a photograph across the street from where the police were breaking up a party. Geraci moved to a vantage point where she could record a protestor's arrest, but did so without getting in the officers' way. If a person's recording interferes with police activity, that activity might not be protected. For instance, recording a police conversation with a confidential informant may interfere with an investigation and put a life at stake. But here there are no countervailing concerns.

In sum, under the First Amendment's right of access to information the public has the commensurate right to record — photograph, film, or audio record — police officers conducting official police activity in public areas.

V. QUALIFIED IMMUNITY

Having decided the existence of this First Amendment right, we now turn to whether the officers are entitled to qualified immunity. We conclude they are.

Government actors are entitled to qualified immunity unless they violated a constitutional right "so clearly established p.361 that '*every reasonable official* would have understood that what he is doing violates that right.'" *Zaloga v. Borough of Moosic,* 841 F.3d 170, 175 (3d Cir. 2016) (quoting *Reichle v. Howards,* 566 U.S. 658, 659, 132 S.Ct. 2088, 182 L.Ed.2d 985 (2012)) (emphasis in original). "In other words, existing precedent must have placed the statutory or constitutional question *beyond debate.*" *Id.* (quoting *Reichle,* 566 U.S. at 664, 132 S.Ct. 2088) (emphasis in original). We do not need Supreme Court precedent or binding Third Circuit precedent to guide us if there is a "robust consensus of cases of persuasive authority in the Courts of Appeals." *L.R. v. Sch. Dist. of Phila.,* 836 F.3d 235, 247-48 (3d Cir. 2016) (alteration and citations omitted). District court decisions, though not binding, also "play a role in the qualified immunity analysis." *Doe v. Delie,* 257 F.3d 309, 321 n.10 (3d Cir. 2001). To determine whether the right is clearly established, we look at the state of the law when the retaliation occurred, here in 2012 (Geraci) and 2013 (Fields). *See id.*

To conduct the clearly established inquiry, we "frame the right 'in light of the specific context of the case, not as a broad general proposition,'" *L.R.,* 836 F.3d at 247-48 (citation omitted), as it needs to be "specific enough to put 'every reasonable official' on notice of it." *Zaloga,* 841 F.3d at 175 (citation omitted). At issue here is Plaintiffs' ability to record the police carrying out official duties in public. We have never held that such a right exists, only that it might. *See Gilles v. Davis,* 427 F.3d 197, 212 n.14 (3d Cir. 2005) ("[V]ideotaping or photographing the police in the performance of their duties on public property may be a protected activity."). In 2010 we held that there was no clearly established right for the public to do so, at least in the context of a police traffic stop. *Kelly,* 622 F.3d at 262 ("We find these cases insufficiently analogous to the facts of this case to have put Officer Rogers on notice of a clearly established right to videotape police officers during a traffic stop [in 2007]."). Only a few years later in 2013, in a non-precedential opinion, we held that "[e]ven if the distinction between traffic stops and public sidewalk confrontations is [] meaningful ... [,] our case law does not clearly establish a right to videotape police officers performing their duties [in 2009]." *True Blue Auctions,* 528 Fed.Appx. at 192-93. So to resolve whether the right has become clearly established after these decisions, we must decide whether a "robust consensus" has emerged that puts the existence of this First Amendment right "beyond debate." *Zaloga,* 841 F.3d at 175.

Plaintiffs contend the absence of Circuit precedent does not end the inquiry, as after the events in *Kelly* and *True Blue* the Philadelphia Police Department adopted official policies recognizing the First Amendment right of citizens to record police in public. As plausible as that may be on the surface, it does not win the argument. With one breath Plaintiffs assert that these policies clearly established their legal right, but for purposes of municipal liability (an issue we remand) they vigorously argue that the policies were utterly ineffective in conveying to the officers that this right clearly existed. And Plaintiffs have compiled evidence indicating this was so. For example, they point out that Captain Francis Healy, the policy advisor to the Police Commissioner, testified that, notwithstanding the adoption of the Department's policies, the "officers didn't understand that there was a constitutional right [to record]." Reply Br. 11 (quoting J.A. 282-83).

As to decisions of other appellate courts relevant to the qualified immunity analysis, Defendants and the District Court argue that those decisions are distinguishable because p.362 they involved expressive intent or an intent to distribute. *See, e.g., Alvarez,* 679 F.3d at 588 ("The ACLU intends to publish these recordings online and through other forms of electronic media."); *Fields,* 166 F.Supp.3d at 538 n.56 ("In *Glik,* the plaintiff expressed concern police were using excessive force arresting a young man in a public park and began recording the arrest on his cell phone[,] and the police then arrested plaintiff.... Notably, the plaintiff in *Fordyce* [*v. City of Seattle,* 55 F.3d 436 (9th Cir. 1995)] claimed he was recording a public protest for a local news station."); *see also* D.O.J. *Amicus* Br. 22 n. 14 ("[I]n those cases, the plaintiffs' objectives or opinions ... [to disseminate] were apparent from context. In this respect, Fields's case in particular is one of first impression."). Indeed, the Fifth Circuit just this year recognized that these other appellate decisions did not clearly establish the constitutional right to record. *See Turner,* 848 F.3d at 687.

Where District Courts in our Circuit have held in favor of the First Amendment right, Defendants also distinguish those cases for requiring expressive act or intent, not just recording alone, once again echoing the reasoning of the District Court here. *See Fields,* 166 F.Supp.3d at 537 ("We find the citizens videotaping and picture-taking in [those district court cases] all contained some element of expressive conduct or criticism of police officers and are patently distinguishable from Fields' and Geraci's activities."). Whether Defendants and the District Court correctly distinguished these cases, we cannot say that the state of the law at the time of our cases (2012 and 2013) gave fair warning so that every reasonable officer knew that, absent some sort of expressive intent, recording public police activity was constitutionally protected. Accordingly, the officers are entitled to qualified immunity.

VI. MUNICIPAL LIABILITY

Because of its First Amendment ruling, the District Court did not reach whether the City could be held liable for its officers' conduct. *See generally Monell v. Dep't of Soc. Servs.,* 436 U.S. 658, 98 S.Ct. 2018, 56 L.Ed.2d 611 (1978). While the City contends that there is no genuine issue of material fact and it cannot be held liable as a matter of law, we follow our usual practice of according our District Court colleague the initial opportunity to resolve these contentions.

* * * * *

We ask much of our police. They can be our shelter from the storm. Yet officers are public officials carrying out public functions, and the First Amendment requires them to bear bystanders recording their actions. This is vital to promote the access that fosters free discussion of governmental actions, especially when that discussion benefits not only citizens but the officers themselves. We thus reverse and remand for further proceedings.

NYGAARD, Circuit Judge, concurring in the part, dissenting in part.

I agree with the majority that the cause must be remanded. Because I conclude that the First Amendment right at issue is and was clearly established, I dissent.

The question of whether a constitutional right is clearly established has to be considered in a real-world context; this is why our analysis is conducted from the perspective of a "reasonable official." *L.R. v. Sch. Dist. of Phila.,* 836 F.3d 235, 247-48 (3d Cir. 2016) (alteration and citations omitted). Such an approach protects public officials — particularly our police officers in the field — from uncertainty about the precise boundary of a particular constitutional right when situations arise that have not yet been considered by the courts. Nonetheless, p.363 we must apply this "reasonable official" analysis consistently, recognizing that there are instances — rare though they may be — when any reasonable official in the circumstance would know the boundaries of a constitutional right well before we have ruled on it. I am confident that this is one of those cases because of the unique combination of a number of factors.

First, as the majority notes, every Circuit Court of Appeals that has considered the issue ruled that there is a First Amendment right to record police activity in public. Four of these decisions were published before the conduct at issue here, and two of them occurred after our decision in *Kelly v. Borough of Carlisle,* 622 F.3d 248 (3d Cir. 2010), in which we posited that the right was not clearly established at that time. *See Am. Civil Liberties Union of Ill. v. Alvarez,* 679 F.3d 583 (7th Cir. 2012); *Glik v. Cunniffe,* 655 F.3d 78 (1st Cir. 2011); *Smith v. City of Cumming,* 212 F.3d 1332 (11th Cir. 2000); *Fordyce v. City of Seattle,* 55 F.3d 436 (9th Cir. 1995).[1] I am convinced that such a "robust consensus," alone, sufficiently grounds a ruling that the right is clearly established. *L.R.,* 836 F.3d at 247-48. However, our record goes far beyond that.

The Police Department's official policies explicitly recognized this First Amendment right well before the incidents under review here took place. Captain Frank Healy of the Department's Research and Planning Unit stated that, in 2011, officers did "not understand the police [were] allowed to be taped in public." App. 119 (2013 Healy dep. at 54). Because there was "some confusion on the street" he testified that there "was a definite need for the policy." App. 121 (2013 Healy dep. at 62). He said that the Department wanted "to be on the forefront rather than on the back end," of educating its officers on this issue, prompting Police Commissioner Charles Ramsey to request that a policy be written requiring police officers to "allow citizens to record the police." App. 118 (2013 Healy dep. at 52). The policy was intended to get "clarification out on the street so the officers knew what their duties [were]." App. 120 (2013 Healy dep. at 59). It issued a memorandum in September, 2011 stating that police should reasonably expect to be photographed, videotaped and or audibly recorded by members of the general public. Commissioner's Memorandum 11-01, issued on September 23, 2011, made clear to all Philadelphia police officers that they "shall not" obstruct or prevent this conduct, and that "under no circumstances" were permitted to disable or damage the devices being used. App. 1185.

In the year that followed publication of the memorandum, Internal Affairs received eight complaints by citizens of retaliation by police for recording police performing their duties. App. 1569. Additionally, the U.S. Department of Justice issued recommendations in May, 2012, that all police departments "affirmatively set forth the First Amendment right to record police activity." App. 1675. As a result, the Commissioner directed Captain Healy and his unit to revise the Memorandum to incorporate the Department of Justice recommendations. The revised document was issued as Departmental Directive 145 on November 9, 2012. Like a Memorandum, a Directive is also official Departmental policy, but it covers a topic in greater depth.

Directive 145 plainly requires officers to allow citizens to make recordings of police activity. The Directive uses, verbatim, the p.364 language of the Department of Justice's recommendation, stating that its purpose was to "protect the constitutional rights of individuals to record police officers engaged in the public discharge of their duties." App. 1187. It said, further, that "observing, gathering, and disseminating of information ... is a form of free speech." *Id.* Police officers were prohibited from "blocking, obstructing, or otherwise hindering" recordings made by persons "unless the person making such recording engages in actions that jeopardize the safety of the officer, any suspects or other individuals in the immediate vicinity, violate the law, incite others to violate, or actually obstruct an officer from performing any official duty." *Id.* As it was published, the Department mandated that a sergeant read it at every roll call, Department-wide. Each police officer also received a copy of the Directive and was required to sign that they received it.

Although the Directives declared a First Amendment right well ahead of this Court, the Philadelphia Police Department Commissioner had a desire to "get out ahead" of what he presciently viewed as an inevitable ruling. With all of this, it is indisputable that all officers in the Philadelphia Police Department were put on actual notice that they were required to uphold the First Amendment right to make recordings of police activity. From a practical perspective, the police officers had no ground to claim ambiguity about the boundaries of the citizens' constitutional right here. Mindful of the established trend among the Circuit Courts of Appeals, this combined with this clear Guidance from the Commissioner sufficiently grounds a conclusion that the right to record official, public police activity was clearly established and "beyond debate." *Zaloga,* 841 F.3d at 175 (quoting *Reichle,* 132 S.Ct. at 2093). However, this, too, ignores another piece of the context of this case that should be considered as part of the "reasonable official" inquiry.

The majority cites to the 2011 article of Seth F. Kreimer,[2] in which he notes that, given the ubiquity of personal electronic devices with cameras, "[w]e live, relate, work, and decide in a world where image capture from life is routine, and captured images are part of ongoing discourse, both public and private. Capture of images has become an adjunct to memory and an accepted medium of connection and correspondence." Seth F. Kreimer, *Pervasive Image Capture and the First Amendment: Memory, Discourse, and the Right to Record,* 159 U. Pa. L. Rev. 335, 337 (2011). If we are to assess the issue from a reasonable officer perspective, we cannot artificially remove him or her from this widespread societal phenomenon. (Indeed, it is not unreasonable to speculate that most — if not all — of the police officers themselves possessed such a personal electronic device at the time that the incidents underlying these cases took place.) A reasonable police officer would have understood, first-hand, the significance of this proliferation of personal electronic devices that have integrated image capture into our daily lives, making it a routine aspect of the way in which people record and communicate events. Apart from any court ruling or official directive, the officers' own lived experience with personal electronic devices (both from the perspective of being the one who is recording and one who is being recorded) makes it unreasonable to assume that the police officers were oblivious to the First Amendment implications of any attempt by them to curtail such recordings.

p.365 As I noted above, I concur with the majority's analysis and conclusions regarding the existence of a First Amendment right to record, and agree that the case against the City of Philadelphia should be remanded for further proceedings. However, in light of the social, cultural, and legal context in which this case arose, I am convinced that — in this unique circumstance — no reasonable officer could have denied at the time of the incidents underlying these cases that efforts to prevent people from recording their activities infringed rights guaranteed by the First Amendment. For these reasons, I dissent from the majority's conclusion that the police officers are immune from suit.

[1] Two more recent decisions reinforce the trend. *See Turner v. Lieutenant Driver,* 848 F.3d 678 (5th Cir. 2017); *Gericke v. Begin,* 753 F.3d 1 (1st Cir. 2014).

[2] Professor, University of Pennsylvania Law School.

FOURTH CIRCUIT DECISIONS

The Affirmative Defense of Qualified Immunity for Law Enforcement

948 F.3d 222 (2020)

Tina RAY, Plaintiff-Appellant,
v.
Michael ROANE, in his individual capacity, Defendant-Appellee.

No. 18-2120.

United States Court of Appeals, Fourth Circuit.
Argued: October 30, 2019.
Decided: January 22, 2020.

Ray v. Roane, 948 F. 3d 222 (4th Cir. 2020)

Appeal from the United States District Court for the Western District of Virginia, at Harrisonburg. Elizabeth Kay Dillon, District Judge. (5:17-cv-00093-EKD).

Dallas S. LePierre, Mario Bernard Williams, NDH LLC, Atlanta, GA, for Plaintiff-Appellant.

Carlene Booth Johnson, Perry Law Firm, PC, Dillwyn, VA, for Defendant-Appellee.

ARGUED: Dallas S. LePierre, NEXUS DERECHOS HUMANOS ATTORNEYS, INC., Atlanta, Georgia, for Appellant. Carlene Booth Johnson, PERRY LAW FIRM, PC, Dillwyn, Virginia, for Appellee. ON BRIEF: Mario B. Williams, NEXUS DERECHOS HUMANOS ATTORNEYS, INC., Atlanta, Georgia, for Appellant.

p.225 Before GREGORY, Chief Judge, KEENAN, and RICHARDSON, Circuit Judges.

Reversed and remanded by published opinion. Chief Judge GREGORY wrote the opinion, in which Judge KEENAN and Judge RICHARDSON joined.

p.224 GREGORY, Chief Judge:

Appellant Tina Ray appeals the dismissal of her claim brought under 42 U.S.C. § 1983, in which she alleged that her Fourth Amendment rights were violated when Officer Michael Roane shot and killed her dog, Jax. According to the complaint, Roane shot Jax when it was in Ray's yard, tethered, and incapable of reaching or harming Roane. Bound by those facts at this stage of the proceeding, we hold that the complaint plausibly states a claim for an unconstitutional seizure of Ray's property for which Roane is not entitled to qualified immunity. Therefore, we reverse and remand for further proceedings.

I.

At the outset, we acknowledge that there is evidence in the record on appeal that appears to contradict some of the allegations in the complaint. However, because Ray's claims were dismissed for failure to state a claim, we "limit our review to the complaint itself." *Braun v. Maynard,* 652 F.3d 557, 559 (4th Cir. 2011). Further, as we do in any case alleging unreasonable use of force under the Fourth Amendment, we focus on the facts and circumstances confronting the officer "immediately prior to and at the very moment" that force was used, and disregard information not known to the officer at that time. *Greenidge v. Ruffin,* 927 F.2d 789, 792 (4th Cir. 1991). With these principles in mind, the relevant factual allegations in the complaint are straightforward.

On September 24, 2017, Roane drove to Ray's property to assist with an arrest warrant that was being served on Ray for domestic abuse. When Roane arrived on Ray's property, four other officers were already present and parked in the driveway. Ray's dog—a 150-pound German Shepard named Jax—was secured by a zip-lead attached to two trees that allowed the animal limited movement within a "play area" of the yard. Rather than park in the driveway like the other officers, Roane parked his truck within the dog's "play area," prompting the other officers on scene to shout and gesture toward Roane, indicating that he should "[w]ait" and "[l]et [Ray] get her dog." Roane exited his vehicle and started walking toward the house.

As Roane emerged from his vehicle, Jax began barking at and approaching Roane. Roane responded by backing away from the dog and drawing his firearm, while Ray ran to the zip-lead and began shouting Jax's name. "In a short moment," Jax reached the end of the zip-lead and "could not get any closer" to Roane. Roane observed that the dog could not reach him, and further observed that Ray was now holding onto Jax's fully-extended lead and continuing to call Jax's name. Roane therefore stopped backing up. Roane then took a step forward, positioning himself over Jax, and fired his weapon into the dog's head. The dog died from the wound.

In her complaint, Ray asserted four claims for relief against Roane—unlawful seizure of Jax in violation of the Fourth Amendment, violation of substantive due process, conversion, and intentional infliction of emotional distress—seeking various categories of damages. Ray later indicated she would not pursue her substantive due process claim. Roane moved to dismiss the entire action against him and answered the p.226 complaint. On September 20, 2018, the district court dismissed Ray's federal claim for unlawful seizure of Jax and declined to exercise supplemental jurisdiction over the remaining two state-law claims. In so doing, the district court concluded Roane's actions had been reasonable under the totality of the circumstances and he would be entitled to qualified immunity.

As to whether Ray sufficiently alleged that Roane's actions were unreasonable, the district court pointed to several facts in the complaint that led it to conclude the seizure was reasonable: (1) Jax was a large dog weighing approximately 150 pounds; (2) Jax was "alarmed" by Roane's arrival; (3) Jax was "barking while approaching Roane," and Roane responded by moving backward, away from him; and (4) the entire incident took only a "short moment." J.A. 362. The district court also pointed to several allegations it distinguished, such as the fact that Jax had reached the end of his zip-lead and could not reach Roane. According to the district court, "an objectively reasonable officer would have felt threatened in the circumstances immediately preceding the shot and ... might not have been sure that Jax no longer posed a threat." J.A. 362-63. The important factor was instead Jax's proximity to Roane.

The district court also held that Roane was entitled to qualified immunity. For the same reasons it concluded that Ray failed to allege an unreasonable seizure, the court concluded that a reasonable officer would not have known it was "clearly unreasonable" to shoot Jax in these circumstances. At worst, this was a "classic case" of a bad guess in a gray area or a reasonable but mistaken judgment. J.A. 370. Accordingly, the district court dismissed the entire action with prejudice. Ray now appeals the district's court dismissal.

II.

We review a district court's grant of a motion to dismiss *de novo. See King v. Rubenstein,* 825 F.3d 206, 214 (4th Cir. 2016) (citing *Simmons v. United Mortg. & Loan Inv., LLC,* 634 F.3d 754, 768 (4th Cir. 2011)). In reviewing a motion to dismiss for failure to state a claim, we must "accept as true all of the factual allegations contained in the complaint and draw all reasonable inferences in favor of the plaintiff." *Id.* at 212. A complaint need only "give the defendant fair notice of what the ... claim is and the grounds upon which it rests." *Tobey v. Jones,* 706 F.3d 379, 387 (4th Cir. 2013) (quoting *Bell Atl. Corp. v. Twombly,* 550 U.S. 544, 555, 127 S.Ct. 1955, 167 L.Ed.2d 929 (2007)). "A Rule 12(b)(6) motion to dismiss 'does not resolve contests surrounding facts, the merits of a claim, or the applicability of defenses.'" *Id.* (quoting *Republican Party of N. Carolina v. Martin,* 980 F.2d 943, 952 (4th Cir. 1992)).

We also review a qualified immunity-based grant of a motion to dismiss *de novo. Id.* at 385 (citation omitted). To determine whether a complaint should survive a qualified immunity-based motion to dismiss, we exercise "sound discretion" in following the two-prong inquiry set forth by the Supreme Court, analyzing (1) whether a constitutional violation occurred and (2) whether the right violated was clearly established. *See Pearson v. Callahan,* 555 U.S. 223, 236, 129 S.Ct. 808, 172 L.Ed.2d 565 (2009); *Saucier v. Katz,* 533 U.S. 194, 200, 121 S.Ct. 2151, 150 L.Ed.2d 272 (2001); *Melgar v. Greene,* 593 F.3d 348, 353 (4th Cir. 2010). A court may consider either prong of the qualified immunity analysis first. *Sims v. Labowitz,* 885 F.3d 254, 260 (4th Cir. 2018).

III.

On appeal, Ray argues the district court erred in analyzing both prongs of the qualified p.227 immunity analysis. First, she asserts the district court erred dismissing the action and concluding the allegations in the complaint were insufficient to allege Roane unreasonably seized Jax in violation of the Fourth Amendment. Ray then contends, assuming the seizure was unconstitutional, the district court also erroneously concluded Roane was entitled to qualified immunity. We agree with Ray.

A.

As an initial matter, it is well-settled that privately owned dogs are "effects" under the Fourth Amendment, and that the shooting and killing of such a dog constitutes a "seizure." *Altman v. City of High Point, N.C.,* 330 F.3d 194, 203-05 (4th Cir. 2003). Thus, we will affirm the district court's conclusion that the shooting of Ray's dog by Roane was constitutional only if we conclude it was reasonable under the circumstances alleged in the complaint.

"To assess the reasonableness of [a government seizure under the Fourth Amendment], '[w]e must balance the nature and quality of the intrusion on the individual's Fourth Amendment interests against the importance of the governmental interests alleged to justify the intrusion.'" *United States v. Jacobsen,* 466 U.S. 109, 125, 104 S.Ct. 1652, 80 L.Ed.2d 85 (1984) (citation omitted). As we held in *Altman,* private interests in dogs—and family pets especially—are highly significant since dogs "have aptly been labeled 'Man's Best Friend,' and certainly the bond between a dog owner and his pet can be strong and enduring." 330 F.3d at 205 ("Many consider dogs to be their most prized personal possessions, and still others think of dogs solely in terms of an emotional relationship, rather than a property relationship."). Likewise, the government undoubtedly has a strong public interest in protecting citizens and officers from dogs that may be dangerous or otherwise a source of public nuisance. *Id.* at 205-06. Thus, "[t]he calculus of reasonableness must embody allowance for the fact that police officers are often forced to make split-second judgments—in circumstances that are tense, uncertain, and rapidly evolving—about the amount of force that is necessary in a particular situation." *Altman,* 330 F.3d at 205 (quoting *Graham v. Connor,* 490 U.S. 386, 396-97, 109 S.Ct. 1865, 104 L.Ed.2d 443 (1989)).

In weighing these competing interests, we focus on the circumstances confronting Roane at the moment he fired his weapon. *Greenidge,* 927 F.2d at 792; *see also Altman,* 330 F.3d at 205-06. Although we view the facts in the light most favorable to Ray, we disregard allegations of subjective intent in the complaint and consider only the information known to Roane at the time of the shooting. *Altman,* 330 F.3d at 205-06; *Greenidge,* 927 F.2d at 792. Our task, as we explained in *Altman,* is to place ourselves in the shoes of Roane and ask whether his actions were objectively unreasonable. *Altman,* 330 F.3d at 205. In other words, we assess whether Roane's asserted justification of officer safety justifies his decision to shoot Jax. *Id.*

Accepting these principles, Roane argues that his actions were objectively reasonable because he was confronted with a 150-pound German Shepard that was "alarmed" by his arrival, barking, and that in a "short moment" had advanced to within a step of him. Under these circumstances, Roane asserts that he reasonably felt threatened by Jax. Roane also cites to numerous cases involving dog shootings in which the officer's conduct was deemed reasonable, despite the fact that the dogs at issue were smaller than Jax or farther from the officer at the time of the shooting. As a result, Roane reasons the district p.228 court properly determined Ray's complaint failed to allege a Fourth Amendment violation. We disagree.

The problem with Roane's argument, and thus with the district court's decision adopting it, is that it requires us to ignore certain factual allegations in Ray's complaint and to draw reasonable inferences *against* Ray on a motion to dismiss. *DePaola v. Clarke,* 884 F.3d 481, 484 (4th Cir. 2018) ("In reviewing the defendants' motions to dismiss, we accept as true the factual allegations set forth in [the] complaint and draw reasonable inferences therefrom in [her] favor."). According to the complaint, Roane stopped backing away from Jax when the dog reached the end of the zip-lead, and then took a step toward the dog before firing his weapon. *See* J.A. 15. These factual allegations yield the reasonable inference that Roane observed that the dog could no longer reach him, and, thus, could not have held a reasonable belief that the dog posed an imminent threat. Taking these factual allegations as true and drawing these reasonable inferences in Ray's favor, Roane's seizure of Jax was unreasonable because Jax no longer posed any threat to Roane.

Tellingly, in reaching the opposite conclusion, the district court relied on cases that were all decided on summary judgment involving one or more dogs that, like here, were barking or advancing toward an officer but, unlike here, were unleashed or unrestrained and posed an immediate danger to the officer. *See, e.g., Stephenson v. McClelland,* 632 F. App'x 177, 179 (5th Cir. 2015) (per curiam); *Schutt v. Lewis,* No. 6:12-CV-1697, 2014 WL 3908187, at *1 (M.D. Fla. Aug. 11, 2014); *McCarthy v. Kootenai Cty.,* No. 08-CV-294, 2009 WL 3823106, at *1-2 (D. Idaho Nov. 12, 2009); *Dziekan v. Gaynor,* 376 F. Supp. 2d 267, 269 (D. Conn. 2005); *Warboys v. Proulx,* 303 F. Supp. 2d 111, 113 (D. Conn. 2004). The district court's extensive reliance on cases decided on summary judgment underscores our conclusion that the district court did not fully credit the allegations in Ray's complaint and the inferences arising therefrom.

Accordingly, we conclude the district court erred in holding that the complaint failed to allege a violation of Ray's Fourth Amendment rights. We next turn to whether Roane is entitled to qualified immunity at this stage of the litigation.

B.

Qualified immunity "shield[s] [officials] from civil damages liability as long as their actions could reasonably have been thought consistent with the rights they are alleged to have violated." *Anderson v. Creighton,* 483 U.S. 635, 638, 107 S.Ct. 3034, 97 L.Ed.2d 523 (1987); *see also Saucier,* 533 U.S. at 201-02, 121 S.Ct. 2151. Thus, although we conclude that Ray has plausibly alleged a violation of her constitutional rights, Roane is entitled to qualified immunity unless we conclude that that a reasonable officer in Roane's position would have understood that his conduct was unlawful at the time of the shooting. *Braun,* 652 F.3d at 561.

The question of whether a right is clearly established is a question of law for the court to decide. *Pritchett v. Alford,* 973 F.2d 307, 312 (4th Cir. 1992). The question of whether a reasonable officer would have known that the conduct at issue violated that right, however, cannot be decided prior to trial if disputes of the facts exist. *Smith v. Ray,* 781 F.3d 95, 100 (4th Cir. 2015). Thus, "while the purely legal question of whether the constitutional right at issue was clearly established is always capable of decision at the summary judgment stage [or on a motion to dismiss], a genuine question of material fact p.229 regarding [w]hether the conduct allegedly violative of the right actually occurred ... must be reserved for trial." *Willingham v. Crooke,* 412 F.3d 553, 559 (4th Cir. 2005) (alteration and omission in original and internal quotation marks omitted) (quoting *Pritchett,* 973 F.2d at 313).

In addition, to determine whether a right was clearly established, we first look to cases from the Supreme Court, this Court, or the highest court of the state in which the action arose. *Owens ex rel. Owens v. Lott,* 372 F.3d 267, 279 (4th Cir. 2004). In the absence of "directly on-point, binding authority," courts may also consider whether "the right was clearly established based on general constitutional principles or a consensus of persuasive authority." *Booker v. S.C. Dep't of Corr.,* 855 F.3d 533, 543 (4th Cir. 2017); *Owens,* 372 F.3d at 279 ("[T]he absence of controlling authority holding identical conduct unlawful does not guarantee qualified immunity."). The Supreme Court has ruled against defining a right at too high a level of generality and held that doing so fails to provide fair warning to officers that their conduct is unlawful outside an obvious case. *White v. Pauly,* ___ U.S. ___, 137 S. Ct. 548, 552, 196 L.Ed.2d 463 (2017).

On appeal, Ray argues that since at least 2003, we have "placed Roane on fair notice/warning that [she] had a clearly established right to enjoy her dog Jax, free from Roane using unreasonable deadly force against Jax," particularly where her dog Jax was secured, controlled, and could no longer reach Roane. According to Ray, Roane's actions—killing a pet while that pet poses no immediate threat of harm to a law enforcement officer—are unreasonable and contravene well-recognized precedents.

In response, Roane contends neither our precedents nor the body of case law involving police-dog shooting address the "particularly unusual circumstances" Roane had faced at Ray's home. According to Roane, there is no authority involving "a 150-pound dog that had advanced toward [an officer] to within a step, 'alarmed' and barking"; a "25-foot zip-lead contraption"; or other relevant facts similar to the ones here. As a result, qualified immunity protects "mistakes in judgment" and gives officers like Roane "breathing room to make reasonable but mistaken judgments." Moreover, this Court should not engage in "Monday morning quarterback[ing]" to find an officer, like Roane, "could have or should have done something different."

We disagree with Roane's contentions with respect to qualified immunity, for the same reasons already set forth in our discussion of whether the complaint states a claim for a violation of the Fourth Amendment. Viewing all facts in the complaint and inferences arising therefrom in Ray's favor, it is clear that Roane shot Jax at a time when he could not have held a reasonable belief that the dog posed a threat to himself or others. Accepting these facts, we hold that a reasonable police officer would have understood that killing Jax under such circumstances would constitute an unreasonable seizure of Ray's property under the Fourth Amendment.

We acknowledge that there is no "directly on-point, binding authority" in this circuit that establishes the principle we adopt today. *Booker,* 855 F.3d at 543. Until now, we have never had the occasion to hold that it is unreasonable for a police officer to shoot a privately owned animal when it does not pose an immediate threat to the officer or others. Still, even without "directly on-point, binding authority," qualified immunity is inappropriate if "the right was clearly established based on general constitutional principles or a consensus of persuasive authority." *Booker,* 855 p.230 F.3d at 543; *Owens,* 372 F.3d at 279-280. This is such a case.

First, we observe that the unlawfulness of Roane's alleged actions was established by the general principles we espoused in *Altman.* In *Altman,* we held that privately owned dogs are protected under the Fourth Amendment, and further established that the reasonableness of the seizure of a dog depends on whether the governmental interest in safety outweighs the private interest in a particular case. 330 F.3d at 203-05. Based on these broader principles alone, it would have been "manifestly apparent" to a reasonable officer in Roane's position that shooting a privately owned dog, *in the absence of any safety rationale at all,* is unreasonable. *Owens,* 372 F.3d at 279.

The consensus of our sister circuits leaves no doubt that this principle was clearly established by September 2017. *See id.* at 279-280. As the D.C. Circuit observed in 2016, prior to Roane's alleged conduct in this case, "[e]very circuit that has considered the issue ... ha[s] invariably concluded that 'the use of deadly force against a household pet is reasonable only if the pet poses an immediate danger and the use of force is unavoidable.'" *Robinson v. Pezzat,* 818 F.3d 1, 7 (D.C. Cir. 2016) (citation omitted); *see also Brown v. Battle Creek Police Dep't,* 844 F.3d 556, 568 (6th Cir. 2016) ("[A] police officer's use of deadly force against a dog ... is reasonable under the Fourth Amendment when... the dog poses an imminent threat to the officer's safety."); *Carroll v. Cty. of Monroe,* 712 F.3d 649, 652 (2d Cir. 2013) (noting that the reasonableness of officers' conduct is contingent on there being "a genuine threat to officer safety"); *Viilo v. Eyre,* 547 F.3d 707, 710 (7th Cir. 2008) ("[C]ommon sense ... counsel[s] that the use of deadly force against a household pet is reasonable only if the pet poses an immediate danger[.]"); *San Jose Charter of the Hells Angels Motorcycle Club v. City of San Jose,* 402 F.3d 962, 977-78 (9th Cir. 2005) (holding that "any reasonable officer [would know] that the Fourth Amendment forbids the killing of a person's dog, or the destruction of a person's property, when that destruction is unnecessary"); *Brown v. Muhlenberg Twp.,* 269 F.3d 205, 210-11 (3d Cir. 2001) ("[T]he state may [not], consistent with the Fourth Amendment, destroy a pet when it poses no immediate danger[.]").

Based on this preexisting consensus of persuasive case law, together with the general principles we announced in *Altman,* we hold that a reasonable officer in Roane's position would have known that his alleged conduct was unlawful at the time of the shooting in this case. *Anderson,* 483 U.S. at 640, 107 S.Ct. 3034; *Booker,* 855 F.3d at 543. Thus, we hold that the district court erred in concluding Roane is entitled to qualified immunity at this stage of the litigation.

Notably, Roane does not contest the legal principle we adopt today, namely, that it is unreasonable for an officer to shoot a privately owned dog when the dog poses no objective threat to the officer or others. Instead, Roane's arguments exclusively focus on the underlying facts, and ultimately amount to the factual assertion that Roane reasonably perceived Jax as a threat at the time of the shooting. But this is an appeal from a motion to dismiss, which tests the sufficiency of the complaint, not its veracity. For the reasons discussed above, we cannot accept Roane's version of the facts at this stage of the proceedings, in which we must grant all reasonable inferences in favor of Ray. *DePaola,* 884 F.3d at 484.

IV.

For the foregoing reasons, we reverse the district court's dismissal of Ray's complaint p.231 and remand for further proceedings consistent with this opinion. REVERSED AND REMANDED.

917 F.3d 763 (2019)

Johnnie WILLIAMS, Plaintiff-Appellee, and
Son Odarious Williams, Plaintiff
v.
Lance Corporal Kyle STRICKLAND, Defendant-Appellant and
Cpl Heroux; Sgt Walter Criddle; Beaufort County Sheriff Office; Raymond S. Heroux, Defendants.
Johnnie Williams, Plaintiff-Appellee, and
Son Odarious Williams, Plaintiff,
v.
Raymond S. Heroux, Defendant-Appellant, and
Cpl Heroux; Sgt Walter Criddle; Beaufort County Sheriff Office; Lance Corporal Kyle Strickland, Defendants.

No. 18-6219, No. 18-6220.

United States Court of Appeals, Fourth Circuit.

Argued: December 13, 2018.

Decided: March 5, 2019.

Williams v. Strickland, 917 F. 3d 763 (4th Cir. 2019)

Appeals from the United States District Court for the District of South Carolina, at Beaufort, (9:15-cv-01118-PMD), Patrick Michael Duffy, Senior District Judge.

ARGUED: Elloree A. Ganes, HOOD LAW FIRM, LLC, Charleston, South Carolina; Mary Bass Lohr, HOWELL, GIBSON & HUGHES, P.A., Beaufort, South Carolina, for Appellants. Jordan Calloway, MCGOWAN, HOOD & FELDER, LLC, Rock Hill, South Carolina for Appellee. ON BRIEF: Whitney B. Harrison, MCGOWAN, HOOD & FELDER, LLC, Columbia, South Carolina, for Appellee.

Before KEENAN, FLOYD, and THACKER, Circuit Judges.

Affirmed by published opinion. Judge Floyd wrote the opinion in which Judge Keenan and Judge Thacker joined.

p.766 FLOYD, Circuit Judge:

Johnnie Williams brought suit under 42 U.S.C. § 1983 against two law enforcement officers: Kyle Strickland and Raymond Heroux. Williams claimed that the officers violated his Fourth Amendment rights by using deadly force while arresting him. The officers moved for summary judgment on the basis of qualified immunity. The district court denied their motions, and the officers now appeal. For the reasons that follow, we affirm.

I.

On June 29, 2012, Williams drove from Georgia to South Carolina to visit a relative. His six-year-old son was with him. When Williams and his son arrived in South Carolina, they stopped at a gas station. There, Williams ran into an acquaintance, Anthony Ancrum, who needed a ride to his apartment. Ancrum's apartment complex was nearby, and Williams offered to drive him.

On the way to the apartment complex, Williams crossed paths with Officer Heroux, who was on duty in a patrol car. Heroux ran Williams's license plate through dispatch and learned that the plate had been stolen. He followed Williams into the parking lot of the apartment complex, where he turned on his blue lights. In response, Williams pulled into a parking space. Heroux got out to approach him. Two other officers, Kyle Strickland and Walter Criddle, arrived on the scene.

What happened over the next several seconds forms the heart of this appeal. When Heroux was about ten feet from Williams's car, Williams shifted the car into reverse and cut the wheel, causing the front end of the car to swivel in Heroux's direction. Heroux, believing himself to be in danger, stepped back and drew his gun. At the same time, Strickland started walking toward Williams's car. Williams then put the car in drive, straightened out, and drove toward Strickland.

Heroux and Strickland opened fire on the car. Crucially, it is not clear—at this stage—how far Williams got before Heroux and Strickland started shooting. He may have been headed toward Strickland. He may have been passing by Strickland, such that Strickland was alongside the car and out of the car's trajectory. Or he may have already driven past Strickland, such that Strickland, like Heroux, was behind the car.

One of Heroux's shots hit Williams in the back.[1] Williams lost control of the car and crashed into a tree. He was airlifted to the hospital for emergency surgery, after which he was placed in a medically induced coma. Despite several subsequent surgeries, p.767 Williams has, among other things, "lost the full and proper function of his bowels, lungs, and other bodily systems." J.A. 45.

Years later, Williams was charged with three counts of assault and battery related to the incident. He pleaded guilty. As part of his plea deal, he admitted that he had deliberately rotated the car in Heroux's direction and that he had driven towards Strickland. Notably, Williams also agreed as part of his plea deal that the officers had started shooting only after his car had driven past them.

In 2015, Williams filed a § 1983 suit against Strickland, Heroux, and other defendants who are no longer parties to the action. He alleged that by firing on him during the course of his arrest, the officers had subjected him to excessive force, violating his rights under the Fourth Amendment.

After discovery, Strickland and Heroux each moved for summary judgment on the basis of qualified immunity. In relevant part, the officers argued that they were entitled to summary judgment because the undisputed facts showed that they had not violated Williams's clearly established rights. More specifically, they argued that when they opened fire on Williams, they believed that Williams was about to hit Strickland with his car; under those circumstances —according to the officers— Williams had no clearly established right to be free from the use of deadly force.

The district court denied the officers' motion. The court determined that a reasonable jury, viewing the evidence in the light most favorable to Williams, could conclude that when the officers discharged their weapons, Williams's car was either (a) in the process of passing Strickland or (b) already past Strickland. According to the district court, if either (a) or (b) were true, then the officers' use of deadly force would have violated rights that we clearly established in *Waterman v. Batton,* 393 F.3d 471 (4th Cir. 2005). Since a reasonable jury could conclude that the officers had acted in a way that violated Williams's clearly established rights, the district court held that the officers were not entitled to summary judgment. The officers now appeal.[2]

II.

Our first task here is to determine whether, and to what extent, we may subject the district court's order to appellate review. Generally, our jurisdiction is limited to final decisions of the district court. 28 U.S.C. § 1291; *Martin v. Duffy,* 858 F.3d 239, 246 (4th Cir. 2017). This means that we cannot normally review a district court's order denying summary judgment, since orders denying summary judgment are interlocutory, not final. *Hensley v. Horne,* 297 F.3d 344, 347 (4th Cir. 2002). There are, however, exceptions. One exception is the "collateral order doctrine," which "permits appellate review of a small class of orders that are conclusive, that resolve important questions separate from the merits, and that are effectively p.768 unreviewable on appeal from the final judgment in the underlying action." *Adams v. Ferguson,* 884 F.3d 219, 223-24 (4th Cir. 2018) (internal quotation marks omitted).

A district court's denial of summary judgment on the basis of qualified immunity is a collateral order and therefore subject to immediate appellate review, despite being interlocutory. *Iko v. Shreve,* 535 F.3d 225, 234 (4th Cir. 2008). Our review of such orders is limited to a narrow legal question: if we take the facts as the district court gives them to us,[3] and we view those facts in the light most favorable to the plaintiff, is the defendant still entitled to qualified immunity? *Id.; see also Brown v. Elliott,* 876 F.3d 637, 641-42 (4th Cir. 2017) ("[W]hen resolving the issue of qualified immunity at summary judgment, a court must ascertain the circumstances of the case by crediting the plaintiff's evidence and drawing all reasonable inferences in the plaintiff's favor." (internal quotation marks omitted)); *Waterman,* 393 F.3d at 473 ("In reviewing the denial of summary judgment based on qualified immunity, we accept as true the facts that the district court concluded may be reasonably inferred from the record when viewed in the light most favorable to the plaintiff."). Significantly, we cannot reach whether the plaintiff has produced enough evidence to survive summary judgment. *Winfield v. Bass,* 106 F.3d 525, 530 (4th Cir. 1997) (en banc).

What this amounts to is: We may review the portion of the district court's order denying Strickland and Heroux's motions for summary judgment on the basis of qualified immunity. But our review may reach only one question: would the officers be entitled to qualified immunity if a jury concluded that they had fired on Williams when they were no longer in the trajectory of Williams's car? We turn to that question now.

III.

Qualified immunity "protects government officials from liability for violations of constitutional rights that were not clearly established at the time of the challenged conduct." *Iko,* 535 F.3d at 233. Given this standard, we must determine two things. First, if Strickland and Heroux fired on Williams after they were no longer in the path of Williams's car, did they violate Williams's Fourth Amendment right to freedom from excessive force? Second, as of June 29, 2012, was it clearly established that using deadly force against Williams after the officers were no longer in the car's trajectory would violate Williams's right to freedom from excessive force?[4] The answer to both questions is yes.

A.

The Fourth Amendment prohibits law enforcement officers from using excessive force to make a seizure. *Jones v. Buchanan,* 325 F.3d 520, 527 (4th Cir. 2003). "Whether an officer has used excessive force is analyzed under a standard of objective reasonableness." *Henry v. Purnell,* 652 F.3d 524, 531 (4th Cir. 2011).

p.769 Because deadly force is extraordinarily intrusive, it takes a lot for it to be reasonable. *See Tennessee v. Garner,* 471 U.S. 1, 9, 105 S.Ct. 1694, 85 L.Ed.2d 1 (1985) ("The intrusiveness of a seizure by means of deadly force is unmatched."). Indeed, an officer may reasonably apply deadly force to a fleeing suspect—even someone suspected of committing a serious felony—only if the officer has "probable cause to believe that the suspect poses a significant threat of death or serious physical injury to the officer or others." *Id.* at 3, 105 S.Ct. 1694.[5] And even a "significant threat of death or serious physical injury" to an officer does not justify the use of deadly force unless the threat is "immediate." *Id.* at 3, 11, 105 S.Ct. 1694; *accord Henry,* 652 F.3d at 532.

Over a decade ago, we applied these principles when deciding *Waterman v. Batton,* a case that bears striking similarities to the one at hand. There, we held that officers who used deadly force against the driver of a car had not violated the Fourth Amendment when, in the after-math of a high-speed chase (during which the driver had reportedly tried to run an officer off the road), the officers were standing in or immediately adjacent to the car's forward trajectory, and the car "lurched forward" and "began to accelerate," such that the officers reasonably believed that the car was going to run them over "in approximately one second." 393 F.3d at 474-76, 475 n.6. We also held that the same officers *had* violated the Fourth Amendment to the extent that they started to use deadly force, or continued to use deadly force, once the car had driven by them—i.e., once it was no longer reasonable for them to believe that the car was about to run them (or their fellow officers) over. *Id.* at 482. This was true even though mere seconds separated the point at which deadly force was lawful from the point at which deadly force was unlawful. *Id.* As we put it then, "force justified at the beginning of an encounter is not justified even seconds later if the justification for the initial force has been eliminated." *Id.* at 481.

Following *Waterman,* we have no difficulty concluding that if Strickland and Heroux started or continued to fire on Williams after they were no longer in the trajectory of Williams's car, they violated Williams's Fourth Amendment right to freedom from excessive force.[6]

B.

Despite having violated a plaintiff's constitutional right, defendants may be entitled to immunity from the plaintiff's suit for damages if, at the time of the violation, the plaintiff's right was not "clearly established." *Williamson v. Stirling,* 912 F.3d 154, 186

(4th Cir. 2018). To determine whether a right was clearly established, we typically ask whether, when the defendants violated the right, there existed either controlling authority (such as a published opinion of this Court) or a "robust consensus of persuasive authority," *Booker v. S.C. Dep't of Corr.,* 855 F.3d 533, 544 (4th Cir. 2017) (internal quotation marks omitted), that would have given the defendants "fair warning that their conduct," under the circumstances, "was wrongful," *Williamson,* 912 F.3d at 187 (internal quotation marks omitted).

p.770 The "clearly established" inquiry has some important guideposts. On the one hand, the Supreme Court instructs us "not to define clearly established law at a high level of generality." *Plumhoff v. Rickard,* 572 U.S. 765, 779, 134 S.Ct. 2012, 188 L.Ed.2d 1056 (2014). On the other hand, defendants can violate clearly established law even under "'novel factual circumstances.'" *Stirling,* 912 F.3d at 187 (quoting *Hope v. Pelzer,* 536 U.S. 730, 741, 122 S.Ct. 2508, 153 L.Ed.2d 666 (2002)); *see also id.* (stating that "clearly established law encompasses not only specifically adjudicated rights, but also those [rights] manifestly included within more general applications of the core constitutional principles invoked" (internal quotation marks omitted)). Thus, although we must avoid ambushing government officials with liability for good-faith mistakes made at the unsettled peripheries of the law, we need not—and should not—assume that government officials are incapable of drawing logical inferences, reasoning by analogy, or exercising common sense. In some cases, government officials can be expected to know that if X is illegal, then Y is also illegal, despite factual differences between the two.

That said, the instant case requires no subtle line-drawing: The right that the officers allegedly violated falls well within the ambit of clearly established law. When we decided *Waterman,* in 2005, we clearly established that (1) law enforcement officers may—under certain conditions—be justified in using deadly force against the driver of a car when they are in the car's trajectory and have reason to believe that the driver will imminently and intentionally run over them, but (2) the same officers violate the Fourth Amendment if they employ deadly force against the driver once they are no longer in the car's trajectory. 393 F.3d at 480-82. *Waterman* obviously and manifestly encompasses the facts of this case. In light of *Waterman,* there can be no question that the right Williams seeks to vindicate was clearly established on the day he was shot.

To summarize: A reasonable jury could conclude that Strickland and Heroux acted in a way that, as a matter of law, violated Williams's clearly established federal rights—specifically, his Fourth Amendment right to freedom from excessive force. Therefore, the officers are not entitled to summary judgment on the basis of qualified immunity, and the district court correctly denied their motions.

IV.

For the foregoing reasons, the judgment of the district court is
AFFIRMED.

[1] Ancrum, too, was injured, but he is not party to this action.

[2] We note that Heroux brings an additional appeal, separate from Strickland. Below, Heroux moved for summary judgment on the ground that Williams's claim

against him was untimely. The district court denied his motion. He asks us to reverse. But a denial of summary judgment on statute-of-limitations grounds is an interlocutory order, and in general, such orders are not immediately appealable. *Cf. Martin Marietta Corp. v. Gould, Inc.,* 70 F.3d 768, 769-70 (4th Cir. 1995) (reviewing order denying summary judgment on statute-of-limitations grounds because the district court had certified its order for appeal). Heroux fails to advance any argument as to why we should—or may—exercise appellate jurisdiction over the district court's rejection of his statute-of-limitations defense in this case. Accordingly, we leave that portion of the district court's order undisturbed.

[3] This is not to say that we are strictly confined to the four corners of the district court's order: we may assume some facts when the district court does not explicitly state them, provided that we draw all inferences in the plaintiff's favor. *See Smith v. Ray,* 781 F.3d 95, 98 (4th Cir. 2015) ("To the extent that the district court has not fully set forth the facts on which its decision is based, we assume the facts that may reasonably be inferred from the record when viewed in the light most favorable to the plaintiff." (internal quotation marks omitted)).

[4] We do not need to answer these questions in sequence. *Pearson v. Callahan,* 555 U.S. 223, 236, 129 S.Ct. 808, 172 L.Ed.2d 565 (2009). But in this case, we see no reason not to.

[5] Nothing in the record or the parties' briefs suggests that Williams posed a significant threat to anyone but the officers at any point during the encounter at issue; therefore, there is no need for us to consider the "or others" portion of the standard.

[6] We note that this conclusion is consistent with our opinion in *Krein v. Price,* 596 F. App'x 184, 189-90 (4th Cir. 2014), which dealt with similar circumstances and applied *Waterman* in substantially the same way.

931 F.3d 307 (2019)

Tiffanie HUPP; R.H., a minor, by and through his next friend, Tiffanie Hupp;
Clifford Myers, Plaintiffs - Appellants,

v.

State Trooper Seth COOK; Colonel C.R. Jay Smithers, Defendants-Appellees, and
West Virginia State Police, Defendant.

No. 18-1845.

United States Court of Appeals, Fourth Circuit.

Argued: April 2, 2019.

Decided: July 25, 2019.

Hupp v. Cook, 931 F. 3d 307 (4th Cir. 2019)

Appeal from the United States District Court for the Southern District of West Virginia, at Charleston, Thomas E. Johnston, Chief District Judge, (2:17-cv-00926).

ARGUED: John Eric Campbell, CAMPBELL LAW, Denver, Colorado; Justin F. Marceau, UNIVERSITY OF DENVER, Denver, Colorado, for Appellants. Michael Deering Mullins, STEPTOE & JOHNSON PLLC, Charleston, West Virginia, for Appellees. ON BRIEF: Alene Anello, ALDF, Cotati, California, for Appellants. Robert L. Bailey, STEPTOE & JOHNSON PLLC, Charleston, West Virginia, for Appellees.

Before GREGORY, Chief Judge, and KING, Circuit Judge.[1]

Affirmed in part, reversed in part, and remanded by published opinion. Chief Judge Gregory wrote the opinion, in which Judge King joined.

p.313 GREGORY, Chief Judge.

Appellant Tiffanie Hupp was arrested for obstruction when she attempted to stop a state trooper from shooting her family's p.314 dog. After her husband video-recorded the incident, the state trooper entered the family's home, without consent and without a warrant, and seized several of the family's electronic devices. Hupp, her minor son, and her father-in-law filed suit against the state trooper, asserting various violations of the Fourth Amendment under 42 U.S.C. § 1983. The district court granted summary judgment to the state trooper and denied Appellants' motion for partial summary judgment. Because issues of fact exist, we affirm the denial of Appellants' partial summary judgment motion but reverse the grant of summary judgment in Trooper Seth Cook's favor and remand for trial on each of Appellants' claims.

I.

A.

Buddy, a 13-year-old husky-Akita mix, lives with his owner, Appellant Clifford Myers, in Waverly, West Virginia. Buddy has been the source of contention between Myers and his neighbor David Wayne, who lives across the street.

On May 9, 2015, the police were called out in response to a dispute earlier that day between the two men over the dog. West Virginia State Troopers Seth Cook and Sean Michael responded to the call. Trooper Cook was there to provide backup to Trooper Michael. Upon their arrival, the troopers spoke with Myers, who was in his front yard drinking a beer. The troopers then went across the street to speak with the Waynes. In speaking with the Waynes, Trooper Cook was told of the "ongoing problem" with Myers over Buddy, that Buddy was, in their mind, "vicious and had killed several of their cats and had chased the children." J.A. 302. Trooper Cook was also told that Buddy had chased Wayne's grandmother back into the house and that Wayne's grandfather had to take a stick with him when he checked the mail "to shoo the dog away." *Id.*[2]

At the time, Myers had another dog, a black Labrador, on a chain in his front yard; Buddy was loose in the yard. According to Myers, Trooper Cook was aware that Buddy was not on a leash. Trooper Cook testified, however, that he did not see Buddy when he first went to speak with Myers. While the troopers spoke with the Waynes, Myers took the Labrador off the chain and placed the chain on Buddy. Myers later explained that it was mere happenstance that he switched the dogs; according to him, it was not because "the black lab was the friendlier of the two dogs." J.A. 82.

After speaking with the Waynes, the troopers returned to Myers's house. Trooper Michael asked Myers for his identification. Myers asked his daughter, Lindsey, to retrieve it for him. As Lindsey headed back toward the house to retrieve the ID, Trooper Cook followed her into Myers's front yard. Trooper Cook testified that he followed Lindsey "because of the people gathering in the door [of Myers's home] and just a general, again, situation awareness." J.A. 208. At that point, Myers had six of his family members at his house, and Trooper Cook wanted to "have a little bit of personal contact with them to, again, determine their nature" and determine if "there were potential other people that [he] needed to be paying closer attention to." J.A. 56, 207-08. Trooper Cook also testified that, due to the slope of Myers's front yard, he wanted to "get closer to where [he] could see better than from down at the road in the driveway looking up at a position of tactical advantage over [him]." J.A. 208.

p.315 Video evidence captured much, but not all, of what happened next.[3] A dog barked as Trooper Cook walked into Myers's yard. J.A. 610 at 1:17-1:20. Trooper Cook, who was trained to identify and "handle" aggressive dogs, took a few steps back after seeing Buddy. J.A. 189, 610 at 1:20-1:22. He then pulled his gun out and, holding it with his left hand, pointed it at Buddy. J.A. 610 at 1:23-1:26. Hupp, Myers's 113-pound daughter-in-law, ran down the front yard from near the house toward Trooper Cook. *Id.* at 1:26-1:27. She stood with her left side next to Trooper Cook's right side, her body perpendicular to Trooper Cook. Buddy was at Hupp's right.

Hupp's arms were at her side and her hands were visibly empty. *Id.* at 1:26-1:28. Within seconds of Hupp's arrival, Trooper Cook grabbed Hupp's left arm with his right hand. *Id.* at 1:29. A brief struggle ensued during which Trooper Cook turned to his left, Hupp moved to her right and directly facing Trooper Cook, all while the two struggled for two seconds with Trooper Cook's grasp on Hupp's arm. *Id.* at 1:29-1:30. As Trooper Cook and Hupp spun around, Hupp fell to the ground. *Id.* at 1:31. When Hupp stood up, Trooper Cook grabbed her arms from behind and walked her to the police car parked a few feet away. *Id.* at 1:34-39. Bending Hupp over the hood of the police car, the troopers handcuffed her. *Id.* at 1:40-2:05.

Though not depicted clearly in the video, Trooper Cook testified that after seeing Buddy as he entered the yard, he yelled for someone to control the dog or to "get a hold of your dog." J.A. 201, 569-70. According to Trooper Cook, he did not at first notice that Buddy was on a chain. Hupp testified that she ran toward Trooper Cook both in response to Buddy's barks but also in response to the trooper's order to control the dog.

Also not clear from the video is what was said by Trooper Cook and Hupp in their brief encounter. Trooper Cook testified that he told Hupp at least twice to back away and that her response was that he could not tell her what to do on her property. Trooper Cook also maintained that Hupp was "cursing" and "screaming profanities" at him. J.A. 210, 509. Hupp testified, on the other hand, that she did not hear any of Trooper Cook's orders and simply told him, "Whoa, whoa, don't do that, stop." J.A. 121.

Hupp's husband, Ryan, recorded the incident with his cell phone from inside Myers's home. As Hupp was being arrested, she asked Ryan, "Did you get that on video?" J.A. 86. Ryan answered, "Don't worry, babe. I've got that shit." J.A. 244. Trooper Cook later testified that he understood that statement to mean that Ryan "was glad he had" the video and "wouldn't get rid of it for his—his possession of it." J.A. 247.

Upon learning that a video had been recorded, Trooper Cook "stepped in" to Myers's home without a warrant and without consent. J.A. 237, 258. He seized four electronic devices: a child's tablet and three cell phones, including Ryan's phone that recorded the incident. J.A. 237, 572.[4] p.316 Trooper Cook explained in his deposition that it is his practice to seize electronic recording devices without first obtaining a warrant if he believes that someone has used the device to capture evidence. The State Police retained the devices for a month before returning them.

B.

Hupp was charged with obstruction under West Virginia Code § 61-5-17(a). She was arraigned, and after the magistrate judge concluded that probable cause existed for her arrest, she was released on bond. Following a jury trial in the Wood County magistrate court, Hupp was acquitted.

Appellants Hupp, Myers, and Hupp's minor son—who witnessed his mother's arrest—filed suit against Trooper Cook, West Virginia State Police Colonel C.R. "Jay" Smithers (the superintendent), and the West Virginia State Police. Appellants brought several claims for violation of their constitutional rights under 42 U.S.C. §

1983 and parallel state law claims. Appellants later amended their complaint, bringing claims against the police officers in their individual and official capacities and against the West Virginia State Police. The district court granted in part a motion to dismiss, dismissing the claims against the West Virginia State Police and those brought against the police officers in their official capacities. As a result, claims remained against only Trooper Cook and Colonel Smithers in their individual capacities. The claims against Trooper Cook included section 1983 claims for false arrest, excessive force, malicious prosecution, unlawful search of Myers's house, unlawful seizure of the electronic devices, and unlawful seizure of Buddy; and state law claims for malicious prosecution, intentional infliction of emotional distress (outrage), and battery. A claim for supervisory liability under section 1983 also remained against Colonel Smithers.

Trooper Cook and Colonel Smithers moved for summary judgment on all of the remaining claims, and Appellants moved for partial summary judgment on the false arrest, excessive force, and unlawful search and seizure claims. The district court granted summary judgment to Trooper Cook and Colonel Smithers and denied summary judgment to Appellants. The district court found that Trooper Cook is entitled to qualified immunity on the false arrest, excessive force, and malicious prosecution claims brought under section 1983 as well as on the common law malicious prosecution claim. The district court granted summary judgment to Trooper Cook on the outrage and battery claims as well. Because the court found that Trooper Cook did not violate Hupp's constitutional rights, it granted summary judgment to Colonel Smithers on the one remaining claim of supervisory liability against him.

The district court also granted summary judgment to Trooper Cook on the unlawful search and seizure claims. The court concluded that exigent circumstances justified the search of Myers's home and the seizure of the electronic devices because an objectively reasonable officer would have believed that Myers's family members would destroy or conceal the video evidence before a warrant could be obtained. With respect to the claim of unlawful seizure of Buddy, the court found that Trooper Cook's actions did not "meaningfully interfere[]" with Appellants' "possessory interest in Buddy." J.A. 636.

Appellants timely appealed the grant of summary judgment on the claims for false arrest, excessive force, malicious prosecution, unlawful entry, and unlawful seizure p.317 of the electronic devices. Appellants also appealed the denial of summary judgment in their favor on the Fourth Amendment claims related to the entry of Myers's home and seizure of the electronic devices. Appellants did not appeal the grant of summary judgment on the supervisory liability claim, claim for unlawful seizure of Buddy, or the state law claims of outrage and battery.

The district court had jurisdiction pursuant to 28 U.S.C. §§ 1331, 1343(a)(3), and 1367, and we have jurisdiction under 28 U.S.C. § 1291.

II.

We review a district court's grant of summary judgment de novo, "applying the same legal standards as the district court, and viewing all facts and reasonable inferences therefrom in the light most favorable to the nonmoving party." *Heyer v. U.S. Bureau of Prisons,* 849 F.3d 202, 208 (4th Cir. 2017) (quoting *T-Mobile Ne., LLC v. City Council of Newport News,* 674 F.3d 380, 384-85 (4th Cir. 2012)). Summary judgment is appropriate "if the movant shows that there is no genuine dispute as to any material fact and the movant is entitled to judgment as a matter of law." *Id.* (quoting Fed. R. Civ. P. 56(a)). "A dispute is genuine if 'a reasonable jury could return a verdict for the nonmoving party.'" *Libertarian Party of Va. v. Judd,* 718 F.3d 308, 313 (4th Cir. 2013) (quoting *Dulaney v. Packaging Corp. of Am.,* 673 F.3d 323, 330 (4th Cir. 2012)). "A fact is material if it 'might affect the outcome of the suit under the governing law.'" *Id.* (quoting *Anderson v. Liberty Lobby, Inc.,* 477 U.S. 242, 248, 106 S.Ct. 2505, 91 L.Ed.2d 202 (1986)).

III.

A.

We first address the district court's determination that Trooper Cook is entitled to qualified immunity on the claims for false arrest, excessive force, and malicious prosecution. "The doctrine of qualified immunity shields government officials from liability for civil damages when their conduct does not violate clearly established constitutional or other rights that a reasonable officer would have known." *Sims v. Labowitz,* 885 F.3d 254, 260 (4th Cir. 2018). The doctrine is intended to "balance[ ] two important interests—the need to hold public officials accountable when they exercise power irresponsibly and the need to shield officials from harassment, distraction, and liability when they perform their duties reasonably." *Smith v. Ray,* 781 F.3d 95, 100 (4th Cir. 2015) (quoting *Pearson v. Callahan,* 555 U.S. 223, 231, 129 S.Ct. 808, 172 L.Ed.2d 565 (2009)). It "gives government officials breathing room to make reasonable but mistaken judgments, and protects all but the plainly incompetent or those who knowingly violate the law." *Stanton v. Sims,* 571 U.S. 3, 5, 134 S.Ct. 3, 187 L.Ed.2d 341 (2013) (internal quotation marks and citation omitted).

An official is not entitled to qualified immunity if he or she deprived an individual of a constitutional right and that right was clearly established at the time of the violation. *Pearson,* 555 U.S. at 231, 129 S.Ct. 808. Our analysis is, therefore, two-fold. We must determine whether the facts, viewed in the light most favorable to Appellants, show that Trooper Cook violated Appellants' constitutional or other rights and whether those rights were clearly established at the time of Trooper Cook's conduct such that a reasonable officer would have known that the conduct was unconstitutional. *Smith,* 781 F.3d at 100. We may consider either prong of the analysis first. *Sims,* 885 F.3d at 260. The p.318 question of whether a right is clearly established is a question of law for the Court to decide. *Pritchett v. Alford,* 973 F.2d 307, 312 (4th Cir. 1992). The question of whether a reasonable officer would have known that the conduct at issue violated that right, on the other hand, cannot be decided on summary judgment if disputes of the historical facts exist. *Smith,* 781 F.3d at 100. Thus, "while the purely legal question of whether the constitutional right at issue was clearly established 'is always capable of decision at the summary judgment stage,' a genuine question of material fact regarding '[w]hether the conduct allegedly violative of the right actually occurred . . . must be reserved for trial.'" *Willingham v. Crooke,*

412 F.3d 553, 559 (4th Cir. 2005) (alteration and omission in original) (quoting *Pritchett*, 973 F.2d at 313).

1. False Arrest

We begin with Hupp's false arrest claim. The Fourth Amendment protects "[t]he right of the people to be secure in their persons . . . against unreasonable searches and seizures." U.S. Const. amend. IV. A seizure is unreasonable under the Fourth Amendment if it is not based on probable cause. *Dunaway v. New York*, 442 U.S. 200, 213, 99 S.Ct. 2248, 60 L.Ed.2d 824 (1979). Thus, "[i]f a person is arrested when no reasonable officer could believe . . . that probable cause exists to arrest that person, a violation of a clearly established Fourth Amendment right to be arrested only upon probable cause ensues." *Rogers v. Pendleton*, 249 F.3d 279, 290 (4th Cir. 2001) (citation omitted).

The district court determined that a reasonable officer would have believed that probable cause existed for Hupp's arrest for obstruction. Appellants, on the other hand, contend that the historical facts material to a probable cause finding are in dispute. "Probable cause is determined by a 'totality-of-the-circumstances' approach." *Smith v. Munday*, 848 F.3d 248, 253 (4th Cir. 2017) (citing *Illinois v. Gates*, 462 U.S. 213, 230, 103 S.Ct. 2317, 76 L.Ed.2d 527 (1983)). The inquiry "turns on two factors: 'the suspect's conduct as known to the officer, and the contours of the offense thought to be committed by that conduct.'" *Id.* (quoting *Graham v. Gagnon*, 831 F.3d 176, 184 (4th Cir. 2016)). While we look to the information available to the officer on the scene at the time, we apply an objective test to determine whether a reasonably prudent officer with that information would have thought that probable cause existed for the arrest. *Graham*, 831 F.3d at 185. Evidence sufficient to secure a conviction is not required, but probable cause exists only if there is sufficient evidence on which a reasonable officer at the time could have believed that probable cause existed for the arrest. *Wong Sun v. United States*, 371 U.S. 471, 479, 83 S.Ct. 407, 9 L.Ed.2d 441 (1963).

Because the probable cause inquiry is informed by the "contours of the offense" at issue, we are guided by West Virginia law in determining the scope of the offense of obstruction proscribed by West Virginia Code § 61-5-17(a)—the offense for which Hupp was arrested. *Rogers*, 249 F.3d at 291; *see Graham*, 831 F.3d at 188 (Although "an actual lack of probable cause is not *dispositive* for qualified immunity purposes[,]. . . [t]he boundaries of the statute [allegedly violated by the plaintiff] are extremely relevant to an assessment of whether [an officer's] mistake was reasonable."). The plain language of the statute establishes that a person is guilty of obstruction when she, "by threats, menaces, acts or otherwise forcibly or illegally hinders or obstructs or attempts to hinder or obstruct a law-enforcement officer, probation officer or parole officer acting in his or p.319 her official capacity." W. Va. Code § 61-5-17(a).

Interpreting this statute, the Supreme Court of Appeals of West Virginia has held that a person is guilty of obstruction when she "check[s] or hamper[s] the action of the officer," does "something which hinders or prevents or tends to prevent the performance of [the officer's] legal duty," or acts in "direct or indirect opposition or resistance to the lawful discharge of [the officer's] official duty." *State v. Johnson*, 134

W.Va. 357, 59 S.E.2d 485, 487 (1950). As West Virginia's high court has "succinct[ly]" explained, to secure a conviction under section 61-5-17(a), the State must show "forcible or illegal conduct that interferes with a police officer's discharge of official duties." *State v. Davis*, 229 W.Va. 695, 735 S.E.2d 570, 573 (2012) (quoting *State v. Carney*, 222 W.Va. 152, 663 S.E.2d 606, 611 (2008)). Because conduct can obstruct an officer if it is either forcible or illegal, a person may be guilty of obstruction "whether or not force be actually present." *Johnson*, 59 S.E.2d at 487. However, where "force is not involved to effect an obstruction," the resulting obstruction itself is insufficient to establish the illegality required by section 61-5-17. *Carney*, 663 S.E.2d at 611. That is, when force is not used, obstruction lies only where an illegal act is performed. This is because "lawful conduct is not sufficient to establish the statutory offense." *Id.*

Of particular relevance to our inquiry here, West Virginia courts have held that "when done in an orderly manner, merely questioning or remonstrating with an officer while he or she is performing his or her duty, does not ordinarily constitute the offense of obstructing an officer." *State v. Srnsky*, 213 W.Va. 412, 582 S.E.2d 859, 867 (2003) (quoting *State ex rel. Wilmoth v. Gustke*, 179 W.Va. 771, 373 S.E.2d 484, 486 (W. Va. 1988)). For example, the Supreme Court of Appeals has found that no obstruction is committed when a property owner asks a law enforcement officer, "without the use of fighting or insulting words or other opprobrious language and without forcible or other illegal hindrance," to leave her property. *Wilmoth*, 373 S.E.2d at 487. This principle is based on the First Amendment "right to question or challenge the authority of a police officer, provided that fighting words or other opprobrious language is not used." *Id.*; *see Graham*, 831 F.3d at 188 ("Peaceful verbal criticism of an officer who is making an arrest cannot be targeted under a general obstruction of justice statute. . . without running afoul of the First Amendment." (citation omitted)).

On the other hand, certain "threats, language, and menacing demeanor" can constitute obstruction. *State v. Davis*, 199 W.Va. 84, 483 S.E.2d 84, 87 (1996). In *Davis*, for example, a police officer responded to a call of shots fired and encountered an intoxicated man who was fighting with his live-in girlfriend. *Id.* The man told the officer that he had a loaded shotgun in the corner of the home, "gestured toward the gun, reminded the officer in a threatening manner that it was loaded, and employed language indicative of both his agitated state and his intention to discharge the gun at any time and any place he chose." *Id.* The police officer exited the home and was forced to call for backup. *Id.* at 86. The court concluded that the "verbal threats and behavior" "had the effect of hindering the police investigation of shots [ ] fired." *Id.* at 87.

With respect to conduct that involves more than mere verbal interactions with law enforcement, obstruction may be found when a person refuses to comply with an officer's order. For example, the Supreme Court of Appeals of West Virginia p.320 upheld a conviction for obstruction where the defendant was told that he was being placed under arrest and then "struggled against arrest." *State v. Forsythe*, 194 W.Va. 496, 460 S.E.2d 742, 745-46 (1995). More recently, the court upheld a conviction for obstruction where the defendant refused to obey a state trooper's numerous orders to stand to be frisked, began a physical altercation with the trooper, and ultimately grabbed the trooper's baton and struck the trooper twice on the head. *State v. Lowery*, No. 17-0210, 2018 WL 2193241, at *1, 5 (W. Va. May 14, 2018) (unpublished).

Applying these principles here, we find that disputes of fact preclude a finding that a reasonable officer in Trooper Cook's position would have believed that probable cause existed for Hupp's arrest. Trooper Cook maintains that Hupp's obstruction began when she approached him in "an aggressive manner" and continued as she failed to comply with his orders and "met [Trooper Cook's order] with a verbal further noncompliance." J.A. 210. First, disputes of fact exist with respect to Hupp's verbal interaction with Trooper Cook. The video evidence shows Hupp running toward Trooper Cook, with her arms to her side and her hands empty, after he pulled a gun on her father-in-law's dog.

She testified that she said only "Whoa, whoa, don't do that, stop." J.A. 121-22.[5] Even if Trooper Cook's testimony is to be believed—that Hupp told him that he could not tell her what to do on her property—such language is a challenge to the trooper's authority and does not constitute the type of menacing language found be to obstructionist in *Davis*. The parties dispute, however, whether Hupp also cursed at Trooper Cook when she approached him. *Compare* J.A. 210 (Trooper Cook's testimony that Hupp was "screaming profanities" at him) *and* J.A. 509 (criminal complaint describing Hupp as "cursing"), *with* J.A. 122 (Hupp's testimony that "[t]here was no cussing") *and* J.A. 140 (Dalton's testimony that Hupp was not cursing). While a reasonable jury could credit Trooper Cook's version of the interaction, it could instead believe Hupp that no "fighting or insulting words or other opprobrious language" were used. *Wilmoth*, 373 S.E.2d at 487.

Disputes of fact also exist with respect to Hupp's alleged failure to comply with Trooper Cook's order to step aside. *See Lowery*, 2018 WL 2193241, at *5. Trooper Cook testified that he gave at least two orders to Hupp to step back, with which she refused to comply. J.A. 570. Specifically, he testified that he told Hupp to "step back"; that Hupp responded, "You can't tell me to f-ing do that"; that he then told Hupp, "Ma'am, I'm not asking you; I'm telling you. Step back"; and that Hupp was "coming back with her opinions and why she's not going to comply." J.A. 215. The defense's expert described *three* orders for Hupp to step back. J.A. 443.[6] Hupp, on the other hand, testified that her only words to Trooper Cook were, "Whoa, whoa, don't do that, stop" and that she "didn't get a chance to hear" any of Trooper Cook's orders. J.A. 121-22. Trooper Cook even acknowledged that Hupp had only "a split p.321 second to comply" with his order before he grabbed her arm. J.A. 604. Clearly, there is a dispute as to whether Hupp refused to comply with Trooper Cook's orders or was even given the opportunity to comply with them before she was arrested mere seconds later.

Indeed, there is evidence to suggest that, rather than defying Trooper Cook's order to step back, Hupp was actually acting to comply with his earlier order to restrain Buddy. Hupp testified in deposition that she approached Trooper Cook and Buddy partly in response to Trooper Cook's undisputed command to "get control of the dog" or "get a hold of your dog." J.A. 121, 201, 569-70. Although Trooper Cook testified that Hupp began to obstruct him when she approached him in an "aggressive manner," J.A. 209-10, Trooper Michael testified that Hupp's "coming down the hill" toward Trooper Cook and Buddy after Trooper Cook's command to control Buddy "could be viewed as complying with his request," J.A. 316.

On this disputed evidence, we cannot conclude that a reasonable officer in Trooper Cook's position would have believed that probable cause existed for Hupp's arrest. With the facts viewed in the light most favorable to Hupp, the record shows that she ran to Trooper Cook to comply with his order to have Buddy controlled. Her arms were down at her side and her hands visibly empty. She told Trooper Cook to stop but did not curse at him. Yet a mere second or two later, before she heard any order to move, Trooper Cook grabbed her arm and flung her to the ground. Such facts do not reasonably support a charge of obstruction under West Virginia law. Accordingly, we reverse the grant of summary judgment on the false arrest claim.[7]

2. Excessive Force

Turning to Hupp's excessive force claim, we also conclude that the district court erred in granting summary judgment to Trooper Cook on qualified immunity grounds. The Fourth Amendment prohibits police officers from "using excessive force to seize a free citizen." *Jones v. Buchanan,* 325 F.3d 520, 527 (4th Cir. 2003); *Graham v. Connor,* 490 U.S. 386, 395, 109 S.Ct. 1865, 104 L.Ed.2d 443 (1989). Rather, police officers are constitutionally permitted to use only that force which is reasonable under the circumstances.

In determining whether excessive force was used, we consider the facts "from the perspective of a reasonable officer on the scene," without the "20/20 vision of hindsight." *Graham,* 490 U.S. at 397, 109 S.Ct. 1865. Therefore, while we do not consider the officer's "intent or motivation," *Jones,* 325 F.3d at 527 (quoting *Elliott v. Leavitt,* 99 F.3d 640, 642 (4th Cir. 1996)), we ask "whether a reasonable officer in the same circumstances would have concluded that a threat existed justifying p.322 the particular use of force," *Elliott,* 99 F.3d at 642 (citing *Graham,* 490 U.S. at 396-97, 109 S.Ct. 1865). In answering this question, we consider several factors, including "the severity of the crime at issue," whether the "suspect pose[d] an immediate threat to the safety of the officers or others," and whether the suspect was "actively resisting arrest or attempting to evade arrest by flight." *Graham,* 490 U.S. at 396, 109 S.Ct. 1865; *Jones,* 325 F.3d at 527. We also consider the extent of the plaintiff's injuries. *Rowland v. Perry,* 41 F.3d 167, 174 (4th Cir. 1994). Ultimately, we must decide "whether the totality of the circumstances justifie[d] a particular sort of . . . seizure." *Smith,* 781 F.3d at 101 (omission in original) (quoting *Tennessee v. Garner,* 471 U.S. 1, 8-9, 105 S.Ct. 1694, 85 L.Ed.2d 1 (1985)).

Here, Hupp alleges that Trooper Cook used unlawful force against her by "grabbing and throwing" her to the ground and "pushing her against the police car." J.A. 25. We first dispense with Hupp's argument that because she was unlawfully arrested, the use of *any* force was necessarily unconstitutional. Certainly, we may consider any lack of probable cause for the arrest as we evaluate the reasonableness of the force used. But we consider the crime that is alleged to have been committed in connection with our overall analysis of *all* of the circumstances surrounding the use of force. *See Graham,* 490 U.S. at 396, 109 S.Ct. 1865; *Jones,* 325 F.3d at 528-31 (explaining that the lack of any crime committed by plaintiff weighed heavily in favor of plaintiff's excessive force claim but nonetheless evaluating remaining *Graham* factors).

Moreover, we do not make any determination as to whether Hupp's arrest was actually unlawful. Our finding that Trooper Cook is not entitled to qualified immunity on the false arrest claim at this stage of litigation does not preclude a finding at a later stage that he lawfully arrested Hupp; a trier of fact could resolve the factual disputes that currently exist in Trooper Cook's favor. Therefore, we cannot agree with Hupp that our evaluation of the grant of qualified immunity on the excessive force claim turns entirely on any lack of probable cause for her arrest. Instead, we evaluate the totality of the circumstances surrounding the use of force against her.

In evaluating those circumstances, we note that the extent of Hupp's injuries is slight. The complaint alleges that Hupp suffered emotional trauma, including anxiety and an inability to sleep, as well as physical injuries. According to her medical records, Hupp suffered from middle and lower back pain and was diagnosed with a contusion and lumbosacral strain two days after the incident with Trooper Cook. J.A. 543-44. The record contains no additional evidence of injury. There is no evidence of serious or permanent physical injuries. *Cf. Rowland,* 41 F.3d at 172, 174 (finding extent of injuries significant where plaintiff suffered torn ligament in his leg, underwent two surgeries, and remained permanently partially disabled).

Hupp's minor injuries, however, are "but one 'consideration in determining whether force was excessive.'" *E.W. by and through T.W. v. Dolgos,* 884 F.3d 172, 185 (4th Cir. 2018) (quoting *Jones,* 325 F.3d at 530). Other factors call into question the reasonableness of the use of force against Hupp. First, the severity of the crime for which she was arrested is slight: obstruction is a misdemeanor. *See* W. Va. Code § 61-5-17(a). When the offense is a "minor one," we have found "that the first *Graham* factor weighed in plaintiff's favor." *Jones,* 325 F.3d at 528 (citations omitted). We see no reason to find otherwise here.

Second, the evidence suggests that Hupp did not "pose[ ] an immediate threat p.323 to the safety of the officers or others." *Graham,* 490 U.S. at 396, 109 S.Ct. 1865; *Jones,* 325 F.3d at 528. The district court found that this factor weighed in favor of qualified immunity, as Hupp positioned herself between Trooper Cook and Buddy, "which could reasonably be construed as hindering Cook's ability to protect himself." J.A. 620. A review of the record, however, suggests otherwise. Hupp is a slender, short, 113-pound female. Trooper Cook, on the other hand, weighs 200 pounds, is a trained police officer, and had undergone training in how to identify and handle aggressive dogs months before Hupp's arrest. Trooper Cook was armed, had his gun drawn, and the video shows that Hupp approached him with her arms down and hands visibly empty. Hupp stood perpendicular to Trooper Cook, did not place herself directly in front of him or his drawn gun, and it was only after Trooper Cook grabbed her arm that she moved in front of his weapon. In light of these facts, we cannot agree with the district court that, as a matter of law, Hupp posed a sufficient threat to tip the scale in Trooper Cook's favor. *See Smith,* 781 F.3d at 102 (finding that second *Graham* factor weighed in favor of section 1983 plaintiff where plaintiff was a "smaller woman," officer was "a pretty good size man" as a "200-something-pound man," and officer had no reason to believe that the plaintiff was armed); *see also Rowland,* 41 F.3d at 174 (finding "no threat to the officer or anyone else" where plaintiff was not armed, officer did not suspect plaintiff was armed, and there was no "real evidence that this relatively passive, retarded man was a danger to the larger, trained police officer").

Third, there is disputed evidence of Hupp's resistance to arrest. The video depicts a brief struggle between Hupp and Trooper Cook lasting mere seconds after he grabbed her arm and before she fell to the ground. Trooper Cook grabbed Hupp's arm mere seconds after she approached him and, according to Hupp, before she had the opportunity to hear any order that he may have given for her to move. She testified that her reaction after having her arm seized was to try to put her arms up in surrender. J.A. 123. We have held that a reasonable officer could not believe that the "initial act of pulling [one's] arm away" when an officer grabs a person "without warning or explanation" justifies the officer's decision to throw the person to the ground. *Smith,* 781 F.3d at 103.

Trooper Cook, on the other hand, testified that Hupp took a "fighting stance" with him and that he "stiff armed" her in order to holster his weapon. J.A. 219, 571. Trooper Cook also testified that immediately before Hupp fell to the ground, she grabbed his clothing and cursed at him.[8] On these disputed versions of the facts, and in light of the other *Graham* factors that are unfavorable to Trooper Cook, we cannot say that a reasonable officer would consider Trooper Cook's use of force reasonable under the circumstances. *See Rowland,* 41 F.3d at 174 (concluding that disputed versions of plaintiff's resistance combined with other "unfavorable" *Graham* factors precluded qualified immunity on excessive force claim).

3. Malicious Prosecution

We next address Hupp's section 1983 malicious prosecution claim. A malicious prosecution claim brought under section 1983 "is properly understood as a p.324 Fourth Amendment claim for unreasonable seizure which incorporates certain elements of the common law tort." *Evans v. Chalmers,* 703 F.3d 636, 646 (4th Cir. 2012) (quoting *Lambert v. Williams,* 223 F.3d 257, 261 (4th Cir. 2000)); *see Manuel v. City of Joliet, Ill.,* ___ U.S. ___, 137 S.Ct. 911, 919, 197 L.Ed.2d 312 (2017) ("If the complaint is that a form of legal process resulted in pretrial detention unsupported by probable cause, then the right allegedly infringed lies in the Fourth Amendment."). To prove such a claim, a plaintiff must show "that the defendant (1) caused (2) a seizure of the plaintiff pursuant to legal process unsupported by probable cause, and (3) criminal proceedings terminated in plaintiff's favor." *Evans,* 703 F.3d at 647.

There is no dispute here that Hupp was arrested, prosecuted, and acquitted. What is disputed is whether probable cause existed for Hupp's prosecution. On this point, the district court determined that probable cause existed for Hupp's arrest and that the magistrate's subsequent finding of probable cause rendered Hupp's prosecution reasonable. J.A. 624. To be sure, we have held that "[o]nce a pretrial seizure has been rendered reasonable by virtue of a probable cause determination by a neutral and detached magistrate, the continuing pretrial seizure of a criminal defendant—either by detention or by bond restrictions—is reasonable." *Brooks v. City of Winston-Salem, N.C.,* 85 F.3d 178, 184 (4th Cir. 1996). We later explained, though, that a finding of probable cause by a neutral magistrate only "weigh[s] heavily *toward* a finding that [the defendant] is immune" from suit. *Merchant v. Bauer,* 677 F.3d 656, 664 (4th Cir.) (quoting *Wadkins v. Arnold,* 214 F.3d 535, 541 (4th Cir. 2000)), *cert. denied,* 568 U.S.

1068, 133 S.Ct. 789, 184 L.Ed.2d 582 (2012). Thus, where a police officer takes certain steps, such as first conferring with a prosecutor about moving forward with a criminal prosecution, and a magistrate judge later affirms the officer's determination that probable cause exists for the prosecution, those steps weigh in favor of a finding of qualified immunity. They do not end the qualified immunity inquiry, however, as they "need only appropriately be taken into account in assessing the reasonableness of [the officer's] actions." *Id.* (internal quotation marks and citation omitted). A grant of qualified immunity still rests on our determination that an officer acted reasonably under the circumstances.

Because a magistrate's finding of probable cause is but a factor in our consideration of the overall reasonableness of the officer's actions, a defendant to a malicious prosecution claim is not absolved from liability when the magistrate's probable-cause finding "is predicated solely on a police officer's false statements." *Manuel,* 137 S. Ct. at 918. An officer who lies to secure a probable-cause determination can hardly be called reasonable. Likewise, where an officer provides misleading information to the prosecuting attorney or where probable cause is "plainly lacking," *McKinney v. Richland Cty. Sheriff's Dep't,* 431 F.3d 415, 419 (4th Cir. 2005), the procedural steps taken by an officer no longer afford a shield against a Fourth Amendment claim. This is because "[l]egal process has gone forward, but it has done nothing to satisfy the Fourth Amendment's probable-cause requirement." *Manuel,* 137 S. Ct. at 918-19.

Hupp contends that the magistrate's finding of probable cause does not afford Trooper Cook qualified immunity on her malicious prosecution claim because the probable-cause finding rested on false statements made by Trooper Cook in the criminal complaint against her. Specifically, Hupp asserts that the criminal complaint falsely stated, *inter alia,* that she p.325 refused to comply with Trooper Cook's orders to "step aside," began cursing at him, "raised her hands towards" him before he grabbed her arm, and then grabbed at him and "began cursing" after he grabbed her arm. J.A. 509; Opening Br. 18, 55.

We agree with Hupp that the district court's finding of qualified immunity on this claim was in error. As we have explained, disputes of fact preclude a finding at this stage that a reasonable officer would have believed that probable cause existed for Hupp's arrest. Those disputes relate to many of the facts set forth in the criminal complaint on which the magistrate relied. For example, there is a dispute as to whether Hupp refused to comply with Trooper Cook's orders for her to move or whether she was instead attempting to obey his order to control Buddy. There is also a dispute as to whether Hupp was cursing at Trooper Cook. Moreover, contrary to Trooper Cook's statement in the criminal complaint, the video clearly depicts Hupp's hands down at her side during the entirety of the few seconds before Trooper Cook grabbed her arm. It was only after he grabbed her arm that she struggled, very briefly, with him.

If we excise the contested statements from the criminal complaint, the additional facts available to the magistrate do not, as the district court found, provide "ample evidence" for a probable-cause determination. J.A. 624. The district court emphasized the fact that Hupp "stepped in between the dog and the undersigned officer," which, according to the district court, showed that Hupp stepped in between Buddy and Trooper Cook as Trooper Cook was attempting to protect himself from the dog. J.A. 509, 624. However, in the criminal complaint, Trooper Cook also clearly stated that Buddy had "reached the end of the tether" and could not "reach" Trooper Cook. J.A. 509. Contrary to showing that Hupp interfered with Trooper Cook's ability to protect himself from Buddy, the complaint established that Trooper Cook knew Buddy was no longer a danger to him. No other basis for Hupp's alleged obstruction of Trooper Cook is identified in the complaint.

Given the disputes of the underlying historical facts, the supported assertion that Trooper Cook's statements in the criminal complaint were not entirely truthful, and the lack of undisputed evidence that otherwise would support a probable-cause finding, we cannot find that Trooper Cook is entitled to qualified immunity on Hupp's malicious prosecution claim under section 1983.

4. Common Law Malicious Prosecution

Trooper Cook's entitlement to immunity on Hupp's common law malicious prosecution claim fares no better. Under West Virginia law, a plaintiff bringing a malicious prosecution claim must show "(1) that the prosecution was set on foot and conducted to its termination, resulting in plaintiff's discharge; (2) that it was caused or procured by defendant; (3) that it was without probable cause; and (4) that it was malicious." *Goodwin v. City of Shepherdstown,* 241 W.Va. 416, 825 S.E.2d 363, 368 (2019) (citation omitted). Where a "want of probable cause for [the] prosecution is shown by a preponderance of the evidence," malice may be inferred. *Truman v. Fid. & Cas. Co. of N.Y.,* 146 W.Va. 707, 123 S.E.2d 59, 68 (1961); *Morton v. Chesapeake & Ohio Ry. Co.,* 184 W.Va. 64, 399 S.E.2d 464, 467 (1990).

The district court determined that, like with the section 1983 malicious prosecution claim, Trooper Cook is entitled to qualified immunity on the common law claim because probable cause existed for p.326 Hupp's arrest. The qualified immunity available against claims brought under section 1983 generally does not extend to common law claims. Nonetheless, West Virginia affords immunity "from personal liability for official acts if the involved conduct did not violate clearly established laws of which a reasonable official would have known." *W. Va. Reg'l Jail & Corr. Facility Auth. v. A.B.,* 234 W.Va. 492, 766 S.E.2d 751, 762 (2014) (citation omitted). The state's qualified immunity doctrine borrows heavily from the analogous federal qualified immunity jurisprudence but also requires an additional finding that the defendant's alleged conduct not be "fraudulent, malicious, or otherwise oppressive" to the plaintiff. *Id.*; *Hutchison v. City of Huntington,* 198 W.Va. 139, 479 S.E.2d 649, 659 (1996).

As discussed above, questions of fact exist that must first be resolved before a court can determine that a reasonable officer in Trooper Cook's position would have believed that probable cause existed for Hupp's arrest and prosecution. Therefore, Trooper Cook is not entitled to immunity on Hupp's common law malicious prosecution claim, and the district court's grant of summary judgment is reversed.

* * *

To summarize, qualified immunity is appropriate at this stage only if there are no disputes of the historical facts underlying the false arrest, excessive force, and malicious prosecution claims. As we have explained, disputes exist. Those disputes must be submitted to a jury. The district court may then "reserve for itself the legal question of whether [Trooper Cook] is entitled to qualified immunity on the facts found by the jury." *Willingham,* 412 F.3d at 560.

B.

We turn finally to Appellants' claims that Trooper Cook unlawfully entered Myers's home and unlawfully seized electronic devices from within the home. Under the Fourth Amendment, "searches and seizures inside a home without a warrant are presumptively unreasonable" and, thus, presumptively unconstitutional. *Payton v. New York,* 445 U.S. 573, 586, 100 S.Ct. 1371, 63 L.Ed.2d 639 (1980); *United States v. Yengel,* 711 F.3d 392, 396 (4th Cir. 2013). This rule is subject to "narrow and well-delineated" exceptions, *Yengel,* 711 F.3d at 396, one of which is when exigent circumstances justify the warrantless entry of a home, *Mincey v. Arizona,* 437 U.S. 385, 392-94, 98 S.Ct. 2408, 57 L.Ed.2d 290 (1978). Exigent circumstances that may justify a warrantless entry include "the imminent destruction of evidence." *United States v. Brown,* 701 F.3d 120, 126 (4th Cir. 2012). That is, police officers may enter a home without a warrant when they "(1) have probable cause to believe that evidence of illegal activity is present and (2) reasonably believe that evidence may be destroyed or removed before they could obtain a search warrant." *United States v. Cephas,* 254 F.3d 488, 494-95 (4th Cir. 2001) (citing *United States v. Turner,* 650 F.2d 526, 528 (4th Cir. 1981)). Likewise, "[w]here law enforcement authorities have probable cause to believe that [property] holds contraband or evidence of a crime," warrantless seizure of the property is permitted under the Fourth Amendment "if the exigencies of the circumstances demand it." *United States v. Place,* 462 U.S. 696, 701, 103 S.Ct. 2637, 77 L.Ed.2d 110 (1983).

Factors to be considered in determining whether exigent circumstances justify a warrantless entry include: "(1) the degree of urgency involved and the amount of time necessary to obtain a warrant; (2) the officers' reasonable belief that the contraband is about to be removed or p.327 destroyed; (3) the possibility of danger to police guarding the site; (4) information indicating the possessors of the contraband are aware that the police are on their trail; and (5) the ready destructibility of the contraband." *Turner,* 650 F.2d at 528. In evaluating these factors, courts consider "[t]he appearance of the scene of the search in the circumstances presented as it would appear to reasonable and prudent men standing in the shoes of the officers." *United States v. Reed,* 935 F.2d 641, 643 (4th Cir. 1991) (alteration in original) (citations omitted).

This case does not present the usual case for exigency; it does not involve a warrantless entry into a home to seize contraband that may be imminently destroyed. *See Cephas,* 254 F.3d at 495-96 (finding exigency where officer had probable cause to believe marijuana was inside apartment and would be destroyed if officer waited to secure warrant); *Brown,* 701 F.3d at 126-27 (finding exigency where probable cause existed to believe that defendant had evidence of child pornography on computers at work that could be deleted before a warrant was obtained). Rather, this case involves a warrantless entry into a home to seize evidence that the police officer understood would *not* be destroyed. The video was taken by Hupp's husband, and

Trooper Cook conceded that he believed Hupp's husband was glad to have the evidence and would not want to part with it. Ryan recorded the video as "[p]roof, if anything were to happen," for his wife's benefit. J.A. 160. That is, he believed that the video could exonerate his wife, not incriminate her. Thus, this case is unlike the "vast majority of cases in which evidence is destroyed by persons who are engaged in illegal conduct, [where] the reason for the destruction is fear that the evidence will fall into the hands of law enforcement." *Kentucky v. King,* 563 U.S. 452, 461, 131 S.Ct. 1849, 179 L.Ed.2d 865 (2011).

1.

Appellants argue that the exigency test cannot be satisfied as a matter of law because there is no evidence that Ryan Hupp intended to destroy or conceal the video. Trooper Cook counters that there is evidence that Ryan intended to destroy or at least conceal the video from the police before a warrant could issue. According to Trooper Cook, Ryan was "glad to have" the video only *before* he realized that Trooper Cook wanted it. Resp. Br. 39 n.150. Trooper Cook points to evidence that after he entered the house and asked about the video, Ryan told him, "Don't worry. I deleted it. It was on this phone." J.A. 258. Additionally, another of Ryan's family members, Dalton, is heard on the video telling Ryan not to let the troopers know that Ryan was recording them. Thus, Trooper Cook asserts, it was reasonable for him to believe that if he did not enter and seize the devices at that time, the evidence would be destroyed or concealed.

The evidence highlighted by Trooper Cook, however, is irrelevant to the exigency analysis. This is because the "existence of exigent circumstances must be determined as of the moment of the warrantless entry of the officers onto the premises." *Reed,* 935 F.2d at 643. Ryan's comments to Trooper Cook about deleting the video footage were made only after Trooper Cook had entered Myers's home and seized three of the electronic devices. According to Trooper Cook's own testimony, he stepped across the threshold into the home, asked Myers's family members that were in the house about the location of the video, received no response, began to seize electronic devices within sight, and only then did Ryan "step[ ] forward from back up the hallway" and tell Trooper p.328 Cook that he had deleted the video from his cell phone. J.A. 258-59. Similarly, Dalton's comments heard in the video were not made in Trooper Cook's presence; an officer would have heard those comments only after seizing the cell phone and watching the video. Thus, before Trooper Cook entered the home and began seizing the devices, his admitted understanding was that Ryan was happy to have the video footage and would not want to destroy it. Of course, we must determine whether a reasonable person in Trooper Cook's position would have believed that Ryan intended to destroy the video. On the facts presented to us, we see no reason to believe that an objective officer would have believed any differently than Trooper Cook did—that Ryan had recorded his wife's arrest, was happy about having recorded it, and would not want to delete that recording.

Trooper Cook's subjective understanding, however, is not the determinative factor. Rather, we must determine whether a reasonable officer in Trooper Cook's position would have believed that Ryan—or another of Hupp's family members present at the time—was likely to destroy or conceal the video. *See Reed,* 935 F.2d at

643. Based on the information available to an officer in Trooper Cook's position at the moment that he entered Myers's home, we cannot say as a matter of law that no reasonable officer would have believed that the video would be preserved while the troopers obtained a warrant. Having heard Ryan yell to his wife not to worry because he recorded her interaction with Trooper Cook, a reasonable officer could conclude, like Trooper Cook initially did, that Ryan was glad to have the video and would not destroy it. On the other hand, Hupp was believed to have committed a crime; the video documenting that crime was recorded by Hupp's husband; and a reasonable officer could have believed that, as Hupp's husband, Ryan would conceal or destroy the video evidence of her crime before handing it over to the police. We are thus hesitant to find that, as a matter of law, Trooper Cook unreasonably believed that the video was likely to be concealed before a warrant could issue. Instead, the question of whether such a belief was reasonable under the circumstances known to the officers at the time of Trooper Cook's entry into Myers's home must be submitted to a factfinder.

Turning to the other exigency factors, we note that there is no evidence regarding the time needed to secure a warrant. The record suggests, though, that there was little to no possibility of danger to the troopers if they stood guard while a warrant was secured. *See Turner,* 650 F.2d at 528. Trooper Cook testified that when he first approached Myers's house, he saw Hupp and Lindsey with a "pistol cross—bow" but saw no arrows and believed that Hupp and Lindsey "were playing with something with [*sic*] the creek" next to the house. J.A. 565-66. Trooper Cook did nothing to secure the crossbow and apparently did not consider it a threat; in fact, there is evidence that the crossbow was a broken plastic toy that belonged to Hupp's three-year-old son. J.A. 85, 128, 141. Buddy, the dog believed to be vicious, was tethered at the time of Hupp's arrest. And although the two troopers were outnumbered by Myers's family members, one of those family members was a toddler, another was pregnant, and there is no evidence that any of them were armed. Therefore, there does not appear to have been any danger to the troopers. *See Yengel,* 711 F.3d at 398 (finding no exigency when officer was informed that there was a grenade in house but other information available to officer indicated "stable nature of the threat"); *United States v. Whitehorn,* 813 F.2d 646, 649 (4th Cir. 1987) (affirming p.329 finding that exigency did not justify warrantless bomb sweep when there was no evidence "that anyone was evacuated from the building or warned of the potential danger, or that the agents had otherwise prepared for the risk of an exploding bomb"); *cf. Reed,* 935 F.2d at 642-43 (finding exigency where police officers saw sawed-off shotgun eighteen inches from man sleeping in a home where another man, known to carry firearms and with past arrests for assault and brandishing weapons, resided).

Nor was the video the only corroborating evidence of Hupp's alleged crime; Trooper Michael was also a witness, as were several of Hupp's family members. That fact, coupled with the minor crime for which Hupp was arrested, suggest that the level of urgency to obtain the video was not high. *See Welsh v. Wisconsin,* 466 U.S. 740, 750, 104 S.Ct. 2091, 80 L.Ed.2d 732 (1984) ("Our hesitation in finding exigent circumstances . . . is particularly appropriate when the underlying offense for which there is probable cause to arrest is relatively minor.").

While these other factors weigh against a finding of exigency, a jury could nonetheless find that Trooper Cook reasonably believed that the video was at risk of being deleted or concealed. Therefore, we decline Appellants' invitation to find that Trooper Cook's entry into Myers's home and his seizure of the electronic devices were unreasonable as a matter of law. Instead, we remand for a trial to determine whether Trooper Cook's actions were reasonable.[9]

2.

We also take a moment to address Trooper Cook's view of the exigency exception to the warrant requirement. In an era in which cell phones are increasingly used to capture much of what happens in daily life, it is important to emphasize the limitations that the Fourth Amendment continues to place on a state's seizure of video evidence.

Trooper Cook testified that his regular practice is to seize any video recording that he believes to contain evidence of a crime he is investigating. J.A. 237-39. But the exigent-circumstances exception does not permit police officers to do what Trooper Cook routinely does: seize video evidence without a warrant even when there is no reason to believe that the evidence will likely be destroyed or concealed. Such a rule would allow officers to seize as a matter of course video-recording devices from not just those involved in an incident, but also from neighbors and other curious bystanders who happen to record the events as they transpire. Under this view, police officers would lawfully be permitted to enter the home of every person living nearby who stands in her doorway or window recording an arrest, to seize her recording device, and to do so without a warrant or her consent—simply because video evidence, by its nature, can be easily deleted.

Such a view finds no support in our Fourth Amendment jurisprudence. While video evidence contained in a cell phone can be easily deleted or concealed, it is not merely the ease with which evidence may be destroyed or concealed that dictates exigency. An officer must also have reason to believe that the evidence will be destroyed or concealed. In short, adopting the broad definition of exigency urged by p.330 Trooper Cook would remove the exigent-circumstances exception to the warrant requirement from the class of "narrow and well-delineated" exceptions permissible under the Fourth Amendment. *Yengel,* 711 F.3d at 396. It would convert exigency from an exception to the rule.

IV.

For the foregoing reasons, we hold that the district court erred in granting summary judgment to Trooper Cook on the false arrest, excessive force, malicious prosecution, and unlawful entry and seizure claims. We also hold that the district court properly denied Appellants summary judgment on the unlawful entry and seizure-of-devices claims. Accordingly, the district court's order denying Appellants' partial summary judgment motion on the search and seizure claims is affirmed and its order granting summary judgment to Trooper Cook is reversed. This matter is remanded to the district court for trial on each of Appellants' claims.

AFFIRMED IN PART, REVERSED IN PART, AND REMANDED

[1] Judge Thacker was unable to participate in oral argument. The decision is filed by a quorum of the panel pursuant to 28 U.S.C. § 46(d).

[2] Myers maintained that Buddy had never harmed a person and simply chased squirrels.

[3] To the extent the video depicts material facts of this case, we review those facts as they are depicted in the video. *Scott v. Harris,* 550 U.S. 372, 380-81, 127 S.Ct. 1769, 167 L.Ed.2d 686 (2007). Where, however, the video "does not 'clearly' or 'blatantly' contradict" Hupp's version of the facts, we adopt her version in reviewing the grant of summary judgment to Trooper Cook. *Witt v. W. Va. State Police, Troop 2,* 633 F.3d 272, 276-77 (4th Cir. 2011) (quoting *Scott,* 550 U.S. at 378, 127 S.Ct. 1769).

[4] Trooper Cook testified that after he "took the phones," Ryan and Tiffanie Hupp gave him the passwords for the phones and signed a property receipt. J.A. 572-73.

[5] The video does not contain clear audio of the incident. Therefore, we must look to the parties' respective deposition testimony and other evidence in the record regarding what was said.

[6] All of these orders, and Hupp's responses and "opinions," are alleged to have been spoken in the incredibly short period of two seconds. Such a back-and-forth exchange would seem to require more than two seconds. At this stage, however, like the district court, we make no determination regarding the credibility of Trooper Cook's testimony.

[7] Appellants presented expert reports and deposition testimony from two expert witnesses, an expert in canine behavior and an expert in police training. Appellants argue that the expert testimony establishes the unreasonableness of Trooper Cook's actions in the way in which he approached Buddy and drew his gun. According to Appellants, the district court's failure to engage with any of their proffered expert testimony constitutes reversible error in itself. As we have explained, the district court's grant of qualified immunity on the false arrest claim is reversed for reasons other than the court's failure to engage with the expert evidence. That being said, we note that the district court did not address the expert testimony in its evaluation of the summary judgment motions. We expect that upon remand, the expert testimony presented by the parties will be appropriately addressed, including any objections to the admissibility of that testimony.

[8] Hupp's alleged grabbing of Trooper Cook is not captured in the video because she allegedly did so when his back was turned to the camera and blocking the camera's view of Hupp.

[9] Because we cannot say as a matter of law that an officer in Trooper Cook's position would reasonably have believed that the video evidence would be concealed or destroyed before a warrant for the video's seizure could be obtained, Trooper Cook is not entitled to qualified immunity on the search and seizure claims. *See Smith,* 781 F.3d at 100.

893 F.3d 213 (2018)

Damon WILSON, Plaintiff-Appellant,
v.
PRINCE GEORGE'S COUNTY, MARYLAND; PFC Gill, ID #3361, Prince George's County Police, Defendants-Appellees.

No. 17-1856.

United States Court of Appeals, Fourth Circuit.
Argued: March 22, 2018.
Decided: June 18, 2018.

Wilson v. Prince George's County, Maryland, 893 F. 3d 213 (4th Cir. 2018)

Appeal from the United States District Court for the District of Maryland, at Greenbelt, William Connelly, Magistrate Judge, (8:16-cv-00425-WGC).

ARGUED: George Aubrey Harper, Law Offices of George Harper, Upper Marlboro, Maryland, for Appellant. Gessesse Teferi, Prince George's County Office Of Law, Upper Marlboro, Maryland, for Appellees. ON BRIEF: Jared M. McCarthy, County Attorney, Andrew J. Murray, Deputy County Attorney, Prince George's County Office Of Law, Upper Marlboro, Maryland, for Appellees.

Before GREGORY, Chief Judge, and KEENAN and FLOYD, Circuit Judges.

p.216 BARBARA MILANO KEENAN, Circuit Judge:

Damon Wilson was shot several times during an encounter with Officer Brendan Gill, a Prince George's County, Maryland, police officer. The incident occurred while Officer Gill was investigating an emergency call that Wilson had committed a burglary of his former girlfriend's dwelling and had assaulted her.

Wilson filed suit under 42 U.S.C. § 1983 against Officer Gill and Prince George's County (collectively, the defendants), alleging excessive force in violation of the Fourth Amendment. Wilson also alleged in his complaint that Officer Gill's conduct violated certain provisions of Maryland state law. The district court awarded summary judgment in the defendants' favor, holding that Officer Gill was entitled to qualified immunity, and that the County was not liable because no constitutional violation occurred.[1]

Upon our review, we hold that the district court erred in determining that Officer Gill's conduct did not violate Wilson's Fourth Amendment rights. Nevertheless, we affirm the district court's determination that Officer Gill is entitled to qualified immunity, because we hold that the constitutional violation was not clearly established when the incident occurred. We also affirm the court's judgment on the common law intentional infliction of emotional distress claim against Officer Gill and on the respondeat superior claim asserted against the County. However, because questions of immunity under state law remain, we vacate the court's award of summary judgment on Wilson's remaining state-law claims against Officer Gill, and remand those claims to the district court for further proceedings.

I.

The parties largely agree on the events that occurred from the moment that Officer Gill first saw Wilson until the time that Officer Gill fired his weapon. We note any disputes of fact below.

On October 7, 2012, late in the afternoon, Wilson walked to the home of his former girlfriend, Mynia Johnson, because he wanted to see his two daughters who were in Johnson's care. After "knocking" and "banging" on Johnson's apartment door and receiving no response, Wilson began shouting that he wanted to see his children. As his anger increased, Wilson "kicked down" the front door of Johnson's p.217 apartment and walked inside, cursing and yelling at Johnson and one of her male guests.

After greeting one daughter, Wilson left the apartment. Johnson followed him outside and, during an argument that ensued, Wilson slapped Johnson. When Johnson threatened to call the police, Wilson attempted to take her phone, which fell into a drain.

Wilson left the area and walked to his brother's home. Because his brother was preoccupied with other matters, Wilson once again became angry, seized a pocket knife, and left his brother's home. Wilson walked back toward Johnson's apartment, intending to commit suicide in front of her so that she would blame herself for his death.

Meanwhile, Johnson had placed a telephone call to a 911 operator and had informed the operator that her ex-boyfriend had broken into her apartment and had assaulted her. Officer Gill arrived at the apartment in response to the 911 call. Johnson showed Officer Gill the damaged apartment door, and informed him that Wilson had assaulted her after breaking into the apartment. Johnson later accompanied Officer Gill outside the building. As Officer Gill and Johnson were leaving the building, Johnson observed Wilson some distance away and identified him to Officer Gill, who directed Johnson to return to her apartment.[2]

Officer Gill began walking toward Wilson, attempting to engage him in a dialogue. Moments later, Wilson pulled a shiny object out of his pocket.[3] However, due to the distance between him and Wilson, Officer Gill was unable to identify the object.

Because Wilson continued walking in Officer Gill's direction, Officer Gill drew his service weapon and commanded Wilson between ten and fifteen times to drop the object in his hands, which object Officer Gill later identified as a knife. After Wilson failed to drop the knife, Officer Gill called for assistance on his radio. Wilson told Officer Gill to leave so that Wilson could "do what [he] wan[ted to] do." Wilson ignored Officer Gill's repeated command that Wilson drop the knife.

Instead, Wilson began directing obscene remarks at Johnson. Rather than drop the knife, Wilson took some steps forward, started "poking" himself with the knife, and "slit his throat." He then took a few more steps toward Officer Gill, and began "stab[bing]" and "poking" himself in the chest, which he testified caused him to "stumble[]" forward about four steps.

According to Wilson, at this point he was about 20 feet away from Officer Gill. Officer Gill, however, disputed Wilson's estimate and stated that he was between 10 and 15 feet away from Wilson. Johnson, who was standing about one or two feet behind Officer Gill, estimated that Wilson stopped eight feet away from Officer Gill. Although Officer Gill stated that Wilson "closed the distance" after stabbing himself in the chest, Officer Gill did not describe Wilson's movement with any particularity. However, sensing that Wilson was "too close," Officer Gill discharged his firearm five times, aiming for the center of Wilson's body. The record does not indicate whether Officer Gill issued a further p.218 warning to Wilson before shooting him. The record also lacks information regarding how quickly Officer Gill deployed the five shots.

Wilson suffered multiple gunshot wounds to the torso, but the record does not indicate which shots, or how many shots, hit Wilson. The gunshot wounds caused Wilson to fall to the ground. With the assistance of another police officer who arrived shortly after the shooting, Officer Gill rolled Wilson away from the knife, placed handcuffs on him, and began performing CPR.[4]

In his complaint filed against Officer Gill and Prince George's County, Wilson asserted a claim under 42 U.S.C. § 1983 alleging excessive force in violation of the Fourth Amendment, as well as several claims under Maryland law.[5] The defendants filed a motion for summary judgment, contending that Officer Gill's conduct was reasonable and that he otherwise was immune from suit under the doctrine of qualified immunity. In granting the defendants' motion, the district court concluded that Officer Gill's use of force was objectively reasonable and, therefore, did not constitute excessive force. Based on this conclusion, the district court also dismissed Wilson's remaining claims against Officer Gill, as well as his claims against Prince George's County.[6] Wilson timely noted this appeal.

II.

A.

We review de novo the district court's award of summary judgment. *Meyers v. Balt. Cty., Md.,* 713 F.3d 723, 730 (4th Cir. 2013). Summary judgment is appropriate only when there are no material facts in dispute, and the moving party is entitled to judgment as a matter of law. Fed. R. Civ. P. 56(a); *Celotex Corp. v. Catrett,* 477 U.S. 317, 322, 106 S.Ct. 2548, 91 L.Ed.2d 265 (1986); *Meyers,* 713 F.3d at 730.

In conducting our review, we construe the evidence in the light most favorable to Wilson, the non-moving party. *Lee v. Town of Seaboard,* 863 F.3d 323, 327 (4th Cir. 2017). We do not weigh the evidence or make credibility determinations. p.219 *See Ray Commc'ns, Inc. v. Clear Channel Commc'ns, Inc.,* 673 F.3d 294, 305 (4th Cir. 2012) (stating that credibility determinations are not part of summary judgment proceedings); *Gray v. Spillman,* 925 F.2d 90, 95 (4th Cir. 1991) (assessing witness credibility and weighing evidence are functions of the jury, not of the trial judge ruling on motion for summary judgment).

B.

Qualified immunity is a doctrine that "balances two important interests—the need to hold public officials accountable when they exercise power irresponsibly and the need to shield officials from harassment, distraction, and liability when they perform their duties reasonably." *Pearson v. Callahan,* 555 U.S. 223, 231, 129 S.Ct. 808, 172 L.Ed.2d 565 (2009). The doctrine of qualified immunity protects from liability officers who commit constitutional violations, but whose conduct does not violate clearly established statutory or constitutional rights known to a reasonable person. *Meyers,* 713 F.3d at 731. The burden of proving the affirmative defense of qualified immunity rests on the party seeking to invoke it. *Id.*

Our application of the qualified immunity doctrine is guided by the Supreme Court's analysis in *Saucier v. Katz,* 533 U.S. 194, 121 S.Ct. 2151, 150 L.Ed.2d 272 (2001), later modified by the Court's decision in *Pearson,* 555 U.S. 223, 129 S.Ct. 808, 172 L.Ed.2d 565. Under the Court's two-step approach, we may first determine whether the facts alleged or shown, taken in the light most favorable to the plaintiff, establish that the officer's conduct violated the plaintiff's constitutional right. *Saucier,* 533 U.S. at 201, 121 S.Ct. 2151. If this initial prong is satisfied, we evaluate whether the right at issue was "clearly established" at the time of the officer's conduct.[7] *Id.* Accordingly, even when the facts in the record establish that the officer's conduct violated a plaintiff's constitutional rights, the officer still is entitled to immunity from suit "if a reasonable person in the [officer's] position could have failed to appreciate that his conduct would violate those rights." *Torchinsky v. Siwinski,* 942 F.2d 257, 261 (4th Cir. 1991) (citation and internal quotation marks omitted).

C.

We first consider whether the facts alleged, taken in the light most favorable to Wilson, show that Officer Gill's conduct violated the Fourth Amendment. *Saucier,* 533 U.S. at 201, 121 S.Ct. 2151. Wilson argues that Officer Gill's conduct of firing his weapon at Wilson constituted excessive force in violation of the Fourth Amendment. In response, Officer Gill contends that his use of deadly force was justified, because he reasonably feared for his safety and the safety of third parties present during his exchange with Wilson. Viewing the facts in the light most favorable to Wilson, we disagree with Officer Gill's argument.

The Fourth Amendment prohibits police officers from using excessive or unreasonable force in the course of making an arrest. *Graham v. Connor,* 490 U.S. 386, 395, 109 S.Ct. 1865, 104 L.Ed.2d 443 (1989). We evaluate whether an officer has used excessive force based on a standard of "objective reasonableness." *Id.* at 396-97, 399, 109 S.Ct. 1865. In applying p.220 this standard, we consider "[1] the severity of the crime at issue, [2] whether the suspect poses an immediate threat to the safety of the officers or others, and [3] whether [the suspect] is actively resisting arrest or attempting to evade arrest by flight." *Id.* at 396, 109 S.Ct. 1865. An officer may not use deadly force against a person who "poses no immediate threat to the officer and no threat to others." *Tennessee v. Garner,* 471 U.S. 1, 11, 105 S.Ct. 1694, 85 L.Ed.2d 1 (1985).

To determine whether a need for force outweighed Wilson's Fourth Amendment rights, we examine each of the three *Graham* factors. We easily resolve the first and third factors. Regarding the first factor, Wilson does not dispute that he "kicked down" Johnson's door, entered her apartment without her consent, and assaulted her. It also is undisputed that Officer Gill knew that Wilson had committed these offenses before his encounter with Wilson. Accordingly, the first *Graham* factor weighs in Officer Gill's favor. *Graham,* 490 U.S. at 396, 109 S.Ct. 1865.

The third *Graham* factor, whether Wilson resisted or attempted to evade arrest, favors Wilson. Officer Gill had not attempted to arrest Wilson, and Wilson was not trying to evade arrest when Officer Gill repeatedly shot Wilson. Thus, this factor weighs against Officer Gill's use of deadly force. *Id.*

The parties' arguments center on whether the second *Graham* factor supported the use of deadly force, namely, whether a reasonable officer could have perceived that Wilson "pose[d] an immediate threat to the safety of the officer[] or others." *Id.* Viewed in the light most favorable to Wilson, the facts show that Wilson did not threaten Officer Gill, Johnson, or any other individual present at the scene during the encounter. Wilson had a small knife in his hand and did not drop the knife when ordered to do so by Officer Gill. However, Wilson testified, and the defendants do not dispute, that Wilson never pointed the pocket knife in the direction of anyone but himself. Neither did Wilson move suddenly or act in a threatening manner toward Officer Gill or others.[8] Additionally, at the time Officer Gill discharged his weapon, Wilson had slit his own throat and had stabbed himself in his chest.

And finally, a key disputed fact further calls into question whether Officer Gill faced an immediate threat. The parties dispute the distance separating Officer Gill and Wilson at the time that Wilson "stumbled" forward and Officer Gill discharged his weapon. The estimates of the three people present ranged between eight feet and 20 feet. A jury could determine that Wilson, standing 20 feet away and armed only with a pocket knife that he was using solely against himself, did not pose an immediate threat to Officer Gill or others, thereby rendering Officer Gill's use of lethal force unreasonable.

Under these alleged facts, therefore, a jury could conclude that Officer Gill violated Wilson's Fourth Amendment right to be free from excessive force. In reaching this conclusion, we emphasize that we do not make credibility determinations in resolving the first prong of the *Saucier* analysis.[9] p.221 *See Ray Commc'ns,* 673 F.3d at 305. Therefore, we conclude that the present record, when viewed in the light most favorable to Wilson, establishes that Officer Gill's use of force was not "objectively reasonable" and, thus, was excessive in violation of the Fourth Amendment. Accordingly, we hold that the district court erred in reaching a contrary conclusion.

D.

Having determined that Officer Gill's actions were an unconstitutional use of excessive force, we turn to consider the second step of the qualified immunity analysis, namely, whether Officer Gill's conduct violated a constitutional right that was clearly established at the time the conduct occurred.[10] *Saucier,* 533 U.S. at 201, 121 S.Ct. 2151. A right is "clearly established" if it would be clear to a reasonable officer that the alleged conduct is unlawful. *Harlow v. Fitzgerald,* 457 U.S. 800, 818, 102 S.Ct. 2727, 73 L.Ed.2d 396 (1982). In other words, the contours of the right must be "sufficiently clear 'that every reasonable official would [have understood] that what he is doing violates that right.'" *Reichle v. Howards,* 566 U.S. 658, 664, 132 S.Ct. 2088, 182 L.Ed.2d 985 (2012) (alteration in the original) (quoting *Ashcroft v. alKidd,* 563 U.S. 731, 741, 131 S.Ct. 2074, 179 L.Ed.2d 1149 (2011)). To determine whether a right is clearly established, we assess whether the law has "been authoritatively decided by the Supreme Court,[11] the appropriate United States Court of Appeals, or the highest court of the state." *Wilson v. Layne,* 141 F.3d 111, 114 (4th Cir. 1998) (citation omitted).

A right need not be recognized by a court in a specific factual context before such right may be considered "clearly established" for purposes of qualified immunity. *See Hope v. Pelzer,* 536 U.S. 730, 739, 122 S.Ct. 2508, 153 L.Ed.2d 666 (2002); *Buonocore v. Harris,* 65 F.3d 347, 356-57 (4th Cir. 1995). However, the Supreme Court has emphasized in recent years that courts are "not to define clearly established law at a high level of generality," and that "[s]pecificity is especially important in the Fourth Amendment context." *Kisela v. Hughes,* ___ U.S. ___, 138 p.222 S.Ct. 1148, 1152, 200 L.Ed.2d 449 (2018) (quoting *City and Cty. of San Francisco v. Sheehan,* ___ U.S. ___, 135 S.Ct. 1765, 1775-76, 191 L.Ed.2d 856 (2015)). Thus, although we often have looked to the general rules articulated in *Graham,* 490 U.S. at 395, 109 S.Ct. 1865, and *Garner,* 471 U.S. 1, 105 S.Ct. 1694, to hold that a right is clearly established, *see, e.g., Clem v. Corbeau,* 284 F.3d 543, 553-54 (4th Cir. 2002), the Supreme Court has cautioned that we should do so only in "obvious case[s]" exhibiting violations of the core of the Fourth Amendment, *Kisela,* 138 S.Ct. at 1153 (citation omitted).

Defined at the level of specificity required by the Supreme Court, we ask here whether it was clearly established law in October 2012 that shooting an individual was an unconstitutional use of excessive force when: (1) the officer had probable cause to believe that the person had committed certain misdemeanors, one of which involved the use of force against another person; (2) the individual was standing about 20 feet from the officer holding a knife and using it to hurt himself, but was not threatening anyone or making any sudden movements; and (3) the individual had ignored the officer's repeated commands to drop the knife. Upon our review of relevant precedent, we hold that it was not clearly established law in October 2012 in the Supreme Court, this Circuit, or in the Court of Appeals of Maryland, that an officer shooting an individual under such circumstances would be engaging in an unconstitutional use of excessive force.

The cases we have examined are not sufficiently analogous to the present case to have placed Officer Gill on such notice. For example, when an individual was armed, we have held that the "mere possession" of a deadly weapon by the individual did not justify the use of deadly force. *See Cooper v. Sheehan,* 735 F.3d 153, 154, 159-60 (4th Cir. 2013) (reviewing the state of the law in 2007 and determining that the right was clearly established). However, when additional facts indicated that an armed person posed a threat of harm to the officers or others, we have held that the use of deadly force was objectively reasonable. *See Anderson v. Russell,* 247 F.3d 125, 128, 132 (4th Cir. 2001) (holding that officers were entitled to qualified immunity for shooting a man suspected of carrying a gun who initially complied with commands, but later lowered his hands and reached into his back left pocket toward a bulge under his clothing); *see also Slattery v. Rizzo,* 939 F.2d 213, 214-17 (4th Cir. 1991) (holding that the shooting of an individual, suspected of narcotics trafficking, was objectively reasonable when the suspect ignored commands to raise his hands and turned in the officers' direction with his hand partially closed around an object).

Here, Wilson was not shot solely because he had a deadly weapon in his possession. Rather, Wilson was suspected of committing two crimes, namely, breaking and entering and battery, and Officer Gill was aware of these crimes before his interaction with Wilson. Wilson also did not comply with Officer Gill's repeated commands to drop the knife he was holding. Thus, our decision in *Cooper* did not put Officer Gill on notice that shooting Wilson would be crossing a bright line in violation of the Fourth Amendment. *See, e.g., Anderson,* 247 F.3d at 128, 132; *Slattery,* 939 F.2d at 214-17.

Cases featuring officer interactions with suicidal individuals or individuals suffering from mental illness likewise are not dispositive. For example, in *Clem,* 284 F.3d at 545-46, two officers responded to a call by a woman explaining that her husband, Robert Clem, was suffering from dementia and various physical problems. Although p.223 Clem was not armed, he grew agitated and began acting erratically after the officers' arrival, causing the officers twice to administer pepper spray in an effort to subdue Clem. *Id.* at 547. Clem began "stomping" forward toward one of the officers with his hands open and in front of his body. *Id.* at 548. Without giving Clem any warning, one of the officers shot him. *Id.* We held that the officer's use of force was unreasonable in violation of the Fourth Amendment. *Id.* at 552.

In contrast, we held in *Sigman v. Town of Chapel Hill,* 161 F.3d 782 (4th Cir. 1998), that an officer was entitled to qualified immunity for shooting an individual who at one point was armed with a knife, and had been drinking, throwing things, and cutting himself. *Id.* at 787. The individual had ignored several commands from the officers, had made threats to the officers and others, and had used the knife to slash at one of the officers through a window before one officer shot him. *Id.*

The conduct at issue here lies somewhere between the officer's unreasonable use of force in *Clem* and the officers' reasonable use of force in *Sigman.* Although *Clem* and *Sigman* both featured a mentally unstable individual, neither case is sufficiently analogous to the circumstances present here. Unlike in *Clem,* Wilson was armed and had been engaged in criminal activity. And unlike in *Sigman,* Wilson never threatened others, either verbally or with the knife, during his interaction with Officer Gill. Therefore, our precedent at the time regarding the use of force on mentally ill individuals did not offer sufficient guidance to place "every reasonable offic[er]" in Officer Gill's position on notice that his conduct would violate the Fourth Amendment. *Ashcroft,* 563 U.S. at 741, 131 S.Ct. 2074 (citation and internal quotation marks omitted).

Our review of Maryland Court of Appeals decisions affirms our conclusion that Officer Gill was not on notice regarding the constitutional violation resulting from his alleged conduct. Decisions by the Maryland Court of Appeals encompass cases that fairly could be deemed "obvious case[s]" of unreasonable uses of force. *See Barbre v. Pope,* 402 Md. 157, 935 A.2d 699, 716 (2007) (holding that officer was not entitled to immunity under the Maryland Tort Claims Act for shooting an individual who was not intoxicated, incapacitated, or threatening the safety of the officer or others, and whose hands were raised in surrender). And decisions by that court have ratified an officer's use of deadly force against individuals who reasonably appear to be armed in dangerous circumstances. *See Richardson v. McGriff,* 361 Md. 437, 762 A.2d 48, 49-50 (2000) (affirming jury verdict in favor of officer when officer shot the plaintiff after the officer's partner quickly opened the door to a closet in a dark kitchen, and officer shined flashlight inside, seeing the plaintiff holding and lowering into firing position what appeared to be a large weapon). However, the Court of Appeals of Maryland has not decided a case with facts sufficiently analogous to those present here such that Officer Gill was on notice that his conduct violated the Fourth Amendment.

A survey of other circuits' case law also illustrates the lack of clear consensus regarding violations of this nature. In some instances, courts have found excessive the use of deadly force against erratically behaving or suicidal individuals who are not otherwise threatening anyone and have not committed any violent acts. *See, e.g., McKenney v. Mangino,* 873 F.3d 75, 79-80, 83 (1st Cir. 2017) (holding that it was excessive force for an officer to shoot a suicidal individual holding a gun in one hand and who ignored officer's commands but who did not point the gun at anyone or p.224 act in a threatening manner toward the officer); *Estate of Escobedo v. Bender,* 600 F.3d 770, 773, 780, 786 (7th Cir. 2010) (holding that the use of tear gas, flash bang devices, and ultimate shooting of an armed suicidal individual under the influence of drugs was excessive when the individual did not threaten anyone). But another out-of-circuit case can be construed as supporting Officer Gill's decision to use deadly force in this case. *See, e.g., Elizondo v. Green,* 671 F.3d 506, 508, 510 (5th Cir. 2012) (holding that officer's shooting of a suicidal teenager not suspected of committing any crimes was reasonable when teenager refused orders to drop the knife in his hand and approached officer with the knife raised). Given the lack of "a consensus of cases of persuasive authority" from other jurisdictions, a reasonable officer in Officer Gill's position would not have known that his actions were unlawful. *Booker v. S.C. Dep't of Corr.,* 855 F.3d 533, 538-39 (4th Cir. 2017) (citation omitted).

Ultimately, this case simply is not an "obvious" one, permitting us fairly to say that the decisions in *Garner* and *Graham,* on their own, clearly established the right at issue. *White v. Pauly,* ___ U.S. ___, 137 S.Ct. 548, 552, 196 L.Ed.2d 463 (2017) (citation and internal quotation marks omitted). As of October 2012, our precedent shed some light on officer interactions with unarmed, mentally ill individuals, *see generally Clem,* 284 F.3d 543, and with armed, actively threatening, mentally unstable individuals, *see generally Sigman,* 161 F.3d 782. Our cases as of that time also addressed the reasonableness of deadly force against armed, but non-threatening individuals. *See generally Cooper,* 735 F.3d 153. And our decisions up to that date provided guidance to officers faced with armed individuals suspected of violent crimes. *See generally, e.g., Anderson,* 247 F.3d 125; *Slattery,* 939 F.2d 213. However, as of October 2012, our precedent and the decisions of the Court of Appeals of Maryland fell short of providing sufficient notice to an officer to bar qualified immunity when the officer used deadly force against an armed, but otherwise non-threatening, self-harming individual suspected of committing misdemeanor offenses.

Accordingly, we hold that in October 2012, it was not clearly established that an officer would violate a suspect's Fourth Amendment right to be free from excessive force by shooting a person who: (1) was suspected of having committed a burglary and a battery; (2) was standing about 20 feet from the officer holding a knife, inflicting harm on himself and stumbling, but not threatening others or making sudden movements; and (3) was refusing to obey the officer's repeated commands to drop the knife at the time he was shot. We therefore conclude that Officer Gill is entitled to qualified immunity. We emphasize, however, that as of the date this opinion issues, law enforcement officers are now on notice that such conduct constitutes excessive force in violation of the Fourth Amendment.

III.

Wilson's remaining claims against Officer Gill involve alleged violations of the Maryland Declaration of Rights Articles 24 and 26, and common law battery. The same standard applies to the Maryland Declaration of Rights claims as to claims asserted under the Fourth Amendment. *See Henry v. Purnell,* 652 F.3d 524, 536 (4th Cir. 2011) (stating that the court's conclusion that the defendant violated the plaintiff's Fourth Amendment rights meant that the defendant also violated the plaintiff's rights under Articles 24 and 26 of the Maryland constitution); *see also Richardson,* 762 A.2d at 56; *Okwa v. Harper,* 360 Md. 161, 757 A.2d 118, 140-41 (2000). Thus, because we have concluded that Officer Gill used excessive force in p.225 violation of the Fourth Amendment, Officer Gill's conduct also violated the Maryland constitution. *See Henry,* 652 F.3d at 536. Additionally, Officer Gill's conduct, if proved, would constitute a battery under Maryland law. *See French v. Hines,* 182 Md.App. 201, 957 A.2d 1000, 1037 (2008) (noting that "[t]o the extent that the officer uses excessive force in effectuating an arrest, the privilege [to commit a battery in the course of a legally justified arrest] is lost").

Because the district court erroneously concluded that Officer Gill's use of force was reasonable, the court did not address fully the question of immunity under Maryland law. "[M]indful that we are a court of review, not of first view," *Lovelace v. Lee,* 472 F.3d 174, 203 (4th Cir. 2006) (citation omitted), we remand these state-law claims against Officer Gill for the district court to consider "in the first instance" whether Officer Gill is entitled to immunity under Maryland law, *Jennings v. University of North Carolina,* 482 F.3d 686, 702 (4th Cir. 2007).

IV.

For these reasons, we affirm the district court's award of summary judgment to Officer Gill on the Section 1983 claim of excessive force and the common law claim of intentional infliction of emotional distress. We also affirm the court's award of summary judgment to the County on the respondeat superior claim. We vacate the portion of the district court's order granting summary judgment to Officer Gill on the remaining state-law claims, and remand those claims for further proceedings consistent with this opinion.

AFFIRMED IN PART; VACATED IN PART; AND REMANDED

[1] Regarding the Section 1983 claim of excessive force, the district court held that Officer Gill's use of deadly force was objectively reasonable. Based on this holding,

the court disposed of the Maryland state-law claims and awarded summary judgment in favor of the defendants on all claims.

[2] Johnson was present for the events that took place following Wilson's re-appearance at her apartment building. It is not clear whether she ignored Officer Gill's request completely or initially obliged but later came out of the building.

[3] It is undisputed that this object was the pocket knife Wilson took from his brother's home.

[4] Wilson's amended complaint alleged that he suffered permanent partial paralysis as a result of his gunshot injuries. However, there is no additional evidence in the record establishing the extent of Wilson's injuries.

[5] The Maryland claims included causes of action under Articles 24 and 26 of the Maryland Declaration of Rights, and the common law torts of battery and intentional infliction of emotional distress. Wilson also originally brought a state-law claim for negligence against Officer Gill and a state-law claim of "unconstitutional custom and practice" against the County, but abandoned both claims in the district court. At oral argument before this Court, Wilson abandoned his appeal regarding his claim for intentional infliction of emotional distress.

[6] We conclude that Wilson has abandoned on appeal any challenge to the district court's dismissal of his claims against the County based on respondeat superior liability. Fed. R. App. P. 28(a)(8)(A) ("[T]he argument . . . must contain . . . appellant's contentions and the reasons for them."); *see also, e.g., Jacobs v. N.C. Admin. Office of the Courts,* 780 F.3d 562, 568 n.7 (4th Cir. 2015). In his briefing to this Court, Wilson asserts that the district court erred in granting summary judgment to the defendants. However, Wilson's brief contains no reference to his claim against the County, much less offers any argument regarding the district court's dismissal of that particular claim. And importantly, Wilson fails to address how any determination that Officer Gill's conduct was unlawful would affect Wilson's claims against the County and to address potential issues of governmental immunity. Accordingly, by failing to raise this issue, Wilson has abandoned it.

[7] Under *Pearson,* we need not conduct the two-step analysis in the sequence set forth in *Saucier.* 555 U.S. at 236, 129 S.Ct. 808. Nonetheless, we exercise our discretion in this case and conduct the qualified immunity analysis in the order provided by the Court in *Saucier. See id.*

[8] As noted previously, Wilson testified in his deposition that he "stumbled" a few steps toward Officer Gill. Drawing a reasonable inference in Wilson's favor, a jury could find such movement non-threatening.

[9] The district court relied on the report of the defendants' expert, Craig Dickerson, in reaching the determination that Officer Gill's use of force was reasonable and justified. Dickerson opined that a person armed with a knife and standing from an officer at a distance of 21 feet could rush toward, and "cut," an officer before the officer would be able to draw his weapon from its holster. Here, however, the facts are undisputed that Officer Gill already had drawn his weapon when Wilson was about 40 feet away from Gill. For this reason, we conclude that Dickerson's expert report is largely irrelevant to our determination of reasonableness. We also observe that it is for the jury to determine whether to credit Dickerson's

opinion. *See Anderson v. Liberty Lobby, Inc.,* 477 U.S. 242, 255, 106 S.Ct. 2505, 91 L.Ed.2d 202 (1986).

[10] The district court did not reach this step of the analysis, concluding that there was no Fourth Amendment violation. Although we could exercise our discretion and first determine whether the right, as alleged, was clearly established without affirmatively holding that there was a violation of the Fourth Amendment when the evidence is construed in the light most favorable to Wilson, we think it is important to recognize the Fourth Amendment violation in this case in order "to further the development of constitutional precedent." *Pearson,* 555 U.S. at 236, 129 S.Ct. 808.

[11] Supreme Court precedent offers little guidance regarding our determination whether the right at issue is clearly established because in many instances, the Court has declined to decide whether an officer's actions constituted a violation of the Fourth Amendment and instead has considered whether the right recognized by a court of appeals was clearly established. *See, e.g., Kisela v. Hughes,* ___ U.S. ___, 138 S.Ct. 1148, 1152, 200 L.Ed.2d 449 (2018) (stating that "the Court need not, and does not, decide whether Kisela violated the Fourth Amendment . . . [f]or even assuming a Fourth Amendment violation occurred[,]" the officer's conduct did not violate clearly established law); *Brosseau v. Haugen,* 543 U.S. 194, 198, 125 S.Ct. 596, 160 L.Ed.2d 583 (2004) ("We express no view as to the correctness of the Court of Appeals' decision on the constitutional question itself.").

885 F.3d 254 (2018)

Trey SIMS Plaintiff-Appellant,

v.

Kenneth E. LABOWITZ, Administrator pursuant to Code of Va. sect. 64.2-454 of the Estate of David E. Abbott, Defendant-Appellee, and Claiborne Richardson, Defendant.

Children's Justice Fund; Child USA, Amici Supporting Appellant.

No. 16-2174.

United States Court of Appeals, Fourth Circuit.

Argued: September 14, 2017.

Decided: March 14, 2018.

Sims v. Labowitz, 885 F. 3d 254 (4th Cir. 2018)

Appeal from the United States District Court for the Eastern District of Virginia, at Alexandria, (1:16-cv-00572-CMH-MSN), Claude M. Hilton, Senior District Judge.

Victor M. Glasberg, Maxwelle C. Sokol, Victor M. Glasberg & Associates, Alexandria, Virginia, for Appellant. Julia Bougie Judkins, Bancroft, McGavin, Horvath & Judkins, P.C., Fairfax, Virginia, for Appellee.

Before KING, KEENAN, and DIAZ, Circuit Judges.

p.257 BARBARA MILANO KEENAN, Circuit Judge:

ON REHEARING

In 2014, David E. Abbott, a detective with the Manassas City Police Department in Virginia, investigated allegations that 17-year-old Trey Sims used his cellular telephone to send sexually explicit photographs and video recordings of himself to his 15-year-old girlfriend. During the p.258 course of the investigation, Abbott obtained a search warrant authorizing photographs of Sims' naked body, including his erect penis. When Abbott executed the warrant, he allegedly demanded that Sims manipulate his penis to achieve an erection. Sims unsuccessfully attempted to comply with Abbott's order. The civil action before us is based on these alleged events.

Abbott died before the present case was filed. Sims therefore initiated this action against Kenneth Labowitz, the administrator of Abbott's estate under Virginia Code § 64.2-454 (the Administrator).[1] Sims asserted claims for damages under 42 U.S.C. § 1983, alleging that the search of his person violated his Fourth Amendment right of privacy or, alternatively, his right of substantive due process under the Fourteenth Amendment.[2] Sims also brought a claim for damages under 18 U.S.C. § 2255 alleging that, as a result of the search, he was the victim of manufactured child pornography in violation of 18 U.S.C. § 2251(a). The district court determined that the Administrator was entitled to qualified immunity on the Section 1983 claims, and accordingly dismissed that portion of Sims' action. The court also dismissed the remainder of Sims' complaint.

Upon our review, we vacate the district court's judgment with respect to the Section 1983 claim alleging a Fourth Amendment violation. Construing the facts in the light most favorable to Sims, a reasonable police officer would have known that attempting to obtain a photograph of a minor child's erect penis, by ordering the child to masturbate in the presence of others, would unlawfully invade the child's right of privacy under the Fourth Amendment. We therefore remand Sims' Section 1983 claim alleging a Fourth Amendment violation to the district court for further proceedings. We also vacate the district court's dismissal of Sims' claim for damages under 18 U.S.C. § 2255 as an alleged victim of child pornography, and remand that claim for consideration by the district court in the first instance. We affirm the district court's dismissal of Sims' remaining claims.

I.

Sims alleged the following facts, which we accept as true in our review of the district court's dismissal of the complaint under Federal Rule of Civil Procedure 12(b)(6). *See Zak v. Chelsea Therapeutics Int'l, Ltd.,* 780 F.3d 597, 601 (4th Cir. 2015). In June 2014, the Commonwealth of Virginia filed felony charges against Sims as a juvenile for manufacturing and distributing child pornography in violation of Virginia Code §§ 18.2-374.1, p.259 18.2-374.1:1. The charges arose based on Sims' conduct of "film[ing] a video of himself and fondling his erect penis" and sending the video to his minor girlfriend using his cellular telephone. After Sims declined to enter into a plea agreement, the Assistant Commonwealth's Attorney for Prince William County, Virginia, Claiborne T. Richardson, II, sought a nolle prosequi, and the juvenile court dismissed the charges against Sims.

The investigation against Sims continued and, at Richardson's direction, Abbott obtained a search warrant from a Virginia magistrate. The warrant authorized a search for "[p]hotographs of the genitals, and other parts of the body of [Sims] that will be used as comparisons in recovered forensic evidence from the victim and suspect's electronic devices. This includes a photograph of the suspect's erect penis."

Richardson and Abbott also obtained a detention order for Sims, which authorized Abbott to transport Sims from his home to a juvenile detention center. In a "locker room" in the center, Abbott and two uniformed, armed officers executed the search warrant. Abbott ordered Sims to "pull down his pants so that photos could be taken of his penis." After Sims complied, Abbott instructed Sims "to use his hand to manipulate his penis in different ways" to obtain an erection. However, Sims was unable to achieve an erection. Nonetheless, Abbott took photographs of Sims' flaccid penis using Abbott's cellular telephone.

The next day, Sims was arraigned on charges of possession and distribution of child pornography. Abbott informed Sims' attorney that Abbott again "proposed to take photographs of [Sims'] erect penis" to be used as evidence. Abbott also stated that if Sims could not achieve an erection, Sims would be taken "to a hospital to give him an erection-producing injection." Abbott obtained a second search warrant from a Virginia magistrate, which authorized additional photographs of Sims' naked body, including his erect penis.

Before the second search warrant was executed, however, the Manassas City Police Department issued a statement explaining that the department's policy did not permit "invasive search procedures of suspects in cases of this nature." Additionally, the Prince William County Commonwealth's Attorney, Paul B. Ebert, condemned the first search of Sims.

Sims' attorney filed a motion to quash the second search warrant. Before the juvenile court ruled on the motion, Richardson informed the court that the Commonwealth "would let the warrant expire without service." Richardson also stipulated that he would not use as evidence the photographs of Sims' penis that had been taken pursuant to the first search warrant.

After the juvenile court reduced the charges to felony possession of child pornography, the court found that the evidence was sufficient to convict Sims but did "not make a finding of guilt[]" and suspended imposition of sentence for one year. The court ordered Sims to comply with certain terms of probation, including performing 100 hours of community service, barring Sims from "access to social media," and prohibiting Sims from sending "text messages." After Sims completed the terms of his probation in August 2015, the court dismissed the charge against him.

The Administrator filed a motion to dismiss with prejudice under Federal Rule of Civil Procedure 12(b)(6). The district court granted the motion, concluding that the Administrator was entitled to qualified immunity on the Section 1983 claims. The district court also dismissed Sims' claim for damages brought under 18 U.S.C. p.260 § 2255. Sims timely filed the present appeal.

II.

A.

We first consider Sims' argument that his right of privacy under the Fourth Amendment was violated when Abbott attempted to obtain a photograph of Sims' erect penis and ordered him to masturbate in the presence of others. Sims contends that any reasonable officer would have known that this conduct violated Sims' Fourth Amendment right of privacy and that, therefore, the Administrator was not entitled to the protection of qualified immunity.

In response, the Administrator maintains that Sims failed to allege sufficient facts to support a Fourth Amendment violation because Abbott's search did not place Sims at risk of physical harm, and because the search did not physically invade Sims' body. The Administrator alternatively contends that even if Abbott's conduct violated the Fourth Amendment, such right was not clearly established at the time of the search because Abbott acted pursuant to a validly issued search warrant. We disagree with the Administrator's arguments.

We review de novo the district court's dismissal of Sims' complaint on the ground of qualified immunity. *Ridpath v. Bd. of Governors Marshall Univ.,* 447 F.3d 292, 306 (4th Cir. 2006). As previously explained, we construe the facts alleged in the light most favorable to Sims. *Id.* at 309.

The doctrine of qualified immunity shields government officials from liability for civil damages when their conduct does not violate clearly established constitutional or other rights that a reasonable officer would have known. *Pearson v. Callahan,* 555 U.S. 223, 231, 129 S.Ct. 808, 172 L.Ed.2d 565 (2009); *Graham v. Gagnon,* 831 F.3d 176, 182 (4th Cir. 2016). Qualified immunity seeks to balance two interests, namely, the "need to hold public officials accountable when they exercise power irresponsibly and the need to shield officials from harassment, distraction, and liability when they perform their duties reasonably." *Graham,* 831 F.3d at 182 (quoting *Pearson,* 555 U.S. at 231, 129 S.Ct. 808). To avoid dismissal of a complaint after a qualified immunity defense is raised, a plaintiff must allege sufficient facts to set forth a violation of a constitutional right, and the court must conclude that this right was clearly established at the time of the alleged violation. *Pearson,* 555 U.S. at 232, 129 S.Ct. 808.

Although we may consider either prong of the qualified immunity inquiry first, we begin by examining the constitutional right advanced by Sims. *See Estate of Armstrong ex rel. Armstrong v. Village of Pinehurst,* 810 F.3d 892, 898-99 (4th Cir. 2016). This approach is beneficial here because our inquiry addresses "questions that do not frequently arise" and, therefore, "promotes the development of constitutional precedent." *Pearson,* 555 U.S. at 236, 129 S.Ct. 808.

The Fourth Amendment protects "[t]he right of the people to be secure in their persons ... against unreasonable searches and seizures." U.S. Const. amend. IV. "The overriding function of the Fourth Amendment is to protect personal privacy and dignity against unwarranted intrusion by the State." *Schmerber v. California,* 384 U.S. 757, 767, 86 S.Ct. 1826, 16 L.Ed.2d 908 (1966).

A search is lawful only when it is reasonable. *Amaechi v. West,* 237 F.3d 356 (4th Cir. 2001). When, as in the present p.261 case, a search involves "movement of clothing to facilitate the visual inspection of a [person's] naked body," the search qualifies as a type of "sexually invasive search." *United States v. Edwards,* 666 F.3d 877, 882-83 (4th Cir. 2011) (citations omitted). To determine whether a sexually invasive search is reasonable, we employ the test adopted in *Bell v. Wolfish,* 441 U.S. 520, 559, 99 S.Ct. 1861, 60 L.Ed.2d 447 (1979). *See King v. Rubenstein,* 825 F.3d 206, 214-15 (4th Cir. 2016); *Edwards,* 666 F.3d at 883.

Under the *Bell* framework, we balance the invasion of personal rights caused by the search against the need for that particular search. 441 U.S. at 559, 99 S.Ct. 1861. Pursuant to *Bell,* we examine the search in its complete context and consider the following factors: (1) the scope of the particular intrusion; (2) the manner in which the search was conducted; (3) the justification for initiating the search; and (4) the place in which the search was performed. *Id.*

In the present case, the scope of the intrusion and the manner in which the search allegedly was performed involve overlapping inquiries. At the outset, we observe that a sexually invasive search "constitutes an extreme intrusion upon personal privacy, as well as an offense to the dignity of the individual." *Wood v. Clemons,* 89 F.3d 922, 929 (1st Cir. 1996) (citation omitted). Courts have described such searches, including strip searches, as terrifying, demeaning, and humiliating. *Mary Beth v. City of Chicago,* 723 F.2d 1263, 1272 (7th Cir. 1983) (citations omitted). When the scope of a search exceeds a visual inspection of an individual's naked body, the magnitude of the intrusion is even greater. *See Amaechi,* 237 F.3d at 363-64.

In *King v. Rubenstein,* we addressed the invasive nature and manner of a search of an inmate who was subjected to surgery to remove penile implants. 825 F.3d at 214-15. We explained that the surgery required cutting "beneath the skin into a sensitive, private body part," and involved "risk, trauma, and pain," as well as emotional anguish. *Id.* at 215. In holding that the inmate sufficiently alleged that the surgery was an unreasonable search under the Fourth Amendment, we stated that the nature of the surgery itself violated the inmate's "interest of bodily integrity," which "involves the most personal and deep-rooted expectations of privacy." *Id.* (citation omitted).

Although the intrusion suffered by Sims was neither physically invasive nor put him at risk of direct physical harm, the search nonetheless was exceptionally intrusive. First, as alleged by Sims, Abbott sought to do more than visually inspect Sims' genitalia. He attempted to photograph Sims' penis in a sexually aroused state. Further, the manner that Abbott employed to execute the warrant, namely, ordering Sims to masturbate to obtain an erection, required that Sims perform a sex act in the presence of three armed officers. Such alleged conduct necessarily invaded Sims' bodily integrity even though no part of Sims' body was penetrated or physically harmed. Abbott's search directed at forcing Sims to achieve an erection intruded "upon an area in which our society recognizes a significantly heightened privacy interest." *See Winston v. Lee,* 470 U.S. 753, 767, 105 S.Ct. 1611, 84 L.Ed.2d 662 (1985). Requiring Sims to masturbate in the presence of others, like searches involving physical penetration of genitalia, constituted "the ultimate invasion of personal dignity." *Amaechi,* 237 F.3d at 363-64; *see also King,* 825 F.3d at 215.

Moreover, we observe that this sexually intrusive search was rendered more egregious p.262 by being conducted in a manner that would instill fear in Sims. *See Edwards,* 666 F.3d at 884-85. Here, Sims alleged that he was "surrounded" by three armed officers as he questioned whether he was required to submit to Abbott's orders. Upon Abbott's insistence, Sims ultimately attempted to comply. Sims further alleged that the search caused him to suffer emotional harm. *Winston,* 470 U.S. at 761-63, 105 S.Ct. 1611 (explaining that intrusions without risk of physical harm nonetheless damage the individual's sense of personal privacy and security). Accordingly, both the outrageous scope of the sexually intrusive search and the intimidating manner in which the search was conducted weigh strongly against any finding that the search was reasonable.

Under the *Bell* framework, we next consider the justification for the search. *See* 441 U.S. at 559, 99 S.Ct. 1861. Abbott sought to obtain photographs of Sims' erect penis for an evidentiary purpose, namely, to compare these photographs with the forensic evidence obtained from the cellular telephones seized from Sims and his girlfriend. However, the Commonwealth ultimately agreed not to use the photographs of Sims' body as evidence, and the juvenile court nevertheless concluded that the evidence was sufficient to find that Sims had committed the offense of possession of child pornography. Thus, the record demonstrates that there was no evidentiary need to seek a photograph of Sims' erect penis. *See Winston,* 470 U.S. at 765-66, 105 S.Ct. 1611 (holding that because the prosecutor had substantial evidence available regarding the origin of the bullets sought to be extracted from the defendant via surgery, the need for surgery was reduced).

We cannot perceive any circumstance that would justify a police search requiring an individual to masturbate in the presence of others. *See id.* at 767, 105 S.Ct. 1611 (explaining that when searches intrude upon heightened privacy interests, a more substantial justification is required). Sexually invasive searches require that the search bear some discernible relationship with safety concerns, suspected hidden contraband, or evidentiary need. *See Logan v. Shealy,* 660 F.2d 1007, 1013 (4th Cir. 1981). Thus, we discern no justification for Abbott's alleged conduct executing the search of Sims' body, and we conclude that the semi-private location of the search did not mitigate the overall circumstances of this exceptionally intrusive search. Accordingly, we hold that Sims sufficiently alleged a violation of his Fourth Amendment right to be free from the sexually invasive search of his person.

We therefore turn to consider the second prong of the qualified immunity analysis, namely, whether Abbott should have known that his combined acts of (1) seeking to obtain a photograph of Sims' erect penis, and (2) demanding that Sims masturbate in the presence of others to achieve an erection, was unlawful under clear precedent at the time the search occurred. *Anderson v. Creighton,* 483 U.S. 635, 640, 107 S.Ct. 3034, 97 L.Ed.2d 523 (1987). To be clearly established, the "contours of the right must be sufficiently clear that a reasonable official would understand what he is doing violates that right." *Id.*

In this analysis, we review "cases of controlling authority in [this] jurisdiction, as well as the consensus of cases of persuasive authority from other jurisdictions." *Amaechi,* 237 F.3d at 363 (internal quotation and citation omitted). We observe that the "exact conduct at issue need not" previously have been deemed unlawful for the law governing an officer's actions to be clearly established. *Id.* at 362 (citing *Anderson,* 483 U.S. at 640, 107 p.263 S.Ct. 3034). Instead, we must determine whether pre-existing law makes "apparent" the unlawfulness of the officer's conduct. *Clem v. Corbeau,* 284 F.3d 543, 553 (4th Cir. 2002) (quoting *Anderson,* 483 U.S. at 640, 107 S.Ct. 3034). "Accordingly, a constitutional right is clearly established for qualified immunity purposes not only when it has been specifically adjudicated but also when it is manifestly included within more general applications of the core constitutional principle invoked." *Id.* (internal quotation and citation omitted).

The Supreme Court and this Court have developed an entire body of jurisprudence establishing limits on sexually intrusive searches. This precedent has made clear that when a search of a person's body would significantly invade that individual's right of privacy, the basis for the search requires greater justification under the Fourth Amendment. *Winston,* 470 U.S. at 767, 105 S.Ct. 1611; *see, e.g., Florence v. Bd. of Chosen Freeholders of Cty. of Burlington,* 566 U.S. 318, 330-38, 132 S.Ct. 1510, 182 L.Ed.2d 566 (2012) (holding that invasive search procedures at jail struck a reasonable balance between inmate privacy and the security needs of the institutions); *Illinois v. Lafayette,* 462 U.S. 640, 645, 103 S.Ct. 2605, 77 L.Ed.2d 65 (1983) (explaining that an officer cannot disrobe an arrestee publicly without justifying factors); *Bell,* 441 U.S. at 558-60, 99 S.Ct. 1861 (holding that practice of conducting visual body-cavity searches of inmates following contact visits did not violate the Fourth Amendment because of significant security interests); *King,* 825 F.3d at 217 (determining that inmate sufficiently alleged Fourth Amendment violation based on surgery to remove penile implants because there was no penological justification); *Edwards,* 666 F.3d at 884-85 (concluding that sexually invasive search was unlawful because dangerous manner in which the officer removed contraband outweighed interest in retrieving contraband); *Amaechi,* 237 F.3d at 365-66 (finding no justification for officer's pat down search to include touching arrestee's buttocks and penetrating her exposed genitalia); *Logan,* 660 F.2d at 1013 (holding that inmate's strip search bore no relationship to security needs at detention center).[3] And here, as we already have explained, there was neither an evidentiary justification for the alleged search to obtain a photograph of Sims' erect penis, nor could there have been a valid reason for demanding that Sims masturbate in the presence of others.

We observe, nevertheless, that there are state and federal district court decisions involving circumstances in which officers lawfully conducted searches to visually inspect a suspect's penis. *See Curtis v. Clarke,* 2012 WL 2342536, at *2 (E.D. Va. June 19, 2012); *Mata v. Hubbard,* 2011 WL 6210668, at *8 (C.D. Cal. Oct. 25, 2011); *Roadcap v. Commonwealth,* 50 Va. App. 732, 653 S.E.2d 620, 622-23 (2007); *Willis v. Commonwealth,* 1997 WL 39801, at *2 (Va. Ct. App. Feb. 4, 1997). However, the searches in these cases were justified by an evidentiary need to confirm certain characteristics of the perpetrator's genitalia, and none of the searches required that the individual achieve an erection or masturbate in the presence of others. Thus, the type of search conducted here by Abbott far exceeded the intrusions into privacy p.264 described in those state and federal district court decisions.

Additionally, the fact that Sims was a minor child at the time of the alleged events should have caused a reasonable officer even greater concern in seeking a warrant and in executing the sexually invasive search. The Supreme Court has explained that minors are more susceptible than adults to influence and psychological damage. *See Eddings v. Oklahoma,* 455 U.S. 104, 115, 102 S.Ct. 869, 71 L.Ed.2d 1 (1982) (recognizing that youth is mitigating factor in defendant's commission of crime). Accordingly, officials taking minors into custody must "preserv[e] and promot[e] the welfare of the child." *Schall v. Martin,* 467 U.S. 253, 265, 104 S.Ct. 2403, 81 L.Ed.2d 207 (1984) (citation omitted). In conducting sexually invasive searches of minors, officials must employ extreme caution because minors are "especially susceptible to possible traumas" affiliated with such searches. *N.G., S.G. ex rel. S.C. v. Connecticut,* 382 F.3d 225, 244 (2d Cir. 2004) (citation omitted). Thus, Abbott should have been aware that any assessment of the legality of a sexually invasive search of a 17-year-old required additional considerations based on the child's age.

Because there was no justification for the alleged search to photograph Sims' erect penis and the order that he masturbate in the presence of others, we conclude that well-established Fourth Amendment limitations on sexually invasive searches adequately would have placed any reasonable officer on notice that such police action was unlawful. *See Amaechi,* 237 F.3d at 365. Thus, the alleged conduct plainly did not qualify as the type of "bad guesses in gray areas" that qualified immunity is designed to protect. *Braun v. Maynard,* 652 F.3d 557, 560 (4th Cir. 2011) (quoting *Maciariello v. Sumner,* 973 F.2d 295, 298 (4th Cir. 1992)).

We further observe that the Administrator is not entitled to invoke qualified immunity simply because no other court decisions directly have addressed circumstances like those presented here. *See Clem,* 284 F.3d at 553. For good reason, most outrageous cases of constitutional violations rarely are litigated. *See K.H. ex rel. Murphy v. Morgan,* 914 F.2d 846, 851 (7th Cir. 1990) (explaining that never before had there been a case accusing welfare officials of selling foster children into slavery, but those officials nevertheless would not be entitled to immunity). Abbott's conduct affronted the basic protections of the Fourth Amendment, which at its core protects personal privacy and dignity against unjustified intrusion by governmental actors. *See Schmerber,* 384 U.S. at 767, 86 S.Ct. 1826.

Our conclusion is not altered by the Administrator's insistence that Abbott's conduct was not unlawful because he first obtained a warrant to take a photograph of Sims' erect penis. As a general matter, search warrants provide officers a "shield of immunity" with respect to challenged searches because a neutral magistrate has considered whether the warrant is supported by probable cause and justifies the intrusion into an individual's privacy. *See Messerschmidt v. Millender,* 565 U.S. 535, 547, 132 S.Ct. 1235, 182 L.Ed.2d 47 (2012). But the fact that a search warrant has been obtained "do[es] not confer immunity if it was objectively unreasonable" for the officer to rely on the warrant. *See Graham,* 831 F.3d at 183 (citations omitted) (discussing arrest warrant). Here, the obvious, unconstitutional invasion of Sims' right of privacy that was required to carry out the warrant rendered reliance on that warrant objectively unreasonable, thereby eliminating the protection that a search warrant typically would have afforded p.265 an executing officer.[4] *See Malley v. Briggs,* 475 U.S. 335, 341, 346 n.9, 106 S.Ct. 1092, 89 L.Ed.2d 271 (1986). For these reasons, we conclude that the district court erred in dismissing Sims' Section 1983 Fourth Amendment claim on the ground of qualified immunity.[5]

B.

Finally, Sims argues that the district court erred in dismissing his claim for damages under 18 U.S.C. § 2255 as a child victim of an enumerated felony offense, namely, sexual exploitation of a child in violation of 18 U.S.C. § 2251(a). Because Section 2255 requires factual allegations supporting a violation of a criminal statute, this separate claim for damages stands in contrast to the civil deprivation of constitutional rights described above and actionable under 42 U.S.C. § 1983.

The district court did not address Sims' claim under Section 2255 in its memorandum opinion, but simply dismissed Sims' complaint in its entirety. Under the procedural posture of this case, we conclude that the district court should consider in the first instance Sims' claim under Section 2255. Accordingly, we vacate the dismissal of that claim, and remand for consideration of that claim by the district court.

III.

For these reasons, we vacate the district court's ruling that the Administrator was entitled to qualified immunity on the Section 1983 claim alleging a Fourth Amendment violation, and we remand this claim to the district court for further proceedings. We also vacate the dismissal of Sims' claim under Section 2255 and remand that claim for consideration by the district court in the first instance. We affirm the district court's dismissal of Sims' remaining claims.

VACATED IN PART, AFFIRMED IN PART, AND REMANDED

KING, Circuit Judge, dissenting:

I write separately to dissent from the majority's denial of Detective Abbott's qualified immunity claim. With great respect for my good colleagues, their decision fails to recognize the controlling facts that undermine the § 1983 claim of plaintiff Sims. That is, Detective Abbott was acting pursuant to the advice of counsel and adhering to a court order. In my view, Abbott's actions were entirely consistent with applicable law and the Fourth Amendment. To explain my position more fully, this dissenting opinion contains three short segments. First, I emphasize the sanctity and importance of court orders. Second, I review the controlling facts and some guiding legal principles. Finally, I explain that Detective Abbott did not contravene any constitutional right and that he is entitled to qualified immunity. Put simply, I would affirm the district court.

A.

A duly issued search warrant is a court order and is entitled to be respected and p.266 complied with, particularly by law enforcement officers, members of the public, and the courts. The simple rule that a court order is to be obeyed is foundational to our legal system and an independent judiciary. *See* Stephen G. Breyer, *Judicial Independence in the United States,* 40 St. Louis U. L.J. 989, 994-96 (1996) (emphasizing importance of court orders in maintaining the rule of law in an orderly society); *see also Cooper v. Aaron,* 358 U.S. 1, 17-19, 78 S.Ct. 1401, 3 L.Ed.2d 5, 3 L.Ed.2d 19 (1958) (holding that courts and public officials are bound by constitutional rulings of Supreme Court). As Alexander Hamilton explained in *The Federalist* papers, the effective administration of justice "contributes, more than any other circumstance, to impressing upon the minds of the people affection, esteem, and reverence toward the government." The Federalist No. 17 (Alexander Hamilton); *see also* Breyer, *Judicial Independence,* 40 St. Louis U. L.J. 989, 995-96 (1996) (emphasizing that "the most important reason to think that a judge's decision will be efficacious is cultural, rather than institutional"). The Supreme Court itself once emphasized, in a proceeding from this Circuit, that "unless we wish anarchy to prevail within the federal judicial system, a precedent of this court must be followed by the lower federal courts no matter how misguided the judges of those courts may think it to be." *See Hutto v. Davis,* 454 U.S. 370, 375, 102 S.Ct. 703, 70 L.Ed.2d 556 (1982).

When a judicial officer — such as a state court magistrate — has issued a search warrant upon probable cause, specifying therein that which is to be searched and seized, it is unreasonable to require the officer charged with executing the warrant to reject the judicial decision and disobey the court's directive. *See United States v. Leon,* 468 U.S. 897, 920 n.21, 104 S.Ct. 3405, 82 L.Ed.2d 677 (1984) (citing Attorney General's Task Force on Violent Crime, Final Report (1981), for the proposition that police officers have a "sworn duty to carry out [the] provisions" of search and arrest warrants). We have consistently recognized and applied these guiding principles. As we explained a few years back, "It would be plainly unreasonable to rule that the [] officers ... must take issue with the considered judgment of an assistant [prosecuting] Attorney and the [] magistrate." *See Wadkins v. Arnold,* 214 F.3d 535, 543 (4th Cir. 2000).

The majority's ruling today — that Detective Abbott can be personally liable for failing to disobey the search warrant requiring Sims to be promptly searched — could lead law officers to second-guess court orders and avoid judgment calls in gray areas. As our friend Judge Wilkinson aptly emphasized more than twenty-five years ago, "If reasonable mistakes were actionable, difficult questions of discretion would always be resolved in favor of inaction, and effective law enforcement would be lost." *See Torchinsky v. Siwinski,* 942 F.2d 257, 261 (4th Cir. 1991).

B.

1.

We have consistently encouraged law enforcement officers to seek and secure search "warrants because magistrates from their detached perspective serve as the essential checkpoint between the Government and the citizen." *See Torchinsky,* 942 F.2d at 261; *see also United States v. Clarke,* 842 F.3d 288, 293 (4th Cir. 2016) ("The Fourth Amendment generally requires police to secure a warrant before conducting a search."). Although unwarranted searches may sometimes properly occur — for example, in exigent circumstances, in searches incident to lawful arrests, in plain view seizures, in vehicular searches, and with consent — a warrant is p.267 generally required by the Fourth Amendment for searches and seizures. In this situation, Detective Abbott complied with that constitutional mandate, and his actions were carried out pursuant to a lawful search warrant.

Detective Abbott personally applied to the Virginia magistrate for the search warrant, but he did so only after consulting with, receiving advice from, and complying with the directives of the Commonwealth's Attorney for Prince William County.[1] We have recognized that, although obtaining a search warrant on the advice of the prosecutor does not automatically render the search reasonable, it is a compelling factor for consideration. *See Buonocore v. Harris,* 134 F.3d 245, 253 (4th Cir. 1998). In our *Wadkins* decision, we explained that, in assessing a detective's qualified immunity claim, the "most compelling aspect of [the] conference [between the detective and prosecutor] is clear: at its conclusion, the Commonwealth's Attorney, on behalf of the Commonwealth of Virginia, authorized warrants for the [search] of [the suspect]." *See* 214 F.3d at 542. We therein also ruled that, even if a warrant is later deemed invalid, law enforcement officers are not required to "secondguess the legal assessments of trained lawyers" and need not disregard the warrant in the first instance. *Id.* at 543.

2.

In his affidavit for the search warrant that he later executed, Detective Abbott sought photos of Sims to "be used as comparisons [to] recovered forensic evidence from the victim and suspect's electronic devices." *See* Supp. J.A. 74-75. Finding probable cause shown, the magistrate in Prince William County issued the search warrant at 5:03 p.m. on June 3, 2014. The warrant provided as follows:

To any authorized officer:

You are hereby commanded in the name of the Commonwealth to forthwith search the following place, person, or thing either in day or night:

Trey Austin Sims, Date of Birth []. A white male, approximately 5'10" tall and approximately 150 pounds.

For the following property, objects and/or persons:

Photographs of the genitals, hands, and other parts of the body of Trey Sims that will be used as comparisons in recovered forensic evidence from the victim and suspect's electronic devices. This includes a photograph of the suspect's erect penis.

See Supp. J.A. 72-75 (emphasis added). Approximately an hour after the magistrate issued the forthwith search warrant, at 6:10 p.m., Detective Abbott and two other officers executed it. On June 5, 2014, Abbott reported to the court in the return that "[t]he following items, and no others, were seized under authority of this warrant: *Photos.*" *Id.* at 73 (emphasis added).

C.

In 2001, the Supreme Court established a two-pronged analysis for a qualified immunity claim interposed by a law enforcement officer. That assessment first requires a determination of whether the p.268 officer's conduct violated a constitutional right. Second, if a constitutional violation has been shown, the court must decide whether the constitutional right was clearly established at the time. *See Saucier v. Katz,* 533 U.S. 194, 200, 121 S.Ct. 2151, 150 L.Ed.2d 272 (2001). In 2009, the Court authorized that analysis to be applied in a sequence reserved to the court's discretion. *See Pearson v. Callahan,* 555 U.S. 223, 236, 129 S.Ct. 808, 172 L.Ed.2d 565 (2009).

1.

In the context of searches and seizures, "the ultimate touchstone of the Fourth Amendment is reasonableness" under the circumstances. *See Brigham City v. Stuart,* 547 U.S. 398, 403, 126 S.Ct. 1943, 164 L.Ed.2d 650 (2006). For example, other than the well-recognized exceptions, "searches conducted outside the judicial process, without prior approval by judge or magistrate, are per se unreasonable under the Fourth Amendment." *See Katz v. United States,* 389 U.S. 347, 357, 88 S.Ct. 507, 19 L.Ed.2d 576 (1967). On the other hand, the existence of a search warrant creates a rebuttable presumption that the search was reasonable. *See Torchinsky,* 942 F.2d at 262. And for the search to be reasonable, it does not have to be conducted flawlessly nor by the least intrusive means. *See Skinner v. Ry. Labor Executives' Ass'n,* 489 U.S. 602, 629 n.9, 109 S.Ct. 1402, 103 L.Ed.2d 639 (1989). There is little deterrent to excluding evidence where "an officer acting with objective good faith has obtained a search warrant from a judge or magistrate and acted within its scope." *See Leon,* 468 U.S. at 920, 104 S.Ct. 3405. Thus, the existence of a search warrant plays a significant role in the determination of whether a search and seizure was reasonable. This principle is important, and it exists because the search warrant mandate insures the reliable and detached scrutiny of a neutral magistrate, rather than the judgment of a single law officer. *See Johnson v. United States,* 333 U.S. 10, 14, 68 S.Ct. 367, 92 L.Ed. 436 (1948). Put succinctly, where a police officer has sought and obtained a search warrant and acted within its scope, the resulting search is presumptively reasonable.

In this situation, the safeguards guaranteed by the Fourth Amendment were carefully observed — i.e., the search of Sims was conducted pursuant to a search warrant issued by the neutral magistrate, and it was supported by probable cause. *See Johnson,* 333 U.S. at 14, 68 S.Ct. 367. This was therefore a warranted search, carried out under the law of Virginia and in compliance with Fourth Amendment jurisprudence. Because Abbott obtained a search warrant and acted within its scope, his search of Sims is presumptively reasonable. *See Torchinsky,* 942 F.2d at 262. Therefore, the § 1983 claim alleged by Sims plainly fails the first prong of *Saucier,* that is, no constitutional right was contravened in these circumstances.

Strikingly, Detective Abbott did not go directly to the Prince William County magistrate seeking the search warrant. He went first to that county's Commonwealth's Attorney and solicited the advice and approval of the prosecutor. We have recognized — in another qualified immunity case arising in the Old Dominion — that an investigating detective's "conference with the Commonwealth's Attorney and the subsequent issuance of the warrants by a neutral and detached magistrate weigh heavily *toward* a finding that [the detective] is immune." *See Wadkins,* 214 F.3d at 541. Our *Wadkins* decision is precedent here, and it drew heavily on Judge Wilkinson's opinion in *Torchinsky.* As that decision adroitly explained:

> p.269 When a police officer protects a suspect's rights by obtaining a warrant from a neutral magistrate, the officer should, in turn, receive some protection from suit under 42 U.S.C. § 1983. Otherwise, the threat of liability would force officers to continuously second-guess the considered decisions of magistrates. This in turn would promote delay in the execution of warrants, and alter the proper allocation of law enforcement functions.

See Torchinsky, 942 F.2d at 262. In executing this search warrant, Detective Abbott was acting pursuant to a court order that he had secured on the advice and direction of the Commonwealth's Attorney. The search was thus reasonable and, in my view, Abbott did not violate any constitutional right.

2.

If Detective Abbott somehow contravened a Fourth Amendment right (as the majority rules today), the § 1983 claim alleged by Sims would nevertheless fail under *Saucier*'s clearly established prong, which requires an assessment of "whether the constitutional violation was of a clearly established right." *See Henry v. Purnell,* 652 F.3d 524, 534 (4th Cir. 2011) (en banc). In making that analysis, we are obliged to conduct an objective "reasonable officer test" of Detective Abbott's actions. *See id.* The doctrine of "[q]ualified immunity operates to ensure that before they are subjected to suit, officers are on notice that their conduct is unlawful." *Hope v. Pelzer,* 536 U.S. 730, 731, 122 S.Ct. 2508, 153 L.Ed.2d 666 (2002). To be true to this central tenet of qualified immunity, the right allegedly violated must be defined "at a high level of particularity." *See Campbell v. Galloway,* 483 F.3d 258, 271 (4th Cir. 2007). As such, "existing precedent must have placed the statutory or constitutional question beyond debate." *Ashcroft v. al-Kidd,* 563 U.S. 731, 741, 131 S.Ct. 2074, 179 L.Ed.2d

1149 (2011). In other words, a constitutional right is clearly established only "when, at the time of the challenged conduct, the contours of a right are sufficiently clear that every reasonable official would have understood that what he is doing violates that right." *Id.* (alterations and internal quotation marks omitted).

As the district court observed when it rejected Sims's § 1983 claim, "even if this conduct violated Plaintiff's rights, the 'clearly established' standard is not satisfied here." *See Sims v. Richardson,* No. 1:16-cv-572, at 9, 2016 WL 5219590 (E.D. Va. Sept. 19, 2016), ECF No. 61. The court decisions relied upon by the majority show that there was no clearly established constitutional right — that every reasonable law officer would have recognized — requiring Abbott to disregard the search warrant. *See Anderson v. Creighton,* 483 U.S. 635, 639-641, 107 S.Ct. 3034 (discussing objective standard imposed on officers executing warrant for purposes of qualified immunity).

In my view, no reasonable police officer or lawyer would have considered this search warrant, duly issued by the Virginia magistrate, to violate a clearly established constitutional right. Indeed, Detective Abbott actually sought and obtained two search warrants — from two different magistrates — at the behest of the Commonwealth's Attorney. The initial search warrant was the only one executed, but two neutral and detached Virginia magistrates separately found probable cause to exist. *See supra* note 1.

Importantly, nine of the ten court decisions relied upon by the majority to support their view of the clearly established prong involved unwarranted searches. Those decisions therefore could not place any reasonable lawyer — much less a reasonable p.270 police officer — on notice that the warranted search carried out by Detective Abbott would violate a clearly established constitutional right.[2]

The majority's ruling — that any reasonable law enforcement officer would have recognized that the search warrant violated a clearly established constitutional right — is not supported by any precedent, much less the compelling precedent that would "have placed the statutory or constitutional question beyond debate." *See al-Kidd,* 563 U.S. at 741, 131 S.Ct. 2074. This lack of precedent fails to even create a "gray area" that would require a reasonable police officer to make a close call. *See Braun v. Maynard,* 652 F.3d 557, 560 (4th Cir. 2011) (observing that qualified immunity "ensures that officials are not unfairly strung up for money damages as a result of bad guesses in gray areas"). Addressing the merits of *Saucier*'s clearly established prong, I agree with the district court that Abbott's conduct did "not violate clearly established statutory or constitutional rights of which a reasonable person would have known." *See Sims,* No. 1:16-cv-572, at 8, 2016 WL 5219590, ECF No. 61.

As we have recognized heretofore, "there is simply no basis for a rule that would require law enforcement officers to take issue with or second-guess the considered judgments of prosecutors and magistrates." *See Wadkins,* 214 F.3d at 543. Put simply, the search warrant at issue here was properly and legally issued, it was complied with, and Detective Abbott is entitled to qualified immunity on Sims's § 1983 claim.[3]

I respectfully dissent.

[1] Sims also named the Assistant Commonwealth's Attorney for Prince William County, Virginia, Claiborne T. Richardson, II, as a defendant. The district court granted Richardson's motion to dismiss, holding that Richardson was absolutely immune from suit because his conduct was performed in the course of his

prosecutorial duties. Sims does not challenge this aspect of the district court's judgment.

[2] Sims also alleged additional Section 1983 claims: (1) that his rights under the Fourth Amendment were violated based on the detention order authorizing the removal from his home to the detention center; and (2) that Richardson and Abbott conspired to interfere with Sims' constitutional rights. Sims does not challenge the district court's dismissal of these claims on appeal. Sims advanced a final Section 1983 claim, namely, that Abbott's threat to forcibly inject Sims with erection-producing medication violated the Fourteenth Amendment's substantive due process clause. We conclude that the district court did not err in dismissing this claim, because mere verbal threats directed toward Sims' attorney did not rise to the level of a constitutional violation with respect to Sims.

[3] As the dissent points out, most of the decisions addressing the legality of sexually invasive searches do not involve searches conducted pursuant to warrants. But this distinction only highlights the plainly unreasonable nature of the search in the present case, because sexually invasive searches typically occur in the context of exigent circumstances.

[4] Additionally, apart from the issue whether the warrant was objectively reasonable, the warrant did not purport to authorize Abbott's conduct of requiring Sims to masturbate in the presence of the officers.

[5] We reject Sims' alternative argument that the Administrator was not entitled to qualified immunity because Abbott's conduct surrounding the search "shocks the conscience," in violation of the Fourteenth Amendment's substantive due process clause. The "Due Process Clause is not the proper lens through which to evaluate law enforcement's pretrial missteps." *Safar v. Tingle,* 859 F.3d 241, 245 (4th Cir. 2017) (considering under Fourth Amendment arrestees' Section 1983 claims against police officers based on allegedly unconstitutional arrest warrant).

[1] On this record, search warrants were issued on June 3, 2014, and again on July 1, 2014, by two different magistrates. *See* Supp. J.A. 72, 76. The June warrant was the only one executed. In executing the June warrant, Abbott was unable to obtain some of the photos being sought. Because the prosecutor and the detective agreed that additional photos were necessary, Abbott was directed to seek the July warrant. That warrant was never executed and was voided. (Citations herein to "Supp. J.A. ___" refer to the contents of the Supplemental Joint Appendix filed by the parties in this appeal.)

[2] Nearly all of the court decisions relied upon the by the majority — for their ruling that the constitutional right contravened by Abbott was clearly established — involved warrantless searches. *See Florence v. Bd. of Chosen Freeholders,* 566 U.S. 318, 132 S.Ct. 1510, 182 L.Ed.2d 566 (2012) (unwarranted strip searches of detainees); *Illinois v. Lafayette,* 462 U.S. 640, 103 S.Ct. 2605, 77 L.Ed.2d 65 (1983) (unwarranted search of shoulder bag); *Bell v. Wolfish,* 441 U.S. 520, 99 S.Ct. 1861, 60 L.Ed.2d 447 (1979) (warrantless searches of pretrial detainees); *King v. Rubenstein,* 825 F.3d 206 (4th Cir. 2016) (coerced consent and unwarranted removal of penile implants); *United States v. Edwards,* 666 F.3d 877 (4th Cir. 2011) (warrantless strip search incident to arrest); *Amaechi v. West,* 237 F.3d 356 (4th Cir. 2001) (warrantless search invading arrestee's genitalia in public); *Logan v. Shealy,* 660 F.2d 1007 (4th Cir. 1981) (unwarranted visual

strip searches of detainees); *Schmerber v. California,* 384 U.S. 757, 86 S.Ct. 1826, 16 L.Ed.2d 908 (1966) (unwarranted blood draw from arrestee); *Wood v. Clemons,* 89 F.3d 922 (1st Cir. 1996) (warrantless search of prison visitors).

The Supreme Court's decision in *Winston v. Lee,* the other case relied upon by the majority, involved a court order that had authorized surgical removal of a bullet. *See* 470 U.S. 753, 105 S.Ct. 1611, 84 L.Ed.2d 662 (1985). That decision, however, is readily distinguishable. It had nothing to do with a § 1983 claim or whether a constitutional right was clearly established.

[3] With respect to Sims's effort to pursue a claim under 18 U.S.C. § 2255, I would affirm the district court's ruling that qualified immunity also bars that claim. Qualified immunity protects a law enforcement officer from civil actions when his conduct does not contravene "clearly established statutory or constitutional rights of which a reasonable person would have known." *See Harlow v. Fitzgerald,* 457 U.S. 800, 818, 102 S.Ct. 2727, 73 L.Ed.2d 396 (1982); *see also Brown v. Elliott,* 876 F.3d 637, 641 (4th Cir. 2017) (same). Because the § 2255 claim is predicated on the same factual scenario, it is — like the § 1983 claim — also barred by qualified immunity.

855 F.3d 533 (2017)

Patrick L. BOOKER, Plaintiff-Appellant,
v.
SOUTH CAROLINA DEPARTMENT OF CORRECTIONS; Sylvia Jones; Ann Sheppard; Thierry Nettles, Defendants-Appellees.

No. 15-7679.

United States Court of Appeals, Fourth Circuit.
Argued: December 6, 2016.
Decided: April 28, 2017.

Booker v. South Carolina Dept. of Corrections, 855 F. 3d 533 (4th Cir. 2017)

p.534 Appeal from the United States District Court for the District of South Carolina, at Charleston. Mary G. Lewis, District Judge, (2:12-cv-01957-MGL).

ARGUED: David Meir Zionts, COVINGTON & BURLING LLP, Washington, D.C., for Appellant. Michael D. Freeman, Sr., GRIFFITH, SHARP & LIIPFERT, LLC, Beaufort, South Carolina, for Appellees. ON BRIEF: Robert A. Long, Jr., COVINGTON & BURLING LLP, Washington, D.C., for Appellant. Hillary G. Meyer, GRIFFITH, SHARP & LIIPFERT, LLC, Beaufort, South Carolina, for Appellees.

Before GREGORY, Chief Judge, and TRAXLER and DIAZ, Circuit Judges.

Vacated and remanded by published opinion. Chief Judge Gregory wrote the majority opinion, in which Judge Diaz joined. Judge Traxler wrote a dissenting opinion.

p.535 GREGORY, Chief Judge:

Patrick Booker, an inmate of the South Carolina Department of Corrections p.536 ("SCDC"), brought a claim under 42 U.S.C. § 1983 alleging that he received a disciplinary charge in retaliation for filing a prison grievance. The district court found that Booker's First Amendment right to be free from retaliation for filing a grievance was not clearly established, and it accordingly held that Appellees were entitled to qualified immunity and granted summary judgment in their favor. Because we find that Booker's right was clearly established, we vacate the judgment and remand to the district court for further proceedings.

I.

Booker mailed a legal document to the Dorchester County Sherriff's Office on November 8, 2010, but it was returned to him at Lieber Correctional Institution because he had not affixed the mailing address. Booker inspected the letter and noticed a slit along the length of the envelope. According to Booker, the sergeant who returned the mail to him indicated that the "confidentiality of its contents had been compromised." J.A. 18.

After learning this information, Booker initiated the prison grievance process by submitting a form known as a Request to Staff Member ("RSM"). The SCDC grievance process consists of several steps. Inmates must first try to "informally resolve a complaint" by either discussing their complaint with the appropriate supervisor or, as Booker did, by submitting an RSM form. J.A. 52. If informal resolution proves unsuccessful, inmates may submit a formal grievance to the Inmate Grievance Coordinator within fifteen days of the incident (known as a Step 1 grievance), with appeals to the SCDC's central Grievance Branch (a Step 2 grievance) and eventually to the South Carolina Administrative Law Court. The SCDC has a policy document titled "Inmate Grievance System," which provides that "[n]o inmate will be subjected to reprisal, retaliation, harassment, or disciplinary action for filing a grievance or participating in the resolution of a grievance." J.A. 57-58.

Booker's RSM, which he addressed to the "Mailroom," made its way to Appellee Sylvia Jones, the mailroom supervisor at Lieber. J.A. 83-84. In his RSM, Booker objected to the prison's opening of and tampering with his legal mail and added that he intended to pursue civil and criminal remedies if he found his mail meddled with again.

Jones contends that in addition to filing the RSM, Booker verbally threatened her regarding the mail incident — a fact that Booker disputes. What is undisputed is that shortly after receiving the RSM, Jones submitted an "Incident Report" recommending that Booker be charged with an "809" disciplinary offense of "Threatening to Inflict Harm on/Assaulting an Employee and/or Members of the Public." J.A. 71, 84. An 809 offense is a Level 2 Disciplinary Offense, which carries penalties of disciplinary detention, loss of accrued good behavior time, and loss of visitation, employment, television, and other privileges. J.A. 67-68, 71. A hearing was later held on the disciplinary charge, at which Booker was found not guilty because he had made "legal threats" against Jones, not physical threats. J.A. 77.

In June 2012, Booker, proceeding pro se, filed suit in state court against Jones, SCDC, and two other SCDC employees, Ann Sheppard and Thierry Nettles. Booker alleged, along with other state and federal claims, that Jones filed a false disciplinary charge against him in retaliation for his submission of the RSM form. J.A. 18-19, 32. Booker identified the First Amendment as the source of this claim: "Sylvia Jones, Ann Sheppard and Thierry Nettles are liable unto Plaintiff in their p.537 individual/personal capacity for violating Plaintiff's First Amendment right to free speech and expression, and to be free from wrongful interference and unlawful retaliation for the exercise of such right." J.A. 32. Appellees removed the case to federal court and later moved for summary judgment.

In its order granting the motion, the district court explained that a First Amendment retaliation claim under § 1983 consists of three elements: (1) the plaintiff engaged in constitutionally protected First Amendment activity, (2) the defendant took an action that adversely affected that protected activity, and (3) there was a causal relationship between the plaintiff's protected activity and the defendant's conduct. J.A. 115 (citing *Suarez Corp. Indus. v. McGraw,* 202 F.3d 676, 686 (4th Cir. 2000)). The court assumed, without deciding, that Booker had engaged in constitutionally protected activity when he filed the RSM form. J.A. 113. The district court still granted Appellees' motion, however, finding Booker had failed to produce sufficient evidence that he had suffered "adverse action as a result of the 809 [disciplinary] charge." J.A. 114.

In the first appeal, this Court vacated the district court's summary judgment order as to Booker's claim that Jones violated his First Amendment rights by submitting a disciplinary charge in retaliation for the grievance Booker submitted. *Booker v. S. Carolina Dep't of Corr.,* 583 Fed.Appx. 43, 45 (4th Cir. 2014). Limiting our review to the second element, as the district court did, we concluded that Booker had "produced sufficient evidence that Jones' conduct would likely deter prisoners of ordinary firmness from exercising their First Amendment rights." *Id.* at 44. We added that the evidence, viewed in the light most favorable to Booker, supported a finding that the disciplinary charge filed against Booker was false. *Id.* We did not decide whether Booker had engaged in constitutionally protected conduct when he filed the RSM form. *Id.* at 44-45.

On remand, Appellees again moved for summary judgment. The district court did not reach the merits of Booker's retaliation claim this time, instead determining that Appellees were protected by qualified immunity. The district court specifically found that a "prison inmate's free speech right to submit internal grievances" was not clearly established. J.A. 136. The court acknowledged that the right was "perhaps sufficiently recognized in other federal circuits." J.A. 136. But because "there has been no published case law from the Supreme Court of the United States, the Fourth Circuit Court of Appeals, or the Supreme Court of South Carolina that squarely establishes" the right at issue, it concluded the right was not clearly established. J.A. 136-37. Accordingly, the court held that Appellees deserved qualified immunity on the retaliation claim and therefore granted their motion for summary judgment.

Booker timely noticed this appeal.

II.

We review de novo a grant of summary judgment on the basis of qualified immunity. *Durham v. Horner,* 690 F.3d 183, 188 (4th Cir. 2012). Summary judgment is proper "only if taking the evidence and all reasonable inferences drawn therefrom in the light most favorable to the nonmoving party," there are no genuine disputes of material fact and the moving party is entitled to judgment as a matter of law. *Henry v. Purnell,* 652 F.3d 524, 531 (4th Cir. 2011) (en banc); *see also* Fed. R. Civ. P. 56(a).

Qualified immunity protects officials "who commit constitutional violations p.538 but who, in light of clearly established law, could reasonably believe that their actions were lawful." *Id.* The doctrine weighs two important values — "the need to hold public officials accountable when they exercise power irresponsibly and the need to shield officials from harassment, distraction, and liability when they perform their duties reasonably." *Pearson v. Callahan,* 555 U.S. 223, 231, 129 S.Ct. 808, 172 L.Ed.2d 565 (2009). In conducting the qualified immunity analysis, "our first task is to identify the specific right that the plaintiff asserts was infringed by the challenged conduct." *Winfield v. Bass,* 106 F.3d 525, 530 (4th Cir. 1997) (en banc). We then engage in a two-step inquiry, asking "whether a constitutional violation occurred" and "whether the right violated was clearly established" at the time of the official's conduct. *Melgar ex rel. Melgar v. Greene,* 593 F.3d 348, 353 (4th Cir. 2010). Courts have discretion to take these steps in either order. *Pearson,* 555 U.S. at 236, 129 S.Ct. 808.

The "clearly established" prong lies at the heart of this case — we do not evaluate the merits of Booker's claim. A "right is clearly established only if its contours are sufficiently clear that 'a reasonable official would understand that what he is doing violates that right.'" *Carroll v. Carman,* ___ U.S. ___, 135 S.Ct. 348, 350, 190 L.Ed.2d 311 (2014) (quoting *Anderson v. Creighton,* 483 U.S. 635, 640, 107 S.Ct. 3034, 97 L.Ed.2d 523 (1987)). The unlawfulness of the official's conduct must be "apparent" in "light of pre-existing law." *Anderson,* 483 U.S. at 640, 107 S.Ct. 3034. To be clearly established, "existing precedent must have placed the statutory or constitutional question beyond debate." *Ashcroft v. al-Kidd,* 563 U.S. 731, 741, 131 S.Ct. 2074, 179 L.Ed.2d 1149 (2011).

We must consider not only "specifically adjudicated rights," but also "those manifestly included within more general applications of the core constitutional principles invoked." *Wall v. Wade,* 741 F.3d 492, 502-03 (4th Cir. 2014) (quoting *Pritchett v. Alford,* 973 F.2d 307, 314 (4th Cir. 1992)). In other words, defendants "can still be on notice that their conduct violates established law even in novel factual circumstances," so long as the law provided "fair warning" that their conduct was unconstitutional. *Hope v. Pelzer,* 536 U.S. 730, 741, 122 S.Ct. 2508, 153 L.Ed.2d 666 (2002).

In conducting the clearly established analysis, we first examine "cases of controlling authority in [this] jurisdiction," *Amaechi v. West,* 237 F.3d 356, 363 (4th Cir. 2001) (quoting *Wilson v. Layne,* 526 U.S. 603, 617, 119 S.Ct. 1692, 143 L.Ed.2d 818 (1999)) — that is, "decisions of the Supreme Court, this court of appeals, and the highest court of the state in which the case arose," *Owens ex rel. Owens v. Lott,* 372 F.3d 267, 279 (4th Cir. 2004) (quoting *Edwards v. City of Goldsboro,* 178 F.3d 231, 251 (4th Cir. 1999)).[1] We "ordinarily" need not look any further than decisions from these courts. *Id.* But when "there are no such decisions from courts of p.539 controlling authority, we may look to 'a consensus of cases of persuasive authority' from *other jurisdictions,* if such exists." *Id.* at 280 (emphasis added) (quoting *Wilson,* 526 U.S. at 617, 119 S.Ct. 1692).

The Supreme Court, in an opinion authored by Chief Justice Rehnquist, articulated that courts may rely on "a consensus of cases of persuasive authority" to determine whether a "reasonable officer could not have believed that his actions were lawful." *Wilson,* 526 U.S. at 617, 119 S.Ct. 1692. Since *Wilson,* the Supreme Court has reaffirmed that "qualified immunity is lost when plaintiffs point either to 'cases of controlling authority in their jurisdiction at the time of the incident' or to 'a consensus of cases of persuasive authority.'" *Ashcroft,* 563 U.S. at 742, 131 S.Ct. 2074 (quoting *Wilson,* 526 U.S. at 617, 119 S.Ct. 1692).[2] And in evaluating whether a right is clearly established in a given circuit, the Supreme Court has looked to precedent from other circuits. *See, e.g., Pearson,* 555 U.S. at 244, 129 S.Ct. 808 (considering decisions from "three Federal Courts of Appeals" and noting officers "were entitled to rely on these cases, even though their own Federal Circuit had not yet ruled on" constitutional issue); *Brosseau v. Haugen,* 543 U.S. 194, 200-01, 125 S.Ct. 596, 160 L.Ed.2d 583 (2004) (discussing Sixth, Seventh, and Eighth Circuit cases in finding right not clearly established in Ninth Circuit).

III.

A.

Before we apply these rules to the instant case, we must first define the right at the "appropriate level of specificity," *Wilson,* 526 U.S. at 615, 119 S.Ct. 1692, keeping in mind that the Supreme Court has cautioned against defining the right at too "high [a] level of generality," *Ashcroft,* 563 U.S. at 742, 131 S.Ct. 2074. *See also id.* (noting, for example, the "general proposition" that whether "an unreasonable search or seizure violates the Fourth Amendment is of little help in determining whether the violative nature of particular conduct is clearly established").

At the outset, we preempt a possible point of confusion — Booker did *not* allege in his complaint that he has an absolute right to file prison grievances pursuant to the First Amendment. Rather, Booker alleged that he has a First Amendment right to be free from retaliation when he does file a grievance pursuant to an existing grievance procedure.[3] *See* J.A. 32.

p.540 More particularly, Booker asserts that this right is rooted in the First Amendment's Petition Clause, which guarantees individuals the right "to petition the Government for a redress of grievances." U.S. Const. amend. I. Booker contends that an inmate's right to petition is violated when he is retaliated against for filing a grievance. Appellees suggest in passing that we should not examine whether the right was established under the Petition Clause, apparently referencing the district court's refusal to consider the right to petition. With minimal explanation, the district court limited its analysis to the Free Speech Clause, stating that an "inmate's free speech right to submit internal grievances" was the right "pressed by the Plaintiff throughout this litigation." J.A. 136.

The district court should not have limited itself so. To the extent the court considered only the free speech right because Booker mentioned that clause in his pro se complaint, we note that Booker also generally alleged a violation of the First Amendment, J.A. 31, and that courts are obligated to "liberally construe[]" pro se complaints, "however inartfully pleaded," *Erickson v. Pardus,* 551 U.S. 89, 94, 127 S.Ct. 2197, 167 L.Ed.2d 1081 (2007) (quoting *Estelle v. Gamble,* 429 U.S. 97, 106, 97 S.Ct. 285, 50 L.Ed.2d 251 (1976)).[4] Booker also directly argued to the district court that "[i]nstead of analyzing the first element to a First Amendment retaliation claim in the context of [] public employee speech, the [magistrate judge] should have realized that the facts in this case related more to a deprivation of Plaintiff's right to petition the government." Pl.'s Objections to Report and Recommendation, Dist. Ct. ECF No. 160, at 5 (May 6, 2015). Booker's detailed factual allegations and his reference to the First Amendment provide a more-than-sufficient basis for us to analyze whether the right was clearly established under the Petition Clause.

B.

The clearly established inquiry asks whether the state of the law gave a reasonable prison official "fair warning" that retaliating against an inmate who files a prison grievance was unconstitutional.

It is "well established" in this Circuit that a "public official may not misuse his power to retaliate against an individual for the exercise of a valid constitutional right." *Trulock,* 275 F.3d at 405. Thus, if an inmate exercises his First Amendment right when he files a prison grievance, retaliation against him for doing so is unconstitutional. The pertinent question in this appeal, then, is whether it was clearly established that an inmate exercises a First Amendment right to petition for redress of grievances when he files a prison grievance. Framed differently, we must determine whether it was clearly established that an inmate's right to petition is violated when he is retaliated against for filing a grievance.

As noted, the first step is to consider cases of controlling authority in this jurisdiction. *See Owens,* 372 F.3d at 279-80. We thus start with Supreme Court, Fourth p.541 Circuit, and Supreme Court of South Carolina decisions that have addressed the asserted right. The parties do not contest the district court's finding that no decision from the United States Supreme Court or Supreme Court of South Carolina explicitly discusses the right. The parties do dispute, however, whether our Court has addressed it. Booker contends that the Fourth Circuit has not discussed in a published opinion whether inmates have a First Amendment right to be free from retaliation for filing grievances. For their part, Appellees appear to agree that this Court has never explicitly considered this right. Nevertheless, they contend that our decision in *Adams v. Rice,* 40 F.3d 72 (4th Cir. 1994), resolves the clearly established analysis in their favor.[5] They understand *Adams* to suggest that inmates do *not* exercise any constitutional right (under the First Amendment or otherwise) when they file a prison grievance. *See* Appellees' Br. 13-14; *see also id.* at 17 (arguing that inmates exercise First Amendment right to petition by accessing the courts, not by filing grievances).

Adams does not stand for — or even imply — that proposition, however. There, an inmate claimed that when he requested protective custody, the prison officials retaliated against him by, among other things, denying him access to the prison's grievance process. *Adams,* 40 F.3d at 75. On appeal, the plaintiff "recast[] his protective custody request as an exercise of a 'right to inform' prison officials of dangerous conditions" incident to the Eighth Amendment. *Id.* In other words, Adams asserted he had a constitutional right "to a particular grievance procedure." *Id.* This Court held that the plaintiff had not exercised any such right by requesting protective custody. *Id.* We went on to state that "the Constitution creates no entitlement to grievance procedures or access to any such procedure." *Id.* (citing *Flick v. Alba,* 932 F.2d 728, 729 (8th Cir. 1991) (per curiam); *Mann v. Adams,* 855 F.2d 639, 640 (9th Cir. 1988) (per curiam)).

Adams establishes a clear rule: inmates have no constitutional entitlement or due process interest in access to a grievance procedure. An inmate thus cannot bring a § 1983 claim alleging denial of a specific grievance process, for example. But *Adams* is entirely silent on the issue in this case — whether an inmate's First Amendment right is violated when he is *retaliated against* for submitting a grievance pursuant to an existing grievance procedure. That a prison is not required under the Constitution to provide access to a grievance process does not mean that prison officials who retaliate against inmates for filing grievances do not violate the Constitution.

As the Eighth Circuit explained nearly three decades ago, there is a very critical distinction between the right of access or entitlement to a grievance process and the right to be free from retaliation for filing a grievance:

> Prison officials cannot properly bring a disciplinary action against a prisoner for filing a grievance that is determined by those officials to be without merit anymore than they can properly bring a disciplinary action against a prisoner for filing a lawsuit that is judicially determined to be without merit. *That the Constitution does not obligate the state* p.542 *to establish a grievance procedure* is, we believe, of no consequence here....

Sprouse v. Babcock, 870 F.2d 450, 452 (8th Cir. 1989) (emphasis added). Indeed, the Eighth Circuit recognizes that (1) an inmate possesses a First Amendment right to be free from retaliation for filing a grievance, *id.,* while simultaneously recognizing that (2) an inmate does not have a due process "liberty interest in access to [a grievance] procedure," *Flick,* 932 F.2d at 729.

The Eighth Circuit is not alone in finding that although inmates do not have a constitutional entitlement to and/or due process interest in accessing a grievance procedure, they have a First Amendment right to be free from retaliation when they do file. *Compare Geiger v. Jowers,* 404 F.3d 371, 374 (5th Cir. 2005) (finding no liberty interest in grievance procedure), *with Bibbs v. Early,* 541 F.3d 267, 272 (5th Cir. 2008) (recognizing First Amendment retaliation right); *compare Mann v. Adams,* 855 F.2d 639, 640 (9th Cir. 1988) (finding inmates have "no legitimate claim of entitlement to a grievance procedure"), *with Hines v. Gomez,* 108 F.3d 265, 269 (9th Cir. 1997) (recognizing First Amendment retaliation right); *compare Bingham, v. Thomas,* 654 F.3d 1171, 1177 (11th Cir. 2011) (holding that inmates have "no constitutionally-protected liberty interest in access to [grievance] procedure"), *with Boxer X v. Harris,* 437 F.3d 1107, 1112 (11th Cir. 2006) (recognizing First Amendment retaliation right). Like our sister circuits, we see no inconsistency between these distinct legal principles.

In short, *Adams* concerns whether inmates have a constitutional entitlement to or liberty interest in accessing grievance procedures. It says nothing about whether a prison official violates an inmate's First Amendment rights by retaliating against the inmate for submitting a grievance. Therefore, contrary to Appellees' suggestion, *Adams* does not speak to the right at issue. As such, neither party has cited cases from courts of controlling authority — the Supreme Court, this Court, or the Supreme Court of South Carolina — that explicitly address an inmate's First Amendment right to be free from retaliation for filing a prison grievance.

To be sure, as discussed at oral argument, there are unpublished opinions in this Circuit that reference *Adams* and/or directly address the right in question. One such decision misconstrued *Adams* to preclude an inmate from bringing a First Amendment claim alleging retaliation in response to his verbal complaints to prison officials. *See Daye v. Rubenstein,* 417 Fed. Appx. 317, 319 (4th Cir. 2011). Others properly applied *Adams. See, e.g., Cameron v. Bonney,* 523 Fed.Appx. 969, 970 (4th Cir. 2013) (applying *Adams* to reject inmate's claim that his constitutional rights were violated when he was denied access to a grievance form). And still more unpublished decisions found that inmates can bring a First Amendment claim alleging retaliation for filing a grievance.[6] *See, e.g., Wright v. Vitale,* 937 F.2d 604, 1991 WL 127597, at *1 (4th Cir. 1991) (unpublished table opinion); *Gullet v. Wilt,* 869 F.2d 593, 1989 WL 14614, at *2 (4th Cir. 1989) (unpublished table opinion). But because these p.543

unpublished opinions "are not even regarded as binding precedent in our circuit," as this Court sitting en banc has explained, they "cannot be considered in deciding whether particular conduct violated clearly established law for purposes of adjudging entitlement to qualified immunity." *Hogan v. Carter,* 85 F.3d 1113, 1118 (4th Cir. 1996) (en banc).

We therefore agree with the district court's conclusion that no published decision from the Supreme Court, this Court, or the Supreme Court of South Carolina squarely addresses whether filing a grievance is protected First Amendment conduct.

The district court, after determining there were no binding cases that squarely established the specific First Amendment right, concluded that the right was not clearly established. J.A. 137. But the clearly established inquiry was not complete: as this Court has stated, and as Booker recognizes, the "absence of controlling authority holding identical conduct unlawful does not guarantee qualified immunity." *Owens,* 372 F.3d at 279. The district court failed to consider whether, despite the lack of directly on-point, binding authority, the right was clearly established based on general constitutional principles or a consensus of persuasive authority. We now proceed to that task.

C.

In the absence of controlling authority that specifically adjudicates the right in question, a right may still be clearly established in one of two ways. A right may be clearly established if "a general constitutional rule already identified in the decisional law [] appl[ies] with obvious clarity to the specific conduct in question." *Hope,* 536 U.S. at 741, 122 S.Ct. 2508 (quoting *United States v. Lanier,* 520 U.S. 259, 271, 117 S.Ct. 1219, 137 L.Ed.2d 432 (1997)); *see also Owens,* 372 F.3d at 279 (stating that a right may be clearly established if it is "manifestly apparent from broader applications of the constitutional premise in question"). A right may also be clearly established based on a "'consensus of cases of persuasive authority' from other jurisdictions." *Owens,* 372 F.3d at 280 (quoting *Wilson,* 526 U.S. at 617, 119 S.Ct. 1692). Here, Booker argues that his First Amendment right was clearly established in both ways.

Arguably, the prohibition on retaliating against inmates for filing grievances was obviously unconstitutional given longstanding principles articulated in controlling authority. It is beyond dispute that prison officials cannot retaliate against inmates for exercising a constitutional right. *Trulock,* 275 F.3d at 405. And Booker presents a logical and compelling argument that, in light of binding Supreme Court precedent, he exercised his constitutional right to petition the government for redress of grievances when he filed an administrative grievance seeking redress for what he believed was the improper handling of his legal mail.[7]

p.544 In addition to Supreme Court precedent, this Court has long held that prison officials may not retaliate against prisoners for exercising their right to access the courts, *Hudspeth v. Figgins,* 584 F.2d 1345, 1348 (4th Cir. 1978), which is a component of the right to petition for redress of grievances, *Hudson v. Palmer,* 468 U.S. 517, 523, 104 S.Ct. 3194, 82 L.Ed.2d 393 (1984). Given the close relationship between an inmate filing a grievance and filing a lawsuit — indeed, the former is generally a prerequisite for the latter — our jurisprudence provided a strong signal that officials may not retaliate against inmates for filing grievances.

Regardless of whether Booker's right was obvious or "manifestly apparent" from broader principles in the decisional law, we find that it was clearly established based on a robust "consensus of persuasive authority." The Second, Sixth, Seventh, Eighth, Ninth, Eleventh, and D.C. Circuits have all recognized in published decisions that inmates possess a right, grounded in the First Amendment's Petition Clause, to be free from retaliation in response to filing a prison grievance. The Second Circuit, for instance, recognized that an inmate can bring a First Amendment right to petition claim when prison officials "intentionally file[] false disciplinary charges against him in retaliation for his cooperation with a state administrative investigation of alleged incidents of inmate abuse at the prison." *Franco v. Kelly,* 854 F.2d 584, 589 (2d Cir. 1988). The court later recognized the right in the context of retaliation against inmates for filing grievances. *Gayle v. Gonyea,* 313 F.3d 677, 682 (2d Cir. 2002) ("An allegation that a prison official filed false disciplinary charges in retaliation for the exercise of a constitutionally protected right, such as the filing of a grievance, states a claim under § 1983.") (citing *Franco,* 854 F.2d at 589-90). The Sixth, Seventh, Eighth, Ninth, Eleventh, and D.C. Circuits have likewise recognized that inmates possess a First Amendment petition right to be free from retaliation for filing grievances. *Herron v. Harrison,* 203 F.3d 410, 414 (6th Cir. 2000) (recognizing claim where inmate alleged that prison officials "impermissibly retaliated against him for exercising his First Amendment right to file grievances and petition the courts for redress"); *Powers v. Snyder,* 484 F.3d 929, 933 (7th Cir. 2007) (recognizing claim where inmate alleged he was retaliated against for "filing grievances against the prison" and noting "[s]uch retaliation violates a prisoner's right, founded on the First Amendment, to petition government for the redress of grievances"); *Dixon v. Brown,* 38 F.3d 379, 379 (8th Cir. 1994) (holding that "filing of a disciplinary charge becomes actionable if done in retaliation for the inmate's filing of a grievance" and stating that such conduct "strikes at the heart of an inmate's constitutional right to seek redress of grievances"); *Brodheim v. Cry,* 584 F.3d 1262, 1266, 1269-72 (9th Cir. 2009) (recognizing First Amendment petition right where inmate alleged retaliation for filing grievances); *Boxer X v. Harris,* 437 F.3d 1107, 1112 (11th Cir. 2006) ("First Amendment rights to free speech and to petition the government for a redress of grievances are violated when a prisoner is punished for filing a grievance...."); *Toolasprashad v. Bureau of Prisons,* 286 F.3d 576, 584-85 (D.C. Cir. 2002) (recognizing that prisoners "undoubtedly" exercise First Amendment petition right when filing grievances and stating that prison "officials may not p.545 retaliate against prisoners for filing grievances").

Even more, the Third, Fifth, and Tenth Circuits have recognized an inmate's right to be free from retaliation for filing a grievance under the First Amendment (albeit without referencing a particular clause). *Mitchell v. Horn,* 318 F.3d 523, 530 (3d Cir. 2003) ("[Inmate's] allegation that he was falsely charged with misconduct in retaliation for filing complaints against Officer Wilson implicates conduct protected by the First Amendment."); *Bibbs v. Early,* 541 F.3d 267, 271 (5th Cir. 2008) (recognizing First Amendment retaliation claim where official filed a disciplinary report "following an inmate's filing of a grievance"); *Williams v. Meese,* 926 F.2d 994, 998 (10th Cir. 1991) ("[T]he district court erred in dismissing plaintiff's claim that

that he was denied particular job assignments or was transferred from one job to another in retaliation for filing administrative grievances or the present civil rights action. Again, although plaintiff has no right to a job or to any particular assignment, prison officials cannot punish plaintiff for exercising his first amendment rights....").

Given the decisions from nearly every court of appeals, we are compelled to conclude that Booker's right to file a prison grievance free from retaliation was clearly established under the First Amendment. Consistent with fundamental constitutional principles and common sense, these courts have had little difficulty concluding that prison officials violate the First Amendment by retaliating against inmates for filing grievances. Rarely will there be such an overwhelming consensus of authority recognizing that specific conduct is violative of a constitutional right. The unanimity among our sister circuits demonstrates that the constitutional question is "beyond debate," and therefore we find that the right at issue was clearly established.

Appellees do not dispute this consensus among the federal appellate courts. They instead argue that there is a "body of case law within the Fourth Circuit that specifically holds prisoners have no constitutional right to file a grievance." Appellees' Br. 13. This "body of case law" consists of three published district court opinions from the Western District of Virginia, two of which were issued by the same district judge and do not even mention the First Amendment. *See id.* at 14. All three decisions erroneously rely on *Adams* in rejecting an inmate's claim that he was retaliated against for filing grievances. *See, e.g., Brown v. Angelone,* 938 F.Supp. 340, 346-47 (W.D. Va. 1996).

These district court decisions do not alter our conclusion that the right was clearly established. First, it is unclear whether we should include district court opinions in the balancing of "persuasive authority." As the Supreme Court has remarked, "[m]any Courts of Appeals [] decline to consider district court precedent when determining if constitutional rights are clearly established for purposes of qualified immunity." *Camreta,* 563 U.S. at 709 n.7, 131 S.Ct. 2020. The Court went on, "[o]therwise said, district court decisions — unlike those from the courts of appeals — do not necessarily settle constitutional standards or prevent repeated claims of qualified immunity." *Id.* Given that published district court opinions, like unpublished opinions from our Court, have no precedential value, it follows that we should not consider them. But even if we classify published district court opinions as relevant "persuasive authority," they are "no match for the Circuit precedents." *Hope,* 536 U.S. at 747, 122 S.Ct. 2508. When weighed against the circuit precedents, there is still an overwhelming "consensus of persuasive authority" p.546 that inmates possess a First Amendment right to be free from retaliation for filing a grievance.

Our "conclusion that 'a reasonable person would have known,' *Harlow* [*v. Fitzgerald,* 457 U.S. 800, 818, 102 S.Ct. 2727, 73 L.Ed.2d 396 (1982)], of the violation is buttressed by" the South Carolina Department of Correction's internal policies. *Hope,* 536 U.S. at 744, 122 S.Ct. 2508. Although officials "do not lose their qualified immunity merely because their conduct violates some statutory or administrative provision," *Davis v. Scherer,* 468 U.S. 183, 194, 104 S.Ct. 3012, 82 L.Ed.2d 139 (1984), the Supreme Court has analyzed prison regulations in combination with case law to determine whether an individual had fair warning, *see Hope,* 536 U.S. at 741-45, 122 S.Ct. 2508 (relying on binding precedent, Alabama Department of Corrections regulation, and Department of Justice report in finding conduct violated clearly established right); *see also Furnace v. Sullivan,* 705 F.3d 1021, 1027 (9th Cir. 2013) (stating that "regulations governing the conduct of correctional officers are also relevant in determining whether an inmate's right was clearly established") (quoting *Treats v. Morgan,* 308 F.3d 868, 875 (8th Cir. 2002) (citing *Hope,* 536 U.S. at 743-744, 122 S.Ct. 2508)); *Okin v. Vill. of Cornwall-On-Hudson Police Dep't,* 577 F.3d 415, 433-34 (2d Cir. 2009).

Here, the SCDC's detailed policy document concerning the "Inmate Grievance System"[8] expressly provides that "[n]o inmate will be subjected to reprisal, retaliation, harassment, or disciplinary action for filing a grievance or participating in the resolution of a grievance." J.A. 57-58. The record further indicates that this prohibition was communicated to prison officials: "As part of the Department orientation program, all newly hired employees will receive written and/or oral explanations of the Department's grievance policy/procedure by a representative of the Inmate Grievance Branch." J.A. 57. Again, the fundamental inquiry for purposes of qualified immunity is whether a reasonable official in Jones's position had "fair warning" that the alleged conduct was unconstitutional. *Hope,* 536 U.S. at 741, 122 S.Ct. 2508. The unequivocal language of SCDC's own policies provides additional support for our finding that Jones had such warning here.

In sum, given the authority discussed above, we conclude that a reasonable prison official had fair warning that retaliating against an inmate who filed a prison grievance was unlawful. Because an inmate's First Amendment right to be free from retaliation for filing a grievance was clearly established, we find that Appellees are not entitled to qualified immunity on that basis and therefore the district court erred in granting their motion for summary judgment.

IV.

For the foregoing reasons, the judgment of the district court is vacated, and we remand for further proceedings consistent with this opinion.

VACATED AND REMANDED.

p.547 TRAXLER, Circuit Judge, dissenting:

Relying on decisions from other circuits, the majority concludes that a prisoner's right to be free from retaliation for filing a grievance was clearly established in 2010, when the actions giving rise to this lawsuit took place. Even assuming that that right may have been clearly established in *other* circuits, the case law from *this* circuit in 2010 could reasonably be understood as foreclosing that claim. *See Adams v. Rice,* 40 F.3d 72 (4th Cir. 1994). Because the controlling law in this circuit did not put the prison officials on notice that their conduct violated Booker's constitutional rights, I believe the prison officials are entitled to qualified immunity. Accordingly, I respectfully dissent.

I.

Qualified immunity works to "avoid excessive disruption of government," *Harlow v. Fitzgerald,* 457 U.S. 800, 818, 102 S.Ct. 2727, 73 L.Ed.2d 396 (1982), by "protect[ing] government officials performing discretionary functions from civil damage suits insofar as the officials' conduct does not violate clearly established rights of which a reasonable person would have known," *Porterfield v. Lott,* 156 F.3d 563, 567 (4th Cir. 1998) (internal quotation marks and alteration omitted). "To be clearly established, a right must be sufficiently clear that every reasonable official would have understood that what he is doing violates that right. In other words, existing precedent must have placed the statutory or constitutional question beyond debate." *Reichle v. Howards,* 566 U.S. 658, 132 S.Ct. 2088, 2093, 182 L.Ed.2d 985 (2012) (internal quotation marks, citations and alteration omitted).

As a general rule, we look only to "the decisions of the Supreme Court, this court of appeals, and the highest court of the state in which the case arose" when determining whether the defendant is entitled to qualified immunity. *Yates v. Terry,* 817 F.3d 877, 887 (4th Cir. 2016) (internal quotation marks omitted). If the case law of this court has addressed the relevant constitutional question, contrary rulings from other circuits are not relevant to the qualified-immunity inquiry. *See Edwards v. City of Goldsboro,* 178 F.3d 231, 251 (4th Cir. 1999) ("If a right is recognized in some other circuit, but not in this one, an official will ordinarily retain the immunity defense." (internal quotation marks and alteration omitted)). In the absence of controlling authority from either the Supreme Court, this court, or the highest state court, however, the existence of "a consensus of cases of persuasive authority" from other jurisdictions can be enough to foreclose a claim of qualified immunity. *Ashcroft v. al-Kidd,* 563 U.S. 731, 746, 131 S.Ct. 2074, 179 L.Ed.2d 1149 (2011) (internal quotation marks omitted); *Owens ex rel. Owens v. Lott,* 372 F.3d 267, 279-80 (4th Cir. 2004).

II.

In the majority's view, there was no controlling authority from this circuit in 2010 addressing whether retaliation against an inmate for filing a grievance violates the inmate's rights under the First Amendment. The majority therefore looks to case law from other circuits, finds a consensus, and holds that an inmate's right to be free from retaliation for participating in the grievance system was clearly established.

I do not disagree that the weight of authority outside this circuit holds that the First Amendment is violated when prison officials retaliate against an inmate for filing a grievance under an established grievance system. Where I disagree with the majority is in its conclusion that case law from this circuit was silent on the relevant p.548 First Amendment question. In my view, this court's decision in *Adams v. Rice* could reasonably be understood as holding that an inmate's use of a prison grievance system does not implicate the First Amendment and that grievance-based retaliation against the inmate likewise does not implicate the First Amendment. Because *Adams* can reasonably be understood to permit the actions of the prison officials at issue in this case, the majority erred by looking outside the circuit to conclude otherwise. *See Edwards,* 178 F.3d at 251.

A.

In *Adams,* a North Carolina inmate requested a transfer to protective custody after he was threatened by other inmates. State prison officials approved that request and directed that the inmate be transferred to the protective custody facility at a different prison. The inmate was never transferred, however, but was instead held in segregation for nine months. He was released from segregation and transferred to another prison after he withdrew his request for protective custody. *See Adams,* 40 F.3d at 73.

Proceeding *in forma pauperis* under the version of 28 U.S.C. § 1915 then in effect, the inmate thereafter filed a lawsuit alleging that prison officials, in retaliation for his protective-custody request, had refused to transfer him to the protective-custody facility, "denied him minimum custody status, failed to schedule a parole eligibility date and hearing, and barred his access to the grievance process." *Adams,* 40 F.3d at 74. The district court concluded that the inmate's claim lacked an arguable basis in law or in fact and therefore dismissed the inmate's claims as frivolous. *See Neitzke v. Williams,* 490 U.S. 319, 325, 109 S.Ct. 1827, 104 L.Ed.2d 338 (1989) ("[A] complaint... is frivolous where it lacks an arguable basis either in law or in fact.").

The inmate appealed, contending that his complaint at least arguably stated claims of retaliation for the exercise of constitutionally protected rights. Because the Eighth Amendment protects inmates "from physical harm at the hands of fellow inmates resulting from the deliberate or callous indifference of prison officials to specific known risks of such harm," *Pressly v. Hutto,* 816 F.2d 977, 979 (4th Cir. 1987), the inmate contended that his reporting of the threats against him and request for protective custody were at least arguably protected by the Eighth Amendment:

> Given that prisoners' right to be protected hinges to a large extent on whether the risks are *known* by the prison officials to exist, it is arguable, that prisoners must perforce have a right to be free from retaliation in *reporting* such risks to those same officials. Freedom to report such incidents would appear to be an essential ingredient to the exercise of the recognized right to be free from harms prison officials know about and are in a position to prevent.

Adams v. Rice, Brief of Appellant, 1994 WL 16014459, at *17.

This court rejected the inmate's arguments. We first agreed with the district court that the inmate's claims were factually frivolous, as there were no allegations in the complaint asserting that the single-cell housing the inmate received was in any way different from the protective custody he requested. *See Adams,* 40 F.3d at 75.

We likewise agreed with the district court's determination that the complaint was legally frivolous. As we explained, "claims of retaliatory actions are legally frivolous unless the complaint implicates some right that exists under the Constitution. p.549 That is, plaintiffs must allege either that the retaliatory act was taken in response to the exercise of a constitutionally protected right or that the act itself violated such a right." *Id.* Applying that standard, we rejected the inmate's claim that he exercised an Eighth Amendment right when he requested protective custody:

> Appellant's assertion of a "right to inform" states only a claim of entitlement to a particular grievance procedure because he seeks, in essence, a means of bringing complaints regarding his incarceration to the attention of prison

officials. As other circuits have recognized, there is no constitutional right to participate in grievance proceedings.

Id. Addressing the specific instances of retaliation by prison officials alleged by the inmate, we explained that the inmate's claims were doomed by the absence of an underlying constitutional right. *See id.* As is most relevant to this case, we explained that the inmate's claim that prison officials prevented him from accessing the prison grievance system was legally frivolous because "the Constitution creates no entitlement to grievance procedures or access to any such procedure voluntarily established by a state." *Id.*

B.

The majority reads *Adams* as holding that "inmates have no constitutional entitlement or due process interest in access to a grievance procedure. An inmate thus cannot bring a § 1983 claim alleging denial of a specific grievance process, for example." *Majority Op.* at 541. According to the majority,

Adams is entirely silent on the issue in this case — whether an inmate's First Amendment right is violated when he is *retaliated against* for submitting a grievance pursuant to an existing grievance procedure. That a prison is not required under the Constitution to provide access to a grievance process does not mean that prison officials who retaliate against inmates for filing grievances do not violate the Constitution.

Id. Because *Adams* does not "explicitly address" the constitutional right being pressed in this case, *id.* at 542, the majority dismisses *Adams* entirely and turns to cases outside this circuit to find the right clearly established.

I believe the majority interprets *Adams* far too narrowly. *Adams* makes two separate holdings addressing prison grievance systems. First, *Adams* holds that an inmate cannot demand a grievance system structured to address whatever complaints he might want to raise. *See Adams,* 40 F.3d at 75 (rejecting inmate's claim of entitlement to "a means of bringing complaints regarding his incarceration to the attention of prison officials"); *id.* ("[T]he Constitution creates no entitlement to grievance procedures...."). Second, *Adams* holds that inmates have no constitutional right to *participate* in a prison's existing grievance system. *See id.* ("[T]here is no constitutional right to participate in grievance proceedings."); *id.* ("[T]he Constitution creates no entitlement to ... access to any [grievance] procedure voluntarily established by a state."). An inmate *participates* in a grievance system, of course, by *filing a grievance*.

When discussing *Adams,* the majority acknowledges the second holding only indirectly, by referring to an unpublished opinion that "properly applied *Adams*" to reject an inmate's constitutional claim based on refusal to supply grievance forms. *Majority Op.* at 542. The majority, however, never grapples with the implications of *Adams'* second holding except to suggest, indirectly, that while there may be no First Amendment right to *file* a grievance, if a grievance is in p.550 fact filed, retaliation based on the grievance violates the First Amendment. *See id.* (discussing unpublished opinion that "misconstrued *Adams* to preclude an inmate from bringing a First Amendment claim alleging retaliation in response to his verbal complaints to prison officials."). I do not believe that *Adams* can be distinguished in this manner.

As we explained in *Adams,* retaliation claims are actionable under § 1983 only if "the complaint implicates some right that exists under the Constitution. That is, plaintiffs must allege either that the retaliatory act was taken in response to *the exercise of a constitutionally protected right* or that the act itself violated such a right." *Adams,* 40 F.3d at 75 (emphasis added). If an inmate has no constitutional right to file a grievance, as *Adams* held, then the inmate exercises no constitutional right by filing a grievance. And if filing a grievance implicates no constitutional right, then retaliation against the inmate because of the grievance does not violate the Constitution. *See id.* ("A claim of retaliation that fails to implicate any constitutional right lacks even an arguable basis in law." (internal quotation marks omitted)). I simply see no basis for concluding, as the majority apparently does, that the act of filing a grievance — an act that is *not* constitutionally protected — somehow imbues the filing with constitutional protections.

Accordingly, it seems to me that this court's decision in *Adams* affirmatively closes the door to the retaliation claim being asserted here. While there may be no single sentence in *Adams* that explicitly states that retaliation based on an inmate's filing of a grievance will not support a constitutional claim under § 1983, the qualified-immunity inquiry does not require that level of specificity. *See, e.g., Odom v. S.C. Dep't of Corr.,* 349 F.3d 765, 773 (4th Cir. 2003) (explaining that the qualified-immunity analysis "must take into consideration not only already specifically adjudicated rights, but those manifestly included within more general applications of the core constitutional principle invoked" (internal quotation marks omitted)). For the reasons outlined above, the conclusion that the retaliation alleged in this case is not sufficient to support a claim of retaliation under § 1983 follows inexorably from *Adams'* clear and explicit holding that inmates have "no constitutional right to participate in grievance proceedings." *Adams,* 40 F.3d at 75.

Even if it were somehow possible to draw the majority's fine, lawyerly line between this case and *Adams,* it still would not be appropriate to deny qualified immunity. The qualified-immunity inquiry focuses on *notice* — whether the existing precedent gives the officials "fair notice that they are acting unconstitutionally." *Mullenix v. Luna,* ___ U.S. ___, 136 S.Ct. 305, 314, 193 L.Ed.2d 255 (2015) (per curiam) (internal quotation marks omitted). Thus, the question is not whether this court can come up with a plausible way of distinguishing *Adams* from the facts of the case at bar; the question is whether, in light of *Adams,* a prison official could "reasonably believe[] that his or her conduct complies with the law." *Pearson v. Callahan,* 555 U.S. 223, 244, 129 S.Ct. 808, 172 L.Ed.2d 565 (2009).

For the reasons outlined above, I believe that a reasonable prison official could read *Adams* as permitting the actions that were taken in this case. Indeed, the reasonableness of such a reading is confirmed by the fact that this court has applied *Adams* in that very way. *See Daye v. Rubenstein,* 417 Fed.Appx. 317, 319 (4th Cir. 2011) (per curiam) (applying *Adams* to reject inmate's claim that prison officials violated his First Amendment rights by retaliating p.551 against him for filing a verbal grievance).[1] While the majority now says that *Daye* "misconstrued" *Adams, Majority Op.* at 542, the question is not whether that reading of *Adams* ultimately proves to be wrong, but whether that reading of *Adams* is *reasonable:*

> In interpreting qualified immunity..., we must appreciate the fact that the direction of the law may be difficult to ascertain. Thus, although public officials

may be charged with knowledge of constitutional developments, they are not required to predict the future course of constitutional law.... The requirement, after all, is that the law be clearly established, not simply possibly established or even probably established. *Since qualified immunity is appropriate if reasonable officers could disagree on the relevant issue, it surely must be appropriate when reasonable jurists can do so.*

Swanson v. Powers, 937 F.2d 965, 968 (4th Cir. 1991) (emphasis added; citation and internal alteration omitted); *see Saucier v. Katz,* 533 U.S. 194, 205, 121 S.Ct. 2151, 150 L.Ed.2d 272 (2001) ("The concern of the immunity inquiry is to acknowledge that *reasonable mistakes* can be made as to the legal constraints on particular police conduct.... If the officer's mistake as to what the law requires is reasonable, ... the officer is entitled to the immunity defense." (emphasis added)), *overruled on other grounds by Pearson v. Callahan,* 555 U.S. 223, 129 S.Ct. 808, 172 L.Ed.2d 565 (2009).

In my view, *Adams* directly, though not explicitly, forecloses Booker's retaliation claim. But even if the distinction between this case and *Adams* that the majority apparently embraces were viable, a reasonable prison official could still conclude that the actions alleged in this case were permissible under this court's decision in *Adams. See Reichle,* 132 S.Ct. at 2093 (qualified immunity should be granted unless the unlawfulness of the challenged action would be apparent to "every reasonable official." (internal quotation marks omitted)). I therefore believe that the defendants are entitled to qualified immunity.

C.

I recognize, of course, that other circuits considering the issue have concluded that prison officials violate the First Amendment if they retaliate against an inmate for filing a grievance. Regardless of how compelling the majority may find the analysis of those cases, they simply are not relevant to our qualified-immunity inquiry.

As this court has frequently explained, "[a] decision of a panel of this court becomes the law of the circuit and is binding on other panels unless it is overruled by a subsequent en banc opinion of this court or a superseding contrary decision of the Supreme Court." *United States v. Collins,* 415 F.3d 304, 311 (4th Cir. 2005) (internal quotation marks omitted). Because *Adams* is binding, controlling authority that rejects Booker's claim, the majority errs by dismissing *Adams* and relying on cases p.552 outside this circuit to deny qualified immunity. *See Owens,* 372 F.3d at 280 (explaining that when performing the qualified-immunity analysis, courts may look to case law from other circuits only if there is no "controlling authority"); *Edwards,* 178 F.3d at 251 ("If a right is recognized in some other circuit, but not in this one, an official will ordinarily retain the immunity defense." (internal quotation marks and alteration omitted)).

If the majority believes *Adams* was wrongly decided,[2] the proper way to correct the error is through en banc proceedings. The majority's chosen path of artificially narrowing the reach of *Adams'* holdings and then dismissing the case as irrelevant because it is not "directly on-point," *Majority Op.* at 543, is disingenuous and inconsistent with our approach to resolving questions of qualified immunity and with our obligation to follow our own precedent.

III.

In *Adams,* this court held that "there is no constitutional right to *participate* in grievance proceedings." 40 F.3d at 75 (emphasis added). Because inmates participate in grievance proceedings by *filing a grievance,* our decision in *Adams* must be understood as holding that inmates have no constitutional right to file a grievance. The filing of a grievance therefore implicates no constitutional right of the inmate and cannot support a retaliation claim against prison officials. *See id.* ("[C]laims of retaliatory actions are legally frivolous unless the complaint *implicates some right that exists under the Constitution.* That is, plaintiffs must allege either that the retaliatory act was taken in response to the exercise of a constitutionally protected right or that the act itself violated such a right." (emphasis added)).

Adams is binding authority that directly rejects the constitutional right asserted in this case. The majority errs by ignoring *Adams* and relying instead on out-of-circuit cases that are inconsistent with our holding in *Adams* in order to declare that an inmate's right to be free from retaliation for filing a grievance was clearly established.

p.553 Accordingly, for the foregoing reasons, I believe that the defendants are entitled to qualified immunity, and I therefore respectfully dissent from the majority's contrary conclusion.

[1] District court opinions, on the other hand, are not decisions of "controlling authority." As the Supreme Court recently explained in an opinion concerning qualified immunity, "[a] decision of a federal district court judge is not binding precedent in either a different judicial district, the same judicial district, or even upon the same judge in a different case." *Camreta v. Greene,* 563 U.S. 692, 709 n.7, 131 S.Ct. 2020, 179 L.Ed.2d 1118 (2011) (quoting 18 J. Moore et al., *Moore's Federal Practice* § 134.02[1][d] (3d ed. 2011)). It is for this reason that "[m]any Courts of Appeals [] decline to consider district court precedent when determining if constitutional rights are clearly established for purposes of qualified immunity." *Id.* (citing *Kalka v. Hawk,* 215 F.3d 90, 100 (D.C. Cir. 2000) (Tatel, J., concurring in part and concurring in judgment) (collecting cases)).

[2] Following the Supreme Court's lead, several of our sister circuits, like us, have recognized that courts may consider decisions from other circuits in the absence of binding precedent. *Werner v. Wall,* 836 F.3d 751, 762 n.28 (7th Cir. 2016) ("We are not alone in looking to trends in the decisional law of other jurisdictions once we are satisfied that controlling precedent in our own circuit does not clearly establish a particular legal right.") (citing *Cox v. Glanz,* 800 F.3d 1231, 1247 (10th Cir. 2015); *Morgan v. Swanson,* 659 F.3d 359, 372 (5th Cir. 2011); *Bame v. Dillard,* 637 F.3d 380, 384 (D.C. Cir. 2011); *Wilson v. City of Boston,* 421 F.3d 45, 56 (1st Cir. 2005); *Turner v. Ark. Ins. Dep't,* 297 F.3d 751, 755 (8th Cir. 2002); *Trulock v. Freeh,* 275 F.3d 391, 407 (4th Cir. 2001)).

[3] Appellees quibble with the right at issue. They contend that the alleged retaliation was in response to Booker's submission of an RSM form — not a grievance. This is simply a matter of semantics. Inmates in the SCDC submit RSM forms to express grievances and initiate the grievance process, and this Court previously classified Booker's submission of the RSM form as "Booker's grievance," *Booker,* 583 Fed.Appx. at 44. The Ninth Circuit rejected a near-identical distinction in *Brodheim v. Cry,* where the defendants suggested that an inmate could not bring a

First Amendment retaliation claim because the alleged retaliation was in response to the inmate's filing of a document called an "interview request form." 584 F.3d 1262, 1271 n.4 (9th Cir. 2009). The court noted that the interview request form was "part of the grievance process" and held that the "applicability of the constitutional right to redress of grievances does not hinge on the label the prison places on a particular complaint." *Id.*

[4] Indeed, courts have liberally construed complaints even where pro se plaintiffs do not reference any source of law, *see Hodge v. Gansler,* 547 Fed.Appx. 209, 210 n.1 (4th Cir. 2013) (construing claim for "racial profiling" as equal protection claim) (citing *Gordon v. Leeke,* 574 F.2d 1147, 1151 (4th Cir. 1978)), or where they cite the wrong part of the Constitution, *see Ambrose v. Roeckeman,* 749 F.3d 615, 618 (7th Cir. 2014).

[5] It is worth noting the change in Appellees' position. Earlier in the litigation, prior to the first appeal, they agreed with Booker that "it has been *clearly established* that a prison official may not retaliate against an inmate for... complaining about a prison official's conduct." Defs.' Reply to Pl.'s Response in Opp. to Mot. for S.J., Dist. Ct. ECF No. 48, at 8 (Jan. 17, 2013) (emphasis added).

[6] We have also found, in an unreported decision, that an inmate could bring a claim alleging he was transferred in retaliation for sending a letter to the mother of a fellow inmate who was severely beaten. *Moore v. Bennette,* 97 Fed.Appx. 405, 406 (4th Cir. 2004). The retaliation claim was later acknowledged in a published decision, *see Moore v. Bennette,* 517 F.3d 717, 724 (4th Cir. 2008), and eventually evaluated by the district court as a First Amendment retaliation claim, *see Moore v. Bennett,* 777 F.Supp.2d 969, 982-85 (E.D.N.C. 2011).

[7] The Supreme Court has long held that prisoners "retain the constitutional right to petition the government for the redress of grievances." *Turner v. Safley,* 482 U.S. 78, 84, 107 S.Ct. 2254, 96 L.Ed.2d 64 (1987). This right "advance[s] personal expression," *Borough of Duryea v. Guarnieri,* 564 U.S. 379, 388, 131 S.Ct. 2488, 180 L.Ed.2d 408 (2011), and "extends to all departments of the Government," including administrative agencies, *California Motor Transp. Co. v. Trucking Unlimited,* 404 U.S. 508, 510, 92 S.Ct. 609, 30 L.Ed.2d 642 (1972). Read together, Booker suggests it is clear that an inmate exercises the petition right when he files a grievance. The Supreme Court has further stated that prisoners retain "protection from arbitrary state action even within the expected conditions of confinement. They may invoke the First and Eighth Amendments and the Equal Protection Clause of the Fourteenth Amendment where appropriate, and *may draw upon internal prison grievance procedures* and state judicial review where available." *Sandin v. Conner,* 515 U.S. 472, 487 n.11, 115 S.Ct. 2293, 132 L.Ed.2d 418 (1995) (emphasis added).

[8] We treat the "Inmate Grievance System" document as a prison regulation. As the South Carolina Court of Appeals recently explained with respect to this exact document, "[a]lthough SCDC's statements concerning the inmate grievance system are within a document entitled 'SCDC Policy/Procedure,' they are 'binding norms' and, thus, more like rules or regulations ... than they are true policy statements." *Ackerman v. S. Carolina Dep't of Corr.,* 415 S.C. 412, 782 S.E.2d 757, 761 n.6 (S.C. Ct. App. 2016). And this Court has previously classified SCDC policy statements as regulations. *See Hines v. S. Carolina Dep't of Corr.,* 148 F.3d 353, 358 (4th Cir. 1998)

(classifying SCDC "Grooming Policy" as "neutral and generally applicable regulation").

[1] The panel of judges deciding Daye included Judge Wilkinson, who wrote the opinion in Adams. That the author of Adams agreed with the analysis in Daye provides an additional indication of the reasonableness of its analysis.

Although unpublished opinions do not clearly establish constitutional rights and thus cannot be relied upon to impose liability on a government official, see Hogan v. Carter, 85 F.3d 1113, 1118 (4th Cir. 1996) (en banc), I do not believe Hogan precludes consideration of unpublished opinions when declining to impose liability, see id. ("We could not allow liability to be imposed upon public officials based upon unpublished opinions that we ourselves have determined will be binding only upon the parties immediately before the court.").

[2] The majority grounds the right at issue in this case in the First Amendment's Petition Clause, and the majority seems to suggest that Adams' determination that inmates have no constitutional right to participate in grievance proceedings is wrong because exhaustion of remedies is generally required before a prisoner can file a civil action challenging his conditions of confinement. See Majority Op. at 543. I disagree.

Adams was decided in 1994, before the PLRA made exhaustion of "available" administrative remedies a mandatory prerequisite for all prison-condition lawsuits. 42 U.S.C. § 1997e(a); see Woodford v. Ngo, 548 U.S. 81, 84-85, 126 S.Ct. 2378, 165 L.Ed.2d 368 (2006) (explaining evolution of exhaustion requirements). Nonetheless, as the Eighth Circuit explained in Flick v. Alba, 932 F.2d 728 (8th Cir. 1991) (per curiam) — a case we relied on in Adams — "the prisoner's right to petition the government for redress is the right of access to the courts." Id. at 729 (emphasis added). If prison officials prevented an inmate from pursuing a grievance through an existing grievance system, then the administrative remedies were not "available" to the inmate, and the PLRA would not bar the inmate from pursuing his claim in court. See, e.g., Kervin v. Barnes, 787 F.3d 833, 835 (7th Cir. 2015) (explaining that if a state creates a grievance system "yet prevents a prisoner from utilizing it he will be excused from having to exhaust the grievance process as a prerequisite to suing in federal court"); Miller v. Norris, 247 F.3d 736, 740 (8th Cir. 2001) ("[A] remedy that prison officials prevent a prisoner from utilizing is not an available remedy under § 1997e(a)...." (internal quotation marks and alteration omitted)). Adams' conclusion that there is no constitutional right to file a grievance, even when considered in light of the PLRA's mandatory exhaustion requirement, does not restrict an inmate's rights under the Petition Clause.

878 F.3d 89 (2017)

Paul Cleveland THOMPSON, Jr., Plaintiff-Appellant,

v.

COMMONWEALTH OF VIRGINIA; Captain Dolan; Lt. R. Thompson; Grievance Coordinator Seay; Blackwell; Ware; Lewis; Baskerville; Jennings; White; Correctional Officer Cooper; Correctional Officer Diming; Virginia Department of Corrections, sued in their official and individual capacities, Defendant-Appellees.

No. 15-7680.

United States Court of Appeals, Fourth Circuit.
Argued: September 15, 2017.
Decided: December 18, 2017.

Thompson v. Commonwealth of Virginia, 878 F. 3d 89 (4th Cir. 2017)

Appeal from the United States District Court for the Eastern District of Virginia, at Norfolk. Rebecca Beach Smith, Chief District Judge, (2:12-cv-00209-RBS-TEM).

Affirmed in part, reversed in part, and remanded with instructions by published opinion. Chief Judge Gregory wrote the opinion, in which Judge Wynn and Judge Diaz joined.

ARGUED: Emily S. Mordecai, Joshua K. Day, UNIVERSITY OF VIRGINIA SCHOOL OF LAW, Charlottesville, Virginia, for Appellant. Trevor Stephen Cox, OFFICE OF THE ATTORNEY GENERAL OF VIRGINIA, Richmond, Virginia, for Appellees. ON BRIEF: Stephen L. Braga, Appellate Litigation Clinic, UNIVERSITY OF VIRGINIA SCHOOL OF LAW, Charlottesville, Virginia, for Appellant. Mark R. Herring, Attorney General, Stuart A. Raphael, Solicitor General, Matthew R. McGuire, Assistant Solicitor General, OFFICE OF THE ATTORNEY GENERAL OF VIRGINIA, Richmond, Virginia, for Appellees.

Before GREGORY, Chief Judge, WYNN, and DIAZ, Circuit Judges.

Affirmed in part, reversed in part, and remanded with instructions by published opinion. Chief Judge Gregory wrote the opinion, in which Judge Wynn and Judge Diaz joined.

p.93 GREGORY, Judge:

Paul Thompson, an inmate of the Virginia Department of Corrections ("VDOC"), brings claims under 42 U.S.C. § 1983, alleging violations of his rights under the First Amendment, Eighth Amendment, and the Fourteenth Amendment by several current and former VDOC officials. He also alleges violations of his rights under the Virginia Constitution by the Commonwealth of Virginia, the VDOC, and those same officials. Claims primarily stem from alleged retaliation by prison officials against Mr. Thompson for filing grievances and lawsuits, most notably by giving him a "rough ride" in a prison van. The district court below granted summary judgment in p.94 favor of the defendants on all claims, relying in part on the doctrine of qualified immunity. We now affirm in part, reverse in part, and remand for further proceedings.

I.

At all relevant times, Appellant Mr. Paul C. Thompson[1] was an inmate at Deep Meadow Correctional Center ("DMCC"), which is run by the VDOC. The case largely centers on whether two correctional officers, Officer Cooper and Officer Diming, gave Mr. Thompson a so-called "rough ride" while transporting him in a van and whether other corrections officials responded inappropriately to the incident.

At around 7 a.m. on April 8, 2010, DMCC began transporting Mr. Thompson to attend a 9:30 a.m. proceeding at the Mecklenburg Circuit Court. Before departure, Officers Diming and Cooper secured Mr. Thompson in handcuffs, leg irons, a belly chain, and a black box.[2]

Diming and Cooper then placed Mr. Thompson in the second row of a van, which was equipped with seatbelts. According to Mr. Thompson, neither officer secured Mr. Thompson's seatbelt, even though his restraints prevented him from doing so himself. Mr. Thompson then specifically requested that his seatbelt be secured, but both Cooper and Diming refused. Cooper and Diming each averred that it was their usual practice to fasten inmates' seatbelts and that they would not refuse seatbelt requests. However, neither officer recalled whether Mr. Thompson in fact had his seatbelt fastened or even made such a request.

Once Mr. Thompson was in the van, Cooper took the wheel, with Diming in the passenger seat. They drove without incident, despite going on windy, sharply-curved roads, for about an hour and a half. By Mr. Thompson's account, the van then made a short stop at a convenience store and turned back around in the direction of DMCC. According to Cooper and Diming, they made no stops during the trip and began the return trip after receiving a phone call from DMCC that the court proceeding had been cancelled.

What happened on the return trip is vigorously disputed. According to Mr. Thompson, the officers intentionally drove the van in a way that caused him to be thrown around the cabin, and they took pleasure in doing so. Cooper reportedly drove erratically, exceeding the speed limit and crossing the white and yellow traffic lines. Because of Cooper's excessive speed on the curved roads and the fact that Mr. Thompson was not belted to his seat, Mr. Thompson was thrown around in the van from one side to the other. The sudden stops and accelerations also caused Mr. Thompson to be thrown forwards and backwards. Meanwhile, Mr. Thompson's restraints prevented him from protecting himself from slamming against the walls of the van. As a result, Mr. Thompson's head and upper body struck the steel mesh covering the windows, causing bleeding and bruising on his forehead, hands, and p.95 arms. Mr. Thompson repeatedly asked Cooper to slow down and to drive carefully, informing both officers that he was getting hurt. Mr. Thompson also specifically asked Diming to intervene. However, Diming did not take any action, even after Mr. Thompson had already sustained visible injuries.

In response to Mr. Thompson's pleas, Cooper and Diming reportedly laughed and taunted him. They said, "So you like to write grievances and take people to court, we know how to deal with inmates ... who create problems." J.A. 476. Since Mr. Thompson's first arrival at DMCC less than six months earlier, he had filed at least 14 complaints, primarily concerning access to the law library and to the notary.

Cooper and Diming joked about how scared Mr. Thompson looked and stated that they were going to make his stay at DMCC a nightmare. Cooper eventually began driving normally again. At some point, Diming called staff at DMCC, stating that Mr. Thompson was banging his own head and being crazy.

Cooper and Diming, unsurprisingly, recounted an entirely different version of events. By their telling, Cooper obeyed all traffic laws. When they were twenty minutes away from DMCC, Mr. Thompson started yelling, shouting profanities, and banging his head on the metal mesh. Mr. Thompson then threatened the officers with lawsuits, saying that he was going to claim they beat him up. Diming called the lieutenant on duty at DMCC, Lt. Thompson, and reported Mr. Thompson's behavior.

Lt. Thompson reported that he heard Mr. Thompson screaming and yelling on speaker-phone during the call. Another officer, K. James, stated that he heard, because the call was on speaker-phone, Mr. Thompson yelling, "I am going to tell them you beat me up," as well as thuds consistent with a head striking a window. J.A. 230.

Mr. Thompson's physical injuries were documented after the ride. Photos were taken, and Lt. Thompson observed a cut that appeared to be a half to three-quarters of an inch long on Mr. Thompson's forehead. An injury report prepared by Cooper and Diming indicated that Mr. Thompson's gash was cleaned and dressed, with no follow-up treatment prescribed.

Mr. Thompson was referred to the prison psychologist for a mental health evaluation. The psychologist, D. Lipscomb, observed Mr. Thompson crying as he recounted the morning's events. Mr. Thompson reportedly expressed concern for his safety, said that he was "scared now[,]" because "they cause[d] [him] to bang [his] head," and that the officers told him, "This will teach you to write grievances ... [and] file litigation." J.A. 451. According to the mental health report, Mr. Thompson also stated, "Don't know if I can do this. Shouldn't have to go through this shit. Now fucking crying like a freaking baby." J.A. 451.

Lt. Thompson issued a disciplinary charge against Mr. Thompson for "lying and giving false information to an employee," specifically for claiming that staff had assaulted him when his injuries were self-inflicted. J.A. 74, 212-214, 513. This resulted in pre-hearing detention, a disciplinary hearing before Hearing Officer Blackwell, and seven days' isolation time (credited by pre-hearing detention).

In addition to the "rough ride," Mr. Thompson also generally alleges that VDOC officials, including Grievance Coordinator Seay, Assistant Warden Jennings, Ombudsman White, and Major Lewis have denied him access to grievance procedures and to the law library and have rejected p.96 grievances without sufficient explanation or after excessive delay.

In 2012, Mr. Thompson, acting *pro se,* filed a 42 U.S.C. § 1983 action in the Eastern District of Virginia, alleging violations of the First Amendment, Eighth Amendment, Fourteenth Amendment, and the Virginia Constitution. The suit named the Commonwealth of Virginia, the Virginia Department of Corrections, Warden Baskerville, Assistant Warden Jennings, Ombudsman White, Major Lewis, Captain Dolan, Lt. Thompson, Grievance Coordinator Seay, Operations Officer Ware, Hearing Officer Blackwell, and Officers Cooper and Diming.

II.

For clarity, we adopt Mr. Thompson's summary of his claims, as referenced by the district court:

> *Claim One.* Defendants named are Baskerville, Jennings, Ware, Lewis, Dolan, Thompson, Seay, Blackwell, White, Cooper and Diming. This is a First Amendment retaliation claim. This claim encompasses more than the transport incident on April 8, 2010, it involves Defendants' actions/inactions prior to and after the transport;
>
> *Claim Two.* Defendants named are Jennings, Dolan, Thompson, Cooper and Diming. This is an Eighth Amendment cruel and unusual punishment claim, that relates directly to the transport incident on April 8, 2010;
>
> *Claim Three.* Defendants named are Jennings, Dolan, Thompson, Cooper, Diming, Lewis, Seay and Blackwell. This is a Fourteenth Amendment claim involving violations of due process concerning the issuance of a false charge, the hearing process, confinement in segregation, extended confinement in segregation and conspiracy to cover up First and Eighth Amendment violations;
>
> *Claim Four.* Defendants named are Baskerville, Jennings, Ware, Lewis, Dolan and White. This is a supervisory responsibility direct involvement claim related to First, Eighth and Fourteenth Amendment violations;
>
> *Claim Five.* Defendants named are Commonwealth of Virginia, VDOC, Baskerville, Jennings, Ware, Lewis, Dolan, Thompson, Seay, Blackwell, White, Cooper and Diming. This is an Article I, Section 12, Virginia Constitution violation involving harassment and retaliation for Plaintiff exercising his First Amendment right;
>
> *Claim Six.* Defendants named are Commonwealth of Virginia, VDOC, Jennings, Dolan, Thompson, Cooper, and Diming. This is an Article I, Section 9, Virginia Constitution violation related to the transport incident on April 8, 2010; and
>
> *Claim Seven.* Defendants named are Commonwealth of Virginia, VDOC, Jennings, Seay, Blackwell, Dolan, Thompson, Lewis, Cooper and Diming. This is an Article I, Section 11, Virginia Constitution violation involving due process violations concerning the issuance of a false charge, hearing process, confinement in segregation, extended confinement in segregation and conspiracy to cover up First and Eighth Amendment violations violating the Fourteenth Amendment.

Thompson v. Dolan, Civ. A. No. 12-209, 2015 WL 13065640, at *1 (E.D. Va. Aug. 10, 2015). The district court granted summary judgment on all seven claims in favor of all defendants.

This court reviews a grant of summary judgment *de novo. Lee v. Town of Seaboard,* 863 F.3d 323, 327 (4th Cir. 2017). We ask "whether any genuine issues of material fact exist for the jury and if not, whether the district court erred in p.97 applying the substantive law." *Id.* In doing so, we "view the evidence in the light most favorable to the nonmoving party." *Id.* "To survive summary judgment, 'there must be evidence on which the jury could reasonably find for the [nonmovant].'" *Id.* (quoting *Anderson v. Liberty Lobby, Inc.,* 477 U.S. 242, 252, 106 S.Ct. 2505, 91 L.Ed.2d 202 (1986)).

For the reasons below, we affirm the grant of summary judgment as to Claims Three and Four but reverse in part as to Claims One, Two, Five, Six, and Seven. Because Claim Two's Eighth Amendment claim goes directly to the transport incident and is the factual epicenter of this case, we address that claim first.

III.

A.

The district court granted summary judgment as to Mr. Thompson's Eighth Amendment claim on qualified immunity grounds. To overcome the qualified immunity defense at the summary judgment stage, the plaintiff must have shown facts that make out a violation of a constitutional right, and the right at issue must have been "clearly established" at the time of the defendant's alleged misconduct.[3] *Pearson v. Callahan,* 555 U.S. 223, 232, 236, 129 S.Ct. 808, 172 L.Ed.2d 565 (2009) (modifying *Saucier v. Katz,* 533 U.S. 194, 121 S.Ct. 2151, 150 L.Ed.2d 272 (2001)). The analysis takes place against the backdrop of two dueling interests: "the need to hold public officials accountable when they exercise power irresponsibly and the need to shield officials from harassment, distraction, and liability when they perform their duties reasonably." *Id.* at 231, 129 S.Ct. 808; *Booker v. S.C. Dep't of Corr.,* 855 F.3d 533, 538 (4th Cir. 2017).

As to the merits prong of the qualified immunity analysis, Mr. Thompson must show a violation of the Eighth Amendment. The Eighth Amendment protects prisoners from "unnecessary and wanton infliction of pain." *Estelle v. Gamble,* 429 U.S. 97, 102, 97 S.Ct. 285, 50 L.Ed.2d 251 (1976). That protection imposes on prison officials an affirmative "obligation to take reasonable measures to guarantee the safety of … inmates." *Whitley v. Albers,* 475 U.S. 312, 319-20, 106 S.Ct. 1078, 89 L.Ed.2d 251 (1986). However, not all Eighth Amendment violations are the same: some constitute "deliberate indifference," while others constitute "excessive force." *Id.* at 319-20, 106 S.Ct. 1078.

The deliberate indifference standard generally applies to cases alleging failures to safeguard the inmate's health and safety, including failing to protect inmates from attack, maintaining inhumane conditions of confinement, or failing to render medical assistance. *See Farmer v. Brennan,* 511 U.S. 825, 834, 114 S.Ct. 1970, 128 L.Ed.2d 811 (1994); *Wilson v. Seiter,* 501 U.S. 294, 303, 111 S.Ct. 2321, 115 L.Ed.2d 271 (1991). The deliberate indifference standard is a two-pronged test: (1) the prisoner must be exposed to "a substantial risk of serious harm," and (2) the prison official must know of and p.98 disregard that substantial risk to the inmate's health or safety. *Farmer,* 511 U.S. at 834, 837-38, 114 S.Ct. 1970. In excessive force cases, on the other hand, courts must determine "whether force was applied in a good-faith effort to maintain or restore discipline, or maliciously and sadistically to cause harm." *Hudson v. McMillian,* 503 U.S. 1, 6-7, 112 S.Ct. 995, 117 L.Ed.2d 156 (1992).

To properly evaluate a prisoner's Eighth Amendment claim, courts ordinarily must choose which standard to apply as to each defendant. The two standards differ significantly, and importantly, deliberate indifference is not always easier to prove than excessive force. While excessive force does require malicious intent, it does not require that the prisoner victim suffer a "significant injury." *McMillian,* 503 U.S. at 9-10, 112 S.Ct. 995 ("When prison officials maliciously and sadistically use force to cause harm, contemporary standards of decency always are violated."). Therefore, a prisoner who suffers a minor, but malicious, injury may be able to prevail on an excessive force claim but not on a deliberate indifference claim.

Under the second prong of qualified immunity, even if an official has violated an inmate's constitutional right, he is still entitled to immunity if the right was not so "clearly established" that "a reasonable official would understand that what he is doing violates that right." *Hope v. Pelzer,* 536 U.S. 730, 739, 122 S.Ct. 2508, 153 L.Ed.2d 666 (2002) (citing *Anderson v. Creighton,* 483 U.S. 635, 640, 107 S.Ct. 3034, 97 L.Ed.2d 523 (1987)). Ultimately, our inquiry is whether "the state of the law [at the time of alleged conduct] gave fair warning that [the officer's] alleged treatment [of the prisoner] was unconstitutional." *Id.* at 741, 122 S.Ct. 2508.

To determine if the right in question was clearly established, we first look to cases from the Supreme Court, this Court of Appeals, or the highest court of the state in which the action arose. *Owens ex rel. Owens v. Lott,* 372 F.3d 267, 279 (4th Cir. 2004). In the absence of "directly on-point, binding authority," courts may also consider whether "the right was clearly established based on general constitutional principles or a consensus of persuasive authority." *Booker,* 855 F.3d at 543; *Owens,* 372 F.3d at 279 ("[T]he absence of controlling authority holding identical conduct unlawful does not guarantee qualified immunity.").

Courts must take care to define the right at an "appropriate level of specificity." *Wilson v. Layne,* 526 U.S. 603, 615, 119 S.Ct. 1692, 143 L.Ed.2d 818 (1999). Ordinarily, "the unlawfulness [of government conduct] must be apparent" "in the light of pre-existing law." *White v. Pauly,* ___ U.S. ___, 137 S.Ct. 548, 552, 196 L.Ed.2d 463 (2017) (citing *Creighton,* 483 U.S. at 640, 107 S.Ct. 3034); *Safar v. Tingle,* 859 F.3d 241, 246 (4th Cir. 2017) (noting that court must identify precedent with sufficiently "similar circumstances" in order to find law is clearly established). However, a "general constitutional rule... may apply with obvious clarity ... even though the very action in question has not previously been held unlawful." *Hope,* 536 U.S. at 741, 122 S.Ct. 2508 (citing *United States v. Lanier,* 520 U.S. 259, 271, 117 S.Ct. 1219, 137 L.Ed.2d 432 (1997)). Thus, "officials can still be on notice that their conduct violates established law even in novel factual circumstances." *Id.* at 741, 122 S.Ct. 2508 (noting that prior cases need not have "fundamentally similar" or even "materially similar" facts).

B.

Mr. Thompson brings his Eighth Amendment claim against Officers Cooper p.99 and Diming, Lt. Thompson, Assistant Warden Jennings, and Captain Dolan. Only Cooper and Diming were directly involved in the transport incident as the driver and the occupant of the passenger seat, respectively. Mr. Thompson's complaint against Lt. Thompson, Jennings, and Dolan sounds in supervisory liability, alleging failures to ensure safe transport and adherence to VDOC procedures. The district court granted summary judgment in favor of all five defendants after finding that Mr. Thompson's right was not clearly established. Because we find that Mr. Thompson has shown facts making out a violation of a clearly established right, we now reverse summary judgment and remand as to Officers Cooper and Diming. However, because Mr. Thompson has not shown sufficient facts for supervisory liability, we affirm the grant of summary judgment in favor of Lt. Thompson, Jennings, and Dolan.

1.

We first address whether Officer Cooper, the driver of the van, is entitled to qualified immunity under the two-step framework. We conclude (1) that Mr. Thompson has presented sufficient facts for a reasonable jury to find that Cooper used excessive force in violation of the Eighth Amendment and (2) that Mr. Thompson's right not to be subjected to such force was clearly established by April 8, 2010, the date of the incident.

a.

Although the district court seemed to assume without expressly deciding that deliberate indifference was the correct standard to apply to Cooper's alleged Eighth Amendment violation, *McMillian* requires application of the excessive force standard in this case. *See* 503 U.S. at 6-7, 112 S.Ct. 995. *McMillian* held that the excessive force standard applied to an officer who punched an inmate during transport for no apparent reason. *See id.* at 4, 6-7, 112 S.Ct. 995. Mr. Thompson essentially claims that Cooper applied force against him without any legitimate purpose, albeit using the transport van's momentum rather than a punch. Those facts do not materially distinguish *McMillian*. *See id.* Accordingly, we must determine whether, viewing the evidence in light most favorable to Mr. Thompson, Officer Cooper used force "maliciously and sadistically to cause harm." *Id.*

We evaluate whether Cooper acted maliciously or "wantonly" by applying a non-exclusive, four-factor balancing test:

(1) the need for the application of force;

(2) the relationship between the need and the amount of force that was used;

(3) the extent of any reasonably perceived threat that the application of force was intended to quell; and

(4) any efforts made to temper the severity of a forceful response.

Iko v. Shreve, 535 F.3d 225, 239 (4th Cir. 2008) (citing *Whitley*, 475 U.S. at 321, 106 S.Ct. 1078). In *Iko* we applied these factors to hold that a prison official used excessive force in violation of the Eighth Amendment by applying pepper spray while removing an inmate from his cell because the official continued to spray even after the inmate attempted to comply. 535 F.3d at 239-40, 243. As discussed below, at least three of the four factors require a similar conclusion here.

First, Officer Cooper never needed to use force on Mr. Thompson during the transport. Unlike Iko, who initially refused to leave his cell as ordered, Mr. Thompson did not disobey any instruction. In fact, the parties do not dispute that Mr. Thompson p.100 fully complied with all instructions at all times leading up to the alleged use of force. *See id.* at 231, 239-40. Moreover, there is no indication in the record that any use of force against Mr. Thompson during transport was justified.

Accordingly, a reasonable jury could credit Mr. Thompson's affidavit and find that Officers Cooper and Diming's intent was malicious — to teach him a lesson for filing grievances. Such a motive, unsupported by any penological interest, is clearly not a legitimate basis for using force.

Second, because there was no need to use force, the force used was necessarily excessive in relation to the need. In *Iko*, we held that the official's use of force became disproportionate once the prisoner began showing signs of compliance. 535 F.3d at 239-40. Here, since there was never a need, the use of force was disproportionate from start to finish. Moreover, even if Mr. Thompson disobeyed instructions, giving a prisoner a so-called "rough ride" in a van does not constitute an acceptable means of securing compliance. *Cf. id.* at 239 (noting that officers are trained to use pepper spray and that pepper spray is allowed for purposes of removing inmates under department's Use of Force Directive). To use force in this manner is a peculiarly cruel means of punishment, as a "rough ride" is designed to place the victim in fear for his life. Not only is the prisoner not able to protect himself, but motor vehicles, unlike a controlled spray or direct applications of force, are not designed for use as a means of securing compliance or otherwise subduing a prisoner. The momentum from the van is not susceptible to precise calibration such that only the amount of force justified by the circumstances is actually deployed. The prospect that neither the victim nor the officer can prevent an instantaneous escalation to a life-or-death situation instills terror. A "rough ride" therefore bears no relationship to any penological need to use force, and even standing alone, its sheer cruelty and impropriety suggest a constitutional violation.

Third, Officers Cooper and Diming do not even assert that Mr. Thompson posed a threat to anyone. In *Iko*, the prisoner posed a minimal threat — he had even lain down on the ground before the officer sprayed him the final time. *Id.* Here, the officers do not, and cannot, argue that Mr. Thompson presented any kind of physical threat, as he was fully restrained with shackles, handcuffs, and a black box. Moreover, he never verbally threatened the officers with violence and was never hostile in any way. Mr. Thompson's only threat, the officers concede, was the threat of future litigation.

Finally, the fourth factor, concerning efforts to temper the use of force, is a draw at best. In contrast to *Iko*, where prison officials failed to provide any medical attention after applying the pepper spray, Cooper and Diming did secure medical assistance upon their return to DMCC. But, they never secured Mr. Thompson's seatbelt, even after he was injured, and they fueled Mr. Thompson's fear for his safety by taunting and threatening him. Even assuming this factor weighs in the government's favor, it alone cannot preclude the conclusion that Mr. Thompson has alleged a constitutional violation. To hold otherwise would allow prison officials to escape liability in excessive force cases simply by rendering medical assistance after the fact.

The extent of Mr. Thompson's injury is not one of the relevant factors and does not, contrary to the government's suggestion, preclude a violation of the Eighth Amendment. Of course, the Eighth Amendment does not prohibit a *de minimis* use of force that is not itself "repugnant p.101 to the conscience of mankind." *McMillian,* 503 U.S. at 9-10, 112 S.Ct. 995 (citing *Whitley,* 475 U.S. at 327, 106 S.Ct. 1078). But when use of force is malicious or repugnant, a plaintiff need not suffer anything significant to establish an excessive force claim. Thus, in *McMillian,* the Supreme Court reversed the Fifth Circuit for rejecting an excessive force claim solely because the inmate had not suffered a "significant injury." 503 U.S. at 4-5, 112 S.Ct. 995. The Court explained:

> When prison officials maliciously and sadistically use force to cause harm, contemporary standards of decency always are violated. *This is true whether or not significant injury is evident.* Otherwise, the Eighth Amendment would permit any physical punishment, no matter how diabolic or inhuman, inflicting less than some arbitrary quantity of injury. Such a result would have been as unacceptable to the drafters of the Eighth Amendment as it is today.

Id. at 9-10, 112 S.Ct. 995 (citing *Whitley,* 475 U.S. at 327, 106 S.Ct. 1078; *Estelle,* 429 U.S. at 102, 97 S.Ct. 285) (emphasis added). The excessive force analysis thus focuses on the maliciousness of the force used, not the severity of the injury that results from that force. *Wilkins v. Gaddy,* 559 U.S. 34, 38, 130 S.Ct. 1175, 175 L.Ed.2d 995 (2010) ("An inmate who is gratuitously beaten by guards does not lose his ability to pursue an excessive force claim merely because he has the good fortune to escape without serious injury."). Here, the momentum from the van was sufficient to cause a gash on Mr. Thompson's forehead, bleeding from his hands and arms and bruising, not to mention significant emotional distress. The force alleged is therefore beyond *de minimis* for Eighth Amendment purposes. *See id.* at 9, 112 S.Ct. 995 (force not *de minimis* when sufficient to cause bruising, swelling, loosened teeth); *see also Wilkins,* 559 U.S. at 35, 40, 130 S.Ct. 1175 (force sufficient to cause bruising, lower back pain, migraines, dizziness, and mental anguish not *de minimis*).

The cases cited by the government and the district court do not support a contrary holding. For example, *Jabbar v. Fischer* merely held that failure to provide inmates with seatbelts, "standing alone," is not an Eighth Amendment violation. *See* 683 F.3d 54, 57 (2d Cir. 2012) (noting no intent to punish and distinguishing reckless-driving case). Other cases are similarly inapplicable because their facts do not involve a prison official acting with malicious intent. *See Spencer v. Knapheide Truck Equipment Co.,* 183 F.3d 902, 907-08 (8th Cir. 1999) (no evidence suggesting intent to punish); *Carrasquillo v. City of New York,* 324 F.Supp.2d 428, 436 (S.D.N.Y. 2004) (car accident due to negligence); *Cooks v. Crain,* 327 Fed.Appx. 493, 493 (5th Cir. 2009) (general failure to install seatbelts on transport vehicles); *Smith v. Sec'y For Dep't of Corr.,* 252 Fed.Appx. 301, 303-04 (11th Cir. 2007) (failure to seatbelt without dangerous driving); *Dexter v. Ford Motor Co.,* 92 Fed.Appx. 637, 640-41 (10th Cir. 2004) (failure to seatbelt standing alone); *Vinson v. U.S. Marshals Serv.,* Civ. A. No. 10-79, 2011 WL 3903199, at *5 (D.S.C. Sept. 2, 2011) (negligent driving and failure to seatbelt do not rise to Eighth Amendment violation), *aff'd,* 459 Fed. Appx. 221 (4th Cir. 2011); *Young v. Dep't of Corr.,* Civ. A. No. 04-10309, 2007 WL 2214520, at *6 (E.D. Mich. July 27, 2007) (no evidence of intent to injure or punish); *Jones v. Collins,* Civ. A. No. 05-663, 2006 WL 1528882, at *2 (S.D. Ill. June 1, 2006) (negligent failure to secure seatbelt).

Because Mr. Thompson has alleged facts from which a reasonable factfinder could conclude that Officer Cooper maliciously subjected him to a rough ride, he has sufficiently alleged an Eighth Amendment p.102 excessive force claim sufficient to survive summary judgment as to Cooper.

b.

We further hold that Mr. Thompson's right was clearly established by April 8, 2010, the date of the incident. Defined at the appropriate level of specificity, prisoners have a right not to be assaulted by their captors. Under the Eighth Amendment, prisoners have the right to be free from malicious or penologically unjustified infliction of pain and suffering. *Rhodes v. Chapman,* 452 U.S. 337, 346, 101 S.Ct. 2392, 69 L.Ed.2d 59 (1981) ("Among 'unnecessary and wanton' inflictions of pain are those that are 'totally without penological justification.'") (citing *Gregg v. Georgia,* 428 U.S. 153, 183, 96 S.Ct. 2909, 49 L.Ed.2d 859 (1976); *Estelle,* 429 U.S. at 103, 97 S.Ct. 285). This principle applies with particular force when inmates have not engaged in wrongdoing, are restrained and compliant and posing no physical threat. Further, no reasonable officer would think that violently tossing a prisoner around in a moving vehicle is an acceptable means of punishment even if the prisoner had engaged in wrongdoing. After examining both controlling and persuasive authority, we conclude that Officer Cooper had fair warning that gratuitously giving an inmate a "rough ride" for no reason other than to retaliate against him for filing lawsuits and grievances is unconstitutional.

A reasonable officer would have known from Supreme Court precedent that the Eighth Amendment prohibits such malicious acts of violence or intentional endangerment. In *McMillian,* one of the seminal cases defining the scope of the right not to be subjected to excessive force, the Supreme Court reversed the dismissal of an Eighth Amendment claim based on a correctional officer's gratuitous punch of an inmate during transport. *See* 503 U.S. at 4, 12, 112 S.Ct. 995. In *Wilkins,* a prison official, angered by the prisoner's request for a grievance form, slammed the prisoner against the ground and physically beat him in response. 559 U.S. at 35, 37, 130 S.Ct. 1175 (citing and reaffirming *McMillian,* 503 U.S. at 9, 112 S.Ct. 995). The Supreme Court reversed the district court's dismissal of the case for failure to state a claim and held that the prisoner would prevail if he proved that the official had in fact acted maliciously. *See id.* at 40, 130 S.Ct. 1175. As in *Wilkins,* if we credit Mr. Thompson's account, the only reason Cooper used force against him was in retaliation for filing grievances. Accordingly, *Wilkins* and *McMillian* are sufficiently similar to Cooper's alleged conduct that a reasonable officer would have known that a retaliatory "rough ride" is unconstitutional.

To be sure, *McMillian* and *Wilkins* involved direct punches and kicks, rather than a "rough ride," but it makes no difference to the constitutional analysis whether Mr. Thompson was slammed against the side of the van by the officer's hands or by the momentum maliciously created by the officer's driving. *See Brown v. Fortner,* 518 F.3d 552, 560-62 (8th Cir. 2008) (holding that prisoner's right not to be endangered by dangerous driving while unbuckled was clearly established despite lack of published authority on those specific facts). The intentionally erratic driving was simply a different means of effectuating the same constitutional violation. To draw a line between these acts would encourage bad actors to invent creative and novel means of using unjustified force on prisoners. Although *McMillian* and *Wilkins* did not reach the qualified immunity question, their holdings provide officers with fair notice that malicious, unprovoked, unjustified force inflicted on inmates who are compliant and restrained, and violates the p.103 Eighth Amendment. In other words, the Eighth

Amendment principle prohibiting such gratuitous violence applies with "obvious clarity" to a malicious "rough ride," just as it does to a malicious direct blow. *See Hope,* 536 U.S. at 741, 122 S.Ct. 2508.

Indeed, two Eighth Circuit cases have held that malicious "rough rides" violate the Eighth Amendment. *See Fortner,* 518 F.3d at 560-62; *Brown v. Morgan,* 39 F.3d 1184, 1994 WL 610993, *1 (8th Cir. 1994) (unpublished). Although these cases applied the deliberate indifference standard, they provided notice to Cooper, because deliberate indifference has a lower intent requirement, and, as discussed *infra,* the injuries here suffice for a deliberate indifference claim. *Fortner* and *Morgan* both involved officers who knowingly refused to fasten a prisoner's seatbelt, drove recklessly, and refused the prisoner's pleas to slow down. *See Fortner,* 518 F.3d at 556, 560-62 (denying qualified immunity); *Morgan,* 39 F.3d 1184, at *1 (finding deliberate indifference). In *Fortner,* the prisoner, like Mr. Thompson, was fully shackled with chains, handcuffs, and a black box such that he could not secure his own seatbelt or brace himself if necessary. *Id.* The driver ignored the prisoner's pleas to stop speeding and eventually caused a car accident. *Id.* Here, Cooper apparently speeded around curves and crossed white and yellow traffic lines, generating enough force to bruise and injure Mr. Thompson.[4] Mr. Thompson not only asked Cooper to slow down, as Brown did in *Fortner,* but also indicated that he had already been injured. Similarly, in *Morgan,* the driver took pleasure in the prisoner's fear and asked, "Are you scared?" before increasing his speed. 39 F.3d at *1. In Mr. Thompson's case, Cooper laughed at him and taunted him for being scared, before stating his intent to teach him a lesson. Cooper's conduct therefore went even further than what was considered unacceptable in *Fortner* and *Morgan,* as Cooper not only disregarded a serious risk of harm, but apparently intended such harm to result. *See Whitley,* 475 U.S. at 320, 106 S.Ct. 1078 (suggesting that malicious intent is more culpable than mere indifference by limiting liability to intentional misconduct). Given the factual parallels, the Eighth Circuit cases are powerful indicators that the officers here had fair notice. *Cf. Pauly,* 137 S.Ct. at 552 (reversing denial of qualified immunity because court failed to identify case with similar circumstances and no general principle applies with obvious clarity).

Although few circuits have addressed specifically an officer's use of a vehicle to injure an inmate, there is a clear consensus among the circuits, including the Fourth, that infliction of pain and suffering without penological justification violates the Eighth Amendment in an array of contexts. Simply put, there are many ways of physically and maliciously assaulting a helpless prisoner, and all of them violate the Eighth Amendment.

The First Circuit denied summary judgment as to an excessive force claim against officers who beat a detainee for requesting permission to finish his meal. *Massey v. Rufo,* 14 F.3d 44, 1994 WL 12326, *2-3 (1st Cir. 1994) (unpublished) (reversing summary judgment).

The Second Circuit has held that retaliating against inmates for taking over a prison after order had been restored would violate the Eighth Amendment. *See Blyden v. Mancusi,* 186 F.3d 252, 258-60, 265, p.104 n.6 (2d Cir. 1999) (affirming jury instructions to that effect); *Al-Jundi v. Mancusi,* 926 F.2d 235, 240 (2d Cir. 1991). The court has also concluded that handcuffing a prisoner for hours without any apparent reason constitutes an unnecessary infliction of pain. *Johnson v. Testman,* 380 F.3d 691,

698, n.6 (2d Cir. 2004); *see also Powell v. Schriver,* 175 F.3d 107, 115 (2d Cir. 1999) (holding that unnecessary disclosure of prisoner's HIV and transsexual status subjected prisoner to unnecessary risk of harm).

The Third Circuit has held that "[n]o reasonable officer could agree that striking and kicking a subdued, nonresisting inmate in the side ... was reasonable or necessary under established law." *Giles v. Kearney,* 571 F.3d 318, 326-28 (3d Cir. 2009); *see also McDowell v. Sheerer,* 374 Fed.Appx. 288, 293 (3d Cir. 2010) ("[B]y 2004, it was established that an officer may not ... use gratuitous force against an inmate who has been subdued.").

This court, in *Iko,* held that using pepper spray on an inmate after he began complying with instructions violated the Eighth Amendment. 535 F.3d at 239-40. Similarly, we have held that the Eighth Amendment prohibits using water hoses, billy clubs, and tear gas against an inmate who was locked in a cell and posed no threat to the prison officials. *Slakan v. Porter,* 737 F.2d 368, 372 (4th Cir. 1984) ("The unjustified striking or beating of a prisoner by police or correctional officials constitutes cruel and unusual punishment which is actionable under 42 U.S.C. § 1983.").

In the words of the Fifth Circuit, "[w]e have little difficulty concluding that in 2009... it was well-established ... that officers may not 'use gratuitous force against a prisoner who has already been subdued... [or] incapacitated.' Reasonable officers had fair notice that [punching and using mace on a non-resisting inmate] violated [the] right to be free from excessive force." *Cowart v. Erwin,* 837 F.3d 444, 449-50, 454-55 (5th Cir. 2016) (holding that law was clearly established as of 2009). The Fifth Circuit also has held that a prison official would "obviously" exceed the protection of qualified immunity if he incentivized other inmates to attack the plaintiff. *See Davis v. Tucker,* 322 Fed.Appx. 369, 370 (5th Cir. 2009) (dismissing claim because inmate had not adduced sufficient evidence to support claim).

Likewise, the Sixth Circuit has "long recognized that a spontaneous assault by a prison guard on an inmate is grounds for an Eighth Amendment excessive force claim." *Coley v. Lucas Cty., Ohio,* 799 F.3d 530, 535, 539-40 (6th Cir. 2015) (clearly established as of 2004); *Pelfrey v. Chambers,* 43 F.3d 1034, 1035, 1037 (6th Cir. 1995) (spontaneously cutting off inmate's hair to scare him and to reinforce dominance violated Eighth Amendment); *Moore v. Holbrook,* 2 F.3d 697, 700-01 (6th Cir. 1993) (inmate's allegations that he was handcuffed and beaten by prison guards would constitute valid Eighth Amendment claim).

In the Seventh Circuit, qualified immunity does not protect an officer who strikes an inmate and slams him against a cell for asking a question. *Hill v. Shelander,* 992 F.2d 714, 715, 718-19 (7th Cir. 1993). The court stated in *Hill* that "an unprovoked assault" is not within "the shadow of legal uncertainty." *Id.* (citing *Whitley,* 475 U.S. at 319, 106 S.Ct. 1078). The Seventh Circuit has also extended the bar against unnecessary infliction of pain and suffering to strip searches that are conducted solely to harass a prisoner, as well as to intentional, gratuitous denials of medication. *E.g., Rodriguez v. Plymouth Ambulance Serv.,* 577 F.3d 816, 828-29 (7th Cir. 2009) (holding that intentionally denying or delaying p.105 access to medical care would violate Eighth Amendment); *Calhoun v. DeTella,* 319 F.3d 936, 939 (7th Cir. 2003) (holding that otherwise lawful strip-search becomes unconstitutional if conducted in manner intended to humiliate and cause psychological pain). If a prison guard may not allow an inmate to suffer a deterioration in health condition without any legitimate penological interest, it seems reasonably clear that a prison guard cannot then directly injure and harm an inmate's health and wellbeing through physical force without justification.

The Eighth Circuit has held that intentionally endangering inmates, such as by exposing them to attack by other inmates, as punishment for filing lawsuits is an "appalling" violation of the Eighth Amendment. *Irving v. Dormire,* 519 F.3d 441, 447-48, (8th Cir. 2008).

The Ninth Circuit has held that *McMillian* clearly established a right to be free from unnecessary and wanton infliction of pain and that officers violated this right by beating and using a Taser on a non-resisting inmate, including after he was handcuffed following a disturbance. *Martinez v. Stanford,* 323 F.3d 1178, 1180, 1183-84 (9th Cir. 2003) (reversing grant of summary judgment).

According to the Tenth Circuit, "an inmate has a constitutional right to be secure in her bodily integrity and free from attack by prison guards." *Hovater v. Robinson,* 1 F.3d 1063, 1068 (10th Cir. 1993) (case of sexual abuse by prison guard).

Finally, the Eleventh Circuit has held that:

> The law of excessive force in this country is that a prisoner cannot be subjected to gratuitous or disproportionate force that has no object but to inflict pain. *This is so whether the prisoner is in a cell, prison yard, police car, in handcuffs on the side of the road, or in any other custodial setting.* The use of force must stop when the need for it to maintain or restore discipline no longer exists. Long before the defendants acted, the law was clearly established that correctional officers could not use force maliciously or sadistically for the very purpose of causing harm.

Skrtich v. Thornton, 280 F.3d 1295, 1304-05 (11th Cir. 2002) (citing *Whitley,* 475 U.S. at 320-21, 106 S.Ct. 1078) (holding that beating prisoner after he was incapacitated by electric shock constituted excessive force) (emphasis added).

As is apparent from the case law of eleven federal courts of appeals, the Eighth Amendment protection against the malicious and sadistic infliction of pain and suffering applies in a diverse range of factual scenarios. That unifying thread provides fair notice to prison officials that they cannot, no matter their creativity, maliciously harm a prisoner on a whim or for reasons unrelated to the government's interest in maintaining order. That principle applies with particular clarity to cases such as this one, where the victim is restrained, compliant, and incapable of resisting or protecting himself, and otherwise presents no physical threat in any way.

The government argues, unpersuasively, that the law is not clearly established because courts have not found a constitutional violation in some failure-to-fasten-seatbelt cases, notwithstanding the Eighth Circuit precedent. However, with one exception, every other seatbelt case cited by the district court and the government involved mere negligence, rather than malice or even recklessness. *See, e.g., Jabbar,* 683 F.3d at 57; *Spencer,* 183 F.3d at 907-08; *Crain,* 327 Fed.Appx. at 493; *Smith,* 252 Fed.Appx. at 304; *Dexter,* 92 Fed.Appx. at 640-41. The one exception is *Young,* an p.106 unpublished district court case that involved reckless driving. 2007 WL 2214520, at *6. However, *Young* took place before *Fortner* was published, and the district court erred by relying purely on negligence cases without recognizing the heightened risk of reckless or malicious endangerment. *See id.* at *5-6. Moreover, even

Young distinguished its facts from a case where the driver drives with the intent to scare an inmate or refuses pleas to slow down. *Id.* Instead, all cases that have squarely dealt with intentional misconduct have found an Eighth Amendment violation.

The government also argues, unpersuasively, that an official's wrongful intent is never relevant to the qualified immunity analysis, even in the context of an Eighth Amendment deliberate indifference or excessive force claim. *See* Appellees' Br. at 31. The government cites *Crawford-El v. Britton* for the sweeping proposition that, under *Harlow v. Fitzgerald,* 457 U.S. 800, 102 S.Ct. 2727, 73 L.Ed.2d 396 (1982), "[e]vidence concerning the defendant's subjective intent is simply irrelevant." *Crawford-El v. Britton,* 523 U.S. 574, 589, 118 S.Ct. 1584, 140 L.Ed.2d 759 (1998). *Crawford-El*'s holding is much more limited and is not itself a decision on qualified immunity. *See* 523 U.S. at 589, 118 S.Ct. 1584 (holding that plaintiff may pursue ordinary discovery into official's intent for claims having intent element notwithstanding irrelevance of intent to qualified immunity defense). Read in context, the Court was merely referring to and reiterating *Harlow*'s holding that "'bare allegations of malice' cannot overcome the qualified immunity defense." *Id.* (quoting *Harlow,* 457 U.S. at 817-18, 102 S.Ct. 2727).

Crawford-El and *Harlow* do not forbid us from considering evidence of intent in Mr. Thompson's excessive force claim. *Harlow* did not involve an Eighth Amendment excessive force claim or a deliberate indifference claim. *See* 457 U.S. at 817-18, 102 S.Ct. 2727 (suit against presidential aides for recommending plaintiff's firing in bad faith). As *Crawford-El* itself recognized, the significance of evidence of intent differs when it "is an essential component of the plaintiff's affirmative case." *See* 523 U.S. at 588-90, 118 S.Ct. 1584.

For claims where intent is an element, an official's state of mind is a reference point by which she can reasonably assess conformity to the law because the case law is intent-specific. Considering evidence of intent in this manner is not foreclosed by *Crawford-El,* as the Supreme Court itself has applied the clearly established prong in reference to retaliatory intent. *See Ortiz v. Jordan,* 562 U.S. 180, 189-91, 131 S.Ct. 884, 178 L.Ed.2d 703 (2011) (holding that law was clearly established that prison guard cannot retaliate against inmate by putting her in solitary confinement) (citing *Crawford-El,* 523 U.S. at 592, 118 S.Ct. 1584).

Thus, in light of the Supreme Court precedent in *McMillian* and *Wilkins,* case law on "rough rides" from our sister circuit, and the overwhelming consensus on the prisoner's right to be free from assault, *i.e.,* malicious infliction of pain and suffering, we conclude that Officer Cooper had fair warning that his actions were unconstitutional and that Mr. Thompson's right was therefore clearly established. Accordingly, we reverse the district court's determination that Officer Cooper is entitled to qualified immunity on the Eighth Amendment excessive force claim.

2.

As to Officer Diming, we agree with the district court that Mr. Thompson has "presented sufficient evidence to create a genuine issue of material fact" as to deliberate indifference but disagree that his right to p.107 reasonable protection from assault was not clearly established as of April 8, 2010. *See Thompson,* 2015 WL 13065640, at *8.

a.

Given the differences in the roles that Officer Cooper and Officer Diming played during the van ride, we hold that deliberate indifference is the correct standard to apply to Officer Diming. Mr. Thompson's affidavits show that Diming refused to buckle his seatbelt, ignored his pleas for help, failed to intervene to stop Cooper's unlawful use of force, and instead verbally taunted and harassed him. Unlike Cooper, who drove the van, Diming did not use unlawful force against Mr. Thompson — rather, he failed to do anything to stop it. Accordingly, the claim against Diming is functionally the same as claims in failure-to-protect or conditions-of-confinement cases, which are evaluated under the deliberate indifference standard.[5] *See Farmer,* 511 U.S. at 834, 114 S.Ct. 1970; *Wilson,* 501 U.S. at 303, 111 S.Ct. 2321. To survive summary judgment, Mr. Thompson must show facts sufficient for a reasonable factfinder to conclude that (1) he was exposed to a "substantial risk of serious harm" and (2) Diming "kn[ew] of and disregard[ed]" that risk. *Farmer,* 511 U.S. at 834, 837-38, 114 S.Ct. 1970.

First, there are sufficient facts for a reasonable jury to conclude that Mr. Thompson was exposed to a "substantial risk of serious harm." An inmate need not show that she in fact suffered serious harm to prevail on this prong because "the Eighth Amendment protects against future harm." *Helling v. McKinney,* 509 U.S. 25, 33-34, 113 S.Ct. 2475, 125 L.Ed.2d 22 (1993). Courts have "plainly recognized that a remedy for unsafe conditions need not await a tragic event." *Id.* Viewing the facts in light most favorable to Mr. Thompson, there was a substantial risk that he would suffer serious harm: he was fully shackled, unable to brace himself for impact, and sitting without a seatbelt, in a vehicle that was speeding and being driven in a way intended to scare and injure him, by a driver who refused both his requests to be seatbelted and to slow down. *See Fortner,* 518 F.3d at 559-60; *Morgan,* 39 F.3d 1184, at *1. In this case, the risk to Mr. Thompson was even greater than the risk involved in *Fortner* and *Morgan,* as neither of the drivers in those cases specifically intended to cause injury.

In arguing to the contrary, the government points to *Vinson,* an unpublished case from the District of South Carolina that involved an unfastened seatbelt and negligent driving. *See* 2011 WL 3903199 (finding no substantial risk of harm). But the court in *Vinson* distinguished its facts from those of *Fortner,* where the Eighth Circuit found an Eighth Amendment violation, because the *Vinson* plaintiff had not alleged reckless driving with specificity, such as by citing speeding and driving over boundary lines. *See Vinson v. U.S. Marshals Serv.,* Civ. A. No. 10-79, 2011 WL 3903057, at *9 (D.S.C. July 29, 2011), *report and recommendation adopted,* 2011 WL 3903199 (D.S.C. Sept. 2, 2011). The plaintiff in *Vinson* made only conclusory statements of recklessness and did not allege that the defendant taunted him or ignored his requests to slow down. *Id.* Because the facts in this case are virtually p.108 identical to those that the court in *Vinson* distinguished, *Vinson* cannot support a grant of summary judgment here. Other cases cited by the government and the district court are similarly inapplicable to the facts of this case. *See, e.g., Jabbar,* 683 F.3d at 57 (failure to seatbelt standing alone); *Spencer,* 183 F.3d at 907-08 (no-seatbelt policy and driver without intent to harm); *Crain,* 327 Fed.Appx. at 493 (failure to install seatbelts); *Smith,* 252 Fed. Appx. at 304 (no dangerous driving); *Dexter,* 92 Fed.Appx. at 640-41 (failure to seatbelt standing alone); *Young,* 2007 WL 2214520, at *5-6 (distinguishing cases where driver ignored pleas to stop and had purpose of harming passenger); *Jones,* 2006 WL 1528882, at *1 (negligent driving); *Oliver v. Georgia Dep't of Corr.,* Civ. A. No. 06-320, 2006 WL 3086792, at *2 (M.D. Ga. Oct. 27, 2006) (negligence and failure to install seatbelts). In sum, we conclude that *Fortner* and *Morgan* are more persuasive in determining a substantial risk of harm because they bear greater factual similarities to this case. *See Fortner,* 518 F.3d at 559-60; *Morgan,* 39 F.3d 1184, at *1.

Under the second prong of deliberate indifference, we must determine whether Diming subjectively knew of and disregarded the substantial risk of harm to Mr. Thompson. Although this element is subjective, a deliberately indifferent state of mind can be proven through "inference from circumstantial evidence." *Farmer,* 511 U.S. at 842, 114 S.Ct. 1970. A prison official is deliberately indifferent if "the official is present at the time of an assault and fails to intervene or otherwise act to end the assault." *Raynor v. Pugh,* 817 F.3d 123, 128 (4th Cir. 2016) (quoting *Williams v. Mueller,* 13 F.3d 1214, 1216 (8th Cir. 1994)). However, prison officials are not liable if taking action would endanger their own lives or if the harm occurred despite their reasonable efforts to prevent it. *Id.; Cox,* 828 F.3d at 236. "But 'completely failing to take any action' to stop an ongoing assault on a prisoner can amount to deliberate indifference." *Raynor,* 817 F.3d at 128 (quoting *Winfield v. Bass,* 106 F.3d 525, 532 (4th Cir. 1997) (en banc)); *see Odom v. S.C. Dep't of Corr.,* 349 F.3d 765, 773 (4th Cir. 2003) ("[A] correctional officer who stands by as a passive observer and takes no action whatsoever to intervene during an assault violates the [Eighth Amendment] rights of the victim inmate.").

We conclude that a reasonable jury could find that Officer Diming subjectively knew of the serious risk to Mr. Thompson's safety. In *Odom,* this court held that prison officials violated the Eighth Amendment for failing to take any steps to protect an inmate from a known attack. 349 F.3d at 767. There, the court found that the prison officer was aware of the risk that the inmate, Odom, would be attacked because Odom (1) had warned the officer, (2) had pleaded for help as the attack was happening, and (3) was experiencing the attack in the officer's presence. *Id.* Here, Mr. Thompson informed Diming that his seatbelt was unfastened, but Diming ignored the request to buckle it, contrary to his normal practice. In addition, Mr. Thompson informed Diming of his concerns for his safety when Cooper began driving erratically, and Cooper's erratic driving of course took place in Diming's presence. Diming was also demonstrably aware of Mr. Thompson's concerns for his safety, as he apparently mocked him for being scared. While it is unclear whether Diming, Cooper, or both indicated to Mr. Thompson that the "rough ride" was intended to teach him a lesson, one could infer that Diming, at minimum, heard that threat. Diming was also aware that Mr. Thompson had been injured, having called the prison to report that Mr. Thompson had banged his head. These facts lead to p.109 the inescapable conclusion that Diming was aware of the risk to Mr. Thompson created by Cooper.

We also conclude that a reasonable jury could find that Diming disregarded a known risk of harm by failing to take any reasonable steps to prevent Mr. Thompson from being hurt. In *Odom,* the officer rejected the inmate's pleas to be let out of the cell where he was being attacked. *Id.* at 767-68. Indeed, he took no action until after the victim had suffered broken ribs. *Id.* In this case, Diming exhibited a similar pattern of disregard in the face of escalating risks to Mr. Thompson's safety. Diming initially dismissed Mr. Thompson's request for a seatbelt. He then dismissed Mr. Thompson's fear of injury and taunted him. Even after Mr. Thompson was visibly injured and began bleeding, Diming took no action, whether to ask Cooper to slow down or to finally secure Mr. Thompson's seatbelt. Moreover, there was nothing that prevented Diming from reasonably taking at least some steps to protect Mr. Thompson. A reasonable factfinder could therefore conclude that Diming was aware of a risk to Mr. Thompson's safety, certainly by the time Mr. Thompson was injured, if not earlier, and that Diming consciously disregarded that risk by failing to intervene. *See Raynor,* 817 F.3d at 128.

In sum, viewing the evidence in the light most favorable to Mr. Thompson, he has alleged sufficient facts to satisfy both prongs of the deliberate indifference test. He adequately asserts that he was exposed to the substantial risk of harm of being physically tossed about in an erratic vehicle and that Diming was aware of that risk and disregarded it by failing to take any preventative measures.

b.

The only remaining question is whether Mr. Thompson's right to reasonable protection from a known threat was clearly established as of April 8, 2010, the date of the incident. As before, we first look to controlling authority in the relevant jurisdiction, specifically cases from the Supreme Court, this Court of Appeals, or the highest court of the state in which the action arose. *Owens,* 372 F.3d at 279. We conclude that Mr. Thompson's right was clearly established.

Odom held that, by June 2000, it was clearly established in the Fourth Circuit that "a correctional officer who stands by as a passive observer and takes no action whatsoever to intervene during an assault violates the rights of the victim inmate." 349 F.3d at 773 (denying qualified immunity). Reasonable officials would understand *Odom* to mean that inmates have an Eighth Amendment right to be protected from malicious attacks, not just by other inmates, but also from the very officials tasked with ensuring their security. *See Hope,* 536 U.S. at 739, 122 S.Ct. 2508 ("[C]ontours [of the right] must be sufficiently clear that a reasonable official would understand that what he is doing violates that right."). Similarly, the Supreme Court has held that the law was "not in controversy," even in 1996, that a prison official could be liable for failing to protect a female inmate from subsequent sexual assault if he were aware of a prior incident. *See Ortiz,* 562 U.S. at 189, 131 S.Ct. 884. That understanding is consistent with and buttressed by the related doctrine of bystander liability, which imposes on officers "an affirmative duty to intervene to protect the constitutional rights of citizens from infringement by other law enforcement officers." *Randall,* 302 F.3d at 203 (2002 decision concerning actions in 2000); *see also Skrtich,* 280 F.3d at 1301 ("[A]n officer who is present at the scene and who fails to take reasonable steps to protect the victim of another officer's use p.110 of excessive force can be held personally liable for his nonfeasance.") (applying bystander liability to corrections officer); *Hovater,* 1 F.3d at 1068 (recognizing inmate's right to be protected from known risk of sexual assault by prison guard).

Because controlling authority clearly establishes an inmate's right to reasonable protection from malicious assault, we look no further and conclude that Mr. Thompson's right was clearly established in this case. Accordingly, we reverse the district court's grant of qualified immunity to Officer Diming.

3.

Mr. Thompson's Eighth Amendment claim also attempts to reach Lt. Thompson, Assistant Warden Jennings, and Captain Dolan. However, Mr. Thompson's appellate brief and argument do not address their liability, nor are there any facts that show how any of the three officials were aware of any risk to Mr. Thompson or how any of their actions contributed to his injuries. Accordingly, we summarily affirm the district court's grant of summary judgment in favor of these three defendants.

IV.

We now turn to Claim One, which is Mr. Thompson's First Amendment retaliation claim. He alleges that Defendants Baskerville, Jennings, Ware, Lewis, Dolan, Lt. Thompson, Seay, Blackwell, White, Cooper and Diming violated his First Amendment rights by retaliating against him before, during, and after the April 8, 2010 incident.

We summarily affirm the district court's grant of summary judgment in favor of Baskerville, Jennings, Ware, Lewis, Dolan, Lt. Thompson, Seay, Blackwell, and White because Mr. Thompson has failed to show any facts that could support an inference that the above officials were aware of his past litigation and grievances or that they acted with retaliatory intent.

However, we reverse the district court's grant of summary judgment as to Cooper and Diming because the record supports an inference that they were acting in response to Mr. Thompson being a frequent filer of grievances and litigation. In deciding to grant summary judgment, the district court relied in part on *Adams v. Rice,* 40 F.3d 72 (4th Cir. 1994). However, since the issuance of the district court's decision, this Court clarified the scope of *Adams* in *Booker. See* 855 F.3d at 541-42. On remand, the district court should proceed in light of this intervening authority.

V.

We now turn to Claim Three, which is Mr. Thompson's due process claim against Jennings, Dolan, Lt. Thompson, Cooper, Diming, Lewis, Seay and Blackwell. He alleges that the defendants conspired to cover up the transport incident and provided a sham disciplinary hearing that was the basis for his being held in segregation.

We summarily affirm the district court's grant of summary judgment as to all defendants because administrative segregation from the general population does not implicate a protected liberty interest absent a showing of specific facts that conditions of confinement are significantly more onerous. *Incumaa v. Stirling,* 791 F.3d 517, 531

(4th Cir. 2015). Mr. Thompson's affidavits do not present specific facts demonstrating such hardship. To the extent that Mr. Thompson alleges that segregation was retaliatory punishment, that argument is better addressed under either the First or Eighth Amendment.

VI.

We now turn to Claim Four, Mr. Thompson's supervisory liability claim against Baskerville, Jennings, Ware, Lewis, p.111 Dolan and White. The district court granted summary judgment as to all defendants. *Thompson,* 2015 WL 13065640, at *10.

We summarily affirm because Mr. Thompson only makes conclusory allegations without any specific facts that these defendants had knowledge that retaliation was taking place and that they acquiesced in the retaliatory acts. *See Randall,* 302 F.3d at 206.

VII.

We now turn to Claims Five, Six, and Seven, which are Mr. Thompson's state law claims. All three claims are in federal court on the basis of supplemental jurisdiction. *Thompson,* 2015 WL 13065640, at *10. The district court declined to exercise jurisdiction and dismissed all three claims because the federal claims, which served as the anchor for the state-law claims, had already been dismissed. *Id.*

Since we reverse summary judgment as to some of the anchoring federal claims, we now reverse the district court's decision to dismiss the state law claims and remand for further proceedings.

VIII.

For the foregoing reasons, we reverse summary judgment as to Officers Cooper and Diming on the Eighth Amendment and First Amendment claims; we reverse the district court's dismissal of the state law claims; we affirm the grant of summary judgment as to all other claims and as to all other defendants; and we remand for further proceedings consistent with this opinion.

AFFIRMED IN PART, REVERSED IN PART, AND REMANDED WITH INSTRUCTIONS

[1] We refer to Appellant Thompson as Mr. Thompson throughout in order to distinguish him from VDOC official, Lt. R. Thompson (no relation).

[2] "A 'black box' is a hard plastic box placed over the lock apparatus that runs between the prisoner's handcuffs which make it more difficult for a prisoner to tamper with his handcuffs. A chain runs through the box and encircles the prisoner's waist. The chain is tightened and then locked in back so that the prisoner's hands, restrained by handcuffs and the black box, are pulled against his stomach." *Peoples v. Davis,* No. Civ. A. No. 08-252, 2009 WL 349171, at *2 (D.S.C. Feb. 10, 2009).

[3] Courts, including the Fourth Circuit, have pointed out a "special problem" that arises when applying the qualified immunity analysis in an Eighth Amendment case.

Appellees' Br. at 19. Specifically, some courts skip the "clearly established" prong entirely upon finding deliberate indifference, because an officer's knowing violation of the law is *per se* unreasonable. *See Cox v. Quinn,* 828 F.3d 227, 238, n.4 (4th Cir. 2016) (raising issue and summarizing other courts' approaches but declining to decide issue). However, as in *Cox,* we do not need to reach this issue because we hold that the clearly established prong is satisfied.

[4] Appellees argue that Mr. Thompson's allegations of reckless driving are too conclusory to be considered. Appellees' Br. at 28. However, they are virtually identical to the statements credited by the Eighth Circuit in *Fortner,* and we conclude that they are sufficiently specific here. *See* 518 F.3d at 559.

[5] Applying the deliberate indifference standard would also create symmetry with the test used to establish bystander liability, which is similar in principle to what Mr. Thompson alleges against Diming. *See Randall v. Prince George's Cty., Md.,* 302 F.3d 188, 204 (4th Cir. 2002) ("[A]n officer may be liable under § 1983, on a theory of bystander liability, if he: (1) knows that a fellow officer is violating an individual's constitutional rights; (2) has a reasonable opportunity to prevent the harm; and (3) chooses not to act.").

FIFTH CIRCUIT DECISIONS

The Affirmative Defense of Qualified Immunity for Law Enforcement

948 F.3d 281 (2020)

Kenneth RATLIFF, Plaintiff-Appellant

v.

ARANSAS COUNTY, TEXAS; Colby Scudder, Individually; Raymond Sheffield, Individually, Defendants-Appellees.

No. 19-40121.

United States Court of Appeals, Fifth Circuit.

FILED January 15, 2020.

Ratliff v. Aransas County, Texas, 948 F. 3d 281 (5th Cir. 2020)

Appeal from the United States District Court for the Southern District of Texas.

Christopher John Gale, Amie Augenstein, Gale Law Group, Corpus Christi, TX, for Plaintiff-Appellant.

Casey Terrance Cullen, Cullen, Carsner, Seerden & Cullen, L.L.P., Victoria, TX, for Defendants-Appellees.

Before JOLLY, SMITH, and COSTA, Circuit Judges.

p.283 E. GRADY JOLLY, Circuit Judge:

Kenneth Ratliff was shot five times when he refused to drop his weapon during an armed confrontation with two sheriff's deputies in Aransas County, Texas. He survived and was later acquitted of criminal assault. He proceeded to sue both deputies, as well as the county, under 42 U.S.C. § 1983, alleging that the deputies used unreasonable and excessive force in violation of the Fourth Amendment. The district court dismissed Ratliff's "official custom" and "failure to train" claims against Aransas County, finding that Ratliff's pleadings failed plausibly to establish municipal liability under *Monell v. Dep't of Soc. Servs.*, 436 U.S. 658, 694, 98 S.Ct. 2018, 56 L.Ed.2d 611 (1978). Later, the court awarded summary judgment to the deputies, holding that Ratliff had failed to rebut their qualified immunity defense. Ratliff appeals; we affirm.

I.

At approximately 3:00 a.m., on March 24, 2015, Aransas County sheriff's deputies were dispatched to a residence in Rockport, Texas, where Kenneth Ratliff was living with Tanya Vannatter, his fiancée. The deputies, Colby Scudder and Raymond Sheffield, had been requested by Vannatter, who reported in a 911 call that Ratliff had beaten her earlier in the evening.

When the deputies arrived, Vannatter explained that Ratliff had been drinking "all day and all night," and that, when she caught him sending text messages to another woman, he went "ballistic." More specifically, Vannatter said that Ratliff had thrown her to the ground, punched her "everywhere," and choked her with such force that she thought she would die. She was reluctant to press charges. But she did request that the deputies ask Ratliff to leave home voluntarily.

As Vannatter and the deputies walked toward Ratliff's front porch, Ratliff began shouting, "Get the f*** off my property." Ratliff was holding a loaded, semi-automatic pistol, but he had not chambered a round. The parties dispute whether the pistol was ever pointed at the deputies, but it is undisputed that the deputies issued five orders to disarm moments before the shooting. Ratliff responded, "shoot me ... shoot me" and "hey, you're on my property." Deputy Scudder fired nine shots, and Ratliff sustained five gunshot wounds. The whole encounter lasted about twenty-five seconds. The deputies called an ambulance p.284 immediately, and paramedics arrived in time to tend to Ratliff, who survived.

II.

Texas authorities charged Ratliff with aggravated assault on a police officer, but he was later acquitted by a jury. Ratliff then sued Deputy Scudder, Deputy Sheffield, and Aransas County under 42 U.S.C. § 1983, alleging that Deputy Scudder violated clearly established law by using deadly force, that Deputy Sheffield violated clearly established law by failing to prevent deadly force, and that Aransas County should be held responsible because the deputies' actions reflect the county's "customary practice[,] ... policy or procedure."[1] The district court quickly dismissed Ratliff's claim against the county, however, holding that Ratliff had failed to plead sufficiently specific facts in support of his "official custom" and "failure to train" theories of *Monell* liability.

Then, on a motion for summary judgment, the district court also disposed of Ratliff's excessive force claims against the deputies. The district court found that Deputy's Scudder's use of deadly force was not objectively unreasonable under the circumstances and that Ratliff could not therefore meet his burden to rebut the defense of qualified immunity. That finding was also fatal to Ratliff's claim against Deputy Sheffield. Ratliff's entire suit was dismissed with prejudice. This appeal followed.

III.

Ratliff raises three issues on appeal. He argues that the district court erred: (1) by granting defendants' motion to dismiss the *Monell* claim against Aransas County, (2) by excluding testimony given by Ratliff in his earlier criminal trial from the summary judgment record in this civil action, and (3) by awarding summary judgment to the deputies on qualified immunity grounds. We will address each issue in turn.

A.

We first consider Ratliff's challenge to the dismissal of his *Monell* claim. Ratliff argues that his pleadings satisfy both the familiar pleading standard established by *Bell Atl. Corp. v. Twombly,* 550 U.S. 544, 127 S.Ct. 1955, 167 L.Ed.2d 929 (2007), and a lower-than-normal pleading standard that, according to Ratliff, applies in the *Monell* context under *Leatherman v. Tarrant County Narcotics Intelligence & Coordination Unit,* 507 U.S. 163, 113 S.Ct. 1160, 122 L.Ed.2d 517 (1993). He can prevail on neither count.

Initially, we note that the ordinary *Twombly* pleading standard applies. It is, of course, true that *Leatherman,* a pre-*Twombly* case, held that courts must not apply a "heightened" pleading standard to *Monell* claims. *See id.* at 168, 113 S.Ct. 1160. Although Ratliff argues otherwise, however, *Leatherman* did not require courts to accept "generic or boilerplate" pleadings in this case or in any other context. Indeed, our precedents make clear that the *Twombly* standard applies to municipal liability claims. *See Peña v. City of Rio Grande City,* 879 F.3d 613, 621-22 (5th Cir. 2018); *Doe ex rel. Magee v. Covington Cty. Sch. Dist. ex rel. Keys,* 675 F.3d 849, 866 n.10 (5th Cir. 2012) (en banc). "To survive a motion to dismiss," Ratliff's *Monell* pleadings "must contain sufficient factual matter, accepted as true, p.285 to state a claim to relief that is plausible on its face." *Ashcroft v. Iqbal,* 556 U.S. 662, 678, 129 S.Ct. 1937, 173 L.Ed.2d 868 (2009) (quotation omitted).

Reviewing *de novo,* we find no error in the district court's conclusion that Ratliff has failed to produce sufficient pleadings. To state a *Monell* claim against Aransas County, Ratliff was required to plead facts that plausibly establish: "a policymaker; an official policy; and a violation of constitutional rights whose 'moving force' is the policy or custom." *Piotrowski v. City of Houston,* 237 F.3d 567, 578 (5th Cir. 2001). The district court held that Ratliff's complaint fails to establish an official custom or policy of excessive force because "[t]he only facts [that Ratliff] allege[d] with any specificity ... relate to his shooting." This assessment is correct.

"[P]lausibly to plead a practice 'so persistent and widespread as to practically have the force of law,' [Ratliff] must do more than describe the incident that gave rise to his injury." *Peña,* 879 F.3d at 622. Ratliff's complaint states that "the assault, beating, and severe injury to citizens, with little or no justification, is a persistent, widespread practice of County employees—namely officers/deputies— that, although not authorized by officially adopted policy, is so common and well settled as to constitute a custom that fairly represents official county policy." But this allegation does not contain any specific facts. Instead, the complaint's only specific facts appear in the section laying out the events that gave rise to this action. Thus, Ratliff's complaint clearly does not satisfy *Twombly* or *Iqbal* with respect to the allegation that excessive force is an Aransas County "custom."

In addition to this theory of widespread and customary police brutality, Ratliff also alleged that "Defendant County is liable for [the] inadequate training of police officers." To prevail on a failure-to-train theory, Ratliff must plead facts plausibly establishing "(1) that the municipality's training procedures were inadequate, (2) that the municipality was deliberately indifferent in adopting its training policy, and (3) that the inadequate training policy directly caused the violations in question." *Zarnow v. City of Wichita Falls,* 614 F.3d 161, 170 (5th Cir. 2010).

Ratliff has failed to carry this burden. Although the district court focused on the first two failure-to-train elements, "we may affirm a district court's [Federal Rule of Civil Procedure] 12(b)(6) dismissal on any grounds raised below and supported by the record." *Cuvillier v. Taylor,* 503 F.3d 397, 401 (5th Cir. 2007). Before the district court, the defendants argued that Ratliff's failure-to-train pleadings were insufficient with respect to the element of causation. It is clear that this argument is meritorious. Ratliff's complaint states in conclusory fashion that a "deficiency in training actually caused Defendants Scudder and Sheffield to violate Plaintiff's constitutional rights." But, absent specific allegations supporting a plausible causation inference, this legal conclusion does not state a claim for relief and warrants dismissal under Rule 12(b)(6).

In short, we hold that the district court did not err in dismissing Ratliff's claim against Aransas County and, consequently, affirm its judgment dismissing the county from this case.

B.

We next examine Ratliff's argument that the district court erred by excluding testimony that Ratliff gave in his earlier criminal trial. He offered the testimony because of a failing memory and to rebut the deputies' p.286 qualified immunity defense in this § 1983 case. This previous testimony was attached, as part of a forty-page exhibit, to Ratliff's response to the defendants' summary judgment motion. The exhibit also included the testimony of other trial witnesses, including Vannatter and Deputy Scudder. The defendants objected only to Ratliff's testimony, arguing that such testimony was inadmissible hearsay to which no exception applied. The district court sustained the objection in a footnote but did not provide analysis or reasoning.

On appeal, Ratliff does not explain why any of the excluded testimony would have been relevant to the issues raised at summary judgment. The testimony could have evidenced only two plausibly-relevant facts: (1) that Ratliff did not know who was approaching his residence when he yelled, "Get the f*** off my property," and (2) that Ratliff did not "raise [his] gun and point it" at anyone, instead holding it "in [his] right hand ... down [at his] side" for the duration of his encounter with the deputies.

"[A]n appeal of a summary judgment presenting evidentiary issues raises two levels of inquiry." *Skotak v. Tenneco Resins, Inc.,* 953 F.2d 909, 916 (5th Cir. 1992) (quotation omitted). First, we review the district court's evidentiary rulings for abuse of discretion. *Id.* Then, once the summary judgment record is "define[d]," we review *de novo* whether summary judgment was appropriately granted. *Id.* Indeed, here, we cannot determine whether the district court's summary judgment order was erroneous until we have "defined" the summary judgment record, *i.e.,* until we have ruled on Ratliff's challenge to the exclusion of his earlier criminal testimony. We thus address Ratliff's evidentiary arguments first, before turning to the merits of the district court's summary judgment order.

We first entertain the defendants' argument that any error in excluding Ratliff's prior testimony was harmless. If it were, we may assume that the exclusion was erroneous and affirm nevertheless. *Saratoga Res., Inc. v. Lexington Ins. Co.,* 642 F. App'x 359, 363 n.10 (5th Cir. 2016) (citing *Matador Petroleum Corp. v. St. Paul Surplus Lines Ins. Co.,* 174 F.3d 653 (5th Cir. 1999)). An error is harmless unless it affects "substantial rights." Fed. R. Civ. P. 61. Ratliff, as the "party asserting... error," bears the burden of proving such prejudice. *Ball v. LeBlanc,* 792 F.3d 584, 591 (5th Cir. 2015).

But no prejudice has been shown. As we have already said, Ratliff's appellate brief does not even explain why the excluded testimony was relevant, let alone demonstrate that its exclusion affected his "substantial rights." Fed. R. Civ. P. 61. On the contrary, none of the points, which we may assume from the excluded testimony, was relevant to the district court's decision to enter summary judgment. Ratliff's testimony that he did not know who was approaching his home on the night of the shooting was irrelevant because, in the context of qualified immunity, the district court assessed the "reasonableness of [Deputy Scudder's] use of force ... from the perspective of a reasonable officer on the scene," not from Ratliff's perspective. Similarly, "the direction of [Ratliff's] gun" was immaterial to the district court's analysis: the district court reasoned that, irrespective of the gun's direction, Deputy Scudder's force was justified because "other facts [had] establish[ed] that the suspect was a threat to the officer[s]," which would include the fact that Ratliff had been accused of a violent crime, the fact that Ratliff was drunk and confrontational, and the fact that Ratliff had ignored five p.287 orders to drop his weapon.[2]

To sum up, we find that, even if the district court erred by excluding testimony from Ratliff's criminal trial, such error was harmless and the testimony's exclusion thus furnishes no basis for reversal.

C.

Finally, we consider the substantive merits of Ratliff's appeal: whether the district court erred by accepting the deputies' qualified immunity defense and awarding them summary judgment. "We review a grant of summary judgment *de novo,* viewing all evidence in the light most favorable to the nonmoving party and drawing all reasonable inferences in that party's favor." *Gonzalez v. Huerta,* 826 F.3d 854, 856 (5th Cir. 2016) (quotation omitted).

Typically, to prevail on a motion for summary judgment, the moving party must show "that there is no genuine dispute as to any material fact." Fed. R. Civ. P. 56(a). However, "[a] good-faith assertion of qualified immunity alters the usual summary judgment burden of proof, shifting it to the plaintiff to show that the defense is not available." *Orr v. Copeland,* 844 F.3d 484, 490 (5th Cir. 2016) (quotation omitted).

So, here, Ratliff was required to adduce summary judgment evidence indicating that the deputies' actions "violate[d] clearly established ... constitutional rights of which a reasonable person would have known." *Mullenix v. Luna,* ___ U.S. ___, 136 S. Ct. 305, 308, 193 L.Ed.2d 255 (2015) (quotation omitted). To determine whether he has done so, we will assume genuinely disputed facts in his favor and engage in a two-pronged inquiry. "The first [prong] asks whether the facts... show [that] the officer's conduct violated a [constitutional or statutory] right." *Tolan v. Cotton,* 572 U.S. 650, 655-56, 134 S.Ct. 1861, 188 L.Ed.2d 895 (2014) (brackets and ellipsis added). The second "asks whether the right in question was 'clearly established' at the time of the violation." *Id.* at 656, 134 S.Ct. 1861. For a right to be clearly established, "its contours must be sufficiently clear that a reasonable official would understand that what he is doing violates that right." *Hope v. Pelzer,* 536 U.S. 730, 739, 122 S.Ct. 2508, 153 L.Ed.2d 666 (2002) (quotation omitted).

The district court focused exclusively on the first prong of the qualified immunity analysis, concluding that the right at issue here, Ratliff's Fourth Amendment right to be free from unreasonable and excessive force, was not violated when Deputy Scudder opened fire. *See Cleveland v. Bell,* 938 F.3d 672, 676 (5th Cir. 2019) ("If the plaintiff fails at either step, [a] federal court can grant qualified immunity by addressing either step or both of them."). To establish a Fourth Amendment violation in this context, Ratliff must establish "(1) [an] injury (2) which resulted directly and only from a use of force that was clearly excessive, and (3) the excessiveness of which was clearly unreasonable." *Freeman v. Gore,* 483 F.3d 404, 416 (5th Cir. 2007). Only the second and third of these elements are at issue. The question is whether Deputy Scudder's resort to deadly force was unreasonable and excessive when the facts are viewed "from the perspective of a reasonable officer on the scene, rather than with the p.288 20/20 vision of hindsight." *Graham v. Connor,* 490 U.S. 386, 396, 109 S.Ct. 1865, 104 L.Ed.2d 443 (1989).

Our recent opinion in *Garza v. Briones* speaks to this question. Prior to *Garza,* our cases had clearly established that deadly force is not unreasonable when an armed suspect has ignored multiple orders to disarm and has either pointed his weapon at a person or used the weapon in such a manner as to make a threatening gesture. *See, e.g., Ramirez v. Knoulton,* 542 F.3d 124, 127-31 (5th Cir. 2008) (officer's use of deadly force was not a Fourth Amendment violation where an armed suspect failed to comply with an order to drop his weapon and then "brought his hands together in front of his waist" as if "in preparation to aim [his gun] at the officers"); *see also Mace v. City of Palestine,* 333 F.3d 621, 624-25 (5th Cir. 2003) (deadly force was not objectively unreasonable when a suspect had "brandish[ed]" an eighteen to twenty inch sword" and failed to "respond to commands to drop his sword or to stop moving toward [police] officers"); *Ballard v. Burton,* 444 F.3d 391, 402-03 (5th Cir. 2006) (deadly force was not unreasonable when a suspect had "refused to put down his rifle, discharged the rifle into the air several times while near the officers, and pointed it in the general direction of [the] officers," even though the suspect was not pointing his gun at anyone when he was shot).

Garza further adds to this line of cases. In *Garza,* police officers received reports that a man was "sitting alone in front of [a] truck stop's bar playing with a pistol and holding what appeared to be a wine bottle and a plastic bag." 943 F.3d at 743. When the officers arrived, they discovered a suspect holding a gun, later revealed to be a BB gun. *Id.* One of the officers ordered the suspect to drop the weapon, but he "did not do so and instead continued to move the firearm around in different directions while making facial gestures." *Id.* "At that time, [the suspect] did not have his finger on the trigger and was not pointing the gun at anyone." *Id.* Nevertheless, the suspect was later shot and killed. *Id.* The administrator of the suspect's estate sued the officers under § 1983, alleging that the officers' resort to deadly force was unreasonable, excessive, and a violation of the Fourth Amendment. *Id.* at 744.

We rejected those allegations. We held that, when "confronting an unpredictable man armed with a dangerous weapon," law enforcement officers "may use deadly force ... without violating the Fourth Amendment." *Id.* at 745. The plaintiff in *Garza* argued, as Ratliff argues now, that "a reasonable jury could find that [the suspect] never pointed his gun at the officers." *Id.* at 746. In support of this argument, the plaintiff relied on an affidavit from one of the officer-defendants, which stated that the suspect "did not at any time point the gun [at the] cops." *Id.* at 747. Although we found that video evidence had conclusively contradicted the affiant's statement, we explained that this fact was not essential to the outcome and further held that a "reasonable officer in any of the defendants' shoes would have believed that [the suspect] posed a serious threat regardless of the direction [of his] gun." *Id.*

Thus, in *Garza,* we found that it is not unreasonable for law enforcement officers to use deadly force against an armed suspect, irrespective of the pointed direction of that suspect's weapon, when the suspect has ignored orders to drop the weapon and has displayed erratic or aggressive behavior indicating that he may pose an imminent threat. We can concede that, here, unlike in *Garza,* the video evidence is inconclusive with respect to the direction of Ratliff's gun. Moreover, we are willing to p.289 accept that the gun's direction is genuinely disputed. But we cannot agree that the pointed direction of Ratliff's gun is material in the context of these facts. Once Ratliff had ignored repeated warnings to drop his weapon, the deputies here, like the officers in *Garza,* had ample reason to fear for their safety.[3]

Thus, we concur in the district court's conclusion that the deputies were entitled to qualified immunity. Ratliff simply has not met his burden to establish a Fourth Amendment violation in the form of unreasonable and excessive force, much less a violation that every reasonable officer in Deputy Scudder's position would appreciate. *See Hope,* 536 U.S. at 739, 122 S.Ct. 2508. The district court was correct to enter summary judgment in favor of both deputies.[4]

IV.

In sum, we hold that the district court committed no reversible error in its dismissal of Ratliff's *Monell* claim against Aransas County, nor in its decision to exclude testimony given in Ratliff's criminal trial, nor in its decision to award summary judgment to both deputies under the doctrine of qualified immunity. The district court's judgment is therefore, in all respects,

AFFIRMED.

[1] Ratliff's complaint also contained a "malicious prosecution" claim that the district court dismissed for failure to "tie [the allegedly malicious prosecution] to rights locatable in constitutional text." *Cf. Castellano v. Fragozo,* 352 F.3d 939, 945 (5th Cir. 2003) (en banc). Ratliff does not challenge the dismissal of that claim on appeal.

[2] As we shall explain later, our cases support the district court's conclusion that, because Ratliff ignored five orders to disarm and engaged in threatening behavior, Deputy Scudder's force was not unreasonable even assuming that Ratliff never raised his gun. *See Garza v. Briones,* 943 F.3d 740, 747 (5th Cir. 2019).

[3] The deputies had been told that Ratliff was drunk and that he had nearly killed a person earlier in the night. When they arrived on the scene, Ratliff dared the deputies to shoot him, cursed at the deputies to get off his property, and ignored the deputies' lawful commands to disarm. Although we accept that it is genuinely disputed whether Ratliff knew that he was dealing with law enforcement, we again note that facts about *Ratliff's* knowledge are beside the point. We examine the reasonableness of Deputy Scudder's force "from the perspective of a reasonable officer on the scene." *Graham,* 490 U.S. at 396, 109 S.Ct. 1865. There is no genuine dispute about whether Deputy Scudder could reasonably have believed that Ratliff knew he was confronting the police. After all, the deputies were in uniform and, although it was dark, the area was illuminated by lights from Deputy Sheffield's squad car.

[4] In his initial brief on appeal, Ratliff does not challenge the district court's dismissal of the claim against Deputy Sheffield, other than to generally assert that summary judgment should not have been awarded to "Appellees." As such, he has waived on appeal any argument that the district court improperly dismissed this

claim. *McKay v. Novartis Pharm. Corp.*, 751 F.3d 694, 702 n.6 (5th Cir. 2014) (issues not raised and argued in an appellant's initial brief are abandoned).

952 F.3d 216 (2020)

Eleanor KELLER, individually and on behalf of all Heirs-at-Law and/or wrongful death beneficiaries of Gerald Simpson, Deceased; The Estate of Gerald Simpson, by and through Glen Simpson, Administrator of Estate, Plaintiffs-Appellees,

v.

Darrin FLEMING, Defendant-Appellant.

No. 18-60081.

United States Court of Appeals, Fifth Circuit.

February 20, 2020.

Keller v. Fleming, 952 F. 3d 216 (5th Cir. 2020)

Appeal from the United States District Court Northern District of Mississippi.

Carlos Eugene Moore, Esq., Moore Law Office, P.L.L.C., Grenada, MS, for Plaintiffs-Appellees.

Daniel J. Griffith, Esq., Jacks Griffith Luciano, P.A., Cleveland, MS, for Defendant-Appellant.

Before STEWART, DENNIS, and WILLETT, Circuit Judges.

p.219 CARL E. STEWART, Circuit Judge:

The original opinion was filed on July 23, 2019 and later WITHDRAWN. *Keller v. Fleming*, 930 F.3d 746 (5th Cir. 2019). We substitute the following:

Following decedent Gerald Simpson's death in which a motorist struck and killed him, Plaintiffs[1] filed suit against, *inter alia,* Deputy Darrin Fleming of the Attala County Sheriff's Department, alleging Fourth and Fourteenth Amendment violations. Fleming filed a motion for summary judgment asserting a qualified immunity defense on each claim. The district court denied the motion, and Fleming timely filed an interlocutory appeal. Concluding that the district court erred in denying qualified immunity as to both the Fourth and Fourteenth Amendment claims, we REVERSE and RENDER judgment in Deputy Fleming's favor.

I.

On January 26, 2015, Gerald Simpson, a mentally infirmed man, was walking in the middle of Highway 12 in Kosciusko, Mississippi.[2] Around 5:00 p.m., an individual witnessed Simpson walking and contacted the authorities. The Kosciusko Police Department responded to the dispatch call. Officer Steve Allan arrived and stopped Simpson and "asked [him] to step out of the highway."[3] He determined that Simpson was outside the city limits and within Attala County's jurisdiction so he alerted the Attala County Sheriff's Department. Waiting for Attala County law enforcement to arrive, Officer Allan attempted to question Simpson, but he was unable to understand Simpson due to his incoherent speech. Simpson continuously pointed westward down the highway.

Kosciusko Police Officer Maurice Hawthorne arrived and replaced Officer Allan, who left to respond to another call. p.220 Simpson then began to resume his walk down the highway. "Officer Hawthorne followed him in his patrol vehicle until he was able to convince Simpson to sit in the backseat of his vehicle."[4] Simpson sat with his feet on the ground with the door still open.

Deputy Fleming of Attala County arrived on the scene, "at which point the officers purportedly decided to take Simpson to his residence, though both officers acknowledge that Simpson was still incoherent."[5] Deputy Fleming put Simpson in the back seat of his vehicle and asked Simpson where he resided. He was unable to articulate the location of his residence and instead pointed west on Highway 12, in the direction of Durant, Mississippi. Deputy Fleming did not ask for Simpson's exact address or identification card. Based on Simpson pointing west, Deputy Fleming transported Simpson in that direction until he reached the Attala County line which was sometime after 5:00 p.m. Deputy Fleming then pulled over, opened the back door of his patrol vehicle, Simpson exited the vehicle, and Simpson continued walking toward Durant on County Road 4101, outside of Attala County's jurisdiction. "Deputy Fleming testified that there was barely enough daylight to see someone walking, but that it was not dark yet."[6] Later that night[7], Simpson was struck by a vehicle and killed as he "was walking east, back toward Kosciusko."[8]

Plaintiffs filed this wrongful death action against City of Kosciusko, Officers Allan and Hawthorne, Attala County, and Deputy Fleming. They alleged, pursuant to 42 U.S.C. § 1983, that the officers' actions violated Simpson's constitutional rights under the Fourth Amendment for wrongful seizure and the substantive due process clause of the Fourteenth Amendment. The district court granted summary judgment in favor of the City of Kosciusko and Officers Allan and Hawthorne.[9] As to Attala County and Deputy Fleming, the court granted only partial summary judgment, finding that genuine issues of material fact existed as to Plaintiffs' constitutional claims. Deputy Fleming appealed.[10]

II.

An interlocutory order denying qualified immunity is immediately appealable "to the extent that it turns on an issue of law." *Gobert v. Caldwell,* 463 F.3d 339, 344 (5th Cir. 2006) (internal quotation marks and citation omitted). Our jurisdiction over such an appeal is limited. *See id.* We must accept the plaintiff's version of events as true, and we may review de novo "only whether the district court erred in assessing the legal significance of the conduct that [it] deemed sufficiently supported for purposes of summary judgment." *Kinney v. Weaver,* 367 F.3d 337, 348 (5th Cir. 2004) (en banc); *Juarez v. Aguilar,* 666 F.3d 325, 331-32 (5th Cir. 2011) ("Where factual disputes exist in an interlocutory appeal asserting qualified immunity, p.221 we accept the plaintiff's version of the facts as true." (quoting *Kinney,* 367 F.3d at 348) (cleaned up)). "[We also] must view the evidence 'in the light most favorable to the opposing party'"— here, Plaintiffs. *Tolan v. Cotton,* 572 U.S. 650, 134 S. Ct. 1861, 1866, 188 L.Ed.2d 895 (2014) (quoting *Adickes v. S.H. Kress & Co.,* 398 U.S. 144, 157, 90 S.Ct. 1598, 26 L.Ed.2d 142 (1970)).

In turn, we accept the district court's determination that genuine "questions of material fact" existed as to whether "Deputy Fleming acted on a custom of picking up those viewed as vagrants and dropping them off in neighboring jurisdictions so as to rid Attala County of the problem." *Keller v. Attala County,* No. 1:16-cv-136-SA-DAS, 2018 WL 615681, at *5 (N.D. Miss. Jan. 29, 2018).[11]

If assuming the version of the disputed events (most favorably to the plaintiff) still does not give rise to a violation of clearly established law, then reversal is appropriate. *Kinney,* 367 F.3d at 347-48.

III.

Plaintiffs bear the burden to rebut Deputy Fleming's qualified immunity defense and demonstrate that there were Fourth and Fourteenth Amendment rights that were clearly established at the time of the constitutional violation. *See, e.g., King v. Handorf,* 821 F.3d 650, 653-54 (5th Cir. 2016) (noting that a "good-faith assertion of qualified immunity alters the usual summary judgment burden of proof") (quoting *Cass v. City of Abilene,* 814 F.3d 721, 728 (5th Cir. 2016)).

In evaluating the qualified immunity defense, the familiar two-step analysis controlling our review is whether (1) "'the facts alleged show the officer's conduct violated a constitutional right'; and [(2)], 'whether the right was clearly established.'" *Trammell v. Fruge,* 868 F.3d 332, 339 (5th Cir. 2017) (quoting *Saucier v. Katz,* 533 U.S. 194, 201, 121 S.Ct. 2151, 150 L.Ed.2d 272 (2001)). We review the district court's resolution of these legal issues— the scope of clearly established law and the objective reasonableness of the defendant government officials' actions—de novo. *See Rockwell v. Brown,* 664 F.3d 985, 991 (5th Cir. 2011); *see also Lytle v. Bexar County,* 560 F.3d 404, 409 (5th Cir. 2009). We have discretion to address either prong of the qualified immunity inquiry first. *See Pearson v. Callahan,* 555 U.S. 223, 236, 129 S.Ct. 808, 172 L.Ed.2d 565 (2009) (noting that "two-step procedure promotes the development of constitutional precedent and is especially valuable for questions that do not frequently arise in cases in which a qualified immunity defense is unavailable").

p.222 We first "answer the constitutional violation question by determining whether the officer's conduct met the Fourth Amendment's reasonableness requirement." *See Lytle,* 560 F.3d at 410.

Fourth Amendment

Plaintiffs' wrongful seizure claim implicates the Fourth Amendment's prohibition on unreasonable seizures as the basis for a constitutional violation. U.S. Const. amend. IV.

Our Fourth Amendment de novo analysis begins with whether Simpson was seized, and assuming a seizure has occurred, we then evaluate the seizure's reasonableness and the clearly established law prong. *McLin v. Ard.,* 866 F.3d 682, 691 (5th Cir. 2017) (reviewing whether a seizure occurred under the qualified immunity framework de novo); *United States v. Cooper,* 949 F.2d 737, 744 (5th Cir. 1991) (stating that "the ultimate question of the legality of the ... seizure is a question of law alone [that this court must answer]" subject to a de novo review).

Seizure. The district court determined that Simpson was seized.[12]

Fleming's position is that the district court erroneously considered his subjective intentions of his encounter with Simpson, rather than applying an objectively reasonable standard. Irrespective of the court questioning Fleming's motive during these events, Fleming is silent on the issue of seizure.[13] Plaintiffs, on the other hand, contend that Fleming improperly seized Simpson in placing Simpson in the back of his patrol vehicle and not allowing him to exit the car without Fleming's authority or assistance. While Fleming is correct that the court analyzes seizure using an objectively reasonable test, it is Plaintiffs who are ultimately correct.

Under the Fourth Amendment, a seizure occurs when, under the totality of the circumstances, a reasonable person would have thought he was not free to leave. *Michigan v. Chesternut,* 486 U.S. 567, 572, 108 S.Ct. 1975, 100 L.Ed.2d 565 (1988) (citation omitted). "[W]henever a police officer accosts an individual and restrains his freedom to walk away, he has seized that person." *Terry v. Ohio,* 392 U.S. 1, 16, 88 S.Ct. 1868, 20 L.Ed.2d 889 (1968) (internal quotations omitted).

Assuming the district court's version of the events to be true, Simpson's freedom of movement was restrained and a reasonable person in Simpson's position would not have felt free to leave. The officers' collective supervision and actions support this finding. Here, when Simpson tried to walk down the highway again[14], p.223 Officer Hawthorne followed him in his patrol car until he had to pull off because there was "no room."[15] Once the vehicle was pulled off to the side, Officer Hawthorne persuaded Simpson to stop and sit in the backseat of his patrol car. In other words, Officer Hawthorne interrupted Simpson's path and "intercept[ed] him to prevent his progress"—which is "probably decisive" in assessing seizure. *United States v. Berry,* 670 F.2d 583, 597 (5th Cir. 1982) (blocking defendant's path at an airport constituted a seizure) (citation omitted). This is likely when the seizure began, and it likely did not end until Simpson was dropped off because as the district court stated, "Fleming [subsequently] put Simpson in the backseat of his vehicle" and drove for several miles, and finally just "pulled over and opened the door of his patrol vehicle" when he reached the county line. *Keller,* 2018 WL 615681, at *1. This is an example of a show of authority restraining Simpson's freedom to leave, triggering the Fourth Amendment. *Florida v. Bostick,* 501 U.S. 429, 434, 111 S.Ct. 2382, 115 L.Ed.2d 389 (1991). ("The encounter will not trigger Fourth Amendment scrutiny unless it loses its consensual nature ... 'Only when the officer, by means of physical force or show of authority, has in some way restrained the liberty of a citizen may we conclude that a 'seizure' has occurred.'") (quoting *Terry,* 392 U.S. at 16 n.16, 88 S.Ct. 1868).

Consequently, we affirm the district court's seizure finding.

Unreasonableness. We now determine whether this seizure was reasonable under the Fourth Amendment.

Absent probable cause, warrantless searches and seizures are presumptively invalid or "*per se*" unreasonable under the Fourth Amendment—subject only to a few specifically established and well delineated exceptions." *Katz v. United States,* 389 U.S. 347, 357, 88 S.Ct. 507, 19 L.Ed.2d 576 (1967); *compare with United States v. Morris,* 477 F.2d 657, 663 (5th Cir. 1973) ("A warrantless arrest is nevertheless valid if the arresting officer has probable cause to believe that the person arrested has committed or is in the act of committing a crime."). As such, Deputy Fleming now bears the burden in proving that the seizure of question was either supported by probable cause or falls within one of the few well-delineated exceptions to the warrant requirement. *United States v. Roch,* 5 F.3d 894, 897 (5th Cir. 1993) ("While in general

... the defendant has the burden of proving ... that the material in question was seized in violation of his constitutional rights, there are several situations where the burden shifts to the government.") (citation omitted).

Here, Deputy Fleming's appellate brief is unclear as to what warrant exceptions justified the seizure of Simpson.[16] Fleming p.224 does not contend that he had probable cause to believe that Simpson was guilty of criminal activity nor does he state that he had a reasonable suspicion of such criminal activity. He continues to rely on his subjective mindset. He also maintains that he was only giving Simpson a courtesy ride and his brief states that "Attala County Sheriff's Department has a history of offering to give pedestrians courtesy rides if there is a need for it or for their own safety."[17] But he goes no further into how this policy or this specific courtesy ride fits within the prism of our well-delineated warrant exceptions. Therefore, Deputy Fleming did not satisfy his burden in justifying this stop because any argument to that effect was forfeited. *See Cinel v. Connick,* 15 F.3d 1338, 1345 (5th Cir. 1994) ("A party who inadequately briefs an issue is considered to have abandoned the claim.").

Accordingly, without a valid exception to the probable cause requirement, the seizure is therefore presumptively unreasonable, and a constitutional violation is present.

Clearly Established Law. Plaintiffs must still demonstrate that there was a clearly established right at the time of the challenged actions. Thus, the question becomes whether there is precedent that put Deputy Fleming on notice that he was committing a constitutional violation when he drove Simpson several miles to the county line and dropped him off.

p.225 For purposes of determining whether the right was clearly established, "[t]he relevant question ... is ... whether a reasonable officer could have believed [his or her conduct] to be lawful, in light of clearly established law and the information the ... officers possessed." *Anderson v. Creighton,* 483 U.S. 635, 641, 107 S.Ct. 3034, 97 L.Ed.2d 523 (1987). In other words, Plaintiffs must point this court to a legislative directive or case precedent that is sufficiently clear such that every reasonable official would have understood that what he is doing violates that law. *Reichle v. Howards,* 566 U.S. 658, 664, 132 S.Ct. 2088, 182 L.Ed.2d 985 (2012) (citing *Ashcroft v. al-Kidd,* 563 U.S. 731, 741, 131 S.Ct. 2074, 179 L.Ed.2d 1149 (2011)).

Here, Plaintiffs' burden is not met. Plaintiffs' clearly established law contentions in their briefing are in fact a narrative as to why Deputy Fleming's seizure was unreasonable. Plaintiffs' narrative argument is of no import of a pre-existing or precedential case. *Kovacic v. Villarreal,* 628 F.3d 209, 214 (5th Cir. 2010) ("Plaintiffs have not referenced a single case in either the district courts or the court of appeals of this circuit in which state actors were held liable for private harm caused to an individual after he was released from custody."). In turn, there is no binding Supreme Court or Fifth Circuit precedent to anchor our de novo review of whether a similarly situated officer violated a constitutional right acting under similar circumstances. *See White v. Pauly,* ___ U.S. ___, 137 S. Ct. 548, 551, 196 L.Ed.2d 463 (2017) (per curiam) ("[F]or a right to be clearly established, 'existing precedent must have placed the statutory or constitutional question beyond debate.'") (quoting *Mullenix v. Luna,* ___ U.S. ___, 136 S. Ct. 305, 308, 193 L.Ed.2d 255 (2015)). Without setting forth a clearly established right for which the analysis can continue, Plaintiffs have not defeated

Deputy Fleming's qualified immunity defense. *Cass,* 814 F.3d at 732-33 (granting qualified immunity because plaintiffs failed to show an existing precedent of the constitutional violation).

Of note, the dissent cites to *Hope v. Pelzer* for the proposition that "general statements of the law are not inherently incapable of giving fair and clear warning" and "general constitutional rule already identified in the decisional law may apply with obvious clarity to the specific conduct in question." 536 U.S. 730, 741, 122 S.Ct. 2508, 153 L.Ed.2d 666 (2002). The dissent argues that Deputy Fleming was on clear notice that the reasonableness of the seizure of Simpson would be subject to a Fourth Amendment balancing test (weighing individual intrusion against legitimate government interests). Weighing the cognizable interests of Simpson against the government interests here, the dissent's position is that the scale tips starkly in Plaintiff's favor in light of *Papachristou v. City of Jacksonville*'s holding that "anti-vagrancy" laws are void for vagueness as they permit "unfettered discretion" in seizing an individual like Simpson. 405 U.S. 156, 171, 92 S.Ct. 839, 31 L.Ed.2d 110 (1972).

Assuming that general statements (under *Hope*) may suffice, the balance of interests here are not so lopsided. As stated herein and by the district court, there is an argument for the community caretaker function (for example) which would be a legitimate government interest as to public safety. *See, supra,* Sect.III n.17 (collecting cases); *see also Keller,* 2018 WL 615681, at *5 ("[T]he initial interaction between Simpson and Deputy Fleming may have been reasonable, given the fact that Simpson possibly posed a danger to himself and the community by standing in oncoming traffic."). Because there are legitimate interests on both sides, this is not a one-sided balancing test where the officer p.226 "do[es] not have any relevant, legitimate interests to put on their side of the[] scales." *Kinney,* 367 F.3d at 372; *cf.* Sect. III n.17.[18]

Accordingly, Deputy Fleming's qualified immunity defense as to Plaintiffs' Fourth Amendment claim prevails because Plaintiffs failed to prove that a reasonable officer like Fleming would have understood his actions violated clearly established law. Judgment is therefore rendered in Deputy Fleming's favor as he is entitled to qualified immunity on this claim.

Fourteenth Amendment

The Due Process Clause of the Fourteenth Amendment provides that "[n]o State shall ... deprive any person of life, liberty, or property, without due process of law." U.S. Const. amend. XIV, § 1.

Plaintiffs submit that Deputy Fleming's conduct created the "special relationship" under *DeShaney v. Winnebago County Department of Social Services* and a "state-created-danger" resulted thereof. 489 U.S. 189, 199-200, 109 S.Ct. 998, 103 L.Ed.2d 249 (1989). The district court held that Fleming was not entitled to qualified immunity under this claim because, *inter alia,* there were genuine issues of material fact as to whether there was a "special relationship" between Fleming and Simpson that deprived Simpson of his liberty. Deputy Fleming argues that the law does not clearly establish that a special relationship would have existed under the facts of this case.

We agree with Fleming because even if a "special relationship" existed, Plaintiffs must show that Simpson's Fourteenth Amendment right was clearly established at the time of the alleged violation.

The Supreme Court has "repeatedly told courts not to define clearly established law at a high level of generality." *Mullenix,* 136 S. Ct. at 308 (quotation omitted) (cleaned up). Again, the dispositive question is "whether the violative nature of particular conduct is clearly established." *Id.*

Here, while Simpson was killed by a motorist after Fleming dropped him off at the county line, the High Court in *DeShaney* held that states and their officials have no affirmative duty to protect individuals from violence by private actors.[19] 489 U.S. at 197, 109 S.Ct. 998. The Court explained

> That the State once took temporary custody of [the child] does not alter the analysis, for when it returned him to his father's custody, it placed him in no worse position than that in which he would have been had it not acted at all; the State does not become the permanent guarantor of an individual's safety by having once offered him shelter.

Id. Some courts have interpreted this language in *DeShaney* as creating a second exception to "the rule against state liability for violence committed by private actors in p.227 situations where the state actor played an affirmative role in creating or exacerbating a dangerous situation that led to the individual's injury." *See Kovacic,* 628 F.3d at 214 (discussing *Davis v. Brady,* 143 F.3d 1021 (6th Cir. 1998) (holding that officers violated a man's substantive due process rights by placing him at risk of harm when they abandoned him in an inebriated condition on an unfamiliar highway against his will)) (internal quotations omitted). But the Fifth Circuit has never recognized this "state-created-danger" exception. *See id.* (concluding that the law did not clearly establish state actors could be liable for private harm to an individual after his release from custody).

Plaintiffs therefore have not demonstrated a clearly established substantive due process right on the facts they allege. Accordingly, we reverse the district court's denial of summary judgment and render judgment that Deputy Fleming is entitled to qualified immunity on Plaintiffs' Fourteenth Amendment claim.

IV.

For these reasons, we REVERSE the district court's judgment denying Deputy Fleming qualified immunity and RENDER judgment granting him qualified immunity from Plaintiffs' Fourth Amendment and Fourteenth Amendment claims.

JAMES L. DENNIS, Circuit Judge, dissenting in part.

The district court found that it was genuinely disputed whether Darrin Fleming picked up and transported Gerald Simpson out of the county pursuant to a local unwritten custom of ousting those perceived as vagrants from the jurisdiction, and we must accept these facts as true at this juncture. *See Cantrell v. City of Murphy,* 666 F.3d 911, 922 (5th Cir. 2012) ("When considering an appeal from the denial of qualified immunity ... our inquiry concerns the purely legal question of whether the defendants are entitled to qualified immunity on the facts that the district court found sufficiently supported in the summary judgment record."). I agree with the majority that, under these facts, Fleming violated Simpson's Fourth Amendment rights. I disagree, however, that Plaintiffs failed to demonstrate that these rights were clearly established.

The district court found that, "[i]n taking Plaintiffs' allegations as true, that [Fleming] wanted to remove Simpson from [his] jurisdiction as a means to rid [Attala County] of a vagrancy problem, it cannot be said that Deputy Fleming did not understand that what he was doing violated the law." The majority holds that this was error because Plaintiffs have failed to demonstrate that the Fourth Amendment rights that Fleming violated were clearly established at the time of the incident. But qualified immunity works only "to ensure that before they are subjected to suit, officers are on notice their conduct is unlawful." *Saucier,* 533 U.S. 194, 206, 121 S.Ct. 2151 (2001). Under this framework, a right may be clearly established even without on-point precedent where a defendant's conduct clearly and obviously violates the Constitution. *See Hope v. Pelzer,* 536 U.S. 730, 741, 122 S.Ct. 2508, 153 L.Ed.2d 666 (2002). The "salient question" is not whether there are previous cases with facts that are "fundamentally similar," but rather, "whether the state of the law [at the time of defendants' conduct] gave [them] fair warning that [plaintiff's] alleged treatment was unconstitutional." *Id.*

At the time the incident at issue here occurred, Supreme Court precedent provided clear notice that "the reasonableness of a seizure under the Fourth Amendment is determined by balancing its intrusion on the individual's Fourth Amendment interests p.228 against its promotion of legitimate government interests." *Hiibel v. Sixth Judicial Dist. Court of Nevada, Humboldt Cty.,* 542 U.S. 177, 187, 124 S.Ct. 2451, 159 L.Ed.2d 292 (2004) (internal quotations omitted). When the question of whether a constitutional violation occurred depends on this sort of balancing of interests, qualified immunity should not apply when, "given the factual disputes identified by the district court and taking the plaintiffs' side of those disputes, [a] case does not require any real balancing at all" because the officers "do not have any relevant, legitimate interests to put on their side of the[] scales." *Kinney,* 367 F.3d at 372. "Our cases show that it is entirely appropriate to deny qualified immunity when the balance of cognizable interests weighs so starkly in the plaintiff's favor" because "the illegality of the Police Official['s] conduct is sufficiently clear that [he] can fairly be said to have been on notice of the impropriety of [his] actions." *Id.*

Accepting the facts that the district court found to be genuinely disputed, there is simply no legitimate government interest against which to balance the significant intrusion posed by Deputy Fleming's decision to seize Simpson and dump him in the next jurisdiction without his valid consent. The Supreme Court has long made clear that the Constitution does not permit police to "roundup ... so-called undesirables" merely because they are "poor people, nonconformists, dissenters, idlers." *Papachristou v. City of Jacksonville,* 405 U.S. 156, 171, 92 S.Ct. 839, 31 L.Ed.2d 110 (1972). With a balance so one-sidedly contrary to an individual's Fourth Amendment rights, every reasonable officer would have understood that seizing Simpson under these circumstances was arbitrary and unreasonable. *See Hope,* 536 U.S. at 741, 122 S.Ct. 2508.

Further, precedent from the Supreme Court provided notice when these events occurred that a law that provides officers with "unfettered discretion" to arrest persons as vagrants merely on suspicion of future criminality is impermissibly vague. *See Papachristou,* 405 U.S. at 163, 168, 92 S.Ct. 839 (invalidating a vagrancy law that criminalized, inter alia, "common night walkers" or "habitual wanderer[s]" and persons "habitually living without visible means of support"); *Kolender v. Lawson,* 461 U.S. 352, 361, 103 S.Ct. 1855, 75 L.Ed.2d 903 (1983) (invalidating a stop-and-identify statute as unconstitutionally vague "because it encourage[d] arbitrary enforcement by failing to describe with sufficient particularity what a suspect must do in order to satisfy the statute"). Given the Supreme Court's well-established jurisprudence limiting an officer's discretion to act pursuant to an established vagrancy or vagrancy-related law, it follows *a fortiori* that an unwritten custom— which would provide even vaguer standards and grant greater discretion—is necessarily unreasonable as a matter of law. When combined with this principle, it is even more apparent that the clearly one-sided balancing of interests served as clear and obvious notice to any reasonable officer in Deputy Fleming's position that seizing Simpson and driving him to the county line violated Simpson's Fourth Amendment rights. *See Hope,* 536 U.S. at 741, 122 S.Ct. 2508.

* * *

Under the facts the district court found genuinely disputed, which we must accept for purposes of this appeal of a denial of qualified immunity, Deputy Fleming's conduct clearly and obviously violated Simpson's Fourth Amendment rights. Accordingly, I would affirm the district p.229 court's denial of summary judgment on Plaintiffs' Fourth Amendment claim.

[1] Plaintiffs are Simpson's estate and Eleanor Keller (Simpson's sister), individually and on behalf of other members of Simpson's family.

[2] Our interlocutory review is based on the facts the district court accepted as sufficient to deny summary judgment which are stated in *Keller v. Attala County,* No. 1:16-cv-136-SA-DAS, 2018 WL 615681, at *1 (N.D. Miss. Jan. 29, 2018); *cf. Cantrell v. City of Murphy,* 666 F.3d 911, 922 (5th Cir. 2012) ("When considering an appeal from the denial of qualified immunity ... our inquiry concerns the purely legal question of whether the defendants are entitled to qualified immunity on the facts that the district court found sufficiently supported in the summary judgment record.").

[3] *Keller,* 2018 WL 615681, at *1.

[4] *Id.*

[5] *Id.*

[6] *Id.*

[7] The operative complaint alleges that it was approximately 8:00 p.m.

[8] *Id.*

[9] Plaintiffs' claims against Kosciusko officers are not the subject of this interlocutory appeal. *Keller,* 2018 WL 615681, at *8-9.

[10] The district court granted a stay pending this appeal because "the disposition of claims against the County are significantly intertwined with the pending resolution of [this appeal]." Order, *Keller v. Fleming*, No. No. 1:16-CV-136-SA-DAS (N.D. Miss. May 2, 2018), ECF No. 103.

[11] While we accept the district court's determination as to the genuineness of this vagrant policy, we do so because we adhere to the interlocutory standard for qualified immunity. *See Wagner v. Bay City*, 227 F.3d 316, 320 (5th Cir. 2000) (stating that on an interlocutory appeal for qualified immunity, we can review the materiality of any factual disputes, but not their genuineness).

It is important to note that upon review of the second amended complaint, and the parties' appellate and district court summary judgment briefing, there are several inconsistencies in what the parties presented to the district court and what the court recognized in its summary judgment order, mainly this anti-vagrant policy theory. Indeed, the operative complaint does not state such a theory, and there is no evidence in support thereof. At summary judgment, Plaintiffs argued that the Attala County policy is that "it is customary for law enforcement officers to give courtesy rides and not to travel beyond their designated jurisdiction"—which the court recognized in its summary judgment order. However, a courtesy ride policy in no way implicates a policy to transport vagrants to neighboring jurisdictions for the purpose of ridding a county of vagrants.

[12] While not expressly stated, the district court clearly infers that Simpson was seized. *Keller*, 2018 WL 615681, at *6. We can draw this inference from the district court's reasonableness holding that the (1) "jury must resolve whether Deputy Fleming was fulfilling his role as a community caretaker and whether that role eventually fell away, leaving only an *improper seizure to remain*"; and (2) "Plaintiff's Fourth Amendment claim is viable, because it is questionable whether Simpson was *improperly seized*—whether Deputy Fleming was acting as a community caretaker, whether Simpson ever felt as though he was free to leave, and whether he was capable of giving his consent to be seized in the first place." *Id.* (emphasis added). Said differently, the district court found that absent a warrant exception or justification (*e.g.*, the community caretaker exception), the jury question was whether Simpson's seizure was unreasonable or improper, not whether Simpson was seized. *Id.*

[13] Of note, Deputy Fleming's appellate brief provides a legal standard for seizure, but he otherwise presents no arguments as to whether Simpson was seized.

[14] We acknowledge that Officer Hawthorne's initial stop of Simpson did not initiate the seizure because "[o]ur cases make it clear that a seizure does not occur simply because a police officer approaches an individual and asks a few questions." *Florida v. Bostick*, 501 U.S. 429, 434, 111 S.Ct. 2382, 115 L.Ed.2d 389 (1991). But it is his actions thereafter that triggered the Fourth Amendment.

[15] In his deposition, Officer Hawthorne states "I shadowed him onto Sand Road; pulled off on Sand Road to where it was a road where I could pull off at, because there wasn't no room ... And asked Mr. Simpson would he like to sit down. And he sat down in the back of my patrol car."

[16] The district court opinion construes Deputy Fleming's courtesy ride statements as a basis for excepting the Fourth Amendment under the community caretaker doctrine and consent warrant exception. *Keller*, 2018 WL 615681, at *7-8.

As to the former, our circuit has yet to explicitly extend this community caretaker doctrine to unlawful detentions, but we have suggested in *dicta* that such seizures may be reasonable. *See United States v. Rideau,* 969 F.2d 1572 (5th Cir. 1992) (en banc). Moreover, a majority of our sister circuits refer to this doctrine as a warrant exception, but we recognize that this doctrine has also been considered as a stand-alone justification. *Taylor v. City of Saginaw,* 922 F.3d 328, 334-35 (6th Cir. 2019) (referring to community caretaker doctrine as an exception to warrant requirement); *United States v. Parks,* 902 F.3d 805, 812-13 (8th Cir. 2018) ("One such exception [to the warrant requirement] applies when police officers engage in a community caretaking function.") (quotation omitted); *Vargas v. City of Phila.,* 783 F.3d 962, 971 (3rd Cir. 2015) ("That community caretaking doctrine ... is an exception to the warrant requirement of the Fourth Amendment."); *MacDonald v. Town of Eastham,* 745 F.3d 8, 13 (1st Cir. 2014) (same); *compare with United States v. Gemma,* 818 F.3d 23, 32 (1st Cir. 2016) (ruling that evidence was admissible because evidence was retrieved in the course of the officer's community caretaker duties).

[17] Of note, there are arguments that can be made with regard to the community caretaker function and consent. As to the community caretaker doctrine, Deputy Fleming could arguably have advanced the public interest because Simpson posed an imminent threat to himself or oncoming traffic. *Cf. Rideau,* 969 F.2d at 1574 ("Police have long served the public welfare by removing intoxicated people from the public streets, where they pose a hazard to themselves and others." (citing *Cady v. Dombrowski,* 413 U.S. 433, 441, 93 S.Ct. 2523, 37 L.Ed.2d 706 (1973))); *Meehan v. Thompson,* 763 F.3d 936, 941 (8th Cir. 2014) ("We have recognized that it may be reasonable under the Fourth Amendment for a police officer, acting in his capacity as community caretaker, to seize an apparently intoxicated individual to ensure the safety of the public and/or the individual.") (internal quotation marks and citations omitted). On the flipside, even if Officer Fleming arrived at the scene as a "community caretaker," a material fact question remains as to whether the procedures he employed (pursuant to that function) were reasonable under the Fourth Amendment. Indeed, community caretaking stops must be both reasonable in their inception and reasonable as conducted. *Cf. United States v. King,* 990 F.2d 1552, 1562 (10th Cir. 1993) (stating that a detention must be justified at its inception and as it proceeds). The same can be said with regard to arguments for and against consent.

But, as mentioned, none of these positions are before us on appeal and are therefore forfeited. *See Cinel v. Connick,* 15 F.3d 1338, 1345 (5th Cir. 1994); *Ragas v. Tenn. Gas Pipeline Co.,* 136 F.3d 455, 458 (5th Cir. 1998) ("Rule 56 does not impose upon the district court a duty to sift through the record in search of evidence [and arguments] to support a party's opposition to summary judgment.").

[18] In other words, denying qualified immunity under the dissent's framework appears to be inappropriate because a "real balancing" of interests would be required here. *Cf. Kinney,* 367 F.3d at 372.

[19] It is worthy to note that the Supreme Court in *DeShaney* also recognized that, in limited circumstances, the State's actions in taking a person into custody and holding him there against his will creates a "special relationship," *id.* at 199-200, 109 S.Ct. 998, such as the relationship between State and prisoners, *Estelle v. Gamble,* 429 U.S. 97, 103-04, 97 S.Ct. 285, 50 L.Ed.2d 251 (1976), involuntarily committed mental

patients, *Youngberg v. Romeo,* 457 U.S. 307, 315-16, 102 S.Ct. 2452, 73 L.Ed.2d 28 (1982), and suspected criminals injured while being apprehended by police, *City of Revere v. Mass. Gen. Hosp.,* 463 U.S. 239, 244, 103 S.Ct. 2979, 77 L.Ed.2d 605 (1983).

952 F.3d 624 (2020)

Maritza AMADOR, Individually and as Representative of The Estate of Gilbert Flores and as Next Friend of Minor R.M.F.; Vanessa Flores; Marisela Flores; Carmen Flores; Rogelio Flores, Plaintiffs-Appellees,

v.

Officer Greg VASQUEZ, Individually and in his Official Capacity; Officer Robert Sanchez, Individually and in his Official Capacity, Defendants-Appellants.

No. 17-51001.

United States Court of Appeals, Fifth Circuit.

FILED March 11, 2020.

Amador v. Vasquez, 952 F. 3d 624 (5th Cir. 2020)

Appeal from the United States District Court for the Western District of Texas.

Matthew J. Kita, Dallas, TX, Robert Paul Wilson, Thomas J. Henry Injury Attorneys, San Antonio, TX, for Plaintiff-Appellee.

Charles Straith Frigerio, Esq., Trial Attorney, Law Offices of Charles S. Frigerio, P.C., San Antonio, TX, for Defendant-Appellant.

Before HIGGINBOTHAM, GRAVES, and WILLETT, Circuit Judges.

p.627 JAMES E. GRAVES, Circuit Judge:

While responding to a domestic violence call, Bexar County Sheriff's Deputies Greg Vasquez and Robert Sanchez shot and killed knife-armed Gilbert Flores after a twelve-minute encounter that ended with Flores standing nearly thirty feet from the deputies, motionless, and with his hands in the air. Flores's wife and other surviving family members (collectively, the "Estate" or "Plaintiffs") brought a 42 U.S.C. § 1983 claim against the deputies, alleging that Vasquez and Sanchez violated Flores's Fourth Amendment right to be free from excessive force. The deputies moved for summary judgment based on qualified immunity. The district court denied the motion, finding that there were genuine issues of material fact. The deputies filed this interlocutory appeal. Because we agree with the district court that genuine issues of material fact exist, we lack jurisdiction to review this appeal. Accordingly, we DISMISS.

SUMMARY JUDGMENT EVIDENCE[1]

In 2015, after a domestic dispute between Flores and his wife at Flores's mother's home, Flores's mother called 9-1-1 for assistance. According to the 9-1-1 call transcript, Flores's mother told the dispatcher that Flores beat up his wife and had "gone crazy". Deputies Vasquez and Sanchez were dispatched to the residence in separate vehicles. While in route, dispatch advised Vasquez and Sanchez that Flores was upset, and that Flores wanted to commit "suicide by cop."[2] Vasquez was also informed that Flores had a knife.

Twelve minutes elapsed between Vasquez's arrival and the officers' fatal shots at Flores.[3] During those twelve minutes, the deputies had a number of encounters with

Flores, and ultimately deescalated the situation. It was only after Flores was standing nearly thirty feet from the deputies, motionless, and with his hands in the air for several seconds that the officers looked at each other and then decided to shoot Flores. The officers each fired a shot, and Flores fell to the ground. Viewing the facts in the light most favorable to the Estate, *Tolan v. Cotton,* 572 U.S. 650, 655-56, 134 S.Ct. 1861, 188 L.Ed.2d 895 (2014), we summarize the encounters.

Encounter #1

Vasquez arrived at the residence first, went into the house, and had an altercation with Flores who was holding a fixed blade p.628 Ozark Trail knife. Vasquez attempted to calm Flores and told him, "put the knife down, you're going to be alright." Flores began approaching Vasquez, and Vasquez retreated out of the residence.

Encounter #2

Not long after Vasquez retreated out-side, Flores exited the residence with the knife in hand and allegedly stabbed at Vasquez, striking Vasquez's protective shield. During this altercation, Sanchez arrived. Flores then began retreating toward the house.

Encounter #3

As Flores retreated toward the house, Sanchez fired one shot at Flores and missed.

Encounter #4

Flores went back to the residence, retrieved two metal folding chairs, and came back outside. While still holding at least one of the folding chairs, Flores allegedly came at Vasquez with the knife. Vasquez blocked the knife with his protective shield and deployed his taser at Flores. The taser missed Flores and hit a chair in Flores's hand, and its wires became entangled with the chair. Vasquez then struck Flores with the taser gun and dropped it from his hand. Flores then went back toward the residence.

At some point around this time, a bystander began videotaping the encounter on a phone.

Encounter #5

For the first few minutes of the video, Flores, wearing only shorts and flip flops, and the officers, each holding a gun, talked and maintained distance from each other: Flores closer to the residence and the officers in or near the street. Around minute marker 4:20, Flores picked up the two metal chairs and walked toward the police officers in the street. The officers retreated, walking backwards away from Flores. Flores picked up the deployed taser that Vasquez dropped, walked back to the lawn, dropped the chairs, and chucked the taser away from the officers. The officers continued to retreat, backing away from Flores.[4] *See* Video at 5:20-24.

Encounter #6

For over a minute, Flores talked and gestured at the officers from the lawn area, remaining some distance away from the officers. During this time, the officers were not in the video and when they reappeared, they were in the street beyond the neighbor's residence. Flores then jogged back toward the house, picked up the chairs on the lawn, and placed the chairs on the porch. Around the seven-minute mark, Flores trotted and walked toward the officers' unlocked patrol SUV, which had an AR-15 inside and keys in the ignition. While Flores was on the other side of the patrol SUV, he was out of view of the video recording. The officers, in view, jogged toward the vehicle and Vasquez pointed his gun at Flores. *See* Video at 7:10.

Flores walked away from the vehicle and toward the officers, talking and gesturing, then went back toward the vehicle. The officers advanced toward Flores. Flores was out of view of the camera until he again walked away from the vehicle. In full view of the video recording, Flores then stood in the driveway of the residence, some steps away from the SUV, and some distance from the officers. At 7:32, Flores moved the knife from his right hand to his left hand. Sanchez had his gun drawn. At 7:33, Flores stood stationary in the driveway.

p.629 Encounter #7

At 7:34, Flores was stationary in the driveway, approximately thirty feet from Vasquez, who was in the street with a protective shield and drawn gun. Sanchez was approximately thirty feet from Flores as well. Flores was closer to the SUV than he was to the officers. At 7:35, Flores, still stationary in the driveway, put both arms up in the air with his hands above his head and the knife in his palm and remained motionless. There was nothing behind the officers hindering their ability to retreat backwards. For about five seconds, Flores did not advance toward the officers, the vehicle, or the home.

Encounter #8

While Flores stood motionless with his hands in the air, Sanchez turned to look toward Vasquez. At about 7:37, Vasquez and Sanchez fatally shot Flores, who stood motionless in a surrender pose. Flores fell backward onto the pavement.

PROCEDURAL HISTORY

The Estate sued the county and the officers under § 1983 for excessive force. The county and the officers moved for summary judgment. The officers argued that they were entitled to qualified immunity. The district court granted the county's motion and denied the officers' motion. In denying the officers' request for qualified immunity, the district court determined there were genuine issues of material fact, and construing the facts in favor of Plaintiffs, the deputies' use of deadly force was objectively unreasonable. The district court found that the deputies' use of deadly force was unreasonable because Flores, "who was stationary for several seconds and put his hands in the air while remaining otherwise motionless, was no longer resisting and had signaled surrender." The officers now appeal.

JURISDICTION AND STANDARD OF REVIEW

This court has jurisdiction over appeals from a district court's final decision. 28 U.S.C. § 1291. "Ordinarily, [this court does] not have jurisdiction to review a denial of a summary judgment motion because such a decision is not final within the meaning of 28 U.S.C. § 1291." *Perniciaro v. Lea,* 901 F.3d 241, 250 (5th Cir. 2018) (citation and internal quotation marks omitted). "However, the 'denial of qualified immunity on a motion for summary judgment is immediately appealable if it is based on a conclusion of law.'" *Id.* (quoting *Palmer v. Johnson,* 193 F.3d 346, 350 (5th Cir. 1999)). "We have no jurisdiction to hear an interlocutory appeal, however, when a district court's denial of qualified immunity rests on the basis that genuine issues of material fact exist." *Michalik v. Hermann,* 422 F.3d 252, 257 (5th Cir. 2005).

"Because of this case's posture ... review is limited to determining whether the factual disputes that the district court identified are material to the application of qualified immunity." *Samples v. Vadzemnieks,* 900 F.3d 655, 660 (5th Cir. 2018) (emphasis omitted); *see also Mitchell v. Mills,* 895 F.3d 365, 369 (5th Cir. 2018) (concluding that the court's "review is limited to evaluating only the legal significance of the undisputed facts").

This court accepts "plaintiff's version of the facts as true and [reviews the facts] through the lens of qualified immunity." *Samples,* 900 F.3d at 660. "If the defendant would still be entitled to qualified immunity under this view of the facts, then any disputed fact issues are not material, the district court's denial of summary judgment was improper, and [this court] must reverse; otherwise, the disputed factual issues are material and [this p.630 court] lack[s] jurisdiction over the appeal." *Lytle v. Bexar County.,* 560 F.3d 404, 409 (5th Cir. 2009). Put another way, "[i]f a factual dispute must be resolved to make the qualified immunity determination, that fact issue is material and we lack jurisdiction over the appeal." *Manis v. Lawson,* 585 F.3d 839, 843 (5th Cir. 2009).

The court reviews materiality and legal conclusions *de novo. Hampton v. Oktibbeha Cty. Sheriff Dep't,* 480 F.3d 358, 364 (5th Cir. 2007). The "scope of clearly established law and the objective reasonableness of those acts of the defendant that the district court found the plaintiff could prove at trial are legal issues we review *de novo.*" *Thompson v. Upshur County.,* 245 F.3d 447, 456 (5th Cir. 2001).

DISCUSSION

"Qualified immunity shields from liability 'all but the plainly incompetent or those who knowingly violate the law.'" *Romero v. City of Grapevine,* 888 F.3d 170, 176 (5th Cir. 2018) (quoting *Malley v. Briggs,* 475 U.S. 335, 341, 106 S.Ct. 1092, 89 L.Ed.2d 271 (1986)). "In determining whether an officer is entitled to qualified immunity, courts engage in a two-step inquiry." *Id.* "The first asks whether the facts, '[t]aken in the light most favorable to the party asserting the injury, ... show the officer's conduct violated a [federal] right [.]'" *Tolan,* 572 U.S. at 655-56, 134 S.Ct. 1861 (quoting *Saucier v. Katz,* 533 U.S. 194, 201, 121 S.Ct. 2151, 150 L.Ed.2d 272 (2001)). The second "asks whether the right in question was 'clearly established' at the time of the violation." *Id.* at 656, 134 S.Ct. 1861 (citing *Hope v. Pelzer,* 536 U.S. 730, 739, 122 S.Ct. 2508, 153 L.Ed.2d 666 (2002)).

I. The Officers Violated Flores's Fourth Amendment Right

The first question in the qualified immunity analysis is whether Officers Vasquez and Sanchez violated Flores's Fourth Amendment right to be free from excessive force.[5] *See Romero,* 888 F.3d at 176. When the facts here are taken in the light most favorable to Plaintiffs, the answer is yes.

"The use of deadly force violates the Fourth Amendment unless 'the officer[s] [have] probable cause to believe that the suspect poses a threat of serious physical harm, either to the officer[s] or to others.'" *Id.* (quoting *Tennessee v. Garner,* 471 U.S. 1, 11, 105 S.Ct. 1694, 85 L.Ed.2d 1 (1985)). To prevail on an excessive force claim, plaintiffs must show that the force employed was objectively unreasonable. *Graham v. Connor,* 490 U.S. 386, 397, 109 S.Ct. 1865, 104 L.Ed.2d 443 (1989). "Excessive force claims are necessarily fact-intensive; whether the force used is 'excessive' or 'unreasonable' depends on the facts and circumstances of each particular case." *Darden,* 880 F.3d at 728 (citation and internal quotation marks omitted). "In making this determination, a court should consider the totality of the circumstances, 'including the severity of the crime at issue, whether the suspect poses an immediate threat to the safety of the officers or others, and whether he is actively resisting arrest or attempting to evade arrest by flight.'" *Id.* at 728-29 (quoting *Graham,* 490 U.S. at 396, 109 S.Ct. 1865). "The 'reasonableness' of a particular use of force must be judged from the perspective of a reasonable officer on p.631 the scene, rather than with the 20/20 vision of hindsight." *Id.* at 729 (citation and internal quotation marks omitted). "The calculus of reasonableness must embody allowance for the fact that police officers are often forced to make split-second judgments—in circumstances that are tense, uncertain, and rapidly evolving—about the amount of force that is necessary in a particular situation." *Id.* (citation and internal quotation marks omitted). However, "[t]he question is one of objective reasonableness, not subjective intent, and an officer's conduct must be judged in light of the circumstances confronting him, without the benefit of hindsight." *Manis,* 585 F.3d at 843 (citation and internal quotation marks omitted).

Further, "[i]t is well-established that '[t]he excessive force inquiry is confined to whether the [officers or other persons were] in danger at the moment of the threat that resulted in the [officers' use of deadly force].'" *Rockwell v. Brown,* 664 F.3d 985, 992-93 (5th Cir. 2011) (quoting *Bazan ex rel. Bazan v. Hidalgo County.,* 246 F.3d 481, 493 (5th Cir. 2001)) (emphasis omitted). So, the focus of the inquiry should be on "the act that led [the officer] to discharge his weapon[.]" *Manis,* 585 F.3d at 845.

Applying that framework, the district court found three genuine disputes of material fact that barred qualified immunity because resolving those facts in Plaintiffs' favor led the court to conclude that shooting Flores was objectively unreasonable. The district court found the relevant, genuine disputes of material fact to be: (1) "whether Flores did open the door or did look inside to see the keys in the ignition or see the weapon that was inside the SUV"; (2) whether Flores tried to activate the taser against the officers; and (3) what occurred in the moments before the deputies shot Flores.

Considering the totality of the circumstances, focusing on the act that led the officers to discharge their weapons, and without reviewing the district court's decision that genuine factual disputes exist, *see Kinney v. Weaver,* 367 F.3d 337, 348 (5th Cir. 2004), we conclude that the genuine issues of material fact identified by the district court are material, and this case should proceed to trial.

Relying on their version of the facts, yet purportedly relying on the video, the officers argue that they reasonably believed that Flores posed a threat of serious harm to the officers or to others.[6] According to the officers, Flores "opened the front passenger door of the Tahoe Patrol vehicle of Deputy Vasquez, [sic] said vehicle had the keys in the ignition and an AR-15 inside the vehicle." They further contend that Flores "picked up Deputy Vasquez' [sic] taser from the street and attempted to activate it against Deputy [sic] Vasquez and Sanchez but was unsuccessful." Most significantly, the officers assert that "Deputies Vasquez and Sanchez were in imminent fear of death or serious bodily injury by the actions of Gilbert Flores *at the time of the fatal shots.*" (emphasis added). However, Plaintiffs assert that at the time Flores was shot, Flores was not next to the patrol car, Flores had "raised both of his hands directly above his head with the knife 'palmed' in his left hand" and "raised his hands in apparent surrender, stood still, his hands were not moving, his feet were not moving, he was not moving or advancing toward the Deputies and no p.632 family members of [sic] neighbors were outside or in the vicinity."

Collectively, these factual disputes are material to resolving whether the officers reasonably believed that Flores posed a threat of serious harm at the time of the shooting. Construing the facts in Plaintiffs' favor, the district court found that a "reasonable officer would have concluded that Flores, who was stationary for several seconds and put his hands in the air while remaining otherwise motionless, was no longer resisting and had signaled surrender." We agree.

Flores had a knife, not a gun; was several feet away from the officers, the house, and the vehicle; had his hands in the air in a surrender position; and stood stationary in the officers' line of sight. Under these facts taken in the light most favorable to Plaintiffs, we conclude that the district court correctly identified material factual disputes as to whether the officers violated Flores's Fourth Amendment rights. Accordingly, we must address the second question of the analysis.

II. Flores's Fourth Amendment Right Was Clearly Established

The second question in the qualified immunity analysis is whether clearly established law prohibited the officers from shooting Flores in these circumstances. *City of Escondido v. Emmons,* __ U.S. ___, 139 S. Ct. 500, 503, 202 L.Ed.2d 455 (2019). Again, the answer is yes.

"A clearly established right is one that is 'sufficiently clear that every reasonable official would have understood that what he is doing violates that right.'" *Mullenix v.*

Luna, ___ U.S. ___, 136 S. Ct. 305, 308, 193 L.Ed.2d 255 (2015) (per curiam) (quoting *Reichle v. Howards,* 566 U.S. 658, 664, 132 S.Ct. 2088, 182 L.Ed.2d 985 (2012)). We cannot "'define clearly established law at a high level of generality,'" *id.* (quoting *Ashcroft v. al-Kidd,* 563 U.S. 731, 742, 131 S.Ct. 2074, 179 L.Ed.2d 1149 (2011)), especially in "the Fourth Amendment context, where the Court has recognized that '[i]t is sometimes difficult for an officer to determine how the relevant legal doctrine, here excessive force, will apply to the factual situation the officer confronts,'" *id.* (quoting *Katz,* 533 U.S. at 205, 121 S.Ct. 2151). "Where constitutional guidelines seem inapplicable or too remote, it does not suffice for a court simply to state that an officer may not use unreasonable and excessive force, deny qualified immunity, and then remit the case for a trial on the question of reasonableness." *Kisela v. Hughes,* ___ U.S. ___, 138 S. Ct. 1148, 1153, 200 L.Ed.2d 449 (2018) (per curiam). "An officer 'cannot be said to have violated a clearly established right unless the right's contours were sufficiently definite that any reasonable official in the defendant's shoes would have understood that he was violating it.'" *Id.* (quoting *Plumhoff v. Rickard,* 572 U.S. 765, 778-79, 134 S.Ct. 2012, 188 L.Ed.2d 1056 (2014)). We do "not require a case directly on point, but existing precedent must have placed the statutory or constitutional question beyond debate." *Id.* at 1152 (citation and internal quotation marks omitted).

"[T]he salient question ... is whether the state of the law in [2015] gave [the officers] fair warning that their alleged treatment of [Flores] was unconstitutional." *Hope,* 536 U.S. at 741, 122 S.Ct. 2508. "[G]eneral statements of the law are not inherently incapable of giving fair and clear warning" to officers. *Id.* In fact, "officials can still be on notice that their conduct violates established law even in novel factual circumstances." *Id.* "[T]here can be the rare obvious case, where the unlawfulness of the officer's conduct is sufficiently clear even though existing precedent does p.633 not address similar circumstances[.]" *Emmons,* 139 S. Ct. at 504 (citation and internal quotation marks omitted).

"In the excessive force context, a constitutional violation is clearly established if no reasonable officer could believe the act was lawful." *Darden,* 880 F.3d at 727. "Our case law makes clear that when an arrestee is not actively resisting arrest the degree of force an officer can employ is reduced." *Id.* at 731; *see Bush v. Strain,* 513 F.3d 492, 502 (5th Cir. 2008) (holding that it was objectively unreasonable for an officer to slam an arrestee's face into a vehicle when the arrestee "was not resisting arrest or attempting to flee"); *Newman v. Guedry,* 703 F.3d 757, 760, 763 (5th Cir. 2012) (holding that it was objectively unreasonable for officers to tase an arrestee when the arrestee's "behavior did not rise to the level of 'active resistance,'" despite the arrestee's alleged noncompliance with orders).

A reasonable officer would have understood that using deadly force on a man holding a knife, but standing nearly thirty feet from the deputies, motionless, and with his hands in the air for several seconds, would violate the Fourth Amendment. The officers argue that they were justified in using deadly force because Flores posed an immediate threat at several instances before their ultimate use of deadly force. However, "an exercise of force that is reasonable at one moment can become unreasonable in the next if the justification for the use of the force has ceased." *Lytle,* 560 F.3d at 413. To say otherwise would grant officers "'an ongoing license to kill an otherwise unthreatening suspect'" who was threatening earlier. *Id.* (quoting *Abraham v. Raso,* 183 F.3d 279, 294 (3d Cir. 1999)).

In *Lytle,* taking the facts in the light most favorable to the plaintiff, we found that the officer could have "had sufficient time to perceive that any threat to him had passed by the time he fired[,]" which was "anywhere from three to ten seconds, perhaps even more" after the perceived threat, rather than "in near contemporaneity" with the perceived threat. 560 F.3d at 414 (citation and internal quotation marks omitted). Here, Vasquez and Sanchez had about five seconds to evaluate Flores, standing thirty feet away from them with a knife and with his hands in the air, before shooting him. At the time of the shooting, Flores's right in this case was "'sufficiently clear that every reasonable official would have understood that what [the officers did] violate[d] that right.'" *Mullenix,* 136 S. Ct. at 308 (quoting *Reichle,* 566 U.S. at 664, 132 S.Ct. 2088).

We find that if a jury accepts Plaintiffs' version of the facts as true, particularly as to what occurred in the moments before the deputies shot Flores, the jury could conclude that the officers violated Flores's clearly established right to be free from excessive force. *See Cole v. Carson,* 935 F.3d 444, 447, *as revised* (5th Cir. Aug. 21, 2019) (en banc) ("We conclude that it will be for a jury, and not judges, to resolve the competing factual narratives as detailed in the district court opinion and the record as to the ... excessive-force claim."). Accordingly, there are factual disputes that must be resolved to make the qualified immunity determination, disputes that are material, and we lack jurisdiction over this interlocutory appeal. *See Manis,* 585 F.3d at 843.

CONCLUSION

Because there are genuine issues of material fact that preclude summary judgment, we lack jurisdiction to review this appeal and DISMISS.

[1] These facts are gleaned from the record on appeal and the district court findings. *See Wagner v. Bay City,* 227 F.3d 316, 320 (5th Cir. 2000) ("In deciding an interlocutory appeal of a denial of qualified immunity, we can review the *materiality* of any factual disputes, but not their *genuineness.*") (emphasis in original). The record contains an audiovisual recording of the encounter filmed by a bystander with a phone. The enhanced video may be accessed via the following internet link: http://www.ca5.uscourts.gov/opinions/pub/17/17-51001.mp4. We analyze the video evidence to determine whether it "utterly discredit[s]" the Estate's version of events such that "no reasonable jury could have believed [the Estate]." *See Scott v. Harris,* 550 U.S. 372, 380, 127 S.Ct. 1769, 167 L.Ed.2d 686 (2007); *see also Carnaby v. City of Houston,* 636 F.3d 183, 187 (5th Cir. 2011) ("A court of appeals need not rely on [a] description of the facts where the record discredits that description but should instead consider the facts in light depicted by the videotape.") (citation and internal quotation marks omitted). We determine that the video does not utterly discredit the Estate's version of events or the district court's determinations regarding the genuineness of facts.

[2] Flores could be heard during the 9-1-1 call saying, "I got a knife and I'm going to suicide by cop, so bring a SWAT team, or uh uh uh or whoever is going to be ready to pull the trigger because I'm going to die today."

[3] Sanchez arrived one minute after Vasquez.

[4] The officers contend that Flores attempted to activate the taser against them.

[5] Because it is alleged that the officers acted in unison, we need not separately address the qualified immunity analysis for each officer. *See Darden v. City of Fort Worth,* 880 F.3d 722, 731 (5th Cir.), *cert. denied sub nom. City of Fort Worth v. Darden,* ___ U.S. ___, 139 S. Ct. 69, 202 L.Ed.2d 23 (2018).

[6] The officers present different "scenarios" that would have justified them using "deadly force." We refuse to speculate on whether it would have been reasonable to kill Flores in those scenarios, which are not before this court.

950 F.3d 245 (2020)

Clarence Dean ROY, Plaintiff-Appellant,
v.
CITY OF MONROE; James Booth, in his official and individual capacities, Defendants-Appellees.

No. 18-31063.

United States Court of Appeals, Fifth Circuit.
FILED February 13, 2020.

Roy v. City of Monroe, 950 F. 3d 245 (5th Cir. 2020)

Appeal from the United States District Court for the Western District of Louisiana.

Ben E. Clayton, Joshua Paul Clayton, Clayton Law Firm, L.L.C., Slidell, LA, Frederick Herbert Nelson, Attorney, American Liberties Institute, Orlando, FL, David Markese, Attorney, Chuluota, FL, for Plaintiff-Appellant.

Brandon Wade Creekbaum, Angie Deal Baldwin, Nanci Stafford Summersgill, City of Monroe, Legal Department, Monroe, LA, for Defendants-Appellees.

Before JOLLY, HO, and ENGELHARDT, Circuit Judges.

p.248 E. GRADY JOLLY, Circuit Judge.

Clarence Dean Roy, a street preacher of the Christian faith, was issued a summons outside a nightclub in Monroe, Louisiana, after a woman accused him of following her and making inflammatory remarks. The summons, which was issued by Sergeant James Booth of the Monroe Police Department, cleared the way for formal charges under the city of Monroe's "disturbing the peace" ordinance, MONROE CITY CODE § 12-153. Roy was tried and acquitted by a municipal court judge. Shortly thereafter, he brought this lawsuit under 42 U.S.C. § 1983, in which he contends that Booth and the city deprived him of numerous constitutional rights under the First, Fourth, and Fourteenth Amendments. Two district court judges denied relief, first in part and then in whole, respectively. We affirm.

I.

On the night of July 17, 2015, Clarence Roy and several others occupied a public street in Monroe, Louisiana. The area was home to bars and nightclubs, including the Corner Bar, Club Neat, and Live Oaks Ballroom and Lounge. Roy viewed the area as a home to sin and thus a rich prospect for his calling, his message, and his other talents. Roy and his cohort arrived with the purpose of conducting what Roy calls "bar ministry" or "street ministry." Roy testified that his ministry typically consists of preaching the gospel by means designed to "startle or stop" nearby bar patrons. Examples given by Roy include warning patrons about the risk of damnation and preaching against "whores," "drunkards," and wayward others who frequent bars. Personally chastising and harassing patrons for their iniquity was his calling card.

On the night in question, Roy was carrying a six-foot cross and wearing an orange jumpsuit. Officers of the Monroe Police Department arrived on the scene after receiving a complaint about an argument between the former owner of the Corner p.249 Bar and a member of Roy's group. One of Roy's "victims," a woman named Jessica Falcon, approached Sergeant James Booth. Falcon reported that Roy had followed her, saying "ugly, lewd things," including that she is a "homosexual," that her "father is the devil," and that she is "going to hell." Roy has denied following Falcon, making these statements, or even "seeing" Falcon on the night of the incident.

Nevertheless, based on Falcon's allegations, Booth issued Roy a summons under the city of Monroe's "disturbing the peace" ordinance. The ordinance reads in relevant part as follows:

> (a) It shall be unlawful to commit an act of disturbing the peace.
>
> (b) Disturbing the peace is the doing of any of the following in such a manner as would foreseeably disturb or alarm the public, or create any dangerous or violent conditions:
>
> ...
>
> (2) Using profane or threatening language or making obscene remarks, gestures, or indecent proposals to or toward another which in the manner uttered has a tendency to incite an ordinary addressee to violent retaliatory action and a breach of the peace;
>
> ...
>
> Disturbing the peace shall also include the commission of any act other than that permitted as an exercise of free speech or free assembly guaranteed by the constitutions of the United States and the State of Louisiana, in such a manner as to disturb or alarm the public, or make such a disturbance imminent, or to provoke another or other to retaliatory action or violence.

MONROE CITY CODE § 12-153.

After issuing the summons, Booth recorded his version of events in this unedited "Probable Cause Narrative":

> On 7-17-2015 at approx 2247 hours I Sgt. Booth, was in the 500 Blk of North 3rd Street dealing with a distance. There was group of people outside Club Neat and the Connor Bar preaching at the customers. While there I was approached by Jessica N. Falcon. Jessica stated while she was crossing the street from Club Neat to The Connor Bar a while male wearing an orange jump suite caring a large wooden cross Followed her across the street. Jessica stated the man called her a homosexual and because of this she was going to hell. Jessica also stated the man told her that her father was the devil. Jessica stated this offended her and it scared her the way he was following her across the street. Jessica pointed out the suspect to me.
>
> The suspect was id as Clarence D. Roy. Roy told me he was not protesting but preaching. Roy was issued a summon (27563) for disturbing the peace.

The city continued with its prosecution, charging Roy in a bill of information. His case was tried to the bench in Monroe City Court, and he was acquitted. Roy resumed his street ministry at the same location, without incident, for nearly a year before retiring from the cause in 2017.

II.

Shortly after his acquittal, however, Roy filed suit in the Western District of Louisiana under 42 U.S.C. § 1983. His complaint alleged that Booth and the city had deprived him of numerous constitutional rights, including the First Amendment rights to free speech and free exercise of religion, the Fourth Amendment right to be free from unreasonable seizures, and the Fourteenth Amendment right to due process of law. Roy sought legal, equitable, and declaratory relief, including a "judgment p.250 and decree declaring [that] the challenged portions of [the ordinance] are unconstitutional on their face and as applied."

Roy's suit was first considered by one district judge before being assigned to a different judge; each judge issued separate rulings. Booth and the city moved for summary judgment on all claims, and the first district judge granted summary judgment in part. The judge rejected Roy's contention that the ordinance is facially unconstitutional under the First and Fourteenth Amendments, reasoning that the ordinance is content neutral and that it satisfies the constitutional requirements for content-neutral regulations of speech. Relying on this same analysis, and adding that Roy failed to meet his burden under *Monell v. Department of Social Services,* 436 U.S. 658, 694, 98 S.Ct. 2018, 56 L.Ed.2d 611 (1978), the court also rejected what Roy calls his "Due Process claim," *i.e.,* his claim that the city violated the Fourteenth Amendment by enforcing an unconstitutional ordinance against him. Finally, deciding that Roy was neither searched nor seized, the court dismissed Roy's Fourth Amendment claims for "malicious prosecution" and "false arrest."

Some of Roy's claims survived, however. Most notably, the district court allowed Roy to proceed on his claims that: (1) Booth's issuance of the summons was unlawful retaliation for Roy's protected expression (the "First Amendment retaliation claim") and (2) the city's ordinance violated the First Amendment as interpreted and enforced against Roy (the "as-applied challenge"). With respect to these claims, the district court declined to award summary judgment because there was a genuine issue of fact as to whether Booth's actions were supported by probable cause.

As noted, the case was then transferred to a second judge. Booth and the city filed a motion to reconsider the first judge's rulings, arguing that the first judge erred by declining to grant summary judgment to Booth on qualified immunity grounds. Roy moved to reopen discovery, but the court denied that motion. Then, on the merits, the district court again held in favor of the defendants, premising Booth's qualified immunity on its finding that "reasonable police officers could [have believed that] probable cause existed." After this second order, Roy was left with only claims for injunctive and declaratory relief. The district court thus struck Roy's jury demand *sua sponte* and conducted a one-day bench trial instead.

Two days after trial, the district court rejected all of Roy's remaining claims. The court first dismissed Roy's claims for injunctive and declaratory relief against Booth, holding that Booth's departure from the Monroe Police Department mooted any claim for prospective relief. Then, addressing Roy's First Amendment claims against the city, the district court further held that Roy had not established a violation of his First Amendment rights because Booth had probable cause to arrest him and, in any event, Booth was not motivated by Roy's protected expression. Finally, the district court held that Roy had failed to make a sufficient showing with respect to his entitlement to injunctive and declaratory relief. A judgment was entered dismissing the entire suit with prejudice. That judgment is now before us.

III.

On appeal, Roy argues that the district court erred by: (1) dismissing his facial and as-applied constitutional challenges to the ordinance, (2) awarding qualified immunity to Booth, (3) denying his motion for additional discovery, (4) rejecting what he calls his "Due Process claim" against the city of Monroe, and (5) dismissing his claims for "malicious prosecution" and p.251 "false arrest" under the Fourth Amendment. Because we (1) reject Roy's challenges to the constitutionality of the ordinance, (2) find that Booth's actions were supported by probable cause, and (3) uphold the district court's denial of the motion to reopen discovery, we find that no error was committed by the district court in its dismissal of the suit.

A.

We first address Roy's facial and as-applied challenges to the ordinance. "Although litigants are permitted to raise both as-applied and [facial] challenges," the "lawfulness of the particular application of the law should ordinarily be decided first." *Serafine v. Branaman,* 810 F.3d 354, 362 (5th Cir. 2016) (quoting *Bd. of Trs. v. Fox,* 492 U.S. 469, 485, 109 S.Ct. 3028, 106 L.Ed.2d 388 (1989)).

Here, however, Roy's as-applied appellate arguments are wholly derivative of his arguments challenging qualified immunity. Indeed, Roy has done no more than cross-reference the qualified-immunity section of his brief: "[f]or the reasons set forth above, the [second] District Court Judge erred in granting Booth qualified immunity, [so] Roy's as-applied claims should be remanded to be addressed on their merits."

For reasons stated *infra,* we have found that Roy's qualified-immunity arguments lack merit. Thus, we decline to make further comment on the district court's disposition of the as-applied challenge. "Failure adequately to brief an issue on appeal constitutes waiver of that argument." *Procter & Gamble Co. v. Amway Corp.,* 376 F.3d 496, 499 n.1 (5th Cir. 2004). Roy has not briefed any non-derivative argument in support of his as-applied challenge and, accordingly, any such further argument is waived.

We thus consider the merits of only Roy's facial challenge to the ordinance, reviewing *de novo* whether the district court erred by granting summary judgment; however, we may "affirm the district court's decision on any ground supported by the record, even if it was not the basis for the judgment." *Gonzalez v. Huerta,* 826 F.3d 854, 856 (5th Cir. 2016) (quotation omitted). "Courts generally disfavor facial challenges, and for good reason." *Voting for Am., Inc. v. Steen,* 732 F.3d 382, 386 (5th Cir. 2013). Facial challenges have been held to "rest on speculation" and "raise the risk of 'premature interpretation of statutes on the basis of factually barebones records.'" *Gibson v. Texas Dep't of Ins.—Div. of Workers' Comp.,* 700 F.3d 227, 238 (5th Cir. 2012) (quoting *Washington State Grange v. Washington State Republican Party,* 552 U.S. 442, 450, 128 S.Ct. 1184, 170 L.Ed.2d 151 (2008)).

The only facial challenge that Roy has adequately briefed pertains to the ordinance's catch-all provision, which prohibits "any act other than [constitutionally protected expression or assembly] in such a manner as to disturb or alarm the public, or make such a disturbance imminent, or to provoke another or other to retaliatory action or violence." MONROE CITY CODE § 12-153. Roy argues that the catch-all provision is unconstitutionally vague and that the district court erred by concluding otherwise.[1]

Though ordinances like the one at issue, which threaten to restrict First p.252 Amendment freedoms, call for a "more stringent vagueness test," Roy nonetheless faces a "daunting" burden given the facial nature of his challenge. *Vill. of Hoffman Estates v. Flipside, Hoffman Estates, Inc.,* 455 U.S. 489, 499, 102 S.Ct. 1186, 71 L.Ed.2d 362 (1982); *Steen,* 732 F.3d at 387. We may reverse the district court only if the city's ordinance "fails to provide people of ordinary intelligence a reasonable opportunity to understand what conduct it prohibits" or "authorizes ... arbitrary and discriminatory enforcement." *Hill v. Colorado,* 530 U.S. 703, 732, 120 S.Ct. 2480, 147 L.Ed.2d 597 (2000). We will not hold that the ordinance is unconstitutionally vague on its face if "it is clear what the ordinance as a whole prohibits" or if the ordinance "is surely valid in the vast majority of its intended applications." *Id.* at 733, 120 S.Ct. 2480.

Roy does not argue that the ordinance fails to provide fair notice of the conduct it prohibits; instead, he argues only that the ordinance "permits 'arbitrary and discriminatory enforcement,' as evidenced by the events in this case." Standing alone, it may be reasonable to suppose that a prohibition on "any act [undertaken] in such a manner as to disturb or alarm the public" fails meaningfully to guide the police and thus poses a substantial risk of arbitrary or discriminatory enforcement. *Cf. Cox v. Louisiana,* 379 U.S. 536, 551-52, 85 S.Ct. 453, 13 L.Ed.2d 471 (1965); *City of Chicago v. Morales,* 527 U.S. 41, 51-55, 119 S.Ct. 1849, 144 L.Ed.2d 67 (1999). But, when entertaining a facial challenge to state or municipal legislation, "[v]agueness can be ameliorated by a state court's authoritative interpretations, if they provide sufficient clarity." *Serv. Emps. Int'l Union, Local 5 v. City of Houston,* 595 F.3d 588, 597 (5th Cir. 2010).

Such is the case, here. The catch-all provision here is substantially similar to language interpreted by the Louisiana Supreme Court in *State v. Jordan,* 369 So.2d 1347 (La. 1979), which addressed an earlier version of the city ordinance at issue in this case. *Id.* at 1350. In *Jordan,* the Louisiana Supreme Court held that conduct is in "a manner which would *foreseeably* disturb or alarm the public" only when that conduct "is violent or boisterous in itself, or ... provocative in the sense that it induces a foreseeable physical disturbance."[2] *Id.* (emphasis added and quotations omitted). Although we are aware that the catch-all provision in the current version of the city's ordinance omits the one word "foreseeably," we find that the *Jordan* construction applies nevertheless. Louisiana courts have tended to apply the construction in similar circumstances. *See Craig v. Carter,* 30625, p.3-4 (La. App. 2 Cir. 9/23/1998), 718 So. 2d 1068, 1071 (applying construction to current version of the city's ordinance in case involving inflammatory speech). And, in any event, we are duty-bound to apply any narrowing construction to which the catch-all provision is "fairly susceptible." *See Netherland v. Eubanks,* 302 F. App'x 244, 246 (5th Cir. 2008) (quoting

City of Lakewood v. Plain Dealer Pub. Co., 486 U.S. 750, 770 n.11, 108 S.Ct. 2138, 100 L.Ed.2d 771 (1988)).

Applying the *Jordan* construction to the catch-all provision, we cannot agree that it is unconstitutionally vague in describing what the "ordinance as a whole prohibits." *Hill,* 530 U.S. at 733, 120 S.Ct. 2480. The p.253 conduct prohibited by the catch-all provision, like the conduct described by the ordinance's enumerated prohibitions, must be violent, or boisterous, or provocative. Although we may question whether, standing alone and without context, a prohibition on "boisterous" conduct would survive an overbreadth challenge, we reiterate that Roy has failed to preserve the issue of overbreadth. *Cf. Hill,* 530 U.S. at 739-40, 120 S.Ct. 2480 (Souter, J., concurring) (a statute is not vague when it "fails to limit very much at all," but rather when it "fails to limit clearly"). We are instead asked to consider whether the catch-all provision's prohibition on violent, boisterous, and provocative conduct is sufficiently clear to satisfy the fair notice requirement of the Due Process Clause of the Fourteenth Amendment. We conclude that it is.

"Violence," "boisterousness," and "provocativeness" are concepts familiar to "common usage and everyday speech." *Doe I v. Landry,* 909 F.3d 99, 118 (5th Cir. 2018). Our circuit has resisted vagueness challenges when the challenged law is couched in "commonly understood" language, *id.,* because such language tends to provide notice to the public and meaningful guidance to the authorities. Here, we are confident that in most cases it will be clear whether a defendant's conduct offends the catch-all provision. To take one example: the Louisiana Supreme Court found in *Jordan* itself that the police lacked probable cause under the ordinance because the suspect had engaged only in non-violent, non-boisterous, non-provocative conduct (sleeping drunkenly in the back of an automobile). 369 So. 2d at 1350.

We also disagree with Roy that the facts of this case illustrate the vagueness of the catch-all provision. Indeed, this case demonstrates that the provision is constitutionally sufficient. Roy testified that the Monroe Police Department allowed him to engage in "street ministry" both before and after the night in question. Booth testified that, on the night Roy did receive a summons, he was perceived to be guilty of conduct and inflammatory speech sufficiently provocative to invite the violent retaliation of those he targeted personally. In the picture that emerges, Monroe police officers make reasonable distinctions between protected expression and forbidden provocation.

Indeed, the Louisiana cases applying the *Jordan* construction have had little difficulty distinguishing between prohibited and permissible conduct. *Compare State v. Stowe,* 93-2020, (La. 4/11/1994) 635 So. 2d 168, 170, 172 n.3 (suspect properly arrested for disturbing the peace after punching through a window, making threats, wandering into traffic, and cursing loudly) *and State v. Heck,* 307 So.2d 332, 333-34 (La. 1975) (defendants properly charged with disturbing the peace after engaging in a fistfight) *with State v. Lindsay,* 388 So.2d 781, 783 (La. 1980) (no disturbance of the peace where defendant was intoxicated on his own property) *and State v. Champagne,* 520 So.2d 447, 451 (La. Ct. App. 1988) (defendant did not disturb the peace by knocking on the window of a squad car to rouse a police dog). The Supreme Court has held that it is evidence of vagueness when courts are unable to converge on a workable standard. *Johnson v. United States,* ___ U.S. ___, 135 S. Ct. 2551, 2558, 192

L.Ed.2d 569 (2015). Here, the courts have not had to struggle to apply the law to a diverse array of factual scenarios.

In sum, we find that the ordinance satisfies the requirements of due process. We thus hold that the ordinance is not unconstitutionally vague.

B.

We next examine whether the district court erred by holding that Booth is entitled p.254 to qualified immunity and, in the process, consider the scope of Roy's appeal, the nature of Roy's claim, the clearly established law applicable to that claim, and the reasonableness of Booth's conduct in the light of that law. The district court held that Booth was entitled to qualified immunity because he "took a firsthand complaint from an alleged victim" after "observing her demeanor and physical manifestations" and thus could not have been "on fair notice" that his "issuance of a citation and summons to Roy would violate Roy's ... rights."

Roy makes three separate arguments that purport to challenge this holding: (1) that the district court defined "clearly established law" with too much specificity, (2) that the district court considered the wrong clearly established right in its qualified immunity analysis, and (3) that the district court erred in determining that Booth's actions could reasonably be thought supported by probable cause.

Typically, to prevail on a motion for summary judgment, the moving party must show "that there is no genuine dispute as to any material fact." Fed. R. Civ. P. 56(a). A fact is "material" if and only if proof of its existence might affect the outcome of the case. *Anderson v. Liberty Lobby, Inc.,* 477 U.S. 242, 248, 106 S.Ct. 2505, 91 L.Ed.2d 202 (1986). There exists a "genuine dispute" about a material fact, as indeed Roy argues, when the evidence would allow a reasonable jury to return a verdict for the nonmovant. *Id.* Notwithstanding: a "good-faith assertion of qualified immunity alters the usual summary judgment burden of proof, shifting it to the plaintiff to show that the defense is not available." *Orr v. Copeland,* 844 F.3d 484, 490 (5th Cir. 2016) (quotation omitted). The burden is thus shifted because qualified immunity "is an immunity from suit rather than a mere defense to liability; and like an absolute immunity, it is effectively lost if a case is erroneously permitted to go to trial." *Mitchell v. Forsyth,* 472 U.S. 511, 526, 105 S.Ct. 2806, 86 L.Ed.2d 411 (1985) (emphasis omitted).

Qualified immunity "protects all but the plainly incompetent or those who knowingly violate the law." *Ashcroft v. al-Kidd,* 563 U.S. 731, 743, 131 S.Ct. 2074, 179 L.Ed.2d 1149 (2011) (quotation omitted). The plaintiff's burden is a formidable one. The plaintiff must show both that the defendant violated the plaintiff's rights and that those rights were "clearly established" at the time of the violation. *Orr,* 844 F.3d at 492. For a right to be clearly established, it must be "beyond debate" that the defendant's conduct was unlawful. *al-Kidd,* 563 U.S. at 741, 131 S.Ct. 2074.

On appeal, Roy asserts only one "clearly established" right to have been violated: in his words, "the right to be free from being arrested for exercising free speech." Roy has thus narrowed the scope of our inquiry solely to whether the district court erred by awarding qualified immunity to Booth on Roy's First Amendment retaliation claim, *i.e.,* the claim that Roy was targeted for harassment and criminal prosecution because Booth opposed his religious expression.[3] *See Gonzalez,* 826 F.3d at 856; *Longoria v. Dretke,* 507 F.3d 898, 901 (5th Cir. 2007) (this court will not "raise and discuss legal issues that [the appellant] has failed to assert").

p.255 To prevail on a First Amendment retaliation claim, however, plaintiffs must plead and prove the absence of probable cause.[4] *Nieves v. Bartlett,* ___ U.S. ___, 139 S. Ct. 1715, 1725, 204 L.Ed.2d 1 (2019). It follows that, at summary judgment, Roy could not rebut Booth's qualified immunity defense without, first, producing evidence that Booth's summons was unsupported by probable cause and, second, establishing that the absence of probable cause would have been apparent to any reasonable officer in Booth's position. *Keenan v. Tejeda,* 290 F.3d 252, 262 (5th Cir. 2002) (holding, in a First Amendment retaliation suit, that "[i]f probable cause existed ... or if reasonable police officers could believe probable cause existed," then the defendants would be "exonerated" from liability).

Roy has principally relied on four cases to establish the absence of probable cause. First, he has attempted to draw an analogy between this case and two non-binding district court decisions, *Harris v. City of Bastrop,* No. CV 15-0761, 2016 WL 3948107, at *6 (W.D. La. July 19, 2016), and *Robertson v. Town of Farmerville,* 830 F. Supp. 2d 183, 188 (W.D. La. 2011). But, in the absence of controlling authority on point, a "*robust* consensus ... of persuasive authority" is necessary to overcome the defense of qualified immunity. *See al-Kidd,* 563 U.S. at 741-42, 131 S.Ct. 2074 (emphasis added). Two non-binding district court opinions hardly constitute a "robust consensus."[5]

Next, Roy relies on a third case, *Evett v. DENTFF,* 330 F.3d 681 (5th Cir. 2003), which, according to Roy, stands for the proposition that an officer lacks probable cause when he fails to search for all available facts "tending to dissipate probable cause." Roy argues that Booth lacked probable cause and should have known it because, like the officer in *Evett,* he failed to investigate further after receiving an uncorroborated statement. But Roy's argument puts more weight on *Evett* than the case allows. In *Evett,* the officer's failure to conduct further investigation meant that the officer's probable cause determination hinged on nothing more than the unsubstantiated statement of another officer—a statement that, even if believed, established only a tenuous connection between the suspect and any criminal activity. 330 F.3d at 687-89.

Here, by contrast, no further investigation was necessary because Booth was relying on the personal knowledge of a witness and victim of the alleged conduct. *Johnson v. Bryant,*[6] No. 94-10661, 1995 p.256 WL 29317, at *3 (5th Cir. Jan. 17, 1995) (unpublished) ("A victim's accusation identifying an individual as the perpetrator is generally sufficient to establish probable cause."); *United States v. Burbridge,* 252 F.3d 775, 778 (5th Cir. 2001) (an eyewitness identification will establish probable cause "unless, at the time of the arrest, there is an apparent reason for the officer to believe that the eyewitness was lying [or mistaken]"). Indeed, we have previously held officers' probable cause determinations reasonable in similar circumstances. *See Bone v. Dunnaway,* 657 F. App'x 258, 261 (5th Cir. 2016) (per curiam) (witness statement made reasonable officer's belief that there was probable cause under a New Orleans disturbing the peace ordinance); *Cooper v. City of La Porte Police Dep't,* 608 F. App'x 195, 200 (5th Cir. 2015) (per curiam) (officer made a reasonable probable cause determination by relying on eyewitness accounts conveyed "over the phone and at the scene"). Roy's analogy to *Evett* fails.

Finally, Roy cites our decision in *Vance v. Nunnery,* 137 F.3d 270 (5th Cir. 1998), to support his theory that Booth clearly lacked probable cause because he failed to corroborate Falcon's allegations. In *Vance,* an officer was found to lack probable cause because he relied on witness statements that did not connect the suspect with the crime under investigation. 137 F.3d at 276-77. Booth, however, relied on Falcon, a victim who claimed personal knowledge and who identified Roy as the perpetrator, a clear connection between the suspect and the relevant offense. Thus, *Vance* does not even apply to the situation here. Moreover, it is far from the kind of "clearly established law" that would make Booth's probable cause determination unreasonable.

In sum, we find that Roy has failed to carry his summary judgment burden.[7] Roy has not shown that Booth's issuance of the summons was unsupported by probable cause or, much less, that a reasonable officer would have known that it was unsupported. On the contrary, our decisions in *Johnson, Burbridge,* and other comparable cases convince us that probable cause supported Booth's summons. His reliance on the purported victim was justified because there was no "apparent reason" to disbelieve her account. We affirm the district court's ruling that Booth is entitled to qualified immunity.

C.

Having addressed the constitutionality of the ordinance and Booth's entitlement to qualified immunity, we find that each of Roy's remaining issues has been resolved. First, Roy challenges the district p.257 court's dismissal of what he calls his "Due Process claim" against the city. The due process violation alleged, however, is that the city deprived Roy of his right to be free from prosecution under an unconstitutional ordinance. We have already rejected Roy's constitutional challenges to the ordinance. His "Due Process claim" has thus been decided by that holding.[8]

Similarly, Roy argues that the district court erred by dismissing his Fourth Amendment claims, which he frames in the language of "malicious prosecution" and "false arrest." But there is "no ... freestanding constitutional right to be free from malicious prosecution" or false arrest. *Castellano v. Fragozo,* 352 F.3d 939, 945, 953 (5th Cir. 2003) (en banc). In this respect, Roy is entitled to relief, if at all, only because Booth's issuance of a summons violated Roy's Fourth Amendment right to be free from unreasonable seizures. The district court held that the issuance of a misdemeanor summons is not a "seizure" implicating Fourth Amendment rights. Perhaps for this reason, Roy's brief addresses only whether Roy's receipt of a summons was a "seizure," not whether the seizure, if any, was unconstitutional.

However, the question of whether a "seizure" occurred is moot because it is plain that any seizure was not "unreasonable." *See* U.S. Const. amend. IV. We have already held that Booth's issuance of the summons was supported by probable cause. Accordingly, even if Booth had made an arrest, the arrest would not have violated the Fourth Amendment. *See Lockett v. New Orleans City,* 607 F.3d 992, 997 (5th Cir. 2010).

IV.

To sum up: in this opinion, we have decided that the city of Monroe's "disturbing the peace" ordinance is not unconstitutionally vague; that, because Sergeant Booth had probable cause to issue a summons under the ordinance, he was entitled to qualified immunity from Roy's First Amendment retaliation claim; and that, in the light of these holdings, Roy cannot prevail on his claims under the Fourth Amendment and Due Process Clause. The judgment of the district court is

AFFIRMED.

[1] Roy has not preserved the question of overbreadth. Roy's brief states in conclusory fashion that the city's ordinance "is unconstitutionally overbroad," but we are not prepared to weigh in on a constitutional question when the party raising it has failed to cite any authority or evidence. *See Procter & Gamble,* 376 F.3d at 499 n.1.

[2] The pedigree of this construction can be traced directly to the Supreme Court's decision in *Garner v. Louisiana,* 368 U.S. 157, 82 S.Ct. 248, 7 L.Ed.2d 207 (1961), which applied the same construction to Louisiana's statewide disturbing the peace statute and held that the statute did not prohibit a peaceful sit-in at a segregated lunch counter. *Id.* at 159-74, 82 S.Ct. 248.

[3] We do not address whether Roy has shown that his constitutional rights were violated because he was targeted for his religious views. For reasons stated in the body of this opinion, this appeal is resolved by our holding that the ordinance is constitutional and our finding that Booth's summons for violating that ordinance was supported by probable cause.

[4] The Supreme Court has recognized a "narrow" exception to this rule where the "plaintiff presents objective evidence that he was arrested [and that] otherwise similarly situated individuals not engaged in the same sort of protected speech had not been." *Nieves,* 139 S. Ct. at 1727. Our review of the record has not turned up any such evidence. On the contrary, the record reveals that Roy, the most "similarly situated" individual of all, was allowed to conduct street ministry both before and after the night in question, without any harassment from the police.

[5] In any event, *Harris* and *Robertson* are distinguishable. In *Harris,* probable cause was not established because genuine factual disputes made it unclear whether the arresting officers had reason to suspect the plaintiff of anything more than "us[ing] a few curse words" that were not "directed at the police officers or anyone else." *Harris,* 2016 WL 3948107, at *1, *6. Similarly, in *Robertson,* there was a genuine dispute whether the police had *any* reason to suspect the plaintiff of various traffic violations. 830 F. Supp. 2d at 188. Here, there is no dispute that Booth relied on the victim's specific statement that Roy had stalked her while making inflammatory remarks. For reasons stated in-text, this allegation was credible enough to create probable cause.

[6] Although *Johnson* is an unpublished opinion, it is precedential because it was issued prior to January 1, 1996. 5th Cir. R. 47.5.3.

[7] Roy complains that he would have been better able to satisfy his summary judgment burden had the district court granted his motion to reopen discovery. But a party moving to reopen discovery must "set forth a plausible basis for believing that specified facts, susceptible of collection within a reasonable time frame, probably

exist and indicate how the emergent facts, if adduced, will influence the outcome of the pending summary judgment motion." *Smith v. Reg'l Transit Auth.,* 827 F.3d 412, 423 (5th Cir. 2016) (citations and quotations omitted). Roy has argued that the district court should have granted him additional discovery so that he could retain "experts showing that a certain case or certain training" would have made Booth aware that he was violating Roy's clearly established rights. But Roy alleged in his complaint that "Booth knew at the time [of the incident that] statements in his [Probable Cause Narrative] did not satisfy the elements of probable cause." Roy thus had ample incentive, during the *original* discovery window, to retain any experts capable of showing that Booth knew he lacked probable cause when he issued the summons. Furthermore, his failure to do so suggests that no facts "susceptible of collection within a reasonable time frame" could have influenced the outcome of the summary judgment proceedings below.

[8] Moreover, and as the district court pointed out, Roy's "Due Process claim" is defeated by his failure to produce evidence satisfying the prerequisites of municipal liability under *Monell.* To establish municipal liability in a § 1983 case, a plaintiff must adduce proof of three elements: "a policymaker; an official policy; and a violation of constitutional rights whose 'moving force' is the policy or custom." *Piotrowski v. City of Houston,* 237 F.3d 567, 578 (5th Cir. 2001). Here, having rejected Roy's challenges to the ordinance and having determined that Sergeant Booth's summons was supported by probable cause, we cannot say that a reasonable trier of fact could find that the Due Process Clause was violated by the city, much less that the violation's moving force was a city policy or custom.

938 F.3d 672 (2019)

Paul A. CLEVELAND; Paris LeBlanc; Mindy Capello, Plaintiffs-Appellees,
v.
Lillian BELL, Defendant-Appellant.

No. 18-30968.

United States Court of Appeals, Fifth Circuit.
FILED September 13, 2019.

Cleveland v. Bell, 938 F. 3d 672 (5th Cir. 2019)

Appeal from the United States District Court for the Middle District of Louisiana.

Franz Nicholas Borghardt, Borghardt Law Firm, Baton Rouge, LA, for Plaintiffs-Appellees.

Arthur Howell Andrews, Parish Attorney's Office for the Parish of East Baton Rouge, Baton Rouge, LA, for Defendant-Appellant.

Before SOUTHWICK, WILLETT, and OLDHAM, Circuit Judges.

p.674 ANDREW S. OLDHAM, Circuit Judge:

Paul Cleveland's survivors sued a prison nurse named Lillian Bell under 42 U.S.C. § 1983 for allegedly violating his Fourteenth Amendment rights. The district court denied qualified immunity to Nurse Bell. We reverse.

I.

Paul Cleveland was seventy-two years old when he was detained at the East Baton Rouge Parish Prison on September 19, 2014. Upon entering the Prison, Cleveland completed a health assessment. According to the assessment, Cleveland had a host of health problems, including diabetes, high blood pressure, rheumatoid arthritis, and peripheral artery disease. During his two months at the Prison, Cleveland received medication for his conditions and had numerous visits with medical staff regarding a variety of health issues.

On the morning of November 10th, Cleveland received emergency medical treatment after he became dizzy and nauseated in the bathroom and fainted. Nurse Ebony White checked his vital signs, treated him for a cut on the back of his head, and put him on a list to see the next available doctor. In the late afternoon, Cleveland said he was "going to pass out." Nurse White visited Cleveland, and Cleveland said he felt dizzy when sitting up or walking long distances. Cleveland demanded to go to the hospital for evaluation and said he wanted "pain medication to knock him out." He reported no chest pains or shortness of breath. Nurse White told Cleveland that he did not exhibit any signs of acute distress, so he would not be sent to the emergency room. Instead, Cleveland would be placed on the list to see the next available doctor for further evaluation.

The nurses brought Cleveland back to the "medical tank," where patients with health issues are kept for observation by medical staff. Nurse White wrote in her notes that Cleveland was "very argumentative" while he was in the medical tank and was banging on the windows. Cleveland was eventually moved from the medical tank to a single cell.

On November 11th, at around 5:54 p.m., Nurse Bell went with Officer Richard Camp to Cleveland's cell to give him his medication. Cleveland was lying in bed, and Nurse Bell told him to get a cup of water so he could take his pills. Cleveland said that he was too weak to get up. Nurse Bell told Cleveland "to stop playing and come get your medication ... there is nothing wrong with you." But Cleveland said that he couldn't get up. Nurse Bell left and said she would come back after completing her "pill call" with the other inmates.

p.675 Around 8:42 p.m., Nurse Bell returned and asked Officer Camp how Cleveland was doing. Camp said he "seems to be sleeping" but had been turning around in his bed and occasionally hit the wall with his fist. Nurse Bell said "okay" and returned to the medical department. Her notes in Cleveland's medical chart indicate that she completed a high-priority "[l]ockdown/trusty sick call" at 11:53 p.m. But to Officer Camp's knowledge, Nurse Bell did not visit Cleveland again to give him his medicine.

At around 2:32 a.m. on November 12th, Officer Camp saw that Cleveland had defecated on himself and his mattress. Officer Camp called Officers Jasmyn Cage and Larry Turner to supervise the cleanup of Cleveland and his cell. The officers told Cleveland to "get up off the floor and come to the bars to be handcuffed so that his cell could be cleaned out." But Cleveland continued to lie on the floor and said that he was "tired." The officers entered Cleveland's cell, removed his dirty mattress and jumpsuit, and allowed staff to clean his cell. Cleveland received a clean jumpsuit, but he declined a chance to use the shower.

During the cleanup, Officer Cage called Nurse Bell. Officer Cage told her that Cleveland was lying "on the floor and talking about [how] he was tired and he couldn't get up." Nurse Bell said she thought he was "faking" and was "trying to get back in the infirmary."

After the call, Officer Camp continued to make his rounds in the Prison. According to his written report, every time he passed by Cleveland's cell, Cleveland "would rollover [sic] or move." If he did not see Cleveland move, he would talk to Cleveland. Officer Camp didn't hold a conversation with Cleveland but would call his name and make sure "he either moved or every now and then ... would answer." Officer Camp paid "extra attention to Mr. Cleveland because of what had occurred." A deputy had advised Officer Camp to keep an eye on Cleveland because Cleveland had just come back from the medical department.

At 4:05 a.m. on November 12th, Officer Camp passed out food to inmates. As he gave the inmates their trays, he made sure they were awake. When Officer Camp went to Cleveland's cell, he noticed Cleveland was unresponsive. He had seen Cleveland just five or ten minutes earlier. Cleveland had no pulse, and attempts to resuscitate him proved unsuccessful.

Cleveland's survivors sued a bevy of medical professionals and law-enforcement officers under 42 U.S.C. § 1983 and various other provisions of law. The district court granted summary judgment to all defendants except Nurse Bell. It refused to grant Nurse Bell qualified immunity from a claim alleging deliberate indifference to Cleveland's medical needs. Nurse Bell timely appealed.

II.

"Qualified immunity is an immunity from suit rather than a mere defense to liability." *Pearson v. Callahan,* 555 U.S. 223, 237, 129 S.Ct. 808, 172 L.Ed.2d 565 (2009) (quotation omitted). "[I]t protects all but the plainly incompetent or those who knowingly violate the law." *Ashcroft v. al-Kidd,* 563 U.S. 731, 743, 131 S.Ct. 2074, 179 L.Ed.2d 1149 (2011) (quotation omitted). "[O]nce properly raised by the defendant, the plaintiff has the burden to negate the assertion of qualified immunity." *King v. Handorf,* 821 F.3d 650, 653 (5th Cir. 2016) (quotation omitted).

To negate qualified immunity, the plaintiff must make two showings. First, the plaintiff must show the defendant violated his constitutional rights. *Pearson,* 555 U.S. at 232, 129 S.Ct. 808. p.676 Second, the plaintiff must show the asserted right was clearly established at the time of the alleged misconduct. *Ibid.* If the plaintiff fails at either step, the federal court can grant qualified immunity by addressing either step or both of them. *See id.* at 236, 129 S.Ct. 808; *Morrow v. Meachum,* 917 F.3d 870, 874 (5th Cir. 2019).

The Supreme Court has said the Eighth Amendment prohibits "deliberate indifference" to a prisoner's medical needs. *Farmer v. Brennan,* 511 U.S. 825, 834-47, 114 S.Ct. 1970, 128 L.Ed.2d 811 (1994). And we've held the same rule applies to pretrial detainees like Cleveland under the Fourteenth Amendment. *Hare v. City of Corinth,* 74 F.3d 633, 648-49 (5th Cir. 1996) (en banc).

To establish a constitutional violation, a plaintiff must show that the defendant: (1) was "aware of facts from which the inference could be drawn that a substantial risk of serious harm exists"; (2) subjectively "dr[e]w the inference" that the risk existed; and (3) disregarded the risk. *Farmer,* 511 U.S. at 837, 114 S.Ct. 1970. In describing the second element, the Supreme Court has emphasized that a "prison official cannot be found liable" unless she "knows of" an excessive risk to inmate health or safety. *Ibid.* A failure to act "unaccompanied by knowledge of a significant risk of harm" is insufficient to establish a constitutional violation. *Id.* at 837-38, 114 S.Ct. 1970. It is not enough to identify a significant risk that the official "should have perceived but did not." *Id.* at 838, 114 S.Ct. 1970.

In this case, the district court failed to provide any analysis of why it denied qualified immunity to Nurse Bell. Instead, it gave a one-sentence conclusory statement: "Taking the facts in the light most favorable to Plaintiffs permits a conclusion that, on the night before and morning of Cleveland's death, she acted with deliberate indifference to Cleveland's welfare." *Cleveland v. Gautreaux,* 2018 WL 3966269, at *16 (M.D. La. Aug. 17, 2018). The court did not identify which facts showed that Nurse Bell: (1) was aware of information that could lead to the inference that Cleveland was experiencing a life-threatening medical emergency; (2) drew the inference and was subjectively aware of how serious the situation was; and (3) disregarded Cleveland's life-threatening medical emergency, despite appreciating its existence.

When the district court fails to identify which facts it relied on, we must review the entire record to determine "what facts the district court, in the light most favorable to the nonmoving party, likely assumed." *Johnson v. Jones,* 515 U.S. 304, 319, 115 S.Ct. 2151, 132 L.Ed.2d 238 (1995). We then review *de novo* the district court's application of the law to those facts. *Hare v. City of Corinth,* 135 F.3d 320, 325 (5th Cir. 1998).

Having reviewed the record, we find no evidence that on November 11th or 12th, Nurse Bell subjectively "dr[e]w the inference" that Cleveland was experiencing a life-threatening medical emergency. *Farmer,* 511 U.S. at 837, 114 S.Ct. 1970. The record contains statements from Nurse Bell indicating that she thought there was nothing wrong with Cleveland and believed he was faking illness. But nothing suggests that these statements reflected anything other than her sincere opinion at the time. Even if we construe her statements in the light most favorable to Plaintiffs, they are insufficient to establish that Nurse Bell knew how serious the situation was. The Supreme Court has made clear that actual knowledge is an essential element of Plaintiffs' burden, as mere negligence cannot establish a constitutional violation. *Id.* at 835-38, 114 S.Ct. 1970. Given the lack of evidence about Nurse Bell's subjective awareness of a substantial risk of serious harm to Cleveland, p.677 Plaintiffs cannot show a constitutional violation at step one of the qualified-immunity analysis.

Plaintiffs have also failed to show a potential violation of clearly established law at step two. The Supreme Court has repeatedly told us "not to define clearly established law at a high level of generality." *Mullenix v. Luna,* ___ U.S. ___, 136 S. Ct. 305, 308, 193 L.Ed.2d 255 (2015) (per curiam) (quotation omitted). The dispositive question in this step of the qualified-immunity analysis is "whether the violative nature of *particular* conduct is clearly established." *Ibid.* (quoting *al-Kidd,* 563 U.S. at 742, 131 S.Ct. 2074). Cases that are "too factually distinct to speak clearly to the specific circumstances here" are not enough to deny qualified immunity. *Id.* at 312.

The district court relied on two of our decisions for the applicable clearly established law. *See Cleveland,* 2018 WL 3966269, at *16 (citing *McCormick v. Stalder,* 105 F.3d 1059 (5th Cir. 1997), and *Fielder v. Bosshard,* 590 F.2d 105 (5th Cir. 1979)). We assume without deciding that our precedent could, in an appropriate case, clearly establish the law. *See, e.g., Taylor v. Barkes,* ___ U.S. ___, 135 S. Ct. 2042, 2045, 192 L.Ed.2d 78 (2015) (per curiam) (summarily reversing the Third Circuit for relying on circuit precedent to deny qualified immunity, but "[a]ssuming for the sake of argument that a right can be 'clearly established' by circuit precedent despite disagreement in the courts of appeals"). Even so, *McCormick* does not fit the bill. That case held that the plaintiff's constitutional claim regarding tuberculosis treatment was "properly dismissed as frivolous." *McCormick,* 105 F.3d at 1062. *McCormick* does not clearly establish anything.

And this case is much different from *Fielder.* While in jail, Fielder began to experience hallucinations, behave erratically, and shake physically. *Fielder,* 590 F.2d at 108. Ten hours after these symptoms began, he said: "Help me. I need a doctor." *Ibid.* Jail staff never brought him to a medical professional, and he was found dead in his cell at 7 a.m. the next day. *Ibid.* Here, by contrast, Cleveland received emergency medical attention two days before he died. The decision not to hospitalize him after he fainted on November 10th was based on a different nurse's medical judgment after she examined Cleveland. Nurse Bell's involvement began only on November 11th. That night, she tried to give Cleveland his medication, but he refused it. A few hours later, she returned to check up on Cleveland but decided not to visit him after being told that he seemed to be sleeping. As we noted in *Fielder,* there "is a vast difference between an earnest, albeit unsuccessful attempt to care for a prisoner" and deliberate indifference. *Ibid. Fielder's* very different facts could not put Nurse Bell on "fair notice" that she was acting unconstitutionally. *Mullenix,* 136 S. Ct. at 314 (quoting *Hope v. Pelzer,* 536 U.S. 730, 739, 122 S.Ct. 2508, 153 L.Ed.2d 666 (2002)).

Our Court has previously held that a "record of extensive medical treatment spanning the final two and one half months" of an inmate's incarceration—combined with "the lack of evidence to establish the necessary culpable intent"—was sufficient for qualified immunity. *Gobert v. Caldwell,* 463 F.3d 339, 351-52 (5th Cir. 2006). Cleveland's case is closer to *Gobert* than to *Fielder.* Nurse Bell is therefore entitled to qualified immunity.

* * *

The district court's denial of summary judgment to Nurse Bell is REVERSED.

935 F.3d 444 (2019)

Randy COLE; Karen Cole; Ryan Cole, Plaintiffs-Appellees
v.
Carl CARSON, Defendant-Appellant.
Randy Cole; Karen Cole; Ryan Cole, Plaintiffs-Appellees
v.
Michael Hunter; Martin Cassidy, Defendants-Appellants.

No. 14-10228, No. 15-10045.

United States Court of Appeals, Fifth Circuit.

August 20, 2019.

As Revised August 21, 2019.

Cole v. Carson, 935 F. 3d 444 (5th Cir. 2019)

Appeals from the United States District Court for the Northern District of Texas.

Rowe Jack Ayres, Jr., Christopher Scott Ayres, Esq., Ayres Law Office, P.C., Dallas, TX, Amir H. Ali, Roderick & Solange MacArthur Justice Center, Washington, DC, James Mark Mann, Mann Firm, Henderson, TX, for Plaintiffs-Appellees.

James Thomas Jeffrey, Jr., Esq., Law Offices of Jim Jeffrey, Arlington, TX, Norman Ray Giles, William S. Helfand, Lewis, Brisbois, Bisgaard & Smith, L.L.P., Houston, TX, for Defendant-Appellant.

Clark McAdams Neily, III, Cato Institute, Washington, DC, for Amicus Curiae Cato Institute.

Gregory Todd Butler, Esq., Phelps Dunbar, L.L.P., Jackson, MS, for Amici Curiae International Municipal Lawyers Association, Texas Municipal League, Texas City Attorneys Association, Texas Association of Counties, Combined Law Enforcement Associations of Texas, City of Arlington, Texas, City of Garland, Texas, City of Grand Prairie, Texas, Mississippi Municipal Service Company, National Association of Police Organizations, Houston Police Officers Union.

Before STEWART, Chief Judge, and HIGGINBOTHAM, JONES, SMITH, DENNIS, CLEMENT, OWEN, ELROD, SOUTHWICK, HAYNES, GRAVES, HIGGINSON, COSTA, WILLETT, HO, DUNCAN, ENGELHARDT, and OLDHAM, Circuit Judges.

p.446 PATRICK E. HIGGINBOTHAM, Circuit Judge, joined by CARL E. STEWART, Chief Judge, and JAMES L. DENNIS, EDITH BROWN CLEMENT, JENNIFER WALKER ELROD, LESLIE H. SOUTHWICK, CATHARINA HAYNES, JAMES E. GRAVES, STEPHEN A. HIGGINSON, GREGG COSTA, and KURT D. ENGELHARDT, Circuit Judges:[1]

The Supreme Court over several years has developed protection from civil liability for persons going about their tasks as government workers in the form of immunity;

not the absolute immunity enjoyed by prosecutors and judges, but a qualified immunity. Today we again repair to issues inherent in the qualification. The doctrine protects at the earliest stage of litigation at which the defense's application is determinable. To that end, courts have developed procedures and pretrial practices, including appellate review of pretrial denials, otherwise interlocutory and unappealable, and a reply to an answer under Rule 7(a) on order of the district court, particularized to address the defense of immunity in a motion to dismiss or for summary judgment. When those processes do not yield pretrial resolution, as with competing factual narratives, the full reach of qualified immunity gives way to a trial, the first point at which its application is determinable. And in obeisance to constitutional mandate, the worker's defense enjoys a right to the protection of a jury—long a bastion interposed between the state and person, and assured by the Founders. And it signifies that today the district judge has multiple ways to present fully the claims and defenses to a jury to ensure the government p.447 worker a full draw upon his immunity defense,[2] including resolution of the competing factual narratives, one of which—or a meld of both—may foreclose liability.[3]

In this case, police officers from Sachse, Texas argue that the district court should have sustained their defense of qualified immunity on their pretrial motions to dismiss and for summary judgment. Ryan Cole and his parents Karen and Randy (collectively "the Coles") sue Officer Carl Carson, Lieutenant Martin Cassidy, and Officer Michael Hunter of the Sachse Police Department under 42 U.S.C. § 1983. The Coles allege that the officers violated Ryan Cole's Fourth and Fourteenth Amendment rights during an incident in which Cassidy and Hunter shot Ryan without warning, and then lied about what happened. The officers filed dispositive pretrial motions in the district court, asserting the defense of qualified immunity. The district court denied these motions, concluding that immunity could not be determined at this stage of the proceeding. In *Cole I,* a panel of our court affirmed the denial of summary judgment as to the Coles' Fourth Amendment excessive-force claim and the denial of the motion to dismiss the Coles' Fourteenth Amendment false-charge claim, but reversed denials of the motion to dismiss the Coles' Fourth Amendment and *Brady* claims attacking the alleged fabrication of evidence.[4] The Supreme Court vacated *Cole I,* and remanded for consideration in light of its intervening decision in *Mullenix v. Luna.*[5] On remand, the panel affirmed the denial of summary judgment as to the excessive-force claim. Because the Coles' other claims were unaffected by the reasoning of *Mullenix,* the panel reinstated *Cole I*'s holdings on the fabrication-of-evidence claims. We reheard this case en banc to reconsider disposition of the Coles' excessive-force claim in light of *Mullenix.*

We conclude that it will be for a jury, and not judges, to resolve the competing factual narratives as detailed in the district court opinion and the record as to the Coles' excessive-force claim. Limited by our jurisdiction to the materiality of factual disputes, we AFFIRM the denial of summary judgment on this claim and DISMISS Cassidy and Hunter's appeal. The Coles' remaining claims are unaffected by the reasoning of *Mullenix,* and so, as in *Cole I,* we AFFIRM denial of the motion to dismiss the Coles' Fourteenth Amendment false-charge claim; REVERSE denial of the motion to dismiss the Coles' Fourth Amendment and *Brady* fabrication-of-evidence claims based on qualified immunity; and return the case to the district court for trial and resolution of issues consistent with this opinion.

I

A.

On October 25, 2010, at around 10:30 a.m., the Sachse Police Department called p.448 available units to the neighboring town of Garland, Texas. There police were searching for Ryan Cole, a seventeen-year-old white male, reported to be walking in the neighborhood with a handgun. Officer Michael Hunter responded by proceeding immediately to the Garland neighborhood. In a statement given on the day of the incident, Hunter related that on arriving in the neighborhood, he overheard a civilian stating that Ryan had given up one of his guns, and that he had unsuccessfully tried to persuade Ryan to not keep his handgun. Hunter searched the area, and saw two officers following Ryan, who was walking away from them holding his gun to his head, approaching a wooded area along Highway 78. Although told by officers that things were under control, Hunter volunteered to go behind the wooded area and possibly intercept Ryan, and suggested that Officer Carl Carson, who was also present, join him.

Four years later, after this litigation had commenced, Hunter for the first time recalled that the civilian he had overheard had described an altercation with Ryan in which Ryan had threatened him. He also then for the first time recalled hearing police-radio transmissions indicating that officers were protecting nearby schools because of "[Ryan]'s dangerous conduct which posed a risk of serious harm to a great many innocent in the vicinity." Hunter otherwise learned nothing "that would cause [him] to believe [Ryan] was violent or wanted to hurt anyone."[6] Hunter understood that Ryan was suicidal, and, four years after the incident, he also raised the possibility that Ryan was using suicide as a pretext to evade the police.

Meanwhile, Lieutenant Martin Cassidy had also heard the original dispatcher's summons. Cassidy called the Sachse Police Department for more information. On the day of the incident, Cassidy swore that he learned "this subject had shown up at [a] residence with a handgun and had just recently been seen walking away." But, four years later, after this litigation had commenced, like Hunter, Cassidy remembered learning more, including that Ryan "had threatened to shoot anyone who tried to take his gun"; had refused an order to drop his weapon; and might be headed for Sachse High School "to possibly engage in violence." Cassidy also decided to intercept Ryan on Highway 78.

The three officers separately arrived at the side of Highway 78 at around the same time. Hunter parked his motorbike and drew his duty weapon; Cassidy also drew his firearm and advised Carson to be ready to use his taser. The officers started walking along the tree line. A steep embankment rose from railroad tracks to the area along Highway 78. Ryan would have to climb this embankment to approach the tree line. Cassidy and Hunter used both the edge of the embankment and the vegetation to conceal themselves as they walked. Hunter also removed his white motorcycle helmet in order to be less conspicuous. Cassidy soon heard a message over the police radio: Ryan was ascending to the tree line. Hunter heard movement in the brush, and signaled to his colleagues.

What occurred next is disputed. Viewing the summary judgment evidence and drawing reasonable inferences in the light most favorable to the non-movant Coles, the district court determined that a reasonable jury could find the following: Ryan backed out from the tree line in front of Hunter and Cassidy, "unaware of the Officers' p.449 presence."[7] Ryan was holding his handgun pointed to his own head, where it remained.[8] "[Ryan] never pointed a weapon at the Officers,"[9] and "never made a threatening or provocative gesture towards [the] Officers."[10] "Officers [Cassidy and Hunter] had the time and opportunity to give a warning" for Ryan to disarm himself.[11] However, the officers provided "no warning ... that granted [Ryan] a sufficient time to respond,"[12] such that Ryan "was not given an opportunity to disarm himself before he was shot."[13] Hunter and Cassidy then shot Ryan multiple times. Officer Hunter's first shot struck Ryan as he was oriented away from the officers at a 90-degree angle—that is, he was not facing Officer Hunter.[14] Following impact of the first shot, as Ryan's body turned or fell towards Hunter, he shot him a second time.[15] As an involuntary reflex to being shot, Ryan pulled the trigger, shooting himself in the temple.[16] But the officers did not know that.

Following the shooting, the three officers remained together at the scene. The Coles allege that during this time the officers conspired to insulate Cassidy and Hunter from liability with a fabricated narrative in which Ryan was facing Hunter and pointed his weapon at the officer, at which point Cassidy and Hunter fired on Ryan in defense. Eventually, members of the Garland Police Department arrived and took control of the scene, but did not follow the standard procedure of separating witnesses to ensure independent recollections. Instead, Cassidy and Hunter were allowed to return to their police station together. Later that day, the officers provided statements to investigators. Hunter stated that he had no chance to issue a command to Ryan. Cassidy and Carson, however, swore that, when Ryan backed out from the brush, they heard Hunter shout a warning to him. Hunter and Cassidy stated that Ryan then turned towards Hunter and pointed his handgun at Hunter, at which point both officers—fearing for Hunter's life—opened fire defensively.[17]

The Dallas County District Attorney presented the officers' narrative to a grand jury, which no-billed the officers and charged Ryan with felony aggravated assault of a public servant. As a result of the charge, Ryan, incapacitated in intensive care, was placed under house arrest. About a month after the indictment, investigators p.450 received a ballistics report from the crime lab. The ballistics analysis, taken together with stippling observed around Ryan's head wound, made clear that Ryan had shot himself in the temple, confounding the officers' account.[18] Dallas County prosecutors then dropped the aggravated assault charge, accepting Ryan's plea to misdemeanor unlawful carry of a weapon, a $500 fine, and forfeiture of his handgun.

Ryan suffered permanent injuries, including cognitive impairment, partial paralysis, and other serious mental and physical disabilities.

B.

The Coles brought, inter alia, four Section 1983 claims against the officers. First, they allege a violation of Ryan's Fourth Amendment right against the use of excessive force arising from the shooting. Second, the Coles allege a violation of Ryan's Fourteenth Amendment right against the imposition of false charges arising from the fabrication of evidence. Third, they allege a violation of Ryan's Fourth Amendment right against unreasonable seizures arising from the fabrication of evidence. Fourth, they allege a *Brady* violation arising from the fabrication of evidence. The officers filed a motion to dismiss these claims under Rule 12(b)(6), asserting qualified immunity defenses. The district court denied the motion in a January 2014 Memorandum Opinion and Order.[19] Carson alone appealed the denial of the motion to dismiss the Coles' three fabrication-of-evidence claims based on qualified immunity. The district court stayed these fabrication-of-evidence claims pending Carson's appeal, allowing the Coles limited discovery against Cassidy and Hunter's qualified immunity defenses to the excessive-force claim. With that discovery complete, the two officers moved for summary judgment, rearguing qualified immunity. The district court denied their motion and Cassidy and Hunter appealed.

The officers' appeals were consolidated. In 2015, in *Cole I,* a panel of this court affirmed the district court's denial of summary judgment on the Coles' excessive-force claim, affirmed denial of the motion to dismiss the Coles' Fourteenth Amendment false-charge claim, and reversed the denial as to the Coles' Fourth Amendment and *Brady* fabrication-of-evidence claims, finding the qualified immunity defense applicable for these claims. The officers petitioned the Supreme Court for a writ of certiorari. In November 2016, the Supreme Court granted certiorari, vacated the panel's judgment, and remanded the case for further consideration in light of *Mullenix v. Luna,*[20] decided in the intervening time.[21]

p.451 On remand from the Supreme Court, recognizing that its jurisdiction was limited to determining the materiality of factual disputes that the district court determined were genuine, the panel once again held that the applicability of qualified immunity for Cassidy and Hunter could not be determined at the summary judgment stage.[22] Finding the Supreme Court's remand order reached no further, the panel reinstated the *Cole I* opinion on the Coles' three fabrication-of-evidence claims.[23] The officers moved for rehearing en banc, which we granted.[24]

II

A.

We hear this case on remand from the Court for further consideration in light of *Mullenix.* We do not reach issues unaddressed by the mandate on remand,[25] and so we hold as in *Cole I* with respect to the Coles' three fabrication-of-evidence claims. First, we affirm the district court's denial of the motion to dismiss the Coles' Fourteenth Amendment claim regarding the imposition of false charges.[26] Second, finding qualified immunity applicable, we reverse the denial of the motion to dismiss the Coles' claim that the alleged fabrication of evidence violated the Fourth Amendment.[27] Lastly, finding qualified immunity applicable, we reverse the denial of the motion to dismiss the Coles' claim that the alleged fabrication of evidence entailed a *Brady* violation.[28]

B.

The qualified immunity inquiry includes two parts. In the first we ask whether the officer's alleged conduct has violated a federal right; in the second we ask whether the right in question was "clearly established" at the time of the alleged violation, such that the officer was on notice of the unlawfulness of his or her conduct.[29] The officer is entitled to qualified immunity if there is no violation, or if the conduct did not violate law clearly established at the time.[30]

p.452 On an appeal of a denial of summary judgment on the basis of qualified immunity, our jurisdiction is limited to examining the materiality of factual disputes the district court determined were genuine.[31] "[I]n an interlocutory appeal we cannot challenge the district court's assessments regarding the sufficiency of the evidence— that is, the question whether there is enough evidence in the record for a jury to conclude that certain facts are true."[32] "[W]e lack jurisdiction to resolve the genuineness of any factual disputes" and "consider only whether the district court erred in assessing the legal significance of the conduct that the district court deemed sufficiently supported for purposes of summary judgment."[33] Like the district court, we must view the facts and draw reasonable inferences in the light most favorable to the plaintiff and ask whether the defendant would be entitled to qualified immunity on those facts.[34] The Supreme Court has summarily reversed this court for failing to take the evidence and draw factual inferences in the non-movants' favor at the summary judgment stage.[35] In doing so, the Court emphasized that the requirement is no less binding "even when ... a court decides only the clearly-established prong of the standard."[36] Within the limited scope of our inquiry, review is de novo.[37]

As instructed, we turn to the guidance provided by the Supreme Court in *Mullenix*. In that case, the Court reviewed a denial of qualified immunity to an officer who had shot and killed a fugitive in a car chase. This court had decided that the officer violated the clearly established rule that deadly force was prohibited "against a fleeing felon who does not pose a sufficient threat of harm to the officer or others."[38] The officer in *Mullenix* reasonably perceived some threat of harm, but we had held the threat was not "sufficient." The Supreme Court reversed our decision. It found that the rule we articulated lacked a referent to define the "sufficiency" of threats.[39] Precedents provided a "hazy legal backdrop," at best.[40] Given these deficient sources, an officer could not reasonably derive an applicable rule to govern his or her conduct in the situation.[41] Finding that we had defined the applicable rule with too much "generality,"[42] the Court reversed our holding that the officer had violated clearly established law.[43]

Under *Mullenix,* application of clearly established law is undertaken with close attention to the relevant legal rule and the particular facts of the case. Here, based on the facts taken in the light most favorable to the non-movant Coles, and p.453 with reasonable inferences drawn in their favor, the district court determined there were genuine factual disputes as to Ryan's and the officers' conduct, upon which a reasonable jury could find "[Ryan] ... did not pose an immediate threat to the officers" when they opened fire.[44] It held that "on October 25, 2010, the date of the shooting, the law was clearly established" that "shooting a mentally disturbed teenager, who was pointing a gun the entire time at his own head and facing away from the officer, in an open outdoor area, and who was unaware of the officer's presence because no warning was given prior to the officer opening fire, was unlawful."[45] As we will detail, the officers ask us to consider a different set of facts, but we cannot do so. We lack jurisdiction to reconsider the district court's factual determinations on an appeal from denial of summary judgment on qualified immunity.

Tennessee v. Garner announced the principle that the use of deadly force is permitted only to protect the life of the shooting officer or others: "Where the suspect poses no immediate threat to the officer and no threat to others, the harm resulting from failing to apprehend him does not justify the use of deadly force to do so."[46] *Garner* also requires a warning before deadly force is used "where feasible,"[47] a critical component of risk assessment and de-escalation. The Supreme Court has repeatedly stated that this rule can be sufficient in obvious cases, and this court has applied it in such cases, without dependence on the fact patterns of other cases.[48]

The summary judgment facts, as determined by the district court, are that Ryan posed no threat to the officers or others to support firing without warning. The "Officers had the time and opportunity to give a warning and yet chose to shoot first instead."[49] This is an obvious case. Indeed, Officer Hunter conceded that he would have had no basis to fire upon Ryan unless Ryan had been facing him and pointing a gun at him.

This case is obvious when we accept the facts as we must. It is also informed by our precedent. Before 2010, *Baker v. Putnal* established clearly that Cassidy's and Hunter's conduct—on the facts as we must take them at this stage— was unlawful. For in *Baker,* members of the public told Officer Michael Putnal, a police officer patrolling a crowded Galveston beach area during spring break, that "someone had entered the crowd with a pistol-gripped shotgun."[50] Minutes later, Officer Putnal heard gunfire and saw the crowd scurrying.[51] There was "a good deal of confusion on the beach."[52] Two people directed the officer to a car in which the p.454 gunman was supposedly sitting.[53] Putnal then saw Wendell Baker Jr. and another man sitting in a truck parked on the beach.[54] The parties disputed what happened next. Putnal stated he saw Baker loading a magazine into a handgun, that he warned Baker to freeze or drop the gun, that Baker instead turned the gun upon Putnal, at which point Putnal fired, killing Baker.[55] However, witnesses "state[d] that [Baker] took no threatening action ... as the officer approached the truck," that Putnal issued no warning to Baker, and that "Baker ... may have barely had an opportunity to see Putnal before [the officer] fired his gun."[56] The parties did not dispute that Putnal had been searching for a gunman, and that a gun had been recovered from Baker's seat, although they disputed whether and how Baker had been holding it, that is, whether he pointed it at Putnal.[57] It was also undisputed that Baker was turning to face Putnal from his seat, although medical reports indicated from "the nature of the wounds ... that Baker... was not facing Putnal when he was shot."[58] Baker's survivors sued the officer, bringing, inter alia, a Fourth Amendment excessive-force claim.[59] The district court granted Putnal qualified immunity, crediting his account that he had fired in response to Baker turning and aiming the gun at him.[60] On appeal, we reversed and remanded the excessive-force claim for trial.[61] Recognizing the dispute as to the officer's warning, Baker's turn, and the position of Baker's gun, we found "simply too many factual issues to permit the Bakers' § 1983 claims to be disposed of on summary judgment."[62] "Chaos on the beach and Baker['s] mere motion to turn and face Putnal are not compelling reasons to find that [the officer's] use of force was not excessive as a matter of law."[63] Viewing the facts and drawing inferences "in the light most favorable to the nonmoving party," we held that "[t]he number of shots and the nature of the wounds raise ... more of a question of fact than a court may dispose of on summary judgment."[64]

The Supreme Court's more recent qualified immunity decisions do not shift this analysis. In *Kisela v. Hughes,* police officers in Tucson, Arizona responded to a call that a woman was behaving erratically with a knife and that she had been hacking at a tree.[65] When officers arrived on scene, the suspect, Amy Hughes, emerged from a house holding a large kitchen knife, and approached to within "striking distance" of a bystander in the driveway.[66] One of the officers, Andrew Kisela, whose further approach was impeded by a chain-link fence, repeatedly ordered Hughes to drop the knife, but Hughes did not follow his commands.[67] Kisela then fired on Hughes p.455 through the fence.[68] Hughes brought a Section 1983 excessive force claim against Kisela.[69] Reviewing a denial of qualified immunity to Kisela, the Supreme Court held that, in light of the officer's limited knowledge of the situation and Hughes's refusal to follow his repeated commands to drop the knife while within striking distance of the bystander—obstinance that heightened the risk of immediate harm to another—the law did not clearly establish that the officer's resort to deadly force was unlawful.[70]

In this case, Officers Cassidy and Hunter found themselves in a search for a suicidal teenager who they knew had already encountered fellow officers and walked away from them with his gun to his head, non-responsive, but without aggressive action. The circumstances of the officers' encounter with Ryan, as in *Baker,* remain heavily disputed: as to whether Ryan was aware of the officers, whether and how he turned and aimed his gun, and whether Hunter warned Ryan to disarm himself. The district court here defined the facts in a 21-page opinion, finding genuine disputes regarding these facts, and, viewing these disputes in a light most favorable to the Coles, concluded that a reasonable jury could find that Ryan made no threatening or provocative gesture to the officers and posed no immediate threat to them. Unlike in *Kisela,* where the officer repeatedly warned an armed suspect to disarm, yet that suspect, facing the officer and hearing his warnings, refused to disarm, here the district court concluded that a reasonable jury could find Cassidy and Hunter opened fire upon Ryan without warning, even though it was feasible. On these facts, the officers' conduct violates clearly established law.

Rather than engage on the facts as we must take them at the summary judgment stage, the officers repeatedly argue from a different set of facts. While the district court found that Ryan was initially facing away from the officers when they fired the first shot, the officers now describe his "armed turn towards Officer Hunter." While the district court found that Ryan kept his gun aimed at his own head and never pointed it at the officers, the officers now suggest that Ryan's gun was "below his head," moving towards Hunter, and then only momentarily turned back towards Ryan's head at the moment he fired (ignoring Hunter's sworn statement that he fired only when the gun was pointed toward him—a story prosecutors accepted until a ballistics report exposed its impossibility). And although the district court found that Ryan was not given an opportunity to disarm himself, the officers contend that he was warned to disarm before being shot. "Had the Officers delayed longer, reaction time lag would have precluded their ability to stop [Ryan] from shooting Officer

Hunter," they argue. Based on this alternative set of facts, echoed again in oral argument to us as a full court, and in the teeth of those found by the district court, the officers now contend Ryan posed a "deadly threat," and no clearly established law in 2010 put the officers' response of firing in self-defense beyond the law.

The Coles and amicus Cato Institute are correct that it is beyond our jurisdiction to consider the officers' set of facts, a narrative evolving over time. "[I]f an excessive force claim turns on which of two conflicting stories best captures what happened on the street," the caselaw "will not permit summary judgment in favor of the defendant p.456 official. ... [A] trial must be had."[71] Whereas the officers will have a chance to present their factual narrative—and to question the Coles'—at trial, they cannot contest the facts in the current appeal.[72]

The dissents also take issue with the disputed facts. Judge Duncan focuses on what he terms "undisputed pre-encounter events." But, particularly in light of the officers' evolving stories, it is disputed whether any of the events recounted were known to Hunter or Cassidy when they fired on Ryan. The dissent cites to the reports and affidavits of other officers and individuals to describe the events occurring before Hunter and Cassidy were called to the scene.[73] But looking at the evidence in the light most favorable to the Coles, Hunter and Cassidy were not aware of the disturbance at the Coles' house the previous night, the alleged cache of weapons left at the Reeds' house, Ryan's alleged suicidal threat, or his threat to shoot anyone who came near him.

And of course, what matters is what the defendant officers knew when they shot Ryan. *See, e.g., White v. Pauly,* ___ U.S. ___, 137 S. Ct. 548, 550, 196 L.Ed.2d 463 (2017) (per curiam) ("Because this case concerns the defense of qualified immunity ... the Court considers only the facts that were knowable to the defendant officers."); *Kingsley v. Hendrickson,* ___ U.S. ___, 135 S. Ct. 2466, 2474, 192 L.Ed.2d 416 (2015) (stressing that "a court must judge the reasonableness of the force used from the perspective and with the knowledge of the defendant officer"). The dissents overlook the fundamental reason most of these facts should not be part of the analysis: we consider only what the officers knew at the time of their challenged conduct. "Facts an officer learns after the incident ends—whether those facts would support granting immunity or denying it—are not relevant." *Hernandez v. Mesa,* ___ U.S. ___, 137 S. Ct. 2003, 2007, 198 L.Ed.2d 625 (2017) (per curiam); *see also Brown v. Callahan,* 623 F.3d 249, 253 ("An official's actions must be judged in light of the circumstances that confronted him, without the benefit of hindsight." (citing *Graham v. Connor,* 490 U.S. 386, 396-97, 109 S.Ct. 1865, 104 L.Ed.2d 443 (1989))). Despite the many "red flags" listed by the dissents as known to others, only those known to Hunter and Cassidy are relevant to the qualified immunity analysis.

Judge Jones's dissent fares no better in addressing some of the key facts of the shooting itself. Contrary to its assertion, the district court found that Ryan was facing at a 90-degree angle away from the officers when he was first shot. *Cole,* 68 F. Supp. 3d at 644. As for the "warning," the district court found that a reasonable jury could conclude that Ryan "was not given p.457 an opportunity to disarm himself before he was shot." *Id.* Relitigating the district court's assessment of factual disputes is not our role on interlocutory review.

What Hunter and Cassidy knew before shooting at Ryan, whether they warned him before doing so, and what actions Ryan took before being shot are all disputed.

The district court must afford Cassidy and Hunter qualified immunity at the earliest point the defense's applicability is determinable. Here, we have not yet reached that point. It will be for a jury to resolve what happened on October 25, 2010. The district court did not err in denying the officers qualified immunity at the summary judgment stage.

III

The district court determined that genuine disputes of fact regarding Cassidy's and Hunter's entitlement to qualified immunity remain. We AFFIRM the district court's denial of summary judgment on the Coles' excessive-force claim and DISMISS Cassidy and Hunter's appeal; AFFIRM denial of the motion to dismiss the Coles' Fourteenth Amendment false-charges claim; REVERSE denial of the motion to dismiss the Coles' Fourth Amendment and *Brady* fabrication-of-evidence claims; and return the case to the district court for trial and resolution of issues consistent with this opinion.

JENNIFER WALKER ELROD, Circuit Judge, joined by CARL E. STEWART, Chief Judge, and EDITH BROWN CLEMENT, CATHARINA HAYNES, STEPHEN A. HIGGINSON, GREGG COSTA, and KURT D. ENGELHARDT, Circuit Judges, concurring:

I concur fully in the majority opinion. Despite the outcry of the dissenting opinions, there is no new law being made or old law being ignored. The majority opinion takes no position on the public policy issues of the day regarding policing and the mentally ill. Rather, it follows the longstanding *en banc* rule that "we lack jurisdiction to review the *genuineness* of a fact issue" on an interlocutory appeal of a denial of summary judgment based on qualified immunity. *Melton v. Phillips,* 875 F.3d 256, 261 (5th Cir. 2017) (*en banc*) (quoting *Allen v. Cisneros,* 815 F.3d 239, 244 (5th Cir. 2016)); *Kinney v. Weaver,* 367 F.3d 337, 341, 346-47 (5th Cir. 2004) (*en banc*). As the able district court determined, the facts are very much in dispute.

EDITH H. JONES, Circuit Judge, joined by SMITH, OWEN, HO, DUNCAN and OLDHAM, Circuit Judges, dissenting:

What "clearly established law" says that only a rogue cop would have shot at this mentally disturbed teenager within 3 to 5 seconds as the teen emerged from dense bushes ten to twenty feet away from Officer Hunter and, with his finger on the trigger of a loaded pistol pointed in the direction of his own head, began turning in the officer's direction? The majority state this is an "obvious case" for the denial of qualified immunity: the officers could not shoot without first announcing themselves to Cole or looking down the barrel of his gun. What is so obvious? Contrary to the majority's dangerously unrealistic proposition, "action beats reaction" every time. *Ontiveros v. City of Rosenberg,* 564 F.3d 379, 384 (5th Cir. 2009). Neither we nor the Supreme Court has ever held that police officers confronted in close quarters with a suspect armed and ready to shoot must hope they are faster on the draw and more accurate. The increasingly risky profession of law enforcement cannot put those sworn to "serve and protect" to a *Hobson*'s choice: place their lives on the line by heroic forbearance or risk their p.458 financial security in defense of lawsuits. The Supreme Court has repeatedly stated in plain terms that the purpose of qualified immunity is to prevent precisely this quandary.

Respectfully dissenting, we are convinced that the Supreme Court's remand from the original panel opinion denying immunity meant something; the governing Supreme Court law is foursquare in the corner of Officers Hunter and Cassidy; and they were entitled to receive summary judgment confirming their immunity from suit, not simply from liability.[1]

I. Background

A. Undisputed facts

The majority opinion paints a picture of the relevant facts that has evolved considerably from the first and second panel opinions to this final majority version. *Compare Cole v. Carson,* 802 F.3d 752, 755-56, 758 (5th Cir. 2015), *vacated sub nom. Hunter v. Cole,* ___ U.S. ___, 137 S. Ct. 497, 196 L.Ed.2d 397 *(Cole I)*, *with Cole v. Carson,* 905 F.3d 334, 337-340 (5th Cir. 2018) *(Cole II)*, *and supra.* Qualified immunity for the use of deadly force is assessed at the moment a law enforcement officer confronts a suspect, *Graham v. Connor,* 490 U.S. 386, 397, 109 S. Ct. 1865, 1872, 104 L.Ed.2d 443 (1989), but the officer's understanding of facts leading up to the event color the question whether "a reasonable officer" could have believed his life or the lives of others were endangered. *White v. Pauly,* ___ U.S. ___, 137 S. Ct. 548, 550, 552, 196 L.Ed.2d 463 (2017). To the majority's picture, it is necessary to add undisputed facts recited in the prior opinions and undisputed evidence from plaintiffs' experts. Hornbook summary judgment law holds that although disputed facts are viewed in the light most favorable to non-movants, the entire record must be considered. *Scott v. Harris,* 550 U.S. 372, 380, 127 S. Ct. 1769, 1776, 167 L.Ed.2d 686 (2007). Further, this court reviews *de novo* the materiality of the relevant facts. *Foley v. Univ. of Houston, Sys.,* 355 F.3d 333, 337 (5th Cir. 2003).

First, both officers who shot at Cole were aware that he had mental issues. Officer Cassidy had learned that Cole "had threatened to shoot anyone who tried to take his gun and had refused an order to drop his weapon." *Cole II,* 905 F.3d at 338. Officer Hunter watched Cole walk steadily down the train tracks ignoring other police who were yelling at him to stop and put down his 9 mm semi-automatic pistol. Both officers were aware that a bulletin had been disseminated about Cole to all law enforcement in Garland and Sachse, and three nearby schools in the vicinity of Highway 78, where Cole was heading, were being protected. *Cole II,* 905 F.3d at 337-38.

Second, Cole emerged from the vegetation, unaware of the officers' presence, within ten to twenty feet of Officer Hunter, and as he turned toward the officers, three to five seconds elapsed. That's less time than it takes to read the preceding sentence. Cole initially stood at a 90 degree angle to the police and then began turning counterclockwise toward them. His movement is conceded by plaintiffs' expert, supported by the ballistic evidence, and p.459 recounted in the district court opinion. *Cole II,* 905 F.3d at 338 ("Cole began to turn counterclockwise."). Plaintiff's expert opines this interval was sufficient for the officers to command Cole to disarm and observe his reaction.

Third, his loaded pistol was pointed within thirty inches toward his head, *Cole I,* 802 F.3d at 756, and Cole's finger was on the trigger.

Next, the officers fired seven shots, two of which hit Cole. Officer Hunter's first shot hit Cole in the left arm, penetrating his body from the left. Another of Hunter's shots merely grazed Cole's left arm as he continued to turn and was facing Hunter. *Cole II,* 905 F.3d at 339. Cole's gun, according to the plaintiffs, involuntarily discharged and hit him in the head, "leaving stippling—gunpowder residue around the wound due to the gun being fired from less than thirty inches away." *Cole I,* 802 F.3d at 756.

Finally, the bodycam evidence shows that some officer began to issue a warning at about the time the shooting started. *Cole II,* 905 F.3d at 338.

B. Prior panel reasoning

The district court denied qualified immunity to Hunter and Cassidy for the shooting[2] and refused to dismiss the allegations of falsified evidence against Hunter, Cassidy, and Carson.

The original panel opinion affirmed,[3] concluding as to the excessive force allegation that "if the Coles' version of the evidence is believed, it was not objectively reasonable to use deadly force against Ryan Cole when the teenager emerged on foot from the wooded area with a gun to his own head and turned left." With regard to immunity, the panel held that by October 2010, "reasonable officers were on notice that they could not lawfully use deadly force to stop a fleeing person who did not pose a *severe and immediate risk to the officers or others,* and they had many examples of the sorts of threatening actions which could justify deadly force. Turning left while unaware of an officer's presence is not among them." *Cole I,* 802 F.3d at 762 (emphasis added) (footnote omitted). The panel's principal support for its legal reasoning was *Luna v. Mullenix,* 773 F.3d 712 (5th Cir. 2014), *rev'd sub nom. Mullenix v. Luna,* ___ U.S. ___, 136 S. Ct. 305, 193 L.Ed.2d 255 (2015). According to the panel, "the central [disputed] issue" is "whether Ryan pointed his gun at Officer Hunter." *Cole I,* 802 F.3d at 762. Absent such a threatening gesture, Cole was said to present no sufficient threat. *Id.*

The next panel opinion was formulated after the Supreme Court reversed us in *Mullenix* on the grounds that "none of our [the Supreme Court's own] precedents 'squarely governs' the facts here. Given [the suspect's] conduct, we cannot say that only someone 'plainly incompetent' or who 'knowingly violate[s] the law' would have perceived a sufficient threat and acted as [the officer] did." 136 S. Ct. at 310. On this second go-round, the panel conceded the deficiency of the "no sufficient threat" rule, but then concluded that, taken in the light most favorable to the plaintiffs, Cole's conduct posed "no threat" when he was shot, p.460 *Cole II,* 905 F.3d at 343, and the officers therefore violated a clearly established "no threat" rule. *Tennessee v. Garner* is cited as the basis for this "bright line" rule.[4] 471 U.S. 1, 105 S. Ct. 1694, 85 L.Ed.2d 1 (1985). This opinion was vacated by a vote to reconsider the case en banc.

C. The Current Majority Opinion

Pivoting yet again, the en banc majority opinion commences with a paean to "the worker's ... right to the protection of a jury," not even bothering to cite Supreme Court authorities that explain why qualified immunity is immunity from suit, not just liability. The majority opinion omits or ignores material undisputed facts recited above—the knowledge of the officers, Cole's turning toward them, the significance of his finger in a loaded pistol, and the three to five second interval—and hides behind the assertion that, relevant to qualified immunity, there are "genuine factual disputes as to Ryan's and the officers' conduct" such that a reasonable jury could find that Cole posed no "immediate threat" to the officers or others. Two paragraphs later, asserting that Cole posed "no threat... to support firing without warning," the majority deem this an "obvious case" for denial of immunity, because the "officers had time and opportunity to give a warning and yet chose to shoot first instead." The "obvious case" rationale again derives, in the majority's view, from *Garner,* fortified only by one Fifth Circuit case and the Supreme Court's decision in *Kisela v Hughes.*[5]

DISCUSSION

The only legal question that needs to be addressed by this court is whether, under the circumstances of this five-second confrontation, *every* reasonable police officer would have reasonably perceived *no* life-threatening danger such that deadly force could be used to incapacitate Cole without a preliminary warning. Put otherwise, as a matter of law, was it clearly established that officers may not fire on a suspect, armed and ready to shoot a pistol, who is turning in their direction with one of their brethren ten to twenty feet away, unless the gun barrel points at them or they first shout a warning and await his response?

The majority deny qualified immunity, seeming to answer on the basis of "disputed fact issues" that Cole posed "no threat." The majority's reasoning is at too high a level of generality. And the majority ignore the critical criterion for qualified immunity in Fourth Amendment cases: the reasonableness of the officers' reasonable perceptions. In sum, the majority here double down on the mistakes that got our court reversed in *Mullenix.*[6]

p.461 Before discussing these problems in detail, it is necessary to recapitulate the reasoning behind the Supreme Court's qualified immunity cases. The majority's bare mention of the standards for qualified immunity ignores the Court's rationale for the defense. Beginning with *Monroe v. Pape* in 1961, the Supreme Court unleashed federal courts to enforce constitutional commands against state actors pursuant to 42 U.S.C. § 1983. *See Monroe v. Pape,* 365 U.S. 167, 187, 81 S. Ct. 473, 484, 5 L.Ed.2d 492 (1961). A foreseeable consequence of facilitating such lawsuits was that a deluge of litigation would follow, at least some of it ill-founded or frivolous. What was to be done to limit claims to those that might have merit? The Court decided in *Pierson v. Ray* that police officers sued under Section 1983 should enjoy qualified immunity accorded at common law. 386 U.S. 547, 556-57, 87 S. Ct. 1213, 1219, 18 L.Ed.2d 288 (1967).

For over fifty years, the Court has developed the standards of qualified immunity, well aware from the beginning that "the local police officer" is "that segment of the executive branch ... that is most frequently and intimately involved in day-to-day contacts with the citizenry, and hence, most frequently exposed to situations which can give rise to claims under Sec. 1983...." *Scheuer v. Rhodes,* 416 U.S. 232, 244-45, 94 S. Ct. 1683, 1691-92, 40 L.Ed.2d 90 (1974). The breadth of this shield represents a deliberate balance between affording a damages remedy for constitutional abuses and the social and personal costs inflicted by meritless claims. *Anderson v. Creighton,* 483 U.S. 635, 638, 107 S. Ct. 3034, 3038, 97 L.Ed.2d 523 (1987). The costs to society include the costs of litigation, the diversion of limited public resources, the deterrence of able people from going into public service, and the danger that fear of being sued will discourage officials from vigorously performing their jobs. *Id.*; *Harlow v. Fitzgerald,* 457 U.S. 800, 814, 102 S. Ct. 2727, 2736, 73 L.Ed.2d 396 (1982). The devastating costs imposed by unfounded lawsuits on officers otherwise entitled to immunity are reputational, potentially employment-related, financial and emotional. For these reasons, the Court has repeatedly explained that qualified immunity shields public officials not just from liability but from suit. *See Mitchell v. Forsyth,* 472 U.S. 511, 526, 105 S. Ct. 2806, 2815, 86 L.Ed.2d 411 (1985); *Pearson v. Callahan,* 555 U.S. 223, 231, 129 S. Ct. 808, 815, 172 L.Ed.2d 565 (2009) ("Qualified immunity is lost if a case is erroneously permitted to go to trial."). Some in the lower federal courts may disapprove of the Court's half century of authorities, but we may not functionally disregard them.

Nearly as venerable as the general defense of qualified immunity are the decisions applying it to Fourth Amendment claims against law enforcement officers. *Anderson v. Creighton* affirmed in 1987 that a law enforcement officer who participates in a warrantless search may be entitled to qualified immunity "if he could establish as a matter of law that a reasonable officer could have believed the search to be lawful." 483 U.S. at 638, 107 S. Ct. at 3038. Justice Scalia's opinion reminded that "qualified immunity protects all but the plainly incompetent or those who knowingly violate the law." *Id.* (internal quotation marks omitted). In determining the objective legal reasonableness of the allegedly unlawful action, "[i]t should not be surprising ... that our cases establish that the right the official is alleged to have violated must have been 'clearly established' in a more particularized, and hence more relevant, sense: The contours of the right must be sufficiently clear that a reasonable official would understand that p.462 what he is doing violates that right." *Id.* at 640, 107 S. Ct. at 3039.

Two years later, the Court clarified that for alleged Fourth Amendment excessive force violations, reasonableness "must be judged from the perspective of a reasonable officer on the scene, rather than with the 20/20 vision of hindsight." *Graham,* 490 U.S. at 396, 109 S. Ct. at 1872. The calculus of "reasonableness must embody allowance for the fact that police officers are often forced to make split-second judgments —in circumstances that are tense, uncertain, and rapidly evolving—about the amount of force that is necessary in a particular situation." *Id.* at 396-97, 109 S. Ct. at 1872. Ultimately, "the question is whether the officers' actions are 'objectively reasonable' in light of the facts and circumstances confronting them...." *Id.* at 397, 109 S. Ct. at 1872. Quoting these statements from *Graham,* the Court later explained that the test for qualified immunity for excessive force "has a further dimension" in addition to the deferential, on-the-scene evaluation of objective reasonableness. *Saucier v. Katz,* 533 U.S. 194, 205, 121 S. Ct. 2151, 2158, 150 L.Ed.2d 272 (2001). Justice Kennedy explained: "The concern of the immunity inquiry is to acknowledge that reasonable mistakes can be made as to the legal constraints on particular police conduct." *Id.* "Qualified immunity operates in this case, then, just as it does in others, to protect officers from the sometimes hazy border between excessive and acceptable force and to ensure that before they are subjected to suit, officers are on notice their conduct is unlawful." *Id.* at 206, 121 S. Ct. at 2158 (internal citation and quotation marks omitted).

Evaluating the qualified immunity defense is thus a two-step process. The first is to determine whether the Fourth Amendment has been violated by conduct that, viewed from the officer's perspective and information at the time, is objectively unreasonable.[7] The second step assesses the objective legal reasonableness of the action, that is, whether every reasonable officer would have known that the conduct in question was illegal. *See Pearson,* 555 U.S. at 232, 129 S. Ct. at 815-16. The illegality must have been apparent, as held in cases that are factually similar to the situation confronting the officer. *White,* 137 S. Ct. at 552. Immunity must be granted to all but the plainly incompetent or those who knowingly violate the law. The Supreme Court has enforced immunity where officers acted negligently, *Anderson,* 483 U.S. at 641, 107 S. Ct. at 3039-40; or when they could have used another method to subdue a suspect, *Mullenix,* 136 S. Ct at 310; or when the law governing their behavior in particular circumstances is unclear. *White,* 137 S. Ct. at 552. The Court emphasizes that the specificity of the applicable "clearly established" rule is especially important in Fourth Amendment cases. *Mullenix,* 136 S. Ct. at 308.

By denying plaintiffs their "day in court" at a preliminary stage, qualified immunity operates as a counterintuitive, albeit vital, defense. Thus, the Supreme Court has regularly reversed denials of qualified immunity where lower courts misapplied the standards. *See Wesby v. District of Columbia,* 816 F.3d 96, 102 (D.C. Cir. 2016) (Kavanaugh, J., dissenting) (citing eleven Supreme Court cases in five years reversing lower courts in the p.463 qualified immunity context including *Mullenix v. Luna,* ___ U.S. ___, 136 S. Ct. 305, 193 L.Ed.2d 255 (2015), *Taylor v. Barkes,* ___ U.S. ___, 135 S. Ct. 2042, 192 L.Ed.2d 78 (2015); *City and County of San Francisco, Calif. v. Sheehan,* ___ U.S. ___, 135 S. Ct. 1765, 191 L.Ed.2d 856 (2015); *Carroll v. Carman,* 574 U.S. 13, 135 S. Ct. 348, 190 L.Ed.2d 311 (2014); *Plumhoff v. Rickard,* 572 U.S. 765, 134 S. Ct. 2012, 188 L.Ed.2d 1056 (2014); *Wood v. Moss,* 572 U.S. 744, 134 S. Ct. 2056, 188 L.Ed.2d 1039 (2014); *Stanton v. Sims,* 571 U.S. 3, 134 S. Ct. 3, 187 L.Ed.2d 341 (2013); *Reichle v. Howards,* 566 U.S. 658, 132 S. Ct. 2088, 182 L.Ed.2d 985 (2012); *Ryburn v. Huff,* 565 U.S. 469, 132 S. Ct. 987, 181 L.Ed.2d 966 (2012); *Messerschmidt v. Millender,* 565 U.S. 535, 132 S. Ct. 1235, 182 L.Ed.2d 47 (2012); *Ashcroft v. al-Kidd,* 563 U.S. 731, 131 S. Ct. 2074, 179 L.Ed.2d 1149 (2011)). Unfortunately, the majority here has fallen into the trap of "letting the jury sort out the truth" despite the gravity of the situation these officers faced.

As explained above, it is undisputed that the two officers confronted and then shot at Cole as he emerged from dense bushes ten to twenty feet from Officer Hunter, unaware of their presence, and began to turn in their direction. This all happened within three to five seconds. While he turned, Cole held a loaded 9mm semiautomatic pistol, finger on the trigger, pointed in the direction of his own head. The officers knew he was mentally distraught, had ignored other police commands to disarm, had issued threats, and proceeded walking in the direction of nearby schools.

For immunity purposes, the question phrased one way is whether *any* reasonable officers could have believed that Cole's split-second turning toward them posed a life-threatening danger such that lethal force was necessary. Alternatively, what "clearly established law" held as of October 2010 that under all of the relevant circumstances, deadly force was not justified unless either a warning was given and the suspect allowed a chance to react, or the suspect actually turned his loaded pistol on the officer? The answer here directly parallels the Supreme Court's reasoning in *Mullenix*, which the majority seriously shortchanged.

In *Mullenix*, this court had denied qualified immunity to a trooper whose shot fatally wounded a suspect fleeing police in a high-speed chase. The Supreme Court's basic criticism of the panel decision was this: "In this case, the Fifth Circuit held that Mullenix violated the clearly established rule that a police officer may not use deadly force against a fleeing felon who does not pose a sufficient threat of harm to the officer or others. Yet this Court has previously considered—and rejected—almost that exact formulation of the qualified immunity question in the Fourth Amendment context." *Mullenix*, 136 S. Ct. at 308-09 (internal quotation marks and citation omitted).

The majority here posit as clearly established law, indeed an "obvious case," that a police officer may not use deadly force— without prior warning—against an armed, distraught suspect who, with finger in the pistol's trigger, posed "no threat" while turning toward an officer ten to twenty feet away. But in *Mullenix*, the Supreme Court reversed this court because "[t]he general principle that deadly force requires a sufficient threat hardly settles this matter." *Id.* at 309. Likewise, here, the majority's "no threat" and "obvious case" conclusions do not settle the matter of clearly established law.[8]

p.464 That the majority here purport to extract clearly established law from *Tennessee v. Garner* was rebuked in *Mullenix*. The Supreme Court corrected this court by summary reversal because the Court itself had summarily rejected applying the general standard of *Tennessee v. Garner* to deny qualified immunity. *Mullenix*, 136 S. Ct. at 309 (*citing Brosseau v. Haugen*, 543 U.S. 194, 199, 125 S. Ct. 596, 599, 160 L.Ed.2d 583 (2004)). Instead, the "correct inquiry" was whether it was clearly established that the Fourth Amendment prohibited the officer's conduct in the precise situation she confronted. *Id.* Including *Mullenix* and *Brosseau*, a series of Supreme Court cases has held that *Tennessee v. Garner* does not state "clearly established law" governing the use of deadly force other than in *Garner*'s precise factual context, the shooting of an unarmed burglary suspect fleeing away from an officer.[9] The confrontation in this case with an armed, ready-to-fire suspect is "obviously" different.

We fail to understand how the denial of qualified immunity to Officers Hunter and Cassidy can be rescued simply by intoning that this is an "obvious case" under *Garner*. *Garner* affirmed the constitutionality of deadly force against suspects when necessary to protect the life of officers or others "if, where feasible, some warning has been given." 471 U.S. at 11-12, 105 S. Ct. at 1701.[10] But *Garner* in no way renders "clearly established" a requirement to give a warning, and await the suspect's response, before shooting. Nor does it mandate that the suspect's weapon be trained on the officer or others. Like the rest of the calculus surrounding Fourth Amendment reasonableness, the "feasibility" of any such potentially deadly delay or factual nuance must be subjected to case-specific balancing with deference paid to the officer's reasonable perceptions in the midst of a tense situation. *Graham,* 490 U.S. at 396, 109 S. Ct. at 1872. Indeed, in describing its holding at the outset, *Garner* states only that "[deadly] force may not be used unless it is necessary to prevent the escape [of an apparently unarmed suspected felon] and the officer has probable cause to believe that the suspect poses a significant threat of death or serious physical injury to the officer or others." 471 U.S. at 3, 105 S. Ct. at 1697.[11] No mention of a warning appears in this introduction, and "probable cause," not a fact-specific test, is the measure of the threat of harm.

Characterizing this case as a "no threat" or "obvious" Fourth Amendment violation is wrong for additional reasons. Whether, under the material undisputed facts, Cole presented "no threat" to a reasonable police officer is the relevant issue to assess a Fourth Amendment violation. But the immunity question, which the majority elides, is whether *every* reasonable officer in this p.465 factual context would have known he could not use deadly force. *See Pearson,* 555 U.S. at 232, 129 S. Ct. at 815-816. The majority's analysis conflates these inquiries. Second, the importance of grounding the inquiry in a specific factual context cannot be overstated. In this case, if Officer Hunter had stood a hundred feet away from Cole, or Cole had not been turning toward the officers, or Cole had put the handgun in his pocket and wasn't touching it, the analysis of qualified immunity could be quite different. Third, describing a situation as posing "no threat" is a conclusion, not an explanation or, as the majority seems to think, an exception to defining clearly established law in a specific context. No doubt there are rare "obvious" cases of Fourth Amendment violations committed by officers who are plainly incompetent or who knowingly violate the law. In the wide gap between acceptable and excessive uses of force, however, immunity serves its important purpose of encouraging officers to enforce the law, in "tense, uncertain and rapidly evolving" split-second situations, rather than stand down and jeopardize community safety.[12]

In their sole, erroneous dependence on *Garner,* the majority, "can cite no case from [the Supreme] Court denying qualified immunity because officers [entitled to apprehend Cole] selected one dangerous alternative over another." *Mullenix,* 136 S. Ct. at 310. The *Mullenix* Court showed that if anything, "clearly established law" was contrary to the plaintiff's position. The Court cited two prior Supreme Court car chase cases that resulted in immunity even though the fugitives—unlike the suspect in *Mullenix*—had not verbally threatened to kill any officers in their path. *Id.* at 310 (*citing Scott,* 550 U.S. at 384, 127 S. Ct. at 1778; *Plumhoff,* 572 U.S. at 777, 134 S. Ct at 2022). And in *Mullenix* itself, as here, the trooper had not warned the fugitive before shooting at his speeding car. These cases "reveal[ed] the hazy legal backdrop against which Mullenix acted," *Id.* at 309. Accordingly, the Court admonished, "[w]hatever can be said of the wisdom of Mullenix's choice, this Court's precedents do not place the conclusion that he acted unreasonably in these circumstances beyond debate." *Id.* at 311 (internal quotation marks omitted).

Not only do the majority cite "no case" in which the Supreme Court denied qualified immunity to an officer who used deadly force against a mentally distraught individual in circumstances like the present case, but to the contrary, the Court required qualified immunity in two somewhat similar cases. In *Sheehan,* officers used deadly force to subdue a mentally ill woman during an armed confrontation. The Court restated that the Fourth Amendment is not violated even if police officers, with the benefit of hindsight, may have made some mistakes, because "[t]he Constitution is not blind to 'the fact that police officers are often forced to make split-second judgments.'" *Sheehan,* 135 S. Ct. at 1775 (quoting *Plumhoff,* 572 U.S. at 775, 134 S. Ct. at 2020).

Even closer to this case is *White v. Pauly,* where an officer arriving at the scene of an armed confrontation shot and killed a suspect without knowing whether his earlier-arrived colleagues had identified themselves as police. 137 S. Ct. at 550-51. In *White,* the Court chastised the lower court for "misunderst[anding]" the "clearly p.466 established" analysis by relying on the generalized pronouncements in *Graham* and *Garner. Id.* at 552. Whether Officer White should have second-guessed the preceding conduct of fellow officers hardly presented an "obvious case" pursuant to *Garner.* The Court speculated that perhaps, given the three-minute delay between when he arrived and when shots rang out, Officer White "should have realized that [a warning about police presence] was necessary before using deadly force." *Id.* There is a world of difference between three minutes and three seconds, which Officer Hunter had here, and between Officer White's securing himself behind a stone wall fifty feet from the suspect and Officer Hunter's standing fully exposed only ten to twenty feet away from Cole. The majority cannot reconcile the Supreme Court's insistence upon qualified immunity in *White* with their denial of the defense to Officers Hunter and Cassidy.

Kisela v. Hughes, cited in support of the majority, in no way articulates clearly established law concerning the necessity of a warning. First, the Court in *Kisela* overturned the Ninth Circuit's denial of qualified immunity without addressing the preliminary Fourth Amendment violation. 138 S. Ct. at 1152. A decision holding only that there was no "clearly established law" cannot itself have defined "clearly established law." The Court also criticized the Ninth Circuit for failing to implement correctly the rule that an officer has not "violated a clearly established right unless the right's contours were sufficiently definite that any reasonable official in the defendant's shoes would have understood that he was violating it." *Id.* at 1153 (internal quotation marks omitted). The Court catalogued all the relevant circumstances of the confrontation that provoked the shooting: a knife-armed, threatening suspect, whose bizarre behavior had been called in to 911, disobeyed officers' commands to disarm for up to one minute before they felt compelled to shoot. *Id.* The Court concluded, "[t]his is far from an obvious case in which any competent officer would have known that shooting Hughes to protect [the third party] would violate the Fourth Amendment." *Id.* Also "far from obvious" is the case before us, in which the officers had five seconds, not a whole minute, in which to decide whether to shoot at Cole.

Finally, the Supreme Court's decision in *Tolan v. Cotton* adds nothing to the substance of the qualified immunity discussion. In *Tolan,* the Court enumerated four critical, disputed evidentiary contentions relating to the officer's perception of danger to himself and thus to qualified immunity. 572 U.S. 650, 657-59, 134 S. Ct. 1861, 1866-67, 188 L.Ed.2d 895 (2014). Because this court had failed to credit the plaintiff's disputed version of these facts, the Court vacated summary judgment for the officer and remanded without deciding any merits issue. *Id.* at 657, 134 S. Ct. at 1866. In contrast, this dissent credits only undisputed material facts and plaintiffs' version of disputable facts.

Like this court's panel in *Mullenix,* the majority here offer no controlling Supreme Court precedent, including *Garner,* to support that "clearly established law" mandated that the officers hold their fire until they had both warned Cole and given him a chance to drop his gun or until he pointed the loaded weapon directly at them.

For good measure, the *Mullenix* Court also considered the potential similarity of lower court decisions that dealt with qualified immunity. 136 S. Ct. at 311. Fifth Circuit case law, the Court noted, did not "clearly dictate the conclusion that Mullenix was unjustified in perceiving grave danger and responding accordingly." *Id.* at 311 *(citing Lytle v. Bexar County,* 560 F.3d 404, 412 (5th Cir. 2009)). But the p.467 Court quoted with approval an Eleventh Circuit case that granted immunity to a sheriff's deputy who fatally shot a mentally unstable individual "who was attempting to flee in the deputy's car, even though at the time of the shooting the individual had not yet operated the cruiser dangerously. The court explained that 'the law does not require officers in a tense and dangerous situation to wait until the moment a suspect uses a deadly weapon to act to stop the suspect ...'" *Id.* at 311 *(quoting Long v. Slaton,* 508 F.3d 576, 581-82 (11th Cir. 2007)). Here, too, the thrust of *Mullenix* contradicts the majority's logic and holding.

Moreover, to the extent it is relevant[13], Fifth Circuit law does not support denying qualified immunity to Officers Hunter and Cassidy. The district court and, inferentially, the majority demand that qualified immunity be granted only if the suspect either disobeys immediate commands to disarm or points his weapon at the officers. The district court described such threatening actions as a *Manis* act.[14] It is true that in previous deadly force cases, this court approved qualified immunity for officers who reasonably believed that a non-compliant suspect was reaching toward where he could retrieve a weapon. *See Manis,* 585 F.3d at 842; *see also Reese v. Anderson,* 926 F.2d 494, 500-01 (5th Cir. 1991); *Young v. City of Killeen, Tx.,* 775 F.2d 1349, 1352 (5th Cir. 1985). The hitch in these particular cases is that there wasn't actually a weapon, yet the officer's objectively reasonable perception was determinative as a matter of law. In another such officer shooting case, this court upheld qualified immunity where the suspect, who was being interrogated for drunk driving at the side of a freeway, turned to walk away from the officer, then appeared to turn around toward him while reaching under his shirttail for what the officer thought could be a concealed weapon. *Salazar-Limon v. City of Houston,* 826 F.3d 272, 278 (5th Cir. 2016). This court added, "[f]urthermore, ... in the context of this case, it is immaterial whether Salazar turned left, right, or at all before being shot. Specifically, we have never required officers to wait until a defendant turns toward them, with weapon in hand, before applying deadly force to ensure their safety." 826 F.3d at 279 n. 6.

While a "*Manis* act" can sustain qualified immunity even where no weapon is visible, it is not logical for an additional "act" to be mandated where the officers confront a suspect armed, ready to shoot his pistol, and turning toward them. An officer may be forced into shooting an unarmed suspect by a *Manis* act, and thus obtain qualified immunity. But it is perverse and inconsistent with Fifth Circuit law to hold that the officer has no qualified immunity because she is constitutionally forbidden to shoot an armed suspect in close quarters without either looking down the barrel of the weapon or awaiting his response to her command.

In fact, that is exactly what this court has not held. In *Ramirez v. Knoulton,* 542 F.3d 124, 127 (5th Cir. 2008), police shot a suspect they believed to be suicidal as he stood in profile to them, with a handgun in his right hand, and "brought his hands together in front of his waist." He "never raised his weapon nor aimed it at the officers." *Id.* at 129. The court held that based on the officers' reasonable perception, no Fourth Amendment violation occurred, because the Constitution "does not require police officers to wait until a suspect shoots to confirm that a serious threat p.468 of harm exists." *Id. at 130. See also Colston,* 130 F.3d at 100; *Ontiveros,* 564 F.3d at 385 (holding no constitutional violation where officer thought suspect was reaching into his boot for a weapon during confrontation in a mobile home). As the Supreme Court put it in *Mullenix,* "the mere fact that courts have approved deadly force in more extreme circumstances says little, if anything, about whether such force was reasonable in the circumstances here." 136 S. Ct. at 312.

The majority describe only one Fifth Circuit police shooting case, out of dozens this court has decided, as an "obvious case." *Baker v. Putnal,* 75 F.3d 190 (5th Cir. 1996). Whether that characterization applies to the claimed Fourth Amendment violation in *Baker,* to qualified immunity analysis, or simply to this court's decision to remand for trial is unclear in the majority opinion. *Baker,* however, says nothing about the merits of the case or about clearly established law, holding instead that "[t]here are simply too many factual issues to permit the Bakers' § 1983 claims to be disposed of on summary judgment." *Baker,* 75 F.3d at 198. Hence, like *Kisela, Baker* cannot support any rule of clearly established law, much less explain what law is "obvious." Significantly, in *Baker,* whether the suspect was holding a gun visible to the officer was an important hotly contested issue, with eyewitnesses contradicting the officer's account of the incident. *Baker,* 75 F.3d at 198. Cole's case, in contrast, does not involve a "chaos on the beach" incident. The undisputed facts are starkly different here. It is undisputed, at a minimum, that Cole was holding a loaded weapon, his finger in the trigger, as he emerged from the woods; he was turning toward the officers; and they had five seconds to react. *Baker* does not show that the officers' conduct in *Cole* violated clearly established law.

To sum up, the majority opinion here repeats every error identified by the Supreme Court when it granted summary reversal in *Mullenix* and sent the instant case back for reconsideration. The majority's "clearly established" rule has changed, but not its errors. *Tennessee v. Garner* does not formulate "clearly established law" with the degree of specificity required by the Supreme Court's decisions on qualified immunity. The majority's "no threat" and "obvious case" statements pose the issues here at an excessive level of generality. The majority has no Supreme Court case law demonstrating that Officers Hunter and Cassidy were either plainly incompetent or had to know that shooting at Cole was unconstitutional under the circumstances before them and with the knowledge they possessed—he was mentally distraught; he was armed with his finger in the pistol's trigger; he was very close to Hunter; he had been walking in the direction of schools for which extra police protection had been ordered; and he had ignored other officers' commands to stop and drop his weapon. And they had three to five seconds to decide how dangerous he could be to them. The majority cites not one case from this court denying qualified immunity under similar circumstances. *Mullenix* aptly summed it up for our purposes: "qualified immunity protects actions in the hazy border between excessive and acceptable force." 136 S. Ct. at 312 (internal quotation marks omitted). "[T]he constitutional rule applied by the Fifth Circuit was not 'beyond debate.'" *Id.*

It is not "clearly established" that police officers confronting armed, mentally disturbed suspects in close quarters must invariably stand down until they have issued a warning and awaited the suspects' reaction or are facing the barrel of a gun. "This was not a belief in possible harm, but a belief in certain harm. The fact that they would later discover this to be a p.469 mistaken belief does not alter the fact that it was objectively reasonable for them to believe in the certainty of that risk at that time." *Carnaby v. City of Houston,* 636 F.3d 183, 188 n.4 (5th Cir. 2011). That is the law in the Fifth Circuit, and the majority has pointed to no clearly established law otherwise. Shooting at Cole may not have been the wisest choice under these pressing circumstances, but the officers' decision, even if assailable, was at most negligent. Hunter and Cassidy were neither plainly incompetent nor themselves lawbreakers. While we are confident a jury will vindicate their actions, they deserved qualified immunity as a matter of law. We dissent.

JERRY E. SMITH, Circuit Judge, dissenting:

This is a "red flag" case if ever there was one. The en banc majority commits grave error, as carefully explained in the dissents by Judge Jones, Judge Willett, Judges Ho and Oldham (jointly), and Judge Duncan. Yet eleven judges join the majority.

Abandon hope, all ye who enter Texas, Louisiana, or Mississippi as peace officers with only a few seconds to react to dangerous confrontations with threatening and well-armed potential killers. In light of today's ruling and the raw count of judges,[1] there is little chance that, any time soon, the Fifth Circuit will confer the qualified-immunity protection that heretofore-settled Supreme Court and Fifth Circuit caselaw requires.

Red flags abound. Judge Duncan cogently details the "rich vein of facts" describing this plaintiff's undisputed actions in the hours leading up to the shooting.[2]

- Red flag: a 9mm semi-automatic handgun and ammunition.
- Red flag: a double-barrel shotgun with shells.
- Red flag: a .44 magnum revolver.
- Red flag: a .38 revolver.
- Red flag: a suspect who had broken into a gun safe and stolen an unknown quantity of weapons and ammunition.
- Red flag: a police visit the night before to the suspect's house because of a disturbance with his parents.
- Red flag: a suspect with a dangerous knife at his parents' house.
- Red flag: a suspect who had a wild look in his eye and was smoking K2.
- Red flag: a suspect, distraught over breaking up with his girlfriend, moving toward the school where she was a student.
- Red flag: a suspect near an elementary school.
- Red flag: a suspect with personal issues including drug abuse.
- Red flag: a suspect seen running through the woods with at least three weapons.
- Red flag: a suspect irate and distraught.
- Red flag: a suspect who said he would shoot anyone who came near him.
- Red flag: a suspect armed with at least one handgun and possibly three.

• Red flag: a suspect who had refused police demands to drop his weapon.

p.470 • Red flag: a suspect who deposited a cache of weapons and ammunition at a friend's house after arguing with his parents.

• Red flag: a suspect who yelled obscenities at an officer.

• Red flag: a suspect who had threatened to kill his girlfriend and himself.

• Red flag: a suspect whom the district court described as troubled.

• Red flag: a suspect described in his complaint as suffering from obsessive compulsive disorder, treated with medications from numerous medical professionals, and having poor judgment and impaired impulse control.

* * * * *

Normally we expect police officers to recognize such red flags and to respond appropriately. Instead of protecting these officers from obvious danger to themselves and the public, however, the en banc majority orders them to stand down. What is the hapless officer to do in the face of today's decision? What indeed is the "clearly established law" that the majority now announces? The judges in the majority do not say.

The law of qualified immunity was poignantly summarized in 2019 by a dissenting judge who is now in the majority. Today's en banc ruling turns those words to dust.[3]

I respectfully dissent.

DON R. WILLETT, Circuit Judge, dissenting:

I repeat what I said last month: The entrenched, judge-invented qualified immunity regime ought not be immune from thoughtful reappraisal.[1]

Qualified immunity strikes an uneasy, cost-benefit balance between two competing deterrence concerns: "the need to hold public officials accountable when they exercise power irresponsibly and the need to shield officials from harassment, distraction, and liability when they perform their duties reasonably."[2] By insulating incaution, p.471 the doctrine formalizes a rights-remedies gap through which untold constitutional violations slip unchecked. The real-world functioning of modern immunity practice—essentially "heads government wins, tails plaintiff loses"—leaves many victims violated but not vindicated. More to the point, the "clearly established law" prong, which is outcome-determinative in most cases, makes qualified immunity sometimes seem like unqualified impunity: "letting public officials duck consequences for bad behavior—no matter how palpably unreasonable—as long as they were the *first* to behave badly."[3]

That said, as a middle-management circuit judge, I take direction from the Supreme Court. And the Court's direction on qualified immunity is increasingly unsubtle. We must respect the Court's exacting instructions—even as it is proper, in my judgment, to respectfully voice unease with them.[4]

I

Qualified immunity protects "all but the plainly incompetent or those who knowingly violate the law."[5] While this bar is not insurmountable, it is sky-high. And it is raised higher when courts leapfrog prong one (deciding whether the challenged behavior violates the Constitution) to reach simpler prong two: no factually analogous precedent. Merely proving unconstitutional misconduct isn't enough. A plaintiff must cite functionally identical authority that puts the unlawfulness "beyond debate" to "every" reasonable officer.[6] Last month, for example, the Eleventh Circuit, noting no "materially similar case" (thus no "clearly established law"), granted immunity to a police officer who fired at a family's dog but instead shot a 10-year-old child lying face-down 18 inches from the officer.[7] Not only that, the court "expressly [took] no position" as to "whether a constitutional violation occurred in the first place."[8] Translation: If the same officer tomorrow shoots the same child while aiming at the same dog, he'd receive the same immunity. *Ad infinitum.*

The Supreme Court demands precedential specificity. But it's all a bit recursive. There's no earlier similar case declaring a constitutional violation because no earlier plaintiff could find an earlier similar case declaring a constitutional violation. "Section 1983 meets Catch-22. Plaintiffs must produce precedent even as fewer courts are producing precedent. Important constitutional questions go unanswered precisely because no one's answered them before. Courts then rely on that judicial silence to conclude there's no equivalent case on the books. No precedent = no clearly established law = no liability. An Escherian Stairwell."[9]

<p.472> ## II

In recent years, individual Justices have raised concerns with the Court's immunity caselaw.[10] Even so, the doctrine enjoys resounding, even hardening favor at the Court. Just three months ago, in a case involving the warrantless strip search of a four-year-old preschooler, a strange-bedfellows array of scholars and advocacy groups—perhaps the most ideologically diverse amici ever assembled—implored the Court to push reset.[11] To no avail. This much is certain: Qualified immunity, whatever its success at achieving its intended policy goals, thwarts the righting of many constitutional wrongs.

Perhaps the growing left-right consensus urging reform will one day win out. There are several "mend it, don't end it" options. The Court could revisit *Pearson*[12] and nudge courts to address the threshold constitutional merits rather than leave the law undeveloped.[13] Even if a particular plaintiff cannot benefit (due to the "clearly established law" prong), this would provide moving-forward guidance as to what the law prescribes and proscribes. Short of that, the Court could require lower courts to explain *why* they are side-stepping the constitutional merits question.[14] Or the Court could confront the widespread inter-circuit confusion on what constitutes "clearly established law."[15] One concrete proposal: clarifying the degree of factual similarity required in cases involving split-second decisions versus cases involving less-exigent situations. The Court could also, short of undoing *Harlow* and reinstating the bad-faith prong, permit plaintiffs to overcome immunity by presenting *objective* evidence of an official's bad faith.[16] Not *subjective* evidence of bad faith, which *Harlow*, worried about "peculiarly disruptive" and "broad-ranging discovery," forbids.[17] And not unadorned *allegations* of bad faith. But objective evidence that the official actually realized that he was violating the Constitution.

p.473 Prudent refinements abound. But until then, as Judge Jones explains in today's principal dissent, the Supreme Court's unflinching, increasingly emphatic application of "clearly established law" compels dismissal.

III

I remain convinced that contemporary immunity jurisprudence merits "a refined procedural approach that more smartly— and fairly—serves its intended objectives."[18] Yet I also remain convinced that a majority of the Supreme Court disagrees. My misgivings, I believe, are well advised. But we would be ill advised to treat the reform of immunity doctrine as something for this court rather than that Court.[19]

For these reasons, I respectfully dissent.

JAMES C. HO and ANDREW S. OLDHAM, Circuit Judges, joined by JERRY E. SMITH, Circuit Judge, dissenting:

Apparently SUMREVs mean nothing.

In *Luna v. Mullenix,* 773 F.3d 712 (5th Cir. 2014), we sent a state trooper to a jury "in defiance" of "the concept and precedents of qualified immunity." 777 F.3d 221, 222 (5th Cir. 2014) (Jolly, J., dissenting from denial of rehearing en banc). The Supreme Court summarily reversed us. *Mullenix v. Luna,* ___ U.S. ___, 136 S. Ct. 305, 193 L.Ed.2d 255 (2015) (per curiam). Then they GVR'd us in *this* case and ordered us to reconsider our obvious error in light of *Mullenix.*

The en banc majority instead doubles down. That is wrong for all the reasons Judge Jones gives in her powerful dissent, which we join in full. We write to emphasize the en banc majority's unmistakable message: Four years after *Mullenix,* nothing has changed in our circuit.

I.

The Supreme Court has not hesitated to redress similar intransigence from our sister circuits—often through the "extraordinary remedy of a summary reversal." *Kisela v. Hughes,* ___ U.S. ___, 138 S. Ct. 1148, 1162, 200 L.Ed.2d 449 (2018) (Sotomayor, J., dissenting) (quotation omitted). *See, e.g., City of Escondido v. Emmons,* ___ U.S. ___, 139 S. Ct. 500, 202 L.Ed.2d 455 (2019) (per curiam) (summarily reversing the Ninth Circuit); *Kisela,* ___ U.S. ___, 138 S. Ct. 1148, 200 L.Ed.2d 449 (per curiam) (same); *District of Columbia v. Wesby,* ___ U.S. ___, 138 S. Ct. 577, 199 L.Ed.2d 453 (2018) (reversing the D.C. Circuit); *White v. Pauly,* ___ U.S. ___, 137 S. Ct. 548, 196 L.Ed.2d 463 (2017) (per curiam) (summarily reversing the Tenth Circuit); *City and County of San Francisco v. Sheehan,* ___ U.S. ___, 135 S. Ct. 1765, 191 L.Ed.2d 856 (2015) (reversing the Ninth Circuit); *Carroll v. Carman,* 574 U.S. 13, 135 S.Ct. 348, 190 L.Ed.2d 311 (2014) (per curiam) (summarily reversing p.474 the Third Circuit); *Wood v. Moss,* 572 U.S. 744, 134 S.Ct. 2056, 188 L.Ed.2d 1039 (2014) (reversing the Ninth Circuit); *Plumhoff v. Rickard,* 572 U.S. 765, 134 S.Ct. 2012, 188 L.Ed.2d 1056 (2014) (reversing the Sixth Circuit); *Stanton v. Sims,* 571 U.S. 3, 134 S.Ct.

3, 187 L.Ed.2d 341 (2013) (per curiam) (summarily reversing the Ninth Circuit); *Reichle v. Howards,* 566 U.S. 658, 132 S.Ct. 2088, 182 L.Ed.2d 985 (2012) (reversing the Tenth Circuit); *Ryburn v. Huff,* 565 U.S. 469, 132 S.Ct. 987, 181 L.Ed.2d 966 (2012) (per curiam) (summarily reversing the Ninth Circuit); *Ashcroft v. al-Kidd,* 563 U.S. 731, 131 S.Ct. 2074, 179 L.Ed.2d 1149 (2011) (same); *Brosseau v. Haugen,* 543 U.S. 194, 125 S.Ct. 596, 160 L.Ed.2d 583 (2004) (per curiam) (same).

In each of these cases, the Supreme Court reminded lower courts that qualified immunity requires us not only to identify a clearly established rule of law, but to do so with great specificity. Everyone agrees, of course, that Ryan Cole has a constitutional right not to be seized unreasonably. But "that is not enough" to subject a police officer to the burdens of our civil litigation system. *Saucier v. Katz,* 533 U.S. 194, 202, 121 S.Ct. 2151, 150 L.Ed.2d 272 (2001). The Supreme Court has "repeatedly told courts ... not to define clearly established law at [that] high level of generality." *al-Kidd,* 563 U.S. at 742, 131 S.Ct. 2074. Rather, "[t]he dispositive question is whether the violative nature of *particular* conduct is clearly established." *Mullenix,* 136 S. Ct. at 308 (citation omitted).

Only by identifying a specific and clearly established rule of law do we ensure that the officer had "fair notice"—"in light of the specific context of the case, not as a broad general proposition"—that his or her *particular* conduct was unlawful. *Brosseau,* 543 U.S. at 198, 125 S.Ct. 596 (citation omitted). *See also, e.g., Sheehan,* 135 S. Ct. at 1776 ("Qualified immunity is no immunity at all if 'clearly established' law can simply be defined as the right to be free from unreasonable searches and seizures."); *Wilson v. Layne,* 526 U.S. 603, 615, 119 S.Ct. 1692, 143 L.Ed.2d 818 (1999) (same); *Anderson v. Creighton,* 483 U.S. 635, 640, 107 S.Ct. 3034, 97 L.Ed.2d 523 (1987) (same).

So where is our clearly established law at issue here? Unbelievably, the en banc majority says we don't need any. That's so, they say, because "[t]his is an obvious case." *Ante,* at 453. That's obviously wrong for three reasons.

First, the Supreme Court to date has *never* identified an "obvious" case in the excessive force context. And the majority thinks this is the first? A case where a mentally disturbed teenager—who has a loaded gun in his hand with his finger on the trigger; who has repeatedly refused to be disarmed; who has threatened to kill anyone who tries to disarm him; who poses such a deadly threat that police have been deployed to protect innocent students and teachers at his nearby high school—turns toward the officers just ten to twenty feet away, giving them only seconds to decide what to do in response. Really?

Second, the Supreme Court has granted qualified immunity in much tougher cases than this one. In *Plumhoff,* for example, officers fired 15 shots and killed two *unarmed* men who fled a traffic stop. In *Brosseau,* an officer shot an *unarmed* man who refused to open his truck window. In *Kisela,* officers shot a woman who was hacking a tree with a kitchen knife. In *Sheehan,* officers shot an old woman holding a kitchen knife in an assisted-living facility. In all of these cases, the Court held the officers were entitled to qualified immunity.

Third, this is *Mullenix* all over again. There our court relied on clearly established p.475 law as articulated in *Tennessee v. Garner,* 471 U.S. 1, 105 S.Ct. 1694, 85 L.Ed.2d 1 (1985). *Garner* involved an unarmed man who fled from police after stealing $10. An officer fatally shot Garner in the back of the head as he attempted to climb a fence. Our court then extended *Garner* to Mullenix's case—which involved a man who led police on a high-speed car chase after violating his probation. A state trooper attempted to end the chase by shooting the speeding car's engine block—but he missed the engine, hit the driver in the face, and killed him. *See Luna,* 773 F.3d at 719-20 (discussing *Garner*). The Supreme Court summarily reversed us because—as should be painfully obvious from the Court's serial reversals in this area—that's not how qualified immunity works. *See Mullenix,* 136 S. Ct. at 308-09 (holding our court erred in our extrapolation of *Garner* to new facts). And they GVR'd us *in this very case* to fix our mistakes in light of *Mullenix.* The Supreme Court's message could not be clearer.[1]

Still, somehow, today's majority does not get it. Here, as in *Mullenix,* the majority attempts to rely on *Garner* to establish the governing rule of law. From *Garner,* the majority somehow divines a rule that an officer cannot shoot a mentally disturbed teenager holding a gun near his school. This is demonstrably erroneous. In fact, one thing that unites the Supreme Court's recent reversals in cases involving qualified immunity and excessive force is the attempt by lower courts to extrapolate *Garner* to new facts. *See Mullenix,* 136 S. Ct. at 308-09; *Scott v. Harris,* 550 U.S. 372, 381-82, 127 S.Ct. 1769, 167 L.Ed.2d 686 (2007) (same); *Allen v. City of West Memphis,* 509 F. App'x 388, 392 (6th Cir. 2012) (extrapolating *Garner*), *rev'd by Plumhoff, supra.*

Moreover, there are additional parallels between *Mullenix* and this case. Consider the supposed requirement that an officer take some sort of non-lethal measure before using lethal force. In *Mullenix,* our court used the power of 20-20 hindsight to say that a reasonable officer should have used spike strips to stop the chase. *See* 773 F.3d at 720-21. The Supreme Court emphatically rebuked us. *See* 136 S. Ct. at 310. They told us that an officer does not have to expose himself or other officers to p.476 harm when the suspect has already refused to be disarmed. That meant Trooper Mullenix did not have to wait to see if the fleeing felon would shoot or run over the officer manning the spike strips. *See id.* at 310-11.

So too here. In this case, the majority complains that the officers did not provide sufficient warning. But there was no clearly established law requiring Officers Cassidy and Hunter to announce themselves— while caught in an open and defenseless position—and hope not to get shot. That is particularly true here because officers previously ordered Cole to put down his gun, he refused, and he threatened to kill anyone who attempted to disarm him.

And in *Mullenix,* as here, we accused the police officers of being cowboys. Earlier on the day of the shooting, Trooper Mullenix received a negative performance review for "not being proactive enough as a Trooper"; so in the aftermath of the shooting, Mullenix said to his supervisor, "How's that for proactive?" 773 F.3d at 717; *see also* 136 S. Ct. at 316 (Sotomayor, J., dissenting). The panel opinions and en banc majority opinion in this case likewise seethe with innuendo that Officers Hunter and Cassidy were wannabe cowboys looking for a gunfight. We are in no position to make such accusations. No member of this court has stared down a fleeing felon on the interstate or confronted a mentally disturbed teenager who is brandishing a loaded gun near his school. And the *Mullenix* Court held that the qualified-immunity standard gives us no basis for sneering at cops on the beat from the safety of our chambers. *See* 136 S. Ct. at 310-11 (majority op.) (citing Brief for National Association of Police Organizations et al. as *Amici Curiae*). Yet here we are. Again.

II.

The majority cannot dodge responsibility for today's decision by pointing to the limits of appellate jurisdiction. *See ante,* at 452-53 (majority op.); *ante,* at 457 (Elrod, J., concurring). We obviously lack interlocutory appellate jurisdiction to review the *genuineness* of an officer's fact dispute. *See, e.g., Johnson v. Jones,* 515 U.S. 304, 313-14, 115 S.Ct. 2151, 132 L.Ed.2d 238 (1995); *Kinney v. Weaver,* 367 F.3d 337, 346-47 (5th Cir. 2004) (en banc) (applying *Johnson v. Jones*).

But that does nothing to defeat jurisdiction where, as here, the factual disputes are *immaterial.* That is why the Supreme Court repeatedly has rejected such no-jurisdiction pleas from those who wish to deny qualified immunity. *See, e.g., Plumhoff,* 572 U.S. at 771-73, 134 S.Ct. 2012; *id.* at 773, 134 S. Ct. 2012 (noting existence of genuine fact dispute did not defeat appellate jurisdiction in *Scott v. Harris*).

All the fact disputes in the world do nothing to insulate this *legal* question: Is this an "obvious case" under *Garner*—notwithstanding a mountain of SUMREVs, GVRs, and pointed admonitions from the Supreme Court? The majority says yes. *Ante,* at 453-54. They obviously must have jurisdiction to say so. With respect, it makes no sense to say we lack jurisdiction to disagree with them.

III.

What explains our circuit's war with the Supreme Court's qualified-immunity jurisprudence? Two themes appear to be at play.

First, the majority suggests we should be less than enthused about Supreme Court precedent in this area, because it conflicts with plaintiffs' jury rights. To quote the panel: "Qualified immunity is a judicially created doctrine calculated to protect an officer from trial before a jury of his or her peers. At bottom lies a perception p.477 that the jury brings a risk and cost that law-enforcement officers should not face, that judges are preferred for the task—a judgment made by appellate judges." *Cole v. Carson,* 905 F.3d 334, 336 (5th Cir. 2018). Or in the words of today's majority: "The Supreme Court over several years has developed protection from civil liability for persons going about their tasks as government workers" (a rather curious way to describe the men and women who swear an oath to protect our lives and communities). *Ante,* at 446. But "the worker's defense" must yield, in cases like this, "in obeisance to [the] constitutional mandate" of a jury trial. *Id.*

We appreciate the majority's candor. But inferior court judges may not prefer juries to the Justices.

Second, some have criticized the doctrine of qualified immunity as a historical and contrary to the Founders' Constitution. *Ante* at 446 (suggesting denial of qualified immunity is commanded by "the Founders"); *compare* William Baude, *Is Qualified Immunity Unlawful?,* 106 CALIF. L. REV. 45, 49-61 (2018), *with* Aaron L. Nielson & Christopher J. Walker, *A Qualified Defense of Qualified Immunity,* 93 NOTRE DAME L. REV. 1853, 1856-63 (2018); *see also Zadeh v. Robinson,* 902 F.3d 483, 498 (5th Cir. 2018) (Willett, J., concurring dubitante), *revised on petition for reh'g en banc,* 928 F.3d 457, 473 (5th Cir. 2019) (Willett, J., concurring in part and dissenting in part).

As originalists, we welcome the discussion. But separate and apart from the fact that we are bound as a lower court to follow Supreme Court precedent, a principled commitment to originalism provides no basis for subjecting these officers to trial.

The originalist debate over qualified immunity may seem fashionable to some today. But it is in fact an old debate. Over two decades ago, Justices Scalia and Thomas noted originalist concerns with qualified immunity. But they also explained how a principled originalist would re-evaluate established doctrines. *See Crawford-El v. Britton,* 523 U.S. 574, 611-12, 118 S.Ct. 1584, 140 L.Ed.2d 759 (1998) (Scalia, J., joined by Thomas, J., dissenting).

A principled originalist would not cherry pick which rules to revisit based on popular whim. A principled originalist would fairly review decisions that favor plaintiffs as well as police officers. As Justice Scalia explained in a dissent joined by Justice Thomas, a principled originalist would evenhandedly examine disputed precedents that *expand,* as well as limit, § 1983 liability:

> [O]ur treatment of qualified immunity under 42 U.S.C. § 1983 has not purported to be faithful to the common-law immunities that existed when § 1983 was enacted .... [But] [t]he § 1983 that the Court created in 1961 bears scant resemblance to what Congress enacted almost a century earlier. I refer, of course, to the holding of *Monroe v. Pape,* 365 U.S. 167, 81 S.Ct. 473, 5 L.Ed.2d 492 (1961), which converted an 1871 statute covering constitutional violations committed "*under color of* any statute, ordinance, regulation, custom, or usage of any State," Rev. Stat. § 1979, 42 U.S.C. § 1983 (emphasis added), into a statute covering constitutional violations committed *without* the authority of any statute, ordinance, regulation, custom, or usage of any State, and indeed even constitutional violations committed in stark violation of state civil or criminal law.

Id. at 611, 118 S.Ct. 1584.

Justices Scalia and Thomas ultimately concluded that it is better to leave things p.478 alone than to reconfigure established law in a one-sided manner. If we're not willing to re-evaluate all § 1983 precedents in a balanced and principled way, then it "is perhaps just as well" that "[w]e find ourselves engaged ... in the essentially legislative activity of crafting a sensible scheme of qualified immunities for the statute we have invented—rather than applying the common law embodied in the statute that Congress wrote." *Id.* at 611-12, 118 S.Ct. 1584.

Translation: If we're not going to do it right, then perhaps we shouldn't do it at all.

Subjecting these officers to trial on originalist grounds is precisely the unprincipled practice of originalism that Justices Scalia and Thomas railed against. And not just for the procedural reasons they identified in *Crawford-El.* What about the original understanding of the Fourth Amendment, which the plaintiffs here invoke as their purported substantive theory of liability in this case? Does the majority seriously believe that it is an "unreasonable seizure," *as those words were originally understood at the Founding,* for a police officer to stop an armed and mentally unstable teenager from shooting innocent officers, students, and teachers?

And make no mistake: Principled originalism is not just a matter of intellectual precision and purity. There are profound practical consequences here as well, given the important and delicate balance that qualified immunity is supposed to strike. As the Supreme Court has explained, qualified immunity ensures that liability reaches only "the plainly incompetent or those who knowingly violate the law." *Mullenix*, 136 S. Ct. at 308 (quotation omitted). And absent plain incompetence or intentional violations, qualified immunity must attach, because the "social costs" of any other rule are too high:

> [I]t cannot be disputed seriously that claims frequently run against the innocent as well as the guilty—at a cost not only to the defendant officials, but to society as a whole. These social costs include the expenses of litigation, the diversion of official energy from pressing public issues, and the deterrence of able citizens from acceptance of public office. Finally, there is the danger that fear of being sued will dampen the ardor of all but the most resolute, or the most irresponsible public officials, in the unflinching discharge of their duties.

Harlow v. Fitzgerald, 457 U.S. 800, 814, 102 S.Ct. 2727, 73 L.Ed.2d 396 (1982) (alterations and quotations omitted); *see also, e.g., Sheehan*, 135 S. Ct. at 1774 n.3 (noting "the importance of qualified immunity to society as a whole").

For those who have expressed concerns about a "one-sided approach to qualified immunity," *Kisela*, 138 S. Ct. at 1162 (Sotomayor, J., dissenting); *see also Zadeh*, 902 F.3d at 499 & n.10 (Willett, J., concurring dubitante) (quoting *Kisela*, 138 S. Ct. at 1162 (Sotomayor, J., dissenting)); 928 F.3d at 480 & n.61 (Willett, J., concurring in part and dissenting in part) (same), look no further than the majority opinion. The majority undoes the careful balance of interests embodied in our doctrine of qualified immunity, stripping the officers' defenses without regard to the attendant social costs.[2]

p.479 Now *that* is a one-sided approach to qualified immunity as a practical matter. And as Justices Scalia and Thomas have observed, it's also a one-sided approach to qualified immunity as an originalist matter: It abandons the defense without also reconsidering the source and scope of officers' liability in the first place. *See Crawford-El*, 523 U.S. at 611-12, 118 S.Ct. 1584 (Scalia, J., joined by Thomas, J., dissenting). To quote Justice Alito: "We will not engage in this halfway originalism." *Janus v. Am. Fed'n of State, Cty., & Mun. Emps., Council 31*, ___ U.S. ___, 138 S. Ct. 2448, 2470, 201 L.Ed.2d 924 (2018). *See also id.* (criticizing litigants for "apply[ing] the Constitution's supposed original meaning only when it suits them"); *Gundy v. United States*, ___ U.S. ___, 139 S. Ct. 2116, 2131, 204 L.Ed.2d 522 (2019) (Alito, J., concurring in the judgment) ("[I]t would be freakish to single out the provision at issue here for special treatment.").[3]

* * *

Our circuit, like too many others, has been summarily reversed for ignoring the Supreme Court's repeated admonitions regarding qualified immunity. There's no excuse for ignoring the Supreme Court again today. And certainly none based on a principled commitment to originalism.

Originalism for plaintiffs, but not for police officers, is not principled judging. Originalism for me, but not for thee, is not originalism at all. We respectfully dissent.

STUART KYLE DUNCAN, Circuit Judge, joined by SMITH, OWEN, HO, and OLDHAM, Circuit Judges, dissenting:

The majority opinion overlooks or omits undisputed material facts showing that any reasonable officer would have viewed Ryan Cole as a severe threat. Before the shooting, the defendant officers: (1) were tracking a distraught suspect wandering through the woods armed with a loaded 9mm semi-automatic handgun; (2) who had earlier that morning off-loaded a cache of weapons and ammunition at a friend's house; (3) who had already refused to give up his pistol when confronted by the police; and (4) who had threatened to "shoot anyone who came near him." Cole did not dispute those facts and, indeed, convinced the district court they were irrelevant. Joining Judge Jones' dissent in full, I respectfully dissent on the additional grounds provided by these pre-encounter facts.

No one doubts some of the events on October 25, 2010—when the officers violently encountered Cole in the woods near Garland, Texas—are disputed. The question is whether those disputes are *material. See, e.g., Bazan ex rel. Bazan v. Hidalgo Cty.,* 246 F.3d 481, 483 (5th Cir. 2001) ("threshold issue" on qualified immunity appeal "is whether the facts the district judge concluded are *genuinely disputed* are also *material*"). Judge Jones' dissent compellingly shows they are not: Resolving p.480 all disputes in Cole's favor, the undisputed facts still show the officers violated no clearly established law. Jones Dissent at 458-59, 463-69. The majority thus errs by concluding that "competing factual narratives" bar it from deciding qualified immunity. Maj. at 446-47.

I write separately to emphasize what led up to the shooting, and also to explain why those undisputed events provide further reasons to reverse. The majority and Judge Jones focus on the shooting itself, as did the district court. But the prelude to the shooting gives unavoidable context for evaluating the officers' actions.[1] Surprisingly, the district court did not even analyze those stage-setting facts, which it mistakenly deemed irrelevant. *See Cole v. Hunter,* No. 3:13-CV-02719-O, 2014 WL 266501, at *13 n.5 (N.D. Tex. Jan. 24, 2014); *Cole v. Hunter,* 68 F. Supp. 3d 628, 642-43 (N.D. Tex. 2014). So, to assess their impact, we must "undertake a cumbersome review of the record." *Johnson v. Jones,* 515 U.S. 304, 319, 115 S.Ct. 2151, 132 L.Ed.2d 238 (1995). That extra work is sometimes imperative, as here, "to ensure that the defendant's right to an immediate appeal on the issue of materiality is not defeated solely on account of the district court's failure to articulate its reasons for denying summary judgment." *Colston v. Barnhart,* 146 F.3d 282, 285 (5th Cir. 1998), *denying reh'g in* 130 F.3d 96 (5th Cir. 1997).

This detailed record review (*see* Part I) compels two conclusions (*see* Part II). First, the district court erred by excluding the undisputed events before the shooting. That error—based on a misreading of our precedent—truncated the qualified immunity analysis. That alone requires reversing the summary judgment denial. Second, in light of those pre-encounter facts, the majority's insistence that this is an "obvious case" collapses. Maj. at 453-54. Given what confronted the officers, the majority cannot say what they did was "obviously" unlawful. The only thing obvious is that no case told the officers, clearly or otherwise, how to respond when they met Cole that morning, emerging from the woods with his finger on the trigger of a loaded gun.

By denying qualified immunity and making the officers run the gauntlet of trial, the majority sets a precedent that "seriously undermines officers' ability to trust their judgment during those split seconds when they must decide whether to use lethal force." *Winzer v. Kaufman Cty.*, 916 F.3d 464, 482 (5th Cir. 2019) (Clement, J., dissenting).

I.

The majority begins "around 10:30 a.m.," less than an hour before the shooting. Maj. at 447-48. But events began to unfold much earlier.[2] Around 2 a.m. that morning, Cole knocked on the door of his friend, Eric Reed Jr., to show him "a 44 magnum revolver." Awakened by the knocking, Eric Jr.'s father (Eric Sr.) left his room, saw Cole with the gun, and told him to leave. Eric Jr. convinced Cole to leave the revolver because "he [did not] need to be carrying a weapon around."

p.481 Around 8 a.m., Eric Jr. gave his father Cole's gun. Eric Sr., a retired Sachse police officer, then notified Officer Vernon Doggett, who came to the Reeds'. Eric Jr. told his father and Doggett that "[Cole] told him there were more guns on the side of the house." There, they found "a double barrel shot gun with some shot gun shells and what appeared to be a plastic bag with 9mm bullets," which Doggett secured. Eric Jr. also explained Cole "had broken up with his girlfriend and was going to kill himself and his girlfriend."

Doggett was a resource officer for Sachse High School, where Cole and his girlfriend attended. He contacted Sergeant Garry Jordan, told him about the guns, and asked to meet at the school. Doggett reported that Cole "may be at school with a 9mm handgun." Another officer checked whether Cole was in class, and Jordan searched the parking areas for Cole.

Not finding him, Jordan went to Coles' and spoke to his parents. He learned that, the previous evening, officers had responded to a disturbance there. Officers had found Cole's father "holding Ryan down" because "he did not want [Cole] to leave the residence with the pocket knife that he had." He said "his son had a wild look in his eye and ... had been smoking K2." While the officers found there had been no assault, all agreed it was "a good idea for Cole to stay the night with a friend." The Coles had not seen Ryan since then but reported he had "apparently returned home during the night and had opened the gun safe, removed an unknown amount [*sic*] of weapons, and reset the combination."

Meanwhile, Eric Jr. noticed Cole was back. He asked Cole if he was armed and Cole showed him a "38 revolver" and a "9mm semiauto." He convinced Cole to give him the revolver, but Cole told him he was not "getting the 9mm." Cole also said that the 9mm was loaded and that he did not "wanna use it on [Eric Jr.]" Cole stated that "he would shoot anyone who came near him." Cole left, and Eric Jr. called his father, who called the police.

Around 10:49 a.m., Officer Stephen Norris radioed "all available Sachse officers" to respond to the area of the Reed residence. He reported Cole was "observed running south of the location with 3 weapons, one a loaded 9mm." He also reported Cole was "irate and distraught and stated he would shoot anyone who came near him." Around the same time, Sachse Officer Michael Hunter was dispatched to assist Jordan at the Coles', but on arrival he was told by Sachse Officer Carl Carson he was not needed. As Hunter was leaving, he heard Norris' call advising Cole was "in the area ... with a gun." Hunter stated he "did not know the specifics of the call at this point," but proceeded to the Reeds' residence. In response to Norris' call, Jordan also left the Coles'.

Sachse Officer Martin Cassidy also received Norris' dispatch and went to the area Norris indicated. He was given Cole's description and advised that Cole was "armed with at least one handgun and possibly three." Cassidy spoke with Norris on the phone about "the proximity of Armstrong Elementary School to the location where [Cole] was last seen." Cassidy therefore went to check on the school and a nearby shopping center for any signs of Cole.

Meanwhile, Hunter arrived at the Reeds', where he met Jordan and Carson. Hunter overheard Eric Jr. say he had gotten "one gun" from Cole but that Cole had left "armed with a 9mm handgun." "Hunter put [Cole's] description out to other officers," and then he and Carson went to search for Cole. After speaking with the officers, Eric Jr. checked for more guns and found "6 firearms around [his] house."

p.482 Jordan then observed Officers Elliott and Sneed pass by in a patrol unit. Those officers found Cole nearby. Elliott reported that "Sneed ... advised [Cole] to show his hands." Instead, Cole "reached into his waist band and pulled a pistol and placed it to his head after about three steps and refused to obey Lt. Sneed['s] commands." When Jordan arrived, Sneed "drew his duty weapon and yelled at [Cole] to drop the weapon," but Cole refused. As Cole continued eastbound towards Highway 78, Sneed "warned [Cole] that [he] would shoot him in the back if he tried to get to the highway or walk toward any innocent bystanders." Cole "would occasionally turn his head and yell obscenities at [Sneed]." Two other officers then parked "directly in front of [Cole's] path." To avoid them, Cole turned "northbound and began walking the railroad tracks." Jordan was constantly updating dispatch about Cole's movements. "Suddenly, [Sneed] observed [Cole] cut eastbound and run up a hill and into the brush towards Highway 78." Dispatch reported that Cole was "off tracks coming through tree lines towards [Highway] 78."

Hunter, Carson, and Cassidy were monitoring Cole's movements from the dispatches. They arrived separately at the part of Highway 78 where Cole was thought to be. Hunter noted "[Cole] appeared to be walking towards the railroad track," and he advised Carson "[they] needed to go out to the highway and intercept [him]." Cassidy advised Carson to get out his taser and follow Cassidy. Hunter "parked further south on Highway 78 as [he] figured [Cole] would be on the railroad track paralleling Highway 78 at about [his] location." He guessed correctly. As Hunter "began to look for cover since [he] was out in the open," Cole "walked out from the brush approximately 10 to 20 feet from [Hunter]."

What followed was the shooting.

II.

Cole did not dispute these stage-setting events in opposing summary judgment. To the contrary, he argued any "prior events" before the shooting were "irrelevant." The district court agreed, excluding from its qualified immunity analysis the "events" from "earlier that morning," *Cole*, 2014 WL 266501, at *13 n.5, and focusing solely on what happened "immediately before and during the shooting." *Cole*, 68 F. Supp.

3d at 644. That mistake skewed the district court's analysis and provides yet another reason why we should reverse.

First, the district court erred by excluding everything that happened before the officers' five-second encounter with Cole. That approach artificially truncates the qualified immunity analysis. In assessing qualified immunity, we "[c]onsider[ ] the specific situation confronting [officers]," *City & Cty. of San Francisco v. Sheehan*, ___ U.S. ___, 135 S. Ct. 1765, 1778, 191 L.Ed.2d 856 (2015), which "must be judged from the perspective of a reasonable officer on the scene[.]" *Graham v. Connor,* 490 U.S. 386, 396, 109 S.Ct. 1865, 104 L.Ed.2d 443 (1989). A "reasonable officer" does not shape his decisions based only on the seconds when he confronts an armed suspect; instead, he acts based on *all* relevant circumstances, including the events leading up to the ultimate encounter. *See, e.g., Escobar v. Montee,* 895 F.3d 387 (5th Cir. 2018) (courts evaluate excessive force claims "from the perspective of a reasonable officer on the scene, paying 'careful attention to the facts and circumstances of each particular case'") (quoting *Graham,* 490 U.S. at 396, 109 S.Ct. 1865). That is precisely how the Supreme Court has instructed lower courts to assess whether force is excessive: The seminal case, *Tennessee v. Garner,* asks whether a seizure was justified, based not only on the immediate p.483 seizure, but on "the totality of the circumstances" facing the officers. 471 U.S. 1, 9, 105 S.Ct. 1694, 85 L.Ed.2d 1 (1985). And qualified immunity cases, both from the Supreme Court and our court, routinely consider the background facts that shaped an officer's confrontation with a suspect in order to evaluate the officer's ultimate use of force.[3]

The district court's sole contrary authority was our statement in *Rockwell v. Brown,* 664 F.3d 985, 991 (5th Cir. 2011), that the excessive force inquiry "is confined to whether the [officer or another person] was in danger *at the moment of the threat.*" But the district court overread *Rockwell.* We made that statement in *Rockwell* to reject the notion that officers' negligence *before* a confrontation determines whether they properly used deadly force *during* the confrontation. *See id.* at 992-93 (rejecting argument that "circumstances surrounding a forced entry" bear on "the reasonableness of the officers' use of deadly force"). The cases *Rockwell* cited say that plainly. *See, e.g., Fraire v. City of Arlington,* 957 F.2d 1268, 1276 (5th Cir. 1992) ("[R]egardless of what had transpired up until the shooting itself, [the suspect's] movements gave the officer reason to believe, at that moment, that there was a threat of physical harm.").[4] And the key case *Rockwell* quoted for the "moment-of-the-threat" point recognized that pre-confrontation events could "set the stage for what followed in the field." *Bazan,* 246 F.3d at 493.

By misreading our cases, the district court blinded itself to a rich vein of facts—facts Cole did not dispute below—that round out the picture of the officers' violent encounter with Cole. At a minimum, that error alone requires reversing the denial of summary judgment and remanding for reconsideration of the officers' actions in light of *all* relevant undisputed facts. *See, e.g., White v. Balderama,* 153 F.3d 237, 242 (5th Cir. 1998) (concluding "limited remand" was appropriate given "lack of specificity in ... district court's order denying summary judgment on the basis of qualified immunity").

Second, the undisputed pre-encounter events underscore why, contrary to the majority's view, this is far from an "obvious case." Maj. at 453-54. An "obvious case," the Supreme Court has explained, is one where an officer's actions are plainly unlawful under a generalized legal test, even if those actions do not contravene a "body of relevant case law." *Brosseau,* 543 U.S. at 199, 125 S.Ct. 596 (citing *Hope v. Pelzer,* 536 U.S. 730, 738, 122 S.Ct. 2508, 153 L.Ed.2d 666 (2002)); *see also, e.g.,* p.484 *White v. Pauly,* ___ U.S. ___, 137 S. Ct. 548, 552, 196 L.Ed.2d 463 (2017) (an "obvious case" means that "in the light of pre-existing law the unlawfulness [of the officer's actions] must be apparent") (citing *Anderson v. Creighton,* 483 U.S. 635, 640, 107 S.Ct. 3034, 97 L.Ed.2d 523 (1987)) (cleaned up). As I understand the majority opinion, it believes this is an obvious case because a jury could find that (1) Cole "posed no threat" to the officers; (2) the officers fired "without warning"; and (3) the officers had "time and opportunity" to warn Cole, but did not. Maj. at 453. According to the majority, this scenario would plainly violate *Garner*'s generalized test that an officer may not use deadly force to apprehend a suspect who "poses no immediate threat to the officer," unless he warns the suspect "where feasible." *Id.* (quoting *Garner,* 471 U.S. at 11-12, 105 S.Ct. 1694).

Judge Jones' dissent shows that, even resolving all disputed facts in Cole's favor, the officers did not "obviously" violate *Garner*'s generalized test during the immediate shooting—that is, when in the space of five seconds at most, the officers met Cole at a distance of 10-20 feet as he backed out of the woods, still armed, and began to turn. Jones Dissent at 463-64. But if we include the undisputed facts leading up to the shooting, the notion that this is an "obvious case" crumbles. To believe that, we would have to blind ourselves to the facts that (1) the officers were searching for an irate, distraught suspect; (2) who was wandering through the woods armed with a loaded semi-automatic handgun; (3) who had refused police demands to turn over his weapon; (4) who had just that morning deposited a cache of weapons and ammunition at his friend's house; and (5) who had threatened to "shoot anyone who came near him." Those were the "totality of the circumstances" facing the officers, *Colston,* 130 F.3d at 100, and they were not disputed by Cole or the district court. Given those circumstances, the officers might have taken any number of actions when they met Cole in the woods that morning—they might have warned him, or shot him, or shot in the air, or retreated, or remained frozen in place to see what he would do. But to say it is "obvious" what they should have done is to denude the concept of an "obvious case" of any meaning.

Once stripped of the conceit that this is an "obvious case," the majority has nothing left to justify its holding. The Supreme Court has bluntly told us that, outside the "obvious case" scenario, "*Garner* ... do[es] not by [itself] create clearly established law[.]" *White v. Pauly,* 137 S. Ct. at 552. And, of course, the majority does not try to claim that the facts of *Garner* are anything like this case. In *Garner,* a police officer shot a fleeing, unarmed burglar in the back of the head. The officer admitted he did not even suspect the burglar was armed. *See* 471 U.S. at 3, 105 S.Ct. 1694 (noting the officer "saw no sign of a weapon" at the time he shot and, afterwards, admitted "[he] was 'reasonably sure' and 'figured' that [the suspect] was unarmed"). Apples and oranges does not capture the chasm between that case and this one.

The majority does claim that our 1996 decision in *Baker v. Putnal,* "clearly established" that the officers' conduct here was unlawful. Maj. at 453-54 (citing 75 F.3d 190, 193 (5th Cir. 1996)). That is mistaken. In *Baker,* Officer Putnal was patrolling a crowded beach area when gunfire erupted. *Id.* Witnesses directed Putnal "toward a red car which they said contained the shooters." *Id.* He approached that car, but then saw two people sitting in another vehicle, a truck. *Id.* One of the truck's passengers, Wendell Baker, "turned in Putnal's direction ... [and] Putnal shot and killed [him]." *Id.* While a pistol was recovered from the truck, the plaintiffs p.485 denied Baker "was holding a pistol" when shot. *Id.* at 196. In other words, a jury could have found Baker was not holding a gun when Putnal killed him.

It is not hard to grasp the key difference between *Baker* and this case. When shot, Baker was *possibly not even holding a gun.* When shot, Cole was *undisputedly holding a gun.* Imagine this conversation between a police officer and the police department's lawyer:

> OFFICER: I heard the Fifth Circuit just decided this *Baker* case. What does it tell me I should or shouldn't do in the field?
> LAWYER: Well, *Baker* says you lose qualified immunity if you shoot someone sitting in a car doing nothing more threatening than just turning in your direction. In other words, someone you don't even see holding a weapon.
> OFFICER: Makes sense. But tell me this. What if the person I approach *is* holding a gun?
> LAWYER: Well, *Baker* doesn't speak clearly to that situation. I mean, the jury in *Baker* could have found the guy didn't even have a gun in his hand when the officer shot him.

In other words, contrary to the majority's view, *Baker* could not have "established clearly that Cassidy's and Hunter's conduct... was unlawful" when they shot Cole as he emerged from the woods with his finger on the trigger of a loaded gun. Maj. at 454. To guide officers in the field, a controlling precedent must be "sufficiently clear that every reasonable [officer] would have understood that what he is doing violates" the Constitution. *Mullenix,* 136 S. Ct. at 308 (cleaned up). *Baker* does not come close.

The officers deserve qualified immunity on the excessive force claims. I respectfully dissent.

[1] Judges Higginbotham and Clement, now Senior Judges of this court, are participating as members of the original panel.

[2] *See* FED. R. CIV. P. 49; Fifth Circuit Civil Pattern Jury Instructions 10.3. *See also McCoy v. Hernandez,* 203 F.3d 371, 376 (5th Cir. 2000).

[3] In any treatment of the jury's role in stepping between state-afforded process and an individual defendant, it bears emphasis that the district judge can impanel a jury of at least six and as many as twelve members whose verdict, absent the parties' agreement otherwise, must be unanimous.

[4] *Cole v. Carson ("Cole I"),* 802 F.3d 752 (5th Cir. 2015), *vacated sub nom. Hunter v. Cole,* ___ U.S. ___, 137 S. Ct. 497, 196 L.Ed.2d 397 (2016).

[5] *Hunter v. Cole,* ___ U.S. ___, 137 S. Ct. 497, 196 L.Ed.2d 397 (2016) (granting certiorari, vacating, and remanding for consideration in light of *Mullenix v. Luna,* ___ U.S. ___, 136 S. Ct. 305, 193 L.Ed.2d 255 (2015) (per curiam)).

[6] In a 2014 declaration, Hunter stated that Cole refused a police officer's order to surrender his weapon. Hunter did not testify that he knew this fact at the time.

[7] *Cole v. Hunter,* 68 F. Supp. 3d 628, 645 (N.D. Tex. 2014). Viewing the evidence in a light most favorable to the Coles, the district court relied on the physical and audio evidence as interpreted by the Coles' expert crime-scene reconstructionist

Thomas Bevel who opined that "no evidence ... would indicate Mr. Cole was or could have been aware of the presence of the police officers prior to the time he was shot."

[8] *Cole,* 68 F. Supp. 3d at 644.

[9] *Cole,* 68 F. Supp. 3d at 644; *id.* at 645 ("[T]he evidence supports Plaintiffs' argument that Cole did not know of the Officers' presence.").

[10] *Cole,* 68 F. Supp. 3d at 645-46.

[11] *Id.* at 645. A reasonable jury could find the officers had up to five seconds during which they could have called out to Cole, sufficient time to make a warning according to Cole's expert.

[12] *Cole,* 68 F. Supp. 3d at 645.

[13] *Id.* 644-45 ("Cole was shot before he had an opportunity to disarm himself.").

[14] *Id.* at 644.

[15] *Cole,* 68 F. Supp. 3d at 644.

[16] *Id.*

[17] Carson stated he could not see Cole's movement because Hunter obstructed his line of sight.

[18] Stippling refers to a discoloration of the skin caused by hot gases and residue released immediately around a discharging firearm.

[19] The Coles filed an initial complaint in September 2012. The officers moved to dismiss or in the alternative requested that the district court order a Rule 7(a) reply to the immunity defense. The district court then afforded the Coles opportunity to file a Rule 7 reply or amended complaint. The Coles filed an amended complaint. The officers then filed a second motion to dismiss.

[20] ___ U.S. ___, 136 S. Ct. 305, 193 L.Ed.2d 255 (2015).

[21] As this court and others have acknowledged, when the Supreme Court grants, vacates, and remands ("GVRs") a case, it does not make a decision on the merits of the case nor dictate a particular outcome. *See Diaz v. Stephens,* 731 F.3d 370, 378 (5th Cir. 2013); *Kenemore v. Roy,* 690 F.3d 639, 641-42 (5th Cir. 2012); *see also Texas v. United States,* 798 F.3d 1108, 1116 (D.C. Cir. 2015); *In re Whirlpool Corp. Front-Loading Washer Prods. Liab. Litig.,* 722 F.3d 838, 845 (6th Cir. 2013); *Gonzalez v. Justices of Mun. Court of Bos.,* 420 F.3d 5, 7 (1st Cir. 2005).

[22] *Cole v. Carson,* 905 F.3d 334, 347 (5th Cir. 2018), *reh'g granted,* 915 F.3d 378, 379 (5th Cir. 2019).

[23] *Id.* at 341-42.

[24] *Cole,* 915 F.3d at 379.

[25] Appellants argue that the Supreme Court's 2017 decision in *Manuel v. City of Joliet,* ___ U.S. ___, 137 S. Ct. 911, 197 L.Ed.2d 312 (2017), changes the legal landscape and justifies revisiting the Coles' Fourteenth Amendment false-charge claim. *Manuel* holds that "pretrial detention can violate the Fourth Amendment not only when it precedes, but also when it follows, the start of legal process in a criminal case," and, therefore, that the plaintiff in that case "stated a Fourth Amendment claim when he sought relief not merely for his (pre-legal-process) arrest, but also for his (post-legal-process) pretrial detention." *Manuel,* 137 S. Ct. at 918-19. It does not hold that the Fourth Amendment provides the exclusive basis for a claim asserting pre-

trial deprivations based on fabricated evidence. We have already so determined in *Jauch v. Choctaw County*: "*Manuel* does not address the availability of due process challenges after a legal seizure, and it cannot be read to mean, as Defendants contend, that *only* the Fourth Amendment is available to pre-trial detainees." *Jauch v. Choctaw Cty.*, 874 F.3d 425, 429 (5th Cir. 2017), *cert. denied sub nom. Choctaw Cty. v. Jauch*, ___ U.S. ___, 139 S. Ct. 638, 202 L.Ed.2d 491 (2018).

[26] *See Cole I*, 802 F.3d at 766-74.

[27] *See id.* at 764-65.

[28] *See id.* at 765.

[29] *Tolan v. Cotton*, 572 U.S. 650, 655-56, 134 S.Ct. 1861, 188 L.Ed.2d 895 (2014) (per curiam).

[30] *Id.*

[31] *Lytle v. Bexar Cty., Tex.*, 560 F.3d 404, 408 (5th Cir. 2009); *see also id.* ("If the determination of qualified immunity would require the resolution of a genuinely disputed fact, then that fact is material and we lack jurisdiction over the appeal.").

[32] *Trent v. Wade*, 776 F.3d 368, 376 (5th Cir. 2015) (quoting *Kinney v. Weaver*, 367 F.3d 337, 347 (5th Cir. 2004) (en banc)).

[33] *Id.* (internal quotations omitted).

[34] *Lytle*, 560 F.3d at 409.

[35] *Tolan*, 572 U.S. at 660, 134 S.Ct. 1861.

[36] *Id.* at 657.

[37] *Trent*, 776 F.3d at 376.

[38] *Mullenix*, 136 S. Ct. at 308-09 (internal quotation marks omitted).

[39] *Id.* at 309.

[40] *Id.* at 309-10.

[41] *Id.*

[42] *Id.* at 311.

[43] *Id.* at 312.

[44] *Cole*, 68 F. Supp. 3d at 645.

[45] *Id.* at 643.

[46] *Tennessee v. Garner*, 471 U.S. 1, 11, 105 S.Ct. 1694, 85 L.Ed.2d 1 (1985).

[47] *Id.* at 11-12, 105 S.Ct. 1694; *see also Colston v. Barnhart*, 130 F.3d 96, 100 (5th Cir. 1997).

[48] *See White v. Pauly*, ___ U.S. ___, 137 S. Ct. 548, 552, 196 L.Ed.2d 463 (2017) (per curiam); *Mason v. Lafayette City-Parish Consol. Gov't*, 806 F.3d 268, 277-78 (5th Cir. 2015); *cf. Hope v. Pelzer*, 536 U.S. 730, 741, 122 S.Ct. 2508, 153 L.Ed.2d 666 (2002); *Newman v. Guedry*, 703 F.3d 757, 764 (5th Cir. 2012).

[49] *Cole*, 68 F. Supp. 3d at 645.

[50] *Baker v. Putnal*, 75 F.3d 190, 193 (5th Cir. 1996).

[51] *Id.*

[52] *Id.* at 198.

[53] *Id.* at 193.

[54] *Id.*

[55] *Id.* at 198.

[56] *Id.*

[57] *Id.*

[58] *Id.*

[59] *Id.* at 193.

[60] *Id.* at 197.

[61] *Id.* at 198.

[62] *Id.*

[63] *Id.*

[64] *Id.* at 198-99.

[65] *Kisela v. Hughes,* ___ U.S. ___, 138 S. Ct. 1148, 1151, 200 L.Ed.2d 449 (2018) (per curiam).

[66] *Id.*; *id.* at 1154.

[67] *Id.* at 1151.

[68] *Id.*

[69] *Id.*

[70] *Id.* at 1153.

[71] *Saucier v. Katz,* 533 U.S. 194, 216, 121 S.Ct. 2151, 150 L.Ed.2d 272 (2001) (Ginsburg, J. concurring). *see also Tolan,* 572 U.S. at 660, 134 S.Ct. 1861; *id.* at 662, 134 S.Ct. 1861 (Alito, J., joined by Scalia, J., concurring in the judgment) (agreeing that "summary judgment should not have been granted" in that case because of the genuine issues of material fact); *Lytle,* 560 F.3d at 408-09.

[72] *Cf. Tolan,* 572 U.S. at 660, 134 S.Ct. 1861 ("The witnesses on both sides come to this case with their own perceptions, recollections, and even potential biases. It is in part for that reason that genuine disputes are generally resolved by juries in our adversarial system. By weighing the evidence and reaching factual inferences contrary to [the plaintiff's] competent evidence, the court below neglected to adhere to the fundamental principle that at the summary judgment stage, reasonable inferences should be drawn in favor of the nonmoving party.").

[73] Recall that Hunter was a late-arriving officer who was not instructed by the Sachse or Garland police departments to pursue Ryan. *See supra* at 447-48.

[1] We do not challenge the majority's decision to leave in place fabricated evidence charges against these two officers and Officer Carson. Only Carson, who was present at the encounter but did not shoot, appealed the district court's refusal to dismiss that claim. The Supreme Court has not been clear on the constitutional basis for such a claim, so we have no ground to criticize the majority. *Compare Manuel v. City of Joliet,* ___ U.S. ___, 137 S. Ct. 911, 197 L.Ed.2d 312 (2017), *with McDonough v. Smith,* ___ U.S. ___, 139 S. Ct. 2149, 204 L.Ed.2d 506 (2019), (refusing to rule on the constitutional grounding of such claims).

[2] Query why Officer Cassidy, whose shots didn't hit the victim, can be sued? This court has held that qualified immunity must be applied individually to each defendant. *Meadours v. Ermel,* 483 F.3d 417, 421-22 (5th Cir. 2007). But no one raised the point here.

[3] The correct disposition if this court agrees there are material fact issues in dispute regarding qualified immunity would be to dismiss the appeal, because our appellate jurisdiction exists only over questions of law. *Mitchell v. Forsyth,* 472 U.S. 511, 529-30, 105 S. Ct. 2806, 2816-17, 86 L.Ed.2d 411 (1985).

[4] The panel curiously described so-called clearly established law in both of its opinions with references to unpublished, non-precedential Fifth Circuit cases. The Supreme Court has expressed uncertainty over whether any circuit court cases, as opposed to its own decisions, may set out "clearly established law." *See Dist. of Columbia v. Wesby,* ___ U.S. ___, 138 S. Ct. 577, 591 n. 8, 199 L.Ed.2d 453 (2018); *Carroll v. Carman,* 574 U.S. 13, 135 S. Ct. 348, 350, 190 L.Ed.2d 311 (2014); *Reichle v. Howards,* 566 U.S. 658, 665-66, 132 S. Ct. 2088, 2094, 182 L.Ed.2d 985 (2012). It is incredible that this court would cite our avowedly non-precedential decisions for that purpose.

[5] This dissent focuses on the majority opinion because Appellees' briefing offered nothing in addition to the meager authorities cited by the majority to support their "clearly established law" theory.

[6] In *Mullenix,* the Supreme Court reversed this court and held an officer entitled as a matter of law to qualified immunity when he shot, and killed, a suspect fleeing from the police in his car at high speed. Following *Mullenix,* the Supreme Court vacated the judgment and remanded *Cole I,* no doubt in part because *Cole I* heavily relied on the reversed panel decision in *Mullenix.*

[7] For present purposes, we "address only the qualified immunity question, not whether there was a Fourth Amendment violation in the first place." *Mullenix,* 136 S. Ct. at 308; *Pearson,* 555 U.S. at 236, 129 S. Ct. at 818 (constitutional violation or qualified immunity may be decided first).

[8] Worse, it treats as a disputed fact issue for immunity purposes what is clearly an issue of law. *See Wyatt v. Fletcher,* 718 F.3d 496, 502-03 (5th Cir. 2013).

[9] *Kisela v. Hughes,* ___ U.S. ___, 138 S. Ct. 1148, 1153, 200 L.Ed.2d 449 (2018); *White,* 137 S. Ct. at 552.

[10] Turning on distinctly different facts, *Garner* alone does not establish pertinent clearly established law here, and the majority does not contend as much.

[11] The majority cites *Colston v. Barnhart,* 130 F.3d 96, 100 (5th Cir. 1997), for the necessity of giving a warning "where feasible" before the use of deadly force. Oddly, *Colston* then immediately holds that the officer there "lying on his back with Colston nearby, had to immediately decide whether to shoot. In light of the totality of the circumstances facing Barnhart, Barnhart's failure to give a warning was not objectively unreasonable." *Id.* The feasibility of a warning is part of the overall Fourth Amendment analysis, not an independent sine qua non of official conduct.

[12] *Compare Wesby,* 138 S. Ct. at 590 ("Of course, there can be the rare obvious case, where the unlawfulness of the officer's conduct is sufficiently clear even though existing precedent does not address similar circumstances. But a body of relevant case law is usually necessary to clearly establish the answer with respect to probable cause.") (internal citation and quotation marks omitted).

[13] *See* fn. 4, *supra.*

[14] *Manis v. Lawson,* 585 F.3d 839 (5th Cir. 2009).

[1] This en banc court consists of the sixteen active judges, plus two senior judges who were on the original panel. Of those sixteen active judges, nine join the majority opinion.

[2] I especially refer the reader to Part I of Judge Duncan's dissent, which sets forth the context and narrative of red-flag facts that easily justify qualified immunity. All three dissents persuasively explain the law of qualified immunity that the majority overlooks.

[3] *Winzer v. Kaufman Cty.,* 916 F.3d 464, 482 (5th Cir. 2019) (Clement, J., dissenting), *petition for rehearing en banc pending*:

The implications of the majority's mistakes cannot be minimized. The majority decides that qualified immunity can be endangered by an affidavit filed at summary judgment that creates a fact issue nowhere else supported by record evidence.

Worse still, it seriously undermines officers' ability to trust their judgment during those split seconds when they must decide whether to use lethal force. Qualified immunity is designed to respect that judgment, requiring us to second-guess only when it clearly violates the law. The standard acknowledges that we judges— mercifully —never face that split second. Indeed, we never have to decide anything without deliberation—let alone whether we must end one person's life to preserve our own or the lives of those around us.

The qualified immunity standard stops this privilege from blinding our judgment, preventing us from pretending we can place ourselves in the officers' position based on a cold appellate record. It prevents us from hubristically declaring what an officer should have done—as if we can expect calm calculation in the midst of chaos.

The majority opinion, written from the comfort of courthouse chambers, ignores that deference. Instead, it warns officers that they cannot trust what they see; they cannot trust what their fellow officers observe; they cannot trust themselves when posed with a credible threat. It instructs them, in that pivotal split second, to wait. But when a split second is all you have, waiting itself is a decision—one that may bring disastrous consequences.

[1] *Zadeh v. Robinson,* 928 F.3d 457, 474 (5th Cir. 2019) (Willett, J., concurring in part, dissenting in part).

[2] *Pearson v. Callahan,* 555 U.S. 223, 231, 129 S.Ct. 808, 172 L.Ed.2d 565 (2009) (flagging these "two important interests").

[3] *Zadeh,* 928 F.3d at 479.

[4] *See, e.g., State Oil Co. v. Khan,* 522 U.S. 3, 118 S.Ct. 275, 139 L.Ed.2d 199 (1997) (overruling prior precedent whose unsoundness had been "aptly described" by the court of appeals).

[5] *District of Columbia v. Wesby,* ___ U.S. ___, 138 S. Ct. 577, 589, 199 L.Ed.2d 453 (2018) (quoting *Malley v. Briggs,* 475 U.S. 335, 341, 106 S.Ct. 1092, 89 L.Ed.2d 271 (1986)).

[6] *Ashcroft v. al-Kidd,* 563 U.S. 731, 741, 131 S.Ct. 2074, 179 L.Ed.2d 1149 (2011); *see also, e.g., Kisela v. Hughes,* ___ U.S. ___, 138 S. Ct. 1148, 1153, 200 L.Ed.2d 449 (2018) (per curiam); *Mullenix v. Luna,* ___ U.S. ___, 136 S. Ct. 305, 308, 193 L.Ed.2d 255 (2015) (per curiam).

[7] *Corbitt v. Vickers,* 929 F.3d 1304, 1307-08 (11th Cir. 2019).

[8] *Id.* at 1323.

[9] *Zadeh,* 928 F.3d at 479-80 (Willett, J., concurring in part, dissenting in part).

[10] Four sitting Justices "have authored or joined opinions expressing sympathy" with assorted critiques of qualified immunity. Joanna C. Schwartz, *The Case Against Qualified Immunity,* 93 NOTRE DAME L. REV. 1797, 1800 (2018) (including Justices Thomas, Ginsburg, Breyer, and Sotomayor, plus recently retired Justice Kennedy); *see, e.g., Ziglar v. Abbasi,* ___ U.S. ___, 137 S. Ct. 1843, 1872, 198 L.Ed.2d 290 (2017) (Thomas, J., concurring in part and concurring in the judgment) ("In an appropriate case, we should reconsider our qualified immunity jurisprudence."); *see also Kisela v. Hughes,* ___ U.S. ___, 138 S. Ct. 1148, 1162, 200 L.Ed.2d 449 (2018) (per curiam).

[11] *Doe v. Woodard,* 912 F.3d 1278 (10th Cir. 2019), *cert. denied,* ___ U.S. ___, 139 S.Ct. 2616, ___, 204 L.Ed.2d 265 (2019). As for congressional reform, Congress's refusal to revisit § 1983 suggests Article I acquiescence.

[12] 555 U.S. at 236, 129 S.Ct. 808.

[13] As observers have cautioned, unfettered *Pearson* discretion contributes to "constitutional stagnation" by impeding the development of precedent. Aaron L. Nielson & Christopher J. Walker, *The New Qualified Immunity,* 89 S. CAL. L. REV. 1, 23-24 (2015).

[14] *Id.* at 7.

[15] *See, e.g.,* RICHARD FALLON, JR., ET AL., HART AND WECHSLER'S THE FEDERAL COURTS AND THE FEDERAL SYSTEM 1047-50 (7th ed. 2015) (noting the difficulties of applying the clearly-established-law test); Karen M. Blum, *Section 1983 Litigation: The Maze, the Mud, and the Madness,* 23 WM. & MARY BILL RTS. J. 913, 925 n.68 (2015) ("[W]hether a right is found to be 'clearly established' is very much a function of which circuit (and I would add, which judge) is asking the question, and how that question is framed.").

[16] *Harlow v. Fitzgerald* prevents plaintiffs from relying on *subjective* evidence of bad faith. 457 U.S. 800, 815-16, 102 S.Ct. 2727, 73 L.Ed.2d 396 (1982).

[17] *Id.* at 817, 102 S.Ct. 2727.

[18] *Zadeh,* 928 F.3d at 481 (Willett, J., concurring in part, dissenting in part).

[19] As for the sidelong critique of me in the dissenting opinion of Judges Ho and Oldham, it is, respectfully, a pyromaniac in a field of straw men. I have not raised originalist concerns with qualified immunity. My concerns, repeated today, are doctrinal, procedural, and pragmatic in nature. Nor has my unease with modern immunity practice led me to wage "war with the Supreme Court's qualified-immunity jurisprudence." I am a fellow dissenter today, notwithstanding my unease, precisely because I believe the Court's precedent compels it. In short, I have not urged that qualified immunity be repealed. I have urged that it be rethought. Justice Thomas— no "halfway originalist"—has done the same. *Ziglar,* 137 S. Ct. at 1872 (Thomas, J., concurring in part and concurring in the judgment) ("In an appropriate case, we should reconsider our qualified immunity jurisprudence.").

[1] The Supreme Court issues GVRs when, as here, legal error infects the judgment below. *See, e.g., Hicks v. United States,* ___ U.S. ___, 137 S. Ct. 2000, 2000-01, 198 L.Ed.2d 718 (2017) (Gorsuch, J., concurring) (defending GVR because "[a] plain legal error infects this judgment" and because petitioner "enjoys a reasonable

probability of success" in getting judgment reversed on the merits); *id.* at 2002 (Roberts, C.J., dissenting) ("[W]ithout a determination from this Court that the judgment below was wrong or at least a concession from the Government to that effect, we should not, in my view, vacate the Fifth Circuit's judgment."). As the cert petition explained, our panel denied qualified immunity "based on the same rationale" on "which this Court reversed in *Mullenix*." Pet. at i, 2016 WL 4987324, ___ U.S. ___, ___ S.Ct. ___, ___ L.Ed.2d ___. We think it obvious the Supreme Court GVR'd because it agreed. And tellingly, the majority does not offer an alternative theory to explain the GVR. We ignore the Court's message at our peril. *See, e.g., Smith v. Mitchell,* 437 F.3d 884 (9th Cir. 2006) (granting habeas relief to a state prisoner because the evidence was insufficient to prove she shook her grandbaby to death); *Patrick v. Smith,* 550 U.S. 915, 127 S.Ct. 2126, 167 L.Ed.2d 861 (2007) (GVR'ing i/l/o *Carey v. Musladin,* 549 U.S. 70, 127 S.Ct. 649, 166 L.Ed.2d 482 (2006)); *Smith v. Patrick,* 519 F.3d 900 (9th Cir. 2008) (again granting habeas relief); *Patrick v. Smith,* 558 U.S. 1143, 130 S.Ct. 1134, 175 L.Ed.2d 967 (2010) (GVR'ing i/l/o *McDaniel v. Brown,* 558 U.S. 120, 130 S.Ct. 665, 175 L.Ed.2d 582 (2010)); *Smith v. Mitchell,* 624 F.3d 1235 (9th Cir. 2010) (again granting habeas relief); *Cavazos v. Smith,* 565 U.S. 1, 132 S.Ct. 2, 181 L.Ed.2d 311 (2011) (SUMREV'ing).

[2] Those social costs are particularly stark today given widespread news of low officer morale and shortages in officer recruitment. *See, e.g.,* Ashley Southall, *When Officers Are Being Doused, Has Police Restraint Gone Too Far?,* N.Y. TIMES, July 25, 2019, at A22; Martin Kaste & Lori Mack, *Shortage of Officers Fuels Police Recruiting Crisis,* NPR (Dec. 11, 2018, 5:05 AM), https://n.pr/2Qrbrnq; Jeremy Gorner, *Morale, Policing Suffering in Hostile Climate, Cops Say; 'It's Almost Like We're the Bad Guys,' Veteran City Officer Says,* CHI. TRIB., Nov. 27, 2016, at 1.

[3] In a footnote, Judge Willett notes that his criticism of the Supreme Court's qualified immunity precedents is not based on originalist grounds. *Ante,* at 473 n.19. To our minds, that makes his criticism harder, not easier, to defend. If his concerns are based on practical and not originalist considerations, then he should address them to the Legislature, rather than attack the Supreme Court as "one-sided." *Zadeh,* 902 F.3d at 499 & n.10 (Willett, J., concurring dubitante) (quoting *Kisela,* 138 S. Ct. at 1162 (Sotomayor, J., dissenting)). He also invokes Justice Thomas's opinion in *Ziglar v. Abbasi,* ___ U.S. ___, 137 S. Ct. 1843, 1872, 198 L.Ed.2d 290 (2017). But that opinion cites Justice Scalia's opinion in *Crawford-El,* which (as we explained above) warns qualified immunity skeptics not to engage in halfway originalism.

[1] *See, e.g., Kingsley v. Hendrickson,* ___ U.S. ___, 135 S. Ct. 2466, 2474, 192 L.Ed.2d 416 (2015) (courts "must judge the reasonableness of the force used from the perspective and with the knowledge of the defendant officer"); *Tennessee v. Garner,* 471 U.S. 1, 9, 105 S.Ct. 1694, 85 L.Ed.2d 1 (1985) (whether a "particular" seizure was justified depends on "the totality of the circumstances").

[2] All of these facts come from reports and transcriptions of radio transmissions made within a day or two of the incident. None come from affidavits submitted by the officers years later. And, as explained below, none of these pre-encounter facts was disputed by Cole or analyzed by the district court.

[3] *See, e.g., Mullenix v. Luna,* ___ U.S. ___, 136 S. Ct. 305, 306, 193 L.Ed.2d 255 (2015) (assessing officer's shooting of suspect during car chase beginning with events preceding the "18-minute chase"); *Plumhoff v. Rickard,* 572 U.S. 765, 768-70, 134 S.Ct.

2012, 188 L.Ed.2d 1056 (2014) (assessing officer's shooting of suspects in Memphis, Tennessee after lengthy car chase beginning with traffic stop in "West Memphis, Arkansas"); *Brosseau v. Haugen,* 543 U.S. 194, 195, 125 S.Ct. 596, 160 L.Ed.2d 583 (2004) (evaluating officer's shooting of fleeing suspect beginning with events "[o]n the day before the fracas"); *Colston,* 130 F.3d at 100 (determining officer's failure to warn was not objectively unreasonable "[i]n light of the totality of the circumstances facing [the officer]") (citing *Garner,* 471 U.S. at 10, 105 S.Ct. 1694).

[4] Our cases continue to apply the *Rockwell* "moment-of-the-threat" principle in this way. *See, e.g., Shepherd v. City of Shreveport,* 920 F.3d 278 (5th Cir. 2019) (explaining that, because the excessive force inquiry is "confined to whether the officer was in danger at the moment of the threat[,] ... [t]herefore, any of the officers' actions leading up to the shooting are not relevant") (emphasis added) (internal quotes and citation omitted); *Harris v. Serpas,* 745 F.3d 767, 772-73 (5th Cir. 2014) (same) (discussing *Rockwell*).

917 F.3d 870 (2019)

Nancy MORROW; Alvin Russell Moon, on Behalf of Estate of Austin Russell Moon, on Behalf of C.D., a Minor; Christa Donahue, on Behalf of A.D., a Minor, Plaintiffs-Appellants,

v.

Jonathan MEACHUM, Defendant-Appellee.

No. 17-11243.

United States Court of Appeals, Fifth Circuit.

FILED March 8, 2019.

Morrow v. Meachum, 917 F. 3d 870 (5th Cir. 2019)

Appeal from the United States District Court for the Eastern District of Texas.

Jeff S. Edwards, David James, Scott Charles Medlock, Edwards Law, Austin, TX, for Plaintiffs-Appellants.

Grant David Blaies, Esq., Jennifer Holland Litke, Blaies & Hightower, L.L.P., Fort Worth, TX, for Defendant-Appellee.

Before DAVIS, COSTA, and OLDHAM, Circuit Judges.

p.872 ANDREW S. OLDHAM, Circuit Judge:

Austin Moon was a young motorcyclist. He liked to ride fast. So fast, in fact, he twice eluded police officers at triple-digit speeds. On officers' third attempt to stop Moon, a Criminal District Attorney Investigator named Jonathan Meachum caused Moon to crash. Moon died. The question presented is whether Meachum is entitled to qualified immunity. The district court held yes. We affirm.

I.

A.

On June 26, 2014, Meachum was patrolling I-20 near the town of Cisco, Texas. He p.873 was driving a marked police SUV. At around 5:30 p.m., Meachum observed motorcyclist Moon speeding at 85 mph and weaving through traffic. Meachum turned on his lights to stop the motorcycle. Moon sped away. Meachum radioed for help.

Having shaken the police SUV from his tail, Moon exited I-20. He stopped at a gas station and hid behind a gas pump. Eastland County Deputy Sheriff Ben Yarbrough drove by the gas station and spotted Moon. Moon likewise spotted Yarbrough. So Moon again sped away—this time performing a "wheelie." Yarbrough turned on his lights and gave chase. Moon again escaped. Yarbrough radioed that Moon was now headed south on US-183.

Meanwhile, Investigator Meachum had also exited I-20 onto southbound US-183. But given Moon's pit stop, Meachum was now in front of him. The relevant stretch of US-183 is a two-lane undivided road with rolling hills. Videos in the record show light but consistent traffic going both directions. Videos also show Meachum was driving approximately 100 mph; motorcyclist Moon was clocked at 150 mph and closing quickly behind Meachum.[1] As Meachum reached the top of a gentle hill, he spotted two vehicles in the oncoming (northbound) lane of US-183. Meachum also spotted Moon approaching from behind.

Thus began the fateful seven seconds at the heart of this case. According to the dashboard camera ("dashcam") on Meachum's police SUV and Moon's expert report, the officer was going approximately 100 mph when he spotted Moon approaching from behind. The dashcam at that moment is timestamped 17:46 and 41 seconds. At 42.3 seconds, Meachum slowed to 93 mph and moved to the right side of his lane. At 43.0 seconds, Meachum slowed to 87 mph. At 44.7 seconds, Meachum slowed to 71 mph. Then, over the next 2.3 seconds —from 44.7 to 47.0—Meachum slowed to 56 mph and moved his SUV leftward and over the center line of US-183. At 47.7 seconds, Moon crashed into the back of Meachum's SUV. The dashcam shows Meachum was traveling 51 mph at impact.[2] Moon died. He was 22.

B.

Moon's survivors and estate sued Meachum under 42 U.S.C. § 1983 for seizing Moon in violation of the Fourth Amendment. They argued Meachum intentionally positioned his SUV to surprise Moon, to prevent him from eluding arrest a third time, and under the circumstances, to kill him.

Meachum described his actions as a "rolling block." Meachum testified he performed a rolling block because he wanted to (1) discourage Moon from passing in the oncoming traffic lane and (2) warn the oncoming traffic of the pursuit. Videos corroborated Meachum's testimony there was northbound traffic on the highway. The p.874 only dispute was whether that traffic was in the northbound lane or on the shoulder. Either way, a witness stated Moon's motorcycle was already in the northbound lane when Meachum crossed the center line.

The district court held Meachum was entitled to qualified immunity and entered summary judgment. It held "the law is clear that '[a] police officer's attempt to terminate a dangerous high-speed car chase that threatens the lives of innocent bystanders does not violate the Fourth Amendment, even when it places the fleeing motorist at risk of serious injury or death.'" *Morrow v. Meachum,* No. 1:16-cv-118, 2017 WL 4124285, at *4 (N.D. Tex. Sept. 18, 2017) (quoting *Scott v. Harris,* 550 U.S. 372, 386, 127 S.Ct. 1769, 167 L.Ed.2d 686 (2007)). Moon's estate and survivors appealed.[3]

II.

Our review is *de novo. Vann v. City of Southaven,* 884 F.3d 307, 309 (5th Cir. 2018) (per curiam). We view the facts in the light most favorable to Appellants and draw all reasonable inferences in their favor. *See ibid.* Even so, they cannot show Meachum violated clearly established law.

A.

Appellants seek money damages from the personal pocket of a law-enforcement officer. The qualified-immunity doctrine makes that task difficult in every case. In this case, it's impossible.

1.

Qualified immunity includes two inquiries. The first question is whether the officer violated a constitutional right. The second question is whether the "right at issue was 'clearly established' at the time of [the] alleged misconduct." *Pearson v. Callahan,* 555 U.S. 223, 232, 129 S.Ct. 808, 172 L.Ed.2d 565 (2009). We can decide one question or both. *See id.* at 236, 129 S.Ct. 808.

The second question—whether the officer violated clearly established law—is a doozy. The § 1983 plaintiff bears the burden of proof. *See Vann,* 884 F.3d at 309. And the burden is heavy: A right is clearly established only if relevant precedent "ha[s] placed the ... constitutional question beyond debate." *Ashcroft v. al-Kidd,* 563 U.S. 731, 741, 131 S.Ct. 2074, 179 L.Ed.2d 1149 (2011). The pages of the *United States Reports* teem with warnings about the difficulty of placing a question beyond debate. From them, we can distill four applicable commandments.[4]

First, we must frame the constitutional question with specificity and p.875 granularity. For example, it is obviously beyond debate the Fourth Amendment prohibits certain "unreasonable ... seizures." U.S. CONST. amend. IV. "Yet that is not enough." *Saucier v. Katz,* 533 U.S. 194, 202, 121 S.Ct. 2151, 150 L.Ed.2d 272 (2001). The Supreme Court has "repeatedly told courts ... not to define clearly established law at [that] high level of generality." *al-Kidd,* 563 U.S. at 742, 131 S.Ct. 2074; *see also City of Escondido, Cal. v. Emmons,* ___ U.S. ___, 139 S.Ct. 500, 503-04, 202 L.Ed.2d 455 (2019) (per curiam). Rather, "[t]he dispositive question is whether the violative nature of *particular* conduct is clearly established." *Mullenix v. Luna,* ___ U.S. ___, 136 S.Ct. 305, 308, 193 L.Ed.2d 255 (2015) (per curiam) (quotation omitted); *see also Bush v. Strain,* 513 F.3d 492, 502 (5th Cir. 2008). That is because qualified immunity is inappropriate only where the officer had "fair notice"—"in light of the specific context of the case, not as a broad general proposition" —that his *particular* conduct was unlawful. *Brosseau v. Haugen,* 543 U.S. 194, 198, 125 S.Ct. 596, 160 L.Ed.2d 583 (2004) (per curiam) (quotation omitted); *accord City & Cty. of San Francisco v. Sheehan,* ___ U.S. ___, 135 S.Ct. 1765, 1776, 191 L.Ed.2d 856 (2015) ("Qualified immunity is no immunity at all if 'clearly established' law can simply be defined as the right to be free from unreasonable searches and seizures."); *Wilson v. Layne,* 526 U.S. 603, 615, 119 S.Ct. 1692, 143 L.Ed.2d 818 (1999) (similar); *Anderson v. Creighton,* 483 U.S. 635, 640, 107 S.Ct. 3034, 97 L.Ed.2d 523 (1987) (similar).[5]

Second, clearly established law comes from holdings, not dicta. *Sorenson v. Ferrie,* 134 F.3d 325, 329 n.7 (5th Cir. 1998) ("The court's language ... is *dictum* that hardly constitutes clearly established law."); *see also Leiser v. Moore,* 903 F.3d 1137, 1145 (10th

Cir. 2018) (concluding Supreme Court precedent did not clearly establish the law because it "express[ed] only dicta"); *Hamilton ex rel. Hamilton v. Cannon,* 80 F.3d 1525, 1530 (11th Cir. 1996) ("The law cannot be established by dicta. Dicta is particularly unhelpful in qualified immunity cases where we seek to identify clearly established law."); *cf. Woods v. Donald,* ___ U.S. ___, 135 S.Ct. 1372, 1376, 191 L.Ed.2d 464 (2015) ("'[C]learly established Federal law' for purposes of [28 U.S.C.] § 2254(d)(1) includes only the holdings, as opposed to the dicta, of this Court's decisions."); *al-Kidd,* 563 U.S. at 741-42, 131 S.Ct. 2074 (holding a district court's "footnoted dictum" did not clearly establish the law for purposes of qualified immunity). Dictum is not law, and hence cannot be clearly established law. *See* BRYAN A. GARNER, ET AL., THE LAW OF JUDICIAL PRECEDENT 44 (2016) (explaining dictum does not "bind future courts" and is "not law per se").[6] And while officers are p.876 charged with knowing the results of our cases—at least when they are so numerous and pellucid as to put the relevant question "beyond debate," *al-Kidd,* 563 U.S. at 741, 131 S.Ct. 2074—officers are not charged with memorizing every jot and tittle we write to explain them.

Third, overcoming qualified immunity is especially difficult in excessive-force cases. This "is an area of the law 'in which the result depends very much on the facts of each case,' and thus police officers are entitled to qualified immunity unless existing precedent 'squarely governs' the specific facts at issue." *Kisela v. Hughes,* ___ U.S. ___, 138 S.Ct. 1148, 1153, 200 L.Ed.2d 449 (2018) (per curiam) (quoting *Mullenix,* 136 S.Ct. at 309). And as this case illustrates, excessive-force claims often turn on "split-second decisions" to use lethal force. *Pasco ex rel. Pasco v. Knoblauch,* 566 F.3d 572, 582 (5th Cir. 2009). That means the law must be *so* clearly established that—in the blink of an eye, in the middle of a high-speed chase— every reasonable officer would know it immediately. *See ibid.*

The fourth and final commandment is we must think twice before denying qualified immunity. The Supreme Court reserves "the extraordinary remedy of a summary reversal" for decisions that are "manifestly incorrect." *Kisela,* 138 S.Ct. at 1162 (Sotomayor, J., dissenting) (quotation omitted). Yet it routinely wields this remedy against denials of qualified immunity. *See Emmons,* 139 S.Ct. at 503-04 (summarily reversing the Ninth Circuit); *Kisela,* 138 S.Ct. at 1153 (majority op.) (summarily reversing the Ninth Circuit); *White v. Pauly,* ___ U.S. ___, 137 S.Ct. 548, 553, 196 L.Ed.2d 463 (2017) (per curiam) (summarily reversing the Tenth Circuit); *Mullenix,* 136 S.Ct. at 312 (summarily reversing our Court); *Stanton v. Sims,* 571 U.S. 3, 5, 134 S.Ct. 3, 187 L.Ed.2d 341 (2013) (per curiam) (summarily reversing the Ninth Circuit). "Because of the importance of qualified immunity to society as a whole, the [Supreme] Court often corrects lower courts when they wrongly subject individual officers to liability." *Sheehan,* 135 S.Ct. at 1774 n.3 (quotation and citation omitted); *accord Carroll v. Carman,* 574 U.S. 13, 135 S.Ct. 348, 190 L.Ed.2d 311 (2014) (per curiam); *Wood v. Moss,* 572 U.S. 744, 764, 134 S.Ct. 2056, 188 L.Ed.2d 1039 (2014); *Plumhoff v. Rickard,* 572 U.S. 765, 778, 134 S.Ct. 2012, 188 L.Ed.2d 1056 (2014); *Reichle v. Howards,* 566 U.S. 658, 663, 132 S.Ct. 2088, 182 L.Ed.2d 985 (2012); *Wesby v. District of Columbia,* 816 F.3d 96, 102 (D.C. Cir. 2016) (Kavanaugh, J., dissenting from the denial of rehearing en banc) ("Indeed, in just the past five years, the Supreme Court has issued 11 decisions reversing federal courts of appeals in qualified immunity cases, including five strongly worded summary reversals."), *rev'd,* ___ U.S. ___, 138

S.Ct. 577, 199 L.Ed.2d 453 (2018). We'd be ill advised to misunderstand the message and deny qualified immunity to anyone "but the plainly incompetent or those who knowingly violate the law." *Malley v. Briggs,* 475 U.S. 335, 341, 106 S.Ct. 1092, 89 L.Ed.2d 271 (1986).

2.

Appellants are seeking an extraordinary remedy. To get it, they must make an extraordinary showing. They have fallen far short. They have not identified a controlling precedent that "'squarely governs' the specific facts at issue." *Kisela,* 138 S.Ct. at 1153. Nor have they identified a controlling precedent rendering it "beyond debate"—such that any reasonable officer would know, even in only seven seconds, and even in the midst of a high-speed p.877 chase—that Meachum's rolling block violated the Fourth Amendment. *See al-Kidd,* 563 U.S. at 741, 131 S.Ct. 2074.

To the extent we can identify clearly established law in excessive-force cases, it supports Meachum, not Moon. In at least three recent cases, the Supreme Court has decided whether officers are entitled to qualified immunity for using deadly force to end high-speed chases. In all three cases, the Court said yes. In *Plumhoff,* the Court held officers were entitled to qualified immunity after firing 15 shots that killed two men who fled a traffic stop at speeds over 100 mph. 572 U.S. at 769-70, 779-80, 134 S.Ct. 2012. In *Mullenix,* the Court held an officer was entitled to qualified immunity after firing six shots and killing a man who evaded arrest at speeds between 85 and 110 mph. 136 S.Ct. at 306-07, 312. And in *Scott,* the Court held an officer was entitled to qualified immunity after ending an 85-mph chase by ramming the suspect's car off the road and paralyzing him. 550 U.S. at 375, 386, 127 S.Ct. 1769. Indeed, in *Scott,* the Court held there was no constitutional violation at all. *Id.* at 386, 127 S.Ct. 1769.

Appellants argue these cases are distinguishable in various ways. True. All that matters here, however, is that three cases affording qualified immunity to officers who used deadly force to end police chases do nothing to *foreclose* using deadly force to end police chases. *See Mullenix,* 136 S.Ct. at 312.

B.

For their part, Appellants attempt to identify clearly established law in three lines of cases. Individually and collectively, they are insufficient.

1.

Appellants first point to *Brower v. County of Inyo,* 489 U.S. 593, 109 S.Ct. 1378, 103 L.Ed.2d 628 (1989). In *Brower,* the Court held a seizure occurred when the police:

(1) caused an 18-wheel tractor-trailer to be placed across both lanes of a two-lane highway in the path of Brower's flight,
(2) "effectively concealed" this roadblock by placing it behind a curve and leaving it unilluminated, and (3) positioned a police car, with its headlights on, between Brower's oncoming vehicle and the truck, so that Brower would be "blinded" on his approach.

Id. at 594, 109 S.Ct. 1378. Appellants interpret *Brower* to hold a "deliberately deadly" roadblock that is "likely to kill [the fleeing suspect]" is *per se* unreasonable and hence unconstitutional.[7]

Brower held no such thing. "The only question in *Brower* was whether a police roadblock constituted a seizure under the Fourth Amendment." *Scott,* 550 U.S. at 384 n.10, 127 S.Ct. 1769; *see also* Brief for Petitioner at i, *Brower v. County of Inyo,* 489 U.S. 593 (1989) (No. 87-248) (setting out the question presented: "Whether the apprehension of decedent by means of a p.878 high speed chase and a 'deadman' roadblock constitutes a seizure within the meaning of the Fourth Amendment."). The Court said nothing about whether the officers could be held personally liable. It said nothing about qualified immunity. And it said nothing about whether the officers had "fair notice" their conduct was unreasonable. Nor did the Court say anything about the *reasonableness* of the seizure. In fact, it remanded for consideration of whether the roadblock was reasonable. *See* 489 U.S. at 599-600, 109 S.Ct. 1378. *Brower* therefore did nothing to clearly establish a prohibition on "deadman roadblocks." And it did not put Meachum on "fair notice" of the reasonableness of anything.

Appellants fall back to *Tennessee v. Garner,* 471 U.S. 1, 105 S.Ct. 1694, 85 L.Ed.2d 1 (1985). In *Garner,* a young man attempted to run from police after stealing a purse and $10. Garner attempted to climb a fence. To stop the purse-snatcher, an officer fatally shot him in the back of the head. From *Garner,* Appellants divine a clearly established prohibition on the use of deadly force "where the suspect poses no immediate threat to the officer and no threat to others." There are at least three problems with that argument. First, the Supreme Court already rejected it. *See Scott,* 550 U.S. at 382, 127 S.Ct. 1769 ("*Garner* did not establish a magical on/off switch that triggers rigid preconditions whenever an officer's actions constitute 'deadly force.'").

Second, the Supreme Court has warned us against extending *Garner.* In fact, that's the one mistake common to the Supreme Court's recent reversals in excessive-force cases. *See Mullenix,* 136 S.Ct. at 308-09 (discussing our Court's erroneous extension of *Garner*); *Scott,* 550 U.S. at 381-83, 127 S.Ct. 1769; *Allen v. West Memphis,* 509 F. App'x 388, 392 (6th Cir. 2012) (extending *Garner*), *rev'd by Plumhoff,* 572 U.S. 765, 134 S.Ct. 2012. We won't repeat that mistake.

Third, and in all events, *Garner* is easily distinguishable. A motorcyclist eluding arrest twice and leading police on a chase at well over 100 mph poses an obvious threat to the pursuing officers and the public. The videos in this case show many other motorists on the road. Moon's "reckless, high-speed flight" therefore endangered the public and officers in ways Garner's fence-hopping never did. *Scott,* 550 U.S. at 384, 127 S.Ct. 1769. That's precisely why the Supreme Court "has ... never found the use of deadly force in connection with a dangerous car chase to violate the Fourth Amendment, let alone to be a basis for denying qualified immunity." *Mullenix,* 136 S.Ct. at 310. And it's why we previously refused to extend *Garner* to high-speed chases. *See Pasco,* 566 F.3d at 580 ("[I]t would be unreasonable to expect a police officer to make the numerous legal conclusions necessary to apply *Garner* to a high-speed car chase."). We refuse again today.[8]

2.

Next, Appellants point to *Lytle v. Bexar County,* 560 F.3d 404 (5th Cir. 2009). In *Lytle,* a police officer shot at a fleeing vehicle and killed a fifteen-year-old passenger in the back seat. *Id.* at 407-08. We held "a jury could conclude [a fleeing car] posed some threat of harm" because "the p.879 chase took place at high speeds within a residential area, there were children playing somewhere nearby, and the [car] had collided with another vehicle." *Id.* at 416. The Court remanded for trial, however, because it did "not agree with [the officer] that the [car] was so menacing under [the plaintiff's] version of the facts that *any* use of force in an attempt to stop it would be objectively reasonable as a matter of law." *Ibid.* (emphasis added).

Even if *Lytle* survives *Mullenix, Plumhoff,* and the Supreme Court's other recent applications of the qualified-immunity doctrine, cases involving gunshots are too factually dissimilar to put the relevant question "beyond debate." *al-Kidd,* 563 U.S. at 741, 131 S.Ct. 2074. "It does not assist analysis to refer to all use of force that happens to kill the arrestee as the application of deadly force." *Mullenix,* 136 S.Ct. at 312 (Scalia, J., concurring in the judgment); *see also Scott,* 550 U.S. at 382, 127 S.Ct. 1769. "A police car's bumping a fleeing [vehicle] is, in fact, not much like a policeman's shooting a gun...." *Scott,* 550 U.S. at 383, 127 S.Ct. 1769 (quoting *Adams v. St. Lucie Cty. Sheriff's Dep't,* 962 F.2d 1563, 1577 (11th Cir. 1992) (Edmondson, J., dissenting)). Therefore, gunshot cases do not "'squarely govern[]' the facts" of a case involving a collision between a police vehicle and a suspect's vehicle. *Mullenix,* 136 S.Ct. at 310.[9]

Even if gunshot cases were relevant, the law is at best ambiguous. Sure, there's *Lytle.* On the other hand, *Mullenix, Plumhoff, Vann, Pasco,* and *Thompson v. Mercer,* 762 F.3d 433, 440-41 (5th Cir. 2014), *all* involved gunshots that ended high-speed chases. And qualified immunity applied in all five. Cases cutting both ways do not clearly establish the law.

3.

Finally, Appellants argue it is unconstitutional for officers to perform a rolling block where a fleeing motorcyclist "posed no immediate danger to anyone." Because there is no binding precedent saying so, they rely on a purported "consensus of persuasive cases from other jurisdictions." *Breen v. Tex. A&M Univ.,* 485 F.3d 325, 339 (5th Cir.), *modified on reh'g,* 494 F.3d 516 (5th Cir. 2007) (per curiam).

We have not previously identified the level of out-of-circuit consensus necessary to put the relevant question "beyond debate." *al-Kidd,* 563 U.S. at 741, 131 S.Ct. 2074. But we know the consensus must be "robust." *District of Columbia v. Wesby,* ___ U.S. ___, 138 S.Ct. 577, 589, 199 L.Ed.2d 453 (2018) (quoting *al-Kidd,* 563 U.S. at 741-42, 131 S.Ct. 2074). And in *McClendon v. City of Columbia,* 305 F.3d 314, 330 (5th Cir. 2002) (en banc), we held recognition of the state-created-danger doctrine in *six circuits* was insufficient to create a robust consensus. We reasoned that, despite widespread acceptance of the doctrine, the circuits were not unanimous in its "contours" or its application "to a p.880 factual context similar to that of the instant case." *Id.* at 331-32.

Appellants fall far short of establishing an out-of-circuit consensus, let alone a robust one. It is true the Sixth Circuit has denied qualified immunity in two motorcycle-chase cases. *See Stamm v. Miller,* 657 F. App'x 492, 495 (6th Cir. 2016); *Walker v. Davis,* 649 F.3d 502, 503 (6th Cir. 2011); *cf. Hawkins v. City of Farmington,* 189 F.3d 695, 702-03 (8th Cir. 1999) (remanding for consideration of whether a "partial roadblock with means of escape" was unreasonable). But for three separate reasons, those cases are irrelevant here.

First, *Stamm* is irrelevant because it was decided after Meachum's chase. *See Anderson,* 483 U.S. at 639, 107 S.Ct. 3034 (qualified immunity turns on "the legal rules that were 'clearly established' at the time [the official action] was taken"); *Pierson,* 386 U.S. at 557, 87 S.Ct. 1213.

Second, and more generally, the Sixth Circuit's approach is infected by the same disease the Supreme Court cured in *Mullenix.* The Sixth Circuit held *Garner* makes it "clearly established law that an officer may not use his police vehicle to intentionally hit a motorcycle unless the suspect on the motorcycle poses a threat to the officer or others." *Stamm,* 657 F. App'x at 496; *see also Walker,* 649 F.3d at 503 (similar). Of course, *Garner* held no such thing. *Garner* involved guns (not police vehicles), and *Garner* involved a $10-thief hopping a fence (not a motorcyclist escaping at triple-digit speed). The only way to use *Garner* for clearly establishing the law in vehicle chases is to identify the constitutional issue from a bird's eye view—an approach the Supreme Court has rejected time and again. *See, e.g., Mullenix,* 136 S.Ct. at 309 (rejecting the "use of *Garner's* 'general' test for excessive force" to identify clearly established law); *see also supra* at 874-75 (collecting cases).

Finally, the Sixth Circuit does not represent a consensus. The Fourth Circuit concluded an officer acted reasonably in hitting a fleeing motorcyclist with his vehicle to end a high-speed chase. *Abney v. Coe,* 493 F.3d 412, 415-18 (4th Cir. 2007). Under Appellants' view, Meachum should be forced to decide—with life-or-death consequences for innocent motorists, in less than seven seconds, and upon pain of personal liability—whether his chase is more like *Abney* and *Mullenix,* or more like a slow-moving motorcycle pursuit "across an empty field in the middle of the night in rural Kentucky," *Walker,* 649 F.3d at 503. Section 1983 does not put Meachum to that choice. Nor do we.

* * *

The judgment of the district court is AFFIRMED.

[1] There is some dispute about Moon's speed after he was clocked by the radar gun. The Texas Department of Public Safety estimated Moon was traveling southbound on US-183 at approximately 170 mph in the seconds before the crash. Moon's expert estimated the motorcycle's speed at impact was between 100 and 110 mph. This dispute is immaterial to our resolution of the case.

[2] The times and speeds in this paragraph come from a frame-by-frame reading of Meachum's dashcam, but they may not be precisely accurate. Moon's expert report posits the speeds displayed on dashcam videos are "substantially delayed" because they are based on GPS data that lags the real-time movement of the police vehicle. Moon's expert argues once that delay is considered, the *actual* speed of Meachum's

SUV at impact was 45 mph not 51 mph. That dispute is immaterial to our resolution of this appeal. We reproduce the dashcam readings only because they illustrate textually what the video depicts visually: the general speed and position of Meachum's vehicle over the course of those seven seconds.

[3] Appellants also sued Eastland County, and the district court also granted summary judgment on those claims. Appellants do not challenge that ruling here.

[4] As Justice Thomas has explained, the qualified-immunity doctrine originated in common-law defenses to torts committed by executive officers. *See Ziglar v. Abbasi,* ___ U.S. ___, 137 S.Ct. 1843, 1870-71, 198 L.Ed.2d 290 (2017) (Thomas, J., concurring in part and concurring in the judgment) (citing *Pierson v. Ray,* 386 U.S. 547, 555-57, 87 S.Ct. 1213, 18 L.Ed.2d 288 (1967)). Some—including Justice Thomas—have queried whether the Supreme Court's post-*Pierson* qualified-immunity cases are "consistent with the common-law rules prevailing [when § 1983 was enacted] in 1871." *Id.* at 1872; *compare* William Baude, *Is Qualified Immunity Unlawful?,* 106 CAL. L. REV. 45, 49-61 (2018), *with* Aaron L. Nielson & Christopher J. Walker, *A Qualified Defense of Qualified Immunity,* 93 NOTRE DAME L. REV. 1853, 1856-63 (2018). Of course, we cannot ask such questions, much less answer them. We apply the Supreme Court's precedents faithfully. *See Hutto v. Davis,* 454 U.S. 370, 374-75, 102 S.Ct. 703, 70 L.Ed.2d 556 (1982) (per curiam).

[5] Of course, "[t]his is not to say that an official action is protected by qualified immunity unless the very action in question has previously been held unlawful." *Hope v. Pelzer,* 536 U.S. 730, 739, 122 S.Ct. 2508, 153 L.Ed.2d 666 (2002). It is to say qualified immunity requires "fair notice" that precedent "squarely governs" the official action. *Mullenix,* 136 S.Ct. at 310, 314 (citing *Brosseau,* 543 U.S. at 201, 125 S.Ct. 596).

[6] Some courts have suggested dicta can clearly establish the law for purposes of qualified immunity. They reason it is "arguably dicta" to find a constitutional violation at step one before granting qualified immunity at step two. But, they say, the very purpose of such "dicta" is to clearly establish the law for future qualified-immunity cases. *Hanes v. Zurick,* 578 F.3d 491, 496 (7th Cir. 2009); *see also Ehrlich v. Town of Glastonbury,* 348 F.3d 48, 56 n.11 (2d Cir. 2003). Since those cases were decided, however, the Supreme Court has clarified that "a constitutional ruling preparatory to a grant of immunity" is "[n]o mere dictum." *Camreta v. Greene,* 563 U.S. 692, 708, 131 S.Ct. 2020, 179 L.Ed.2d 1118 (2011). As a result, these cases do not stand for the proposition dicta can clearly establish the law.

[7] Supreme Court precedent renders irrelevant whether Meachum "deliberately" caused a fatal collision. "An officer's evil intentions will not make a Fourth Amendment violation out of an objectively reasonable use of force...." *Graham v. Connor,* 490 U.S. 386, 397, 109 S.Ct. 1865, 104 L.Ed.2d 443 (1989); *see also Anderson,* 483 U.S. at 641, 107 S.Ct. 3034. "[D]etermining whether [a defendant] violated the Fourth Amendment requires us to ask, not whether it was reasonable to kill [the suspect] but whether it was reasonable to [act as the defendant did] in light of the risk to [the suspect]." *Mullenix,* 136 S.Ct. at 313 (Scalia, J., concurring in the judgment); *see also Scott,* 550 U.S. at 383, 127 S.Ct. 1769 ("[A]ll that matters is whether [the officer's] actions were reasonable."). For the same reasons, it is irrelevant whether Meachum subjectively believed "deadly force" was necessary.

[8] In assessing a threat to the public, we consider not only the safety of those present at the moment of collision but also "the safety of those who could have been harmed if the chase continued." *Pasco,* 566 F.3d at 581 (citing *Scott,* 550 U.S. at 383-84, 127 S.Ct. 1769). For this reason, it does not matter whether the oncoming vehicles were in the northbound lane of US-183 (as Meachum testified) or the shoulder of the highway (as Appellants argued). Either way, they were in harm's way.

[9] Appellants also rely on our original opinion in *Vann,* which we have withdrawn, *see* 884 F.3d at 309, and numerous cases from our sister courts of appeals that involved firearms. *See Rodriguez v. Passinault,* 637 F.3d 675 (6th Cir. 2011); *Tubar v. Clift,* 286 F. App'x 348 (9th Cir. 2008) (per curiam); *Kirby v. Duva,* 530 F.3d 475 (6th Cir. 2008); *Adams v. Speers,* 473 F.3d 989 (9th Cir. 2007); *Murray-Ruhl v. Passinault,* 246 F. App'x 338 (6th Cir. 2007); *Jones v. City of Atlanta,* 192 F. App'x 894 (11th Cir. 2006); *Sigley v. City of Parma Heights,* 437 F.3d 527 (6th Cir. 2006); *Smith v. Cupp,* 430 F.3d 766 (6th Cir. 2005); *Vaughan v. Cox,* 343 F.3d 1323 (11th Cir. 2003); *Cowan ex rel. Cooper v. Breen,* 352 F.3d 756 (2d Cir. 2003); *McCaslin v. Wilkins,* 183 F.3d 775 (8th Cir. 1999); *Abraham v. Raso,* 183 F.3d 279 (3d Cir. 1999); *Estate of Starks v. Enyart,* 5 F.3d 230 (7th Cir. 1993). These decisions did not clearly establish the law for the same reasons *Lytle* did not.

922 F.3d 590 (2019)

Angie WALLER, Individually and in her Capacity as Independent Executrix of the Estate of Kathleen Margaret Waller; Chris Waller, Plaintiffs-Appellees.

Terry Wayne Springer; Gayla Wynell Kimbrough, Intervenor Plaintiffs-Appellees

v.

Benjamin B. HANLON; Richard Hoeppner; B. S. Hardin, Defendants-Appellants.

No. 18-10561.

United States Court of Appeals, Fifth Circuit.

FILED April 24, 2019.

Waller v. Hanlon, 922 F. 3d 590 (5th Cir. 2019)

Appeals from the United States District Court for the Northern District of Texas.

Arthur John Brender, Law Offices of Art Brender, Fort Worth, TX, for Plaintiffs-Appellees ANGIE WALLER, CHRIS WALLER.

Michael Ware, Fort Worth, TX, for Intervenor Plaintiff-Appellee TERRY WAYNE SPRINGER, GAYLA WYNELL KIMBROUGH.

James Thomas Jeffrey, Jr., Esq., Law Offices of Jim Jeffrey, Arlington, TX, for Defendant-Appellant BENJAMIN B. HANLON.

Kenneth E. East, Esq., Foster & East, North Richland Hills, TX, Dee Lee Thomas, Jr., Law Office of D. Lee Thomas, Fort Worth, TX, for Defendant-Appellant RICHARD HOEPPNER.

Stephen Chamberlain Maxwell, Bailey & Galyen, Fort Worth, TX, for Defendant-Appellant B. S. HARDIN.

Before KING, SMITH, and WILLETT, Circuit Judges.

p.595 KING, Circuit Judge:

Fort Worth Police Officer Richard Hoeppner fatally shot 72-year old Jerry Waller in Waller's own garage. Hoeppner insists he did so only out of reasonable fear for his life. Seeking recompense for Waller's death, Waller's survivors came to the district court alleging that forensic evidence substantially undermines Hoeppner's version of events. The district court concluded that the plaintiffs pleaded enough facts to plausibly allege that Hoeppner did not reasonably fear for his safety when he shot Waller. It likewise concluded they pleaded enough facts to allege that defendant police officers Benjamin Hanlon and B. S. Hardin conspired with Hoeppner to veil the true circumstances of Waller's death. It accordingly denied the defendants' motions for a judgment on the pleadings.

The defendants appeal that ruling. Exercising appellate jurisdiction under the collateral-order doctrine, we AFFIRM in part and REVERSE in part. We agree with the district court that the plaintiffs plausibly allege Waller was unarmed—and thus posed no reasonably perceivable threat—when Hoeppner killed him. But we conclude the plaintiffs' claims alleging the defendants denied them access to the courts are currently unripe. We also conclude the plaintiffs do not have standing to seek declaratory (as opposed to retrospective) relief for the past injury to Waller.

I.

A.

We draw the following facts from the plaintiffs' pleadings and the attachments thereto.

Defendants Richard Hoeppner and Benjamin Hanlon, both Fort Worth police officers on patrol during the early morning of May 28, 2013, were dispatched to 409 Havenwood Lane North to investigate a residential burglary alarm. Hoeppner and Hanlon arrived in separate vehicles and parked down the street from 409 Havenwood Lane North, so they could approach surreptitiously. The officers proceeded on foot to 404 Havenwood Lane North, erroneously believing it was 409 Havenwood Lane North, which was across the street. The officers looked around the outside of the house and noticed the garage door was open. Hanlon then went to knock on the front door while Hoeppner stayed by the open garage. Meanwhile, the officers' flashlights roused Jerry and Kathleen Waller, the residents of 404 Havenwood Lane North. Jerry Waller attributed the lights to his car alarm, so he went out to the garage to investigate.

What happened next is the subject of dispute. Hoeppner and Hanlon, the only surviving witnesses to the encounter, recounted the following version of events in a series of statements to investigators.[1] Holding a small gun, Waller entered the garage through a door that led in from the house. Hoeppner shined his 600-lumen flashlight in Waller's eyes specifically to conceal himself, drew his service weapon, and repeatedly ordered Waller to drop the gun. Hoeppner did not identify himself as a police officer, but Hanlon, upon hearing Hoeppner shouting in the garage, rushed to the garage while yelling "Fort Worth PD."

Waller ignored Hoeppner's repeated commands to drop his gun. Instead, Waller became combative and demanded that Hoeppner get the light out of his eyes. Waller eventually did put the gun down on the back of a car parked in the garage. Hoeppner moved toward the gun, but Waller p.596 suddenly lunged for the gun, retrieved it, and pointed it at Hoeppner. Fearing for his life, Hoeppner shot Waller five or six times, and Waller fell forward on top of the gun. Hanlon did not fire his weapon.

The plaintiffs accuse Hoeppner and Hanlon of fabricating this story to cover up an unjustified use of force. They allege that physical evidence shows that Waller could not have been holding a gun when he was shot. Rather, they say the autopsy report and blood-splatter patterns suggest that Waller was holding both his hands over his face when he was shot.

The autopsy report, which the plaintiffs attach to their pleadings, shows that one of Hoeppner's bullets went through Waller's left thumb and struck several of his fingers on his left hand. The plaintiffs maintain that the bullet's path through Waller's fingers and the blood on the palm of his left hand suggest that he could not have been gripping a gun with his left hand when it was struck. Further, they say that Waller's gun was not damaged in the shooting and crime-scene photographs do not reveal any blood on the gun's handle, making it unlikely it was in Waller's left hand when he was struck.

Likewise, Waller had blood splatter on the palm of his right hand, which the plaintiffs cite as evidence that when he was shot, he was not holding anything in his right hand either. Waller also had blood splatter around his left ear, which, the plaintiffs posit, means he must have been holding his left hand above his face when the bullet hit it, likely because he was trying to shield the light from his eyes. And if the blood splatter on his right hand also came from the wound on his left hand, then his right hand must have also been at eye level when he was shot.

The events that allegedly followed further animate the plaintiffs' suspicions. They allege that defendant B. S. Hardin, another Fort Worth officer, arrived at the scene a few minutes after the shooting and conspired with Hoeppner and Hanlon to cover up Hoeppner's culpability. Hardin told investigators that he went to administer aid to Waller when he arrived on scene because he had prior experience as an EMT. Hardin said that Hoeppner told him there was a gun underneath Waller, so he lifted Waller's body and laid the gun off to the side before administering aid in case Waller could still fire the weapon. It was not until after removing the gun, Hardin said, that he discovered Waller did not have a pulse.

The plaintiffs allege that Hardin lied about finding a gun under Waller's body. The plaintiffs assert that Hardin had no legitimate reason to move the gun from underneath Waller to about a foot from Waller's head, where it is later depicted in crime-scene photographs. They also point to inconsistent statements about the positioning of Waller's arms as evidence that Hardin fabricated his story. Hardin told investigators that Waller's arms were tucked underneath his chest when Hardin found him. But Kathleen Waller, who, according to Hardin, entered the garage around the same time as he arrived (and thus before he removed the gun), recalled that Jerry Waller's hands were at his sides in a "pushup"-like position. Subsequent crime-scene photographs show Waller with his left arm stretched perpendicular to his body and his right arm laying parallel at his side.

The plaintiffs additionally allege several procedural irregularities in the early stages of the investigation, which they contend to be further evidence of a conspiracy. They allege that the defendants took more than five hours to call the medical examiner in violation of a state law that requires police officers to report an unnatural death to the medical examiner "immediately" p.597 upon its discovery.[2] Tex. Code Crim. Proc. Ann. art. 49.25 § 7(a). They likewise argue that one of the officers violated state law by moving Waller's body without permission from the medical examiner. *See id.* § 8. And they allege someone stepped in Waller's blood and tracked it throughout the garage, further contaminating the crime scene.

B.

Waller's survivors[3] brought 42 U.S.C. § 1983 claims against Hoeppner, Hanlon, Hardin, the City of Fort Worth, and several officers involved in the investigation into Waller's death. As relevant to this appeal, they alleged that Hoeppner used excessive force against Waller in violation of his Fourth and Fourteenth Amendment rights to be free from unreasonable seizures. They also claimed that Hoeppner, Hanlon, and Hardin conspired to cover up Hoeppner's use of excessive force in violation of their constitutional right to access the courts. And they sought declaratory relief for violations of analogous rights under the Texas Constitution.

Hoeppner, Hanlon, and Hardin each answered with a qualified-immunity defense to the § 1983 claims. On the district court's order, the plaintiffs then filed a reply addressing qualified immunity. Hoeppner, Hanlon, and Hardin subsequently moved for judgment on the pleadings, arguing that the plaintiffs' pleadings were insufficient to overcome their qualified-immunity defenses. The district court determined that the defendants were not entitled to qualified immunity based on the plaintiffs' well-pleaded allegations and thus denied the defendants' motions in relevant part.[4] Specifically, it concluded that the plaintiffs' allegations, taken as true, established that Waller was not holding a weapon when Hoeppner shot him. Thus, it ruled that the plaintiffs plausibly alleged Hoeppner did not reasonably perceive a threat when he shot Waller in violation of clearly established law. The district court also concluded that the plaintiffs plausibly alleged the defendants conspired to tamper with the crime scene and give false statements in a manner that could prove fatally detrimental to the plaintiffs' claims against Hoeppner. These acts, the district court explained, violated the plaintiffs' clearly established rights to access the courts. Lastly, the district court ruled that state law authorized the plaintiffs to pursue declaratory relief for violations of the Texas Constitution. The defendants appeal these rulings.

II.

Before turning to the merits of the defendants' appeal, we must assure ourselves of our appellate jurisdiction. Congress has granted us jurisdiction over "final decisions of the district courts" within this circuit. 28 U.S.C. § 1291. Under the collateral-order doctrine, the Supreme Court has interpreted "final decisions" to include certain decisions that "finally determine claims of right separable from, and collateral to, rights asserted in the action, too important to be denied review p.598 and too independent of the cause itself to require that appellate consideration be deferred until the whole case is adjudicated." *Cohen v. Beneficial Indus. Loan Corp.,* 337 U.S. 541, 546, 69 S.Ct. 1221, 93 L.Ed. 1528 (1949). An order denying an officer's qualified-immunity defense is generally a collateral order subject to immediate appeal. *See Hinojosa v. Livingston,* 807 F.3d 657, 663 (5th Cir. 2015).

Despite the general rule, the plaintiffs argue that we do not have jurisdiction to review the district court's order denying the defendants' motions for a judgment on the pleadings because, in denying those motions, the district court determined that "genuine issues of material fact" precluded dismissal. This argument confuses the procedural posture of this case. In hearing an appeal from an order denying summary judgment on qualified-immunity grounds, we have jurisdiction to "review the materiality of any factual disputes, but not their genuineness." *Hogan v. Cunningham,* 722 F.3d 725, 731 (5th Cir. 2013) (quoting *Juarez v. Aguilar,* 666 F.3d 325, 331 (5th Cir. 2011)). But this appeal comes to us on the defendants' motions for judgment on the pleadings, not summary judgment. In reviewing the defendants' motions for judgment on the pleadings, the district court did not (and could not) consider whether the evidence created a genuine factual dispute. *See Bosarge v. Miss. Bureau of Narcotics,* 796 F.3d 435, 439 (5th Cir. 2015). We possess —and routinely exercise— jurisdiction to review a district court's determination at the pleadings stage that a plaintiff has alleged sufficient facts to overcome a qualified-immunity defense. *Id.* at 438-39; *see also, e.g., Shaw v. Villanueva,* 918 F.3d 414, 416 (5th Cir. 2019); *Doe v.*

Robertson, 751 F.3d 383, 386-87 (5th Cir. 2014). Accordingly, we have jurisdiction to review the district court's rulings on the defendants' qualified-immunity defenses to the plaintiffs' § 1983 claims.

Whether we have jurisdiction to review the portion of the district court's order addressing the plaintiffs' state-law declaratory-judgment claims is a separate question. As the plaintiffs point out, the defendants do not assert immunity from these claims—nor could they because qualified immunity applies only to claims for money damages. *See Morgan v. Swanson,* 659 F.3d 359, 365 n.3 (5th Cir. 2011) (en banc). We thus agree with the plaintiffs that, normally, the denial of a motion to dismiss a declaratory-judgment claim is not immediately appealable. But we may exercise pendent jurisdiction over interlocutory orders when, inter alia, "addressing the pendent claim will further the purpose of officer-immunities by helping the officer avoid trial" or "the claims involve precisely the same facts and elements." *Escobar v. Montee,* 895 F.3d 387, 392-93 (5th Cir. 2018) (footnotes omitted). Both situations are present here. It would undermine the purpose of qualified immunity if the defendants here were subject to trial on the declaratory-judgment claims despite immunity from the § 1983 claims. *Cf. Melton v. Phillips,* 875 F.3d 256, 265 n.9 (5th Cir. 2017) (en banc) ("[Q]ualified immunity is an immunity from suit that 'is effectively lost if a case is erroneously permitted to go to trial.'" (quoting *Pearson v. Callahan,* 555 U.S. 223, 231, 129 S.Ct. 808, 172 L.Ed.2d 565 (2009))). Further, the plaintiffs identify no differences between the facts or elements needed to prove their declaratory-judgment claims and those needed to prove their § 1983 claims. Accordingly, we have jurisdiction to review the district court's rulings on the plaintiffs' declaratory-judgment claims.

III.

We review the defendants' motions for judgment on the pleadings de p.599 novo. *Edionwe v. Bailey,* 860 F.3d 287, 291 (5th Cir. 2017). The standard for Rule 12(c) motions for judgment on the pleadings is identical to the standard for Rule 12(b)(6) motions to dismiss for failure to state a claim. *See Doe v. MySpace, Inc.,* 528 F.3d 413, 418 (5th Cir. 2008). To survive a motion for a judgment on the pleadings, "a complaint must contain sufficient factual matter, accepted as true, to 'state a claim to relief that is plausible on its face.'" *Ashcroft v. Iqbal,* 556 U.S. 662, 678, 129 S.Ct. 1937, 173 L.Ed.2d 868 (2009) (quoting *Bell Atl. Corp. v. Twombly,* 550 U.S. 544, 570, 127 S.Ct. 1955, 167 L.Ed.2d 929 (2007)). This involves a two-step inquiry. *See Robertson,* 751 F.3d at 388, 390. First, we must identify the complaint's well-pleaded factual content. *See id.* at 388. In doing so, we set aside "any unsupported legal conclusions," the truth of which "we cannot assume." *Id.; see also Iqbal,* 556 U.S. at 678-79, 129 S.Ct. 1937. Second, we ask whether the remaining allegations "are sufficient to nudge the [plaintiff's] claim across the 'plausibility' threshold." *Robertson,* 751 F.3d at 390 (quoting *Iqbal,* 556 U.S. at 678, 129 S.Ct. 1937). In other words, we ask whether we can reasonably infer from the complaint's well-pleaded factual content "more than the mere possibility of misconduct." *Iqbal,* 556 U.S. at 679, 129 S.Ct. 1937. This is "a context-specific task that requires the reviewing court to draw on its judicial experience and common sense." *Id.*

Section 1983 provides a cause of action to an individual harmed by a state official's violation of federal law. A state official sued under § 1983 is entitled to qualified immunity from damages, which protects the official from liability for any act that was not objectively unreasonable at the time of the act. *See Lincoln v. Turner,* 874 F.3d 833, 847 (5th Cir. 2017). "The basic steps of our qualified-immunity inquiry are well-known: a plaintiff seeking to defeat qualified immunity must show: '(1) that the official violated a statutory or constitutional right, and (2) that the right was "clearly established" at the time of the challenged conduct.'" *Id.* at 847-48 (quoting *Morgan,* 659 F.3d at 371). When confronted with a qualified-immunity defense at the pleadings stage, the plaintiff must plead "facts which, if proved, would defeat [the] claim of immunity." *Westfall v. Luna,* 903 F.3d 534, 542 (5th Cir. 2018) (quoting *Brown v. Glossip,* 878 F.2d 871, 874 (5th Cir. 1989)).

A.

We first consider whether the plaintiffs allege sufficient facts to overcome Hoeppner's qualified-immunity defense to their excessive-force claim. The parties appear to agree that that Hoeppner did not violate Waller's rights if Waller was holding the gun at the time he was shot but did violate Waller's clearly established rights if Waller was not holding the gun. Neither party makes an argument under the second prong of the qualified-immunity test. Thus, only the first prong is at issue here, and the sole question is whether the plaintiffs' pleadings plausibly allege that Waller was unarmed when Hoeppner shot him.

We conclude the plaintiffs' claim is plausible based on the specific and detailed factual allegations they advance in support of their theory of events. Most notably, the plaintiffs' allegations about Waller's left-hand wounds and blood-spatter patterns support the reasonable inference that Waller was unarmed when he was shot. The path of the bullet through Waller's fingers appears to suggest his hand was not clenched, as it would have been if he had been holding a gun. Further, if Waller was holding a gun when the bullet struck his left hand, it seems unlikely the bullet p.600 would have hit three of his fingers without at all damaging the gun. Moreover, it is not clear how unsmeared blood splatter could have ended up on Waller's right palm if Waller was holding a gun in his right hand.

Hoeppner raises two specific challenges to the sufficiency of these allegations. First, he insists that the plaintiffs pleaded themselves out of court by attaching the autopsy report to their pleadings. On the face of their pleadings, the plaintiffs allege that the autopsy report shows Waller could not have been holding a gun when he was shot. But Hoeppner observes that the autopsy report does not opine on whether Waller could have been holding a gun when he was shot. Therefore, Hoeppner says, the autopsy report conflicts with the plaintiffs' pleadings and takes precedence over the pleadings. *Cf. Smit v. SXSW Holdings, Inc.,* 903 F.3d 522, 528 (5th Cir. 2018) ("[W]hen an 'allegation is contradicted by the contents of an exhibit attached to the pleading, then indeed the exhibit and not the allegation controls.'" (quoting *United States ex rel. Riley v. St. Luke's Episcopal Hosp.,* 355 F.3d 370, 377 (5th Cir. 2004))).

We disagree. Hoeppner misunderstands the plaintiffs' reliance on the autopsy report. The plaintiffs do not allege that the autopsy report itself concluded that Waller could not have been holding a gun at the time he was shot. Rather, they allege that such an inference can be drawn from the information contained within the autopsy report—specifically, the descriptions of Waller's left-hand wounds. The contents of the autopsy report are consistent with the plaintiffs' allegations, so at this stage of the litigation, we accept those allegations as true.

Second, Hoeppner argues that these allegations raise only the possibility that he was not justified in shooting Waller. He asserts the plaintiffs' allegations about Waller's left-hand wounds and right-hand unsmeared blood spatter only show Waller was unarmed when he was hit by one of Hoeppner's five bullets. If Waller was armed when Hoeppner began to fire but dropped the gun sometime between being struck by Hoeppner's first and final shots, then Hoeppner argues his use of force would have been reasonable. In making this argument, Hoeppner ignores his own statement to investigators—attached to and quoted verbatim in the plaintiffs' pleadings—that he fired multiple shots specifically because Waller did not drop the gun and thus remained a threat. He explained:

> I know there was one delayed shot [be-]cause I put rounds on him at first I kind of noticed he kind of ... I mean, like he was taking them like that and then he kind ... kind of hunched over. And I'm not sure if he was falling over or if he was bending over [be]cause it hurt so ... and I saw *he still had the gun in his hand* and so I ... so I ... I put ... I put one more round on him and that's when he fell forward.

(ellipses in original) (emphasis added).

Furthermore, even if Waller might have dropped the gun at some point during the shooting, this possibility, when weighed against the plaintiffs' detailed and specific factual pleadings, does not render implausible their allegation that Waller was unarmed when shot. Hoeppner demands too much at the pleadings stage; allegations need "not conclusively establish" the plaintiffs' theory of the case. *Robertson,* 751 F.3d at 389. For now, it suffices that the plaintiffs' allegations "are not 'naked assertions devoid of further factual enhancement.'" *Id.* (quoting *Iqbal,* 556 U.S. at 678, 129 S.Ct. 1937).

p.601 Hoeppner tries to compare the present facts to those in several police-shooting cases in which we held for the officers because the plaintiffs' evidence only permitted us to speculate about whether the officers' descriptions of events leading up to the shootings were untruthful. None of these cases is an apt comparison. In each case, the plaintiffs sought to rely on certain circumstantial evidence to create a genuine factual dispute on summary judgment, but the court in each instance found that the plaintiffs' evidence was consistent with the officers' versions of events. *See Small ex rel. R.G. v. City of Alexandria,* 622 F.App'x 378, 382-83 (5th Cir. 2015) (unpublished) (per curiam) (affirming summary judgment for officer because "no record evidence call[ed] into question [the officer's] testimony about [the decedent's] behavior immediately prior to the shooting"); *Thomas v. Baldwin,* 595 F.App'x 378, 382 (5th Cir. 2014) (unpublished) (explaining that autopsy report suggesting decedent was shot in his side did not support plaintiffs' "bare assertion that [the decedent] was fleeing at the time he was shot"); *Manis v. Lawson,* 585 F.3d 839, 844 (5th Cir. 2009) (reversing denial of qualified immunity on summary judgment because plaintiffs did "not dispute the *only* fact material to whether [the officer] was justified in using deadly force: that [the decedent] reached under the seat of his vehicle and then moved as if he had obtained the object he sought"); *Ontiveros v. City of Rosenberg,* 564 F.3d 379, 383

(5th Cir. 2009) (explaining that plaintiffs were "attempting to use ... undisputed facts to imply a speculative scenario that ha[d] no factual support"). Here, by contrast, the hand wounds and blood splatter provide at least some support for the plaintiffs' allegation that Waller was not holding a gun, which, if true, contradicts Hoeppner's and Hanlon's explanations for the shooting.

In sum, the plaintiffs' specific and detailed factual pleadings about the crime-scene evidence make plausible their allegation that Waller followed Hoeppner's commands, put down his weapon, and was unarmed when Hoeppner shot him. If this allegation is true, then qualified immunity would not shield Hoeppner from the plaintiffs' excessive-force claim. *See, e.g., Bazan ex rel. Bazan v. Hidalgo County,* 246 F.3d 481, 493 (5th Cir. 2001). Accordingly, we affirm the district court's order denying Hoeppner's motion for judgment on the pleadings on the plaintiffs' excessive-force claim.

B.

We next consider whether the plaintiffs sufficiently allege that Hoeppner, Hanlon, and Hardin conspired to cover up the true circumstances of Waller's death in violation of the plaintiffs' clearly established right to access the courts. We have recognized a right of access to the courts, which is founded in the Article IV Privileges and Immunities Clause, the First Amendment Petition Clause, and the Fifth and Fourteenth Amendment Due Process Clauses. *See Ryland v. Shapiro,* 708 F.2d 967, 971-73 (5th Cir. 1983). Denial-of-access claims take one of two forms: forward-looking claims alleging "that systemic official action frustrates a plaintiff or plaintiff class in preparing and filing suits at the present time," and backward-looking claims alleging that an official action has "caused the loss or inadequate settlement of a meritorious case, the loss of an opportunity to sue, or the loss of an opportunity to seek some particular order of relief." *Christopher v. Harbury,* 536 U.S. 403, 413-14, 122 S.Ct. 2179, 153 L.Ed.2d 413 (2002) (citations omitted). The plaintiffs alleged both forward- and backward-looking denial-of-access claims against each of the defendants, but only the backward-looking p.602 claims are at issue on this appeal.

"To maintain a backward-looking claim, a plaintiff must identify (1) a nonfrivolous underlying claim; (2) an official act that frustrated the litigation of that claim; and (3) a remedy that is not otherwise available in another suit that may yet be brought." *United States v. McRae,* 702 F.3d 806, 830-31 (5th Cir. 2012). From our conclusion above that the plaintiffs state a claim against Hoeppner for excessive force, it follows that the plaintiffs have satisfied the first of these elements. For present purposes, although disputed, we will assume the plaintiffs' allegations satisfy the second element as well by alleging that the defendants conspired to sabotage the crime scene and lie to investigators to cover up the fact that Waller was unarmed when Hoeppner shot him. Nevertheless, the plaintiffs' claims fail on the third element: they have not explained what relief the defendants' alleged misdeeds have cost them. The plaintiffs premise their backward-looking denial-of-access claims on the theory that the defendants' alleged coverup frustrated their excessive-force claim against Hoeppner. Yet the plaintiffs are actively—and, so far, successfully—litigating that claim. They filed hundreds of pages of pleadings in the district court supported by dozens of exhibits containing detailed forensic evidence in support of their claim. They survived Hoeppner's pleadings-stage assertion of qualified immunity first in the district court and now on appeal. In short, there is no reason to believe the remedy the plaintiffs seek "is not otherwise available" in their active lawsuit against Hoeppner. *Id.* at 831.

In reaching the contrary conclusion, the district court explained that the plaintiffs' "ability to prove their [excessive-force claim] may have been permanently compromised." That might turn out to be the case, but it is too early to say. *See Christopher,* 536 U.S. at 414, 122 S.Ct. 2179 ("These cases do not look forward to a class of future litigation, but backward to a time when specific litigation ended poorly, or could not have commenced, or could have produced a remedy subsequently unobtainable." (footnotes omitted)). Unless and until the plaintiffs' claim against Hoeppner suffers some concrete setback traceable to the defendants' alleged coverup, their allegation that the defendants impaired their effort to bring that claim is no more than speculation about an event that may or may not come to pass. *See id.* at 415, 122 S.Ct. 2179 ("There is, after all, no point in spending time and money to establish the facts constituting denial of access when a plaintiff would end up just as well off after litigating a simpler case without the denial-of-access element.").

The plaintiffs argue that their delay in bringing this lawsuit can, on its own, constitute the prejudice necessary to state their denial-of-access claims. We disagree. True, we have suggested in dicta that "[c]onduct by state officers which results in delay in the prosecution of an action in state court may cause such prejudice." *Ryland,* 708 F.2d at 974. But as we later clarified:

> *Ryland* stands for the proposition that if state officials wrongfully and intentionally conceal information crucial to a person's ability to obtain redress through the courts, and do so for the purpose of frustrating that right, and that concealment and the delay engendered by it *substantially reduce the likelihood of one's obtaining the relief* to which one is otherwise entitled, they may have committed a constitutional violation.

Crowder v. Sinyard, 884 F.2d 804, 812 (5th Cir. 1989) (emphasis added), *abrogated on other grounds by Horton v. California,* 496 U.S. 128, 110 S.Ct. 2301, 110 L.Ed.2d 112 p.603 (1990). Thus, showing delay alone is not enough; the plaintiffs must likewise show the delay caused some further harm to their cause of action. And here the plaintiffs run into a familiar problem—any harm caused by the delay in filing their excessive-force claim has yet to manifest.

Therefore, the plaintiffs are left with pleadings that do not adequately allege a necessary element of their backward-looking denial-of-access claims. But the possibility remains that they will be able to state such claims in the future if their excessive-force claim goes south in later stages of this litigation. Faced with similar facts, the Ninth Circuit has repeatedly ordered backward-looking denial-of-access claims dismissed without prejudice as unripe. *See Delew v. Wagner,* 143 F.3d 1219, 1222-23 (9th Cir. 1998) ("To prevail on their claim, the Delews must demonstrate that the defendants' cover-up violated their right of access to the courts by rendering 'any available state court remedy ineffective.' However, because the Delews' wrongful death action remains pending in state court, it is impossible to determine whether this has in fact occurred." (citation omitted) (quoting *Swekel v. City of River Rouge,* 119 F.3d 1259, 1264 (6th Cir. 1997))); *Karim-Panahi v. L.A. Police Dep't,* 839 F.2d 621, 625 (9th Cir. 1988) ("Because the ultimate resolution of the present suit remains in doubt, Karim-Panahi's cover-up claim is not ripe for judicial consideration."); *cf. Lynch v.*

Barrett, 703 F.3d 1153, 1157 (10th Cir. 2013) (concluding denial-of-access claim ripened once plaintiff lost underlying lawsuit). We agree this is the proper resolution. *See Choice Inc. of Tex. v. Greenstein,* 691 F.3d 710, 715 (5th Cir. 2012) ("[A] case is not ripe if further factual development is required." (quoting *New Orleans Pub. Serv., Inc. v. Council,* 833 F.2d 583, 587 (5th Cir. 1987))). Accordingly, we reverse the district court's order declining to dismiss the plaintiffs' denial-of-access claims and remand with instruction to dismiss those claims without prejudice.[5]

IV.

Lastly, we conclude the plaintiffs do not have standing to seek declaratory relief for violations of Waller's rights under the Texas Constitution. "'In a case of actual controversy within its jurisdiction,' the Declaratory Judgment Act allows a federal court to 'declare the rights and other legal relations of any interested party seeking such declaration.'" *Hosein v. Gonzales,* 452 F.3d 401, 403 (5th Cir. 2006) (quoting 28 U.S.C. § 2201). But the Declaratory Judgment Act does not vest the federal courts with jurisdiction broader than Article III's "case or controversy" limitation. *Id.* "In order to demonstrate that a case or controversy exists to meet the Article III standing requirement when a plaintiff is seeking injunctive or declaratory relief, a plaintiff must allege facts from which it appears there is a substantial likelihood that he will suffer injury in the future." *Bauer v. Texas,* 341 F.3d 352, 358 (5th Cir. 2003). "To obtain [declaratory] relief for past wrongs, a plaintiff must demonstrate either continuing harm or a real and immediate threat of repeated injury in the future." *Id.*

The plaintiffs here allege only past injury to Waller. Faced with similar circumstances, the Supreme Court ruled that a plaintiff had no standing to seek declaratory relief finding his son was fatally p.604 shot by police in violation of the Fourth Amendment. *See Ashcroft v. Mattis,* 431 U.S. 171, 172, 97 S.Ct. 1739, 52 L.Ed.2d 219 (1977) (per curiam). Accordingly, we reverse the portion of the district court's order declining to dismiss the plaintiffs' claims for declaratory relief and remand with instruction to dismiss those claims without prejudice.

V.

For the foregoing reasons, we AFFIRM the portion of the district court's order denying Hoeppner's qualified-immunity defense against the plaintiffs' excessive-force claim, but we otherwise REVERSE and REMAND with instructions to dismiss the plaintiffs' denial-of-access and declaratory-judgment claims without prejudice.

[1] The plaintiffs attach these statements to their pleadings but disavow their accuracy.

[2] In contrast, the plaintiffs allege that a police-union attorney was "on the scene within minutes" of Waller's death.

[3] The original plaintiffs consist of Waller's two children, one of whom is acting in a dual capacity as the executrix of Kathleen Waller's estate, who died while this case was pending below. Waller's two additional children joined as intervenors. We

refer to the plaintiffs and intervenors collectively as the "plaintiffs" throughout this opinion.

[4] The district court granted the motions as to several claims not at issue in this appeal and granted Officer A. Chambers's motion in its entirety.

[5] The parties do not address this issue in terms of ripeness. But because ripeness implicates the district court's subject-matter jurisdiction, we raise it sua sponte. *See Elam v. Kan. City S. Ry. Co.,* 635 F.3d 796, 802 (5th Cir. 2011); *Lopez v. City of Houston,* 617 F.3d 336, 341 (5th Cir. 2010).

928 F.3d 457 (2019)

Doctor Joseph A. ZADEH; Jane Doe, Patient, Plaintiffs - Appellants,
v.
Mari ROBINSON, in her individual capacity and in her official capacity; Sharon Pease, in her individual capacity; Kara Kirby, in her individual capacity, Defendants - Appellees.

No. 17-50518.

United States Court of Appeals, Fifth Circuit.

FILED July 2, 2019.

Zadeh v. Robinson, 928 F. 3d 457 (5th Cir. 2019)

Appeals from the United States District Court for the Western District of Texas.

Meagan Elizabeth Hassan, William Pieratt Demond, Demond & Hassan, P.L.L.C., Houston, TX, Delonia Anita Watson, Law Office of Delonia A. Watson, Fort Worth, TX, for Plaintiff-Appellant Doctor Joseph A. Zadeh.

Meagan Elizabeth Hassan, William Pieratt Demond, Demond & Hassan, P.L.L.C., Houston, TX, for Plaintiff-Appellant Jane Doe, Patient.

Bill L. Davis, Assistant Attorney General, Office of the Attorney General, Office of the Solicitor General, Adam Arthur Biggs, Assistant Attorney General, Office of the Attorney General for the State of Texas, Austin, TX, for Defendants-Appellees.

Andrew Layton Schlafly, Far Hills, NJ, for Amicus Curiae Association of American Physicians & Surgeons.

Before JOLLY, SOUTHWICK, and WILLETT, Circuit Judges.

p.461 ON PETITION FOR REHEARING EN BANC

LESLIE H. SOUTHWICK, Circuit Judge.

No member of the panel nor judge in regular active service requested that the p.462 court be polled on rehearing en banc. The petition for rehearing en banc is therefore DENIED. *See* FED. R. APP. P. and 5th Cir. R. 35. Treating the petition for rehearing en banc as a petition for panel rehearing, the petition is GRANTED. We withdraw our prior opinion, *Zadeh v. Robinson,* 902 F.3d 483 (5th Cir. 2018), and substitute the following.

The Texas Medical Board executed an administrative subpoena on Dr. Joseph Zadeh's medical office. Thereafter, Dr. Zadeh and one of his patients sued several Board members under 42 U.S.C. § 1983, claiming that the Board's actions violated the Fourth Amendment. The district court partially granted the defendants' motion to dismiss and later granted their motion for summary judgment rejecting all remaining claims. We AFFIRM.

FACTUAL AND PROCEDURAL BACKGROUND

Plaintiff Dr. Joseph Zadeh appeals the dismissal of his Section 1983 claim against several members of the Texas Medical Board who he claims violated his constitutional rights through a warrantless search of his office and medical records. Dr. Zadeh, an internal medicine doctor, owns and operates a medical practice in Euless, Texas. One of his patients, Jane Doe, is also a plaintiff-appellant in this case.

Dr. Zadeh was the subject of an administrative proceeding before the State Office of Administrative Hearings ("SOAH") for violations of the Board's regulations. The Drug Enforcement Agency ("DEA") also was investigating him. Indeed, it appears the Board first learned about allegations against Dr. Zadeh when the DEA filed a complaint with the Board about his prescribing practices in September 2013. The DEA investigator emailed a representative of the Board, stating, "I'm at a point in the criminal case that I need to interview Dr. Zadeh and review his patient files." The Board then initiated an investigation.

As part of this investigation, Defendants Sharon Pease and Kara Kirby, who were investigators with the Board, served an administrative subpoena on Dr. Zadeh on October 22, 2013. The subpoena had the electronic signature of Defendant Mari Robinson, who was the Executive Director of the Board. The subpoena was for the immediate production of the medical records of sixteen of Dr. Zadeh's patients. Two DEA agents who were investigating related criminal allegations accompanied Kirby and Pease.

The district court found the "facts surrounding the execution of the subpoena" to be "largely undisputed." Dr. Zadeh was not present when the investigators arrived. The subpoena was handed to the doctor's assistant. The investigators sat in the medical office waiting room to give the doctor time to appear. While they waited, the assistant spoke on the phone with Dr. Zadeh, his lawyer, and his brother who also is a lawyer. The assistant testified that after these calls had occurred but no permission to proceed had been given, the investigators told her they would suspend Dr. Zadeh's license if the records they sought were not produced. The investigators admit something was said that was akin to a promise of some vague "disciplinary action." What was said at that point is at least unclear. The assistant eventually complied, taking the defendants into a conference room and delivering the requested records to them. Although most of their time was spent inside the public waiting area or conference room, the investigators also approached the medical assistant to ask for help while she was in exam rooms and later in a storage room.

As a result of that search, Dr. Zadeh and his patient, Jane Doe, sued Robinson, p.463 Pease, and Kirby in their individual capacities and Robinson in her official capacity in the United States District Court for the Western District of Texas. They alleged the defendants' actions violated their Fourth Amendment, due process, and privacy rights. The plaintiffs sought monetary damages under 42 U.S.C. § 1983 as well as declaratory relief. The defendants moved to dismiss the claims on these grounds: (1) the plaintiffs lacked standing; (2) the *Younger* abstention doctrine barred the requests for declaratory relief; (3) the claim against Robinson in her official capacity was barred by the doctrine of sovereign immunity; (4) the doctrine of qualified immunity applied to the claims against the defendants in their individual capacities.

In ruling on the motion to dismiss, the district court held Dr. Zadeh had standing to pursue declaratory relief, but Jane Doe did not. Nonetheless, the district court concluded that "the *Younger* abstention doctrine require[d] [it] to abstain from adjudicating Plaintiff Zadeh's claims for declaratory relief." The district court also held that sovereign immunity barred the plaintiffs' claims for monetary damages against Robinson in her official capacity. Finally, the court concluded that the defendants were entitled to qualified immunity for the privacy and due process claims. The only part of the suit left, then, was Dr. Zadeh's claim that the defendants violated his clearly established Fourth Amendment rights during the search of his office.

The defendants moved for summary judgment on "whether Defendants exceeded their statutory subpoena authority by searching and inspecting Plaintiff's office and records." Although the plaintiffs alleged that the investigators performed a thorough search of Dr. Zadeh's office, the district court found that the record did not support this allegation. Instead, the district court determined that the "Defendants' presence at Plaintiff's office was solely to execute the subpoena instanter." The district court also held that Robinson was not liable as she neither affirmatively participated in the alleged search nor implemented unconstitutional policies that caused the alleged constitutional deprivation. Further, there was "no evidence Defendants Pease and Kirby inspected Plaintiff's office or searched his records." The plaintiffs timely appealed.

DISCUSSION

The plaintiffs appeal both the order granting the motion to dismiss in part and the order granting the motion for summary judgment. Although we review both *de novo,* a different legal standard applies to each:

> In the former, the central issue is whether, in the light most favorable to the plaintiff, the complaint states a valid claim for relief. In the latter, we go beyond the pleadings to determine whether there is no genuine issue as to any material fact and that the movant is entitled to judgment as a matter of law.

St. Paul Mercury Ins. Co. v. Williamson, 224 F.3d 425, 440 n.8 (5th Cir. 2000) (citations omitted).

We first address the plaintiffs' challenge to the district court's grant of qualified immunity, evaluating whether clearly established law prohibited the defendants' conduct. Next, we discuss whether the district court erred in abstaining from deciding the plaintiffs' claims for declaratory judgment. Finally, we analyze whether Robinson was liable in her supervisory capacity.

I. Grant of qualified immunity

"The doctrine of qualified immunity protects government officials from civil damages liability when their actions could reasonably have been believed to be p.464 legal." *Morgan v. Swanson,* 659 F.3d 359, 370-71 (5th Cir. 2011). Officials are entitled to qualified immunity "unless (1) they violated a federal statutory or constitutional right, and (2) the unlawfulness of their conduct was 'clearly established at the time.'" *District of Columbia v. Wesby,* ___ U.S. ___, 138 S. Ct. 577, 589, 199 L.Ed.2d 453 (2018) (quoting *Reichle v. Howards,* 566 U.S. 658, 664, 132 S.Ct. 2088, 182 L.Ed.2d 985 (2012)).

Using this framework, we analyze the plaintiffs' arguments that clearly established law prohibited the defendants' execution of the subpoena instanter. The plaintiffs offer two theories for why the defendants' conduct was unconstitutional. First, they argue it was a warrantless search that did not satisfy the administrative exception. Second, they argue it was a pretextual search and thus unconstitutional.

a. Warrantless search

The plaintiffs argue the Board violated the Fourth Amendment when it demanded immediate compliance with its administrative subpoena. We have previously considered a challenge to a subpoena instanter executed by the Texas Medical Board. *See Cotropia v. Chapman,* 721 F. App'x 354 (5th Cir. 2018). In that nonprecedential opinion, we held: "Absent consent, exigent circumstances, or the like, in order for an administrative search to be constitutional, the subject of the search must be afforded an opportunity to obtain precompliance review before a neutral decisionmaker." *Id.* at 358 (quoting *City of Los Angeles v. Patel,* ___ U.S. ___, 135 S. Ct. 2443, 2452, 192 L.Ed.2d 435 (2015)).

In that case, the physician at the center of a Board investigation pled sufficient facts to overcome qualified immunity. *Id.* at 361. The doctor alleged that a Board member "violated the clearly established right to an opportunity to obtain precompliance review of an administrative subpoena before a neutral decisionmaker" when he took documents from the physician's office over objections from the office receptionist. *Id.* at 357. Relying on Supreme Court precedent, we held that it was clear at the time that "prior to compliance, Cotropia was entitled to an opportunity to obtain review of the administrative subpoena before a neutral decisionmaker." *Id.* at 358 (citing *See v. City of Seattle,* 387 U.S. 541, 545, 87 S.Ct. 1737, 18 L.Ed.2d 943 (1967); *Donovan v. Lone Steer, Inc.,* 464 U.S. 408, 415, 104 S.Ct. 769, 78 L.Ed.2d 567 (1984)). Similarly, the demand to turn over Dr. Zadeh's medical records immediately did not provide an opportunity for precompliance review. We agree, then, that a requirement of precompliance review in many, if not most, administrative searches had been clearly established by Supreme Court precedent prior to the search here.

The defendants acknowledge this law but maintain there was no constitutional violation because this search fell into an exception to the general rule requiring precompliance review. We next examine that argument.

i. Closely regulated industry

No opportunity for precompliance review is needed for administrative searches of industries that "have such a history of government oversight that no reasonable expectation of privacy" exists for individuals engaging in that industry. *Marshall v. Barlow's, Inc.,* 436 U.S. 307, 313, 98 S.Ct. 1816, 56 L.Ed.2d 305 (1978). Even so, warrantless inspections in closely regulated industries must still satisfy three criteria: (1) a substantial government interest, (2) a regulatory scheme that requires warrantless searches to further the government interest, and (3) "a constitutionally p.465 adequate substitute for a warrant." *New York v. Burger,* 482 U.S. 691, 702-03,

107 S.Ct. 2636, 96 L.Ed.2d 601 (1987) (quoting *Donovan v. Dewey,* 452 U.S. 594, 603, 101 S.Ct. 2534, 69 L.Ed.2d 262 (1981)).

Cotropia did not resolve whether the Board's use of administrative subpoenas satisfied the *Burger* criteria because the issue was not raised until oral argument. *Cotropia,* 721 F. App'x at 360 & n.6. As a result, the panel's holding was expressly limited to concluding that the Board's demand for immediate compliance with the subpoena did not satisfy the general administrative exception to the warrant requirement. The argument has timely been raised here, though. Thus, we must discuss whether the *Burger* exception permitted the Board's administrative subpoena and whether that law was clearly established at the time of its execution.

To categorize industries under *Burger,* courts consider the history of warrantless searches in the industry, how extensive the regulatory scheme is, whether other states have similar schemes, and whether the industry would pose a threat to the public welfare if left unregulated. *See Burger,* 482 U.S. at 704, 107 S.Ct. 2636; *Patel,* 135 S. Ct. at 2454. The defendants characterize the relevant industry in two different ways. We evaluate first whether the practice of medicine is a closely regulated industry and then whether the practice of prescribing controlled substances is closely regulated.

Acknowledging that the medical profession is subject to close oversight, the district court emphasized the absence of a history of warrantless inspections to conclude that the medical profession was not a closely regulated industry. Important to its conclusion was the confidential nature of the doctor-patient relationship: "It strains credibility to suggest that doctors and their patients have no reasonable expectation of privacy." On appeal, the defendants all but concede that there is not a lengthy history of warrantless searches. They instead emphasize the extensive regulatory scheme governing the practice of medicine and the risk that the industry could pose to the public welfare.

There is no doubt that the medical profession is extensively regulated and has licensure requirements. Satisfying the *Burger* doctrine requires more. The Supreme Court instructs "that the doctrine is essentially defined by 'the pervasiveness and regularity of the federal regulation' and the effect of such regulation upon an owner's expectation of privacy." *Burger,* 482 U.S. at 701, 107 S.Ct. 2636 (quoting *Dewey,* 452 U.S. at 605-06, 101 S.Ct. 2534). Another key factor is "the duration of a particular regulatory scheme." *Id.* (quoting *Dewey,* 452 U.S. at 606, 101 S.Ct. 2534).

The Board cites several laws or regulations governing the behavior of doctors. Outside of citing Texas's licensure requirement for physicians, the regulations the Board cites do not apply to the entire medical profession. Instead, they target the practice of prescribing controlled substances. As examples, the Board states that doctors must register with the DEA to prescribe controlled substances, TEX. HEALTH & SAFETY CODE § 481.061; that prescriptions of controlled substances are monitored by several law enforcement agencies, *id.* §§ 481.067, 481.075, 481.076; and that pain management clinics must register as such, which allows the Board to inspect them from time to time, TEX. OCC. CODE §§ 168.101, 168.052; 37 Tex. Reg. 10079, 10079-80 (2012), *adopted* 38 Tex. Reg. 1876, 1876-77 (2013), *amended* 39 Tex. Reg. 297, 297-98 (2014) (former 22 TEX. ADMIN. CODE § 195.2); 35 Tex. Reg. 1924, 1925-26 (2010), *adopted* 35 Tex. Reg. 3281, 3281-82 (2010), *amended* 43 Tex. p.466 Reg. 768, 768-74 (2018) (former 22 TEX. ADMIN. CODE § 195.3). The Board also refers us to laws and regulations that similarly regulate anesthesia. These, though, do not amount to pervasiveness and regularity of regulation over the medical industry as a whole as *Burger* requires. Instead, only specific groups of doctors may have been put on notice that the Board may perform some inspections.

We also do not see in the medical profession an entrenched history of warrantless searches. Its absence is relevant, though not dispositive, to our issue. *Burger,* 482 U.S. at 701, 107 S.Ct. 2636. For example, when the Court held that the liquor industry was closely regulated, it mentioned that English commissioners could inspect brewing houses on demand in the 1660s, and that Massachusetts passed a similar law in 1692. *Colonnade Catering Corp. v. United States,* 397 U.S. 72, 75, 90 S.Ct. 774, 25 L.Ed.2d 60 (1970). It then referred to a 1791 federal law that has continued in various forms, permitting federal officers to perform warrantless searches of distilleries and imposing an excise tax on distilled liquor. *Id.* Because the focus there was "the liquor industry long subject to close supervision and inspection," the Court concluded that the Fourth Amendment did not prohibit the warrantless searches authorized by Congress. *Id.* at 77, 90 S.Ct. 774. Here, there is no such history.

In considering the reasonable expectation of privacy, we also consider the sensitive nature of medical records. The Ninth Circuit explained that "the theory behind the closely regulated industry exception is that persons engaging in such industries, and persons present in those workplaces, have a diminished expectation of privacy." *Tucson Woman's Clinic v. Eden,* 379 F.3d 531, 550 (9th Cir. 2004). We agree with that court's observation that in medical contexts, the expectation of privacy likely is heightened. *Id.*

Admittedly, federal regulations do exempt the Board from the privacy requirements of the Health Insurance Portability and Accountability Act ("HIPAA"). 45 C.F.R. § 164.512. Further, the Board cites Texas laws providing that where the Board does obtain information, it is subject to confidentiality requirements. *See* TEX. OCC. CODE §§ 159.002; 159.003(a)(5); 164.007(c). That HIPAA permits disclosure to the Board and that the regulations governing the Board continue to protect that information from disclosure does not mean that the Board is entitled to access to that information through an administrative search without allowing an opportunity for precompliance review.

We conclude, then, that the medical industry as a whole is not a closely regulated industry for purposes of *Burger.* Still, even if the medical profession at large cannot be said to fall within these *Burger* factors, it is possible that a subset, such as those who prescribe controlled substances, would do so. Because the parties focus their analysis of whether there is a closely regulated industry on the medical profession as a whole and not on pain management clinics, we assume only for purposes of our analysis today that pain management clinics are part of a closely regulated industry and that Dr. Zadeh was operating such a clinic even if his clinic was not certified as one. Such assumptions are appropriate in this case because ultimately our resolution turns on whether the relevant law was clearly established. At this point, we can at least say that the law was not clearly established whether pain management clinics are part of a closely regulated industry. The remaining relevant law, established with clarity or not, is analyzed below.

p.467 ii. *Burger* exception requirements

Even were we to accept the defendants' argument that doctors prescribing controlled substances are engaging in a closely regulated industry with less reasonable expectations of privacy, administrative searches of such industries still must satisfy the three *Burger* criteria. There is no meaningful dispute in this case as to the first two factors, namely, that the State has a substantial interest in regulating the prescription of controlled substances and that the inspection of a doctor's records would aid the Government in regulating the industry. We thus analyze only whether the statutory scheme is a proper substitute for a search warrant. The Board relies on its authority to issues subpoenas and to inspect pain management clinics. The principal response from plaintiffs is that neither provides a constitutionally adequate substitute for a warrant.

In order for a warrant substitute authorized by statute to be constitutionally adequate, "the regulatory statute must perform the two basic functions of a warrant: it must advise the owner of the commercial premises that the search is being made pursuant to the law and has a properly defined scope, and it must limit the discretion of the inspecting officers." *Burger,* 482 U.S. at 703, 107 S.Ct. 2636. The relevant statute provides: "The board may issue a subpoena or a subpoena duces tecum to compel the attendance of a witness and the production of books, records, and documents." TEX. OCC. CODE. § 153.007(a). The Board argues that the statute, when considered with the following regulation, limits the discretion of the officials. The regulation provides that after a "request by the board or board representatives, a licensee shall furnish to the board copies of medical records or the original records within a reasonable time period, as prescribed at the time of the request." 22 TEX. ADMIN. CODE § 179.4(a). The regulation defines "reasonable time" as "fourteen calendar days or a shorter time if required by the urgency of the situation or the possibility that the records may be lost, damaged, or destroyed." *Id.*

The district court held that a search using the Board's subpoena authority did not satisfy the third factor of the *Burger* test as it was "purely discretionary," allowing the Board "to choose which doctors to subpoena and to do so at a frequency it determines." To evaluate that holding, we consider the limits that do exist: only licensees are subject to the subpoena; only medical records must be produced; and it is the Board or its representatives who will be asking for the records. As the district court stated, though, there is no identifiable limit on whose records can properly be subpoenaed.

As to inspections of pain management clinics, the Board argues that some limits to its authority are set by the statute permitting it to inspect pain management clinics. Specifically, the statute allows it to examine "the documents of a physician practicing at the clinic, as necessary to ensure compliance with this chapter." TEX. OCC. CODE. § 168.052(a). Providing more specific guidance, the regulation in effect at the time provided:

> The board may conduct inspections to enforce these rules, including inspections of a pain management clinic and of documents of a physician's practice. The board may contract with another state agency or qualified person to conduct these inspections.

35 Tex. Reg. 1925, 1925-26 (2010), *adopted* 35 Tex. Reg. 3281, 3281-82 (2010), *amended* 43 Tex. Reg. 768, 768-74 (2018) (former 22 TEX. ADMIN. CODE § 195.3).

The district court found this inspection authority, like the subpoena authority, to p.468 be "purely discretionary." The governing criteria for an inspection is that the target be a pain management clinic, that the Board performs the inspection, and that the purpose for the search be to determine compliance with pain management rules. We agree with the district court, though, that these requirements suffered from the same fatal *Burger* flaw as the subpoena authority: they did not limit how the clinics inspected are chosen.

In summary, there are insufficient limits on the discretion of the Board to satisfy the *Burger* requirements, whether considering the medical profession in general or as to pain management clinics. What is left is the question of whether the law on these points was clearly established and, regardless, whether the search was invalid as pretextual.

iii. Clearly established law for qualified immunity

To summarize, we have concluded there was a violation of Dr. Zadeh's constitutional rights. That is true even with our twin assumptions that pain management clinics are part of a closely regulated industry and that Dr. Zadeh operated a pain management clinic. Nonetheless, the defendants are entitled to qualified immunity unless the constitutional requirements they violated were clearly established at the time of their actions. *Reichle,* 566 U.S. at 664, 132 S.Ct. 2088. We hold that it was clearly established at the time of this search that the medical profession as a whole is not a closely regulated industry, meaning that governmental agents violate the Constitution when they search clinics that are not pain management clinics without providing an opportunity for precompliance review. We also hold, even assuming that pain management clinics are part of a closely regulated industry, that on-demand searches of those clinics violate the constitution when the statutory scheme authorizing the search fails to provide sufficient constraints on the discretion of the inspecting officers. We need to analyze, though, whether that last statement of law was clearly established when this search occurred.

Our analysis of the clarity of relevant law is objective, meaning it does not focus on the specific defendants' knowledge. "The touchstone of this inquiry is whether a reasonable person would have believed that his conduct conformed to the constitutional standard in light of the information available to him and the clearly established law." *Goodson v. City of Corpus Christi,* 202 F.3d 730, 736 (5th Cir. 2000). "[E]ven law enforcement officials who 'reasonably but mistakenly [commit a constitutional violation]' are entitled to immunity." *Glenn v. City of Tyler,* 242 F.3d 307, 312-13 (5th Cir. 2001) (quoting *Goodson,* 202 F.3d at 736). For the law to be clearly established, there must be a close congruence of the facts in the precedent and those in the case before us. *Wesby,* 138 S. Ct. at 589-90. "The precedent must be clear enough that every reasonable official would interpret it to establish the particular rule the plaintiffs seek to apply." *Id.* at 590.

Defendants rely on one of our precedents that reviewed an administrative search of a dentist's office by agents of the Texas State Board of Dental Examiners, accompanied by Department of Public Safety officials. *Beck v. Tex. State Bd. of Dental*

Exam'rs, 204 F.3d 629, 632 (5th Cir. 2000). Dentist Beck was a target because of complaints filed against him for prescribing controlled substances. *Id.* We concluded that the search did not violate the plaintiff's clearly established rights. *Id.* at 638-39. We applied the *Burger* exception and determined there was a significant state interest in regulating dentists' p.469 use of controlled substances; the search was conducted pursuant to two regulatory schemes; and there was an adequate substitute for a warrant where the statute permitted the official to conduct inspections during "reasonable times" after "stating his purpose" and presenting his credentials to the owner. *Id.* at 638-39. In light of *Beck,* the Board argues that reasonable investigators could have believed the *Burger* exception permitted the execution of the subpoena as they too were investigating prescriptions of controlled substances within the medical industry.

The plaintiffs insist that *Beck* is "patently distinguishable" for the same reason argued in the separate opinion here. The clarity of any possible distinction, though, must be viewed through the lens that the law, including a distinction, must be "sufficiently clear that every reasonable official would understand that what he is doing is unlawful" at that time. *Wesby,* 138 S. Ct. at 589 (quotation marks omitted). That means "existing law must have placed the constitutionality of the officer's conduct 'beyond debate." *Id.* Perhaps most relevant, the "legal principle [must] clearly prohibit the officer's conduct *in the particular circumstances before him.* The rule's contours must be so well defined that it is 'clear to a reasonable officer that his conduct was unlawful in the situation he confronted.'" *Id.* at 590 (emphasis added).

The claimed sufficient distinction here is that the regulations and statutes under which the investigators in *Beck* acted explicitly permitted inspections without prior notice. *See Beck,* 204 F.3d at 639. The *Beck* court discussed that point at the end of the opinion, as it addressed several questions regarding whether what occurred was a valid administrative search of a closely regulated industry. *Id.* The final subject the court discussed was that one of the statutes under which the inspection was conducted did not require that prior notice be given. *Id.* (quoting Section 5.01(c) of the Texas Controlled Substances Act.) That is no small distinction, and we conclude today that absent similar statutory or perhaps regulatory authority that dispenses with prior notice, a search such as occurred here cannot be conducted without prior notice. The issue for us, though, is whether that law was clearly established at the time of the search we are reviewing today.

As we already stated, the right is not clearly established unless it is beyond debate using an objective test. We have discussed the intricacies of *New York v. Burger,* which permit warrantless searches when they satisfy a three-factor test. Our *Beck* decision held that the search there was of a closely regulated industry, and therefore went through the three *Burger* factors. The discussion of the specific statutory authorization for no-notice inspections was to show that the third *Burger* factor was satisfied, which is that an adequate substitute for a warrant existed. We did not say in *Beck* that the only sufficient substitute under *Burger* was a statute authorizing no-notice searches. We did hold that "under these circumstances, Beck does not show a violation of a clearly established constitutional right." *Beck,* 204 F.3d at 639.

Instead of clearly establishing the principle that prior notice of a regulatory search must be given unless the authorizing statute explicitly announces it is unnecessary, *Beck* applied the general *Burger* principle to the facts of that case that a warrant substitute authorized by a "regulatory statute must perform the two basic functions of a warrant: it must advise the owner of the commercial premises that the search is being made pursuant to the law and has a properly defined scope, and it must limit the discretion of the inspecting p.470 officers." *Burger,* 482 U.S. at 703, 107 S.Ct. 2636. In the *Beck* situation, that factor was satisfied with the statutory language already discussed. We cannot see, though, that every reasonable official prior to conducting a search under the circumstances of this case would know this *Burger* factor was not satisfied. We think some, even many, reasonable officers would believe under the third *Burger* factor that the owner of the premises was charged with knowledge that a statute authorized the search, and the officers would reasonably believe the scope of the search and the discretion of the officials was validly limited. We have held that the statute fails this standard, but we do not hold that all reasonable officers would have known that, until now.

Therefore, although *Beck* does not control the constitutionality of the Board's actions in this case, it does weigh in favor of the defendants' receiving qualified immunity. We find more guidance from cases where a statute did not clearly limit the official's discretion in selecting who would be subject to an administrative search. In one, we held that the statute provided a constitutionally adequate substitute for a warrant where the statute provided:

> The licensing agency shall make or cause to be made inspections relative to compliance with the laws and regulations governing the licensure of child care facilities. Such inspections shall be made at least once a year but additional inspections may be made as often as deemed necessary by the licensing agency.

See Ellis v. Miss. Dep't of Health, 344 F. App'x 43 (5th Cir. 2009) (citing MISS. CODE. ANN. § 43-20-15). Though that opinion is not precedential, we agree with its reasoning.

We also upheld an administrative search where, despite limits on the conduct of an officer after a traffic stop, there were not clear limits on an officer's discretion as to whom to stop. *See United States v. Fort,* 248 F.3d 475, 482 (5th Cir. 2001). Because we have not so far required there to be a clear limit on determining whom officials select for an administrative search, the defendants reasonably could have believed that the administrative scheme here provided a constitutionally adequate substitute for a warrant.

Finally, the plaintiffs argue that even if qualified immunity might apply to defendants who conducted a proper search, the defendants did not follow the statutory scheme. Therefore, they assert, caselaw in which the legal requirements for the search were followed is inapplicable. The claims of overstepping authority, though, are minor. First, while the medical assistant was waiting for Dr. Zadeh to appear, there is evidence one of the investigators approached the assistant at her desk, then followed her into two exam rooms. While in one of the rooms, the investigator asked if controlled substances were kept in the room. Second, there is evidence this same investigator also approached the assistant while the latter was in a storage room and asked if the investigators could use the medical office's copy machine. The district court said there was no evidence the investigator ever looked at any files or went somewhere in the medical office without the assistant. Finally, as soon as the investigators were asked to leave the office, they did so. We agree with the district court that there is "no support in the record" to sustain the allegation the investigators did a "thorough search and inspection." The factual basis for deviations from search protocols is insubstantial.

In conclusion, the unlawfulness of the defendants' conduct was not clearly established at the time of the search.

p.471 b. Pretextual searches

The plaintiffs also argue that the search was a pretext for uncovering evidence of criminal wrongdoing, not a valid administrative search. According to the plaintiffs, the DEA brought Dr. Zadeh's possible misdeeds before the Medical Board. A DEA agent then was present during the search. To finish the story, though, the Medical Board proceeded against Dr. Zadeh. Before there was a full hearing on the merits, the Board entered an agreed order. In the order, the panel found that Dr. Zadeh was operating a pain management clinic without registering it. There is nothing in this record indicating whether the DEA's investigation resulted in a criminal prosecution or any other action.

"Even under a valid inspection regime, the administrative search cannot be pretextual." *Club Retro, LLC v. Hilton,* 568 F.3d 181, 197 (5th Cir. 2009). It is incorrect, though, to use the label "pretext" simply because of an overlap between an administrative search and a criminal search. The *Burger* Court remarked that "a State can address a major social problem *both* by way of an administrative scheme *and* through penal sanctions." *Burger,* 482 U.S. at 712, 107 S.Ct. 2636. To determine whether the search there was constitutional, the Court looked to whether the administrative scheme really "authorize[d] searches undertaken solely to uncover evidence of criminality." *Id.*

Similarly, the Supreme Court dismissed a defendant's argument "that because the Customs officers were accompanied by a Louisiana State Policeman, and were following an informant's tip that a vessel in the ship channel was thought to be carrying marijuana," the Government could not rely on the administrative search exception. *United States v. Villamonte-Marquez,* 462 U.S. 579, 584 n.3, 103 S.Ct. 2573, 77 L.Ed.2d 22 (1983).

We have applied these principles to a search of an automobile salvage yard. *United States v. Thomas,* 973 F.2d 1152, 1155-56 (5th Cir. 1992). There, an investigator with the Texas Department of Public Safety tracked a vehicle to an auto salvage business and there conducted an inventory inspection under Texas statute. *Id.* at 1155. Even though the inventory inspection was prompted by suspicion of criminal conduct, the investigator still was entitled to use information gained during the inspection to obtain a search warrant for the salvage-yard owner's residence. *Id.* "Administrative searches conducted pursuant to valid statutory schemes do not violate the Constitution simply because of the existence of a specific suspicion of wrongdoing." *Id.* at 1155-56.

Beck has similar analysis. As here, the administrative search in *Beck* was initiated after a tip. Dental Board member Michael Pitcock "stated in his deposition that information was forwarded to him alleging that Beck had ordered unusually high volumes of controlled substances." *Beck,* 204 F.3d at 632. The Dental Board suspected Beck of violating criminal statutes, and a law enforcement officer accompanied the board agent in its inspection of the dental office. *Id.* The dentist argued that the search was conducted to uncover criminal wrongdoing and thus was not conducted pursuant to a valid administrative scheme. *Id.* at 638. We held that the suspicions of criminal wrongdoing "did not render the administrative search unreasonable," citing *Villamonte-Marquez* and *Thomas. Id.* at 639.

As to Dr. Zadeh, the DEA was closely involved with the Board's investigation. Under *Burger,* though, we look to whether the search that occurred was under a scheme serving an administrative purpose. The Board's purpose is demonstrated by p.472 the subsequent administrative action against Dr. Zadeh. The search was not performed "solely to uncover evidence of criminality." *See Burger,* 482 U.S. at 698, 107 S.Ct. 2636. Thus, the search was not pretextual.

II. Declaratory Judgment

Dr. Zadeh argues that the district court erred in abstaining from deciding the declaratory judgment claims following *Younger.* Dr. Zadeh asked the district court to make declaratory judgments on several laws implicating the Board. The district court did not resolve any.

"In *Younger,* the Supreme Court 'instructed federal courts that the principles of equity, comity, and federalism in certain circumstances counsel abstention in deference to ongoing state proceedings.'" *Wightman v. Tex. Supreme Court,* 84 F.3d 188, 189 (5th Cir. 1996) (citations omitted). Following Supreme Court precedent, this court follows "a three-part test describing the circumstances under which abstention [is] advised: (1) the dispute should involve an 'ongoing state judicial proceeding;' (2) the state must have an important interest in regulating the subject matter of the claim; and (3) there should be an 'adequate opportunity in the state proceedings to raise constitutional challenges.'" *Id.* (citation omitted).

The district court applied the reasoning of one of our unpublished cases, *Perez v. Tex. Med. Bd.,* 556 F. App'x 341 (5th Cir. 2014). There, we held that *Younger* barred the plaintiffs' suit seeking to enjoin the Board from pursuing any causes of action against them. *Id.* at 342-43. We agree with that panel's determination that Texas had a strong interest in regulating the practice of medicine, and the *Perez* plaintiffs could raise their constitutional challenges in the state court because the law provided for judicial review of the administrative decision. *Id.* at 342. Following *Perez,* the district court concluded that Dr. Zadeh had an ongoing administrative action pending; the state had a significant interest in regulating medicine in Texas; and Dr. Zadeh could appeal his administrative action in state court and raise constitutional challenges there. Accordingly, the district court abstained from adjudicating the requests for declaratory relief.

Dr. Zadeh claims *Younger* is inapplicable because the Board argued that the lawsuit did not implicate the underlying investigation. Dr. Zadeh also argues that there will be no adequate opportunity in the state proceedings to raise any constitutional challenges. He claims that "[d]octors do not have the power to file an appeal concerning the findings of fact and conclusions of law contained in a final decision (but the TMB does)."

Dr. Zadeh was subject to an ongoing state administrative proceeding, and that qualifies as a judicial proceeding for this analysis. *See Middlesex Cnty. Ethics Comm. v. Garden State Bar Ass'n,* 457 U.S. 423, 432, 102 S.Ct. 2515, 73 L.Ed.2d 116 (1982). As we stated in *Perez*, Texas has a strong interest in regulating the practice of medicine. Finally, despite plaintiffs' contrary view, Texas law does permit judicial review by either party of an administrative decision.[1] "A person who has exhausted all administrative remedies available within a state agency and who is aggrieved by a final decision in a contested p.473 case is entitled to judicial review under this chapter." TEX. GOV'T CODE. § 2001.171.

The district court did not abuse its discretion in abstaining from deciding the declaratory judgment claims.

III. Director Robinson's potential supervisory capacity liability

The plaintiffs argue that Robinson should be held liable in her supervisory capacity. "A supervisory official may be held liable under § 1983 only if (1) he affirmatively participates in the acts that cause the constitutional deprivation, or (2) he implements unconstitutional policies that causally result in the constitutional injury." *Gates v. Tex. Dep't of Protective and Regulatory Servs.*, 537 F.3d 404, 435 (5th Cir. 2008). A failure to train claim requires that the plaintiff show (1) the supervisor's failure to train; (2) the failure to train resulted in the violation of the plaintiff's rights; and (3) the failure to train shows deliberate indifference. *Id.* For deliberate indifference, "there must be 'actual or constructive notice' 'that a particular omission in their training program causes ... employees to violate citizens' constitutional rights' and the actor nevertheless 'choose[s] to retain that program.'" *Porter v. Epps,* 659 F.3d 440, 447 (5th Cir. 2011) (citation omitted).

The plaintiffs argue that Robinson improperly delegated her subpoena authority to subordinates whose training she knew nothing about. Therefore, the subpoena did not comply with Texas law because the Executive Director of the Board is not permitted to delegate her subpoena authority. The district court did not determine whether the delegation was permissible. "In light of the express regulatory authority for the delegation, the precedent set by her predecessors, and the sheer volume of subpoenas issued every year by the TMB," Robinson's actions did not amount to deliberate indifference.

In Texas administrative law, a rule of statutory construction presumes that where a statute grants specific authority to a designated public officer, the legislature intended only that officer to have that authority. *Lipsey v. Tex. Dep't of Health,* 727 S.W.2d 61, 64 (Tex. App.-Austin 1987, writ ref'd n.r.e.). Still, *Lipsey* recognized "the authority to 'subdelegate' or transfer the assigned function may be *implied* and the presumption defeated owing to the nature of the assigned function, the makeup of the agency involved, the duties assigned to it, the statutory framework, and perhaps other matters." *Id.* at 65.

In this case, a statute permits the Board to subpoena records. TEX. OCC. CODE. § 153.007. Section 153.007(b) permits the Board to delegate subpoena authority "to the executive director or the secretary-treasurer of the board." By administrative rule, the executive director may "delegate any responsibility or authority to an employee of the board." 22 TEX. ADMIN. CODE § 161.7(c).

In resolving this issue, we start with the fact the rule articulated in *Lipsey* is only a presumption. Even assuming that the plaintiffs could show that Robinson failed to train her subordinates and that failure resulted in a constitutional violation, Robinson was not deliberately indifferent in delegating her subpoena authority in light of the fact she was acting pursuant to the regulations in the same way as her predecessors and the numerous subpoenas issued each year. To the extent the plaintiffs seek to impose Section 1983 liability on Kirby and Pease through the subdelegation argument, that law also was not clearly established.

AFFIRMED.

p.474 DON R. WILLETT, Circuit Judge, concurring in part, dissenting in part:

State investigators, without notice and without a warrant, entered a doctor's office and demanded to rifle through the medical records of 16 patients. Or else. The doctor was not in, and the investigators, after being told that the doctor contested the subpoena, warned his assistant that if she didn't produce the patient files at once, there would be grave repercussions. According to her, the investigators threatened to suspend the doctor's medical license. They demanded compliance—immediately.

The Fourth Amendment forbids such roughshod rummaging. The Framers cared deeply about We the People's right "to be secure in [our] persons, houses, papers, and effects against unreasonable searches and seizures."[1] The Fourth Amendment was the Founding generation's "response to the reviled 'general warrants' and 'writs of assistance' of the colonial era, which allowed British officers to rummage through homes in an unrestrained search for evidence of criminal activity."[2] In fact, outrage over unchecked searches was "one of the driving forces behind the Revolution itself."[3]

The majority opinion correctly diagnoses Dr. Zadeh's injury but refuses to prescribe a remedy: His rights were violated, but since the law wasn't clearly established, Dr. Zadeh loses. I originally agreed with this violation-without-vindication result.[4]

But deeper study has convinced me that the officials' constitutional misstep violated clearly established law, not a previously unknown right. And it has reaffirmed my broader conviction that the judge-made immunity regime ought not be immune from thoughtful reappraisal.

I

To rebut the officials' qualified-immunity defense and get to trial, Dr. Zadeh must plead facts showing that the alleged misconduct violated clearly established law.[5] He has done so.

A

The Supreme Court held 40-plus years ago in *See* that the Fourth Amendment requires precompliance review.[6] An administrative subpoena "may not be made and enforced by the inspector in the field...."[7] Almost 20 years later, the Court in *Lone Steer* elaborated that although an agency "may issue an administrative subpoena without a warrant," it must give the subpoenaed person an opportunity "to question the reasonableness of the subpoena... by raising objections in an action in district court" before suffering any penalties for noncompliance.[8] The Court reaffirmed this settled precompliance-review requirement again just four years ago in *Patel.*[9]

p.475 Here, Texas officials gave Dr. Zadeh no time to question the subpoena's reasonableness. That's a violation. Plain and simple.

B

But there are exceptions to most every rule. Under the Supreme Court's 1981 decision in *Burger,* officials don't have to give people time to comply if:

- the business is part of a closely regulated industry;
- there's a substantial government interest;
- warrantless searches are necessary; and
- there's a "constitutionally adequate substitute for a warrant."[10]

This search whiffs two requirements. So I agree with the majority opinion: The *Burger* exception doesn't apply.

1

Medical practices—including pain-management clinics—aren't "closely regulated" industries. In both *Burger*[11] and *Patel,*[12] the Supreme Court considered the history of warrantless searches, then-current regulations, and the public interest. Take *Patel.* The Court held that hotels aren't a closely regulated industry—no history of regular, warrantless searches.[13] Public-accommodation laws require hotels to serve all paying customers. That just doesn't equate to state officials knocking down doors.[14]

Likewise, state officials haven't historically rummaged through pain-management clinics without warrants. If anything, it's the opposite. The law has consistently protected doctor-patient confidentiality. In 2011, the Supreme Court in *Sorrell* noted that "for many reasons, physicians have an interest in keeping their prescription decisions confidential."[15] Ten years earlier, the Court in *Ferguson* recognized medical patients' "reasonable expectation of privacy"—that no one will share their records without permission.[16]

It's not just our Nation's highest court. Lower courts recognize this too. The district court here emphasized that "warrantless inspections of doctors' offices" don't often happen.[17] In 2017, another Texas federal district court stressed a stark distinction between medicine and "closely regulated" industries. The court noted that the government has long treated liquor and guns very differently than doctors.[18]

True, we held in *Schiffman* that pharmaceuticals are a "pervasively" regulated industry.[19] But that was in 1978. And the Supreme Court has since clarified things. As the Court said in *Patel,* the closely-regulated-industry p.476 exception is very much that—"the exception."[20] So *Schiffman* doesn't control.

In sum, the law strongly protects privacy in medicine. Pain management is a medical field. So pain-management clinics aren't closely regulated.

Unfortunately, the majority opinion assumes without deciding that pain-management clinics *are* closely regulated. In doing so, the majority blurs constitutional contours.[21] Our legal system serves the public best when it provides clear rules, consistently applied—bright lines and sharp corners. We owe clarity to the courts below us, the litigants before us, and the cases beyond us. Thankfully, our court has at least established that medicine generally isn't closely regulated.

2

Setting aside the "closely regulated" issue, the *Burger* exception still doesn't apply. The laws here aren't a constitutionally adequate substitute for a warrant. In *Burger,* the Court explained that a statute has to notify the public that the government can search on-demand. And it must limit officer discretion.[22] These statutes neither notify nor limit.[23]

Our 2000 decision in *Beck* sheds light on what counts for notice.[24] There, the Controlled Substances Act explicitly authorized officers to search dental offices "upon stating [their] purpose[s]" and showing their credentials.[25] That was clear statutory notice. And so we upheld an on-demand search. In other words, there had to be notice that no notice is necessary.[26]

Consider our 2001 opinion in *Fort* too.[27] There, we stamped our approval on a statute that allowed officers to inspect vehicles "after stating the purpose of the inspection."[28] The law put Texas drivers on notice that their cars could be searched. Eight years later in *Club Retro,* we again enforced the notice requirement.[29] That time, a SWAT team had raided a nightclub—replete with "physical assault, threats at gunpoint, and prolonged detention."[30] But the supposed authorizing statute p.477 notified owners only of periodic fire-safety and alcohol compliance checks.[31] So we held that the search failed to meet the notice requirement.[32]

Here, the statutes don't notify business owners of on-demand searches. These statutes allow "a reasonable time" to produce records.[33] And they define "reasonable time" as "fourteen calendar days"; less only if there's an emergency or a risk "that the records may be lost, damaged, or destroyed."[34] That's not notice of routine, on-the-spot searches.

Lastly, the statutes don't limit officer discretion. The only limits: who can subpoena things (the Board);[35] who the Board can subpoena (licensees);[36] and what the Board can demand (medical records).[37] But that's it. Otherwise, there's total discretion.

Thus, the *Burger* exception doesn't apply. And so all that's left to decide is if the violation was clearly established.

C

It was. Just last year in *Wesby,* the Supreme Court explained that "clearly established" means "settled law."[38] "[C]ontrolling authority" must explicitly adopt the principle; or else there must be "a robust consensus of cases of persuasive authority."[39] Mere implication from precedent doesn't suffice.[40]

What's more, the Court in *Wesby* reiterated that the legal principle must be specific—not general. The rule must "prohibit the officer's conduct in the particular circumstances before him."[41] The Court doesn't require "a case directly on point."[42] But it does require a case "where an officer acting under similar circumstances ... violated the Fourth Amendment."[43]

The Supreme Court in *See,*[44] *Lone Steer,*[45] and *Patel*[46] made clear the need for precompliance review of administrative subpoenas. That's controlling law.

Summing up: The Board violated Dr. Zadeh's Fourth Amendment rights. No exception p.478 applies. And the law was clearly established. The state officials are thus not immune. On this basis alone, Dr. Zadeh deserves his day in court.

II

Respectfully, I think that the majority opinion is wrong for two reasons. First, this court shouldn't determine whether exceptions to violations are clearly established. Second, even if we should, Dr. Zadeh should win anyway.

A

The majority concedes that the statutes here don't limit the discretion of the inspecting officers as *Burger* requires. The court also acknowledges that statutes must provide notice. Yet the court holds that these requirements weren't—themselves— clearly established.

I understand the impulse. After all, qualified immunity is supposed to protect "all but the plainly incompetent or those who knowingly violate the law"—that's what the Supreme Court remarked in *Wesby*.[47] So if reasonably competent officers wouldn't necessarily know that they're violating the law, they shouldn't be liable. For example, the majority says that since we haven't yet enforced the limited-discretion requirement, reasonable officials could've thought that the subpoena satisfied *Burger*. Thus, they wouldn't necessarily realize they're breaking the law.

But that hyperspecific take snubs the Supreme Court's time-worn test: Was there a clearly established violation?[48] Yes, it's a violation to conduct a warrantless search without precompliance review. Sometimes there's an exception to this test. But not here. No exception applies. And it's only when an exception applies that the general rule doesn't.

B

Yet even if we should ask whether the *Burger* exception was clearly established, Dr. Zadeh still ought to win. Controlling law dictates that there must be statutory notice.

Recall *Beck*. In that case, the law authorized on-demand, warrantless searches. And so we upheld the search.[49] Don't forget *Fort*[50] or *Club Retro*[51] either, in which we similarly enforced the notice requirement. Then of course there's *Burger* itself. In upholding a warrantless search, the Supreme Court emphasized that the statute "set[ ] forth the scope of the inspection and, accordingly, place[d] the operator on notice as to how to comply with the statute."[52]

Those cases control. They require statutory notice. So the *Burger* exception's notice element is clearly established. And the Texas laws don't provide notice for on-demand inspections.

For that reason, the limited-discretion requirement shouldn't matter. The notice requirement would govern. No matter how you shake it, the officials shouldn't be immune.

III

Yet here we are—Dr. Zadeh still loses; there and back again. Everyone agrees his Fourth Amendment rights were violated. But owing to a legal *deus ex machina*— p.479 the "clearly established" prong of qualified-immunity analysis—the violation eludes vindication. At first I agreed with the panel majority that the government violated the law but not *clearly established* law. I was wrong. Beyond this case, though, I must restate my broader unease with the real-world functioning of modern immunity practice.

To some observers, qualified immunity smacks of unqualified impunity, letting public officials duck consequences for bad behavior—no matter how palpably unreasonable—as long as they were the *first* to behave badly. Merely proving a constitutional deprivation doesn't cut it; plaintiffs must cite functionally identical precedent that places the legal question "beyond debate" to "every" reasonable officer.[53] Put differently, it's immaterial that someone acts unconstitutionally if no prior case held such misconduct unlawful. This current "yes harm, no foul" imbalance leaves victims violated but not vindicated. Wrongs are not righted, and wrongdoers are not reproached.

Today the majority opinion says Dr. Zadeh loses because his rights weren't clearly established. But courts of appeals are divided—intractably—over precisely what degree of factual similarity must exist. How indistinguishable must existing precedent be? On the one hand, the Supreme Court reassures plaintiffs that its caselaw "does not require a case directly on point for a right to be clearly established."[54] On the other hand, the Court admonishes that "clearly established law must be 'particularized' to the facts of the case."[55] How to square these abstract instructions? Take Dr. Zadeh. Effectively, he loses since no previous panel has ever held this exact sort of search unconstitutional. In day-to-day practice, the "clearly established" standard is neither clear nor established among our Nation's lower courts.

Two other factors perpetuate perplexity over "clearly established law." First, many courts grant immunity without first determining whether the challenged behavior violates the Constitution.[56] They avoid scrutinizing the alleged offense by skipping to the simpler second prong: no factually analogous precedent. Forgoing a knotty constitutional inquiry makes for easier sledding, no doubt. But the inexorable result is "constitutional stagnation"[57]—fewer courts establishing law at all, much less *clearly* doing so. Section 1983 meets Catch-22. Plaintiffs must produce precedent even as fewer courts are producing precedent. Important constitutional questions go unanswered precisely because no one's answered them before. Courts then rely on that judicial silence to conclude there's no equivalent case on the books. No precedent = no clearly established law p.480 = no liability. An Escherian Stairwell. Heads government wins, tails plaintiff loses.

Second, constitutional litigation increasingly involves cutting-edge technologies. If courts leapfrog the underlying constitutional merits in cases raising novel issues like digital privacy, then constitutional clarity—matter-of-fact guidance about what the Constitution requires—remains exasperatingly elusive. Result: gauzy constitutional guardrails as technological innovation outpaces legal adaptation.

Qualified immunity aims to balance competing policy goals: "the need to hold public officials accountable when they exercise power irresponsibly and the need to shield officials from harassment, distraction, and liability when they perform their duties reasonably."[58] And I concede that the doctrine enjoys special favor at the Supreme Court, which seems untroubled by any one-sidedness.[59] The Court recently declined to take up a closely watched case challenging the warrantless strip search of a four-year-old preschooler.[60] A strange-bedfellows alliance of leading scholars and advocacy groups of every ideological stripe—perhaps the most diverse amici ever assembled—had joined forces to urge the Court to fundamentally reshape immunity doctrine. Even in this hyperpartisan age, there is a growing, cross-ideological chorus of jurists[61] and scholars[62] urging recalibration of contemporary immunity jurisprudence.

Indeed, it's curious how this entrenched, judge-created doctrine excuses constitutional p.481 violations by limiting the statute Congress passed to redress constitutional violations.[63] Count me with Chief Justice Marshall: "The government of the United States has been emphatically termed a government of laws, and not of men. It will certainly cease to deserve this high appellation, if the laws furnish no remedy for the violation of a vested legal right."[64]

Doctrinal reform is arduous, often-Sisyphean work. Finding faults is easy; finding solutions, less so. But even if qualified immunity continues its forward march and avoids sweeping reconsideration, it certainly merits a refined procedural approach that more smartly—and fairly—serves its intended objectives.

[1] The plaintiffs note that the administrative law judge in the SOAH proceeding declined to address the constitutional questions. Even so, all the law requires is that the issue have been preserved for the appeal to the state court. *See Ohio Civil Rights Comm'n v. Dayton Christian Schs., Inc.,* 477 U.S. 619, 629, 106 S.Ct. 2718, 91 L.Ed.2d 512 (1986).

[1] U.S. CONST. amend. IV.

[2] *Riley v. California,* 573 U.S. 373, 134 S. Ct. 2473, 2494, 189 L.Ed.2d 430 (2014).

[3] *Id.*

[4] *Zadeh v. Robinson,* 902 F.3d 483, 498 (5th Cir. 2018) (Willett, J., concurring dubitante).

[5] *Ashcroft v. al-Kidd,* 563 U.S. 731, 735, 131 S.Ct. 2074, 179 L.Ed.2d 1149 (2011).

[6] *See v. City of Seattle,* 387 U.S. 541, 87 S.Ct. 1737, 18 L.Ed.2d 943 (1967).

[7] *Id.* at 544-45, 87 S.Ct. 1737.

[8] *Donovan v. Lone Steer, Inc.,* 464 U.S. 408, 415, 104 S.Ct. 769, 78 L.Ed.2d 567 (1984).

[9] *City of Los Angeles v. Patel,* ___ U.S. ___, 135 S. Ct. 2443, 2452, 192 L.Ed.2d 435 (2015) ("[T]he subject of the search must be afforded an opportunity to obtain precompliance review before a neutral decisionmaker.").

[10] *New York v. Burger,* 482 U.S. 691, 702-03, 107 S.Ct. 2636, 96 L.Ed.2d 601 (1987).

[11] *See id.* at 704, 107 S.Ct. 2636.

[12] *See Patel,* 135 S. Ct. at 2454.

[13] *Id.* at 2455.

[14] *Id.*

[15] *Sorrell v. IMS Health Inc.,* 564 U.S. 552, 572, 131 S.Ct. 2653, 180 L.Ed.2d 544 (2011).

[16] *Ferguson v. City of Charleston,* 532 U.S. 67, 78, 121 S.Ct. 1281, 149 L.Ed.2d 205 (2001).

[17] *Zadeh v. Robinson,* No. 1:15-CV-598, Dkt. No. 40, at *10 (W.D. Tex., Apr. 26, 2016), *aff'd,* 902 F.3d 483 (5th Cir. 2018).

[18] *Barry v. Freshour,* No. H-17-1403, 2017 WL 4682176, at *6-7 (Rosenthal, J.) (S.D. Tex. Oct. 18, 2017), *rev'd on other grounds,* 905 F.3d 912 (5th Cir. 2018).

[19] *United States v. Schiffman,* 572 F.2d 1137, 1142 (5th Cir. 1978).

[20] 135 S. Ct. at 2455.

[21] *See* discussion *infra* Section III.

[22] *Burger,* 482 U.S. at 703, 107 S.Ct. 2636 ("[Statutes must] perform the two basic functions of a warrant: it must advise ... that the search is being made pursuant to the law and has a properly defined scope, and it must limit the discretion of inspecting officers.").

[23] TEX. OCC. CODE § 153.007 ("[T]he board may issue a subpoena or a subpoena duces tecum to compel the attendance of a witness and the production of books, records, and documents."); TEX. OCC. CODE § 168.052 (allowing the Board to examine "the documents of a physician practicing at the clinic, as necessary to ensure compliance with this chapter"); 22 TEX. ADMIN. CODE § 179.4 ("Upon the request by the board or board representatives, a licensee shall furnish to the board copies of medical records ... within a reasonable time period ...."); 22 TEX. ADMIN. CODE § 195.3 ("The board may inspect a pain management clinic certified under this chapter, including the documents of a physician practicing at the clinic, to determine if the clinic is being operated in compliance with applicable laws and rules.").

[24] Beck v. Tex. St. Bd. of Dental Exam'rs, *204 F.3d 629, 639 (5th Cir. 2000).*

[25] *Id.* at 639.

[26] *Id.* ("Thus, [the statute] did not require that prior notice be given.").

[27] *United States v. Fort,* 248 F.3d 475, 482 (5th Cir. 2001).

[28] *Id.* (citing TEX. TRANSP. CODE § 644.104(b)).

[29] *Club Retro, L.L.C. v. Hilton,* 568 F.3d 181, 200 (5th Cir. 2009).

[30] *Id.*

[31] *Id.*

[32] *Id.*

[33] TEX. ADMIN. CODE § 179.4(a).

[34] *Id.*

[35] *Id.* ("Upon the request *by the board* or board representatives, a licensee shall furnish to the board copies of medical records ... within a reasonable time period ...." (emphasis added)).

[36] *Id.* ("Upon the request by the board or board representatives, *a licensee shall furnish* to the board copies of medical records ... within a reasonable time period ...." (emphasis added)).

[37] *Id.* ("Upon the request by the board or board representatives, a licensee shall furnish to the board *copies of medical records* ... within a reasonable time period ...." (emphasis added)).

[38] *Wesby,* 138 S. Ct. at 589 (2018) (quoting *Hunter v. Bryant,* 502 U.S. 224, 228, 112 S.Ct. 534, 116 L.Ed.2d 589 (1991) (per curiam)).

[39] *Id.* at 590 (cleaned up) (quoting *Ashcroft v. al-Kidd,* 563 U.S. 731, 741-42, 131 S.Ct. 2074, 179 L.Ed.2d 1149 (2011)).

[40] *Id.*

[41] *Id.*

[42] *Id.* (quoting *al-Kidd,* 563 U.S. at 741, 131 S.Ct. 2074).

[43] *Id.* (quoting *White v. Pauly,* ___ U.S. ___, 137 S. Ct. 548, 552, 196 L.Ed.2d 463 (2017) (per curiam)). *But cf.* discussion *infra* Section III.

[44] 387 U.S. at 544-45, 87 S.Ct. 1737.

[45] 464 U.S. at 415, 104 S.Ct. 769.

[46] 135 S. Ct. at 2452.

[47] 138 S. Ct. at 589 (quoting *Malley v. Briggs,* 475 U.S. 335, 341, 106 S.Ct. 1092, 89 L.Ed.2d 271 (1986)).

[48] *See* discussion *infra* Section III.

[49] 204 F.3d at 639.

[50] 248 F.3d at 482.

[51] 568 F.3d at 200.

[52] 482 U.S. at 711, 107 S.Ct. 2636.

[53] *Ashcroft,* 563 U.S. at 741, 131 S.Ct. 2074; *see also, e.g., Kisela v. Hughes,* ___ U.S. ___, 138 S. Ct. 1148, 1153, 200 L.Ed.2d 449 (2018) (per curiam); *Mullenix v. Luna,* ___ U.S. ___, 136 S. Ct. 305, 308, 193 L.Ed.2d 255 (2015) (per curiam).

[54] *Kisela,* 138 S. Ct. at 1152 (quoting *White v. Pauly,* ___ U.S. ___, 137 S. Ct. 548, 551, 196 L.Ed.2d 463 (2017)).

[55] *Pauly,* 137 S. Ct. at 552 (quoting *Anderson,* 483 U.S. at 640, 107 S.Ct. 3034).

[56] *See Pearson v. Callahan,* 555 U.S. 223, 227, 129 S.Ct. 808, 172 L.Ed.2d 565 (2009).

[57] Aaron L. Nielson & Christopher J. Walker, *The New Qualified Immunity,* 89 S. CAL. L. REV. 1, 12 (2015) ("Because a great deal of constitutional litigation occurs in cases subject to qualified immunity, many rights potentially might *never* be clearly established should a court skip ahead to the question whether the law clearly established that the officer's conduct was unlawful in the circumstances of the case. The danger, in short, is one of constitutional stagnation." (cleaned up)).

[58] *Pearson,* 555 U.S. at 231, 129 S.Ct. 808 (flagging these "two important interests").

[59] That said, four sitting Justices "have authored or joined opinions expressing sympathy" with various doctrinal, procedural, and pragmatic critiques of qualified immunity. Joanna C. Schwartz, *The Case Against Qualified Immunity,* 93 NOTRE DAME L. REV. 1797, 1800 (2018) (including Justices Thomas, Ginsburg, Breyer, and Sotomayor, plus recently retired Justice Kennedy).

[60] *Doe v. Woodard,* 912 F.3d 1278 (10th Cir. 2019), *cert. denied,* No. 18-1173, ___ U.S. ___, 139 S.Ct. 2616, 204 L.Ed.2d 265, 2019 WL 1116409, at *1 (May 20, 2019).

[61] *See, e.g., Kisela,* 138 S. Ct. at 1162 (Sotomayor, J., dissenting) (fearing the Supreme Court's "one-sided approach to qualified immunity transforms the doctrine into an absolute shield for law enforcement officers, gutting the deterrent effect of the Fourth Amendment" and signaling "that palpably unreasonable conduct will go unpunished"); *Ziglar v. Abbasi,* ___ U.S. ___, 137 S. Ct. 1843, 1872, 198 L.Ed.2d 290 (2017) (Thomas, J., concurring in part and concurring in the judgment) ("In an appropriate case, we should reconsider our qualified immunity jurisprudence."); *Thompson v. Clark,* No. 14-CV-7349, 2018 WL 3128975, at *11 (E.D.N.Y. June 26, 2018) (Weinstein, J.) ("The Supreme Court's recent emphasis on shielding public officials and federal and local law enforcement means many individuals who suffer a constitutional deprivation will have no redress....").

[62] Last year's symposium issue of the Notre Dame Law Review gathers several scholarly essays that scrutinize qualified immunity and discuss potential refinements given mounting legal and empirical criticism. Symposium, *The Future of Qualified Immunity,* 93 NOTRE DAME L. REV. 1793 (2018); *see also, e.g.,* William Baude, *Is Qualified Immunity Unlawful?,* 106 CALIF. L. REV. 45, 88 (2018) (claiming the doctrine "lacks legal justification, and the Court's justifications are unpersuasive"); Joanna C. Schwartz, *How Qualified Immunity Fails,* 127 YALE L.J. 2, 70 (2017) (concluding that "the Court's efforts to advance its policy goals through qualified immunity doctrine has been an exercise in futility"); John C. Jeffries, Jr., *What's Wrong with Qualified Immunity?,* 62 FLA. L. REV. 851, 869 (2010) ("Today, the law of qualified immunity is out of balance .... The Supreme Court needs to intervene, not only to reconcile the divergent approaches of the Circuits but also, and more fundamentally, to rethink qualified immunity and get constitutional tort law back on track."). The essays in Notre Dame Law Review feature lively disagreement, including a nuanced pro-immunity piece by Professors Aaron Nielson and Christopher Walker, *A Qualified Defense of Qualified Immunity,* that addresses two principal anti-immunity arguments— that qualified immunity (1) is unlawful as a matter of positive law and (2) fails to advance its purported policy objectives. Aaron L. Nielson & Christopher J. Walker, *A Qualified Defense of Qualified Immunity,* 93 NOTRE DAME L. REV. 1853 (2018).

[63] *Cf. United States v. Ugalde,* 861 F.2d 802, 810 (5th Cir. 1988) ("We must ensure that for every right there is a remedy." (citing *Marbury,* 5 U.S. at 163)).

[64] *Marbury v. Madison,* 5 U.S. (1 Cranch) 137, 163, 2 L.Ed. 60 (1803). In *Little v. Barreme,* Chief Justice Marshall's opinion declined to "excuse from damages" Captain George Little for unlawfully capturing a Danish vessel, though it was "seized with pure intention." 6 U.S. (2 Cranch) 170, 179, 2 L.Ed. 243 (1804).